KT-568-925

Third Edition

Estimation of the Time Since Death

Third Edition

Estimation of the Time Since Death

Edited by

Burkhard Madea, MD
Professor, Director, Institute of Forensic Medicine
University of Bonn, Germany

CRC Press
Taylor & Francis Group
Boca Raton London New York

CRC Press is an imprint of the
Taylor & Francis Group, an **informa** business

CRC Press
Taylor & Francis Group
6000 Broken Sound Parkway NW, Suite 300
Boca Raton, FL 33487-2742

© 2016 by Taylor & Francis Group, LLC
CRC Press is an imprint of Taylor & Francis Group, an Informa business

No claim to original U.S. Government works

Printed on acid-free paper
Version Date: 20150728

International Standard Book Number-13: 978-1-4441-8176-0 (Pack - Book and Ebook)

This book contains information obtained from authentic and highly regarded sources. While all reasonable efforts have been made to publish reliable data and information, neither the author[s] nor the publisher can accept any legal responsibility or liability for any errors or omissions that may be made. The publishers wish to make clear that any views or opinions expressed in this book by individual editors, authors or contributors are personal to them and do not necessarily reflect the views/opinions of the publishers. The information or guidance contained in this book is intended for use by medical, scientific or health-care professionals and is provided strictly as a supplement to the medical or other professional's own judgement, their knowledge of the patient's medical history, relevant manufacturer's instructions and the appropriate best practice guidelines. Because of the rapid advances in medical science, any information or advice on dosages, procedures or diagnoses should be independently verified. The reader is strongly urged to consult the relevant national drug formulary and the drug companies' and device or material manufacturers' printed instructions, and their websites, before administering or utilizing any of the drugs, devices or materials mentioned in this book. This book does not indicate whether a particular treatment is appropriate or suitable for a particular individual. Ultimately it is the sole responsibility of the medical professional to make his or her own professional judgements, so as to advise and treat patients appropriately. The authors and publishers have also attempted to trace the copyright holders of all material reproduced in this publication and apologize to copyright holders if permission to publish in this form has not been obtained. If any copyright material has not been acknowledged please write and let us know so we may rectify in any future reprint.

Visit the Taylor & Francis Web site at
http://www.taylorandfrancis.com

and the CRC Press Web site at
http://www.crcpress.com

Contents

Preface to the Third Edition

Estimation of the time since death is a practical task in daily forensic casework. Already the physicians of the 19th century were familiar with the difficulties in estimating the time since death. As a historical review will indicate, the problem of determining the postmortem interval has absorbed doctors and scientists for at least one century and a half, yet accuracy still remains beyond our grasp. Since the 1960s, forensic scientists have tried hard to solve the problem of estimating the time since death by developing methods that would permit the determination of the exact time of death. But the results of all these often very extensive studies clearly show that the moment of death can only be determined within certain limits of probability. According to Francis E. Camps, the establishment of the time since death must have a true scientific backing both on an experimental and on a statistical basis. Otherwise the evidence might possibly be useless to the aims of justice. The main aim should be to obtain a figure with the smallest range of error as possible. In fact, it would be better to prove without contradiction that death could have occurred at a time when a certain person was present rather than that it occurred at a certain exact time.

This book is based on basic research, and this basic research should always be the background for time since death estimation in practice. However, an actual case does sometimes not fit into the experimental background of scientific research. Instead of analyzing a case and evaluating which information is possible to obtain, some practitioners rely only on environmental evidence instead of seeking an intellectual challenge to find solutions based on an examination of the scene of death and the body.

Relying just on environmental evidence is often for the convenience or even because of the laziness of the forensic pathologist, who may feel uncomfortable with studying the results of research. Since the last edition of this book, numerous papers on estimation of the time since death have been published. Most of them have in common that they are of no value for practice. The main criterion for the quality of any new method is that it helps to solve a case better, easier and with greater accuracy compared to traditional methods.

Progress in the field of death time estimation usually requires long-lasting research. Real progress will not be achieved by just writing a paper. Research must focus for **years** on a special problem arising from the basic idea to validate the method over field studies to prove the accuracy and reliability of the method.

In practice, estimating the time of death is not always an exact science. The best we can achieve is often only a reasoned guess, taking into account all known factors. Our aim should be to limit the margin of error inherent in assessing the effects of these factors. The aim of the methods of estimating the time since death is according to Camps to give true scientific evidence and to avoid at all costs a miscarriage of justice. However, in some cases the time of death resembles somewhat the value attributed in some peoples' minds to the lie detector. It is hoped that this new book edition will continue to be the main work in English to provide up-to-date data and references on this important subject.

In this third edition, we have included new developments in death time estimation. All chapters of the previous edition were revised and new chapters were added. These new chapters include forensic aspects of decomposition, such as how immunohistochemistry and magnetic resonance spectroscopy can contribute to death time estimation. Also discussed is the estimation of duration of immersion based on decomposition in relation to the actual water temperature. Entomology and the radiocarbon test have been included as well since they may be of importance already in the early postmortem period. Because of the increasing importance of postmortem imaging, a chapter on cross-sectional imaging and the postmortem interval is included as well. Furthermore, a new mathematical approach to narrow down the postmortem interval derived from the compound method (conditional probability in death time estimation) is described in detail.

I have to thank all contributors to the third edition and hope that the book will be a valuable source of information for forensic practitioners and scientists dealing with the estimation of the time since death. Many thanks to my secretary Elke Weinland and the staff of the Institute of Forensic Medicine in Bonn for continuous support.

Burkhard Madea

Authors

Elke Doberentz, MD
Forensic Pathologist
Institute of Forensic Medicine
University of Bonn
Bonn, Germany

Doris Döppes, PhD
Scientific Collaborator, Head of the
    3D-Laboratory
Reiss-Engelhorn-Museen
Curt-Engelhorn-Center for Archaeometrie
Mannheim, Germany

Claus Henssge, MD
Professor Emeritus of Forensic Medicine
Berlin, Germany

Michael Hubig, PhD
Mathematician, Biomechanics
Institute of Forensic Medicine
Jena University Hospital – Friedrich Schiller
    University Jena
Jena, Germany

Gerhard Kernbach-Wighton, MD
Professor
Institute of Forensic Medicine
University of Bonn
Bonn, Germany

Bernard Knight, MD
Professor Emeritus of Forensic Medicine
University of Wales
College of Medicine
Cardiff, United Kingdom

Thomas Krompecher, MD
Professor Emeritus of Forensic Medicine
Institute of Legal Medicine
University of Lausanne
Le Mont-sur-Lausanne, Switzerland

Burkhard Madea, MD
Professor, Director
Institute of Forensic Medicine
University of Bonn
Bonn, Germany

Gita Mall, MD
Professor, Director
Institute of Forensic Medicine
Jena University Hospital – Friedrich Schiller
    University Jena
Jena, Germany

Bruno Morgan, MA, PhD, BM, BCh, MRCP, FRCR
Professor and Honorary Consultant Radiologist
University of Leicester Department of Radiology
Leicester Royal Infirmary
Leicester, United Kingdom

Holger Muggenthaler, PhD
Computer Scientist, Biomechanics
Institute of Forensic Medicine
Jena University Hospital – Friedrich Schiller
    University Jena
Jena, Germany

Frank Musshoff, PhD
Professor
Forensic Toxicologist Centre (FTC)
Munich, Germany

Stefan Potente, MD
Forensic Pathologist
Institute of Legal Medicine
University of Frankfurt
Frankfurt am Main, Germany

Saskia Reibe, PhD
Biologist
Institute of Forensic Medicine
University of Bonn
Bonn, Germany

Wilfried Rosendahl, PhD
Director rem gmbH
Head German Mummy Project
Reiss-Engelhorn Museum
Mannheim, Germany

Guy Rutty, MD
Professor
Division of Forensic Pathology
Leicester Royal Infirmary
Leicester, United Kingdom

1 General Remarks on Estimating the Time Since Death

Burkhard Madea and Claus Henssge

1.1 Estimation of the time since death

Bernard Knight [12] began the general introduction to the previous edition with the following words:

'The importance of estimating the time since death must have been appreciated for centuries, probably millennia. Even in the most unsophisticated societies, when homicides took place the community would inevitably have correlated the location and movements of the prime suspects with the apparent time of death – however crude that comparison might have been – to test what would later become the defence of alibi.

Little has changed from those early days, except that their data acquisition equipment was merely the back of a hand to test the coolness of the corpse's skin, and their eyes and nose to evaluate decomposition. We now have multichannel thermometry with thermocouples sensitive to a fraction of a degree, enzyme methods, vitreous chemistry, muscular reactivity and several other avenues for collecting data. Regrettably, the accuracy of estimating the postmortem interval has by no means kept pace with the enormous strides made in technological sophistication.'

Estimation of the time since death is a practical task in daily forensic casework. The main objective is to give the police a first estimation of the time since death already at the place where the body was found. Methods of estimating the time since death should of course be as precise as possible, but even more important is its reliability. Reliability as the most important principle can only be provided empirically by statistical analysis of mistakes (deviation between calculated and real time since death) in field studies. The demands of practice are to be precise, to be reliable and to give an immediate result. The main principle of determining the time since death is the calculation of a measurable date along a time-dependent curve back to the starting point. Characteristics of the curve (e.g. the slope) and the starting point are influenced by internal and external, antemortem and postmortem conditions.

Therefore, the estimation of the time since death will never reveal a time point, but rather an interval.

Methods of estimating the time since death are based on two different approaches:

1. Which antemortem changes, either physiological or pathological, can be detected and allow, together with police investigations, a conclusion on the time since death (survival time)? Methods such as wound age estimation and gastric emptying when time and volume of the last meal are known follow this approach.
2. Which postmortem changes allow a conclusion to be made on the time since death? Most methods used in practice follow this second approach.

There is an extensive literature on methods proposed for estimating the time since death. However, most of these methods have never gained practical importance. Many papers on 'estimating the time since death' simply describe the time dependence of an analyte or parameter. However, the search for new analytes on postmortem changing parameters does not make any sense because nearly all parameters are changing more or less with an increasing postmortem interval. Furthermore, just applying new technologies ('time since death markers have lagged behind the advance in technology over the past 50 years') does not involve any breakthrough for the practical purposes of death time estimation.

The various methods proposed for estimating the time since death are completely different from each other:

- Predominantly physical processes such as body cooling and hypostasis.
- Metabolic processes such as concentration changes of metabolites, substrates and activity of enzymes.
- Autolysis (loss of selective membrane permeability, diffusion according to Fick's law with increase or decrease of analytes in various body fluids, morphological changes).
- Physicochemical processes (supravital reagibility, rigor mortis, immunological reactivity).
- Bacterial processes (putrefaction).

Furthermore, the methods for estimating the time since death are not only different but also have widely varying scientific value in terms of the underlying scientific background, the mode of investigation and the validation of the method (Table 1.1).

Methods of the highest scientific value do of course comprise methods with a quantitative measurement of postmortem changes and a mathematical description that takes into account influencing factors quantitatively. Clear data

Table 1.1 Grading of methods of estimating the time since death regarding mode of registration of postmortem changes, description, considering influencing factors; calculation of confidence limits

1. Quantitative measurement, mathematical description, taking into account influencing factors quantitatively, declaration of precision, proof of precision on independent material. Examples: body cooling (nomogram method); potassium in vitreous humour.

2. Subjective description (grading), considering influencing factors, declaration of precision, proof of precision on independent material. Example: supravital reactions.

3. Subjective description of postmortem changes; influencing factors known 'in principle', empirical estimations instead of statistically evaluated reference values. Examples: rigor mortis, lividity.

4. Subjective description; analogous conclusions based on empiricism and assumptions instead of statistically evaluated reference values. Example: gastric contents.

5. Subjective description, velocity of progression of postmortem changes entirely depending on ambient factors; because of the broad spectrum of ambient factors, no sound empirical estimation possible. Example: putrefaction.

on the precision of the method are available, and the data on precision have been proved on independent material and in field studies.

Conversely, the evidence for death time estimation of the lowest scientific value involves methods with only a subjective description of the postmortem change. The progression of a postmortem change is entirely dependent on ambient factors. However, these ambient factors cannot be taken into account quantitatively.

The estimation of the time since death at the scene of crime has, as already mentioned, two different objectives (Table 1.2):

1. To give the police a preliminary idea of the time of an assault. The time since death gives information on the time of an assault only in those instances in which the survival period after an injury was short.

2. To check whether the time since death is consistent or inconsistent with the alibi of a suspect. Only in rare cases does the time of death play a major role in court as the only evidence for or against the guilt of a suspect.

Table 1.2 Objectives of estimating the time since death

1. To give the police a preliminary idea on the time of an assault in criminal connotations.

2. To check whether the time since death is consistent with the alibi of a suspect.

3. When two deaths occur, especially of spouses or siblings, the order of deaths and hence survivorships.

4. Registration purposes: 'Enquire where, when and by what means a person came to death'.

However, the coroner, medical examiner or other authority needs to know the time date of death for registration purposes. Indeed, the legal basis of the English coroner's jurisdiction is to 'enquire where, when and by what means a person came to his death'.

Other matters besides usual criminal connotations concern insurance and contract and culpability issues, as well as situations in which two deaths, especially of spouses or siblings, occur close together, and the order of those deaths – and hence survivorship – may have profound effects on the transfer of estate and property [12].

Before any suspect is questioned or charged, knowledge of the approximate time of death is essential if the investigating officers are to direct their enquiries in the appropriate direction. The relationship of the time of death with other events, with persons in the vicinity and with those who could not have been in the vicinity, will automatically channel investigative efforts along certain lines. When several suspects are being considered, the best estimate of the time of death forms a primary screening procedure to eliminate some putative killers, who could not have had access to the deceased at the material time, and it may strengthen suspicion against others whose movements coincided with an estimated time. There is thus a heavy responsibility on the doctor who offers an opinion as to the probable time of death – if he or she is significantly in error, an investigation may be dislocated at its earliest and perhaps most vulnerable stage.

To offer an unreasonably accurate time of death is worse than providing such a wide range of times that the police can derive no help from it. In the latter situation, police officers do at least then know that they have to use other methods in their investigations, but to mislead the police by some outrageously precise time runs the risk of excluding the true culprit, as well as falsely implicating an innocent party [12].

For estimating the postmortem interval, different sources are used [21]:

1. Evidence from the body of the deceased (postmortem changes).

2. Information from the environment in the vicinity of the body (date of the newspaper, open television programme).

3. Anamnestic factors concerning the deceased's habits (leaving a flat, arriving at work, day to day activities).

For the forensic investigation of the time since death, all sources of information on the time since death always should be kept in mind. In forensic medicine much research has been carried out on postmortem changes. The progression of all postmortem changes is influenced by many internal or external factors, mainly the ambient temperature. The longer the postmortem interval, the less accurate is the estimation of the time since death based on postmortem changes [21].

Postmortem changes, especially body cooling, have been investigated with sophisticated methods, and formulas developed to calculate the time since death are full of mathematics. Despite the high level of research in estimating the time since death, in practice we can often achieve not more than a reasoned guess on the time elapsed since death.

■ Design of study (methodology)

If new parameters are studied, the following should be kept in mind: What is the nature of the underlying process studied [6,17] (Figure 1.1)?

- Predominantly physical processes (body cooling, hypostasis).
- Metabolic processes (e.g. concentration of metabolites and substrates, activity of enzymes).
- Autolysis (loss of selective membrane permeability, diffusion, morphological changes).
- Physicochemical processes (supravital reagibility, rigor mortis, immunological reactivity).
- Bacterial process (putrefaction).

Analyzing the underlying process may already prevent wrong expectations. In theory, it could be expected that a parameter with just a postmortem increase that is solely caused by diffusion would correlate much more strongly with the time since death than would a parameter that increases as a result of vital/postmortem degradation (metabolic process) and diffusion [19]. Furthermore, a clear definition of the site of measurement or site of sample acquisition is necessary. Postmortem changes should preferably be investigated in longitudinal studies with objective measurements of these changes, although it should be kept in

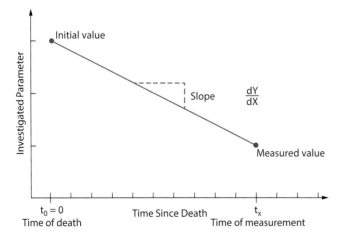

Figure 1.1 Main principle of the determination of the time since death (calculation from a measured value along a curve back to the initial value).

mind that the objective measurement contributes only in a small part to a more accurate death time estimation.

For the early postmortem interval with body cooling and supravital reactions, standards in practice have been established, and applicability and reliability were confirmed in field studies that can hardly be improved by other studies [1,4–10,14–19]. Therefore, research should focus on the later postmortem interval. However, investigations on the time course of any analyte do not make any sense without also verifying the variability because it is often the interindividual variability that prevents the application of a parameter in practice (besides the fact that *in corpore* measurements at the scene are, from the standpoint of practicability, always of higher value compared with *in vitro* measurements).

Therefore, at some different times (10, 20, 30,…, hpm), postmortem (time-dependent) investigations and taking samples from some bodies should be carried out; however, the ambient temperature or temperature history of the bodies should differ markedly (e.g. differing ambient temperature for identical postmortem intervals). This time-saving procedure already allows a first estimation of the variability in comparison with established methods. If new parameters or methods are recommended for death time estimation, their reliability and accuracy should always be compared with those of methods developed for the same postmortem period. Besides the same postmortem interval, a comparison of methods should always address the practicability and the time interval until results are available. Influencing factors governing the change of an investigated parameter should be studied (preferably in longitudinal studies), and they should be taken into account for the death time estimation quantitatively. Without considering influencing factors, a wide period will result. Control studies on independent case material must be carried out to prove the accuracy of the method. Furthermore, field studies on cases with a known time since death are necessary to check the practicable applicability, reliability and accuracy compared with standard methods. Additionally, the combination of different methods for a common result of death time estimation should be investigated [9,15].

Case material

The case material should comprise different causes of death; diseases and the duration of the terminal episode may be vital points for the strength of correlations between investigated parameter and time since death, and they must be addressed [16,18].

Analyses of results

For statistical analysis, it is not sufficient to present only mean values of the correlation between investigated parameters and time since death or correlation coefficients.

Instead, statistical parameters of the deviation of single values from the mean correlation such as confidence limits are necessary.

■ Conclusions

The huge amount of literature, especially on chemical methods of estimating the time since death [23], is still increasing. However, most of these methods have never gained any practical relevance because they do not meet the demands of practice (being precise, being reliable and giving immediate results). Field studies are good indicators of the practical value of a method, but, to our knowledge, field studies on most methods of estimating the time since death are nearly completely missing in the literature compared, for instance, with studies of body cooling or supravital reactions [1,8,9,15]. Thus, most methods proposed for an estimation of the time since death are of only academic interest because they describe just postmortem changes. These methods gain practical relevance only if the following criteria are fulfilled: quantitative measurements, mathematical descriptions, taking into account influencing factors quantitatively, declarations of precision and proof of precision on independent material.

Without validation of a method and field studies, the application of novel approaches in practice may be misleading, a miscarriage of justice and irresponsible.

1.2   Errors in estimating the time since death

Camps [2] stated that estimating the time of death is not an exact science: 'The best we can achieve is a reasoned guess taking into account all the known factors and our aim should be to limit the margin of error inherent in assessing the effect of these factors. Aim of estimating the time since death is to give true scientific evidence and avoid at all costs a miscarriage of justice. … in other words, I feel that at present the time of death resembles somewhat the value in some people's minds to the lie detector' [2].

Van den Oever [24] proposed that for greater accuracy in the estimation of the time since death, it seems that the proper way is to find a suitable combination of the most efficient known methods. Using different methods with a different background concerning postmortem changes and analytical approach increases the reliability of the estimation of the time since death and the self-confidence of the investigator. Therefore, in the protocol of a medico-legal autopsy, as in the report of the crime scene investigation, it is better to describe 10 findings that prove to be of no significance than to omit a single finding that may be critical [20].

In his famous paper on classical mistakes in forensic pathology, Alan R. Moritz [20] summarized some errors of omission in the collection of evidence required for establishing the time of death:

1. Failure to record the rectal temperature of the body.
2. Failure to observe changes that may occur in the intensity and distribution of rigor mortis – before, during and after autopsy.
3. Failure to observe the ingredients of the last meal and its location in the alimentary tract.

A further classical mistake, especially concerning estimating the time since death, may be to talk too soon, too much or to the wrong people. This was outlined by Moritz [20] with an illustrative case example. The danger of releasing opinions prematurely is illustrated by the following case: Because the dead woman's body was still warm and there was no rigor, Dr X, the pathologist, told the district attorney, who was eager to know the time of death, that the woman probably died early that morning. Dr X provided this information before the autopsy had actually been started. The district attorney immediately passed this information to news reporters. Shortly before the noon edition of the newspapers reached the streets, the pathologist realized that he had talked too soon. The degree of autolysis of the parenchymatous organs, together with the presence of intravascular haemolysis, indicated a considerably longer postmortem interval than he originally thought. The noon edition of the newspaper carried two items on the first page: the district attorney's news release to the effect that Dr X had established that the woman was murdered early that morning, and a recent news bulletin stating that the murderer had just confessed that he killed the woman during the evening of the preceding day. Approximately 12 hours after the murder, and 2 hours before the body was found, the murderer moved the woman's body from the warm room where the crime occurred to the cool basement where the police found the victim. The interior of the body was warm because it had been in a warm place during most of the postmortem period. There was no rigor because rigor had developed and regressed. If the murderer had not confessed, and if he had been able to establish an alibi for the time that the murder was supposed to have been committed, he could have used the pathologist's premature and incorrect guess to support his innocence.

General problems in estimating the time since death can be summarized as follows:

- Most methods are of help only in the first 1 or 2 days post mortem.
- Does the actual case meet the requirements of experimental investigations (e.g. unusual cooling conditions with no reference values)?
- High ambient temperature is a problem.

- Is experimental reference material with calculation of the margin of error available or not (e.g. preservation of decomposing bodies in plastic bags)?
- Being unfamiliar with the scientific background, the requirements and limitations of a method is a problem.

The main errors in estimating the time since death can be summarized as follows:

- Not taking into account the postmortem temperature plateau.
- Using rules of thumb.
- No careful examination of the scene of the crime (severe changes of cooling conditions).
- Calculation of a mean value without confidence limits.
- Using a wrong temperature site for calculation (e.g. outer ear temperature is used as body core temperature in the nomogram).
- Not taking into account influencing factors.
- Postmortem changes not seen in a context.

Factors that can introduce errors into the calculation of the time since death by body cooling include the following:

- The ambient temperature can vary widely and rapidly in certain conditions and can swing both higher and lower than the final temperature as measured on discovery of the body. The temperature of the environment is, of course, partly determined by some of the other factors.
- Wind and draughts affect body temperature by increasing convection and conduction from the surface and by evaporating moisture.
- Rain, humidity and snow, apart from the direct temperature effect, alter the evaporative properties of the skin and clothing.
- The body posture alters the rate of heat loss, by varying the effective exposed surface area per unit mass available for convection and conduction.
- The body size also alters the mass/surface area ratio. Infants and children cool more quickly for this reason because the heat gradient from the core is steeper.
- Naturally, clothing (or its lack) makes a very great difference to cooling rates. Other coverings, such as bedclothes, other fabrics, even debris or another adjacent body, can dramatically alter the cooling characteristics.
- In the same way as clothing, body fat acts as an insulator, and its deficiency or absence accelerates cooling, and *vice versa*.
- However debatable the applicability of Newton's law of cooling may be to human cooling, there is no doubt that the original body temperature at the time of death affects the progress of heat loss. This is partly by the Newtonian principle of a higher cooling rate where the excess of body temperature above ambient is large, but also from the smaller fall of temperature remaining above ambient.
- Further problems are the result of fever at death, a longer agonal period and hypothermia.

One of the few published accounts of an estimation of actual errors was made by James and Knight [11,13]. In this investigation, 110 bodies with a known time of death were examined by of 2 experienced forensic pathologists, each pathologist making the estimation alternately with no knowledge of the real time of death. The estimates were then compared with the true interval to evaluate the errors.

Of the 100 bodies, the true time since death was correctly estimated in only 11 cases, whereas underestimations occurred in 57 cases and overestimations in 32 cases. In 35 of the 100 cases, the error was less than 10 per cent, in 54 cases less than 20 per cent, in 70 cases less than 30 per cent, in 90 cases less than 40 per cent and in 95 cases less than 50 per cent. In 2 cases, there was an error of 100 per cent. The absolute error increased as the interval grew longer, but, in percentage terms, appreciable errors can also exist even near the time of death.

The general experience gained from this investigation was that in deaths occurring less than 4 hours before estimation, the major problem was the variable 'plateau'. Seven bodies had rectal temperatures at or even above 37°C up to 4 hours post mortem – a phenomenon constantly encountered since the early days of research in the mid-nineteenth century.

References

1. Albrecht A, Gerling I, Henssge C, Hochmeister M, Kleiber M, Madea B, Oehmichen M, Pollak S, Püschel K, Seifert D, Teige K. Zur Anwendung des Rektaltemperatur-Todeszeit-Nomogramms am Leichenfundort. *Z Rechtsmed* 1990;**103**:257–278.
2. Camps F. Establishment of the time since death: a critical assessment. *J Forensic Sci* 1959;**4**:73–76.
3. Henssge C. Todeszeitbestimmung: eine Methodenkritik. *Beitr Gerichtl Med* 1986;**44**:109–116.
4. Henssge C. Rectal temperature time of death nomogram: dependence of corrective factors on the body weight under stronger thermic isolation conditions. *Forensic Sci Int* 1992;**54**:51–56.
5. Henssge C. Temperature-based methods II. In: Henssge C, Knight B, Krompecher T, Madea B, Nokes L (eds.). *The Estimation of the Time Since Death in the Early Postmortem Period.* 2nd ed. London, Edward Arnold, 2002.
6. Henssge C, Madea B. Methoden zur Bestimmung der Todeszeit an Leichen. In: *Arbeitsmethoden der medizinischen und naturwissenschaftlichen Kriminalistik,* vol. 18. Lübeck, Schmidt-Römhild, 1988.
7. Henssge C, Madea B. Estimation of the time since death in the early post-mortem period. *Forensic Sci Int* 2004;**144**:167–175.
8. Henssge C, Althaus L, Bolt J, Freislederer A, Haffner HT, Henssge CA, Hoppe B, Schneider V. Experiences with a compound method for estimating the time since death. I. Rectal temperature nomogram for time since death. *Int J Legal Med* 2000;**113**:303–319.

9. Henssge C, Althaus L, Bolt J, Freislederer A, Haffner HT, Henssge CA, Hoppe B, Schneider V. Experiences with a compound method for estimating the time since death. II. Integration of non–temperature-based methods. *Int J Legal Med* 2000;**113**:320–331.

10. Henssge C, Knight B, Krompecher T, Madea B, Nokes L. (eds.). *The Estimation of the Time Since Death in the Early Postmortem Period*. London, Edward Arnold, 1995 (2nd ed., 2002).

11. James E, Knight B. Errors in estimating the time since death. *Med Sci Law* 1965;**5**:111–116.

12. Knight B. General introduction. In: Henssge C, Knight B, Krompecher T, Madea B, Nokes L (eds.). *The Estimation of the Time Since Death in the Early Postmortem Period*. 2nd ed. London, Edward Arnold, 2002, pp 1–2.

13. Knight B. Errors in estimating the time since death. In: Henssge C, Knight B, Krompecher T, Madea B, Nokes L (eds.). *The Estimation of the Time Since Death in the Early Postmortem Period*. 2nd ed. London, Edward Arnold, 2002, pp 30–31.

14. Madea B. Is there recent progress in the estimation of the post-mortem interval by means of thanatochemistry? *Forensic Sci Int* 2005;**151**:139–149.

15. Madea B, Henssge C. Electrical excitability of skeletal muscle postmortem in casework. *Forensic Sci Int* 1990;**47**:207–227.

16. Madea B, Henssge C. Eye changes after death. In: Henssge C, Knight B, Krompecher T, Madea B, Nokes L (eds.). *The Estimation of the Time Since Death in the Early Postmortem Period*. 2nd ed. London, Edward Arnold, 2002, pp 103–133.

17. Madea B, Henssge C. Time since death. In: Payne-James J, Busuttil A, Smock W (eds.). *Forensic Medicine: Clinical and Pathological Aspects*. London, Greenwich Medical Media Limited, 2003, pp 91–114.

18. Madea B, Henssge C, Hönig W, Gerbracht A. References for determining the time of death by potassium in vitreous humor. *Forensic Sci Int* 1989;**40**:231–243.

19. Madea B, Käferstein H, Hermann N, Sticht G. Hypoxanthine in vitreous humor and cerebrospinal fluid: marker of postmortem interval and prolonged (vital) hypoxia? *Forensic Sci Int* 1994;**65**:19–31.

20. Moritz AR. Classical mistakes in forensic pathology. *Am J Clin Pathol* 1956;**26**:1383–1392.

21. Pounder D. Postmortem changes and time since death. Department of Forensic Medicine, University of Dundee, Scotland, 1995.

22. Sabucedo AJ, Furton KG. Cardiac troponin I: a time since death marker. *Forensic Sci.. Int..* 2003;**134**:11–16.

23. Schleyer F. Determination of the time since death in the early postmortem interval. In: Lundquist F (ed.). *Methods of Forensic Sciences*, vol. 2. London, Interscience Publishers, 1963, pp. 253–295.

24. Van den Oever R. A review of the literature as to the present possibilities and limitations in estimating the time of death. *Med Sci Law* 1976;**16**:269–276.

2 Historical Review on Early Work on Estimating the Time Since Death

Bernard Knight and Burkhard Madea

■ Temperature measuring scales

Fahrenheit

This scale was devised in about 1714 by the German instrument maker Gabriel Fahrenheit (1686–1736). He used a mixture of ammonium chloride and ice for his 0 degrees and his own body temperature for the 100-degree mark. On this scale, the freezing point of water was 32 degrees, and its boiling point was 212 degrees.

Centigrade

This scale is divided into 100 degrees, with the freezing point of water as 0 and its boiling point at 100. It is often misnamed 'Celsius', after Anders Celsius (1701–44), a Swedish astronomer, who proposed a 100-degree scale in 1742. However, he placed the freezing point of water at 100 and the boiling point at 0 degrees; it was reversed 8 years later by his pupil Martin Stromer.

Réaumur

This scale was devised in France in 1731 by René Réaumur (1683–57). He used an alcohol thermometer, with the freezing point of water as 0, then graduating the stem into degrees, each of which contained one-thousandth of the volume of the bulb and stem up to the 0-degree mark. Arbitrarily, the boiling point of water lay at 80 degrees on his scale.

■ Early work on temperature and time of death

Although the general principle that corpses cool progressively after death has been appreciated since time immemorial, the first attempts to place the phenomenon on a scientific footing appeared towards the middle of the nineteenth century, as far as writings in English are concerned [30,31].

In 1839, a book was published in London by Dr John Davey [10], titled *Researches, Physiological and Anatomical*, in which Chapter 13 dealt with 'Observations on the Temperature of the Human Body after Death'. In this chapter,

the author described his experiments in thermometry conducted on the bodies of 8 British soldiers in Malta in 1828 and subsequently on 10 others after his return to the cooler climate of the British Isles. Considering that Davey was such a pioneer in this field, and also considering the primitive facilities of his day, Davey's methodology and his insight into the results were remarkably modern. In Malta, the bodies were placed, soon after death, on a wooden table in a large room and were covered only with a sheet, thus ensuring relatively uniform environmental conditions. Davey recorded the ambient temperature in all cases. No details of his thermometer are given, other than it had a (presumably mercury) bulb and was calibrated in degrees Fahrenheit. Unlike many workers who followed him, Davey did not confine his measurements to only one body site, but rather he recorded the temperatures in various places within the tissues. No skin, mouth, axillary or rectal temperatures were taken, and it seems obvious that the measurements were recorded during the course of autopsies. They were taken between 3 and 29 hours after death, and most were later than 12 hours post mortem. Davey made no attempt to estimate the time of death from his data – much of the discussion in relation to the Malta bodies concerned the very high temperatures discovered in some corpses, which reached 108°F and even 113°F some hours after death. Davey decided that the hot climate and the common infective causes of death contributed to this phenomenon, but he also began the long-running speculation about postmortem production of heat in the organs and tissues. However, Davey rejected this hypothesis after some discussion. Following his return to England, Davey decided to continue his measurements in a more temperate climate, and he conducted similar tests on soldiers dying in Chatham General Hospital in Kent. In his preamble to this section, Davey offered the first mention of the forensic use of body temperature:

'It may often be a question, how long a body has been dead. By attention to its temperature, particularly of the deep-seated parts, taking into consideration the circumstances affecting temperature, probably in most instances an answer may be given approximating to the truth and which may be of considerable use in evidence'.

Davey's final comments are worth recording, because although in hindsight the first part has proved overly optimistic, his last caution is as true today as when first written, more than 150 years ago:

'These observations may enable the enquirer, instituting similar trials and reasoning analogically, to arrive at a tolerably positive conclusion, in doubtful cases of death, as to the time which may have elapsed between the fatal event and the postmortem examination. Much judgement, however, and nice discrimination may be requisite on the part of the medical man in appreciating the circumstances likely to modify temperature, so as to enable him, when called on for his opinion, to give one which will be satisfactory to the legal officers and to himself, on reflection'.

Soon after Davey, there were some brief records published in the United States, in the journal *The Medical Examiner* of Philadelphia, although this general clinical publication has no medico-legal connection with the modern office of Medical Examiner. In June 1845, this journal published an abstract from an article in the *Western Journal of Medicine and Surgery* for June and October 1844 by Dr Bennett Dowler of New Orleans, concerning his temperature measurements of a variety of corpses. This abstract was followed, in August, September and October 1845, by letters from Dr Dowler with further information. His main interest was again the 'postmortem caloricity' noted by John Davey – the frequent marked rise in body temperature after death. Dowler took temperatures at different sites, both on the body surface and internally, and he also measured these temperatures at intervals. His records are a mixture of Fahrenheit and Réaumur, but he does not describe his thermometer. However, he seems to have had not the slightest interest in using his data for medico-legal purposes [30].

Dowler's publications stimulated another letter to *The Medical Examiner* of Philadelphia in January 1846, this time from a Dr Benjamin Hensley [18], who gave an address in Marietta, Ohio. He said that he used the thermometer mentioned by Dr Dowler, which was composed of a large glass cylinder with a bulb at one extremity, the large cylinder enclosing a smaller one, which was graduated in degrees Réaumur. The boiling and freezing points were found to be correct to within less than half a degree on the scale.

Hensley took many temperatures from various sites, including the skin, axilla, rectum, vagina, antecubital fossae, muscle and under internal organs. He repeated these measurements at varying intervals and built up quite a mass of data, although he seems to have made no real use of it. He also took the temperature of the 'dead-house' and in some cases, measured the body temperature several hours before death, presumably in those of his patients whom he knew were going to die.

After these rather futile beginnings, as far as a postmortem interval is concerned, there was a gap of some 17 years before the subject was tackled again. In 1863, a substantial paper was published in London, which is often cited as if it had been the very first in the field, in spite of its quoting Davey, Dowler and Hensley. However, it was the first English-language paper to concentrate on the forensic aspects of the topic. It was a long article by Taylor and Wilkes [68] from Guy's Hospital in London and was published in the *Reports* of that institution.

Alfred Swaine Taylor was a Lecturer in Medical Jurisprudence at Guy's Hospital and was the author of the famous book *Taylor's Principles and Practice of Medical Jurisprudence,* which was first published in 1865 and was for a century the premier textbook of forensic medicine in the English language. The article had a typically lengthy title for that era, being called 'On the Cooling of the Human Body after Death – Inferences Respecting the Time of Death: Observations of Temperature made in 100 Cases'. The 30-page paper is largely anecdotal and discursive and, although very interesting, is rather disappointing from the scientific aspect. It begins with several pages devoted to putrefaction, a subject hardly relevant to the title.

Taylor and Wilkes' experimental results are marked by several major faults, which cannot be blamed on the facilities available in the middle of the nineteenth century. First, almost all the hundreds of temperature measurements were made 'by placing the naked bulb of a good thermometer uncovered on the skin of the abdomen'. This is highly unsatisfactory because the thermometer readings must have varied with air temperature, stray draughts, humidity and also with the inconstant area of contact of the curved bulb with the abdomen – to say nothing of the variable relationship of any such small area of skin with the deep tissue temperature.

The other error, which is admitted in the paper, was that for the first 27 cases of the series of 100, the authors omitted to record when the bodies were brought from the hospital wards to the 'dead-house', so it was quite unknown for how long there was a different environmental temperature.

All but 4 of the hundreds of measurements were taken on the skin surface, and the results were grouped into four ranges: 2 to 3, 4 to 6, 6 to 8 and 12 or more hours after death. Because the variation of temperature within each group was very wide, and also because the size of each group varied from 29 to 76 people, the statistical value of the results is very limited. As with previous authors, Taylor and Wilkes made no effort to derive any formula from their data, to assist in calculating the time of death.

Among the generalizations and numerous anecdotal cases, there are some interesting observations and speculations. Like previous writers, Taylor and Wilkes noted that there is sometimes a postmortem rise in temperature, and they discussed possible mechanisms for this increase. These included, of course, the frequent infections that were a common cause of death. They also noted, although without giving it a name, the temperature 'plateau' that still gives rise to controversy and that was to become so important in later research. Other aspects discussed were the effect of environmental temperature, clothing and the effect of immersion in hastening cooling. The first concept of a heat gradient from the interior to the surface is discussed, as well as the obvious fact that the interior of the body can remain warm after the skin is cold.

Two other phenomena were quoted from other authors, which have passed into forensic mythology and still appear, without any scientific foundation, in some textbooks today – although to be fair to Taylor and Wilkes, they were partly dismissive of the claims. The first phenomenon was quoted from Dr W. B. Richardson, who also wrote in 1863, although the reference is not offered. Richardson stated that 'a loss of blood, as in cases of death from haemorrhage, whether the blood is effused externally or internally or even temporarily withdrawn from the heart as in syncope, is a cause of rapid cooling of the body'. Taylor and Wilkes point out that 'the sudden cold of collapse is here confounded with the slow and progressive cooling of the dead body'. To Richardson's claim that 'if the body is left dead from direct and absolute loss of blood, cooling to the temperature of the surrounding medium is completed in regard to the external surface in two hours', they comment that 'this may lead to a serious error and implicate an innocent person in a charge of murder'.

The second myth is quoted from Nysten, although again no reference is provided. Nysten claimed that 'the bodies of persons who have died from asphyxia by hanging or suffocation or from the inhalation of carbonic acid gas, do not cool until from 2–48 hours after death and that sometimes, even three days have elapsed before the body has become completely cold'. Taylor and Wilkes disparaged this statement by saying 'Too much importance must not be attached to this statement, since it is quite certain that in some cases of fatal asphyxia, the body has cooled just as rapidly as in death from other causes'. However, this justifiable criticism is contradicted elsewhere in the paper, when the authors are describing the death of the Prince of Conde, Duke of Bourbon, who was found hanging by his cravat from a window shutter. Here they say 'As in asphyxia from hanging, the warmth of the body is preserved longer than under common circumstances'. They also made the unfounded assertion that 'Where death has taken place suddenly, as from accident or acute disease or apoplexy, a body has sometimes been found to retain its heat for a long period'.

To summarize, although the article of Taylor and Wilkes has been acclaimed as the earliest paper on postmortem temperatures, it is in fact neither the earliest nor particularly erudite, although it has great interest in other ways, such as a record of a hundred common causes of death in mid-nineteenth century London and a series of Victorian anecdotes, which throw a fascinating light on both patients and doctors of that era.

In the German-speaking countries it was R. Seydeler [64] who wrote on 'Nekrothermometrie'. Like the others, he measured the temperature of the axilla. Temperature measurements were not made for the purpose of estimating the time since death but to prevent apparent deaths. Seydeler wanted to determine which temperature increase or decrease could be found in various causes of death. However, he also developed a method to determine the time since death.

The next important contribution to the literature came 3 years later, and it was of a different scientific calibre altogether. It was written in 1868 by Harry Rainy [60], Professor of Medical Jurisprudence at the University of Glasgow, who wrote with a clarity of thought and the use of mathematics that at least equal many modern papers on the subject. Rainy acknowledged the publications of previous authors and credited the collection of his own data to Dr Joseph Coates of Glasgow Royal Infirmary. They measured abdominal skin and rectal temperatures on 100 bodies but sensibly discarded all the surface readings in favour of those from the rectum. They also rejected 54 cases because the temperature of the mortuary was not constant during their experiments. Four, and sometimes 5, serial temperatures were measured on each body, between limits of 30 minutes and 63 hours after death. Rainy then calculated the 'ratio of cooling per hour' for each measurement, by expressing the proportion that the excess of temperature above the ambient at the end of an hour bore to the excess at its commencement, the latter being taken as unity. Rainy was the first to mention Newton's law of cooling, but he rightly declared that it was not absolutely correct when applied to dead bodies. 'Bodies recently dead are not found to cool in conformity with this law', he stated, and went on to recount that some temperatures actually rise after death, again quoting Davey, Dowler, Taylor and Wilkes in this respect. 'We scarcely hesitate to ascribe this rise in temperature in these cases to physiological processes which are continued after the action of the heart ceases'. Rainy commented on the 'plateau', although again he did not name it as such. He said 'It follows that the cooling may be retarded in the earlier stages by the continuance of obscure vital processes ... these processes must be kept in view in estimating the time which has elapsed since death'.

Like Fiddes and Patten [14], Marshall and Hoare [43–48] and others in the twentieth century, Rainy stated categorically that more than one temperature reading is needed to determine the time since death:

'It will be obvious that it is important to ascertain, not merely the relative temperature of the body and the surrounding medium when the body is found, but also the rate at which the process of cooling is going on during that period. This requires two observations at an interval of an hour, or if possible, two or three hours.'

He went on to state another truth, which is still disregarded by many pathologists and police surgeons even today: '... having obtained these data, though we cannot exactly calculate the period which has elapsed since death, we can almost always determine a minimum and a maximum of time within which that period will be included'. This is a statutory warning, from well over a century ago, for doctors not to be so rash as to volunteer a single time of death, but rather to give a preferred range within which they consider that death occurred.

Rainy was the first to offer a formula for calculating the central point of that range of time since death.

'Let the excess of temperature of the rectum at the first observation be t, and at one hour later t − n: and let the excess of temperature of the body at death be n + D, where D = the rectal temperature at death minus environmental temperature. Further, let t/t1 = R and because t is greater than n and consequently will be greater than unity, then:

$$\frac{\log D - \log t\mathit{l}}{\log R} = x$$

which is the number of hours that have elapsed since death. The number of hours, x, determined by this calculation will in almost every case be less than the actual time which has elapsed since death. This arises from the fact that in the early stages, the cooling proceeds more slowly than the assumed (Newton's) law and that the calculation furnishes us with a minimum time'.

Here, Rainy was acknowledging the plateau: he went on to say

'It is more difficult to fix a maximum time with precision, but a careful comparison of recorded cases will show that in all cases in which the temperature of the rectum is found to be below 85°F, the time elapsed since death has been less than the minimum multiplied by 1.5'.

Rainy then offered the delightful comment, still often appropriate in respect of the mathematical ability of many doctors, that 'Persons unacquainted with logarithms may make the necessary observations when the body is found – and the proper inferences may be deduced by competent parties afterwards!'

This article was the first that can truly be recognized as a proper scientific contribution to the subject, and in spite of its relatively early date, the style and content compare favourably with many modern publications.

Indeed: The theoretical content of Rainy's publications was more important than that of many publications that were published 100 years later. He transferred the Newton rule of cooling to the cooling of corpses and thus he considered the environmental temperature. By measuring the temperature several times he could even determine experimentally the individual steepness of the temperature drop curve according to the Newton coefficient. Additionally, Rainy already identified the postmortal temperature plateau as declination of the single-exponential model (Newton) and consistently designated the calculated death time as minimum time.

Interest increased in the topic, both in English and Continental journals. In 1870, Goodhard [16] published a report, although he contributed little that was useful.

Wilkie Burman [6], a medical officer at a mental asylum in Wiltshire, published papers in 1874 and 1880, describing his experiments with a special thermometer that he had designed. This thermometer was bent at right angles so that the bulb could be left in the axilla while the mercury level was read. Burman first reviewed the writings of Hensley [18] and Dowler [30] (whom he called 'Fowler') and of Taylor [68], on whose failure to record the time of removal to the mortuary he seized. In his own experiments, all of which were carried out on skin temperatures, Burman found no plateau – again showing that the delay in the fall of core temperature must be the result of the interval needed for the establishment of a heat gradient. Burman tested a number of cases from a 'lunatic asylum' in Yorkshire and pointed out that 'his results were of greater value than those of Taylor and Wilkes', because his special thermometer could be read without disturbing its position in the axilla and also because all his estimations began either at the moment of death or even before death took place. Burman's article was the first to exhibit a graph of results, which indicates an almost linear fall over the first 12 hours, with no trace of a plateau. He calculated that the mean drop in temperature was 1.6°F per hour. One of his deaths showed a slight postmortem temperature increase and, in common with the material of many of the early writers, the temperatures at death are often markedly elevated, presumably because of infective disease.

Burman stated that cooling was much faster in the immediate postmortem period because there was no plateau in skin measurements. The mean rate of cooling for hyperthermic bodies was 4.4°F per hour. As a recommendation for calculating the time since death, he advocated dividing the observed drop in temperature in degrees Fahrenheit by his factor of 1.6, which is really the same rule-of-thumb method recommended right up to the present day by some authors. In fact, Burman suggested, in 1880, that the factor be rounded down to 'one and a half' – exactly the figure given in standard books for so many years. To give credit to Burman, he added all the usual cautions and advocated modifying the result according to environment, clothing, etc.

The first author writing in English to move to the Centigrade system was Womack [72], in 1887. Womack used a special mercury thermometer with a flattened bulb of very thin glass, which he strapped to the abdominal wall with white adhesive tape. This obviously gave better results than the Taylor and Wilkes method because it reduced cooling of the bulb by draughts and convection. However, Womack claimed that the thermometer could be read to an accuracy of 'better than a fortieth of a degree', which seems unrealistic even by today's standards, and for 1887, it seems unlikely that comparably exact calibration could have been available.

Womack used sophisticated mathematics, including calculus, to apply Newtonian theory to his 118 cases, and he illustrated his article with several graphs. These he referred to as 'woodcuts', as they were white on a black background – perhaps an early precursor of our 'reverse video'!

Once again, Womack found no initial plateau, as a result of his choice of the skin as a measuring site. Although Womack's paper is an impressive piece of mathematics, it is marred in retrospect by the unrealistic accuracy with which he computed the time of death. In his first illustrative case, he apologized for estimating the time of death as minutes to 5 o'clock, whereas it was really 5 minutes past 5... yet the first temperature reading was not taken until half past 12. In his second example, Womack again calculated to within a few minutes of the true time, more than 5 hours after the death, from 2 skin temperatures taken 30 minutes apart. Over his series of 118 cases, he recorded an accuracy of better than 25 minutes from the true time for 57 deaths – an impossible result given the method used.

One of the best-known of the 'modern' publications in the field of temperature and time of death is that of De Saram et al. [11,12], who carried out their research in Sri Lanka (at that time Ceylon). This work appeared in 1955 and began a new era of investigation in the subject. Some of the interest stemmed possibly from the rather macabre fact that the work was carried out on victims of judicial execution, but the intrinsic worth of the research is undoubted, even though the algorithm produced has never enjoyed widespread use in practice.

De Saram and his collaborators worked in a tropical country where the ambient temperature was high, so their results were not readily applicable to temperate climates. They investigated the cooling rates of 41 executed criminals under strictly observed conditions, by taking hourly rectal temperatures beginning usually an hour after execution.

These investigators noted a 'lag period' or plateau of about 45 minutes and added this to their estimates of time since death arrived at from their calculations. De Saram et al. recommended using a formula that incorporated all the known variables, rather than the use of a general calculation followed by further modifications according to local circumstances. The actual submission is that: 'The time of death (should) be estimated, not, as at present, by a

generalised formula where the influence of modifying factors are assessed, so as to say, empirically, but by the use of a formula which itself embodies the influence of these factors'. De Saram et al. included the humidity of the environment, which in Ceylon varied between 70 and 90 per cent saturation, considering that this was a potent factor in altering the cooling rate. The presence of thick cotton overalls on the bodies was dismissed as having little influence because five of the bodies from a different prison were measured unclothed.

The De Saram formula combined heat losses from convection, radiation and conduction, and the mathematical principles of his methods are discussed in a later chapter of this review. His discussion from first principles is an excellent review of the whole problem and well repays study even from this distance of many years.

In 1956, Lyle and Cleveland [37] entered the scene with new technology in the form of a six-channel thermocouple device that continuously recorded temperatures at a number of sites, these being plotted on a strip chart every minute. These sites were from the skin of the chest, forehead, rectum, liver, brain and thigh muscle. Valuable data were acquired, demonstrating that the rate of heat loss was widely different at different sites, but that extrinsic variables had less effect on brain than on rectal temperature. These investigators also pointed out the well-known fact that time of death could not be determined satisfactorily after 24 hours or where the difference in environmental and body temperature was only a few degrees. Lyle and Cleveland did not derive any practical formula from their work, and the main legacy of this research is some of the actual data from the recordings.

Karl Sellier [63] from the Bonn Institute, published a paper of considerable mathematical complexity in 1958, based on the concept of the infinite cylinder. Most of his work was pure mathematics and heat mechanics, and it was a very useful dissection of the theoretical basis of the problems. Sellier was obviously very much influenced by the work of De Saram et al. [11,12], to whom he referred constantly. He stated that the experimental material in his own Institute was not usable because the environmental temperature was too variable and the bodies did not stay long enough, so he used the data of De Saram for his manipulations.

Sellier made the interesting assertion that the retardation of cooling in fat bodies was not the result of the insulating effect of the 'fatty pads', as he called them, but rather was caused by the fact that the excess adipose tissue increased the radius of his cylinder.

Also in 1958, the seminal paper of Fiddes and Patten [14] appeared, which, like that of De Saram et al. [11,12] is still held up as one of the models of theorizing about the use of temperature in time-of-death estimation. Fiddes and Patten pinned their hopes on assessing the rate of fall of the temperature, by using two or more temperature measurements. They also developed the concept of 'virtual cooling time', this being the time taken to cool through 85 per cent of the difference between normal body temperature (not defined, but assumed to be 37°C) and the environmental temperature. This is discussed in more detail in Chapter 3.

Fiddes and Patten devised a 'percentage cooling rate', in which the fall in temperature from 'normal' is expressed as a percentage of the difference in temperature between 37°C and the ambient. This is calculated for two or more points separated in time, and the postmortem interval calculated by applying the data to a standard graph offered by the authors from 100 known cases. The method can be applied only if the ambient temperature remains constant throughout the whole investigation and if the initial body temperature is assumed to be 37°C (or some other fixed assumption). It may also be noted that when James and Knight [25] used the Fiddes and Patten double-measurement method in their research into errors, they found it to give no added accuracy compared with a simple single-exponential method.

Professor T. K. Marshall [43–48] of Belfast is one of the most prolific writers of recent years (up to the 1970s) and, with several collaborators, produced a doctorate thesis and six other publications on temperature and time since death. The best-known paper is that by Marshall and Hoare [48], published in 1962. The paper showed that a dead body did not cool according to Newtonian principles during the first 12 hours after death. These authors suggested that the deviation from Newton's law is caused by postmortem metabolism and the development of temperature gradients in the surface layers of the body, resulting in a sigmoid rather than single exponential cooling curve. However, after about 12 hours, the curve approximates to an exponential expression and is then amenable to use for postmortem interval calculation because the rate of heat loss is then directly proportional to the excess of temperature of the body over its surroundings.

The rate of cooling per degree of temperature difference (the 'cooling factor') was then said by Marshall to be proportional to the ratio of the effective radiating surface of the corpse to its mass (the 'size factor').

Marshall and Hoare devised a formula, discussed later in this chapter, which expressed two exponential terms: first, the cooling proportional to the excess of the temperature excess of the body over its environment; and second, the influence of modifying factors.

By reference to many experimental results, which provided 'standard cooling curves', the use of this formula was held to provide satisfactory results. Their data have been re-worked several times by other investigators, although with conflicting results. The more recent computer and nomogram methods of Henssge et al. [19–21] described at length in later chapters of this book are substantially based

on Marshall and Hoare material. In the many other papers by Marshall, with and without collaborators, the basic theory was discussed and refined. Perhaps one of the most useful comments of this prolific author is contained in the very last sentence of an article in the *Journal of Forensic Sciences*: 'It would seem that the timing of death by means of temperature can never be more than an approximation' [44].

■ Postmortem electrical excitability of skeletal muscle – historical review

Studies on the electrical excitability of skeletal muscle post mortem began with Luigi Galvani's discovery of 'animal electricity' [15].

The great period of electrophysiology during the nineteenth century was accompanied by many studies on the postmortem electrical excitability of skeletal muscle, studies that were performed mainly by physiologists, but also by French and German pathologists. At the beginning of the nineteenth century, the aim of these studies was mainly to exclude apparent death (Table 2.1), and only those bodies in which electrical excitability had ceased completely were buried [9].

As late as 1872, Rosenthal [62] wrote that the loss of electrical excitability was the most reliable sign of death. However, as early as 1811, Nysten [52] described (in analogy to the onset of rigor mortis – Nysten's rule) the regular loss of electrical excitability in different regions of the body, 'In musculis trunci citius periit irritabilitas, quam in musculis membrorum; musculi extremitatum inferiorum eam citius perdunt quam musculi extremitatum superiorum'. This rule proved to be quite exact in succeeding investigations.

Table 2.1 Development of electrical excitability of skeletal muscle post mortem in the nineteenth century

Galvani	1780 —	Animal electricity.
Klein	1794	
Creve	1796	
Hüpsch	1800	Studies on electrical excitability of
Heidmann	1804	skeletal muscle post mortem to detect
Struwe	1805	and prevent apparent death.
Sommer	1833	
Rosenthal	1872	
Bichat	1800	
Nysten	1811	
Devergie	1841	Studies on electrical excitability of
Harless	1851	skeletal muscle post mortem that
Kölliker	1851	provide some knowledge for
Rosenthal	1871	determining the time since death.
Onimus	1880	

Several papers on anatomical and physiological investigations in executed bodies provided information on the duration of electrical excitability [17,32]. According to these authors, indirect electrical excitability of skeletal muscle ceases some minutes after death. However, Du Bois Reymond (in Kölliker and Virchow) and Kölliker and Virchow [32] saw intensive muscle contractions after exciting the nerve at 1.5 hours post mortem. This finding was confirmed more than 100 years later by Krause *et al.* [34] on amputated limbs. Figure 2.1 shows experiments by Aldini on human bodies after decapitation. Aldini examined the electrical excitability of the muscles of the trunk, limbs and facial muscles of two criminals decapitated in Bologna in 1804 [70].

On direct excitation, excitability remained preserved for several hours, according to Nysten [52], up to 26 hours post mortem. In several executed bodies (decapitation) he was able to detect the following intervals of electrical excitability:

1. Left chamber of the heart: 'short'.
2. Bowel and stomach: 45 minutes.
3. Right chamber of the heart: 3 hours.
4. Oesophagus: 1.5 hours.
5. Iris: 1.75 hours
6. Muscles of the trunk shorter than muscles of the lower limbs shorter than muscles of the upper limbs.

Nysten [52] investigated the influence of the cause of death on electrical excitability in 40 hospital cases and found a loss of electrical excitability after:

- 2.75 hours in cases with peritonitis.
- 3 to 6 hours in cases with phthisis, scirrhus, carcinoma.
- 9 hours in cases of fatal haemorrhage or injuries of the heart.
- 12 hours in cases with apoplexy with paralysis.
- 10 to 15 hours in cases with 'adynamic fever'.
- 13 to 15 hours in cases with pneumonia.
- 5 to 27 hours in cases with aneurysm of the heart.

In 1872, Rosenthal [62] stated that the sphincter palpebrarum remains the longest excitable muscle; this finding was confirmed more than 100 years later by Klein and Klein [27].

The fact that Rosenthal was working in the 1870s indicates that it was recognized quite early that electrical excitability of skeletal muscles may be a suitable method for determining the time since death in the early postmortem interval. This conclusion was also reached by Onimus [53] and Tidy [69]. However, Lochte [36] and Puppe [56] rejected electrical excitability as a method of death-time estimation – Lochte having no experimental experience and Puppe working with already outdated time intervals.

The renaissance of postmortem electrical excitability of skeletal muscles began with investigations stimulated by Prokop [55]. Several papers on the construction of square-wave generators and a large series on human bodies followed [1,4,26–29,33–35,38,49,54,57–59,61,71,73].

Rigor mortis

In 1964 and 1971, Mallach [41,42] published his well-known table on the time course of rigor mortis based on potations in the classical textbooks of forensic medicine. He used also the data of Eduard von Hofmann (1876/77) [22,23], which were some of the rare data from the nineteenth century that could be used for statistical analysis of the time course of rigor mortis. In 1964, Mallach had already calculated mean values and standard deviations for the various degrees of rigor mortis published by von Hofmann. These data are still actual more than 100 years later. At the same time, Niderkorn (1872) [51] published his observation on the time course of rigor mortis. He noticed the time until complete development of rigor mortis. These data could also be used for a statistical analysis and recalculated mean values and standard deviations. The random sample consisted of 113 cases; complete rigor mortis was established after 5.6 hours. The variation was between 2 and 13 hours, and the 95 per cent limits of confidence were between 1.2 and 10.1 hours post mortem. The variations in 95 per cent limits of confidence are quite similar in the case material of von Hofmann and Niderkorn; however, the mean value for complete development of rigor mortis in the case material of von Hofmann is, at 8 hours, much higher than in the material of Niderkorn, at 5.6 hours. One reason may reflect the composition of the case material and the influencing factors on the time course of rigor mortis [39].

Vitreous potassium as a measure of the postmortem interval

Chemical tests for determining the postmortem interval have been largely developed since the 1950s. Among these tests, the most widely used worldwide is the vitreous potassium concentration. Naumann [50], in 1959, was the first who studied extensively the human postmortem vitreous fluid, and he demonstrated a rise in the vitreous potassium values but did not attempt to correlate this increase with the postmortem interval. Since then numerous papers have been published [24], and in 1963 Sturner [67] published his observation on the postmortem rise of vitreous potassium with very narrow 95 per cent limits of confidence in the postmortem interval up to 1 hour post mortem. The development of formulae on vitreous potassium as a measure of the postmortem interval was summarized by Coe [8].

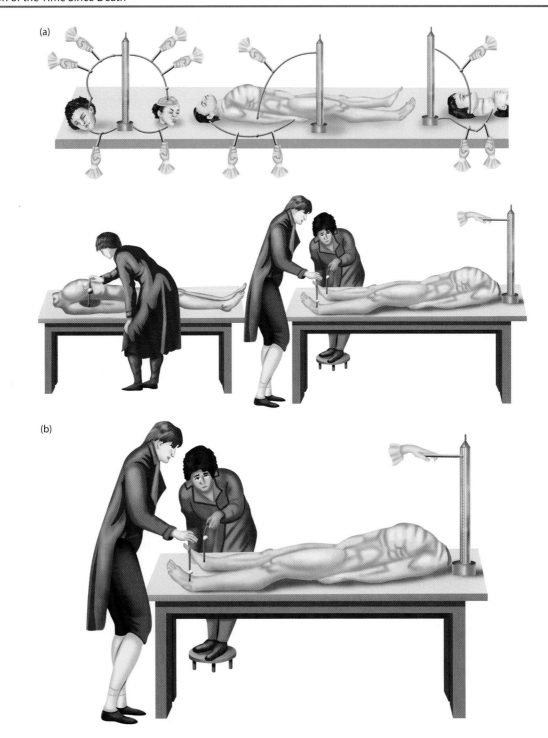

Figure 2.1 (a), (b) and (c) Experiments on electrical excitability of skeletal muscles post mortem conducted after decapitation, by J. Aldini in 1804. Aldini (1762–34) was a nephew of Galvani. After having performed animal experiments he wanted to study further questions regarding 'animal electricity' on human bodies. He thought that the bodies of persons dying of chronic diseases were not suitable for his experiments because the diseases would destroy the 'fibre structure of muscles'. Therefore, he used bodies whose vital force would be preserved after death. 'Therefore I stood so to speak near the scaffold to receive from the hangman's hand the exsanguinated bodies … It was for advantage to me that two criminals in Bologna were decapitated and the government understood my physical curiosity'. The copperplate print shows the experiments being carried out. (*Continued*)

(c)

Figure 2.1 (*Continued*) (a), (b) and (c) Experiments on electrical excitability of skeletal muscles post mortem conducted after decapitation, by J. Aldini in 1804. Aldini (1762–34) was a nephew of Galvani. After having performed animal experiments he wanted to study further questions regarding 'animal electricity' on human bodies. He thought that the bodies of persons dying of chronic diseases were not suitable for his experiments because the diseases would destroy the 'fibre structure of muscles'. Therefore, he used bodies whose vital force would be preserved after death. 'Therefore I stood so to speak near the scaffold to receive from the hangman's hand the exsanguinated bodies … It was for advantage to me that two criminals in Bologna were decapitated and the government understood my physical curiosity'. The copperplate print shows the experiments being carried out.

References

1. Berg S. Nervensysteme und Totenstarre. *Dtsch Z Gerichtl Med* 1948/49;**39**:429–434.

2. Bichat X. *Recherches physiologiques sur la vie et la mort* (1800). German trans. Barth JA, Leipzig, 1912.

3. Billroth T, Fick A. Postmortale Temperatursteigerung. *Vierteljahresschr Naturforsch Ges (Zürich)* **VIII B**, 1863.

4. Böhm E. Anmerkungen zu Reizbarkeit und Starreeintritt der Skelettmuskulatur. *Beitr Gerichtl Med* 1986;**44**:439–450.

5. Brown A, Marshall T. Body temperature as a means of estimating the time of death. *Forensic Sci Int* 1974;**4**:125–133.

6. Burman J. On the rate of cooling of the human body after death. *Edinb Med J* 1880;**25**:993–1003.

7. Casper J. *Praktisches Handbuch der gerichtlichen Medizin.* Berlin, 1857.

8. Coe JI. Vitreous potassium as a measure of the postmortem interval: an historical review and critical evaluation. *Forensic Sci Int* 1989;**42**:201–213.

9. Creve CC. *Vom Metallreize, einem neuentdeckten untrüglichen Prüfungsmittel des wahren Todes.* Leipzig und Gera, Germany, 1796.

10. Davey J. Observations on the temperature of the human body after death. *Res Physiol Anat (Lond)* 1839;**1**:228–248.

11. De Saram G. Estimation of death by medical criteria. *J Forensic Med* 1957;**4**(2):47.

12. De Saram G, Webster G, Kathirgamatamby N. Post-mortem temperature and the time of death. *J Crim Law Criminol Police Sci* 1955;**1**:562–577.

13. Dittrich, Gerlach, Herz. Beobachtungen an den Leichen von 2 Hingerichteten. *Prag Vierteljahresschr* 1851;**31B**.

14. Fiddes F, Patten TA. Percentage method for representing the fall in body temperature after death. *J Forensic Med* 1958;**5**:2–15.

15. Galvani L. Cited by Rothschuh KE. In: *Physiologie. Der Wandel ihrer Konzepte, Probleme und Methoden vom 16. bis 20. Jahrhundert.* Freiburg-München, Germany, Karl Alber, 1968.

16. Goodhard JF. Thermoelectric observations in clinical medicine. *Guy's Hosp Rep* 1870;**15**:365–419.

17. Harless E. Untersuchungen an einem Hingerichteten. *Jenaer Analen II* 2, 1850; Zit. nach *Schmids Jahrbuch* 1851;**72**:10–11.

18. Hensley B. Experiments on the temperature of bodies after death. *The Medical Examiner (Philadelphia)* 1846;**2**:149–152.

19. Henssge C. *Methoden zur Bestimmung der Todeszeit-Leichenabkühlung und Todeszeitbestimmung.* Dissertation B. Berlin, Humboldt University, Berlin, 1982.

20. Henssge C. Death time estimation in case work. I. The rectal temperature time of death nomogram. *Forensic Sci Int* 1988;**38**:209–236.

21. Henssge C, Madea B, Gallenkemper E. Death time estimation in casework; integration of different methods. *Forensic Sci Int* 1988;**38**:77–87.

22. Hofmann E v. Die forensisch wichtigsten Leichenerscheinungen. *Vierteljahresschr Gerichtl Med* 1876;**25**:229–261.

23. Hofmann E v. Die forensisch wichtigsten Leichenerscheinungen. *Vierteljahresschr Gerichtl Med* 1877;**26**:17–40.

24. Jaffe FA. Chemical post-mortem changes in the intraocular fluid. *J Forensic Sci* 1962;**7**:231–237.

25. James W, Knight B. Errors in estimating time since death. *Med Sci Law* 1965;**5**:111–116.

26. Joachim H, Feldmann U. Eine quantitative Methode der Todeszeitbestimmung durch Untersuchung der galvanischen Reizschwelle. *Z Rechtsmed* 1980;**85**:5–22.

27. Klein A, Klein S. *Die Todeszeitbestimmung am menschlichen Auge.* Medical Dissertation, B, Dresden, Germany, Medical Academy, 1978.

28. Klein A, Krause D, Hamann B. Praktische Erfahrungen mit einem neuen elektronischen Reizgerät zur Todeszeitbestimmung. *Kriminal Forens Wiss* 1975;**19**:126.

29. Kliese U, Henssge C, Madea B. Reizgenerator zur Prüfung der elektrischen Erregbarkeit der Skelettmuskulatur. Unpublished manuscript, 1985.
30. Knight B. The evolution of methods for estimating the time of death from body temperature. *Forensic Sci Int* 1988;**36**:47–55.
31. Knight B. *Forensic Pathology.* London, Edward Arnold, 1991.
32. Kölliker A, Virchow R. Über einige an der Leiche eines Hingerichteten angestellte Versuche und Beobachtungen. *Wiss Zool* 1851;**III**:37–52.
33. Krause D, Klein A, Mattig W, Waltz H. Praktische Erfahrungen mit dem Reizgerät D 76 zur Todeszeitbestimmung. *Kriminal Forens Wiss* 1980;**40**:83–86.
34. Krause D, Klein A, Zett L. Todeszeitbestimmung mittels indirekter Muskelreizung über den N. ischiadicus und N. radialis. *Kriminal Forens Wiss* 1976;**26**:66–67.
35. Krause D, Schöning R, Kuchheuser W. Stimulator M 85 – Ein kommerzielles Reizgerät zur Todeszeitbestimmung. In: Liebhardt E, Schuck M, Eisenmenger W (eds.). *Medizin und Recht. Festschrift fur Wolfgang Spann.* Berlin, Springer, 1986, pp 639–644.
36. Lochte Th. Über die Absterbeerscheinungen der Skelettmuskulatur, insbesondere über die Totenstarre in gerichtlich-medizinischer Beziehung. *Z Ges Gerichtl Med* 1923;**2**:169–190.
37. Lyle H, Cleveland F. Determination of the time since death by heat loss. *J Forensic Sci* 1956;**1**:11–24.
38. Madea B. *Supravitale elektrische Erregbarkeit der Skelettmuskulatur: Längsschnittuntersuchungen zur Objektivierung der muskulären Reaktion an 70 Leichen.* Cologne, Germany, Habil. Schrift, 1989.
39. Madea B, Henssge C. Historisches zur Todeszeitbestimmung. *Z Rechtsmed* 1985;**95**:19–25.
40. Madea B, Henssge C, Honig W, Gerbracht A. References for determining the time of death by potassium in vitreous humor. *Forensic Sci Int* 1989;**8**:231–243.
41. Mallach HJ. Zur Frage der Todeszeitbestimmung. *Berl Med* 1964;**18**:577–582.
42. Mallach HJ, Mittermeyer HJ. Totenstarre und Totenflecke. *Z Rechtsmed* 1971;**69**:70–78.
43. Marshall T. *The Cooling of the Body After Death.* MD thesis. Leeds, University of Leeds, 1960.
44. Marshall T. Estimating the time of death. *J Forensic Sci* 1962;**7**:189–210.
45. Marshall T. Estimating the time of death. *J Forensic Sci* 1962;**7**:210–221.
46. Marshall T. Temperature methods of estimating the time of death. *Med Sci Law* 1965;**5**:224–232.
47. Marshall T. The use of body temperature in estimating the time of death and its limitations. *Med Sci Law* 1969;**9**:178–182.
48. Marshall T, Hoare F. Estimating the time of death: the rectal cooling after death and its mathematical representation. *J Forensic Sci* 1962;**7**:56–81.
49. Nagy J. The postmortem excitability of the skeletal muscles. *Acta Med Leg Soc (Liege)* 1968:177–178.
50. Naumann HN. Postmortem chemistry of the vitreous body in man. *Arch Ophthalmol* 1959;**62**:356–363.
51. Niderkorn PF (1872). Zitiert nach Tidy CM. The period of cadaveric rigidity (rigor mortis). *Legal Medicine,* vol. 1. London, Smith Elder, 1882, pp 62–69.
52. Nysten PH. Von der Erstarrung, welche die Körper der Menschen und Tiere nach dem Tode befällt. *Recherches de physiologie et chemie pathologique,* Paris, 1811. German trans. and with additional material by Mayer AC, Bern. *Huieland-Journal* 1816;43.
53. Onimus M. Modification de l'excitabilité des nerfs et des muscles après la mort. *J Anat Physiol Normale Pathol* 1880:629.
54. Popwassilew J, Palm W. Über die Todeszeitbestimmung in den ersten 10 Stunden. *Z Arztl Fortbild* 1960;**54**:734–737.
55. Prokop O. *Lehrbuch der gerichtlichen Medizin.* Berlin, Verlag Volk und Gesundheit, 1960.
56. Puppe G. Der Scheintod und seine Diagnose. *Med Wochenschr* 1920;14/**15**:383–385.
57. Radam G. Ein elektronisches Reizgerät zur Todeszeitbestimmung. *Gesundheitswes* 1963;**18**:1400–1401.
58. Ravache-Quiriny J. The time of death: some thoughts on the trustworthiness of our response. *Int Acad Leg Med Soc Med* 1982;**1**(Newsletter):9–11.
59. Ravache-Quiriny J. *Les moments de la mort. Cahiers de médicine légale, droits medicales no. 3: Association Lyonnaise Médicine legale.* Lyon, Editions Alesandre Lacasagne, 1986.
60. Rainy H. On the cooling of dead bodies as indicating the length of time since death. *Glasg Med J* 1868;**1**:323–330.
61. Raszeja S, Bardzik S. Studies on the "intralethal" excitability of muscles following stimuli obtained from an electronic stimulator. *Bull Pol Med Sci Hist* 1971;**14**:93.
62. Rosenthal M. Untersuchungen und Beobachtungen über das Absterben der Muskeln und den Scheintod. *Wiener Medizinisches Jahrbuch* 1872:389–413.
63. Sellier K. Determination of the time of death by extrapolation of the temperature decrease curve. *Acta Med Leg Soc* 1958;**2**:279–301.
64. Seydeler R. Nekrothermometrie. *Prag Vierteljahresschr* 1869;**104B**:137–148.
65. Shapiro H. Medico-legal mythology: the time of death. *J Forensic Med* 1954;**1**(3) 1–159.
66. Shapiro H. The post-mortem temperature plateau. *J Forensic Med* 1965;**12**:137–41.
67. Sturner WQ. The vitreous humour: post-mortem potassium changes. *The Lancet* 1963;**1**:807–808.
68. Taylor A, Wilkes D. On the cooling of the human body after death. *Guy's Hosp Rep* 1863;**9**:180–211.
69. Tidy CM. Changes in the muscle and in the general condition of the body after death. *Legal Medicine.* Part 1. London, Smith-Elder, 1882.
70. Vogt H. *Das Bild des Kranken.* Munich, Germany, JF Bergman, 1980.
71. Waltz H, Mattig W. Elektrische Messungen an Leichen für die Konstruktion eines elektronischen Reizgerätes zur Todeszeitbestimmung. *Kriminal Forens Wiss* 1974;**16**:159–178.
72. Womack F. The rate of cooling of the body after death. *St Barts Hosp Rep* 1887;**23**:193–200.
73. Zink P, Reinhardt G. Die Todeszeitbestimmung bei der ärztlichen Leichenschau. *Bayer Arztebl* 1972;**27**:109–115.

3 Supravitality in Tissues

Burkhard Madea

As far as we know, the last review in the English literature on determination of the time since death in the early postmortem interval (dealing also in detail with supravital reactions) was published by Schleyer in 1963 in Volume II of Lundquist's *Methods of Forensic Science* [64]. Since then, much work has been carried out on supravital reactions, and some progress has been made. This, and the fact that many scientific papers in this field have been published in German, may justify a new review on supravital reactions in English. Those supravital reactions that are of practical value in casework (mechanical excitability of skeletal muscles, electrical excitability of skeletal muscle with subjective grading of muscular contraction, chemical excitability of the iris) are mentioned briefly again in Chapter 10.

The objective of this chapter is to present some basic considerations on supravitality, to review the work on mechanical and electrical excitability of skeletal muscles and to present some recent longitudinal studies on electrical excitability that have no current practical value in casework but may be of some heuristic interest and may also form the basis of future work on influencing factors. A complete summary of supravital reactions was published in German in 1988 by Henssge and Madea [15].

3.1 Definitions

Irreversible circulatory arrest represents the starting point for a period of survival of some tissues under the condition of global ischaemia; this is called the 'supravital period' or 'intermediary life'.

Investigations on global ischaemia in various organs have been performed mainly with regard to the survival period and to the resuscitation period (Figure 3.1) [5,9,21,30,47–49,63,65,66].

The *latency period* is defined as an undisturbed period characterized by continuing aerobic energy production.

The *survival period* is the interval up to the point after which every aspect of life ceases. During the survival period, there is still spontaneous activity of organs (e.g. spontaneous but decreasing myocardial contractility), as well as reagibility (e.g. the response of muscles to stimulation) on excitation (e.g. evoked potentials on acoustic stimulation, nerve action potentials on electrical stimulation of nerves) [13,16–20,72].

The *resuscitation period* is the duration of global ischaemia after which the ability to recover expires. The resuscitation period is mainly defined as the interval when

complete recovery of morphological, functional and biochemical parameters in the postischaemic period is possible. The time required for complete recovery of these parameters is the 'recovering time'. The latency period is limited by the oxygen reserve as the basis of aerobic energy production characterized biochemically by the exhaustion of creatinine phosphate and a small decrease of adenosine triphosphate (ATP). During the resuscitation period, there is a breakdown of ATP to less than 60 per cent of the normal value and a steep increase in lactic acid (Figure 3.2) [9,70].

Ischaemia, resulting in cessation of nutrition and waste product removal, not only causes reversible consequences – 'effects' – but also, after a longer duration, results in irreversible changes – 'damage'.

The end of the resuscitation period demarcates both these steps of deficiency – reversible effects and irreversible damage [5,47,49,65].

Although 'survival period' and 'resuscitation period' are terms of great importance in physiology, organ preservation and transplantation because they describe the maximal ischaemic damage that is completely reversible in terms of structure and function, forensic medicine is also interested in the subsequent period – the period characterized by increasingly irreversible damage to structures and functions.

Although the definition of the resuscitation period of organs and tissues is based on complete recovery of different functional and biochemical parameters in the post-ischaemic period, supravitality is mainly defined by reagibility on excitation in the ischaemic period itself, irrespective of whether the damage to function is reversible (Figure 3.3).

As a result, the data on the duration of the resuscitation period on the one hand, and the supravital period on the other, are not comparable. The resuscitation period of skeletal muscles under normothermic conditions is 2 to 3 hours; supravital reagibility of skeletal muscles may be maintained in some cases for up to 20 hours post mortem [8,25,33,40].

The resuscitation period of the heart under normothermia is 3.5 to 4 minutes (without cardiac massage in the postischaemic period), but supravital electrical excitability of cardiac muscle, according to Raule *et al.* [59], is preserved for up to 100 to 120 minutes post mortem.

One difference between the resuscitation period and the supravital period is described by the 'reversibility/irreversibility' of damage. Another important difference is that physiologists and experimental surgeons are working on the restoration of the function of organs after ischaemic

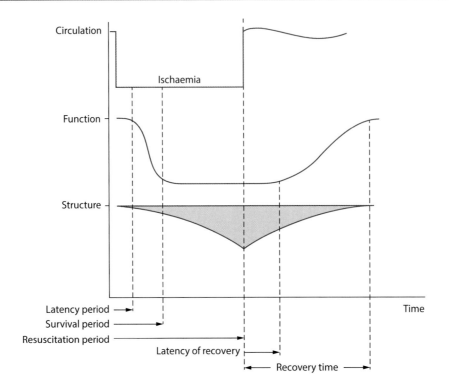

Figure 3.1   Survival and resuscitation periods of organs after temporary global ischaemia and reperfusion.

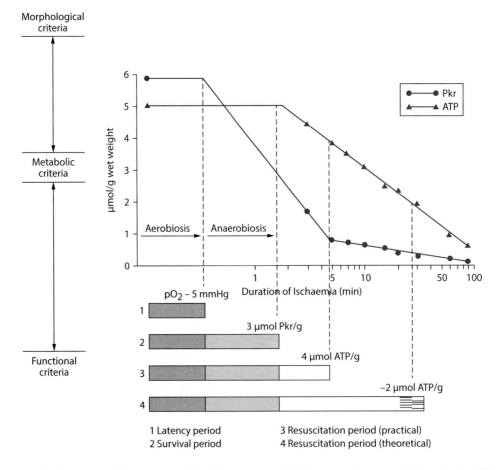

Figure 3.2   Latency, survival and resuscitation periods of the heart compared with the state of energy-rich phosphates. ATP, adenosine triphosphate; [18]Pkr, phosphocreatine.

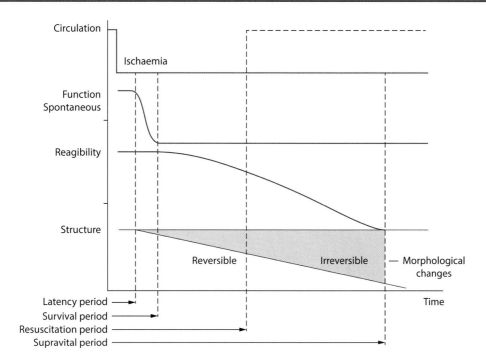

Figure 3.3 Postmortem course of functions (spontaneous function and reagibility) and structures after continuous global ischaemia (compare this with Figure 3.1).

damage within an intact organ system, whereas forensic medicine is concerned with the functions of tissues because organ functions cannot be restored after an irreversible loss of the function of the major systems and their coordination.

Supravitality is compared with the resuscitation period the longer the survival on a morphologically deeper step of organization. On a yet deeper step (the cell) reagibility of the myofibrils may be preserved even longer than in tissues.

Up to 104 days post mortem, muscle cells in frozen muscle pulp may react to ATP administration with strong contractions; weak contractions end after 5 minutes [50].

■ Spontaneous supravital activity

These introductory definitions are not only of theoretical value but may also be of great practical importance, for instance, in cases where spontaneous supravital activity is in question.

This can be illustrated by a short case history published in *Medicine, Science and the Law* [46]. A 78-year-old woman – cause of death spontaneous cerebral haemorrhage – displayed coordinated motor movements of her right lower limb, especially of the right foot, for 2 hours post mortem. These motor movements were thought to be coordinated by the spinal cord and are analogous to movements of the decapitated chicken. However, this interpretation of the authors requires that, at 2 hours post mortem, spontaneous activity of the spinal cord and of peripheral

nerves is still preserved. According to all basic investigations on the supravital period and resuscitation period of spinal cord and nerves, spontaneous activity of spinal cord tissue is impossible 2 hours post mortem [6,28,63,72].

In my opinion, there was no spontaneous supravital activity; this was the spontaneous activity of a woman still alive but who was declared dead.

■ Supravital reagibility

From the definition of supravital reactions – obtainable vital reaction patterns of special tissues on proper excitations beyond individual death – it becomes evident that no fixed postmortem interval can be given for the supravital period.

The supravital period is specific for each tissue; it depends on the tissue-specific metabolism (enzymes, substrates) under the condition of global ischaemia. Within the same tissue, it depends on the topographical localization within the body (different cooling velocity at different sites of the body depending on the diameter). Finally, the postmortem duration of supravital reagibility depends on the mode of excitation and recording of the reaction (Figure 3.4). For instance, Popwassilew and Palm [51] reported the maximum duration of electrical excitability of the thenar muscles to be 5.5 hours post mortem, whereas in my own investigations, with different modes of excitation and by objectifying muscular contractions of thenar muscles, reactions could be obtained up to 13 to 15 hours post mortem (see page 32).

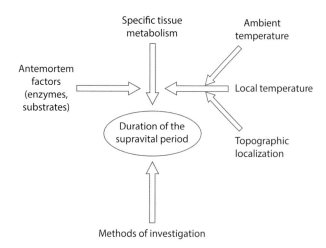

Figure 3.4 Factors determining the time course of supravitality.

■ Supravital metabolism

The basis of supravital reactions is the vital metabolism, which, after death, runs down until substrates (e.g. glycogen) are exhausted or (and just as important) until reaction-limiting changes of the milieu intérieur cease (e.g. cessation of anaerobic glycolysis at pH 6.3).

Postmortem anaerobic glycolytic metabolism proceeds at a high rate during the first 10 hours post mortem, but only at a low rate thereafter. Correspondingly, lactic acid shows its steepest increase within the first 6 to 8 hours post mortem, as shown by Schourup [67] in cerebrospinal fluid (Figure 3.5). In contrast, the pH shows its steepest

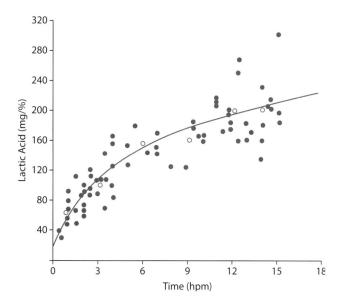

Figure 3.5 Lactic acid in mg per cent of cerebrospinal fluid over the postmortem interval. Closed circles, single values; open circles, mean values. hpm, hours post mortem. (From Schourup K. *Determination of the Time Since Death* (Danish, English summary). Medical dissertation, Copenhagen, 1950.)

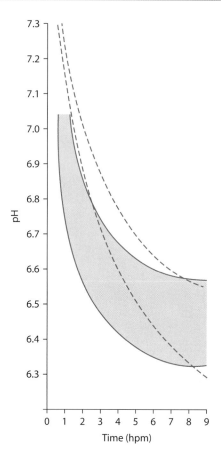

Figure 3.6 pH of cerebrospinal fluid (dashed lines) and heart blood (shaded area) in the first 9 hours post mortem (hpm). (From Dotzauer G, Naeve W. Wasserstoffionenkonzentration im Liquor post mortem. *Zentralbl Allg Pathol Anat* 1959;**100:**516–524.)

decrease in the same time interval (Figure 3.6) [12], the decrease of the blood in the heart being steeper than that of the blood in the peripheral veins. This finding can be attributed to the higher glycogen content of heart muscle and to the different cooling velocity at central and peripheral measuring points, as shown by Dotzauer and Naeve [11].

During the first 10 hours post mortem, the partial pressure of carbon dioxide (pCO_2) shows its steepest increase, as well as the accumulation of lactic acid, as was shown in vitreous humour by Klein and Klein [25]. After 10 hours post mortem, the pCO_2 is decreasing very slowly by diffusion; even after 120 hours post mortem, it has not yet reached its original level.

Although blood gases and substrates and metabolites of anaerobic glycolytic metabolism show the most marked changes of concentration within the first 10 hours post mortem, all authors agree that these parameters are of only limited value for determining the time since death because of the great interindividual variability.

The interindividual variability of supravital reactions cannot, of course, be smaller than that of the substrates and metabolites of the basic metabolic processes [15].

▪ Physiological peculiarities of supravital reagibility

The smooth iris muscle is reactive to electrical and pharmacological stimulation for a longer time period than skeletal muscles. Klein and Klein [25] presented extensive experimental data on death time estimation using the smooth iris muscle (electrical and pharmacological stimulation). These authors examined 18 different pupillomotor drugs in different concentrations. The onsets of reactions vary between 5 and 30 minutes; the reactions lasted at least 1 hour. The drug concentrations had no influence on the durations and strengths of reaction. The onsets of reaction were later with increasing postmortem intervals, the maximum reactions being reached later; the intensities of reactions (pupil dilatation in millimetres) decreased with an increasing postmortem interval (Table 3.1 and Figure 3.7). The postmortem pharmacological excitability to adrenaline, atropine and cyclopentolate covers three different postmortem intervals; additionally, adrenaline and acetylcholine have the longest postmortem efficiencies (Table 3.2). For practical use of pharmacological excitability of the iris in casework, see Chapter 10.

The strongest and longest postmortem effects of acetylcholine and noradrenaline, as the natural transmitters of cholinergic and adrenergic fibres, reflect Cannon and Rosenblueth's law of denervation. According to this law, each denervated structure becomes supersensitive to the humoral mediator. This supersensitivity also becomes evident from the concentration of the drugs used in the cadaver experiments, which would cause no change or only a small change in the pupillary diameter in living individuals.

The physiological mechanism of supersensitivity of denervated smooth muscles to adrenergic drugs is related to the loss of the main mechanism for the regulation of adrenergic drugs at the receptor–neuronal re-uptake. It is a presynaptic specific supersensitivity (Figure 3.8).

For acetylcholine, the physiological mechanism of supersensitivity after denervation is a decrease in activity of the cholinesterase.

Discussing Cannon and Rosenblueth's law of denervation, we have seen that denervated structures may be supersensitive to physiological excitations; however, other tissues, with increasing postmortem intervals, need much stronger excitations than vital tissues. Although impulses 0.2 millisecond in duration are a common means of excitation in clinical neurophysiology, skeletal muscle fails to react 2 hours post mortem to a stimulus of such a short duration, whereas impulses 1 second in duration stimulate muscular contractions (Figure 3.9) (see page 23).

Table 3.1 Pharmacological excitability of the iris

Investigation of 5765 eyes from bodies.

Subconjunctival injection instead of injection into the anterior chamber; reaction after 5–30 minutes.

Duration of reaction at least 1 hour.

Concentration of drugs has no influence on the intensity and duration of reaction.

Data from Klein A, Klein S. *Die Todeszeitbestimmung am menschlichen Auge.* Dresden, Germany, Medical Academy, Dresden University, MD thesis, 1978.

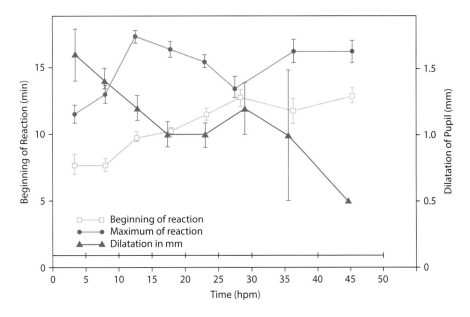

Figure 3.7 Postmortem excitability of the iris after injection of noradrenaline. x axis = hours post mortem (hpm); left y axis = beginning of the reaction after injection (in minutes); right y axis = dilatation of pupil (in millimetres). For each classified time interval the mean value and 95 per cent confidence limits are given. (The figure is designed using original data from Klein A, Klein S. *Die Todeszeitbestimmung am menschlichen Auge.* Dresden, Germany, Medical Academy, Dresden University, MD thesis, 1978.)

Table 3.2 Pharmacological excitability of the iris: postmortem duration of excitability after injection of different drugs*

		Number of bodies postmortem excitability (h)	Subconjunctival (n)	Anterior chamber (n)
Mydriatica				
Noradrenaline/ adrenaline	1.00%	14–46	573	737
Tropicamide	0.25%	5–30	307	320
Atropine/ cyclopentolate	1%/0.50%	3–10	131	145
Miotica				
Acetylcholine	5.00%	14–46	586	721

* In two cases there was no mydriasis in the interval 3 to 12 hours post mortem.

Although muscular contractions on mechanical excitation in the early postmortem interval are characterized by contraction of the whole muscle (i.e. propagated excitation), with an increasing postmortem interval the contraction is confined to the place of excitation; a local contraction called 'idiomuscular contraction' or 'idiomuscular pad' then results [10,23,27,44,69]. This change from propagated excitation to local contraction can also be seen after electrical excitation in both skeletal and smooth muscles [25].

For instance, on electrical excitation, in the early postmortem interval the smooth iris muscle reacts by a miosis (propagated excitation), but in the later postmortem interval there is only a drawing out of muscle fibres into the direction of the electrodes – a local contraction (Figure 3.10).

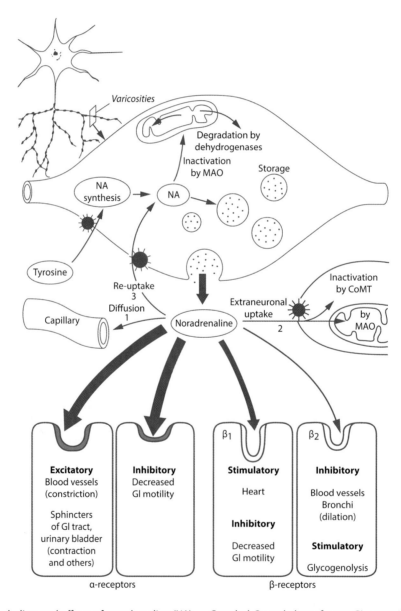

Figure 3.8 Synthesis, metabolism and effects of noradrenaline (NA). Neuronal re-uptake (3) is the main mechanism for the regulation of adrenergic activity at the receptor; it ceases after denervation. CoMT, Catechol-O-methyltransferase; GI, gastrointestinal; MAO, monoamine oxidase. (Data from Silbernagel S, Despopoulos A. *Taschenatlas der Physiologie,* 3rd ed. Stuttgart, Germany, Thieme, 1988.)

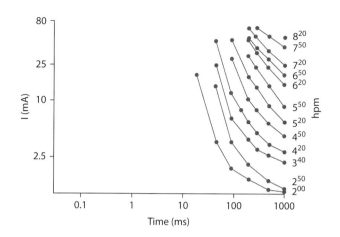

Figure 3.9 Strength-duration curve. y axis = current intensity (in In milliamperes); x axis = duration of stimulus in milliseconds. At the right: time of death in hours and minutes. Using stimuli with a duration of less than 10 milliseconds, at 2 hours post mortem (hpm) no muscular reaction can be obtained.

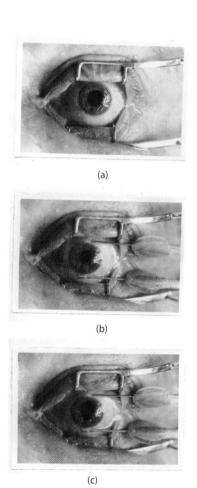

(a)

(b)

(c)

Figure 3.10 Electrical excitability of the iris. (a) Pupil before excitation. (b) Miosis after excitation (propagated excitation). (c) Drawing out of the pupil in the direction of the electrodes (local contraction). (From Klein A, Klein S. *Die Todeszeitbestimmung am menschlichen Auge*. Dresden, Germany, Medical Academy, Dresden University, MD thesis, 1978.)

Decreasing ciliary motility of nasal cells or cells of the respiratory tract, as well as motility of spermatozoa, as supravital phenomena with potential importance for estimating the time since death have already been described in the older literature. More recently, the working group around Romanelli and Solarino *et al.* [62] carried out *in vitro* experiments on nasal ciliary motility. These investigators evaluated the diagnostic usefulness of ciliary motility as a potential tool in estimating the time since death. Specimens of ciliated epithelium from 100 consecutive bodies were obtained by scraping the nasal mucosa at three different postmortem intervals. The samples were then smeared on a slide, and an *in vitro* evaluation of ciliary movement was analyzed by phase-contrast microscopy. Postmortem nasal ciliary motility was observed, and a statistically significant relationship between decreasing ciliary movements and increasing postmortem interval was detected even in the presence of putrefactive changes to nasal ultrastructure integrity. Some peculiar causes of death seemed to influence ciliary motility in the early postmortem interval, whereas no significant correlations with gender or age were observed. According to the results of this study by Romanelli *et al.* [62], postmortem evaluation of nasal ciliary motility should be studied further.

These few comments on supravitality can be summarized as follows:

1. Supravitality, especially reagibility on excitation, covers a much longer postmortem period than latency, survival and resuscitation times. Clinically oriented investigations on latency, survival and resuscitation periods may form the only scientifically safe basis for the explanation of spontaneous supravital activity, but they do not provide an explanation for the upper margin for vital actions and reactions beyond the end of the resuscitation period. The portion of the supravital period beyond the end of the resuscitation period requires further scientific investigation.

2. The correlation of functional and biochemical parameters, which have been investigated for the latency, survival and resuscitation periods, should be extended over the whole supravital period. The aim of these investigations would be to improve the precision of death time estimation using supravital reactions, by narrowing the great interindividual variability of supravital reagibility by considering complementary parameters of metabolism.

3. With an increasing postmortem interval, the supravital reaction pattern differs not only quantitatively but also qualitatively from physiological conditions. Investigations of supravital reagibility should address this issue, with the aim of extending the investigations over a postmortem period for as long as possible.

3.2   Postmortem mechanical excitation of skeletal muscle

Zsako's phenomenon [74,75] and the idiomuscular contraction [10] are different phases of the postmortem mechanical excitability of skeletal muscles. Whereas Zsako's phenomenon seems to be a propagated excitation of muscle fibres, the idiomuscular contraction or idiomuscular pad is a local contraction of the muscle.

Investigations on postmortem mechanical excitability of skeletal muscles were mainly carried out during the nineteenth century and during the first half of the twentieth century [10,44,51,53,68,74,75] (the more recent investigations are listed in Table 3.3).

In these older investigations, different muscles were investigated and different modes of excitation were used (including pinching and hitting with the hand, the back of the hand, the back of a knife or a chisel). The heavier the blow, the stronger is the reaction. Different names were used for the same phenomenon, for instance 'Zsako's muscle phenomenon', which is just a propagated contraction of the muscle after mechanical excitation in the very early postmortem interval. Some authors confined their experiments to the very early postmortem period [74,75], and they recommended as many as eight different locations to examine this phenomenon (Figure 3.11); however, clear values for the duration of postmortem excitability of these different muscles are lacking. Therefore, the literature on mechanical excitation of skeletal muscles is somewhat confusing, and different studies are hardly comparable. For practical use, the extensive studies on idiomuscular contraction by Dotzauer [10] and by Popwassilew and Palm [51] should be considered because they present relatively detailed information on the mode of excitation and the results obtained (Table 3.4 and Figure 3.12; see also Figure 3.11).

According to Dotzauer [10] and the detailed review of Joachim [23] on postmortem mechanical excitability of skeletal muscle, three phases or degrees of mechanical excitability of skeletal muscles can be distinguished (see Figure 3.11; Table 3.5):

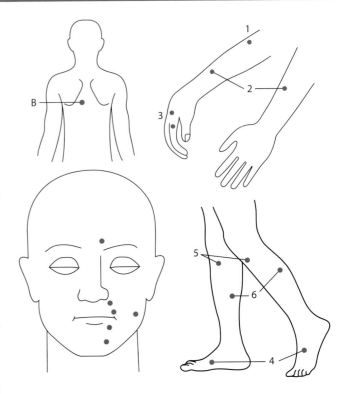

Figure 3.11   Examining Zsako's phenomenon (mechanical excitability of skeletal muscle in the very early postmortem interval). The points give the places where optimum reactions can be obtained. (From Joachim H. Mechanische und elektrische Erregbarkeit der Skelettmuskulatur. In: Henssge C, Madea B (eds.). *Methoden zur Bestimmung der Todeszeit an Leichen.* Lübeck, Schmidt-Römhild, 1988, pp 32–82.)

1. In the first phase, mechanical excitation of the muscle reveals a contraction of the whole muscle (propagated excitation). This first phase of idiomuscular contraction is identical to Zsako's muscle phenomenon [74,75]. Zsako himself gave eight methods of examining the mechanical excitability of skeletal muscles at different regions of the body (see Figure 3.11). Although these methods are quoted in the literature, very few investigators seem to have experience with Zsako's methods, as stated by Dotzauer [10]. Prokop [53] recommended the following procedure for

Table 3.3   **Investigations on idiomuscular pad with random samples, muscles investigated and results obtained**

Reference	Random sample	Results	Muscles investigated
Näcke [44]	20 mentally ill men	Mechanical excitability of skeletal muscles expired after 3–4 hours.	Mimic muscles, neck muscles, limb muscles
Dotzauer [10]	595 examinations on 176 bodies	Idiomuscular pad can be induced up to 12 hpm; $\bar{x} = 6.9$ hpm.	M. pectoralis M. deltoideus M. biceps brachii
Popwassilew and Palm [51]	60 examinations	Idiomuscular pad can be induced in the interval of 1.5–8 hpm; $\bar{x} = 4.25$ hpm.	M. biceps brachii
Semmler [68]	102 bodies	2 hpm idiomuscular pad positive in 90.3%, 8 hpm negative in all cases; $\bar{x} = 4.21$ hpm.	Right thigh

hpm, hours post mortem; M., musculus; $\bar{x}$, mean value.

Table 3.4 Postmortem mechanical excitability

Zsako's phenomenon/idiomuscular pad	Grading	
	++	+
Idiomuscular pad	0–5.5	1.5–8
(Musculus biceps brachii)	$\bar{x} = 2.25$	$\bar{x} = 4.25$
	n = 77	n = 60
Zsako's phenomenon		0–2.5
Hitting on the musculi interossei at the back of the hand		$\bar{x} = 1.5$
Hitting on the musculus quadriceps femoris		n = 41

+, only weak reaction, idiomuscular pad just to touch; ++, stronger reaction, idiomuscular pad is good, visible; $\bar{x}$, mean value.

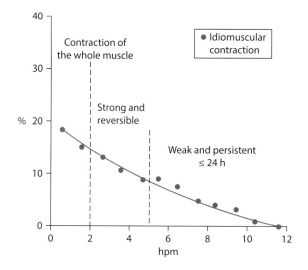

Figure 3.12 Percentage frequency of positive results in mechanical excitability of skeletal muscles. The mechanical excitability is graded in three phases (see also Table 3.5). hpm, hours post mortem.

Zsako's method: Hit the lower third of the thigh with four to five cross-fingers above the patella. This first degree of idiomuscular contraction (propagated excitation) can be seen up to 1.5 to 2.5 hours post mortem [10,23]. Figures 3.13 and 3.14 show the frequency of idiomuscular contraction post mortem within three temperature classes.

2. In the second phase, a strong and typically reversible idiomuscular pad develops. This phase may be seen

Table 3.5 Mode of excitation and grading of the three phases of postmortem mechanical excitability of skeletal muscles

Mode of excitation: hitting vigorously with the back of a knife or a chisel on the musculus biceps brachii at a right angle to the arm axis	
Phase one	Contraction of the whole muscle; 1.5–2.5 hpm.
Phase two	Strong and typical reversible idiomuscular pad; 4–5 hpm.
Phase three	Weak idiomuscular pad which may persist for a longer period (up to 24 hours); 8–12 hpm.

as long as 4 to 5 hours post mortem. The mechanical excitation of the muscle causes membrane depolarization. The shortening of the muscle spreads very slowly, at only 0.2 cm/second, over the whole length of the muscle; the duration of shortening is 0.7 second. Shortening is initiated by action potentials. The local excitation and contraction comprise a relatively stable process, with mechanical excitability lasting longer than electrical excitability, according to older literature as referenced by Dotzauer [10].

3. In the last phase, a weak idiomuscular pad develops which may persist over a rather long period (up to 24 hours). The weak idiomuscular pad can be seen in the time interval up to 8 to 12 hours post mortem.

Semmler [68], working on the influence of ambient temperatures on the duration of electrical excitability also examined idiomuscular contractions and Zsako's phenomenon. The idiomuscular pad was examined by hitting on the right thigh with a reflex hammer. At about 2 hours post mortem, an idiomuscular pad was present in 90.3 per cent of the bodies investigated; at 8 hours post mortem it was absent in all of the 102 bodies (median value, 4.21 hours post mortem). No temperature dependency of the idiomuscular pad could be demonstrated (see Figure 3.13). The shorter time period in which an idiomuscular pad could be demonstrated in Semmler's study compared with Dotzauer's study [10] may reflect the composition of the samples. Dotzauer worked on forensic pathology material, and Semmler studied clinical pathology material.

Zsako's phenomenon was also investigated by hitting the interosseous muscles between metacarpals 3 and 4 with a reflex hammer. At 2 hours post mortem, Zsako's phenomenon was seen in 35.5 per cent of all bodies, but at 3 hours post mortem only two bodies showed positive results, and at 4 hours post mortem, none had positive results for this phenomenon. (Figure 3.14 shows the frequency of Zsako's phenomenon.) For practical use regarding death time estimation in casework, we recommend that the data in Table 3.5 should be used.

3.3 Postmortem electrical excitability of skeletal muscles in casework

■ Current state

The renaissance of postmortem electrical excitability of skeletal muscles began with investigations stimulated by Prokop [52]. These studies were followed by several papers on the construction of square-wave generators [7,29,43,45,51,55–57,71,73] and a large series on human bodies [22–29,33,35–38,58–61].

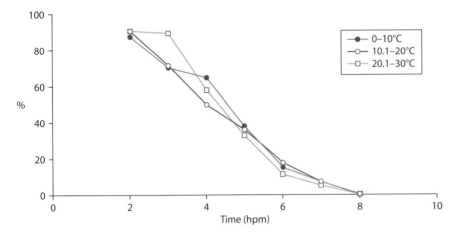

Figure 3.13 Percentage frequency of positive results in mechanical excitability of skeletal muscles (idiomuscular pad and Zsako's phenomenon). There is no obvious temperature dependency for the duration of mechanical excitability. The reason for the shorter postmortem period in which idiomuscular pad could be induced, compared with Figure 3.12, is probably that Semmler used hospital cases, whereas Dotzauer (see Figure 3.12) used coroner cases for his investigations. hpm, hours post mortem. (Diagram was drawn using original data from Semmler [68].)

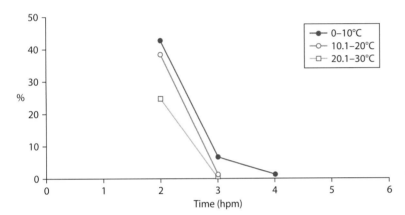

Figure 3.14 Percentage frequency of Zsako's phenomenon within three temperature classes. Mode of excitation: hitting onto the musculi interossei between metacarpal 3 and 4 with a reflex hammer. hpm, hours post mortem. (Drawn using original data from Semmler J. *Einfluss der Umgebungstemperatur auf die Todeszeitbestimmung durch elektrische Reizung der Oberlidmuskulatur menschlicher Leichen.* Magdeburg, Germany, Magdeburg University, MD thesis, 1979.)

Most investigators of the postmortem electrical excitability of skeletal muscles have worked with a verbal description and subjective grading of the muscular response to excitation – the muscular contraction – according to:

1. The strength of contraction.
2. The spread of movement to areas distant from the electrodes.

For example, the results of the first large study on electrical excitability of orbicularis oculi muscle, orbicularis oris muscle and muscles of the hand and forearm on 102 bodies are shown in Figure 3.15 and Table 3.6. The muscle contraction is graded into three degrees [51].

During the early postmortem interval there is strong contraction of the muscles, and the excitation also spreads to muscles distant from the electrodes (+++; Figure 3.16). Conversely, with an increasing postmortem interval, muscle contraction becomes weaker, and the muscular response is confined to the place of excitation (+). Table 3.7 gives the results of this first major investigation (mean values for the special degree, ranges of scatter and number of cases).

Succeeding investigations modified the subjective grading of electrical excitability for the electrode positions in the orbicularis oculi muscle: the three degrees by Popwassilew and Palm [51] were changed to six degrees by Klein and Klein [25] and to four degrees by Krause *et al.* [26,27,29] (Table 3.8).

Not only was the subjective grading changed, but also the position of electrodes was altered, even for the same investigated muscle (Table 3.9). Most investigators use puncture electrodes; only Zink and Reinhardt [73] recommend surface electrodes.

The depth of insertion of the puncture electrodes varies between 3 mm and 2 cm.

Finally, the physical parameters of excitation also differ (Table 3.10). Some authors work with differing repetition rate-voltage combinations [25,27], for example, rectangular-like impulses of some milliseconds duration, a repetition rate of 10, 30, 70 and 120 per second, and a voltage of 10, 30 or 50 V, which means 12 repetition rate-voltage combinations [25]. Together with the 6 (7) degrees of muscular reaction, 75 combinations between mode of excitation and degree of reaction result. In this way, examining electrical

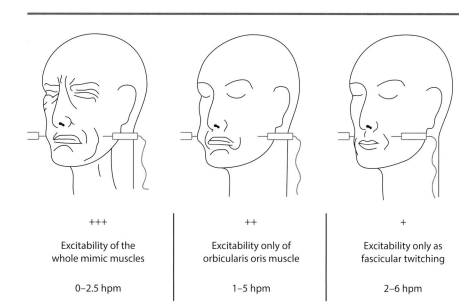

+++

Excitability of the
whole mimic muscles

0–2.5 hpm

++

Excitability only of
orbicularis oris muscle

1–5 hpm

+

Excitability only as
fascicular twitching

2–6 hpm

Figure 3.15 Positions of electrodes and grading of muscular contractions of the orbicularis oris muscles according to Popwassilew and Palm [51] with the postmortem duration of electrical excitability for the special degree. +, This degree is found in any case up to 2 hours post mortem (hpm) and in some cases up to 6 hours post mortem. [51]

Table 3.6 Grading by Popwassilew and Palm

	Grading		
	+++	++	+
Orbicularis oculi	Contraction of the whole mimic muscles.	Contraction of the eyelids.	Fibrillar twitching.
Orbicularis oris	Contraction of orbicularis oris, neck muscles and eyelids.	Contraction of orbicularis oris.	Fibrillar twitching.
Hand	Contraction of the whole arm.	Contraction of the hand and the forearm.	Fibrillar twitching.

Data from Popwassilew J, Palm W. Über die Todeszeitbestimmung in den ersten 10 Stunden. *Z Arztl Fortbildg* 1960;**54**:734–737.

excitability becomes very complicated, without any rise in the precision of the death time estimation.

These few tabular summaries show that all elements of methods (position of electrodes, parameters of excitation, grading of muscular contraction) have been modified. Therefore, it is not surprising that the results of different authors are hardly comparable (Table 3.11). For instance, the Popwassilew and Palm [51] three degrees are comparable to the six degrees of Klein and Klein [35]; however, according to the parameters of excitation and the position of electrodes, the mean values and ranges of scatter for the degrees differ widely. The same is the case for the results on the orbicularis oris muscle.

In practice, there arises the question of which investigation (mode of excitation and results) to use as a reference. If experts wish to use different studies as references, they must apply different square-wave generators.

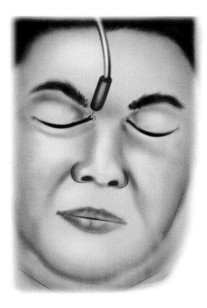

Figure 3.16 Contraction of the whole mimic muscles on excitation. Degree +++ according to Popwassilew and Palm [51] or degree VI according to Klein and Klein [25] (see Tables 3.7 and 3.8).

Table 3.7   Random sample of 102 cases of Popwassilew and Palm*

	Grading		
	1	2	3
	+++	++	+
Orbicularis oculi			
Range	0–2.5 h	1–5 h	2–8 h
Mean	1.25 h	2.25 h	4.25 h
N	64	79	75
Orbicularis oris			
Range	0–2.5 h	1–5 h	2–6 h
Mean	1 h	1.75 h	3.75 h
N	56	67	56
Hand			
Range	0–2.5 h	1–4 h	1–5.5 h
Mean	0.75 h	1.25 h	3.25 h
N	53	55	51

* For grading, see Table 3.6.

Data from Popwassilew J, Palm W. Über die Todeszeitbestimmung in den ersten 10 Stunden. *Z Arztl Fortbildg* 1960;**54**:734–737.

Table 3.8   Subjective grading of muscular responses to excitation for the orbicularis oculi muscle

Popwassilew and Palm [51]	Klein and Klein [25]	Krause *et al.* [27]
+++ Whole mimic muscles.	VI upper and lower eyelid and forehead and cheek.	IV heavy contraction spreading to the surrounding muscles.
	V upper and lower eyelid and forehead.	III contraction in whole length of the excited muscle.
++ Upper and lower eyelid.	IV upper and lower eyelid. III whole upper eyelid.	II incomplete contraction of the excited muscle.
+ Fibrillar twitching.	II 1/3–2/3 upper eyelid. I local upper eyelid.	I fibrillar twitching.

Recommendations for practical use

One of the most extensive investigations was presented by Klein and Klein [25], on case material of 447 bodies. The position of electrodes and the grading of muscular contraction are seen in Tables 3.8 and 3.9 and in Figures 3.17 and 3.18. From this extensive case material, Henssge [15] calculated the 95 per cent confidence limits for the six degrees of muscular contraction.

The data originally referred to stimulation by rectangular-like impulses of some milliseconds duration, with a repetition rate of 30 to 70 per second, a voltage of 50 V and resistance of 1 kOhm. These data are completely transferable to excitation with constant-current rectangular impulses of 30 mA, of 10 milliseconds duration and a repetition rate 50

Table 3.9   Positions of electrodes in the orbicularis oculi muscle according to different authors

Positions of electrodes	Reference
Puncture electrodes in a horizontal distance of 10 mm in the medial part of the left upper eyelid 3 mm deep or Puncture electrodes in a vertical distance of 10 mm into the right upper eyelid, inner angle, 3 mm deep	Krause *et al.* [27]
Surface electrodes beside the eye angles of the same eye	Zink and Reinhardt [75]
Puncture electrodes from lateral into the upper eyelid (musculus orbicularis oculi, pars palpebralis)	Popwassilew and Palm [51]
Needle electrodes in a distance of 15 to 20 mm into the nasal part of the upper eyelid 5 to 7 mm deep	Klein and Klein [25]
Like Popwassilew and Palm – 2 cm deep	Walz and Mattig [71]

per second. At the scene of a crime, we use a small, self-constructed generator (Figure 3.19), with the previously mentioned physical parameters of excitation.

The 95 per cent confidence limits for the six degrees of electrical excitability of the orbicularis oculi muscle were calculated on forensic pathology case material. In cases with a longer terminal episode (clinical pathology), the duration of electrical excitability is shorter (see Table 3.10).

In cases with haematomas or emphysema of the eyelid, electrical excitability may last much longer than that corresponding to the upper 95 per cent confidence limits for the special degree of the forensic pathology case material (Table 3.12 and Figure 3.20). This response may result from aerobic glycolysis in these cases, with a 19-fold greater energy profit [1,2,4,33] and a postmortem Feng effect [33].

Re-examination of the data of Klein and Klein

My colleagues and I performed investigations on 30 bodies (traumatic or sudden natural death without long-lasting terminal episodes) with about 300 excitations, to re-examine whether the calculated 95 per cent confidence limits for the different degrees are valid.

The time period investigated ranged from 2 to 13 hours post mortem. The mode of excitation was constant-current rectangular impulses of 1 second duration at 30 mA. The boxes represent the upper and lower 95 per cent confidence limits for the special degree (Figure 3.21).

In spite of the slightly differing mode of excitation, the 95 per cent confidence limits proved to be valid (see Figure 3.21). Each point represents one single excitation and all points are within the boxes, except some points for the degrees IV to VI, which represent several excitations in

Table 3.10   Differing parameters of excitation according to different authors

Parameters of excitation	Investigated muscles	Reference
Probably rectangular impulses of 6 ms duration, 9 V, repetition rate 100/s; voltage peaks >4000 V.	M. orbicularis oculi M. orbicularis oris Flexors of the forearm	Popwassilew and Palm [51]
Rectangular impulses of some ms duration, repetition rate 10 to 120/s; 10, 30, 50 V; resistance 1 kOhm.	M. orbicularis oculi M. orbicularis oris	Klein and Klein [25] Klein et al. [26]
Triangular impulses; repetition rate probably 50/s; 10 voltage steps between 9 and 70 V.		Mattig and Waltz [43]
Rectangular impulses of 'a few ms duration', 10 to 50 V, repetition rate between 10 and 100/s.	M. orbicularis oculi M. orbicularis oris M. biceps brachii M. brachioradialis	Krause et al. [27]
Constant-current rectangular impulses of 10 ms duration, 30 mA, repetition rate 50/s.	M. orbicularis oculi M. orbicularis oris	Henssge and Madea [14,35]
Rectangular impulses of 1 s duration; 200 V; current intensities according to the muscular threshold.	Different muscles	Joachim and Feldmann [24] Madea [33] Madea and Henssge [40] Ravache-Quiriny [60,61]
Rectangular impulses of 30 V; repetition rate 50/s.		Waltz and Mattig [71]
Non sinus-like voltage with voltage peaks up to 1000 V.	M. orbicularis oculi	Zink and Reinhardt [73]
Constant-current rectangular impulses of 1 s duration, current intensity between 0.1 and 80 mA according to muscular threshold or definite supraliminal strength.	Thenar, hypothenar, M. biceps brachii, M. quadriceps, M. orbicularis oculi	Madea [33]

M, musculus.

Table 3.11   Mean values and 95 per cent limits of confidence (Klein and Klein) or ranges of scatter (Popwassilew and Palm) of differing degrees of electrical excitability (in hours)*

		Klein and Klein [25]		Popwassilew and Palm [51]	
		x	95% limits	x	Range of scatter
Musculus orbicularis oculi					
I	Upper eyelid, nasal part	13.5	5–22		
II	1/3–2/3 upper eyelid	10.5	5.16 J+++	4.25	2–8
III	Whole upper eyelid	8.25	3.5–13		
IV	Plus lower eyelid	5.5	3–8.00 J+++	2.25	1–5
V	Plus cheek	4.5	2–7		
VI	Plus forehead	3.5	1–6 J+	1.25	0–2.5
Musculus orbicularis oris		7	3–11	3.25	2–6

* The three degrees of Popwassilew and Palm are comparable to the six degrees of Klein and Klein. Different time values according to position of electrodes and mode of excitation.

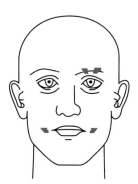

Electrical excitability of mimic muscles

Eye: puncture electrodes in a distance of 15 to 20 mm in the nasal part of the upper eyelid 5 to 7 mm

Mouth: puncture electrodes on both sides 10 mm besides angle of the mouth

Figure 3.17   Positions of electrodes for the stimulation of mimic muscles (musculus orbicularis oculi, musculus orbicularis oris) according to Klein and Klein [25].

two cases of fatal hypothermia. In hypothermia, electrical excitability may last much longer.

■ Conclusions

Examining the electrical excitability of skeletal muscles post mortem is a very easy procedure, which can be performed at the scene of a crime. It takes less than 1 minute to perform, and information on the time since death is available immediately.

Because, in almost all previous papers, either the mode of excitation or the grading of muscular contraction has changed, the investigator must adhere to one method.

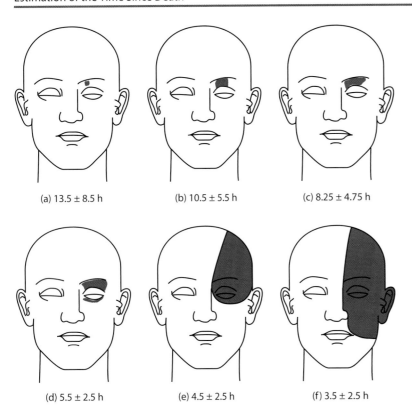

(a) 13.5 ± 8.5 h   (b) 10.5 ± 5.5 h   (c) 8.25 ± 4.75 h

(d) 5.5 ± 2.5 h   (e) 4.5 ± 2.5 h   (f) 3.5 ± 2.5 h

Figure 3.18   (a) to (f) Degrees of a positive reaction for stimulating the orbicularis oculi muscles according to Klein and Klein [25] with mean values and 95 per cent limits of confidence (in hours) for the special degree (calculated by Henssge from data of Klein and Klein [25]).

I recommend examining electrical excitability using a square-wave generator with rectangular impulses of 10 milliseconds duration, 30 mA and a repetition rate of 50 per second. The positions of electrodes and the grading of muscular contractions are according to Klein and Klein, with the 95 per cent confidence limits calculated by the method of Henssge. These times are valid for forensic cases (exceptions: fatal hypothermia; haematoma or emphysema of the eyelid, where longer times are possible) (Table 3.13).

By combining electrical excitability with the nomogram method of Henssge *et al.* in the early postmortem interval, the precision and the accuracy of the death time estimation may be raised considerably (see Chapter 6, part 6.1). Using two independent methods to obtain a common result increases the investigator's confidence for the calculation of the time since death. When the temperature method cannot be used, examining electrical excitability alone may provide valuable additional information on the time of death. In my opinion, the examination of electrical excitability should be included in the minimum standard of methods used in the early postmortem interval for determining the time since death. In those countries where, for legal reasons, the insertion of needle electrodes before autopsy is not permitted, the use of surface electrodes may be an alternative.

Figure 3.19   Self-constructed generator for examining electrical excitability at the scene of a crime. The output consists of constant-current rectangular impulses of 30 mA, 10 milliseconds duration, at a repetition rate of 50/second.

Table 3.12   Upper and lower 95 per cent limits of confidence for the six degrees of electrical excitability in two different random samples: forensic pathology and clinical pathology*

Degree		Forensic pathology (hours)	Clinical pathology (longer-lasting terminal episode) (hours)
I	Local upper eyelid	5–22	3–16
II	1/3–2/3 upper eyelid	5–16	0–16
III	Whole upper eyelid	3.5–13	1.5–9
IV	Upper and lower eyelid	3–8	1–7
V	Upper and lower eyelid and forehead	2–7	1–7
VI	Upper and lower eyelid and forehead and cheek	1–6	1–6

* In clinical pathological cases (longer lasting terminal episode), the duration of electrical excitability is shorter.

(a)   (b)

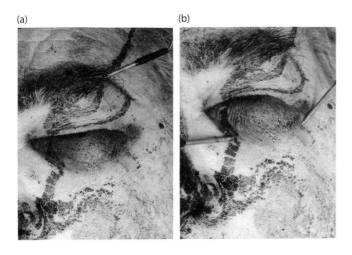

Figure 3.20 Electrical excitability of the upper eyelid (a) at 16 hours post mortem while the whole bloodshot lower eyelid is still contracting (b).

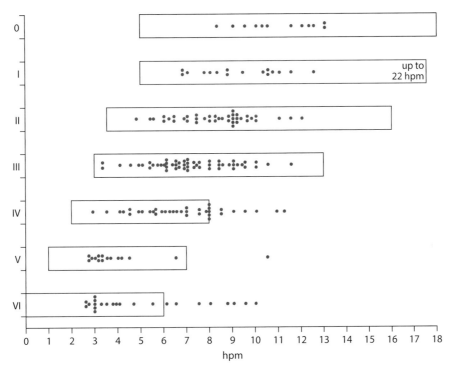

Figure 3.21 Re-examination of the calculated 95 per cent limits of confidence for the forensic pathology case material. I to VI: The degree of electrical excitability according to grading by Klein and Klein. The boxes represent the upper and lower 95 per cent limits of confidence.

Each point corresponds to one excitation (about 300 excitations on 30 bodies). The points outside the boxes (the upper 95 per cent limits of confidence) for degrees IV to VI were observed in 2 cases of fatal hypothermia. hpm, hours post mortem.

However, this would require further investigations if the 95 per cent confidence limits for the six degrees are to be valid for this modified mode of excitation.

Table 3.13 Duration of electrical excitability in cases of traumatic emphysema, postmortem artificial emphysema and traumatic haematoma of the eyelid

Circumstances	Duration of electrical excitability (hpm)
Traumatic emphysema (vital)	Up to 29
Postmortem emphysema (air insufflation into the eyelid)	27.3–52
Traumatic haematoma of the eyelid	Up to 32

hpm, hours post mortem.

3.4 Longitudinal studies of electrical excitability

One of the main reasons for the unsatisfactory comparability among different studies on electrical excitability of skeletal muscle is that the subjective grading of muscular contractions was made only by visual perception of the muscular reactions or their intensity (spread). The first improvement must therefore be the introduction of a method for objectifying muscular contraction. Another reason for the lack of comparability among different studies is that different authors worked with:

- Different modes of excitation.
- Insufficiently defined physiological parameters of excitation.

This second point for improvement must therefore be the introduction of well-defined electrical stimuli.

An electrical stimulus is defined, according to its biological efficiency, by:

1. Strength or intensity.
2. Rise.
3. Duration in one direction.
4. Repetition rate.

■ Objectifying supravital muscular contraction

The preceding studies showed variation in all elements of excitation. The aim of the present study was to analyze the objectified muscular contraction in relation to electrical stimuli. Therefore, according to the practice in clinical neurophysiology, we used only constant-current rectangular impulses of 1 second duration as single impulses. These impulses are characterized by an infinitely high rise, sufficient duration in one direction and a defined strength. Our experimental studies with a much shorter duration of stimulus – for instance, 0.2 millisecond, as it is usual in physiology – revealed that even by 2 hours post mortem the muscle failed to give any response on excitation.

The third defect in preceding investigations was that longitudinal studies on the electrical excitability of the same muscle, until excitability expired, were virtually non-existent (with the exception of the postmortem rise of galvanic threshold).

After an encouraging pilot study in 1984 that avoided these three defects of the preceding investigation [14], an accurate, standardized and reproducible method was developed for assessing the contractions of skeletal muscles after death by means of electrical stimulation, by assessing this phenomenon serially and then relating it to the time elapsed since death [14,33,36–38,31,41,42

For objectifying muscular contractions, we used a sensitive force transducer (originally constructed for investigations in experimental cardiac surgery [31,32]) inserted in a hypodermic needle. Below the top of the force transducer is a lateral window, in which a flexural bar can be seen (Figure 3.22 (a)).

When the force transducer was inserted into the muscle, the contracting muscle fibres pressed on the flexural bar and caused it to lose its axial position in the force transducer; this signal will be quantified by the strain gauge. The signal measured the centripetal force acting on the bar in response to the contracting muscle fibres (Figure 3.22 (c)).

The measured force of the muscle fibres compressing the bar and the electrical stimulus were registered by a two-channel writer (Figure 3.22 (d)).

The force transducer was pricked into the muscle, and puncture electrodes were inserted on either side (Figure 3.23). Investigations were performed mainly on the thenar and hypothenar muscles. The muscle was stimulated half hourly, using rectangular impulses of 1 second duration at 2, 4, 8, 16, 32, 64 and/or 80 mA, by use of a commercial square-wave generator (Siemens Neurotron 726 S) until the electrical excitability expired for the applied or for highest current intensity (Table 3.14).

Electrical excitation and registration were usually performed at contralateral positions. When electrical excitability expired at one position, the electrodes and the force transducer were inserted into another muscle. The random sample consisted of 50 cases of sudden natural or traumatic death. Afterward, a control group of 21 cases was also investigated. The experiments took place in a constant ambient temperature of 20°C (Table 3.15). Continuous measurement of the deep rectal temperature was made, as well as the local temperature at the location of measurement.

Two graphical forms of muscular contraction must be distinguished:

1. A two-peak shape during the first hours after death.
2. A one-peak shape in the later postmortem interval (Figure 3.24).

The continuous change of the shape of muscular contraction could be studied in some cases where the start of investigation could be made very soon after death, with a long duration of electrical excitability (Figure 3.25 (a)).

In the early postmortem interval, the muscular contraction is characterized by a two-peak shape: a closing and opening contraction at the beginning and the end of the 1-second electrical stimulus (see Figure 3.25). The closing and opening contractions have their own contraction and relaxation periods.

In the early postmortem interval, the closing contraction has a higher maximum force than the opening contraction (see Figure 3.25 (a)). When the relaxation period of the closing contraction becomes weaker, the opening contraction begins at a higher force level and shows a higher force maximum (see Figure 3.25 (d)). This results in a superimposition of the closing contraction on the opening contraction.

As the contraction velocity of the closing contraction decreases, the contraction period of the closing contraction is continued through the contraction period of the opening contraction. Consequently, a one-peak shape of

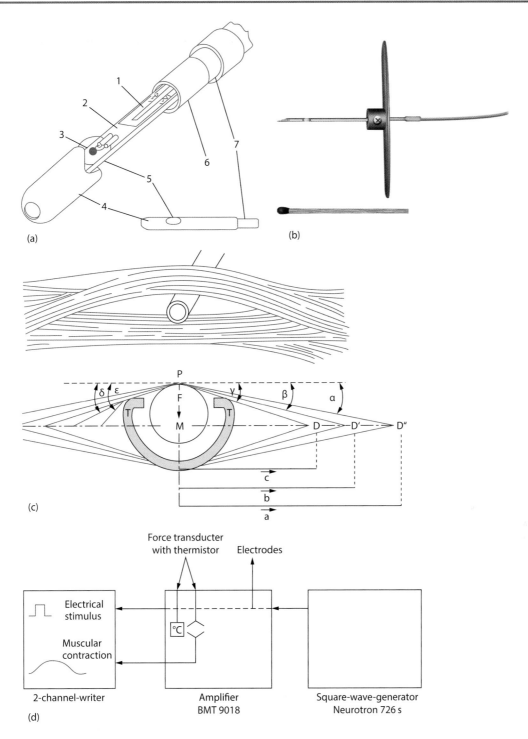

Figure 3.22 (a) Schematic presentation of the force transducer: 1, DMS (strain gauge); 2, flexural bar; 3, thermistor; 4, outer tube; 5, lateral window; 6, bar support; 7, PE-catheter. (b) Size of the force transducer compared with a match. (c) Schematic drawing of the force transducer pricked into a skeletal muscle. The resulting force measured is the centripetal on the bar (M) acting force (F) of different layers of the contracting muscle fibres. (d) Schematic drawing of the experimental design.

muscular contraction results. At 80 mA current intensities, the one-peak shape appears, on average, at 5 hours post mortem.

This one-peak shape of muscular contraction becomes increasingly weaker with the increasing postmortem interval (see Figure 3.25 (f to h)). The reason that this pattern of muscular contraction has not yet been described in the literature may be that long-lasting stimuli, such as used here, are not normally used for physiology investigations.

The first appearance of a one-peak shape of muscular contraction depends not only on the current intensity used for stimulation but also on the temperature history of the

(a)

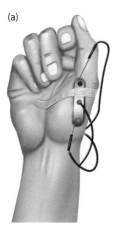

(b) (3) (4)   (2) (1)

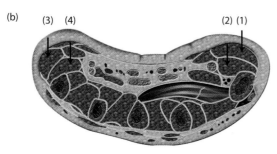

Figure 3.23 (a) *In corpore* insertion of force transducer and puncture electrodes on the right thenar. (b) Cross-section of the hand with muscles investigated: thenar (musculus abductor pollicis brevis (1)); musculus opponens pollicis (2); hypothenar (musculus abductor digiti minimi) (3); musculus opponens digiti minimi (4).

body. The deeper the rectal temperature is at the beginning of the investigations, the later the one-peak shape of muscular contraction will appear.

With this method the following criteria for extrapolating the time since death from the objectified muscular contraction could be derived:

- Decrease of the maximum force of the muscular contraction after excitation with various current intensities (Figure 3.26).
- Increase of the relaxation time (Figure 3.27).
- Increase of the galvanic threshold (Figure 3.28).

Table 3.14 Experimental procedure and equipment

Measurement mostly at contralateral positions (thenar, hypothenar, biceps of right and left side).
Mode of excitation: rectangular impulses of 1 second duration of supraliminal strength (2, 4, 8, 16, 32, 64, 80 mA) each half hour until electrical excitability expired for the applied or highest current intensity. Then change to another location (of the same muscle) or to another muscle.
Puncture electrodes (steel, 2-mm diameter, 10 mm long) were pricked into the muscle at a distance of 3 to 4 cm, 5 to 7 cm deep.
Generator: Neurotron 726 S (Siemens).
Objectifying muscular contraction by a force transducer pricked into the muscle (see text).

Table 3.15 Composition of the reference and control samples

Reference sample	Control sample
50 cases of sudden natural or traumatic death with a short terminal episode.	21 cases of sudden natural or traumatic death with a short terminal episode.
Male: 26; $\bar{x}$ 54.2 years (21–80 years)	10; $\bar{x}$ 38.3 years (19–69 years)
Female: 24; $\bar{x}$ 53.5 years (16–76 years)	11; $\bar{x}$ 66.3 years (40–79 years)
Beginning of the experiments	
2 to 11 hpm ($\bar{x}$ 3.9 hpm)	2 to 8 hpm ($\bar{x}$ 4.3 hpm)
Duration of the experiments	
1 to 9 h ($\bar{x}$ 4.9 h)	1 to 9 h ($\bar{x}$ 4.3 h)

hpm, hours post mortem; $\bar{x}$, mean value.

The original investigations were carried out on different muscles: biceps brachii, thenar and hypothenar. The consecutive cases 1 to 50 were used as reference – the following 21 cases comprised the control sample. It could be shown that a decrease of the maximum force after stimulation with definite current intensities, an increase of the relaxation time in the form of force related relaxation time and an increase of the galvanic threshold were suitable criteria for extrapolating the time since death.

In the original investigation, consecutive cases were used as references or control sample. Because they were not matched concerning beginning of the investigations, duration of electrical excitability, age and other factors, a matched reference and control sample was remodelled from the original data set [42] (Table 3.16). On the remodelled references and control sample, the calculations described after this list were performed to answer the following questions:

1. Is there an increase in the precision of death time estimation by using the postmortem interval as dependent variable? From statistical calculations on the correlation between analyte concentrations in vitreous humour and time since death, it is known that using the analyte concentration as an independent variable reveals a statistically significant higher precision of death time estimation compared with its use as a dependent variable.
2. Are there systematic differences between contralateral muscles?
3. Are there differences among muscles (biceps brachii muscle, thenar, hypothenar muscles) in the duration of the electrical excitability?
4. Can the original data on precision of death time estimation be confirmed on the remodelled reference and control sample?

From the original data set of 71 cases, 2 reference and control groups, each comprising 28 cases, were remodelled and matched concerning postmortem beginning of the experiments, duration of electrical excitability and ambient temperature until beginning of the experiments. The relevant data for the reference and control samples are

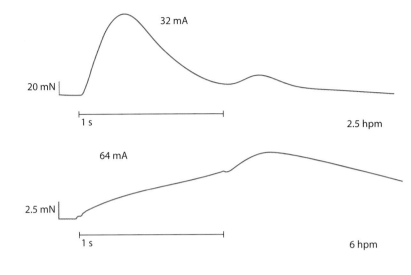

32 mA

20 mN

1 s   2.5 hpm

64 mA

2.5 mN

1 s   6 hpm

Figure 3.24 Two principal graphical forms of muscular contraction after stimulation with rectangular impulses of 1 second duration and supraliminal strength. Top, Two-peak-shaped contractions corresponding to a closing and opening contraction at beginning and end of the stimulus. Fast relaxation of the closing, as well as the opening contraction. Bottom, One-peak-shaped muscular contraction. The maximum force is achieved following the end of the stimulus; an opening contraction is missing. Return of the contracted muscle fibres to the starting tension is retarded. hpm, hours post mortem.

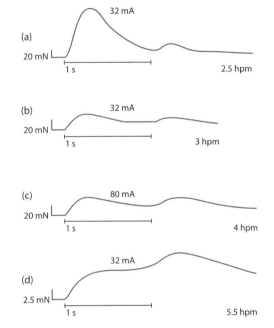

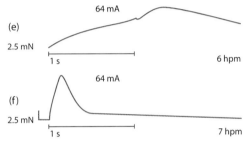

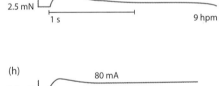

Figure 3.25 Postmortem change in the shape of muscular contraction. Left, force in millinewtons; bottom, duration of the 1-second electrical stimulus in relation to the time course of muscular contraction; current intensities; time since death in hours. The curves (a) to (e) were registered at 100 mm/second, the curves (f) to (h) at 10 mm/second paper speed. hpm, hours post mortem.

shown in Table 3.10. Questions 1 to 4 were checked on the reference group. The precision of death time estimation is always given as 95 per cent confidence limits in hours. The calculations were performed for various criteria of objectified muscular contraction (decrease of maximum force, increase of relaxation time, increase of galvanic threshold). To achieve a clear structure, the results for one criterion (e.g. decrease of maximum force) are presented when questions 1 to 4 are addressed, although calculations have been carried out with other criteria (e.g. increase of galvanic threshold), also with the same results. The results were checked against those of the control group (e.g. by calculation of the accuracy of death time estimation on the data of the control sample in comparison with the reference group).

■ Is there a higher precision of death time estimation when using the time since death as dependent variable?

For the regression between time since death and decrease of the maximum force on the left thenar muscle after stimulation with a current intensity of 80 mA, the hypothesis was checked for using the postmortem interval as a dependent variable or for using it as an independent variable. This revealed a higher precision of death time estimation. Thus, if in the regression analysis the postmortem interval was used as a dependent variable, the precision of death time estimation was much greater with a standard

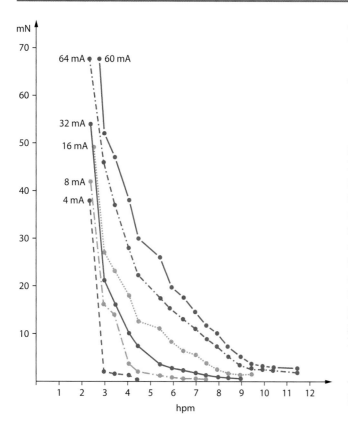

Figure 3.26   Decrease of maximum force (in millinewtons, mN) on the right thenar over the postmortem interval for current intensities from 4 to 80 mA (one case). Exponential decrease of the maximum force for the same current intensity over the postmortem interval. hpm, hours post mortem.

deviation [SD] of ± 1.93 hours compared with a linear regression with the postmortem interval as an independent variable (SD ± 3.4 hours) (Table 3.17). The precision of

death time estimation calculated on the reference sample was confirmed on the control sample.

■ Are there any differences between contralateral muscle groups?

Contralateral muscle groups normally show a very similar pattern, for instance, for the decrease of the maximum force after stimulation with the same current intensity or the increase of the galvanic threshold. When the 95 per cent confidence limits of precision of death time estimation (e.g. for the increase of the galvanic threshold or the decrease of the maximum force after stimulation with the same current intensity) were compared for contralateral muscle groups, nearly identical data were revealed (Figures 3.29 (a) and 3.30 (a)). Furthermore, the data on the precision of death time estimation for contralateral muscle groups could be confirmed for the control samples (see Figures 3.29 (b) and 3.30 (b)).

■ Are there differences among muscle groups?

The mean duration of electrical excitability for different muscle groups for current intensities between 2 and 80 mA was calculated. The duration of electrical excitability was systematically shorter for the biceps brachii muscle compared with the thenar and hypothenar muscles. For the highest current intensity of 80 mA, thenar and hypothenar muscles showed a nearly identical duration of electrical excitability (Figure 3.31).

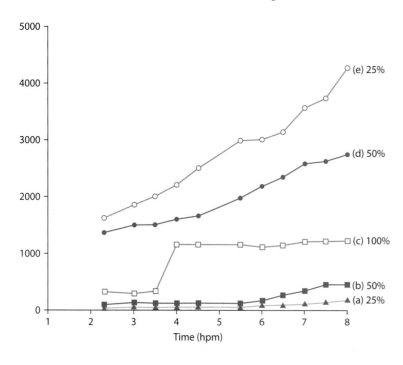

Figure 3.27   Contraction and relaxation time over the postmortem interval. Contraction time up to 25 per cent (a), 50 per cent (b), 100 per cent (c) of the maximum force; relaxation time up to 50 per cent (d) or 25 per cent (e) of the maximum force achieved during muscular relaxation. The relaxation time up to 25 per cent of the maximum force shows the steepest increase over the postmortem interval. Each point is a mean value for at least three muscular contractions registered at the same time post mortem after excitation with different current intensities. hpm, hours post mortem.

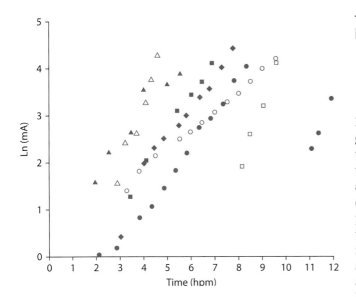

Figure 3.28 Postmortem rise of galvanic threshold (ln mA) for eight cases marked with different symbols. Linear relationship between natural logarithm (ln) of galvanic threshold (rheobase) and time since death. hpm, hours post mortem.

Table 3.16 Remodelled reference and control sample at the beginning of the experiments (minutes post mortem) and duration of electrical excitability (minutes post mortem).

	Reference sample	Control sample
N	28	28
Age (in years)	21–80; $\bar{x}$ 52.86	16–78; $\bar{x}$ 53.64
Beginning of the experiments (min pm) $\bar{x}$ ± SD	269.21 ± 126.71	233.21 ± 91.46
Duration of electrical excitability (min) $\bar{x}$ ± SD	282.71 ± 116.43	306.07 ± 118.72

SD, standard deviation.

Table 3.17 Calculation of precision of death time estimation using the postmortem interval as a dependent or an independent variable in correlation between decrease of maximum force and time since death

	Reference sample	Control sample
N (number of cases)	28	28
n (number of measurements)	130	154
PMI residues*		
PMI as dependent variable	1.93	2.01
PMI as independent variable	3.41	3.96

* Standard deviation in hours.

PMI, postmortem interval.

Could the original data on the precision of death time estimation be confirmed on the remodelled reference and control sample?

For the criteria decrease of maximum force, increase of the galvanic threshold and increased force-related relaxation time, 95 per cent confidence limits of death time estimation between ± 2.69 hours (force-related relaxation time) and ± 4.27 hours (decrease of maximum force) were calculated for the original reference group. These data on the precision of death time estimation could be confirmed for the decrease of the maximum force and the increase of the force related relaxation time on the remodelled reference sample. For the increase of the galvanic threshold, systematically higher 95 per cent confidence limits were calculated on the remodelled reference sample (Table 3.18).

Conclusions

For regression analysis between analytical parameters and time since death, the analytical parameters should always be used as independent variables because this approach reveals a higher precision of death time estimation compared with a change of variables.

There is no difference in duration of electrical excitability between contralateral muscle groups. Thus, investigations can be carried out at either side.

The thenar and hypothenar muscles are much more suitable for examination of electrical excitability compared with the biceps brachii muscle, perhaps because of the higher tension of the biceps brachii muscle during development of rigor mortis compared with the thenar or hypothenar muscles (the greater the tension, the higher is the oxygen demand). Another point is the higher local temperature of the biceps brachii muscle compared with the thenar and hypothenar muscles (greater diameter of the upper arm compared with thenar or hypothenar; the greater the diameter, the more slowly the temperature will drop).

The original data on the precision of death time estimation using different criteria of objectified muscular contraction were proved to be valid for the decrease of the maximum force and the increase of the force related relaxation time, but not for the increase of the galvanic threshold. Therefore, the results of the original work were confirmed on the matched remodelled reference and control samples. Different criteria of the objectified muscular contraction allow a much more precise estimation of the time since death than do other criteria of electrical excitability, especially subjective grading. However, great interindividual variability in the duration of electrical excitability still remains. Main factors determining the time course of the supravital period of skeletal muscles are the glycogen content of the muscles at the moment of death

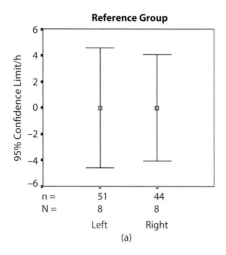
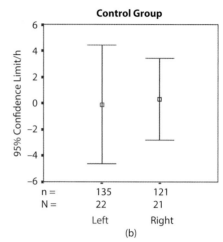

Figure 3.29 (a) and (b) 95 per cent confidence limit for estimating the time since death using the increase of the galvanic threshold on the left and right thenar muscles. N = number of cases; n = number of measurements.

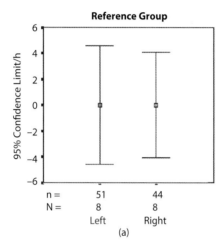
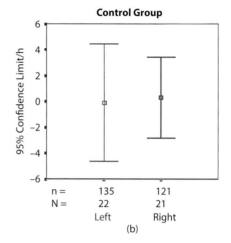

Figure 3.30 (a) and (b) Precision of estimating the time since death based on the decrease of the maximum force after stimulation with a current intensity of 80 mA on the right and left thenar muscles.

Precision calculated on the reference sample confirmed on the control sample N = number of cases; n = number of measurement.

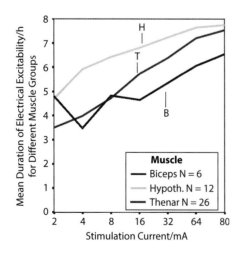

Figure 3.31 Mean duration of electrical excitability (hour) for different muscle groups (biceps brachii, hypothenar, thenar) and current intensities.

Table 3.18 Precision of death time estimation (95 per cent confidence limits in hours) of the original reference sample and of the remodelled reference sample

		Original reference sample	Remodelled reference sample
Decrease of maximum force	95% confidence limit	± 4.27	± 3.68
	n	445	280
	N	35	28
Increase of galvanic threshold	95% confidence limit	± 3.27	± 4.15
	n	267	182
	N	17	15
Increase of force related relaxation time	95% confidence limit	± 2.69	±2.87
	n	346	150
	N	35	16

N, number of cases; n, number of measurements.

and the environmental and, of course, local temperatures at the places of excitation. With the described method of objectifying muscular contraction, the role of the glycogen content at the moment of death and the ambient temperature should be examined in further investigations.

■ Current recommendations

1. Objectifying of supravital muscular contractions reveals a higher precision of death time estimation compared with the subjective grading of muscular excitability.
2. For regression analysis between the analytical parameters and death time estimation, the analytical parameters should always be used as independent variables because they reveal a higher precision of death time estimation compared with a change of variables.
3. In contralateral muscle groups, the duration of electrical excitability is almost identical; however, among different muscles of the same body, the duration of electrical excitability differs widely (in the thenar and hypothenar muscles, it is longer than in the biceps brachii muscle).
4. Differences in the duration of electrical excitability among different muscles of the same body may be the result of the variations in the glycogen content of different muscles, the varying cooling velocity depending on the diameter of the muscles and their topographical localization and the extension of the muscles (the greater the extension, the sooner the electrical excitability will expire). These influence factors have to be taken into consideration in further studies.

References

1. Bate-Smith EC, Bendall JR. Rigor mortis and adenosine-triphosphate. *J Physiol* 1947;**106**:177–185.
2. Bate-Smith EC, Bendall JR. Factors determining the time course of rigor mortis. *J Physiol.*1949;**110**:47–65.
3. Bedford PJ, Tsokos M. The occurrence of cadaveric spasm is a myth. *Forensic Sci Med Pathol* 2013;**9**(2):244–248.
4. Bendall JR. Postmortem changes in muscle. In: Bourne DH (ed.). *The Structure and Function of Muscle,* vol. II. *Structure,* part 2. London, Academic Press, 1973, pp 244–309.
5. Blasius W. Allgemeine Physiologie des Nervensystems. In: Rosemann H, (ed.). *Lehrbuch der Physiologie des Menschen,* vols. 2, 28 Munich, Germany, Urban und Schwarzenberg, 1962, pp 629–662.
6. Blasius W, Zimmermann H. Comparative studies on the functional, structural and histochemical changes of the anterior horn ganglion cells of rabbit spinal cord in gradually receding ischemia [in German]. *Pflugers Arch Physiol* 1957;**264**(6):618–650.
7. Böhm E. Anmerkungen zu Reizbarkeit und Starreeintritt der Skelettmuskulatur. *Beitr Gerichtl Med* 1986;**44**:439–450.
8. Bohn HJ. *Status energiereicher Phosphate und glykolytischer Metabolite in der Extremitälenmuskulatur der Ratte bei Ischämie und in der postischämischen Erholung.* Cologne, Germany, University of Cologne, MD thesis, 1974.
9. Bretschneider HJ, Hübner G, Knoll D, Lohr B, Nordbeck H, Spieckermann PG. Myocardial resistance and tolerance to ischaemia: physiological and biochemical basis. *J Cardiovasc Surg* 1975;**16**:241–260.
10. Dotzauer G. Idiomuskulärer Wulst und postmortale Blutung bei plötzlichen Todesfällen. *Dtsch Z Gerichtl Med* 1958;**46**:761–771.
11. Dotzauer G, Naeve W. Die aktuelle Wasserstoffionenkonzentration im Leichenblut. *Zentralbl Pathol* 1955;**93**:360–370.
12. Dotzauer G, Naeve W. Wasserstoffionenkonzentration im Liquor post mortem. *Zentralbl Allg Pathol Anat* 1959;**100**:516–524.
13. Gerard RW. The response of nerve to oxygen lack. *Am J Physiol* 1930;**92**:498–541.
14. Henssge C, Lunkenheimer PP, Salmon O, Madea B. Zur supravitalen elektrischen Erregbarkeit der Muskulatur. *Z Rechtsmed* 1984;**93**: 165–174.
15. Henssge C, Madea B. *Methoden zur Bestimmung der Todeszeit an Leichen.* Lübeck, Schmidt-Römhild, 1988.
16. Hirsch H. Recovery of the electrocorticogram after incomplete and complete ischaemia of the brain. *Acta Neurochir* 1982;**66**:147–158.
17. Hirsch H, Hohmann V, Kaegler M, Sickel B. Auditory evoked potentials during and after complete ischaemia of the brain. *Adv Neurosurg* 1986;**14**:364–367.
18. Hirsch H, Hohmann V, Kaegler M, Sickel B. Recovery of auditory evoked potentials after long-term complete brain ischaemia. *Neurosurg Rev* 1989;**12**(Suppl 1):313–316.
19. Hirsch H, Kaegler M, Hohmann V, Mues B. Latency of recovery and electrical silence of auditory potentials and the electrocorticogram after peracute complete brain ischaemia of 2–30 minutes duration. *Adv Neurosurg* 1989;**17**:254–258.
20. Hirsch H, Tesch P. Recovery of the electrocorticogram of canine brains after complete cerebral ischaemia at 37 and 32°C. *Neurosurg Rev* 1982;**5**:49–54.
21. Isselhard W. Akuter Sauerstoffmangel und Wiederbelebung. *Dtsch Med Wochenschr* 1965;**90**:349–355.
22. Joachim H. *Probleme der frühen Todeszeitbestimmung und die sogenannten supravitalen Reaktionen des Muskels im Tierversuch.* Freiburg, Germany, Habil Schrift, 1976.
23. Joachim H. Mechanische und elektrische Erregbarkeit der Skelettmuskulatur. In: Henssge C, Madea B (eds.). *Methoden zur Bestimmung der Todeszeit an Leichen.* Lübeck, Schmidt-Römhild, 1988, pp 32–82.
24. Joachim H, Feldmann U. Eine quantitative Methode der Todeszeitbestimmung durch Untersuchung der galvanischen Reizschwelle. *Z Rechtsmed* 1980;**85**:5–22.
25. Klein A, Klein S. *Die Todeszeitbestimmung am menschlichen Auge.* Dresden, Germany, Medical Academy, Dresden University, MD thesis, 1978.
26. Klein A, Krause D, Hamann B. Praktische Erfahrungen mit einem neuen elektronischen Reizgerät zur Todeszeitbestimmung. *Kriminal Forens Wiss* 1975;**19**:126.
27. Krause D, Klein A, Mattig W, Waltz H. Praktische Erfahrungen mit dem Reizgerät D 76 zur Todeszeitbestimmung. *Kriminal Forens Wiss* 1980;**40**:83–86.
28. Krause D, Klein A, Zett L. Todeszeitbestimmung mittels indirekter Muskelreizung über den N. ischiadicus und N. radialis. *Kriminal Forens Wiss* 1976;**26**:66–67.
29. Krause D, Schöning R, Kuchheuser W. Stimulator M 85 – Ein kommerzielles Reizgerät zur Todeszeitbestimmung. In: Liebhardt E, Schuck M, Eisenmenger W (eds.). *Medizin und Recht. Festschrift für Wolfgang Spann.* Berlin, Springer, 1986, pp 639–644.

30. Lochte T. Über die Absterbeerscheinungen der Skelettmuskulatur, insbesondere über die Totenstarre in gerichtlich-medizinischer Beziehung. *Z Gesamte Gerichtl Med* 1923;**2**:169–190.

31. Lunkenheimer PP, Lunkenheimer A, Stroh N, Köhler F, Welham K, Graham G, Kirk E, Sonnenblick E, Kröller J. Vergleich klassischer und neuer Zugänge zum intramyokardialen Kraftverteilungsmuster. *Zentralbl Vet Med A* 1982;**29**:557–601.

32. Lunkenheimer PP, Lunkenheimer A, Torrent-Guasp F. *Kardiodynamik: Wege zur strukturgerechten Analyse der Myokardfunktion. Beiträge zur Kardiologie*, vol. 33. Erlangen, Germany, Perimed-Fachbuch-Verlagsges, 1985.

33. Madea B. *Supravitale elektrische Erregbarkeit der Skelettmuskulatur – Längsschnittuntersuchungen zur Objektivierung der muskulären Reaktion an 70 Leichen.* Cologne, Germany, Habil Schrift, 1989.

34. Madea B. Postmortem electrical excitability of skeletal muscle in casework. In: Henssge C, Knight B, Krompecher T, Madea B, Nokes L. (eds.). *The Estimation of the Time Since Death in the Early Postmortem Period.* London, Arnold, 2002, pp 164–206.

35. Madea B. Zum postmortalen Verhalten von Reizzeit – Reizstromstärkekurven. *Beitr Gerichtl Med* 1991;**49**:233–246.

36. Madea B. Estimating time of death from measurement of the electrical excitability of skeletal muscle. *J Forensic Sci Soc* 1992;**32**:117–129.

37. Madea B. Längsschnittuntersuchungen zur supravitalen elektrischen Erregbarkeit der Skelettmuskulatur. I. Objektivierung der supravitalen Muskelkontraktion. *Z Rechtsmed* 1992;**2**:107–121.

38. Madea B. Längsschnittuntersuchungen zur supravitalen elektrischen Erregbarkeit der Skelettmuskulatur. II. Quantifizierung der supravitalen Muskelkontraktion. *Z Rechtsmed* 1993;**3**:44–50.

39. Madea B. Cadaveric spasm. *Forensic Sci Med Pathol* 2013;**9**:249–250.

40. Madea B, Henssge C. Electrical excitability of skeletal muscle postmortem in casework. *Forensic Sci Int* 1990;**47**:207–227.

41. Madea B, Henssge C. Zum postmortalen Verhalten der Rheobase. *Z Rechtsmed* 1990;**103**: 435–452.

42. Madea B, Rödig A. Precision of estimating the time since death using different criteria of supravital muscular excitability. *Forensic Sci Med Pathol* 2006;**2**(2):127-133.

43. Mattig W, Waltz H. Untersuchungen zur Todeszeitbestimmung mittels elektrischer Reizung. *Kriminal Forens Wiss* 1976;**26**:68–71.

44. Näcke P. Die Dauer der postmortalen mechanischen Muskulaturerregbarkeit bei chronisch Geisteskranken, speziell Paralytikern. *Z Gesamte Neurol Psychiatr* 1911;**7**:424–446.

45. Nagy J. The postmortem excitability of the skeletal muscles. *Acta Med Leg Soc (Liege)* 1968:177–178.

46. Nokes LD, Barasi S, Knight BH. Case report: co-ordinated motor movement of a lower limb after death. *Med Sci Law* 1989;**29**:265.

47. Opitz E. Physiologie der Erstickung und des Sauerstoffmangels. In: Ponsold A (ed.). *Lehrbuch der Gerichtlichen Medizin.* Stuttgart, Germany, Thieme, 1950, pp 174–218.

48. Opitz E. Der Stoffwechsel des Gehirns und seine Veränderungen bei Kreislaufstillstand. *Verh Dtsch Ges Kreislaufforsch* 1953;**19**:26–44.

49. Opitz E, Schneider M. Über die Sauerstoffversorgung des Gehirns und den Mechanismus von Mangelwirkungen. *Ergebn Physiol* 1950;**46**:126–260.

50. Partmann W. Zur Frage der postmortalen Reaktionsfähigkeit des kontraktilen Mechanismus der Muskulatur. *Naturwissenschaften* 1955;**42**:161–162.

51. Popwassilew J, Palm W. Über die Todeszeitbestimmung in den ersten 10 Stunden. *Z Arztl Fortbild* 1960;**54**:734–737.

52. Prokop O. *Lehrbuch der gerichtlichen Medizin.* Berlin, Verlag Volk und Gesundheit, 1960.

53. Prokop O. *Forensische Medizin.* Berlin, Verlag Volk und Gesundheit, 1975.

54. Puppe G. Der Scheintod und seine Diagnose. *Med Wochenschr* 1920;**14/15**:383–385.

55. Radam G. Ein elektronisches Reizgerät zur Todeszeitbestimmung. *Gesundheitswes* 1963;**18**:1400–1401.

56. Ramme H, Staak M. Vergleichende Untersuchungen zur Methodik der Todeszeitschätzung. *Beitr Gerichtl Med* 1983;**41**:365–369.

57. Rampitsch D. *Todeszeitbestimmung im frühpostmortalen Stadium.* Graz, Austria, University of Graz, Medical dissertation, 2010.

58. Raszeja S, Bardzik S. Studies on the "intralethal" excitability of muscles following stimuli obtained from an electronic stimulator. *Bull Pol Med Sci Hist* 1971;**14**:93.

59. Raule P, Forster B, Joachim H, Ropohl D. Tierexperimentelle Untersuchungen zur Erregbarkeit des absterbenden Herzmuskels. *Z Rechtsmed* 1974;**74**:99–110.

60. Ravache-Quiriny J. The time of death: some thoughts on the trustworthiness of our response. *Int Acad Leg Med Soc Med* 1982;**1**(Newsletter):9–11.

61. Ravache-Quiriny J. *Les moments de la mort. Cahiers de Médiane légale, Droits medicales,* no. 3. Association Lyonnaise Médicine legale. Lyon, Editions Alesandre Lacasagne, 1986.

62. Romanelli MC, Gelardi M, Fiorella ML, Tattoli L, Di Vella G, Solarino B. Nasal ciliary motility: a new tool in estimating the time of death. *Int J Legal Med* 2012;**126**(3):427-433.

63. Rotter W. Über die postischämische Insuffizienz überlebender Zellen und Organe, ihre Erholungszeit und die Wiederbelebungszeit nach Kreislaufunterbrechung. *Thoraxchir* 1958/59;**6**:107–124.

64. Schleyer F. Determination of the time of death in the early postmortem interval. In: Lundquist F. (ed.). *Methods of Forensic Science*, vol. 2. London, Interscience, 1963, pp 253–293.

65. Schneider M. Über die Wiederbelebung nach Kreislaufunterbrechung. *Thoraxchir* 1958;**6**:95–106.

66. Schneider M. Die Wiederbelebungszeit verschiedener Organe nach Ischämie. *Langenbecks Arch Klin Chir* 1964;**308**:252–264.

67. Schourup K. *Determination of the Time Since Death* (Danish, English summary), Copenhagen, Medical dissertation, 1950, Dansk Videnskabs Kobenhavn.

68. Semmler J. *Einfluss der Umgebungstemperatur auf die Todeszeitbestimmung durch elektrische Reizung der Oberlidmuskulatur menschlicher Leichen.* Magdeburg, Germany, Magdeburg University, MD thesis, 1979.

69. Silbernagel S, Despopoulos A. *Taschenatlas der Physiologie*, 3rd ed., Stuttgart, Germany, Thieme, 1988.

70. Spieckermann PG. *Überlebens – und Wiederbelebungszeit des Herzens. Anaesth and Resuscit 66.* Berlin, Springer, 1973.

71. Waltz H, Mattig W. Elektrische Messungen an Leichen für die Konstruktion eines elektronischen Reizgerätes zur Todeszeitbestimmung. *Kriminal Forens Wiss* 1974;**16**:159–178.

72. Wright EB. A comparative study of the effects of oxygen lack on peripheral nerve. *Am J Physiol* 1946;**147**:78–89.

73. Zink P, Reinhardt G. Die Todeszeitbestimmung bei der ärztlichen Leichenschau. *Bayer Ärztebl* 1972;**27**:109–115.

74. Zsako S. Die Bestimmung der Todeszeit durch die muskelmechanischen Erscheinungen. *Munch Med Wochenschr* 1916;**3**:82.

75. Zsako S. Die Bestimmung des Todeszeitpunktes. *Psychiatr Neurol Wochenschr* 1941;66–69.

4 Rigor Mortis
Estimation of the Time Since Death by Evaluation of Cadaveric Rigidity

Thomas Krompecher

Rigor mortis is certainly the most fascinating cadaveric sign. Because it gives the deceased person a petrified appearance, rigor mortis is noticed by everybody who encounters a corpse. It is therefore often used to estimate the time since death, even (and especially) by the non-initiated. It is generally accepted that a watch must be tested, perhaps even under various circumstances, before it is used to measure time. In addition, one is expected to read the user's manual. Alas, I fear we lack such a user's manual in the case of rigor mortis – and, if this is so, it is certainly not for want of related literature; in fact, publications about cadaveric rigidity abound. A brief summary of our present knowledge concerning this phenomenon is presented here.

■ Explanation of the mechanism of rigor mortis

According to our current understanding, rigor mortis is the result of postmortem muscle contraction. Therefore, to understand the development of rigidity, we must first study the mechanism of muscle contraction and hence the structure of the muscle.

In the 1940s, Szent-Györgyi [86,87], whose laboratory gave us numerous basic data concerning the composition and the function of the muscle, described the muscle fibre as, 'the loveliest toy ever provided by nature for the biochemist ... like most children, the biochemist, when he finds a toy, usually pulls it to pieces ...'

Szent-Györgyi's attempts to pull the muscle fibre to pieces resulted in the discovery of two proteins, which he named actin and myosin. These two proteins form interdigitating thick (myosin) and thin (actin) filaments, which build the sarcomere, the contractile unit of the muscle. The sarcomeres are organized from head to tail in series (4000 per cm) that form the fibrils. The muscle cell is a fibre composed of 1000 to 2000 fibrils (Figure 4.1).

The contraction of the muscle can be explained by the adenosine triphosphate (ATP) theory of Erdös [18] and the sliding filament model of contraction proposed by Hanson and Huxley [28]. According to this sliding filament model, contraction or tension in the muscle is achieved by the contrary motion of the interdigitating filaments. The myosin filament carries myosin heads on both ends. These heads attach to the actin filament and act as cross-bridges to form the actin-myosin complex. During contraction, the heads swivel and the thin filament is pulled past the thick filament. As the heads on each end of the myosin filament swivel in opposite directions, the Z-lines approach each other and the sarcomere shortens. The limit of contraction is reached when the thick myosin filaments butt against the Z-line (see Figure 4.1).

Both filaments slide without changing their length. Motion is achieved by cyclical formation and breaking of the cross-bridges. The fibrils may shorten by 30 to 50 per cent, thus requiring that the swivel cycle be repeated many times.

The driving force for the sliding motion comes from the myosin heads. The kinetic energy is derived from chemical processes. The myosin heads bind ATP and form myosin-ATP, which in turn has a very high affinity for actin, resulting in the actin-myosin complex. When the actin-myosin complex is formed, the low ATPase activity displayed by free myosin heads is increased, and ATP is hydrolyzed. The energy released through ATP hydrolysis is used for the dissociation of the actin-myosin complex.

The ATP used is almost immediately regenerated. This may be achieved through three different processes:

1. The hydrolysis of creatine phosphate, which furnishes rapidly available energy within short time limits. As a consequence, brief but violent exercise may be accomplished (e.g. a 100-metre sprint). The creatine phosphate used in this process is restored by means of the energy generated by anaerobic glycolysis.

2. For continued exercise, the glycogen content of the muscle must be used. Glycogen can be transformed entirely to lactic acid by anaerobic hydrolysis. This process is limited by the accumulation of lactic acid.

3. Oxidative phosphorylation is the combustion of glucose in the presence of oxygen. It results in the production of carbon dioxide and water and, although it liberates great amounts of ATP, it is a relatively slow process.

If ATP is not regenerated, as is the case when ATP is consumed after death, the actin-myosin complex is not split; rather, it persists and the muscle remains inextensible. This stable actin-myosin complex is the basis for the development of rigor mortis in the postmortem state.

In summary, rigor mortis is a normal muscle contraction occurring after death and fixed by lack of ATP.

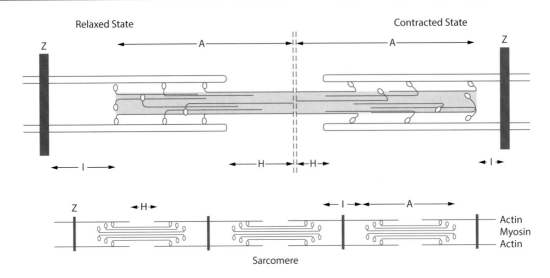

Relaxed State   Contracted State

Sarcomere

Figure 4.1 Schematic representation of the contraction and relaxation of an isolated sarcomere. The cross-bridges (myosin heads) pull the actin filaments and the attached Z-lines towards each other.

The swivel cycle is repeated until the myosin filaments butt against the Z-line. The H zone and I band shorten, and the A band remains constant.

The *in vitro* experiments of Erdös [18] and Krause and Zett [40,41] demonstrated that rigidity disappears after the addition of ATP or oxygen. Consequently, the onset of rigor mortis can be considered a supravital phenomenon; in fact, it is the last evident vital event in the muscle.

Given this explanation, it is easy to understand the mechanism of development of cadaveric rigidity, which unfolds in four different phases.

First phase: delay period

After clinical death, the muscle survives in a normal state for a short time and stays relaxed as long as the ATP content remains sufficiently high to permit the splitting of the actin-myosin cross-bridges. This fact was first proven by Erdös [18], who compared the hardness of the muscle with its ATP concentration. The two curves showed mirror images: the decrease in ATP levels was matched by an increase in hardness (confirmed by Bate-Smith and Bendall [3]). The rate of ATP depletion depends on its content at the time of death, on the possibility of postmortem ATP production and on the rate of ATP hydrolysis.

Second phase: onset period (reversible)

The ATP content of the muscle falls below a critical threshold. The cross-bridges remain intact and rigidity appears. However, this state is still reversible: the addition of ATP (reported by Erdös [18] and confirmed by Bendall [6]) or oxygen [40] results in relaxation, indicating that the muscle is still able to function.

According to Bendall [6], the rigor-tension development of postmortem muscles is very feeble compared with a living muscle; the maximal tension is about 150 g/cm^2 compared with about 4000 g/cm^2 in tetanus.

Third phase: rigor (irreversible)

Rigidity is fully developed and becomes irreversible. Postmortem modifications of muscle fibres destroy their ability to relax.

Fourth phase: resolution

Rigidity disappears and the muscle becomes limp. The cause of resolution is not definitely established. Nevertheless, I believe that, according to our present knowledge, one can accept the suggestions of Erdös [18] and Szent-Györgyi [86] that resolution is a denaturation process. Morphological evaluations confirm this hypothesis [13,17,42,69].

Bendall [6] proposed that the process is strongly pH dependent and added, 'Thus there may be no further need to search about, apparently hopelessly, for a protease (cathepsin) which could break the rather specific linkages probably involved'.

The foregoing phases are valid only for isolated fibres. In everyday practice, one is confronted with muscles that are made up of a multitude of fibres. The timing of the onset of rigor mortis cannot be determined precisely because rigor mortis is a progressive event, evolving from less apparent to more pronounced. The progression can be explained by the coexistence of fibres at different stages of developing rigidity.

Although the timing of the onset of rigor mortis in a fibre may depend on its ATP content, there are other reasons for heterogeneity.

The human skeletal muscles contain two types of fibre:

- Type I (red): rich in mitochondria, with a predominantly oxidative metabolism and slow myosin.
- Type II (white): relatively poor in mitochondria, with a predominantly glycolytic metabolism [10,19,60] and fast myosin [9].

The onset of rigor mortis in these two types of fibres is expected to occur at different times.

During a given period of time after the onset of rigor mortis, rigidity that is broken (by forcing the movement of a joint) is restored. This re-establishment of rigor mortis can be explained as follows: those fibres that are still slack, and perhaps those that are not fully contracted, retain their capacity for reversible binding of the myosin heads to the actin filaments. The contraction of such fibres causes the re-establishment of rigor mortis.

The progressive nature of the resolution of rigor mortis may be caused by a similar phenomenon. The different fibres relax at different times as the number of fibres destroyed by postmortem reactions increases.

The development of rigor mortis in canine cardiac muscle has been also investigated [56,80,91]. Seelye *et al.* [80] found that 'at 37°C the physical onset of rigor mortis commenced after 40 min … and complete rigor was attained at 100 min. The onset of rigor mortis commenced when the adenine content of the muscle had fallen by 62 per cent and was complete when a 75 per cent loss had occurred'.

Evidence for rigor in smooth muscle was described by Wuytack and Casteels [94] in guinea pig taenia coli and in rabbit aorta, mesenteric artery and vena portae. These investigators concluded that 'this contracture occurring during metabolic depletion corresponds to a rigor mortis of smooth muscle'.

■ Description of cadaveric rigidity in the literature

Description based on subjective examinations

Nysten's law

In 1811, the French physician and chemist P. H. Nysten [66] published the first scientific description of rigor mortis. The law named after him states: ' The rigidity in humans begins in the trunk and the neck, followed by the upper extremities and after that by the lower limbs. It follows the same order during the resolution'. The development of rigor mortis is thus descending, a finding thought to be related to the varying distances between the different muscles and the central nervous system (CNS). However, Nysten himself noticed that the destruction of the CNS did not affect the order of the development of rigidity.

Although Naumann [64] confirmed the descending development of rigor mortis, he added that in some special cases (e.g. in weak individuals or those diminished by illness), rigidity may show an ascending pattern.

Based on 271 protocols carried out by the same forensic pathologist, Mittmeyer [61] concluded that: 'With increasing time interval from death, the joints were seen absolutely rigid and completely released in the following order: nape, elbow, jaw, knee and leaping joints'.

Shapiro [81,82] wrote:

'It is difficult to understand why a physico-chemical process which takes place in recently dead tissues should follow the sequence usually described. It appears more likely that, because we are dealing with a physico-chemical process in what is virtually a lump of clay, this will take place *simultaneously* in all the recently dead muscles. If that be the case, it would be reasonable to expect that small masses of muscle would be involved completely much more rapidly than large masses of muscle.

The account of the invariable progression of death stiffening from the top to the bottom of the body as generally given in the textbooks must, therefore, be modified. The explanation may have to be sought along the lines indicated, viz., that rigor mortis does not progress from the upper end to the lower end of the body in a well-defined fashion, but occurs simultaneously in the recently dead muscles; and that the fixation of a joint depends, among other things, on the involvement by rigor mortis of the quantity of muscle which controls that joint. Variations in the sizes of different joints and in the muscle masses which control them determine the surface, from where further heat loss occurs to the atmosphere by radiation and convection'.

I found a possible confirmation of this hypothesis in the paper of Tarrant and Mothersill [89]. These investigators found that in beef carcasses the pH values decreased with distance from the surface and as muscle temperature increased. The time required for the pH to fall to 6.0 in six major hindquarter muscles ranged from 2.2 to 13.6 hours, and it varied with the muscle and depth in the carcass. Moreover, these investigators observed a good correlation between the rate of ATP turnover and muscle temperature.

Much of our knowledge of the chemical changes underlying the rigor process was discovered in laboratories working for the meat industry because the tenderness (i.e. the quality of the meat) depends on this process. New data are continually emerging, and they help create a better understanding of this phenomenon [26,85]. For example, one article is titled 'Meat toughening does not occur when rigor shortening is prevented' [39]. Reading some of these articles [33,36,37], we can appreciate the complexity of the physicochemical and structural changes that occur during the conversion of muscle to meat.

Textbooks of forensic medicine often suggest exceptions to Nysten's law, implying that:

- Nysten's law is often valid.
- Considering the exceptions, we must not rely on it.

The chronology of the development of rigor mortis

In this respect, it is interesting to recall the observations of Niderkorn [65], who in 1872 determined the times

Table 4.1   Time course of cadaveric rigidity

| Rigor phase | Mean with standard deviation(s)* | Hours post mortem | | | | Number of publications evaluated |
| | | Limits of 95.5% probability (2 s) | | Variations | | |
		Lower limit	Upper limit	Lower limit	Upper limit	
Delay period	3 ± 2	—	7	<1/2	7	26
Re-establishment possible	Up to 5	—	—	2	8	—
Complete rigidity	8 ± 1	6	10	2	20	28
Persistence	57 ± 14	29	85	24	96	27
Resolution	76 ± 32	12	140	24	192	27

* Mean and standard deviation calculated from the literature data of 150 years (1811 to 1960) by Mallach 1964.

Modified from Schleyer F. Leichenveränderungen. Todeszeitbestimmung im früh postmortalen Intervall. In: Muller B (ed.). *Gerichtliche Medizin*, vol. 1. Berlin, Springer, 1975.

necessary for the completion of rigor mortis in 113 bodies. In 76 corpses (67 per cent), rigor mortis was fully established after 4 to 7 hours (in 31 cases, after 4 hours; in 14 cases, after 5 hours; in 20 cases, after 6 hours; and in 11 cases, after 7 hours). In 2 cases, rigidity was complete 2 hours post mortem, and in 2 others, only 13 hours after death.

Mallach's chronology of the development of rigor mortis [57,58], which was based on a survey of the literature from 1811 to 1960, is shown in Table 4.1 [76].

This summary has been criticized, however [30]. Indeed, it is hazardous to compare and evaluate 'feelings' statistically: the observations are highly subjective and were gathered by examiners over 150 years (1811–1960). Moreover, these observations were not codified: various authors often used different classifications in their determination of the state of development of cadaveric rigidity. Nonetheless, we lack a better survey.

In spite of the subjective nature of the information, I believe that every individual estimate is highly valuable. In fact, our predecessors, with observation as the sole method at their disposal, used this simple means expertly, and their conclusions are of great worth. In our own work on cadaveric rigidity, we often base our experiments on statements provided by ancient authors. If our measurements happen to contradict these statements, we regard the results with scepticism. Once an experiment is repeated, and if our results are confirmed, we always seek a valid explanation for the discrepancy.

If these observations are valid (and in my mind, they are indeed in most cases), what are the reasons for the great differences in the development of rigor mortis between one corpse and another? The answer stems from the realization that the process is biological or, more precisely, biochemical, and that it can be affected by a number of intrinsic and extrinsic factors.

First, we must consider the physical condition of the individual before death (i.e. the factors that influence the energetic reserves).

H. A. Husband [34], in his 1877 *Student's Hand-Book of Forensic Medicine*, summarized such factors as follows:

- 'Effects of enfeebling disease before death: rapid in its invasion, passing off rapidly.
- Effects of a robust frame at period of death: the accession may be prolonged, but, other things being equal, it is more strongly manifested and continues longer.
- Effects of violent exercise before death: supervenes and disappears rapidly.
- Effects of poison. Poisons that cause violent contractions for some time before death (e.g. strychnine) influence the rapid invasion of the rigor mortis, its short duration and the subsequent putrefaction.
- Where death in poisoning by strychnine is almost instantaneous, with a short convulsive stage, the rigor mortis comes on rapidly and remains for a long time.'

Today, more than 100 years later, textbooks include very similar statements.

In 1984, Vock *et al.* [93] published a case of tetany involving instantaneous rigor. Electrocution may also hasten the onset of cadaveric rigidity. In the three electrocution cases reported by Schneider in 1985 [77], stiffness was complete after 1 hour 40 minutes, 1 hour 45 minutes and 2 hours 5 minutes after death. In one of our cases [44], rigidity was fully established 1 hour post mortem in the upper limbs located in the path of the electrical current, but no rigidity was observed elsewhere. Another individual who was found in the bath tub with a hairdryer was in a state of complete rigidity only 3 hours after being seen alive for the last time.

Several cases of accelerated rigidity after certain intoxications have been reported, with organophosphate compounds [59] and strychnine [50].

Re-establishment

According to Mallach's [57] chronology of the development of rigor mortis, the re-establishment of the rigidity is possible between 2 and 8 hours post mortem, with a mean time up to 5 hours. In current textbooks and publications [31,32,38,75], we found the same upper limit (i.e. 8 hours, sometimes 8 to 12 hours [72,88]).

In a more recent publication, Anders *et al.* [1] examined 314 joints (elbow and knee) of 79 deceased persons. These investigators found that re-establishment – tested manually – occurred in 38.5 per cent of joints at 7.5 to 19 hours post mortem.

The influence of temperature

Considering that the onset of rigor mortis depends on biochemical processes, and that its resolution results from the degradation of cellular structures, it is easy to understand that its overall development is affected by the temperature of the body and consequently by that of the surroundings.

Naturally, this fact was noticed long ago. In 1811, Nysten [66] stated that rigidity persists longer in cold, dry air than in warm, wet air.

In 1856, Kussmaul [54] wrote: 'The corpses of strong persons can stay stiff till 8 to 10 and more days in air of 2.5 to 7.5°C, while at 18.8 to 30°C the last traces of rigidity disappear in 4 to 6 days'.

In his 1877 textbook, Husband [34] summed up the effect of low temperature as follows: '[Rigor mortis is] prolonged by dry cold air and cold water'.

In 1888, Bierfreund [8] examined the influence of temperature on the development of cadaveric rigidity on the lower limbs of rabbits. His observations are shown in Table 4.2.

Morgenstern's [62] experiments in 1927 on rabbits and cats of various ages showed that temperature has spectacular effects on the development of rigor mortis. These experiments also revealed differences related to the species studied and the various ages of the animals. Morgenstern also recorded an important acceleration in the onset of rigidity when human corpses were immersed in warm water (35°C to 37°C).

In 1974, Forster *et al.* [23] observed the duration of cadaveric rigidity in the lower limbs of human corpses kept at low temperatures (4°C to 11°C). Based on the observations made during the entire period when the corpses were available, the following conclusions were made:

'If we address the question raised in the beginning specifically the persistence of complete rigidity 130 hours after death, we must come to the conclusion that at low temperatures, rigidity can be demonstrated well after this period, even if we take into account slight fluctuations in temperature and a possible error (of a few hours) in the estimate of time of death'.

In one of Forster's cases, a corpse kept at +4°C exhibited strong rigidity, even after 234 hours.

Duncan *et al.* [15] published a case of malignant hyperthermia (42°C) in a dog secondary to ingestion of hops where 'the onset of rigor mortis was evident in <15 minutes'.

Varetto and Curto [92] tested the mobility of the knee on corpses kept at a constant temperature of +4°C. These investigators found a persistence of complete rigor lasting for 10 days in all the cadavers, and in one case, rigor lasted for 16 days.

In our practice, the opposite situation was illustrated by the case of two corpses found on an exceptionally hot summer day (40°C) in a closed car exposed to the sun. At the examination, carried out less than 8 hours after death, the corpses appeared strongly affected, with parts that were blackened and, naturally, without the faintest sign of rigidity. At the other temperature extreme, an interesting observation was made by Bendall [6]: 'If a muscle is frozen in the pre-rigor state while ATP and PC [phosphocreatine] levels are high, after thawing out rigor sets in'. However, because this experiment was carried out on very thin strips of muscle, which were rapidly frozen at −20°C, it is difficult to imagine the occurrence of this phenomenon in the forensic practice.

Table 4.2 Effect of temperature on the development of rigor mortis on the lower limbs of rabbits

Number	Temperature of air (°C)	Beginning of the onset of rigidity post mortem		Complete development of rigidity		Beginning of resolution post mortem		Complete resolution post mortem	
		Hours	Min	Hours	Min	Hours	Min	Hours	Min
1	4.0	1	30	7	—	38	—	48	—
2	20.0	1	—	5	15	26	—	36	—
3	22.5	1	—	4	20	—	—	36	—
4	29.0	—	50	3	20	24	—	28	—
5	37.5	—	35	2	—	2	25	4	10
6	41.0	—	45	1	5	1	22	2	30
7	52.5	—	15	—	45	1	—	1	40
8	54.0	—	—	—	50	1	—	1	50
9	55.0	—	2–5	—	37	—	40	1	40
10	60.0	Almost instantly		—	10	—	35	1	10

Data from Bierfreund M. Untersuchungen über die Totenstarre. *Pflügers Arch* 1888;**43:**195–216.

The influence of the central nervous system

As noted earlier, the descending pattern in the development of rigor mortis was thought to be caused by the varying distances from the CNS. In 1904, Fuchs [25] described the brain as the initial site of death, followed by the proximal part of the spinal cord, and suggested that the process then progressed towards the caudal spinal cord: the presumed impulsions arose from catabolic changes in the nerve cells.

In 1819, Busch [11] observed that the removal of the brain and spinal cord resulted in an early onset of rigidity; moreover, rigidity was more pronounced and lasted longer.

In experiments conducted on animals, Eiselberg [16] in 1881 demonstrated that when the sciatic nerve was sectioned on one side, in more than 70 per cent of the cases rigidity developed later than on the other side.

Gendre [27] and Aust [2] confirmed this finding. Aust, in particular, obtained this result in 12 of a total of 13 experiments. Having conducted *in vivo* sectioning of the left side of the spinal cord in rabbits (underneath the pyramidal crossing), Bierfreund [8] in 1888 made the following statement: 'I was very surprised to find that after a few hours following death, the right half of the body became very rigid, while the left half remained almost normally mobilisable'. Bierfreund thought that the 'accelerating' effect of the CNS on the appearance of cadaveric rigidity was the result of weak excitation of the muscular system, and if this excitation really did exist, it was too weak to cause a visible contraction. To prove this hypothesis, Bierfreund conducted animal experiments that involved weak irritation by the sciatic nerve. The results were the very opposite of what he had hoped for.

In the 1940s, Berg [7] determined that, following death, cholinesterase retains its full or partial activity in the muscle until an advanced stage of muscular degradation. Moreover, during the delay period, the muscular system was found to release small amounts of acetylcholine. The onset of cadaveric rigidity was found to be hastened by the inhibition of acetylcholinesterase, by the addition of acetylcholine or by thermal irritation of the contralateral motor region. The inhibition of transmitters retarded the onset of rigidity.

In 1976, Krause *et al.* [42] made the following interesting observation: 'The irritation of sciatic and radial nerves in amputated arms and legs caused violent muscular reactions for up to two hours, but action potentials in the nerves were detectable even after this period of time'.

The experimental results described in this section are partially contradictory. Therefore, it remains unclear what role the nervous system may play in the development of cadaveric rigidity.

Instantaneous rigor or cadaveric spasm

Instantaneous rigor is defined as complete rigor mortis occurring at the moment of death and involving a hand, limb or even the entire body. In 1923, Baumann [4] surveyed the literature on this subject and concluded that most of the reported cases of instantaneous rigor mortis involving lesions in the head, brain, brainstem and thorax were caused by death from internal lesions and also probably by gas embolism. Laves [55] and Prokop [73,64] proposed that the cause could be decerebrate rigidity as also suggested by Sherrington in 1908 [83].

Polson and Gee [71] cited many such instances in the literature, but during their 20-year practice in Leeds, they reported only two cases. In our own practice, I have never encountered an example of truly instantaneous rigor mortis, nor have I been able to gather acceptable examples in my colleagues' cases.

Some of the cases published in the literature, especially the more spectacular ones, were based on observations made during war time [71,73]. Interestingly, Mueller [63], a German forensic pathologist, searched but failed to observe a case of instantaneous rigor during the Second World War, in spite of his surveys of military medics.

My colleagues and I have encountered numerous cases of electrocution in which the body apparently remained in the position of the spasm caused by the electric shock [77]. In these cases, the facies was also found to be contracted. However, the term 'instantaneous rigidity' does not apply here. Indeed, in all our observed cases [44], the body remained in direct or indirect contact with the electrical current up to the moment of discovery of the cadaver. Because of the accelerated onset of rigor mortis (see earlier), it is reasonable to assume that rigor mortis fixed the body in a given position while the spasm was still occurring.

Pirch *et al.* [70] presented the case of a young woman found dead in an upright standing position. These investigators concluded that 'Whereas the position of the body is most unusual, a detailed analysis reveals that it is a stable position even without rigor mortis. Therefore, this case does not further support the controversial concept of IR'.

In our practice, my colleagues and I encountered an identical case.

Ultimately, we believe that even if instantaneous rigor mortis does exist, it is a very rare event. Consequently, before accepting such an explanation, it is important to study all the other possibilities (e.g. changes in the position of the body and/or of the surrounding objects, electrocution).

Objective measurements of rigor mortis

Rigor mortis, the stiffening of the muscles after death, immobilizes the joints. The resistance in the joints can be used to make a qualitative or even a quantitative estimate of the degree of rigor.

In the situations described so far, the conclusions were drawn on the basis of estimates of the force necessary to bend a knee or an elbow immobilized by cadaveric rigidity. Such manual estimates are necessarily subjective and cannot be compared among different observers. Moreover, this method is not applicable when the degree of rigidity rises above a certain level. For example, one feels the same when asked to lift 200 or 500 kg – the weight makes no difference because one cannot move either. The same situation can be found in the case of rigidity. When rigidity in a knee or jaw joint cannot be broken, it is not clear whether rigidity increases or decreases until its intensity falls down to the levels commensurate with human strength.

It is, of course, desirable to determine the exact degree of rigidity, to obtain reproducible numerical values that can be compared and to extend the measurements in situations where human strength is insufficient.

As far as we know, the first objective measurements of rigidity were reported in 1919, by Oppenheim and Wacker [67], who gave a detailed description of their method to measure the force necessary to bend a leg with a knee joint immobilized by rigidity; this is referred to as 'breaking' the rigidity of a joint. Oppenheim and Wacker expressed their results relative to the mass of the relevant muscles. They discussed the influence of the cause of death on the development of rigor mortis, so their results could not be used to estimate the time of death.

Subsequently, two German research teams further developed methods to measure the force necessary to break the cadaveric rigidity of a knee joint. One team was headed by Forster in Freiburg, and the other by Beier in Munich. However, before reviewing their findings, a few general comments about the development of cadaveric rigidity may be useful.

In forensic practice, one examines the degree to which muscular rigidity fixes or immobilizes a joint. Hence, the measure of cadaveric rigidity is a measure of the force necessary to move a joint. The development of rigidity is the process of change in the intensity of rigidity over time. This intensity is weak at first, but it then increases, reaches a maximum, decreases and finally practically disappears after a variable period of time. This process can be represented by a curve, although such a curve is valid only for one given corpse under clearly defined conditions.

Although only two points are necessary (and sufficient) to define a straight line, multiple points are needed to define a curve, which cannot be determined by a single point. This is the basis of the difficulty in attempting to characterize the development of cadaveric rigidity by using a single measurement (it is not even possible to make two measurements because the development of cadaveric rigidity is different in the two lower limbs of the same corpse; this is discussed later). Forster et al. [24] proposed standardizing the measurements using the following formula:

FRR (Freiburger Rigor Index) = $p \cdot I_1/U^2 \cdot I_2 \times 100$

where p is the traction force (kp), I_1 is the length of the leg (cm), I_2 is the distance from the rotation axis of the knee joint to the anterior surface of the knee cap (cm) and U is the circumference of the thigh (cm) (Table 4.3).

Table 4.3 Proposed standardized measurements of cadaveric rigidity

Rigor index	Degree of rigidity	Subjective observation
>5.5	1	Complete rigidity
<5.5–4.0	2	Very difficult to break
<4.0–2.5	3	Relatively easy to break
<2.5–1.3	4	Soft
<1.3–0.2	5	Weak
<0.2	6	Complete resolution

This formula may be used to correct (at least partially) for the differences among individual cases. However, it does not take into account individual factors, such as the difference in muscle mass between two thighs with the same circumference.

The actual worth of this formula remains unknown. Although Forster et al. published the formula on several occasions [20,21,24], they did not communicate any numerical data to justify the entries made in their table. They also published a schematic curve of the development of rigor mortis [20,21,24], which was apparently based on the results calculated using their formula, but without explaining how they obtained it. Lacking conclusive reports, these conclusions should be treated with great caution.

Beier et al. [5] relied on a similar approach to measure the intensity of cadaveric rigidity. The experiments consisted of determining the torque necessary to break the rigor mortis of arms and legs. The measurements were made on 17 female and 35 male cadavers stored at a temperature of 4°C. The authors concluded that:

'The values show differences between male and female cadavers to an extent that both groups have to be treated separately. Relating the torque to the diameter of the cross-section of the limb does not eliminate the difference. Frequently, considerable differences between left and right limbs were obtained, however, without preference for one side over the other. There is no direct functional relationship between postmortem time and the intensity of rigor mortis, but the values occasionally allow estimates on the maximum time postmortem'.

In a second series of reports [78,79], the following observations were made:

'The torque to overcome rigor mortis was determined for each leg by bending the lower leg of the prone cadaver toward the fixed thigh. The device ensures that the force is kept perpendicular to the tibia. The force is read from a spring balance with an accuracy of 5 Nm. For the lever arm, the distance from the knee joint, or the epicondylus lateralis, to the site of attachment of the spring balance was taken. Torque values ranging from 10 to 500 Nm were measured to

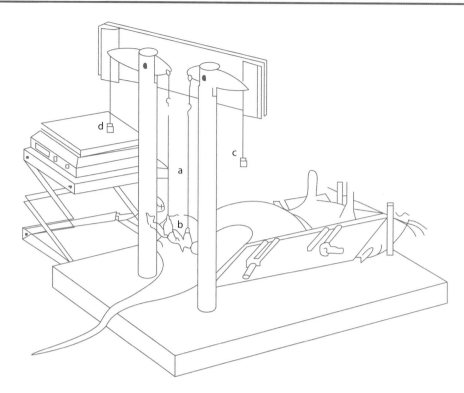

Figure 4.2 Apparatus for the measurement of rigor mortis intensity: cord attached to hind limb (a), steel hooks permitting attachment of cord to limbs (b), hook supporting weights (previous technique) (c), hook attached to a digital balance (d).

an accuracy of 3 Nm and, above 100 Nm, to 3 per cent. Before measurement the cadavers were kept in storage rooms at 4–6°C.

The rigor mortis of the legs of 101 male human cadavers were investigated. These were selected from the cadavers brought to the Institute by the following criteria: age at least 14 years, no pathological findings at the investigated extremities, time of death known exactly to within one hour.

There seems to exist an upper limit for the torque of rigor mortis, depending on the lay-time, above which no value was found. Below this limit, however, every value could be found. By calculating the 90% tolerance limits of lay-times grouped at 12-hourly intervals, this upper limit was found to decrease exponentially with lay-time. This plot may be used for the estimation of maximum lay-times from rigor mortis measurements'.

Serial objective measurements to follow the development of rigor mortis

Beier's investigations and results have probably reached the limits of the possibilities offered by this method. Considering that only a single measurement can be made per joint (or limb), and that the obtained value represents a random time point in the development of rigor mortis, one can appreciate the large degree of freedom in constructing a curve depicting the development of rigidity.

Given these limitations, I developed a different method for the objective measurement of the intensity of cadaveric

rigidity in rats [45–48]. The apparatus used is shown in Figure 4.2. The principle of the method is to determine the force necessary to cause a movement of small amplitude (4 mm) in the limb under examination.

Because this movement does not break rigor mortis, serial measurements can be taken. Our apparatus measured the resistance caused by rigor both in the knee and in the hip joints.

Initially, the force was measured by hooking successively heavier weights to obtain the standardized movement of the limb [45–48]. Subsequently, a slight modification was introduced: the hook was attached to the plate of a digital balance, which was placed on a jack (see Figure 4.2, label d). When the balance was lowered to produce the standardized small amplitude movement of the limb, the resistance caused by rigidity could be read directly from the balance (a negative value, as traction was exerted).

All the experiments were conducted on male albino rats. Each study involved animals of the same age and weight.

We reproduce here the curve of the development of the rigor mortis as first obtained on a rat at a temperature of 24.5°C (Figure 4.3).

Effect of difference in the muscle mass

In the following experiment [46], we demonstrated that there is essentially no difference in the time course of the development of rigor mortis in the hind and front limbs, even though the muscular mass of the hind limbs is 2.89 times greater than that of the front limbs. At the same time,

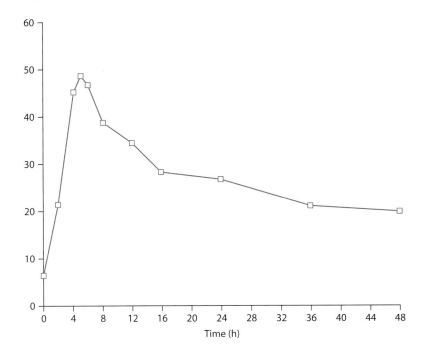

Figure 4.3 Evolution of the intensity of rigor mortis in the hind limb of a rat weighing 350 g.

in the initial phase, rigor mortis was more pronounced in the front limbs. Moreover, resolution was initially faster in the front limbs, although both hind and front limbs reached complete resolution at the same time.

The development of rigor mortis was also studied in rats of varying ages and weights [48]. Although the time course of the development was always the same, the intensity of rigor was found to be directly proportional to the increase in the animal's body weight.

Effect of physical exercise

Because the method appeared to be suitable for studying the development of rigor mortis in rats, we decided to determine the effects of physical exercise before death [47]. The animals were subjected to a treadmill exercise lasting 1 hour, with the distance covered being approximately 1020 metres. For rats raised in small cages, a 1000-metre run must represent a considerable effort, but the experimental animals tolerated it quite well. The results of this experiment are presented in Figure 4.4.

The development of rigor mortis in rats that had exercised before death differed from that of the control. The following features were noted for the exercised animals:

- There was a higher intensity in the initial phase.
- Maximum development was reached at the same time as in the controls.

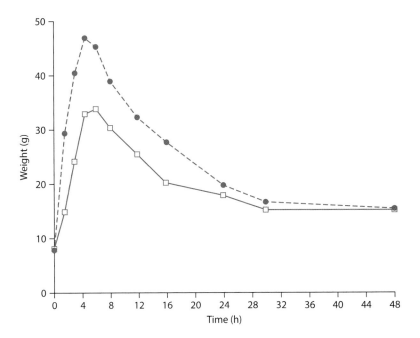

Figure 4.4 The evolution of rigor mortis in the hind limbs of rats in control (solid lines) and exercised (dashed lines) groups. Values given are always an average for 10 animals (20 hind limbs).

Table 4.4   **Evolution of rigor mortis in the two groups relative to the maximum value of the control group (33.8 g) taken as 100 per cent**

	Time post mortem (h)						
	1.66	**3**	**4.5**	**6**	**8**	**12**	**16**
Treadmill exercise (%)	86.5	119.5	139.2	134.6	115.8	95.6	82.3
Control (%)	44.4	72.3	97.8	100.0	89.8	76.0	60.3

- Higher maximum values were reached (in our experiments, 1.39 times the maximum values in the controls).
- The higher values were maintained from 100 minutes to 16 hours, with statistically significant differences.
- Resolution occurred at the same time.

Table 4.4 summarizes the development of rigor mortis in the exercised and in the control groups, relative to the maximum value of the control group (33.8 g) normalized to 100 per cent. The results illustrate the types of errors that can occur when a single, manual estimate of rigor made on a cadaver with an unknown history is used to establish the time of death. For example, the values obtained at 100 minutes and 16 hours in the exercised group are both very close to 100 per cent, which could be interpreted, erroneously, as fully developed rigidity (compared with the control group).

Effect of different temperatures

The development of rigor mortis at different temperatures is shown in Figure 4.5. Figure 4.6 illustrates the development of rigor at 6°C. By transferring the cadavers to 24°C for 24 hours between 216 and 240 hours post mortem, we wished to accelerate decomposition, thus causing the possible remnants of rigor mortis to disappear. The consecutive transfer to 6°C for 24 hours was made to determine whether the decrease in temperature alone could cause rigidity. Indeed, a marked increase in resistance could be seen between the measurements taken at 240 hours post mortem at 24°C and those taken 24 hours later at 6°C. The only difference between the specimens at these two time points was the decrease in rectal temperature from 24°C to 6°C (note that the muscles were not frozen). The increase in resistance (from 17.3 to 27.6 g) led us to conclude that a decrease in temperature alone enhances the stiffness of the muscles and perhaps the resistance in the joints as well, thus leading to what can be called 'cold rigidity'. The increase in our case was 59.53 per cent, which was highly significant [49].

Effect of intoxication

Figure 4.7 illustrates the effects of fatal intoxication by strychnine, carbon monoxide and curare on the development of intensity of rigor mortis [50]. Our findings can be summarized as follows:

- Strychnine intoxication hastens the onset and the passing of rigor mortis.
- Carbon monoxide intoxication delays the resolution of rigor mortis.
- The intensity of rigor may vary depending on the cause of death.

Effect of electrocution

In one of our electrocution cases, our first investigation at the scene of death revealed that the arms of the victim,

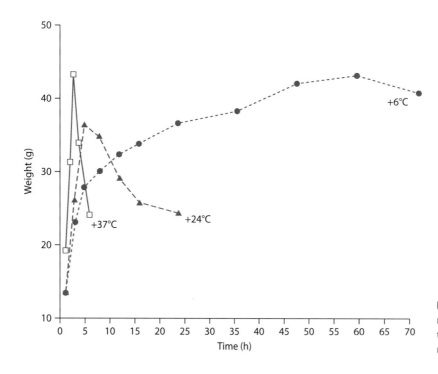

Figure 4.5   The evolution of the intensity of rigor mortis in the hind limbs of rats at different temperatures. Values given are always an average for 10 animals (20 hind limbs).

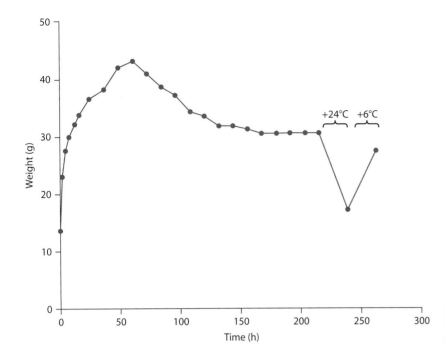

Figure 4.6 The evolution of the intensity of rigor mortis in the hind limbs of rats at +6°C. Values given are always an average for 10 animals (20 hind limbs).

which were in direct contact with the electrical current, displayed severe rigor. The victim's husband, suspected of the murder of his wife, asserted that he had left her alive 1 hour earlier.

Our experiments on electrocution [44] were conducted on rats as follows:

- Group 1, a control set killed in the usual manner by nitrogen asphyxia.
- Group 2, electrocution with 140 V, 50 Hz alternating current applied for 50 seconds, with the electrodes clamped on the left front and the right hind limb of the animal.

- Group 3, same as group 2, but electrocution for 90 seconds.
- Group 4, animals killed by nitrogen asphyxia, followed by electrocution (same as group 3), 10 minutes later.

The results of this experiment, shown in Figure 4.8, led to the following conclusions:

1. Electrocution hastens the onset of rigor mortis. After a 90-second electrocution, rigor mortis developed as rapidly as 1 hour post mortem, compared with 5 hours for the controls.

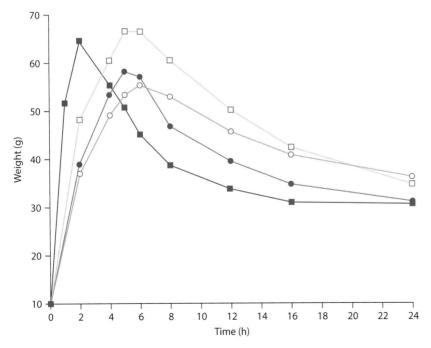

Figure 4.7 Evolution of the intensity of rigor mortis in the hind limbs of rats in the case of nitrogen asphyxia (open squares); fatal intoxication by strychnine (closed squares); carbon monoxide (open circles); and curare (closed circles). Mean values are for 10 animals (20 hind limbs).

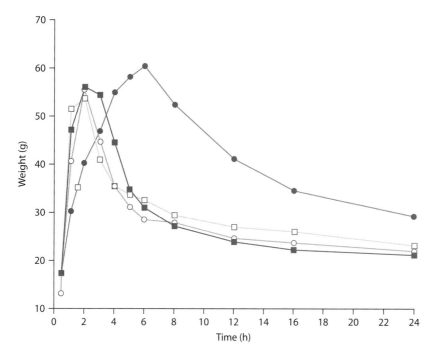

Figure 4.8 Evolution of the intensity of rigor mortis in the hind limbs of rats in the case of nitrogen asphyxia (closed circles); 'direct' electrocution for 50 seconds (open circles); 'direct' electrocution for 90 seconds (open squares); 'direct' postmortem electrocution for 90 seconds (closed squares). Mean values are for 10 animals (20 hind limbs) in the control group and for 10 animals (10 hind limbs) in the 'electrocution' groups.

2. Electrocution hastens the disappearance of rigor mortis.
3. In the case of postmortem electrocution, the observed changes were slightly less pronounced.

The changes in the development of rigor mortis were less pronounced in the limbs that were not directly affected by the electrical current (left hind limbs in our experiments).

Our results were confirmed by different authors [12,14,68]. For example, Owens and Sams [68] wrote: 'Electrical stimulation accelerated rigor mortis development'.

Moreover, we have found a good explanation for the rapid resolution of the rigidity in case of electrocution in the article of Iwamoto *et al.* [35]. They wrote: '...the gas stunned chickens maintained a good fibre structure for

4 h or more, but the electrically stunned had already lost intact fibre structure at 4 h'.

Effect of breaking

The influence of the breaking (mechanical solution) is shown in Figures 4.9 and 4.10.

Our experiments [53] showed that:

- Cadaveric rigidity can re-establish after breaking.
- Significant rigidity can reappear if the breaking occurs before the process is complete.
- Rigidity is considerably weaker after the breaking.
- The time course of the intensity does not change in comparison with the controls:

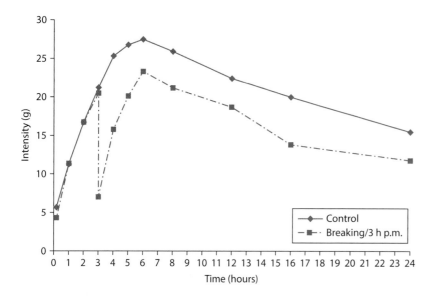

Figure 4.9 Influence of breaking on rigor mortis. Breaking 3 hours post mortem.

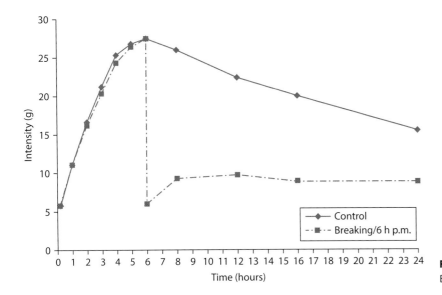

Figure 4.10 Influence of breaking on rigor mortis. Breaking 6 hours post mortem.

- The re-establishment begins immediately after the breaking.
- Maximal values are reached at the same time as in the controls.
- The course of the resolution is the same as in the controls.

To explain the phenomenon of the re-establishment of rigor mortis after 'breaking', our hypothesis is the following:

In the course of the development of rigidity, muscle fibres enter the rigid state progressively (i.e. one by one according to their different metabolism). The less fibres are rigid, the more easily rigor mortis can appear anew. When full rigor is installed, there remain no more muscle fibres which could reproduce rigidity after the breaking.

After the breaking at 6 hours post mortem (i.e. after the rigor was fully established), we still observed an increase in resistance, but the maximal values were lower than those measured in the control group 24 hours post mortem, after complete resolution. We thus conclude that this resistance is not caused by rigor mortis. Every person dealing with dead bodies can observe that, on human corpses, after resolution of rigor mortis – which requires 2 to 3 days depending on the ambient temperature – in spite of complete resolution, the joints are not as mobile as during the initial few minutes post mortem. Certain rigidity remains, and it can be easily broken. We believe that this residual rigidity is not caused by muscular rigidity *per se,* but rather by the resistance of all the periarticular tissues. We base our opinion also on the finding that when the rigidity was broken after 6 hours post mortem, there was a significant rise in the resistance after breaking, but no more changes were noted in the resistance after the maximal values were reached (i.e. no 'resolution').

In a paper already mentioned, Anders *et al.* [1] found that on human corpses the re-establishment of rigor mortis after breaking occurred up to 19 hours post mortem (i.e. after full installation of rigor mortis). There is a contradiction between our results and explanations and this observation.

It is difficult to understand the re-establishment of a 'real muscular' rigidity at 19 hours post mortem, taking in consideration the postmortem cellular decay as well. Moreover, our experimental work was made on standardized animal groups, and we used objective measurements. In their study, Anders *et al.* [1] made their observations on 79 different corpses and used subjective (manual) estimation.

To clarify the question of re-establishment of rigor mortis on human corpses studies made by objective measurement would be necessary.

For daily forensic practice, we recommend taking into consideration the possibility of the higher upper limit of the possible re-establishment of rigor mortis proposed by Anders *et al.,* being that in practice we use manual estimation.

Nysten's law: does it apply to rats?

We tried to determine the validity of Nysten's law in the case of rats. For this purpose, we adapted our method to perform parallel measurements in the masticatory muscles, the neck, the front limbs and the hind limbs in rats, while respecting the same principles of measurements [52].

- In group 1: hind limbs, the maximal values of the intensity of rigor mortis were reached at 5 hours post mortem.
- In group 2: front limbs, at 5 hours post mortem.
- In group 3: neck, at 3 hours post mortem.
- In group 4: masticatory muscles, at 2 hours post mortem.

No significative differences were found concerning the resolution of rigor mortis among the four groups.

Consequently, Nysten's law seems to apply to rats as far as the onset of rigor mortis is concerned.

Effect of the central nervous system

To evaluate the possible influence of the CNS on the evolution of rigor mortis, the following experiments were conducted on four groups of rats [51]:

- Group 1: control.
- Group 2: section of the sciatic nerve.
- Group 3: destruction of the spinal cord with a needle introduced in the spinal canal.
- Group 4: section of the medulla oblongata.

No significant difference was found in the development of rigor mortis among the four groups. We can thus state that in a 'normal' condition the CNS has no significant influence on the intensity or on the time course of the rigor mortis. These experiments do not exclude the possibility of the influence of the CNS on the development of cadaveric rigidity in some pathological conditions.

Although it is clear that the results of our experiments are not directly applicable to humans, our method is the only means to evaluate the effects of different intrinsic and extrinsic factors on the development of rigor mortis, under a set of well-defined conditions. Moreover, these experiments do provide us with an overall idea on the time course of the various changes.

In terms of practical applications based on our experiments, if the stage of rigidity is used to estimate the time of death, it is necessary to perform a succession of objective measurements of the intensity of rigor mortis and to verify the possible presence of factors that can play a role in the modification of the development of rigor mortis.

Estimation of the time since death by repeated measurements of the intensity of rigor mortis

We applied these two principles and tested our method by deriving an estimate of time elapsed since death [43]. The experiment consisted of monitoring the development of the intensity of rigor mortis in nine groups of six rats each. The animals were killed by nitrogen asphyxia at an ambient temperature of 24°C. Measurements were initiated after 2, 4, 5, 6, 8, 12, 15, 24 and 48 hours post mortem and lasted 5 to 9 hours, which would be the usual procedure when a corpse is discovered.

The results of these experiments are shown in Figure 4.11 and Table 4.5. The measurements, which were initiated 2 hours post mortem and covered a period of 9 hours, resulted in a curve composed of a rising portion, a plateau and a descending slope. When the measurements were started 4 hours post mortem, the rising portion was small, and this was followed by a long descending slope. At the later time points, the rising part was absent: after 8 hours post mortem, for example, the curve showed a plateau and a descent.

Thus, three different phases were observed that can help estimate the time since death:

1. If an increase in intensity is observed, measurements are made no later than 5 hours post mortem.
2. If a decrease in intensity is observed, measurements are made no earlier than 7 hours post mortem.
3. At 24 hours post mortem, the resolution is complete; there are no more changes in intensity.

It should also be noted that the totality of the curves assembled in Figure 4.11 gives a form very similar to that of a normal curve (compare this with Figure 4.3).

The results presented here demonstrate that, in comparison with the single measurement method used earlier, repeated measurements of the intensity of rigor mortis in rats allow the derivation of a more accurate estimate of the time since death.

The question remains whether this method is applicable to human corpses. In theory, it should be, and although we

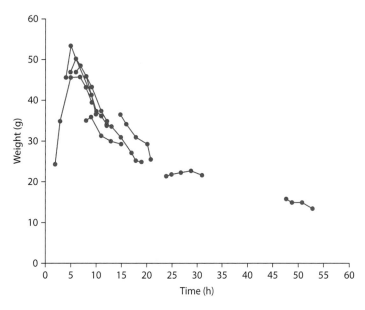

Figure 4.11 Changes in the intensity of rigor mortis in rats in different postmortem periods.

Table 4.5 Experimental evaluation of rigor mortis

Time post mortem (h)	Intensity changes
2–9	2↑3↑ 5 — 7↓8↓ 9
4–10	4↑5 — 7 ↓ 9↓10
5–12	5↑6 — 8 ↓ 10 — 11↓12
6–12	6 — 7 ↓ 9 ↓ 11↓12
8–15	8 — 9 ↓ 11 — 13 — 14 — 15
12–19	12 — 13 ↓ 15 ↓ 17↓18 — 19
15–21	15 — 16 ↓ 18 — 20↓21
24–31	24 — 25 — 27 — 29 — 31
48–53	48 — 49 — 51 ↓ 53

↑, Increase.
↓, Decrease. } Significant changes.
—, No significant changes.

can attest that its practical realization is not simple, we are nevertheless attempting to build a measuring device.

In terms of objective methods of evaluation of rigor mortis, two more methods deserve mention. Hasan and Mason [29] described a technique for measuring the propagation velocity of a mechanical pulse along a muscle. The pulse was generated by piezoelectric crystals (bimorph benders). They used this method for the evaluation of the mechanics of rigor.

Vain *et al.* [90] used the myotonometer to grade rigor mortis. The instrument gives a mechanical impact against the muscle. The muscle responds with a damped vibration, which is registered and treated mathematically. The method gives quantitative information on the muscular stiffness and can be used, according to the authors, when estimating the time of death. We do not have enough data to evaluate the practical value of this method.

■ Recommendations for practice

First, I would like to quote a remark made by Keith Simpson [84]: 'Rigor mortis is the best known, though the most uncertain and unreliable postmortem event'.

I hope that this chapter has convinced readers of the validity of this statement, and that they should exercise great caution if they use cadaveric rigidity to estimate the time since death.

Having studied cadaveric rigidity for a long time, I have come to believe that it is not the 'good method', or not 'the method' to estimate the time since death. Indeed, it requires experience (i.e. regular examinations of corpses made over a long period of time). Moreover, one must remember that there are no tables with values necessarily applicable to a given case.

Nevertheless, I am sure that rigor mortis could be a useful complement to the estimation of the time since death. Under such circumstances, I can make only the following recommendations:

1. We must base estimates on our own personal experience.
2. It is important to consult the data in the literature, in particular the descriptions of individual experiences made by a number of persons.
3. In Mallach's table (see Table 4.1), the extreme values, and not the averages, must be considered.
4. We must always seek and appreciate factors that may affect the development of rigor mortis.

Finally, I hope that the method of repeated measurements of the intensity of rigor mortis, once adapted to the human corpse, will permit a better use of this phenomenon for the estimation of time since death.

References

1. Anders S, Kunz M, Gehl A, Sehner S, Raupach T, Beck-Borholdt HP. Estimation of the time since death: reconsidering the re-establishment of rigor mortis. *Int J Legal Med* 2013;**127**:127–130.
2. Aust G. Zur Frage über den Einfluss des Nervensystems auf die Todtenstarre. *Pflugers Arch* 1886;**39**:241–244.
3. Bate-Smith EC, Bendall JR. Rigor mortis and adenosine triphosphate. *J Physiol* 1947;**106**:177–185.
4. Baumann J. Ueber kataleptische Totenstarre. *Dtsch Z Gesamte Gerichtl Med* 1923;**2**:647–670.
5. Beier G, Liebhardt E, Schuck M, Spann W. Totenstarremessungen an menschlichen Skelettmuskeln *in situ*. *Z Rechtsmed* 1977;**79**:277–283.
6. Bendall JR. Postmortem changes in muscle. In: Bourne GH (ed.). *The Structure and Function of Muscle*, vol. II, *Structure*, part 2. London, Academic Press, 1973, pp 24–309.
7. Berg S. Nervensystem und Totenstarre. *Dtsch Z Gesamte Gerichtl Med* 1948/49;**39**:429–434.
8. Bierfreund M. Untersuchungen über die Totenstarre. *Pflügers Arch* 1888;**43**:195–216.
9. Billeter R, Weber H, Lutz H, Howald H, Eppenberger HM, Jenny E. Myosin types in human skeletal muscle fibres. *Histochemistry* 1980;**65**:249–259.
10. Brooke MH, Kaiser KK. The use and abuse of muscle histochemistry. *Ann N Y Acad Sci* 1974;**228**:121–144.

11. Busch. *Experimenta quaedam de morte.* Halae, 1819. Cited by Bierfreund M. Untersuchungen über die Totenstarre. *Pflugers Arch* 1888;**43**:195–216.

12. Cavitt LC, Sams AR. Evaluation of physical dimension changes as nondestructive measurements for monitoring rigor mortis development in broiler muscles. *Poultry Sci* 2003;**82**:1198–1204.

13. David H, David S. Submikroskopische Veränderungen der Skelettmuskulatur während der postmortalen Autolyse. *Acta Biol Med Ger* 1965;**14**:423–435.

14. Devine CE, Payne SR, Peachey BM, Lowe TE, Ingram JR, Cook CJ. High and low rigor temperature effects on sheep meat tenderness and ageing. *Meat Sci* 2002;**60**:141–146.

15. Duncan KL, Hare WR, Buck WB. Malignant hyperthermia-like reaction secondary to ingestion of hops in five dogs. *J Am Vet Med Assoc* 1997;**210**:51–54.

16. Eiselberg AV. Zur Lehre von der Todtenstarre. *Pflugers Arch* 1881;**24**:229–231.

17. Eisenmenger W, Peschel O, Bratzke H, Welsch U, Herzog V. Electronenoptische Untersuchungen zur Totenstarre. In: Bauer G (ed.). *Gerichtsmedizin: Festschrift für W. Holczabek.* Vienna, F. Deuticke Verlag, 1988, pp 251–266.

18. Erdös T. Rigor, contracture and ATP. *Studies from the Institute of Medical Chemistry, University, Szeged* 1943;**3**:51–56.

19. Essen B, Jansson E, Henriksson J, Taylor AW, Saltin B. Metabolic characteristics of fibre types in human skeletal muscle. *Acta Physiol Scand* 1975;**95**:153–165.

20. Forster B. Der Arzt am Tatort. Todeszeitbestimmung. *Hippokrates* 1978;**49**:22–40.

21. Forster B, Ropohl D. *Rechtsmedizin 2.* Stuttgart, Germany, Ferdinand Enke Verlag, 1979.

22. Forster B, Ropohl D. *Medizinische Kriminalistik am Tatort.* Stuttgart, Germany, Ferdinand Enke Verlag, 1983.

23. Forster B, Ropohl D, Prokop O, Riemer K. Tierexperimentelle und an menschlichen Leichen gewonnene Daten zur Frage der Dauer der Totenstarre. *Kriminal Forens Wiss* 1974;**13**:35–45.

24. Forster B, Ropohl D, Raule P. Eine neue Formel zur Beurteilung der Totenstarre. Die Feststellung des FRR-Index. *Z Rechtsmed* 1977;**80**:51–54.

25. Fuchs. *Z Allg Physiol* 1904;**4**:359. Cited by Berg S. Nervensystem und Totenstarre. *Dtsch Z Gesamte Gerichtl Med* 1948/49;**39**:429–434.

26. Geesink G, Sujang S, Koohmaraie M. Tenderness of pre- and post-rigor lamb longissimus muscle. *Meat Sci* 2011;**88**:723–726.

27. Gendre AV. Ueber den Einfluss des Nervensystems auf die Todtenstarre. *Pflugers Arch* 1885;**35**:45–48.

28. Hanson J, Huxley HE. The structural basis of contraction in striated muscle. *Symp Soc Exp Biol* 1955;**9**:228–264.

29. Hasan H, Mason P. Pulse propagation in muscle. *Phys Med Biol* 1978;**23**:917–927.

30. Henssge CI, Madea B. *Methoden zur Bestimmung der Todeszeit am Leichen.* Lübeck, Schmidt-Römhild, 1988.

31. Henssge C, Madea B. Estimation of the time since death in the early post-mortem period. *Forensic Sci Int* 2004;**144**:167–175.

32. Henssge C, Madea B. Leichenerscheinungen und Todeszeitbestimmung, In: Brinkmann B, Madea B (eds.). *Handbuch gerichtliche Medizin,* vol. 1. Berlin, Springer, 2004, pp 79–225.

33. Huff Lonergan E, Zhang W, Lonergan SM. Biochemistry of postmortem muscle: lessons in mechanism of meat tenderization. *Meat Sci* 2010;**86**:184–195.

34. Husband HA. *The Student's Hand-Book of Forensic Medicine and Medical Police.* Edinburgh, E. and S. Livingstone, 1877.

35. Iwamoto H, Ooga T, Moriya T, Miyachi H, Matsuzaki M, Nishimura S, Tabata S. Comparison of the histological and histochemical properties of skeletal muscles between carbon dioxide and electrically stunned chickens. *Br Poultry Sci* 2002;**43**:551–559.

36. Kemp CM, Parr T. Advances in apoptotic mediated proteolysis in meat tenderization. *Meat Sci* 2012;**92**:252–259.

37. Kemp CM, Sensky PL, Bardsley RG, Buttery PJ, Parr T. Tenderness: an enzymatic view. *Meat Sci* 2010;**84**:248–256.

38. Knight B (ed.). *The Estimation of the Time Since Death in the Early Postmortem Period.* 2nd ed. London, Edward Arnold, 2002.

39. Koohmaraie M, Doumit ME, Wheeler TL. Meat toughening does not occur when rigor shortening is prevented. *J Anim Sci* 1996;**74**:2935–2942.

40. Krause D, Zett L. Experimentelle Untersuchungen über den Einfluss von Sauerstoff auf Mechanogramm und Membranpotential bei der Ausbildung der Totenstarre. *Beitr Gerichtl Med* 1973;**30**:252–257.

41. Krause D, Zett L. Physiologische und morphologische Untersuchungen zu Mechanismus und Verlauf der Totenstarre. *Z Rechtsmed* 1973;**72**:245–254.

42. Krause D, Klein A, Zett L. Todeszeitbestimmung mittels indirekter Muskelreizung über den N. ischiadicus und N. radialis. *Kriminal Forens Wiss* 1976;**26**:66–67.

43. Krompecher T. Experimental evaluation of rigor mortis. VIII. Estimation of the time since death by repeated measurements of the intensity of rigor mortis on rats. *Forensic Sci Int* 1994;**68**:149–159.

44. Krompecher T, Bergerioux C. Experimental evaluation of rigor mortis. VII. Effect of ante- and postmortem electrocution on the evolution of rigor mortis. *Forensic Sci Int* 1988;**38**:27–35.

45. Krompecher T, Fryc O. Experimentelle Untersuchungen an der Leichenstarre. II. Das Entstehen der Leichenstarre unter Einfluss von körperlicher Anstrengung. *Beitr Gerichtl Med* 1978;**36**:345–349.

46. Krompecher T, Fryc O. Experimental evaluation of rigor mortis. III. Comparative study of the evolution of rigor mortis in different sized muscle groups in rats. *Forensic Sci Int* 1978;**12**:97–102.

47. Krompecher T, Fryc O. Experimental evaluation of rigor mortis. IV. Change in strength and evolution of rigor mortis in the case of physical exercise preceding death. *Forensic Sci Int* 1978;**12**:103–107.

48. Krompecher T, Fryc O. Zur Frage der Todeszeitbestimmung auf Grund der Leichenstarre. *Beitr Gerichtl Med* 1979;**37**:285–289.

49. Krompecher T, Fryc O. Experimental evaluation of rigor mortis. V. Effects of temperature on the evolution of rigor mortis. *Forensic Sci Int* 1981;**17**:19–26.

50. Krompecher T, Bergerioux C, Brandt-Casadevall C, Gujer HR. Experimental evaluation of rigor mortis. VI. Effect of various causes of death on the evolution of rigor mortis. *Forensic Sci Int* 1983;**22**:1–9.

51. Krompecher T, Gilles A, Brandt-Casadevall C, Horisberger B, Mangin P. Experimental evaluation of rigor mortis: the influence of the central nervous system on the evolution of the intensity of rigor mortis. *Proc Am Acad Forensic Sci* 2005;**11**:261.

52. Krompecher T, Gilles A, Brandt-Casadeval C, Mangin P. Experimental evaluation of rigor mortis. Nasten's law: does it apply to rats? *Proc Am Acad Forensic Sci* 2004;**10**:255–256.

53. Krompecher T, Gilles A, Brandt-Casadevall C, Mangin P. Experimental evaluation of rigor mortis IX. The influence of the breaking (mechanical solution) on the development of rigor mortis. *Forensic Sci Int* 2008;**176**:157–162.

54. Kussmaul A. Ueber die Todtenstarre und die ihr nahe verwandtem Zustande von Muskelstarre, mit besonderer Berücksichtigung auf die Staatsarzneikunde. *Vierteljahrsschr prakt Heilk (Prag)* 1856;**13**:67–115.

55. Laves W. Ueber die Totenstarre. *Dtsch Z Gerichtl Med* 1948/49;**39**:186–198.

56. Lowe JE, Jennings RB, Reimer KA. Cardiac rigor mortis in dogs. *J Mol Cell Cardiol* 1979;**11**:1017–1031.

57. Mallach HJ. Zur Frage des Todeszeitbestimmung. *Berlin Med* 1964;**18**:577–582.

58. Mallach HJ, Mittmeyer HJ. Totenstarre und Totenflecke. *Z Rechtsmed* 1971;**69**:70–78.

59. Maresch W. Die Vergiftung durch Phosphor säureester. *Arch Toxikol* 1957;**16**:285–319.

60. Meijer AEFH, Elias EA. The value of enzyme histochemical techniques in classifying fibre types of human skeletal muscle. I. Adult skeletal muscles with no apparent disease of the neuromuscular system. *Histochemistry* 1976;**48**:257–267.

61. Mittmeyer HJ. Abhängigkeit der Totenstarre und Totenflecke vom Leichenalter. *Beitr Gerichtl Med* 1971;**28**:101–107.

62. Morgenstern S. Experimentelle Ergebnisse zur Frage des Temperatureinflusses auf die Leichenstarre. *Dtsch Z Gesamte Gerichtl Med* 1927;**9**:718–722.

63. Mueller B. *Gerichtliche Medizin.* Berlin, Springer, 1953.

64. Naumann E. Untersuchungen über den Gang der Totenstarre. *Pflugers Arch* 1917;**169**:517–536.

65. Niderkorn PF. Cited by Polson CJ. *The Essentials of Forensic Medicine.* Oxford, Pergamon Press, 1962.

66. Nysten PH. *Recherches de physiologie et de chimie pathologiques, pour faire suite à celles de Bichat sur la vie et la mort.* Paris, J.A. Brosson, 1811, pp 384–420.

67. Oppenheim F, Wacker L. Das Ausbleiben der postmortalen Saurebildung im Muskel als Ursache der verschiedenen Intensität der Totenstarre menschlicher Leichen. *Berl Klin Wochenschr* 1919;**42**:990–994.

68. Owens CM, Sams AR. Muscle metabolism and meat quality of pectoralis from turkeys treated with postmortem electrical stimulation. *Poultry Sci* 1997;**76**:1047–1051.

69. Peschel O, Bratzke H, Eisenrnenger W, Welsch U. Zur Mikromorphologie der Totenstarre im menschlichen Skelettmuskel. *Beitr Gerichtl Med* 1989;**47**:31–42.

70. Pirch J, Schutz Y and Klintschar M. A case of instantaneous rigor? *Int J Legal Med* 2013;**127**:971–974.

71. Polson CJ, Gee DJ. *The Essentials of Forensic Medicine.* Oxford, Pergamon Press, 1973.

72. Pounder DJ. Postmortem interval. In: Payne-James J, Byard RW, Corey TS, Henderson C (eds.). *Encyclopedia of Forensic and Legal Medicine,* vol. 3. Oxford, Elsevier, 2005, pp 382–488.

73. Prokop O. Supravitale Erscheinungen. In: Prokop O, Göhler W (eds.). *Forensische Medizin.* Berlin, Volk und Gesundheit Verlag, 1975, pp 16–27.

74. Prokop O. Die Totenstarre (Rigor Mortis). In: Prokop O, Göhler W (eds.). *Forensische Medizin.* Stuttgart, Germany, G. Fischer Verlag, 1976.

75. Saukko P, Knight B. *Knight's Forensic Pathology.* London, Arnold, 2004.

76. Schleyer F. Leichenveränderungen. Todeszeitbestimmung im früh postmortalen Intervall. In: Muller B (ed.). *Gerichtliche Medizin,* vol. 1. Berlin, Springer, 1975.

77. Schneider V. Zum Elektrotod in der Badewanne. *Arch Kriminol* 1985;**176**:89–95.

78. Schuck M, Beier G, Liebhardt E, Spann W. On the estimation of lay-time by measurement of rigor mortis. *Forensic Sci Int* 1979;**14**:171–176.

79. Schuck M, Beier G, Liebhardt E, Spann W. Zur Schätzung der Liegezeit durch Messungen der Totenstarre. *Beitr Gerichtl Med* 1978;**36**:339–343.

80. Seelye RN, Nevalainen TJ, Gavin JB, Webster VJ. Physical and biochemical changes in rigor mortis of cardiac muscle. *Biochem Med* 1979;**21**:323–332.

81. Shapiro HA. Rigor mortis. *Br Med J* 1950;**2**:304.

82. Shapiro HA. Medico-legal mythology: some popular forensic fallacies. *J Forensic Med* 1953/54;**1**:144–169.

83. Sherrington CS. *The Integrative Action of the Nervous System.* London, A. Constable and Co, 1908.

84. Simpson K. *Forensic Medicine.* London, Edward Arnold, 1974.

85. Swatland HJ. Observations on rheological, electrical, and optical changes during rigor development in pork and beef. *J Anim Sci* 1997;**75**:975–985.

86. Szent-Györgyi A. Studies on muscle. *Acta Physiol Scand* 1945;**9**(Suppl 25).

87. Szent-Györgyi A. *Chemistry of Muscular Contraction.* New York, Academic Press, 1947.

88. Tacqui A. Time since death. In: Siegel JA, Saukko PJ, Knupfer GC (eds.). *Encyclopedia of Forensic Sciences,* vol. 3. London, Academic Press, 2000, pp 1357–1363.

89. Tarrant PV, Mothersill C. Glycolysis and associated changes in beef carcasses. *J Sci Food Agric* 1977;**28**:739–749.

90. Vain A, Kauppila R, Humal LH, Vuori E. Grading rigor mortis with myotonometry: a new possibility to estimate time of death. *Forensic Sci Int* 1992;**56**:147–150.

91. Vanderwee MA, Humphrey SM, Gavin JB and Armiger LC. Changes in the contractile state, fine structure and metabolism of cardiac muscle cells during development of rigor mortis. *Virchows Arch (Cell Pathol)* 1981;**35**:159–167.

92. Varetto L, Curto O. Long persistence of rigor mortis at constant low temperature. *Forensic Sci Int* 2005;**147**:31–34.

93. Vock R, Hein PM, Metter D. Tod im tetanischen Anfall. *Z Rechtsmed* 1984;**92**:231–237.

94. Wuytack F, Casteels R. Evidence for rigor in smooth muscle. *Arch Int Physiol Biochim* 1975;**83**:340–341.

5 Postmortem Lividity
Hypostasis and Timing of Death

Burkhard Madea and Bernard Knight

■ Definition

Hypostasis is one of the most obvious postmortem changes; alternative names are 'postmortem lividity' and the older term, 'suggillation'.

Hypostasis is the staining of the skin surface – and of internal organs – by the settling of blood under the influence of gravity after circulation has ceased [2–5,7–9].

After irreversible circulatory arrest, postmortem lividity develops early and therefore is one of the initial postmortem changes. Following circulatory arrest, in blood vessels the hydrostatic pressure becomes the leading force within the parallelogram of forces consisting of blood pressure, structural barriers, tissue turgor and pressure of underlying surfaces. 'Hypostasis' means the movement of body fluids according to gravity. All fluid compartments are involved in hypostasis, both intravascular and transcellular fluids. Hypostasis in internal organs has misled inexperienced pathologists into regarding hypostasis in the intestines and myocardium as true infarctions, as a result of the dark, congested appearance in organs. Influenced by gravity, blood is sinking into the lowest parts within the vascular system of the body, in a supine position toward the back, the buttocks, thighs, calves and back of the neck. Where the body is pressed onto a firm supporting surface, these contact areas remain pale because the vascular channels are obliterated by pressure; this is commonly seen over the buttocks and the shoulder blades. Irregular pink patches over the face, especially over the cheeks in the agonal period, are caused by local stasis and in German are called 'Kirchhofrosen' (Table 5.1). Postmortem lividity visible on the skin is a result of the sinking of blood into the capillaries of the corium. Postmortem lividity may be visible within 20 to 30 minutes after death, in the early stages as pink patches that regularly and gradually become confluent with an increasing postmortem interval. Because of consumption of oxygen, the pink colour of lividity changes to dark pink and then to bluish (Figure 5.1).

In the areas of deep hypostasis, cutaneous petechial haemorrhages secondary to capillary rupture may develop; these are called 'vibices' (see Figure 5.1 (b)). Of diagnostic and criminal investigation relevance is not only the development but also the colour of lividity, its distribution over the body and the phenomena of fixation (disappearance after turning the body) and disappearance (blanching) on blunt thumb pressure.

The colour of hypostasis varies; it is darker red or blue when the contained haemoglobin is less oxygenated. In hypothermia, or if the body has been in refrigeration or other cold environmental surroundings, the colour may be bright pink.

In cases of intoxication such as with carbon monoxide and cyanides, the colour of hypostasis usually appears cherry pinkish, and in methaemoglobin intoxication it is brownish (Table 5.2; see also Figure 5.1 (d)). Because of the lack of dissociation of oxyhaemoglobin, a bright pink colour of lividity may be seen in cases of hypothermia as well. If a body is transferred from a cold environment to normal room temperature, a typical zonal segmentation of hypostasis may be seen, with the colour turning dark blue in the rewarmed areas (see Figure 5.1 (c)).

True postmortem hypostasis develops at very variable rates following cardiac arrest. The standard forensic medicine textbooks offer a wide range of the time of onsets (Table 5.3).

Several authors have attempted to use subjective measurements of hypostasis, by using stages such as 'beginning, confluence, maximum intensity, displacement by slight pressure, complete shifting and incomplete shifting'. Mallach [10] analyzed such data, but the wide scattering of results and the doubtful specificity of such subjective descriptions make the results of little practical value in casework, other than to add a further general corroboration to better results obtained by other techniques.

Given these wide ranges, it is obvious that the use of hypostasis in estimating the time of death is of little evidential use. All that can be said about hypostasis is that it usually appears between 30 minutes and 4 hours after death, it reaches maximum intensity in up to about 12 hours following death and it persists in an undisturbed corpse until putrefactive changes set in, usually a number of days later. Under tropical conditions, hypostasis may be destroyed by decomposition on the first day after death, if the body undergoes rapid dissolution.

Apart from the initial time of the onset of hypostasis, it has been claimed over a long period of time that its permanent fixation is time related. Numerous textbooks have stated that, after a certain (but very variable) time, primary hypostasis becomes fixed and will not move again under the influence of gravity, even if the body position is altered.

Of predominant criminal investigation significance regarding lividity are the phenomena **disappearance on pressure** and **disappearance after turning the body.** In early stages, lividity completely disappears on soft thumb pressure. With an increasing postmortem interval, the pressure must increase as well. Later on, lividity disappears

Table 5.1 Lividity: causes, consequences and phenomena checked on the body

Cause	Consequence(s)	Phenomenon
Decrease of intensity of myocardial contraction	Stasis	'Kirchhofrosen', local stasis with patchy discolouration during the agonal period resulting from centralization of the circulation.
Cardiac arrest, hydrostatic pressure	Hypostasis	Livores with a 'shifting' quality and 'disappearance on pressure'.
Vascular permeability	Haemo-concentration	Decrease of shifting and disappearance on pressure.
Autolysis, putrefaction	Diffusion of haemoglobin	No shifting, no disappearance on pressure.

Table 5.2 Postmortem lividity discolouration

Etiology	Colour	Mechanism
Normal	Blue-purplish	Venous blood.
Carbon monoxide	Pink, cherry-red	Carboxyhaemoglobin.
Cyanide	Pink, cherry-red	Excessively oxygenated blood resulting from inhibition of cytochrome oxidase.
Fluoroacetate	Pink, cherry-red	Same as above.
Refrigeration/ hypothermia	Pink, cherry-red	Oxygen retention in cutaneous blood by cold air left shifting of the haemoglobin-oxygen dissociation curve.
Sodium chloride/ nitrite, nitrate	Brown	Methaemoglobin.
Hydrogen sulphide	Green	Sulfhaemoglobin.

Modified from Spitz WU. *Spitz & Fisher's Medicolegal Investigation of Death*. 3rd ed. Springfield, Illinois, Charles C Thomas, 1993.

only incompletely on blunt pressure, and finally, it does not disappear at all.

If the body is turned in the early postmortem interval, some or all of the hypostasis may move down to the most dependent areas as a result of gravity. In a comparatively later postmortem interval, only some of the hypostasis will slip down to the newly dependent area, and only faint blanching of the lividity will be noted in the formerly dependent areas (Figure 5.2).

With an increasing postmortem interval, disappearance of hypostasis on thumb pressure and relocation after shifting decrease and then cease completely. This effect is caused by an increasing haemoconcentration of intravascular erythrocytes in response to transcapillary extravasation of plasma. The intravascular haemoconcentration is the main reason that the disappearance of hypostasis gradually decreases on thumb pressure and after shifting. In a comparatively later postmortem interval, haemolysis and haemoglobin diffusion into the perivasal tissues start, but these are only secondary mechanisms contributing to the fixation of hypostasis.

All different elements of hypostasis such as beginning, confluence, maximum, disappearance on thumb pressure

Table 5.3 Time of onset of hypostasis

Textbook authors	Onset	Maximum hours
Adelson	30 min–4 h	8–12
Polson and Gee	30 min–2 h	6–12
Spitz and Fisher	2–4 h	8–12
Taylor (ed. Simpson)	0 h	12
Taylor (ed. Mant)	1 h	12
Gradwohl (ed. Camps)	20–30 min	6–12
Glaister	—	8–12
DiMaio	30 min–2 h	8–12
Sydney Smith	0 h	12
Mant	0 h	12
Gordon and Shapiro	'Few' h	12

and complete or incomplete disappearance after shifting change with an increasing postmortem time interval.

Longitudinal studies of these criteria in large random samples are lacking, and cross-sectional studies are of only

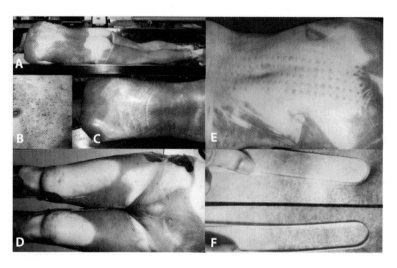

Figure 5.1 Postmortem lividity. (a) Postmortem lividity in a supine position, with pink colour resulting from storage in a refrigerator. (b) Petechial-like haemorrhages secondary to capillary ruptures in areas of deep hypostasis (vibices). (c) Zonal segmentation of hypostasis: partly dark blue, partly red. (d) Brownish colour of hypostasis in case of methaemoglobin intoxication. (e) Patterned hypostasis of the back resulting from the underground. (f) Complete disappearance of lividity on light blunt pressure.

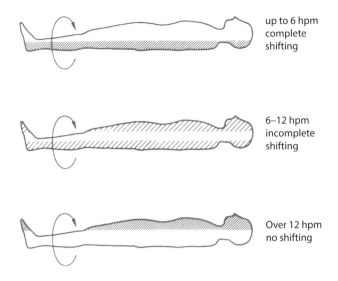

up to 6 hpm
complete
shifting

6–12 hpm
incomplete
shifting

Over 12 hpm
no shifting

Figure 5.2 Shifting of lividity after turning the body. (Modified from Patscheider/Hartmann, Leitfaden der Rechtsmedizin, 3rd ed., Göttingen, Verlag Hans Huber, 1993.)

limited value. The best statistical data available were summarized by Mallach [10], who calculated mean values, standard deviations and 95 per cent limits of confidence based on a number of textbook reports (Table 5.4). Because better data are lacking, these data are still undisputed. However, these data do not represent absolute threshold values. Investigations using a quantitative measurement of livor mortis have not yet gained practical importance.

■ Attempts to objectify postmortem blanching

Crude methods of detecting fixation have been used in which local pressure is applied to the hypostatic skin, to determine whether the colour can be blanched.

Suzutani *et al.* [12] examined 430 bodies by pressing the side of forceps against the dependent skin. These authors discovered that hypostasis could not be squeezed out in about 30 per cent of cases where death had occurred 6 to 12 hours previously. More than 50 per cent of cases were fixed after a postmortem interval of 12 to 24 hours, and no fading took place in about 70 per cent of those who had died 1 to 3 days earlier.

Suzutani *et al.* [12] also found a significant number of cases in which hypostasis was not fixed for up to at least 3 days. In addition, there was some seasonal variation, with less movement in the summer months; cases of asphyxial deaths and those with intracranial lesions also had delayed fixation rates.

Fechner *et al.* [1] examined 28 cases of sudden death in which the bodies were stored at different temperatures and found a variation of hypostatic fixation with temperature, but no linear relationship and very wide individual variation relative to the time of death.

Although the foregoing commentary seems to indicate that hypostasis is almost valueless in the determination of time since death, more recent research – some of which is still in progress – is attempting to improve this situation with the use of sophisticated optical equipment.

Schuller *et al.* [11] began to use colorimetry on hypostasis. When examining seven corpses over a period from 3 to 35 hours after death, these investigators observed an increasing paleness of the hypostasis between 3 and 15 hours post mortem. These authors concluded that there was a colour change from a wavelength of 575 nm at 3 hours at an average rate of 2 nm per hour.

Ongoing research by Vanezis [13] uses a tri-stimulus colorimeter. A standard xenon light source and filter illuminate the bodies, conforming to standard illumination D 65, which resembles daylight. A constant, small area of hypostasis on each corpse is illuminated, and the reflected light is split into blue, green and red for measurement. The body,

Table 5.4   Time course of different criteria of lividity: statistical calculations by Mallach based on textbook reports*

| | $\bar{x}$ | SD | 2 SD | | Range of scatter | | |
			Lower limit	Upper limit	Lower limit	Upper limit	Number of quotations
Development	¾	½	—	2	¼	3	17
Confluence	2½	1	¾	4¼	1	4	5
Greatest distension and intensity	9½	4½	½	18¼	3	16	7
Disappearance							
1. Complete on thumb pressure.	5½	6	—	17½	1	20	5
2. Incomplete on sharp pressure (forceps).	17	10½	—	37½	10	36	4
Displacement after turning the body							
1. Complete.	3¾	1	2	5½	2	6	11
2. Incomplete.	11	4½	2¼	20	4	24	11
3. Only little pallor.	18½	8	2½	34½	10	30	7

* The statistical calculations are not based on cross-sectional or longitudinal studies but on empirical knowledge quoted in textbooks.

$\bar{x}$, mean value; SD, standard deviation. Data from Mallach HJ. Zur Frage der Todeszeitbestimmung. *Berlin Med* 1964;**18:**577–582.

which had developed primary hypostasis in the supine position, was turned to a prone position, and an area of lumbar skin was examined at 30-minute intervals to determine changes in colour as secondary movement took place over a period of 3 to 8 hours.

In a pilot study of 41 corpses, Vanezis [13] claimed that there is a linear relationship between the fading colour of the hypostasis and time during the first 24 hours, after which the relationship is unpredictable.

In 1996, Vanezis and Trujillo [14] reported further on the use of colorimetry in measuring the hypostasis from 93 corpses. Measurements were taken over a 4-hour period, and the rate of change of colour intensity of the hypostasis was plotted over a postmortem interval. A regression formula was reported with a correlation coefficient r of 0.538. These authors commented that the shift in hypostasis was marked during the first 12 hours and decreased thereafter. They also claimed that hypostasis could be a useful means for determining the postmortem period up to 48 hours.

Methods to replace the subjective examination of postmortem lividity by objectifying postmortem blanching had been previously unsuccessful [6].

■ Stages of postmortem lividity

Beginning is stated if mottled patches at lower parts of the body (e.g. over the neck in a supine position) are observed.

Confluence is stated if separate areas of discolouration of moderate intensity are noted.

Maximum can be stated if during death scene investigation and autopsy hypostasis did not increase.

The criterion **thumb pressure** is positive if lividity disappears completely on soft thumb pressure.

Complete relocation is given when all hypostasis shifts down to the newly dependent areas. This may be observed at the scene when a body is turned from a face-down into a supine position.

In **incomplete shifting,** hypostasis remains in the formerly dependent areas, but it also shifts to a greater or lesser extent to the newly dependent areas.

References

1. Fechner G, Koops E, Henssge C. Cessation of livor in defined pressure conditions. *Z Rechtsmed* 1984;**93**:238–287.
2. Henssge C, Madea B. *Methoden zur Bestimmung der Todeszeit an Leichen.* Lübeck, Schmidt-Römhild, 1988.
3. Henssge C, Madea B. Leichenerscheinungen und Todeszeitbestimmung. In: Brinkmann B, Madea B (eds.). *Handbuch Gerichtliche Medizin*, vol. I. Berlin, Springer, 2004, pp 79–150.
4. Henssge C, Madea B. Estimation of the time since death in the early postmortem period. *Forensic Sci Int* 2004;**144**(2–3):167–175.
5. Henssge C, Madea B. Estimation of time since death. *Forensic Sci Int* 2007;**165**:182 184.
6. Hunnius PV, Mallach HJ, Mittmeyer HJ. Quantitative pressure measurements of livores mortis relative to the determination of the time of death. *Z Rechtsmed* 1973;**73**:325–244.
7. Madea B. Death: time of. In: Jamieson A, Moenssens A (eds.). *Wiley Encyclopaedia of Forensic Sciences,* vol. 2. Chichester, John Wiley and Sons, 2009, pp 697–716.
8. Madea B. Time of death determination. In: Jamieson A, Moenssens A (eds.). *Wiley Encyclopaedia of Forensic Sciences,* vol. 5. Chichester, John Wiley and Sons, 2009, pp 2466–2479.
9. Madea B, Henssge C. Timing of death. In: Payne-James J, Busuttil A, Smock W (eds.). *Forensic Medicine: Clinical and Pathological Aspects.* London, Greenwich Medical Media, 2003, pp 91–114.
10. Mallach HJ. Zur Frage der Todeszeitbestimmung. *Berlin Med* 1964;**18**:577–582.
11. Schuller E, Pankratz H, Liebhardt E. Farbortmessungen an Totenflecken. *Beitr Gerichtl Med* 1987;**45**:169–73.
12. Suzutani T, Ishibashi H, Takatori T. Studies on the estimation of the post-mortem interval. 2 The post-mortem lividity. *Hokkaido Zasshi* 1978;**52**:259–267.
13. Vanezis P. Assessing hypostasis by colorimetry. *Forensic Sci Int.*1991;**52**:1–3.
14. Vanezis P, Trujillo O. Evaluation of hypostasis using a colorimeter measuring system and its application to the assessment of the post-mortem interval (time of death). *Forensic Sci Int* 1996;**78**:19–28.

6 Postmortem Body Cooling and Temperature-Based Methods

6.1 Basics and application of the 'nomogram method' at the scene

■ *Claus Henssge*

The main topic of this chapter is the rectal temperature 'nomogram method' for determining the time of death, which was developed for practical use at the scene of death. It provides a time range immediately at the scene, and it may considerably assist criminal investigations at their earliest stage. Beyond that, evidence may be provided regarding the guilt or innocence of a suspect as a result of the denial or corroboration of an alibi.

The main object is to be able to use the method in a wide spectrum of casework. For that purpose, the circumstances at the scene of death must be analyzed thoroughly and the findings taken into account. This process requires personal experience. Additional rapid methods used at the scene are helpful for reducing the range of the interval limited by the nomogram, and these methods are described in Chapter 10.

Part 6.1 of this chapter is divided into two main sections. The first section discusses basic physical considerations, including mathematically modelling body cooling by two exponential equations and verifying them on experimental body and dummy cooling under various controlled conditions. The second section describes the practical means of applying the nomogram method in casework, with references to the first section where essential.

■ Scientific investigation of experimental body cooling under controlled conditions

Basic conditions

Body cooling results from non-stationary heat conduction inside a body of low thermal diffusivity.

1. With failure of circulation, convectional transport of heat inside the body ceases. (In hanged bodies, hypostasis could theoretically distort rectal temperature by warm blood descending from above, but this has no practical significance.)
2. Exchange of heat between the core and the surface of the body takes place only by conduction. Heat transfer inside the body by radiation and convection is negligible.
3. The postmortem rate of heat production is very low. Heat is produced mainly by anaerobic glycolysis, which is ongoing for about the first 10 hours post mortem, in a non-linear fashion. Lundquist [93] calculated roughly that heat release per gram of glycogen was 0.4 kcal, so the glycogen store of the body (350 g) corresponds to 140 kcal heat release. A body of about 70 kg and a specific heat of 0.8 kcal/kg would be heated by 2.5°C over the first 10 hours after death. With that, one sixth of the postmortem temperature plateau could be explained as a rough estimation. The rate of heat release from autolysis and putrefaction is even lower during the early postmortem phase of cooling the body to ambient temperature, so that its influence on cooling is negligible. Fulminant putrefaction in the early postmortem period may markedly decelerate the cooling.
4. The thermal diffusivity of body tissues is much lower than that of metals. (Thermal diffusivity of water is 0.00143; that of fat is 0.001; and that of aluminium is 1.0 [10^{-4} m^2 per s^{-1}]. Note the small difference between water and fat.) Given its lower thermal conductivity, fat conducts heat more slowly than muscle. Because of its lower specific heat and specific weight, the fall in temperature is greater when leaving a hotter object. Because the thermal diffusivity is the quotient from thermal conductivity and specific heat times specific weight, only a small difference results between water and fat (e.g. [138]).
5. The cooling of a body is nearly 'non-stationary' and unsteady. As a consequence, the 'thermal diffusivity' is the measure of any heat transfer inside the body, but not the 'thermal conductivity'.
6. The body is not 'thermally thin'.
7. Newton's law of cooling is not adequate to describe the cooling curve of any central probe site.
8. With the start of cooling, a temperature gradient develops from the surface to the core of any part of the body.
9. First, heat is lost from the most superficial layers of the body, whereas the deeper layers are initially unaltered. Because of the low velocity of heat transport inside the body, it takes some time for heat to be conducted from the deeper layers to the more superficial (colder) layers, until, eventually, the temperature gradient reaches the core.
10. The temperature gradient has an almost radial direction. The cooling curve of any central temperature probe site has a sigmoidal shape, with the physically determined 'postmortal temperature plateau' occurring during the first cooling phase.

Cooling dummy

Any solid body consisting of a substance of low thermal diffusivity and without significant heat release cools in the same manner. Thus, a body configured like a human trunk, consisting of a layer of coated material or caoutchouc (natural rubber) and filled with a gel mixture of glycerine (47.5 per cent), water (47.5 per cent) and agar (5 per cent) (Figure 6.1) provides cooling curves that resemble those of cadavers, including the plateau (Figure 6.2). Similarly, the two exponential equations (see equation 6.14), although investigated empirically on dead human bodies, also apply to the dummy (Figure 6.3). This is because of the similar thermal diffusivity and the similar relationship between surface area and volume of both dead human bodies and dummies. Therefore, a dummy cools under controlled conditions as does a cadaver of a specified body weight, depending on its cross-sectional dimensions (Table 6.1 and Figure 6.4.) The conformity of cooling curves of bodies and dummies has been confirmed in numerous experiments conducted under different conditions (see Figure 6.18). Therefore, in test cooling, dummies can replace bodies [61,71,72,90,100,143,160].

Heat exchange to surroundings

The actual mechanisms of heat exchange between body and surroundings (conduction, convection, radiation, evaporation) depend on the individual circumstances at the scene and therefore cannot be stated in generally valid terms for any cooling conditions.

Conductive heat exchange results from the temperature difference between the body and the surroundings, from the intermediate material between the body surface and the surroundings (e.g. clothing, covering) and from the

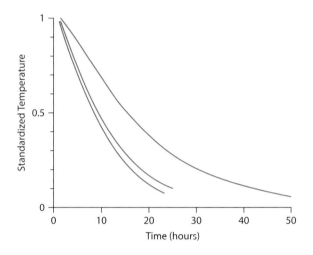

Figure 6.2 Cooling curves of two different-sized dummies. Abscissa: time (hours) after taking the 37°C heated dummy out of the incubator. Ordinate: standardized temperature (central temperature of the dummy – ambient temperature) divided by (37°C – ambient temperature). Each of six test coolings occurred under chosen standard conditions at each of three different places in nearly constant ambient temperatures between 0.1°C and 14.1°C. The upper cooling curves are as good as the curve of a 73-kg body, and the lower curves are as accurate as the curve of a 42-kg body when cooling under comparable 'standard' conditions. Even the 'postmortal temperature plateau' is equally developed. The model curves of a 73-kg body and a 42-kg body computed according to equation 6.14 would fit into the middle of each of the six curves (see Figure 6.3).

surrounding medium (e.g. water, air). At the contact zones of the body with the supportive surface, conductive heat exchange plays the decisive role. The heat capacity and the thermal conductivity of the supporting surface must be noted (see Figures 6.19 to 6.21).

At non-contact areas of naked bodies, the convectional mechanism of heat exchange dominates, even without forced convection such as wind. In the case of a naked body, the heat exchange at the non-contact surface usually exceeds that of the contact surface (see Figures 6.7, 6.8 and 6.22), unless the supporting base conducts heat exceptionally well (see Figure 6.19).

Under standard conditions, heat exchange by radiation is extensive for the first hour post mortem, but it decreases during the later process of cooling, depending on the rapid decrease in skin temperature [97,98]. However, under special conditions, such as sun radiating on the body, the net exchange of heat between body and surroundings is influenced to a large degree. There are no reports about this in the literature.

The loss of heat from the dry surface of the body by evaporation does not have any significant influence on cooling. The loss of heat would correspond to 580 kcal/l of evaporated water. The weight of the body does not diminish during the early postmortem interval to such an extent that considerable acceleration of cooling would result from such fluid loss.

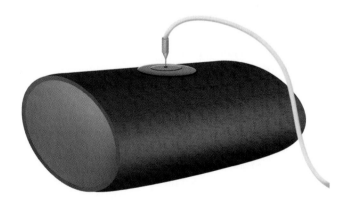

Figure 6.1 Example of a cooling dummy. The 1.5-mm-thick wrap is made of caoutchouc. It is filled with a gel mixture (Wirodouble, BEGO, Bremen, Germany: 47.5 per cent glycerine and water, 5 per cent agar) at 90°C, at which it is molten. At lower temperatures the consistency becomes solid and elastic. The dimensions are 19 cm (sagittal), 38 cm (transverse) and 50 cm (longitudinal). The real weight is 31 kg. The temperature probe is inserted in the middle, 9.5 cm deep, corresponding to half of the sagittal diameter.

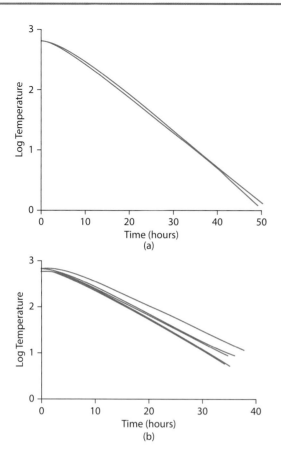

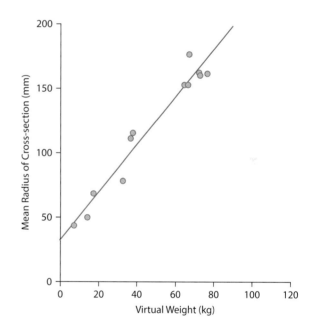

Table 6.1 Mean radius of cross-section of some different-sized dummies and the resulting body weight ('virtual weight') calculated from the Newtonian coefficient *B* of the cooling curves according to equation 6.3 (see Figure 6.4)

Real weight (kg)	Mean radius (mm)	Virtual weight (kg)	Wrap
0.70	42.8	6.9	0.5-mm-thick
1.02	49.6	14.3	PVC-coated
2.82	67.8	17.3	material
3.35	78.1	32.8	or
8.20	110.9	36.8	0.5-mm-thick
10.00	115.6	38.0	transparent
21.80	152.9	64.8	PVC foil.
22.00	152.9	66.5	
27.50	161.2	72.5	
24.00	162.3	72.4	
25.00	162.3	76.5	
31.00	177.0	67.0	1.5-mm-thick caoutchouc.

PVC, polyvinyl chloride.

Figure 6.3 Experimental cooling curves of dummies and their modelling by the two exponential equations using the figures of constants investigated on bodies (equations 6.5 and 6.14) 10 years before the dummies were 'born'. Abscissa: time (hours); ordinate: logarithm of (central temperature of the dummy – ambient temperature). (a) Cooling curve of the dummy in Figure 6.1. The 36.5°C heated dummy cooled in a nearly constant mean ambient temperature of 20.1°C. The stars without connecting lines are the original values of measurements. The crosses linked by connecting lines represent the model curve of a 67-kg dead human body. The differences between the real and the model-computed cooling times do not exceed –0.8 to 1.1 hours up to the fortieth hour. After this time, the differences increase to 1.8 hours. (b) Experimental cooling and model curves of a dummy and two bodies under identical circumstances. Naked bodies lying on a wooden board in a closed room:

	Uppermost body	Intermediate body	Lowest dummy
Ambient temperature (°C)	19.5	20.5	20.6
First measurement hpm	3	1	0
°C	35.7	37.6	36.5
Real body weight (kg)	80.8	67.0	—
Calculated body weight (equation 6.3)	78.0	69.8	64.6
Cooling coefficient	−0.0558	−0.0618	−0.0663

hpm = hours post mortem.

Noting the almost radial direction of heat conduction inside the body, it is essential to take into account which parts of the body contribute to total heat transfer.

Figure 6.4 Close relationship between mean radius of cross-section and 'virtual weight' of some different-sized dummies (see Table 6.1). The virtual weight results from the Newtonian coefficient *B* of the cooling curves set in equation. 6.3.

Heat flow measurements on body surfaces

By using new, highly sensitive heat flow sensors (HY-CAL Engineering Sensable; Santa Fe Springs, California; types used: BI-6 and LO-6) (Figure 6.5), the heat exchange on both the contact and the non-contact surfaces can be investigated in combination with superficial and central temperatures (Figures 6.6 to 6.8). Using the analogy of Ohm's law, the heat flow corresponds with the power of an electric current. With the temperature measurements corresponding to the voltage,

Figure 6.5 Heat flow sensor. The active thermoelectric sensor transduces the whole absorbed or emitted heat flow of a surface area into a voltage. The sensitivity of the two sensors was 149 and 46 mV per 500 Btu ft^{-2} h^{-1}. The range of measurements was limited from minus to plus 11.38 Btu ft^{-2} h^{-1} and the discrimination was set to 0.01 Btu ft^{-2} h^{-1}. Into each heat flow sensor a thermocouple (10 mV/°C) is integrated to measure the surface temperature beside the heat flow. The gauge can be attached easily using double-sided tape.

the resistance can be calculated as the third, but unknown, quantity of Ohm's law. Thus, a complete circuit of the heat exchange between body and environment can be established (Figure 6.9). Heat flow measurements on body surfaces support the incorporation of influencing factors of body cooling such as clothing, wetness or supporting surfaces [90,100,160].

Rectal temperature probe sites

Keeping the non-stationary heat conduction inside a body of low 'thermal conductivity' in mind, the time course of any body temperature depends first of all on the temperature probe site. Because surface temperatures may be susceptible even to transient, minute alterations of the actual cooling circumstances, they seem to be unsuitable for measuring 'the' body temperature. (The measurement of surface temperatures is problematic [e.g., Newitt C, Green MA. J *Forensic Sci Soc* 1979;**19**:179–181]. In addition, surface temperatures approach the ambient temperature more quickly and complicate the procedure once more.) At present, the deep rectal temperature and central brain temperature are the most thoroughly investigated probe sites. Because of the greater radius of the trunk compared with the radius of the head, the cooling curve of the rectal temperature probe site has a shallower slope and therefore gives information about the time since death over a longer postmortem interval than the steeper cooling curve of the brain. Conversely, in general, the steeper the cooling curve, the more exact the calculated time since death will be. Therefore, temperature probe sites on different parts of the body having a different radius are not alternative methods but can complement each other (e.g. brain and rectal probe site [70] as well as multiple probe sites).

Besides the location of the temperature probe, another question should be discussed: the infliction of injuries by measuring brain temperature and the disturbance of traces

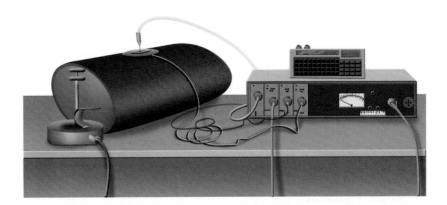

Figure 6.6 Experimental arrangement for measurements of ambient temperature (air and base), the central temperature of the dummy, surface temperatures and heat flow on both the contact and non-contact surfaces. To control and store the seven automatic measurements, the hand-held computer HP 71B is used. This picks up the measurements in optional intervals from the data logger at the right. After the programmed end of measurements the HP 71B is connected to a plotter, a printer and a digital cassette drive. To analyze the data, special algorithms corresponding to the given equations are used. Development of the device including construction of the probes, integration of thermocouples into the heat flow sensors (seen in Figure 6.5) and calibration: BMT Messtechnik GmbH – Dr Ing F. Wallner, Berlin.

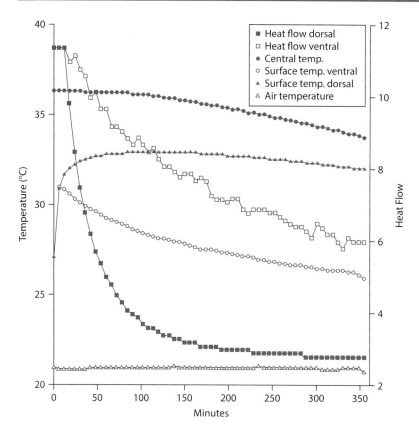

Figure 6.7 Heat flow measurements on the surfaces of the dummy of Figure 6.6. Central temperature, ventral (non-contact) and dorsal (contact), both surface temperatures and heat flow curves of a 36.5°C heated dummy during the first 6 hours of cooling in still air of 21°C. The supporting base was a wood board 2 cm thick. Left ordinate: temperature (°C); right ordinate: heat flow Btu ft^{-2} h^{-1}. Abscissa: cooling time (min). Interval of measurements: 6 minutes. The initially great heat flow at the contact surface (dorsal) heats the base quickly (see the curve of dorsal surface temperature). The subsequent very low dorsal heat flow is combined with a very slow decrease of the dorsal surface temperature, indicating that the wood board has a low thermal conductivity. The curves of ventral heat flow and surface temperature initially show the heating of the bound layer, and afterward, with the start of thermic air movement (convectional heat exchange), the greater heat loss combined with a steeper fall of the ventral surface temperature compared with the dorsal surface. Note the more irregular curve of the ventral ('naked') heat flow in comparison with the dorsal flow.

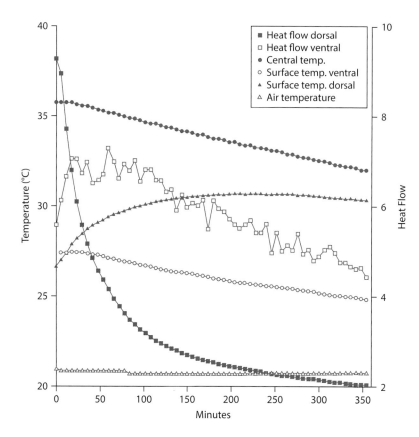

Figure 6.8 Heat flow measurements on the surfaces of a body. Rectal and ambient temperatures, dorsal and ventral surface temperatures and heat flows of a naked 69.5-kg body lying on a wood board 2 cm thick in still air at 20.7°C. Left ordinate: temperature (°C); right ordinate: heat flow (Btu ft^{-2} h^{-1}). Abscissa: cooling time after the start of measurements 3.1 hours post mortem with a rectal temperature of 35.8°C. Interval of measurements 6 minutes. Considering the death time of 3.1 hours at the beginning of measurements with advanced postmortal plateau, the curves agree well with those of the dummy in Figure 6.7. The more irregular curve of the ventral heat flow curve is apparent, indicating that it is unsuitable for short interval analysis, at least on naked surfaces.

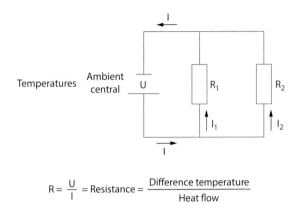

$$R = \frac{U}{I} = \text{Resistance} = \frac{\text{Difference temperature}}{\text{Heat flow}}$$

Figure 6.9 Circuit of heat exchange between body and environment analogous to Ohm's law. Calculating both the total and the parts of resistance (R_1, R_2) and flow (I_1, I_2) at lying and non-lying surfaces, the parts of their surface areas must be taken into account.

such as semen during measurement of rectal temperature. The injuries caused by central brain temperature measurements are minute and discernible [20,21,68,122].

The disturbance of traces by rectal temperature measurement can be avoided by taking a swab before inserting the temperature probe into the sphincter. The securing of micro-traces by the criminal investigators must be finished before any removal of the clothing or cutting through the crotch area of trousers can be done. Co-operation is required with other investigators to avoid conflict of interests.

In my opinion, the rectal probe site provides the most reliable determination of the time since death, compared with other probe site measurements.

Nevertheless, there is some discussion concerning the exact probe site in the rectum. Joseph and Schickele [80] suggested that variation of the exact location of thermometers in the rectum from body to body (and from one experiment to another) could explain the wide variation of Marshall and Hoare's cooling curves [101–103]. They criticized the rectal probe site for not being at the centre of the body, and they proposed a convenient standardized location – a more defined point 2.5 cm (1 inch) above the symphysis – at which the thermometer would be inserted through an incision to a depth half the distance of the anteroposterior diameter. However, this impracticable procedure could cause injury (e.g. of the bladder, possibly followed by an outflow of urine into the peritoneal cavity).

The site of a straight, non-flexible probe inserted at least 8 cm inside the anal sphincter [101–103] is in fact not at the centre of the lower trunk but at a level corresponding to the junction between the posterior third and anterior two thirds of the anteroposterior diameter of the trunk, at a longitudinal level that is not defined exactly [74]. If a straight, non-flexible probe is inserted deep into the rectum via the anal sphincter without undue force, a convenient standardized point is given; a great variation of the 'location

factor' (so-called by Joseph and Schickele) from body to body is not of practical significance, in our opinion.

Hiraiwa *et al.* [75] analyzed the location of the rectal probe by computed tomography in 10 patients after inserting the thermometer about 10 to 15 cm beyond the anus close to the anterior wall of the sacrum. The ratio of the length between the centre of the rectum and the middle of the back to the distance between the surface of the lower abdomen and the middle of the back was found to have a mean of 0.27. Our own simple measurements of the sagittal and transverse diameter of the lower trunk at the level of the greater trochanter and the anterior inferior iliac spine (corresponding to the actual level of a straight rigid temperature probe when inserted via the anus into the rectum as deep as possible without resort to force) resulted in ratios between 0.42 and 0.47, depending on whether the insertion was more ventral or more dorsal.

Standardization of the temperature probe site is absolutely necessary and is much more important than its exactly central location. All experience of death time estimation from body cooling is limited to a distinct probe site. Experience can be extended more by systematic measurements based on a few standardized probe sites than by a surfeit of 'new' temperature probe sites. I therefore decided to adhere to Marshall and Hoare's procedure [101–103], including the rectal probe site as described earlier, when I started my studies of body cooling in 1975.

The rectal temperature and the ambient temperature were measured online by an electronic device within an accuracy of 0.1°C.

Mathematically modelling the rectal cooling curve by the two exponential formulae of Marshall and Hoare

In 1962, Marshall and Hoare [101–103] published a formula for modelling rectal body cooling mathematically by using different notation:

$$Q = \frac{Tr - Ta}{To - Ta}$$
$$= A \times \exp(B \times t) + (1 - A) \times \exp\left(\frac{A \times B}{A - 1} \times t\right) \quad (6.1)$$

where Q is the standardized temperature; Tr is the rectal temperature at any time t; To is the rectal temperature at death ($t = 0$); Ta is the ambient temperature; A is the constant; B is the constant; and t is the time of death.

There are two exponential terms: the first (with the constant B as exponent) expresses the exponential drop of the temperature after the plateau according to Newton's law of cooling (Figure 6.10). The second (with the constant A as a part of the exponent) describes the 'postmortal temperature plateau'.

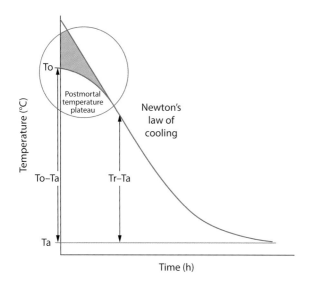

Figure 6.10 Sigmoidal shape of cooling curve. A single exponential term such as Newton's law of cooling is insufficient to describe this mathematically. The two-exponential term (equation 6.1) of Marshall and Hoare provides a close mathematical description. The quotient Tr-Ta/To-Ta (standardized temperature) is a good measure of the progress of cooling.

The formula by Marshall and Hoare is the ultimate success in modelling body cooling for the purpose of estimation of the time since death. The formula requires only two constants besides the body temperature at death, but it nevertheless provides a sufficient mathematical description of real cooling curves of different parts of the body (e.g. rectum, brain), as well as of the cooling dummy. As demonstrated by Brown and Marshall [23], more than two exponential terms complicate the model without improving results.

Although there are some difficulties in identifying the individual values of the only two constants in any specific case, the solution is not to look for a better model, but rather for the best way to identify the individual values of the constants A and B. They depend on the body build and the ambient cooling conditions, including the thermal factors on the surface of the body. Besides great variation of body build, the cooling conditions at the scene may vary over a wide range. In addition, some of the actual influencing factors at the scene may be unknown to the forensic pathologist. Furthermore, the ambient conditions can change between the time of death and the time of investigation. The question of identifying the representative values of the required constants seems to be insoluble.

First, we must accept that the problem cannot be solved in all cases. Second, we must accept that the problem cannot be solved *exactly* in many cases. However, we can at least *approximate* the value of the required constants.

There are two different ways to identify the individual values of the constants. The first is to estimate the values by analyzing the whole experimental cooling curve. Then

we can decide whether a short part of the cooling curve is able to give representative values of the constants for the whole curve. The second way uses the effect of the constants on whole cooling curves, as a means to find rules approximating the representative individual values of the constants indirectly by taking the most important features of body build and ambient cooling conditions into account.

Theoretically, both ways have some inherent advantages and disadvantages. The decision whether the first or the second way is better can only be made under the conditions of practice at the scene in many cases.

Although the formulae of Marshall and Hoare validate the earlier observation of Rainy in 1868 [121] that bodies would cool more slowly in the first phase after death than expected by Newton's law of cooling, and even though the excellent papers of Marshall and Hoare gave an adequate and easily applied mathematical expression of postmortem cooling, including the postmortal plateau, progress concerning their application to the important field of forensic practice was incomprehensibly insignificant. Instead, for example, pathologists continued to use simplistic methods such as the rule of thumb that bodies would cool 1°C per hour: this persisted as if Rainy [121] and Marshall and Hoare [101–103] had not existed. Only James and Knight [78] reported errors in estimating the time since death in coroners' cases, and Prokop [120] stated that Marshall and Hoare's data would be much more useful than the earlier data of Schwarz and Heidenwolf [137], who produced a sigmoidal curve of rectal body cooling in 1953.

As has been said, the main question is to identify the individual values of the constants A and B in individual cases at the scene where the circumstances do not allow extensive measurements. The constant B has greater significance for the reproduction of the cooling curve from the measurement at the scene to the moment of death because it describes the cooling rate for as long as there is a difference of temperature between the body and the ambient. In comparison, the constant A is of less significance; it expresses the relative duration of the plateau phase and ceases its function after that. Both these constants are discussed here.

The individual value of the constant *B* (the Newtonian cooling coefficient)

Estimation of *B* by multiple temperature measurements

The individual value of *B* can be exactly computed by a linear regression line with time *t* (hours) as the independent variable *(X)* and logarithm of temperature difference between rectum and ambient ln *(Tr − Ta)* as the dependent variable *(Y)* of the cooling curve after the plateau (Figure 6.11 (c)). The exact estimation of *B* as the slope of the regression line (regression coefficient b_{yx}) requires a long period of temperature measurements after the plateau,

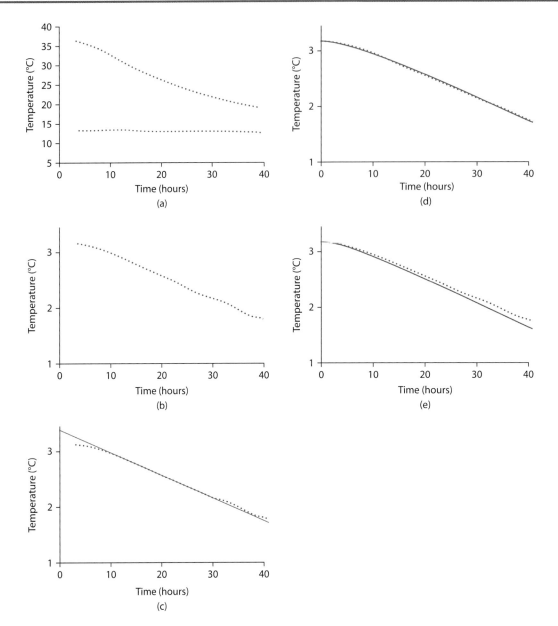

Figure 6.11 The cooling of a body and its modelling. Hourly measurements of rectal (Tr) and ambient (Ta) temperatures from the beginning of the third hour post mortem of a naked body of 99.5 kg lying extended on the back on a thermally indifferent base in a closed room. Abscissa: time since death (t) in hours; ordinate: temperature (°C). Compare with Table 6.2. (a) Data points of rectal and ambient temperatures in linear measures. The mean of the ambient temperature is 13.3°C (Ta). (b) Logarithm of temperature differences 'rectal–ambient'. There is apparently a linear relationship between 'time' and 'ln temperature difference' from the 8th to the 28th hour post mortem. (c) Regression line 'time' (X) against 'ln temperature difference' (Y) computed from the data points between the 8th and the 28th hour post mortem: ln (Tr – Ta) = a_{yx} + b_{yx} × t. Regression coefficient b_{yx} = B (slope) = –0.0408 'Newtonian cooling coefficient'. Intercept a_{yx} = ln (Tr – Ta) at t_0 = 0 = 3.3677; exp (a_{yx}) = 29.01 (°C). Correlation coefficient r = 0.9996. (d) Model curve according to equation 6.2. B = –0.0408 as computed from all the data points between the 8th and the 28th hour; therefore called 'direct examined B'. A = 1.25 as an empirically investigated constant. To = 37.2°C as a chosen constant;

Ta = 13.3°C. The computed death times are estimations. The errors (see Table 6.2) are caused by the inevitable use of empirically investigated constants (A and T_o) and not by the use of an insufficient model. (e) Model curve according to equations 6.1 and 6.2. Instead of the use of the real existing figure of B (–0.0408), which can only be known exactly by many hourly data points after the postmortal plateau and without any tendency change of cooling conditions, B = –0.0439 is used as calculated from the real body weight (99.5 kg) according to the empirically investigated equation 6.2; therefore called 'indirect estimated B'. The real figure of B (–0.0408) would be calculated (equation 6.2) from a body of 106.6 kg according to equation 6.3. The difference between the real, direct examined figure of B (–0.0408) and the body weight–related, indirect estimated figure of B (–0.0439) causes additional errors in computation of the time of death (see Table 6.2). The error increases with the progress of cooling, as in this case. This disadvantage yields a great gain for practical application in casework. Now, the time of death can be computed from a single measurement of rectal temperature at any time in the process of cooling.

without any change of the cooling conditions (including constant ambient temperature). The more slowly the body cools (e.g. high body weight, covering with thick clothing or bedclothes), the more the requirement has to be met. Shorter periods of temperature measurement of the order of 1 to 4 hours and/or actual changes of the cooling conditions shortly before or during the measurements may result in erroneous values of B. The inability to estimate reliably the representative cooling rate B to the whole period between death and time of investigation by multiple temperature measurements within a few hours at the scene is the main reason that these methods give unsatisfactory results in estimating the time since death (Table 6.2).

Without any question, it would be an important breakthrough, similar to that of Marshall and Hoare [101–103], to obtain a measurement of the individual slope of the temperature drop of any case, instead of evaluating it indirectly from the 'size factor' [101–103] or the body weight with 'corrective factors' for particular circumstances (nomogram method; see later).

The methods of De Saram *et al.* [35], Fiddes and Patten [42], Marshall and Hoare [101–103] and Green and Wright [48,49] are based on the principle of measurement of the individual slope, by measuring the temperature at least twice. The most sophisticated method of this type is that published by Green and Wright [48,49].

We therefore examined these methods, especially that of Green and Wright [48,49], on all our experimental material, as well as on the more problematic part of our casework [65].

Experiments on a series of 30 cooling curves of dummies under different, but controlled, constant conditions [91] gave the same results as in body cooling [51] – we obtained worse results than with the nomogram method (see later).

In my opinion, there are three main reasons for these inferior results from multiple temperature measurements:

1. There is only a small decrease in the rectal temperature over an interval of 1 to 3 or 4 hours, especially in cases of obesity, thick clothing or high ambient temperature: thus, even a small mismeasurement of either one or both rectal temperatures, of the order of 0.1°C, may lead to a relatively large error in the cooling rate. In computing the time of death, this small error in the rate is multiplied and may result in a large error in the calculated time of death. To reduce this source of error, Marshall and Hoare [101–103] recommended taking the second measurement 3 or 4 hours apart. To avoid any inaccuracy of the rate by small mismeasurements, Green and Wright [48,49] used, in addition to a double measurement, an 11-fold measurement of the rectal temperature, with measurements taken at intervals of 6 minutes over a period of 1 hour for computing a regression line, but without success, as demonstrated by the experiments of Koppes-Koenen [91].

Table 6.2 The cooling of a body and its modelling*

Time (h)	Real temperatures (°C)		Model error (h)	
	Rectal	1n difference	$B = -0.0408$ (Figure 6.11(d))	$B = -0.0439$ (Figure 6.11(e))
0	—	—	—	—
1	—	—	—	—
2	—	—	—	—
3	36.1	3.1274	0.9	0.6
4	35.7	3.1097	0.7	0.4
5	35.4	3.0962	0.2	−0.1
6	35.0	3.0780	−0.1	−0.5
7	34.6	3.0594	−0.4	−0.9
8	34.2	3.0405	−0.8	−1.3
9	33.4	3.0015	−0.5	−1.1
10	32.8	2.9712	−0.6	−1.2
11	32.0	2.9293	−0.4	−1.1
12	30.9	2.8687	0.3	−0.5
13	30.3	2.8341	0.3	−0.6
14	29.7	2.7982	0.2	−0.7
15	28.9	2.7482	0.6	−0.5
16	28.3	2.7090	0.6	−0.6
17	27.7	2.6682	0.6	−0.6
18	27.1	2.6257	0.7	−0.6
19	26.5	2.5813	0.8	−0.5
20	26.1	2.5506	0.6	−0.8
21	25.7	2.5189	0.4	−1.1
22	25.1	2.4693	0.7	−0.9
23	24.7	2.4349	0.5	−1.1
24	24.1	2.3809	0.9	−0.9
25	23.7	2.3432	0.8	−1.0
26	23.5	2.3238	0.3	−1.5
27	22.9	2.2633	0.8	−1.2
28	22.5	2.2208	0.8	−1.2
29	22.3	2.1989	0.4	−1.7
30	21.9	2.1535	0.5	−1.6
31	21.7	2.1300	0.1	−2.1
32	21.5	2.1059	−0.4	−2.5
33	21.1	2.0560	−0.1	−2.4
34	20.9	2.0301	−0.5	−2.8
35	20.5	1.9761	−0.2	−2.6
36	20.1	1.9191	0.2	−2.3
37	19.7	1.8586	0.7	−1.9
38	19.7	1.8586	−0.3	−2.9
39	19.5	1.8269	−0.5	−3.2
40	19.3	1.7942	−0.7	−3.4

* Mean ambient temperature = 13.3°C.

Data from Figure 6.11.

2. The actual measured rate of the decrease in rectal temperature is valid only for the cooling conditions during the period of measurement. When the cooling

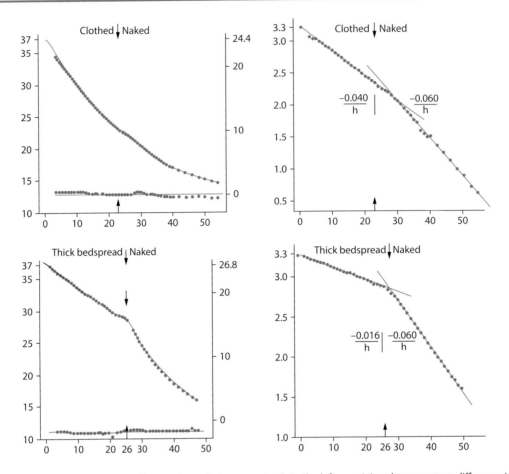

Figure 6.12 'Broken' cooling experiments. Change from clothes to naked (upper graphs) and from being covered by a thick bedspread to naked (lower graphs). On the left: rectal and ambient temperature (scale in the left margin) and temperature difference 'rectum–ambient' (scale in the right margin) in linear measures. On the right: logarithm of the temperature difference 'rectal–ambient' [58,60].

conditions* – including the ambient temperature – have been changed, even shortly before, the body cooling rate also changes. Nevertheless, it is used multiplicatively for the whole period between time of death and time of investigation. There is no way to take into account even well-recognized changes of the cooling conditions* – including the ambient temperature. Figures 6.12 and 6.13 illustrate the great change in the cooling rate *B* after the cooling conditions had been altered. The cooling conditions inevitably change at the scene of death, because the forensic pathologist is never the first to arrive. The question is whether we can recognize and reconstruct the changes in cooling conditions more or less approximately. If not, no temperature-based method can be applied. If this is possible, the method used

should be able to take the changes into account, even approximately (compare the recommended strategy of the nomogram method; see Figure 6.38). Therefore, the main advantage of the enlightened method of Green and Wright [48,49] – measuring instead of evaluating the individual factors – is reduced by the impossibility of taking into account even known changes of the cooling conditions.

3. The plateau must have ended before estimating constant *B*. In casework at the scene, the doctor cannot decide whether the plateau is over or not. Only the method of Green and Wright [48,49] avoids this particular problem, which could introduce great errors during the very early phase after death.

The real inability to estimate reliably the representative cooling rate *B* by multiple temperature measurements within a few hours at the scene led to the concept of indirect estimation of the individual values of the constants *A* and *B* by ascertaining rules from a mass of experimental body cooling under various controlled conditions. This took the main influencing factors of body cooling into account in calculating the time since death at the scene of death.

---

* Common situations at the scene: a thick bedspread was taken off the body; the ambient temperature is changed by the investigators opening windows and doors or using special lamps, which generate heat, or by the sun rising and shining on the body. Such changes can occur before the temperature measurements of the body can be made.

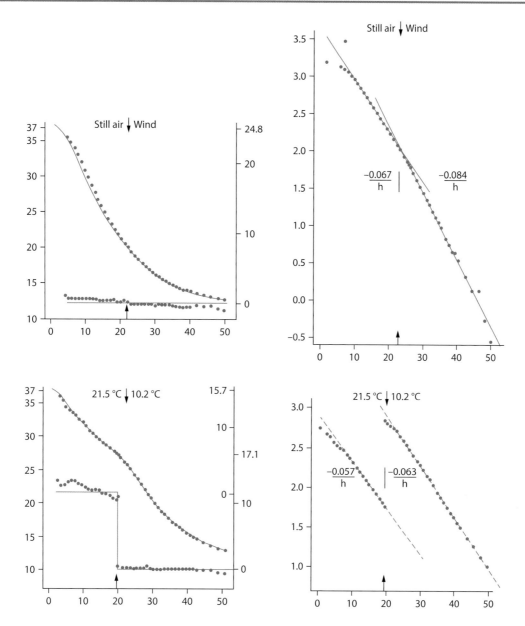

Figure 6.13 'Broken' cooling experiments. Change from cooling in still air to permanently moving air ('wind'; upper graphs). As a control experiment (lower graphs): change of the ambient temperature only, from 21.5°C to 10.2°C [58,60]. For further details, see Figure 6.12.

Indirect estimation of *B* under chosen standard conditions of cooling

As said earlier, the values of the constants *A* and *B* depend on the body build and the ambient cooling conditions, including the thermal factors on the surface of the body. To investigate empirically the dependency of the constants on the body build, I at first kept the other influencing factors uniform, except for the ambient temperature, which was relatively constant during a single experiment but was at different levels (between 5.8°C and 22°C) in different experiments.

The chosen standard conditions (Figure 6.14) of the cooling used in this sequence of experiments are the same as described by Marshall and Hoare [101–103]:

- Naked body – lying extended – on the back – on a thermally indifferent base – in still air – in a closed room – without any sources of strong heat radiation.

In the first sequence of experimental body cooling under almost identical conditions of the chosen standard (same investigator, room and random circumstances), I estimated the true value of *B* by the procedure shown in Figure 6.11 (c) and investigated it in relation to some measures of body build. The strongest correlation was found between the 'body weight to the power of −0.625' and the 'directly estimated' value of *B* (see Figure 6.14 and equation 6.1).

The correlation between the 0.8-fold of the quotient 'body surface/body weight' ('size factor' according to

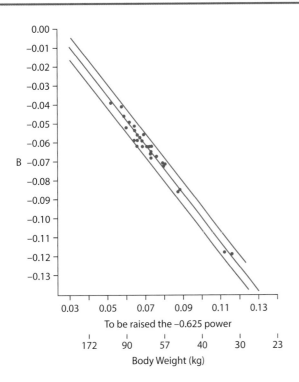

Figure 6.14   Relation between the exponent B (equation 6.2) and the body weight to the power of −0.625 under chosen standard conditions of cooling. Regression line and permissible variation of 95 per cent [58,60].

Marshall and Hoare [101–103]) and the value of B was less strong but not significantly so in this sample of 29 bodies, which ranged between 30 and 112 kg body weight [48,57]. I concluded that the body build described as the relation of height and weight (by the size factor) does not give a more precise estimation of the cooling coefficient B than the more simple measure of the body weight (bw) in kilograms only. Therefore, I preferred the simpler procedure of calculating the value of B from the body weight. In addition, the quantity of fatty tissue of a body had no apparent influence on the value of B, in accordance with theoretical aspects [138] (see footnote 4, earlier).

A combined series of 53 body-cooling experiments by different investigators conducted at different places (though under the chosen standard conditions of cooling) confirmed this correlation. The variance was greater than in the first series because of similar, but not identical, cooling conditions [146]. In consequence, the individual value of B can be computed under 'chosen standard conditions' of cooling by:

$$B = -1.2815(bw^{-0.625}) + 0.0284 \qquad (6.2)$$

The power of −0.625 seems to be an analogy to the 'rule of surface': the surface is proportional to the body weight to the power of 0.67 according to the cubic root of the squared body weight. If the individual value of B is investigated experimentally from the whole cooling curve of the body

(Figure 6.11 (c)), the body weight can be computed [65] by solving for the variable body weight *(bw)* in equation 6.2:

$$bw\,(\text{kg}) = \left[\frac{-1.2815}{B - 0.0284}\right]^{1.6} \qquad (6.3)$$

In 46 cases, this agreed with the real body weight within a standard deviation of ± 6.1 kg. That means that body weight–related estimation of the value of B results in a rather moderate inaccuracy, compared with the direct estimation by multiple temperature measurements over a period of a few hours, possibly after a change in the cooling conditions. Nevertheless, this moderate inaccuracy can lead to a moderate systematic error in computing the time since death, which increases with progress of cooling related to the standardized temperature, Q.

A typical but pronounced example is the case of Figure 6.11. The body of 99.5 kg cooled somewhat slower than expected compared with the body weight-related value of B according to equation 6.2, which would be −0.0439, so providing a progressive overestimation of the calculated time since death, as can be seen by comparing Figure 6.11 (d) and Table 6.2 with Figure 6.11 (e) and Table 6.2. The actual observed value of B (−0.0408) would correspond to a body weight of 106.6 kg according to equation 6.3.

Indirect estimation of *B* under cooling conditions differing from the chosen standard

See Figures 6.12 and 6.13.

Investigations on bodies

For a clear decision as to whether there is a significant influence of clothing, covering and wind on the body cooling [101–103,58] or not [108,138], I performed some special 'broken' experiments (see Figures 6.12 and 6.13). A body was allowed to cool for the first few hours clothed or covered, the covering was removed and the body then cooled naked in still air (chosen standard) (see Figure 6.12). The graphs on the left show the original points of measurement with the computed cooling curves (lines) according to equations 6.1 and 6.2 using the individual calculated values of the constant B, which can be seen in the graphs on the right. These graphs demonstrate the cooling curves as the logarithm of the temperature difference between the rectum and the surroundings. Here, the given lines are the regression lines and the given figures are the slopes, which are identical to the constant B of each of the two parts of the cooling curves (see Figure 6.11 (c)).

Figure 6.12 clearly illustrates the results. The clothed body (upper graphs) cools with a slope of B = −0.04, which corresponds to the slope of a naked body of 109 kg according to equation 6.3. After taking the clothing off the body, the same body now cools with a slope of B = −0.06, corresponding to 72 kg. The actual body weight was 76 kg.

The influence of the clothing (underwear, shirt, suit and thicker coat) is significant. The influence of a covering such as a thick bedspread (lower graphs of Figure 6.12) is much more pronounced: the body cools with $B = -0.016$, corresponding to 217 kg. After taking the covering off the body, it cools with $B = -0.06$, corresponding to 72 kg. The actual body weight was 73 kg. In analogy (see Figure 6.13, upper graphs), if a body first cools naked in still air (chosen standard), then later in permanently moving air (by switching on a small fan; 25 watts, mounted on the ceiling at a distance of about 2 m from the body surface, thus giving only a very slight air movement), the slope B equals -0.067 (64 kg) under the chosen standard conditions (still air) and is closely related to the real body weight of 65 kg. This changes to $B = -0.084$ under the conditions of moving air corresponding to 49 kg. The conclusion of this experiment indicates that even a slight but permanent air movement results in a significant acceleration of the cooling of a naked body.

Conversely (see lower part of Figure 6.13), there is no significant change in the slope of the cooling curve when the ambient temperature changes only rectangularly. As a control experiment, this naked body of 71 kg body weight cooled in still air, first in an ambient temperature of about 21.5°C and later, after a quick transfer to another room, in about 10°C ambient temperature. The slope B changed from -0.057 (76 kg) to -0.063 (68 kg), which is insignificant.

The principle of corrective factors of the body weight

Taking as an example the upper part of Figure 6.12, a clothed body cools like a naked body 1.4 times heavier: 109 kg/76 kg = 1.4. This corrective factor of the body weight *(C)* equals the body weight calculated according to equation 6.3 from B of the cooling curve *(bw calc)* divided by the real body weight *(bw):*

$$C = \frac{bw\,calc}{bw} \qquad (6.4)$$

So, equation 6.2 is now:

$$B = -1.2815(C \times bw)^{-0.0625} + 0.0284 \qquad (6.5)$$

where C = corrective factor of the body weight taking into account any difference of the cooling conditions from the chosen standard.

In the case of the lower part of Figure 6.12 (thick bedspread):

$$C = \frac{217\,kg}{73\,kg} = 3.0$$

In the case of the upper part of Figure 6.13 (wind):

$$C = \frac{49\,kg}{65\,kg} = 0.75$$

In the case of the lower part of Figure 6.13 (chosen standard; rectangular change of the ambient temperature only):

$$C = \frac{76\,kg}{71\,kg} = 1.07, \quad \text{and} \quad \frac{68\,kg}{71\,kg} = 0.96$$

In comparison with the chosen standard ($C = 1$), thermic insulation conditions result in a corrective factor greater than 1. Conditions that cause an acceleration of the cooling result in a corrective factor less than 1.

After the pilot experiments, we made several series of cooling experiments under various cooling conditions, all differing from the chosen standard, using naked bodies in constantly moving air, different types of dry clothing and covering [146,166], wet clothing, wet, naked body surface with or without wind [64] and body cooling in still water [69]. From each experimental body cooling curve, the real value of B (analogous to the graphs on the right in Figures 6.12 and 6.13), the corresponding body weight according to equation 6.3 and the resulting corrective factor according to equation 6.4 were calculated.

Body cooling in constantly, even slightly moving, air The cooling curves of 10 naked bodies of actual body weight between 52 and 89 kg, lying extended on the back beneath a 25-watt fan mounted at a distance of 2 m on the ceiling of the room and producing a slight movement of air, provided values of B equal to 0.75 times the real body weight on average (Table 6.3). The corrective factor varied only a little, from 0.66 to 0.81, corresponding to lower errors of computed death times (standard deviation ± 0.9 hours) in comparison with body cooling in still air (standard deviation ± 1.3 hours) in the same series of body coolings [58].

The cooling of clothed bodies The data of experimental cooling of clothed bodies in still air (Table 6.4) show the relationship between the verbal description of clothing and the corrective factor. However, they also show that this relationship is not without exception, and therefore it is not possible to estimate a corrective factor true to within ± one tenth from a verbal description. A further

Table 6.3 Body cooling in permanently moving air*

Case	Body weight	B_{wind}	bw_{calc}	Corrective factor
01	52.0	−0.095	42.3	0.81
02	57.0	−0.098	40.7	0.71
27	65.0	−0.094	42.8	0.66
28	65.0	−0.084	49.1	0.76
29	66.5	−0.082	50.5	0.76
30	89.0	−0.063	68.4	0.77
38	56.0	−0.091	44.3	0.79

* Body weight calculated (bw_{calc}) according to equation 6.3.

From Henssge C. Estimation of death-time by computing the rectal body cooling under various cooling conditions (German, English summary). *Z Rechtsmed* 1981;**87**:147–178.

Table 6.4   Corrective factors for clothed bodies lying on a 'thermally indifferent' base in still air

Case number	Whole clothing	Clothing of lower trunk	Real body weight	Calculated body weight	Corrective factor
B61	Work jacket, trousers displaced upward, downward, vest, short pants.	Short pants.	92.0	92.0	1.0
B63	Vest, panties.	Panties.	110.0	121.0	1.1
H66	Sweater, vest, drawers, short pants.	Drawers, short pants.	92.5	94.4	1.02
B64	Shirt, displaced upward, vest, short pants, trousers.	Short pants, trousers.	82.0	90.2	1.1
B58	Trousers, thin sweater, two vests, short pants.	Trousers, short pants.	68.0	74.8	1.1
B37	Open anorak, sweater, trousers, drawers.	Trousers, drawers.	79.0	85.3	1.08
B57	Anorak, jacket, sweater, vest, trousers, drawers.	Trousers, drawers.	76.5	86.4	1.26
H2	Jacket, sweatshirt, shirt, vest, short pants, trousers.	Trousers, drawers.	84.5	110.7	1.31
H6	Sweater, shirt, vest, trousers, two drawers.	Trousers, two drawers.	68.0	72.8	1.07
B53	Parker, jacket, waistcoat, shirt, vest, trousers, drawers.	Parker, trousers, drawers.	79.0	104.3	1.32
H4	Jacket, vest, roll-on panty, two short pants, trousers.	Trousers, roll-on panty, two short pants.	86.5	102.9	1.19
B60	Waistcoat, shirt, two vests, short pants, trousers, corselet, tights.	Trousers, corselet, tights, short pants.	55.5	79.4	1.43
B54	Jacket, shirt, long cardigan, vest, trousers, thick drawers.	Long cardigan, trousers, thick drawers.	63.5	91.4	1.44
B36	Woollen coat, jacket, waistcoat, vest, shirt, short pants, trousers.	Woollen coat, trousers, short pants.	85.0	126.7	1.49
B59	Jacket, sweater, vest, drawers, trousers, truss with pad.	Trousers, drawers, truss with pad.	78.5	125.6	1.6
B60	Lining trench coat, thick woollen dress, slip, short panty, tights.	Lining trench coat, thick woollen dress, slip, short panty, tights.	52.0	93.6	1.8

Data from Henssge C, Madea B. *Methodenzur Bestimmung der Todeszeit an der Leiche*. Lübeck, Schmidt-Römhild, 1988; and Stipanits E, Henssge C. Präzisionsvergleich von Todeszeitrückrechnungen ohne und mit Berücksichtigung von Einflussfaktoren (German, English summary). *Beitr Gerichtl Med* 1985;**43**:323–329.

conclusion is that only the clothing of the lower trunk is relevant for the retardation of rectal body cooling. The almost radial direction of heat transfer inside the body and the rectal temperature probe site theoretically support this conclusion.

Clothed bodies in moving air[33]   A study of Table 6.3 (naked bodies in moving air) and Table 6.4 (clothed bodies in still air) shows that the influence of moving air on clothed bodies becomes less as the clothing or covering becomes thicker. Moving air accelerates cooling in very thinly clothed bodies (Table 6.5; H12, H15), compensates the slightly decelerating influence of thin clothing (H14, H11) and seems to be without any accelerating influence on thicker-clothed bodies (B66, B67). Moving air accelerates the cooling by forced convection of heated air from the body surface. Clothing decelerates the cooling, mainly by fixation of a layer of heated air at the surface of the body. This principle should be borne in mind when estimating a corrective factor in cases of clothed bodies lying in moving air.

Covered bodies in still air   The corrective factors for taking usual coverings into account are rather uniform, although

Table 6.5   Corrective factors for clothed bodies in permanently moving air

Case number	Clothing of lower trunk	Real body weight	Calculated body weight	Corrective factor
H12	Nightwear, short panty.	73.3	55.7	0.76
H15	Short panty.	67.5	60.8	0.9
H14	Trousers, drawers.	78.0	75.6	0.97
H11	Trousers, drawers.	73.0	80.3	1.10
B66	Thin trench coat, short panty, trousers.	78.5	110.7	1.41
H13	Dress, slip, short panty, roll-on panty, truss.	63.7	77.7	1.21
B67	Thick coat, skirt, slip, corselet, tights, short panty.	83.5	138.7	1.66

From Henssge C, Madea B. *Methodenzur Bestimmung der Todeszeit an der Leiche*. Lübeck, Schmidt-Römhild, 1988.

Table 6.6 Corrective factors for covering of naked and partly clothed bodies, respectively

Case number	Clothing	Covering	Real body weight	Calculated body weight	Corrective factor
		Thinner covering – thermically indifferent supporting base			
B62	Naked.	Simple cover.	66.0	79.2	1.2
B51	Naked.	Double cover.	91.0	106.2	1.17
B56	Drawers, short panty.	Simple cover.	92.5	119.3	1.29
B52	Drawers, short panty.	Simple blanket.	74.0	100.2	1.34
		Bed-like covering – mattress on supporting base			
B33	Short panty.	Thick bedspread.	73.0	157.7	2.16
H08	Naked.	Two thick blankets.	77.0	110.4	1.44
H07	Nightwear.		93.0	124.0	1.33
H10	Trousers, drawers.		113.0	152.2	1.35
H06	Skirt, drawers.		64.5	127.0	1.97
H09	Two napkins,		6.3	16.4	2.6
	short panty.		6.25	25.0	4.0

From Henssge C, Madea B. *Methodenzur Bestimmung der Todeszeit an der Leiche.* Lübeck, Schmidt-Römhild, 1988.

it is pointed out that the cooling experiments listed in Table 6.6 were made by laying the bodies on 'thermally indifferent' bases (e.g. on a simple covered stretcher). When bodies are lying on more thermally insulating bases (couch, divan, bed), somewhat higher corrective factors may be required, even in covered bodies. The corrective factors of bed-like covered bodies are rather non-uniform. In Table 6.6, the different corrective factors for cases H09 and H06, and H08 and H10 may be explained by the great difference in body weight because the cooling conditions were nearly identical in these cases. This is one clue that lower corrective factors are necessary for higher thermic insulation conditions (e.g. a bedspread) on heavier bodies, and vice versa (see later).

Body cooling in still water Nineteen bodies (body weights between 48.5 and 108.5 kg) were suspended undressed in a tub holding 1000 l of almost still water at temperatures of approximately 20 and 10°C, from the third hour post mortem (Table 6.7). The rectal temperature was measured, usually until the 33rd hour post mortem. The bodies cooled as quickly as naked bodies of half the real body mass in still air of the same temperature, corresponding to a corrective factor of 0.5 as a mean (ranging from 0.36 to 0.63). However, 10 further bodies (body weights between 44 and 95 kg), suspended in nearly still water at approximately 0°C, yielded a distinctly smaller temperature decrease, which was especially marked at rectal temperatures lower than about 11°C in all bodies, without regard to body mass. In bodies of great body weight and small body surface in proportion to body mass, the lower cooling rate was pronounced, the cooling curve corresponding to corrective factors tending to 1.0. This can be explained by a decrease in the thermal conductivity of the subcutaneous adipose tissue with a decrease in tissue temperature [69].

Body cooling in flowing water Brown and Marshall [23] characterized the cooling curve of a very small body (size factor: 320 cm²/kg) suspended in flowing water (velocity 5 m/hour) by a four-exponential model. Transcribed to the two-exponential equation 6.1 and the body weight relation of *B* according to equation 6.2, this would result in a corrective factor of the body weight in order of 0.35, which relates well to all the other corrective factors.

Body cooling in cases of wet clothing or covering, or unclothed wet body surface Some cooling experiments of 'wet-through' clothed or covered bodies, and of naked bodies with a wet body surface were made in a closed room, and by night in the open air under a cloudless sky when reconstructing a special case [64].

According to the accused husband, his wife had fallen from a boat into the water and drowned. The real time of death could not have been earlier than 22:10 hours and not later than 22:20 hours, averaging 22:15 hours according to his declaration. Some 15 minutes later, the body was detected by the husband and salvaged by witnesses. The body was laid on a lawn. At 00:23 hours, the deep rectal temperature was measured as 28°C, and at 00:40 hours as 27.5°C. The law court decided on a 28.3°C rectal temperature at 00:23 hours after examining the thermometer. The body weight of the woman was 53 kg, and her height was 159 cm. Until the temperature measurement, the body was clothed with a slip, a corselette, Silastic trousers, a shirt, a brassiere and a long waterproof anorak. The day in August was sunny. During the windless night there was a cloudless sky. The weather station stated the following temperatures: 20.7°C (16:00 hours), 20.1°C (19:00 hours), 15.6°C (21:00 hours), 14.3°C (22:00 hours), 13.8°C (23:00 hours), 12.6°C (00:00 hours) and 11.9°C (01:00 hours). From these data there resulted a mean temperature of 12.8°C between 23:00 and 01:00 hours. The water temperature within the

Table 6.7 **Body cooling in still water**

Case number	Body weight (kg)	$B_{standard}$* calculated	Water temperature (°C)	B_{water} real	bw_{calc} (kg)	Corrective factor
01	65.0	−0.066	19.3	−0.128	28.9	0.445
20	68.0	−0.063	20.0	−0.107	36.5	0.536
21	59.5	−0.071	20.3	−0.137	26.6	0.447
22	84.5	−0.052	20.2	−0.091	44.6	0.528
24	108.5	−0.040	20.2	−0.074	57.4	0.529
25	100.5	−0.043	19.8	−0.082	50.5	0.502
27	97.5	−0.045	19.7	−0.084	49.0	0.503
28	77.5	−0.056	19.9	−0.113	34.1	0.439
30	71.5	−0.061	20.5	−0.111	35.0	0.489
						0.491
						±0.036
02	92.0	−0.048	9.8	−0.074	57.4	0.623
03	48.5	−0.085	9.8	−0.156	22.2	0.457
04	75.0	−0.058	10.0	−0.098	40.7	0.543
05	58.5	−0.063	9.9	−0.104	36.4	0.631
08	88.0	−0.050	10.2	−0.103	38.2	0.435
10	70.0	−0.062	10.2	−0.127	29.2	0.417
11	83.5	−0.052	10.0	−0.099	40.2	0.482
12	77.5	−0.056	8.3	−0.133	27.5	0.355
13	56.5	−0.075	10.0	−0.150	23.5	0.415
14	85.5	−0.051	9.1	−0.092	44.3	0.518
						0.488
						±0.086
06	44.2	−0.092	0.6	−0.140	25.8	0.583
07	75.5	−0.058	0.0	−0.071	60.3	0.798
09	83.5	−0.052	0.0	−0.079	52.9	0.633
15	95.5	−0.046	0.0	−0.044	99.7	1.040
16	79.0	−0.055	0.0	−0.092	44.0	0.557
17	80.0	−0.054	−0.1	−0.055	79.0	0.988
18	49.0	−0.084	−0.1	−0.121	31.1	0.638
19	69.5	−0.062	0.0	−0.073	57.6	0.828
23	58.0	−0.073	0.0	−0.090	44.9	0.775
29	66.5	−0.065	1.2	−0.082	50.6	0.761
						0.760
						±0.155

* $B_{standard}$ according to equation 6.2; body weight$_{calculated}$ (bw_{calc}) according to equation 6.3; corrective factor according to equation 6.4.

From Henssge C, Brinkmann B, Püschel K. Determination of time of death by measuring the rectal temperature in corpses suspended in water (German, English summary). *Z Rechtsmed* 1984;**92**:255–276.

harbour measured approximately 20°C. The decisive question was whether the rectal body cooling to 28.3°C at 00:23 hours could be compatible with a death time at 22:15 hours.

To solve this question, some cooling experiments were made (Table 6.8), which led to the following conclusions:

1. Naked bodies suspended in water for a short time (~10 minutes) cool in still air as a result of their wet body surface at the same rate as bodies 0.75 times the real body weight.
2. Bodies with thin but 'wet-through' clothing/covering seem to cool in moving air like bodies of 0.7 times the real body weight.

3. Bodies with more layers of wet-through clothing/covering seem to cool in moving air like bodies of the real body weight without any corrective adjustment.
4. One layer of thin, wet-through clothing/covering does not seem to have a marked influence on the velocity of body cooling in still air, compared with cooling under chosen standard conditions. Therefore, no corrective adjustment of the real body weight is necessary. Conversely, thick, wet-through clothing/covering, especially of several layers, provides a reduced velocity of body cooling in still air that is similar to dry clothing/covering and corresponding to corrective factors between 1.1 and 1.4.

Table 6.8 Body cooling under wet-through clothing/covering and respective wet body surface

Case number	Cooling conditions	Real body weight	Corrective factor
	Closed room, still air, wet body surface		
50		45.0	0.77
52		65.0	0.75
	Wet-through covering or clothing		
41	One smock.	84.5	1.00
42	Two smocks.	57.2	1.10
51	Roll-on panty, trousers, three smocks.	69.5	1.10
44	Roll-on panty, trousers, three smocks.	65.0	1.30
	Permanently moving air		
68	Drawers, trousers, skirt, pullover, jacket.	64.5	0.7
55	Drawers, trousers, pullover, coat.	91.0	0.9
47	Three smocks.	91.5	0.7
	Under cloudless sky, wet lawn, still air		
80	Drawers, dress, one smock.	59.5	1.2
81	Drawers, skirt, one smock.	67.5	1.4
82	Drawers, dress, one smock.	58.0	1.4

From Henssge C, Brinkmann B. Todeszeitbestimmung aus der Rektaltemperatur. *Arch Kriminol* 1984;**174**:96–112.

On the basis of these results, corrective factors from 1.1 to 1.4 were used to test the husband's account of events. However, another technical expert maintained that the body would have cooled more because of the influence of radiation against the cloudless sky at night, which would be equal to a corpse at −30°C. To examine this argument, the cooling experiments of cases 80, 81 and 82 in Table 6.8 were made by night in the open air under a cloudless sky by laying the bodies on a wet lawn. The results were the same as for a closed room, showing that radiation from the surface of the body to the cloudless sky by night had no marked influence on body cooling. The computation was made using the following:

- Mean ambient temperature 12.8°C.
- Body weight 53 kg.
- Averaged corrective factor 1.2.
- Rectal temperature 28.3°C.
- Rectal temperature at death 36.5°C (as agreed by the law court).

This equals (according to equations 6.1 and 6.5) 9.4 hours before 00:23 hours as a mean value. Using the range of corrective factors from 1.0 to 1.4, which could be possible according to the special cooling experiments (see Table 6.8), the time of death ranges between 5.6 hours (corrective factor = 1.0) and 13.5 hours (corrective factor

= 1.4), corresponding to 3.8 hours around the mean of 9.4 hours, which is in close agreement with three times the experienced standard deviation of cooling experiments under various conditions (see Figures 6.29 and 6.30 and Table 6.14). Therefore, a time of death at 22:15 hours (22:10 to 22:30 hours) could be excluded.

Investigations on dummies

Using dummies to replace bodies of average weight, we obtained results that correspond well with the corrective factor for various cooling conditions. An exception was experiments with wet-surfaced dummies and dummies suspended in water, where somewhat lower corrective factors were found compared with bodies (Figure 6.15).

Dependence of corrective factors on the body weight

Although the corrective factors established on bodies include a wide spectrum of frequently occurring cooling conditions, nearly all these experiences resulted from bodies of average body weight [61,143]. Only a few cases support the assumption that bodies of a very high body weight and, at the same time, strong thermic insulation conditions (see Table 6.6) would require lower corrective factors and, conversely, bodies of a low body weight would require higher corrective factors. To correct these deficiencies, 98 cooling experiments on 5 different-sized dummies under 5 different cooling conditions, besides standard ones, were made. The dummies were cooled under standard conditions equivalent to human bodies of 14, 33, 41, 83 and 104 kg, respectively.

Characteristics of the cooling conditions

The dummies were laid on a thick, foam-upholstered supported base and exposed permanently to a slightly moving air, produced by a small fan (25 watts) mounted on the ceiling at a distance of approximately 2 m.

- Clothing I: two layers. One layer was thin (cotton textile, like pants), and the second layer was rather thick (blue jeans).
- Clothing II: three layers. Additional to 'clothing I', a second thin layer was applied.
- Covering I: A wool blanket, loose-fitting.
- Covering II: A thick feather eiderdown. The dummies were laid on an additional mattress, which was placed on the upholstered support base used for the other dummies.

After repeated test cooling measurements under chosen standard conditions, the coefficient B was calculated. From these 'experimental' values of B, 'virtual' weights were calculated according to equation 6.3. The virtual weight represents the weight of a body whose cooling curve is identical to cooling under standard conditions.

Just as under standard conditions of cooling, a close linear relationship results between 'experimental' B and 'virtual weight' to the power of −0.625 for each condition differing from the standard (Figure 6.16 and Table 6.9).

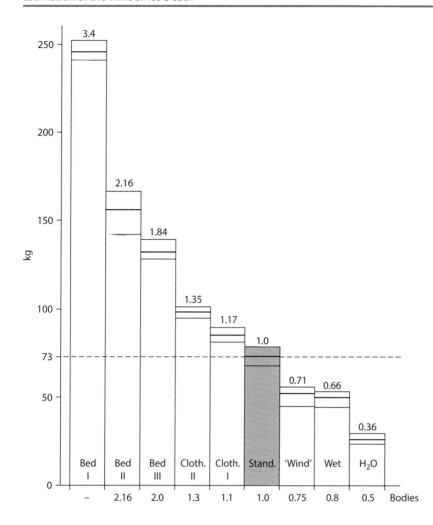

Figure 6.15 Comparison of corrective factors investigated on bodies and on a dummy cooling under various, but very similar, conditions. The dummy replaces a body of 73 kg. The corrective factors resulting from dummy experiments are given at the top of the columns. Beneath the baseline the corrective factors of bodies are shown as they resulted from the previously reported experimental body investigations. (Data from Henssge C, Madea B, Schaar U, Pitzken C. Die Abkühlung eines Dummy unter verschiedenen Bedingungen im Vergleich zur Leichenabkühlung (German, English summary). *Beitr Gerichtl Med* 1987;**45**:145–149.)

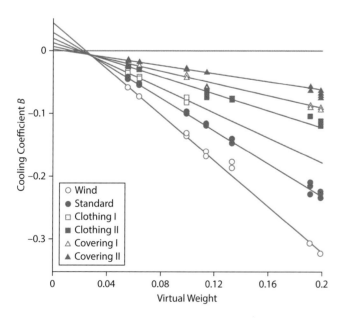

Figure 6.16 Regression lines (see Table 6.9) of the dependence of cooling coefficient *B* (ordinate) on virtual weight to the power of −0.625 (abscissa) for the various cooling conditions. The common point of intersection has the coordinates Y = −0.007 and X = 0.028 [61,143].

Table 6.9 Regression lines of cooling coefficient *B* (ordinate) against virtual weight to the power of −0.625 (abscissa) for the various cooling conditions (see Figure 6.16)

Condition	Number of experiments	Regression line	
		Slope 'S'	Intercept
Wind	20	−1.8083	0.0436
Standard	24	−1.2815	0.0289
Clothing I	07	−0.9591	0.0199
Clothing II	12	−0.6431	0.0110
Covering I	17	−0.4828	0.0065
Covering II	18	−0.3218	0.0020

Data from Henssge C. Rectal temperature time of death nomogram: dependence of corrective factors on the body weight under stronger thermic insulation conditions. *Forensic Sci Int* 1992;**54**:51–56; and Stadtmüller K. *Zur Todeszeitbestimmung aus der Leichenabkühlung: Die Normierung der Abkühlgeschwindigkeit unterschiedlicher Körper auf verschiedene äussere Bedingungen.* Cologne, Germany, University of Cologne, MD thesis, 1991.

Because of the common point of intersection, the dependence of B for each cooling condition is differentiated only by the slope S. Therefore, the coefficient B can be calculated for each cooling condition, depending on the body weight (standard) according to its own slope S:

$$B_{\text{condition}} = [(bw^{-0.625} - 0.028)S_{\text{condition}}] - 0.007 \qquad (6.6)$$

$B_{\text{condition}}$ can be used to calculate the body weight (kg) by:

$$bw_{\text{condition}} = [-1.2815/B_{\text{condition}} - 0.0284] [61,143] \qquad (6.7)$$

The bw condition represents the weight that is apparently changed by the special cooling conditions. Dividing the virtual weight (standard) by the apparently changed weight, the corrective factor can be determined. Conversely, the virtual weight of the dummy (standard) multiplied by the corrective factor provides for a special cooling condition.

The corrective factors of the investigated cooling conditions can be calculated universally for any virtual weight (Figure 6.17):

$$\frac{\left[\dfrac{-1.2815}{(S_{\text{condition}} \times bw_{\text{standard}} + I_{\text{condition}})}\right]^{1.6}}{bw_{\text{standard}}} = F \qquad (6.8)$$

where $S_{\text{condition}}$ is the slope; $I_{\text{condition}}$ is the intercept from Table 6.9; and bw_{standard} is the virtual weight under standard conditions.

The dependence of the corrective factors on the virtual dummy weight (acting for body weight) is evident. If the dependence on body weight did not exist, the lines for all the cooling conditions in Figure 6.17 would have to be horizontal, just as they are for the standard condition and, approximately, for the cooling condition 'wind'. The dynamics of the dependence on body weight become pronounced with the power of the thermic insulation. The curves of Figure 6.17 demonstrate a non-linear regularity of the cooling conditions. The dependence between virtual weight and the corrective factor of the investigated cooling conditions can also be used to interpolate the relation to non-examined cooling conditions of any distinct weight, as shown in Figure 6.18 for an average body weight of 70 kg. The 'best fit' curve of the measurement points drawn is expressed mathematically:

$$S = 3.24596 \times \exp(-0.89959 \times C_{70}) \qquad (6.9)$$

where S is the slope to calculate the cooling coefficient B from body weight to the power of -0.625 (see Figure 6.16), and C_{70} is the corrective factor valid for a special cooling condition to a body of 70 kg.

The interpolation can only be made, in the first instance, on the range of the actually investigated cooling conditions (from wind to thick bedspread) and for those corrective factors (from 0.75 to 3.0) valid for 'average' body weights.

Using the same principle, the corrective factor *(C)* can be calculated for any actual body weight (kg) according to equation 6.8, provided that the corrective factor for an 'average body weight' of 70 kg (C_{70}), for any actual cooling condition, is known:

$$\frac{\left[\dfrac{-1.2815}{(bw^{-0.625} - 0.028)(-3.24596 \times \exp(-0.89959 \times C_{70})) - 0.0354}\right]^{1.6}}{\text{kg}} = C \qquad (6.10)$$

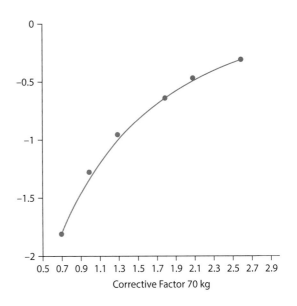

Figure 6.18 The relation between corrective factors (abscissa) and slope S of the correlation between cooling coefficient and weight according to Figure 6.16 and Table 6.9 (ordinate) for a dummy of approximately 70 kg. The points represent, from below: wind, standard, clothing I, clothing II, covering I, covering II. (Data from Henssge C. Rectal temperature time of death nomogram: dependence of corrective factors on the body weight under stronger thermic insulation conditions. *Forensic Sci Int* 1992;**54:**51–56.)

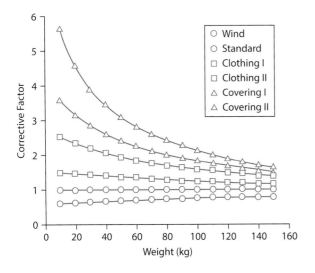

Figure 6.17 Generalization of the dependence of the corrective factors on the virtual weight of dummies (acting for body weight) for the investigated cooling conditions [61,143].

Using equation 6.10, the corrective factors were calculated for body weights ranging from 4 to 150 kg, related to the corrective factors of 70 kg (see Table 6.17).

Equation 6.10 can be used to demonstrate that special thermic insulating conditions, which require a corrective factor of 2.0 on a dummy of 70 kg virtual weight, would require a higher corrective factor of approximately 3.2 on a dummy of virtual 10 kg; and, in the case of a 110-kg dummy, a lower corrective factor of 1.7. In these experiments, the corrective factor for one of the different-sized dummies of one of the applied cooling conditions can be calculated by equation 6.10 if the corrective factor of a different-sized dummy is known.

Because of the close conformity of the previous investigations in comparing the cooling of dummies and bodies under various conditions (see Figure 6.15) it is concluded that the result of the dependence of corrective factors on the body weight is applicable to bodies.

Intuitively, it appears obvious that, in the case of a 150-kg body, a special bedspread does not cause a deceleration of cooling proportional to the body weight corresponding to 525 kg (3.5 × 150 kg), such as in a case of a 4-kg body corresponding to 14 kg (3.5 × 4). The physical explanation for this effect is, however, more difficult. The model of a cylinder of infinite length [50] applied to body cooling [74,75,138] may be helpful. A special bedspread has a distinct layer thickness. The enlargement of the radius is, in the case of a 4-kg body, relatively much greater than in the case of a 150-kg body; it is not proportional to the radius of the body, but it enlarges the radius cumulatively. In addition, the bedspread causes a deceleration of heat loss by its comparatively smaller heat conductivity against body tissues. The effect of this component on the velocity of body cooling is proportional to the surface area of the body. The surface area itself is proportional to the body weight to the power of 0.67 (see Figure 6.4; 'geometric likeness'). Therefore, it may be concluded that the deceleration of body cooling by a bedspread is provided by the enlargement of the radius of a body as an additive component, as well as by the low heat conductivity as a proportional component [61,143].

However, although these considerations may be helpful in understanding, they do not lead to practicable solutions useful for casework.

Influence of the type of supporting base on body cooling

In a series of cooling experiments utilizing heat flow sensors (see Figures 6.5 to 6.9), 'naked' dummies were lain on supporting bases with very different thermic features [90,100,160] (Table 6.10 and Figures 6.19 to 6.21).

Related to a 'thermally indifferent base', insulating bases slow down the cooling rate by corrective factors of up to 1.3. As may be seen in Table 6.10, it was not possible to slow down the cooling beyond this level by adding more insulating material (see experiment numbers 200 to 310) but not covering the dummies' flanks. Conversely, some

bases accelerate the cooling, requiring corrective factors in the order of 0.75 to 0.5.

Figure 6.19 (a) (b) and (c) demonstrates not only the dependence of the heat flow at the contact surface but also the slope of central temperature on that type of base. Even the heat flow at the non-contact surface is slightly influenced by the type of base, which is comprehensible in view of the parallel circuit of the surfaces in Figure 6.9. This also explains why the cooling cannot be further decelerated by adding more insulating features to the supporting base. Finally, the heating of the ground by the heat flow from the contact surface of the dummy to the base itself, immediately after contact, causes a more reduced temperature difference between base and contact surface, as can be clearly seen in the first parts of the curves in Figures 6.7 and 6.8. In accordance with this, there is a linear relationship between central temperature *(X)* and heat flow at the contact surface *(Y)* during cooling after the plateau. The slope of this regression line best characterizes the influence of the type of base on the cooling velocity, because there is a strong correlation with the cooling coefficient *B* (see Figure 6.21), which means the slope of logarithm of temperature difference against cooling time (see Figure 6.11 (c)).

In a second series of experiments by Unland [160] with different-sized dummies, it was shown that this relation depends on the size of dummy (see Figure 6.21). According to Figure 6.21, the cooling coefficient *B* can be computed for any body weight and any kind of base by:

$$B = (bw \times 0.4774 + 13.3462)^{-0.725}$$
$$\times sFT - (bw \times 0.3210 + 1.5299)^{-0.98} \quad (6.11)$$

where *bw* is body weight in kg, and *sFT* is the slope of central temperature against the heat flow at the lying surface.

The importance of equation 6.11 is the replacement of the estimation of a corrective factor for any cooling condition, by the measurement of the heat flow at surfaces, in addition to the measurement of ambient and central (rectal) temperatures and body weight.

Body cooling under the condition of lying on leaves and covered by leaves

Cooling experiments of two different dummies were carried out using first 'standard conditions of cooling', second with a 2-cm-thick compressed layer of leaves on the floor and third covered by a 10-cm-thick layer of leaves additionally [6]. Under chosen standard conditions of cooling, the dummies cooled like bodies of virtual weights of 60.4 kg and 67.6 kg (calculation according to equation 6.3). When the dummies were lying on wet-through leaves at the beginning of the measurements, cooling was not different from standard conditions. Over a period of several days, the leaves became drier and drier, and the cooling retarded, corresponding to

Table 6.10   Type of supporting base and its influence of cooling of a 'naked' dummy related to a 'thermally indifferent base' as used at 'standard conditions'*

Experiment number	Supporting base	Real B	Body weight calculated	Corrective factor
	Thick foam-upholstered base			
200		−0.0514	84.9	1.31
201		−0.0524	83.3	1.29
202		−0.0528	82.6	1.28
270	Thick foam-upholstered base + polystyrene (Styropor) plate.	−0.0529	82.4	1.27
300	Thick foam-upholstered base + polystyrene (Styropor) plate + cushion.	−0.0514	85.0	1.31
310	Armchair.	−0.0526	82.9	1.28
	Table + cover 'indifferent'.			
210		−0.0646	66.4	1.03
211		−0.0669	63.9	0.99
212		−0.0659	65.1	1.01
225		−0.0672	63.6	0.98
	Floor of a room covering with PVC.			
230		−0.0840	49.1	0.76
231		−0.0838	49.2	0.76
232		−0.0829	49.9	0.77
	Loft.			
	Ground of cellar.			
240		−0.0859	47.8	0.74
250		−0.0863	47.5	0.73
251		−0.0864	47.5	0.73
252		−0.0953	42.1	0.65
260	Stone slab outside.	−0.0867	47.3	0.73
	Steel plate on concrete-ground wash round.			
290		−0.1095	35.4	0.55
291		−0.1106	34.9	0.54
292		−0.1116	34.5	0.53

* Calculation of the body weight according to equation 6.3. Calculation of the corrective factor according to equation 6.4 with an average 'standard' weight of 64.7 kg. The nearly constant ambient temperatures ranged between 14°C and 19°C, except in experiment number 260, where it was 6.1°C [90].

PVC, polyvinyl chloride.

higher virtual body weights related to corrective factors of about 1.3 (calculation according to equation 6.4). When the dummies were lying on totally dry leaves, corrective factors of the order of 1.5 are adequate (Table 6.11). In contrast, corrective factors greater than 1.3 could not be achieved in the experiments of Table 6.10 when using smooth and rigid insulating bases that did not cover the flanks of the dummies. In the experiments using leaves, the material is flexible and adapts itself to the body surface. In consequence, the insulating area is enlarged by the flanks of the dummy, thus providing corrective factors up to 1.5. When the dummies were lying on leaves and covered by a nearly 10-cm-thick layer of leaves, corrective factors of 1.8 to 2.7 were determined (Table 6.12). The great variability of the

insulating effect of apparently identical layers of leaves can be explained by different amounts of enclosed air.

The individual value of the plateau-related constant A

Estimation of A on bodies

The empirical investigation of the dependency of the constant A in experimental body cooling was much more difficult than that of the constant B, because A describes the 'postmortal temperature plateau' [139], and the temperature at death was really unknown in our cases, given that the bodies investigated came in between 0.8 and 6 hours post mortem. In the first series of experiments, the

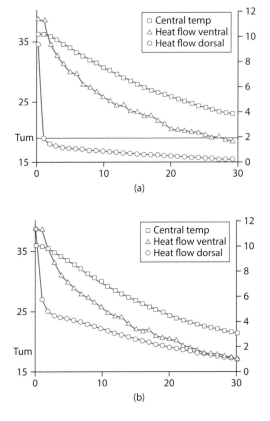

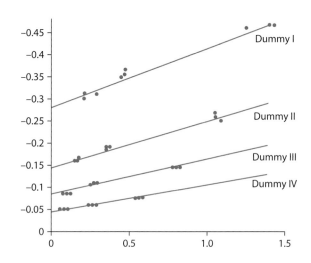

Figure 6.19 Heat flow on the contact and the non-contact surfaces of a 'naked' dummy in still air lying on different supporting bases. Abscissa: cooling time (hours); ordinate: heat flow (Btu ft^{-2} h^{-1}) [90]. (a) Isolating base. Experiment number 201 from Table 6.10. (b) Indifferent base. Experiment number 211 from Table 6.10. (c) Well-conducting base. Experiment number 292 from Table 6.10.

duration of the plateau varied from 5 to 14 hours, which is equivalent to a period without any drop of the rectal temperature between 1 and 6 hours [57]. Nevertheless, there was a significant relationship between the duration of the plateau and the rate of the temperature drop after the plateau. Bodies with a low rate (high body weight) also had a longer plateau phase than bodies with a high rate (low

body weight). There is a relationship between the values of the exponent of the first and second terms of the model (see equation 6.2). Within the investigated range of the ambient temperature, between 5°C and 22°C, the value of the second exponent was found to be five times the value of the first exponent *(B)*, resulting in an approach of $A = 1.25$ as a mean [57]. In the example of the body in Figure 6.11,

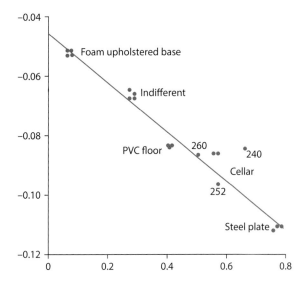

Figure 6.20 Relationship between the slope of central temperature against heat flow on the contact surface (abscissa) and cooling coefficient B (ordinate) of the experiments with different thermal features of the base listed in Table 6.10. (Data from [90].)

Figure 6.21 Relationship between the slope of heat flow against central temperature (abscissa) and cooling coefficient B (ordinate) investigated in four different-sized dummies (I = 6.9 kg; II = 17.3 kg; III = 36.8 kg; IV = 72.5 kg) and three thermally different bases (double-covered table; thick, foam-upholstered base; concrete cellar floor). (Data from [160].)

Table 6.11 Corrective factors determined by experiments using leaves on the floor

Virtual weight under standard conditions of cooling [kg]	Virtual weight lying on leaves [kg]	Humidity of the leaves	Resulting corrective factor
67.6	68.1	Wet through	1.01
67.6	86.5	More or less dry	1.28
67.6	84.7	More or less dry	1.25
60.4	88.0	Totally dry	1.46
60.4	93.7	Totally dry	1.55
60.4	93.4	Totally dry	1.54

the temperature measurement began 3 hours after death. The intercept of the regression line (Figure 6.11 (b)) was 3.3677, corresponding to 29.01°C above ambient temperature (13.3°C) in a linear measure. The best fit of the curve was made using a value of *A* equal to 1.25, assuming a starting temperature at death of 37.2°C (see Figure 6.11 (d)).

If the value of *A* really equals 1.25, then the starting temperature must have been 36.5°C, because (29.01/1.25) + 13.3 gives 36.5°C. In contrast, if the starting temperature was 37.2°C, then the value of *A* must equal 1.21 (29.01/[37.2 − 13.3]). This example demonstrates the difficulties in investigating the 'true' value of *A* in bodies where the starting temperature at death is unknown.

Marshall and Hoare [101–103] did not discover any distinct relation between the first exponent *(B)* and the second one (inherent in *A*). In practice, they set the value of the second exponent at a fixed value of −0.4 for all bodies, independent of its general cooling velocity. This procedure leads to additional errors in calculating the time

Table 6.12 Corrective factors using leaves on the floor and covered by leaves

Virtual weight under standard conditions of cooling [kg]	Virtual weight laying on and covered by leaves [kg]	Resulting corrective factor
67.6	120.0	1.77*
67.6	154.6	2.28
67.6	136.7	2.02
67.6	159.2	2.35
67.6	165.5	2.45
67.6	177.2	2.62
67.6	155.8	2.30
60.4	142.3	2.35
60.4	140.9	2.33
60.4	136.7	2.26
60.4	146.2	2.41
60.4	154.0	2.54
60.4	164.5	2.72
60.4	147.0	2.43

* The factor could have been influenced by low humidity of the leaves.

since death, especially in cases of a greater or a lower cooling rate *B*. This error is avoidable by linking the second exponent to the first one, which is provided by a distinct value of *A*.

Using the value 1.25 for *A*, the rectal cooling curves published in 1955 by De Saram *et al.* [35] (which were obtained in ambient temperatures between 26°C and 31°C) systematically overestimated the time of death. The reason for this was solely an overestimation of the relative length of the plateau related to *A* = 1.25. By means of an approach of *A* = 1.11 (where the value of the second exponent is 10 times that of the first), corresponding to a relatively shorter length of the plateau, the overestimation was removed. Theoretically, the plateau also depends on the magnitude of the difference in temperature between the rectum and surroundings at death [80], so that the empirical result in modelling De Saram's cooling curves would establish a real dependency of the value of *A* (relative length of the postmortal temperature plateau) on the ambient temperature. The ambient temperatures of our own experimental body coolings (*A* = 1.25) did not usually exceed 23°C. In De Saram's material it ranged between 26°C and 31°C (*A* = 1.11). The dependency of *A* on the ambient temperature seems to be non-linear but pronounced in ambient temperatures above 23°C. Certainly, a jump in the value of *A* from 1.25 to 1.11 at 23°C, or at any other level of an ambient temperature, is not to be expected but, lacking more experimental data of rectal cooling curves in higher ambient temperatures, we were unable to pursue the matter any further.

Determination of *A* on dummies

The rule of the close relationship between the first exponent *(B)* and the second exponent of equation 6.1, corresponding to the value of *A* according to:

$$\text{Second exponent} = A \times B/A - 1 \qquad (6.12)$$

can be better studied on dummies than on bodies because of the exact measurement of the starting point of cooling *(To)* immediately after removing the dummy from the incubator because:

$$A = \exp(a_{yx})/To - Ta \qquad (6.13)$$

whereas the *To* of bodies is usually unknown.

By extrapolation of the later part of the cooling curves to *t* = 0 according to the procedure shown in Figure 6.11 (c), the value of 'exp (a_{yx})' is easy to obtain.

Dividing exp (a_{yx}) by *To* − *Ta* gives the value of *A*.

Cooling curves of a dummy corresponding to a body weight of 70 kg in ambient temperatures of 2°C and 28°C (Figure 6.22) show an identical duration of the plateau if the value of *A* remains the same at 1.25. The plateau is equivalent to a period of 3.7 hours without any drop of the central temperature, independent of the ambient temperature. However, the cooling curves of two dummies of

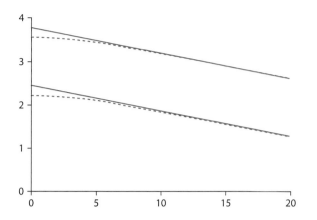

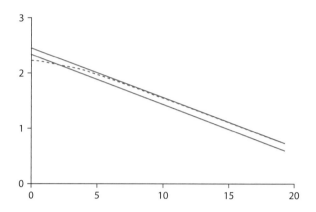

Figure 6.22 Cooling curves equivalent to a 70-kg body (B = −0.0617) starting at 37.2°C in ambient temperatures of 2°C (upper curve) and 28°C (lower curve) with identical values of A (1.25). The regression lines reach 37.2°C at the same time of 3.7 hours. Abscissa: time (hours); ordinate: ln (Tr − Ta).

Figure 6.24 The figure of A and its influence on the duration of postmortal plateau in model curves. Model cooling curves of a 50-kg body (B = −0.0827) starting at 37.2°C in an ambient temperature of 28°C. Modelling with A = 1.25 (upper curve); modelling with A = 1.11 (lower curve). The time till regression lines reach 37.2°C is different: 2.7 hours (A = 1.25) and 1.3 hours (A = 1.11), respectively. After the end of the plateau the curves proceed in parallel with a time difference of 1.4 hours.

different body weights (10 and 110 kg) show a different duration of their plateaux (Figure 6.23), equivalent to periods of 6.3 hours (110 kg) and 0.8 hours (10 kg) without any drop of central temperature, assuming the same value of A (1.25). These data are comparable to those of our first sequence of cooling experiments on 29 bodies with real body weights between 30 and 112 kg, which led to the best fit of the actually observed durations of the plateau using 1.25 as value of A. If the plateau is really shorter (Figure 6.24), as it is in De Saram's cooling curves, a value of A lower than 1.25 must be chosen (e.g. 1.11), for best fitting the plateau.

From 216 cooling experiments conducted on dummies corresponding to body weights of between 7 and 104 kg, and under different ambient temperatures and a wide

range of different cooling conditions (including variable conditions such as clothing, covering, wind, wet surface, grounds of very different thermal conductivity and capacity), a mean value of A of 1.16 with a standard variation of ± 0.14 was found. A systematic analysis [4] could not confirm any dependence of the figure of the constant A on the ambient temperature as supposed in body cooling. Nevertheless, the magnitude of A showed a slight dependence on the virtual weight of dummies in cooling experiments under standard conditions. The magnitude of A also varied with the magnitude of B resulting from the virtual weight and the corrective factor for various cooling conditions differing from standard. The cooling curves could not be modelled more accurately mathematically using these 'new' results than using the 'old' value of 1.25 for the constant A.

The value of A may also depend on the homogeneity of body temperature when death occurs. If the superficial layers of the body are already cool because of the peripheral vasoconstriction (e.g. during haemorrhagic shock without any central hypothermia), a gradient in body temperature, directed from the shell to the core of the body, is present when death occurs; the postmortem temperature plateau, so to speak, has started during life. The real postmortem plateau will be shorter in such cases than in cases with a short duration of agony. This particular event cannot be reproduced by dummies.

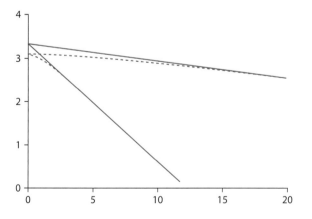

Figure 6.23 Postmortal temperature plateau dependent on the body weight. Cooling curves are equivalent to a 110-kg body (B = −0.0395; upper curve) and a 10 kg body (B = −0.2755; lower curve) both starting at 37.2°C in 15°C ambient temperature. The value of A is 1.25. The regression line of the 110-kg body reaches 37.2°C as late as 5.7 hours after the start of cooling, but that of the 10-kg body reaches 37.2°C 0.9 hours after start of cooling. Abscissa: time (hours); ordinate; ln (Tr − Ta).

The temperature at death

The temperature at death, To, is the third constant of Marshall and Hoare's formula [101–103]. Any temperature-based method for calculating the time since death needs a distinct value of this constant. If the rectal temperature at death is unknown, as is usual in casework at the scene, it is necessary to use a fixed value. Because the central body temperature has a circadian rhythm, a detailed discussion about the 'true' value of To, which should be used as the fixed value in the formula, is meaningless – the more so as physiological mechanisms can change the central temperature (e.g. the menstrual cycle or strong physical activity shortly before death). We used the same fixed value (37.2°C) as used by Marshall and Hoare [101–103].

In giving evidence at court, one can extrapolate the rectal temperature to limiting values of the physiological range of rectal temperature (36.5°C to 37.5°C), instead of using the fixed value. Actually, this would be an unimportant part of the overall range of uncertain factors (mean ambient temperature, corrective factor of the body weight, approximation of the constants B and A) in calculating the time since death in any particular case. In addition, the overall limits of error resulting from many investigated body coolings include the partial errors resulting from the physiological range of rectal temperature. One of the most widely discussed sources of error in calculating the time since death by extrapolating the body temperature is 'fever at death'. Equation 6.1 is open for electing a greater value than 37.2°C if there is actual information concerning a fever of the decedent (this usually comes from the physician, other witnesses and/or as a result of autopsy) (examples in Figure 6.25). Nevertheless, this is an exception to the rule.

Conversely, an unrecognized rise of temperature ante mortem during agony may be present in certain cases (especially in intracranial injuries, certain poisonings, febrile illness without any pathomorphological findings, struggle or physical work shortly before death). What errors can be expected in cases of unrecognizable fever? The error caused by fever is greatest during the first hours post mortem and decreases with time. Because of the higher gradient between the rectal and the ambient temperature, the drop of the rectal temperature is at first steeper than the stated value of 37.2°C at death (Figure 6.26 and Table 6.13). As long as the measured rectal temperature is 37.2°C or higher, the decedent is 'still alive' according to the formula's value of 37.2°C. When the rectal temperature falls to 37.1°C, the real possibility of an error caused by a fever exists. In the example of Table 6.13, the death time is 0.8 hours in a case of 37.2°C at death. In a case with a real starting point of 40.2°C, the death time would be 4.8 hours and, in using equation 6.1 with the stated starting point of 37.2°C, an error of −4 hours would result. This is the maximum error in this case. However, this error should be recognized by rigor mortis, hypostasis and the reduced mechanical and electrical excitability after a real time since death of about 5 hours (see Chapter 10).

Later on, when the rectal temperature decreases further, the error caused by a fever diminishes to a level of about 2.5 to 2 hours (see Table 6.13).

More serious, in relation to large errors of calculated time since death, is a fall of rectal temperature during the period between fatal injury and death (or general hypothermia). This is because an antemortal decrease of rectal temperature can become greater than any increase caused by fever. As long as the antemortal decrease of rectal temperature is of the same order, but with changed sign, the overestimation of the calculated death time is also of the same order (see Table 6.13 and Figure 6.26). Nevertheless, if there is any suspicion of general hypothermia, any temperature method of calculating the time since death must not be used. Hypothermia should be suspected if a long agonal period

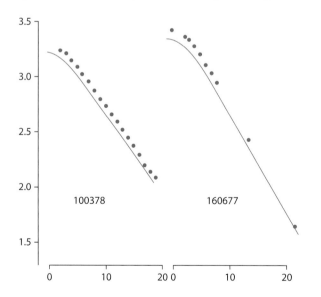

Figure 6.25 Real cooling curves and model curves according to equation 6.2 with stated 37.2°C as 'To' of two bodies with fever at death [65]. Abscissa: time of death in hours; ordinate: ln (rectal – ambient temperature). Case 100378: measured temperature 37.8°C 2 hours post mortem and 37.0°C 3 hours post mortem, respectively. Result of autopsy: acute tuberculosis of the lungs with pneumonia and pleuritis. Case 160677: chronic leukaemia with final blast crisis. Last measured temperature 4 hours before death occurred was 39.6°C.

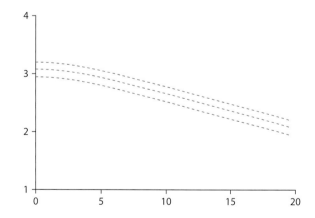

Figure 6.26 Errors caused by fever or slight hypothermia at death. Model cooling curves of a 70 kg body (B = −0.0617) in 15°C ambient temperature starting at 40.2°C (upper curve), 37.2°C (middle curve) and 34.2°C (lower curve), respectively. The errors of computed death times according to equation 6.2 using 37.2°C as the value for To are seen in Table 6.13.

Table 6.13 Errors caused by fever or slight hypothermia at death*

Measured rectal temperature (°C)	Stated 37.2°C at death Time of death	Really 40.2°C at death Calculated	Really 40.2°C at death Error	Really 34.2°C at death Calculated	Really 34.2°C at death Error
37.2	0.0	4.6	−4.6	—	—
37.1	0.8	4.8	−4.0	—	—
34.2	5.0	7.6	−2.6	0.0	5.0
34.0	5.4	7.8	−2.4	1.2	4.2
28.0	12.2	14.4	−2.2	9.8	2.4
22.0	22.4	24.4	−2.0	20.0	2.4

* Errors of computed death times (equation 6.1) using 37.2°C as the value for T_0 if the temperature at death is really 40.2°C and 34.2°C, respectively. Example of a 70-kg body in 15°C ambient temperature (see Figure 6.28) [146].

existed under ambient conditions conducive to hypothermia. In the very early postmortem interval of the first 10 hours, a threatened error can be avoided by applying other tests of death time estimation (especially the examination of mechanical and electrical excitability of skeletal muscle), which gives results inconsistent with the low rectal temperature in cases of hypothermia (see Chapter 10).

Accuracy of calculated time since death

When plotting the errors in calculated death time against the postmortem time scale, there was first a decrease in error, which reached a minimum about 16 to 22 hours post mortem in a series of 28 bodies between 31 and 112 kg body weight [57]. This phenomenon is mainly caused by the use of a fixed (but actually unknown) value of rectal temperature at death To of 37.2°C, which provides larger errors in the early cooling phase than later on, as discussed earlier (see Table 6.13). A second reason was the usually unknown cooling conditions between death and the beginning of examination, before the body had been transported to the mortuary. This was called 'preanalytic error' [68].

After the minimum phase of error, there is a continuous increase in error because the mean value of the constants A (1.25) and B (equations 6.2 and 6.5, respectively) and the low accuracy of temperature measurements become progressively more disturbing as the temperature difference between body and ambient temperature decreases. In addition, even small changes of ambient temperature, as well as of any other cooling condition, cause larger errors, as the difference between body and ambient becomes lower.

Plotting the errors against the progress of death time is not a good way of obtaining information about errors because of the great variation in the time taken to reach the ambient temperature, which depends on the body weight (Table 6.14). The body of a baby reaches the ambient temperature corresponding to increased errors in a much shorter time than does the obese body of an adult, where the larger errors develop much later.

In summarizing cases of different body weights, the errors of computed death time should not be plotted against the progress of death time, but against the progress of cooling

– which is the real cause of the increase in errors. A good measure of the progress of cooling is the standardized temperature Q (see Figure 6.10 and equation 6.1). Its value is 1 at death, and 0 when the rectal temperature has reached the ambient temperature. So, a value of 0.5 means that the original difference between the rectal and the ambient temperature at death has been reduced to 50 per cent. Dependent on the body weight, a defined value of Q corresponds to different times of death (see Table 6.14). Relating the errors of calculated time since death to the standardized temperature, Q, the values from bodies of very different weights become comparable. In our own experiments under controlled conditions in ambient temperatures between 5°C and 22°C, the computed time of death, according to equations 6.1 and 6.2 (see equation 6.14), had errors that could be classified into three groups (Figures 6.27 and 6.28 and Table 6.15). These corresponded to values of Q between 1 and 0.5 – the permissible variation of 95 per cent is ± 2.8 hours. For more progressive cooling, corresponding to values of Q between 0.5 and 0.3, the permissible variation of 95 per cent is ± 3.2 hours. For values of Q between 0.3 and 0.2, the permissible variation of 95 per cent is ± 4.5 hours [146]. Below a Q value of 0.2, we obtained very large errors in some cases. Therefore, and in compliance with Fiddes and Patten [42], the reliability of computing the time since death cannot be assessed.

Computing the time since death of the cooling curves reported by De Saram et al. [35] in ambient temperatures between 26°C and 31°C according to equation 6.15, the standard deviation was ± 1 hour [57], which corresponded to the permissible variation of 95 per cent of about ± 2 hours. Nevertheless, we recommend the use of the given

Table 6.14 Death time at defined levels of the standardized temperature 'Q' dependent on the body weight

Level of Q	Body weight (kg) 30	50	70	90	100
0.5	7	11	15	19	23
0.3	12	17	23	29	36
0.2	15	22	30	38	46

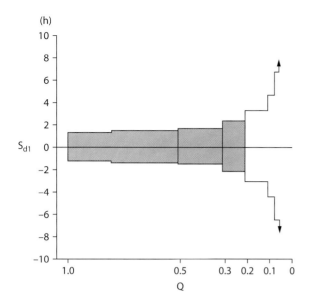

Figure 6.27   Standard deviation s_{dt} of calculated death time dependent on the progress of cooling Q. Chosen standard conditions of cooling. Fifty-three bodies were used; body weights of 9 to 112 kg; age 1 to 87 years; ambient temperature 5.8°C to 22°C; start of temperature measurement 0.8 to 6 hours post mortem to end 10 to 75 hours post mortem. Most bodies were cases of a sudden unexpected death, all of them with time of death known to within some minutes. Calculation of the death time according to equations 6.1 and 6.2 [60,146].

permissible variation of 95 per cent of our own experimental cooling curves in lower ambient temperatures because the computation of death time ended at 8 hours post mortem in the material of De Saram *et al.*

In computing the time since death of the experimental body cooling under various cooling conditions, and the resulting error statistics (Table 6.16), we assumed a variation in the corrective factor of ± 0.1 around the real one. If the investigated corrective factor was, for example, 1.4

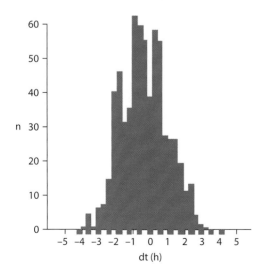

Figure 6.28   Histogram of the errors of calculated death time for 1 > Q > 0.5 in addition to Figure 6.27. Standard conditions of cooling [60,146].

Table 6.15   Standard deviation of 'calculated-real death time' dependent on the progress of cooling Q of 53 bodies under chosen standard conditions of cooling*

Q range	n	Equations 6.1 and 6.2	Rule of thumb
1.0 > Q > 0.90	117	1.3	1.4
0.9 > Q > 0.80	126	1.3	2.0
0.8 > Q > 0.70	142	1.4	2.5
0.7 > Q > 0.60	140	1.4	3.2
0.6 > Q > 0.50	155	1.4	4.0
0.5 > Q > 0.40	181	1.6	5.1
0.4 > Q > 0.30	208	1.6	6.7
0.3 > Q > 0.20	208	2.2	10.8
0.2 > Q > 0.10	224	3.1	16.1
0.1 > Q > 0.07	67	4.5	18.1

* In comparison with the calculation of death time according to the two exponential formulae, the figures are also given for calculation of the death time according to the rule of thumb '1°C decrease of rectal temperature per hour plus 3 hours' [146].

Table 6.16   Standard deviation of 'calculated-real death time' dependent on the progress of cooling Q of 26 bodies under various cooling conditions*

Q range	n	Equations 6.1 and 6.5	Rule of thumb
1.0 > Q > 0.5	464	1.3	3.9
0.5 > Q > 0.3	142	2.2	9.2
0.3 > Q > 0.2	42	3.4	18.3

* For the 'rule of thumb' see Table 6.15.

in a case, we also supplied 1.3 and 1.5. This was done in casework where the selection of a corrective factor is really somewhat uncertain. Depending on the progress of cooling *Q*, we obtained the listed permissible variations (see Table 6.16; Figures 6.29 and 6.30) [57].

How is the death time obtained?

To apply all the basic considerations raised by mathematical modelling of the body cooling, and the experience of experimental body and dummy coolings to casework, a simple means is required for the quick calculation of the interval of death at the scene without any mental arithmetic.

The basis for calculating the time of death is equation 6.1, which has the three constants *To*, *B* and *A*, and the two measures *Tr* (rectal temperature) and *Ta* (ambient temperature). As discussed earlier, we defined:

- *To* as 37.2°C.
- *B* as [−1.2815 × (corrective factor × body weight)$^{-0.625}$ + 0.0284] (equation 6.5).
- *A* for ambient temperatures up to 23°C as 1.25.

Table 6.17 Data of instructive cases of a field study

Case number	Cooling conditions	Correction factor		Real body weight (kg)	Ambient temperature (°C)		Rectal temperature (°C)	Time estimated lower limit (hpm)	Time estimated upper limit (hpm)	Time ascertained lower limit (hpm)	Time ascertained upper limit (hpm)	Comment
		Mean	Range		Measured	Used						
11	Outside, LB on asphalt, trousers, pants, short panty, moving air*.	1.1	1.0–1.2	60	16.0/16.3	14.0*/16.3	22.1	16.7	25.7	?	?	*According to local weather station for the period in question.
13	Room, floor, LB, open trousers, short panty.	1.1	1.0–1.2	98	19.8/19.8	16.0*/18.0	33.2	07.2	12.8	08.3	†08.3	*Reconstruction of the room temperature by night 1 day later with automatically turned off central heating system. The body was found in the morning. †Stop of destroyed wrist watch.
15	Street, LL, wet-through track-suit trousers, short panty, rain, moving air.	0.7	0.6–0.8	76	12.8/12.8	11.8/13.8	35.0	00.3	05.9	04.3	04.5	
22	Outside, soil, LP, wet-through work trousers, short panty, wind, rain.	0.7	0.6–0.8	93	09.9/09.9	08.9/10.9	36.2	00.0	04.9	02.7	02.9	
25	Room, floor, LB, pyjamas, briefs, temporarily moving air.	1.0	0.9–1.1	56	15.7/17.2	15.7/17.2	25.4	10.7	17.1	12.9	13.0	
26	Concrete staircase ground floor, LB, jeans, short panty.	1.0	0.9–1.1	82	07.3*/11.1†	04.2†/11.1	30.2	06.3	11.9	07.4	07.4	*Ground floor near the body. †Staircase second floor. ‡Outside, open front door.
27	Metal road, LL, jeans pulled down to knee-joints, moving air.	0.7	0.5–0.9	68	14.2/14.2	07.0*/14.2	30.6	02.8	08.4	01.5	6.3	*Lowest temperature at night before finding in the morning.
31	Outside, soil, LL, remnants of carbonized* clothing, wet body surface, moving air.	0.7	0.6–0.8	57	06.2†/10.3‡	06.2/10.3	33.3	00.3	05.9	03.8	04.3	*Some minutes after inflammation of the person extinguishing began, first with dry fire-fighting equipment, subsequently with water. †Soil. ‡Air.
	Second measurement 1 hour later:						31.2	01.4	07.0	04.8	05.3	

(Continued)

Table 6.17 (Continued) Data of instructive cases of a field study

Case number	Cooling conditions	Correction factor Mean	Correction factor Range	Real body weight (kg)	Ambient temperature (°C) Measured	Ambient temperature (°C) Used	Rectal temperature (°C)	Time estimated lower/upper limit (hpm)	Time ascertained lower/upper limit (hpm)	Comment
								Method not used.		Estimation of the period since death by non-temperature-based methods only; see Table 6.7
33	LB on bed covered with thick blanket, trousers, boxing shorts, short panty.	2.2	2.0–2.4	62	18.5/18.5		41.6	(04.7 / 10.3) Not used (lack of expertise) 12.1*	00.5 35.3* / 25.5	*On the supposition of malignant hyperthermia with temperature at death of 43.5°C. Subtraction of 6.3°C from the measured rectal and ambient temperatures as the difference between the supposed rectal temperature at death (43.5°C) and the 37.2°C-norm of the formula (nomogram).
42	Room of attic flat, floor, open skylight*, jeans, short panty.	1.1	1.0–1.2	57	22.5/22.5	12.8*/22.5	24.8	12.6 / 33.0	15.4 / 16.2	*Mean temperature at night outside: 12.8°C (weather station). Examination at noon (summertime).
43	Room, floor, LL, naked, temporarily moving air*.	0.9	0.75–1.0	67	19.0/21.0	18.0/22.0	34.5	02.1 / 07.7	02.7 / ?	*Open windows.
44	Room, floor, carpet, LB, trousers, short panty, moving air*.	1.0	0.9–1.1	71.5	15.4*/21.3‡	15.4/21.3	35.5	01.1 / 06.7	03.6 / 04.3	*Open windows and doors †At time of examination beside body. ‡Within cupboards, beneath carpets near the body.
45	Situation at finding: outside, head-stand-like position within a big bale of straw, jeans, short panty.	1.8?	1.5–2.0?	83	18.6* 11.5† 12.2‡			32.8 / Method not used: no experience as to particular cooling condition.	04.5 / 07.5	*Within straw. †Air at examination. ‡Soil at examination. §Air for the period in question (weather station) Estimation of the time since death by non-temperature-based methods only; see Table 6.7.
	4 hours before examination: Outside soil, LB, jeans, short panty, temporarily moving air.	1.0	0.9–1.1		16.0–18.0§					

(Continued)

Table 6.17 (Continued) Data of instructive cases of a field study

Case number	Cooling conditions	Correction factor Mean	Range	Real body weight (kg)	Ambient temperature (°C) Measured	Used	Rectal temperature (°C)	Time estimated lower upper limit (hpm)		Time ascertained lower upper limit (hpm)		Comment
48	Room, LL on sofa with his back in contact with the back-rest of sofa, blanket between tights, short underpants.	1.2	1.1–1.3	78	27.3/27.3	25.0*/27.3	33.3	08.8	14.4	11.0	14.0	*According to crime police on coming to the scene 2 hours before examination.
49	Outside, soil, LB, jeans, trousers, leggings, panty, moving air	1.35	1.3–1.4	45.5	16.6*/20.3†	13.0†/20.3	25.4	11.2	21.6	16.3	16.8	*Soil. †Air. ‡Mean temperature at night before finding the body at the early afternoon.
54	Room, LL on couch, tracksuit, short panty, moving air*	1.05	0.9–1.2	77	21.5/21.5	17.0*/20.0†	29.8	10.5	16.4	04.8	13.8	*Open window. †The open window of the very small room was closed by investigators 1 hour before examination. At this time the room temperature was 18.5°C measured by crime police.
55	Street, LL on asphalt, jeans, short panty, moving air.	0.9	0.8–1.0	80	05.5*/07.2†	05.5/07.2	33.2	02.2	07.8	03.8	05.2	*Asphalt. †Air.
56	Room, LL on bed, trousers, short panty, moving air*.	1.05	0.9–1.2	78	15.7/16.2	10.0†/16.2	26.9	11.2	19.1	04.7	20.7	*The window was open at finding the body 4.5 hours before examination. Then it was closed. It was opened again for 30 minutes a short time before examination and was closed again. †The temperature outside at night before examination at noon was around 0°C
64	Outside LP* on lawn, jeans, short panty, temporarily moving air.	1.0	0.9–1.1	98	10.3/11.0	10.3/11.0	33.8	03.9	09.5	06.3	06.6	*Found LP, changed to LB by first aid doctor.
62	LB on bed, naked.	1.15	1.0–1.2	60	18.0/20.5	18.0/20.5	27.5	10.9	17.3	13.2	19.7	

(Continued)

Table 6.17 (*Continued*)   Data of instructive cases of a field study

Case number	Cooling conditions	Correction factor		Real body weight (kg)	Ambient temperature (°C)		Rectal temperature (°C)	Time estimated upper limit (hpm)	Time estimated lower limit (hpm)	Time ascertained lower limit (hpm)	Time ascertained upper limit (hpm)	Comment
		Mean	Range		Measured	Used						
66	Room, LB on bed, covered with eiderdown until 2.5 hours before examination, boxer shorts.	1.8	1.6–2.0*	116	26.9†/26.9†	26.4/27.4	33.0	24.1	34.2	24.8	?	*Because of strong insulation condition and high body weight adaptation to 1.4 to 1.7 according to [61]. †Temperature at any place in the near and wider surrounding of bodies.
72	Behind open entrance-door of shop, floor, LL, trousers, short panty, temporarily moving air.	1.0	0.9–1.1	82	17.1/17.5	17.1/17.5	33.9	03.9	09.5	05.1	05.4	

hpm, hours post mortem; LB, lying back; LL, lying laterally; LP, lying prone.

From Henssge C, Althaus L, Bolt J, Freislederer A, Henssge CA, Hoppe B, Schneider V. Experiences with a compound method for estimating the time since death. I. Rectal temperature nomogram for time since death. *Int J Legal Med* 1999;**113**:303–319.

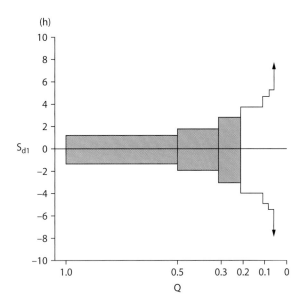

Figure 6.29 Standard deviation S_{dt} of calculated death time dependent on the progress of cooling Q. Various cooling conditions differing from the chosen standard. Twenty-six bodies were used. Calculation of the death time was according to equations 6.2 and 6.6. For further details see Figure 6.30 [60,146].

Equation 6.1 can now be written as:

$$Q = \frac{Tr - Ta}{37.2 - Ta} = 1.25 \times \exp(B \times t) - 0.25 \exp(5 \times B \times t) \tag{6.14}$$

The cooling curves published by De Saram *et al.* [35] were obtained in ambient temperatures between 26°C and 31°C and could be better fitted by $A = 1.11$, giving:

$$Q = \frac{Tr - Ta}{37.2 - Ta} = 1.11 \times \exp(B \times t) \\ - 0.11 \exp(10 \times B \times t) \tag{6.15}$$

Equations 6.14 and 6.15 cannot be solved to time t, and therefore an approximation is necessary. There are two

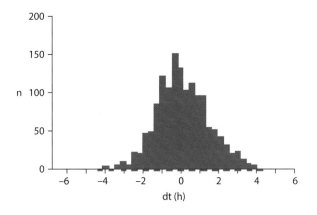

Figure 6.30 Histogram of the errors of calculated death time for 1 > Q > 0.5 in addition to Figure 6.29. Various cooling conditions differing from the chosen standard [60,146].

ways to calculate the time since death at a scene of death, neither of which requires the use of any mental arithmetic:

1. By means of a computer program. 'Professor, I get thanks from the whole world for putting the formulae that you worked out into a computer form that police officers now carry on their cell phones', wrote Ed Friedlander MD (Kansas City) to the author. His free online program (Java) calculates the time since death following this method (http://www.pathguy.com/TimeDead.htm). The self-explanatory program (Figure 6.31) operates on the basis of Table 6.18. It

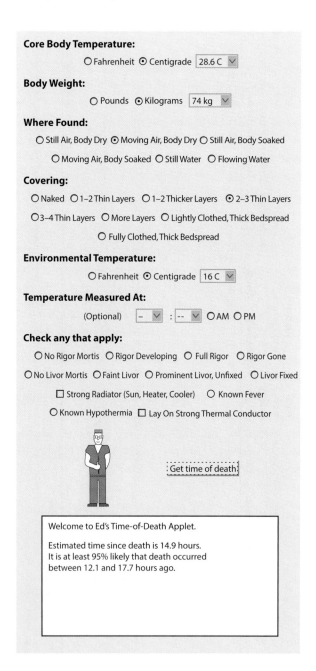

Figure 6.31 Computation of a case example by Ed Friedlander's computer program. (Courtesy of E. Friedlander, http://www.pathg uy.com/TimeDead.htm)

Table 6.18 Empirical corrective factors of the body weight for cooling conditions differing from the chosen standard*

Dry clothing/covering	Air	Corrective factor	Wet-through clothing/ covering wet body surface	In air	In water
		0.35	Naked.		Flowing
		0.5	Naked.		Still
		0.7	Naked.	Moving	
		0.7	One to two thin layers.	Moving	
Naked.	Moving	0.75			
One to two thin layers.	Moving	0.9	Two or more thicker layers.	Moving	
Naked.	Still	1.0			
One to two thin layers.	Still	1.1	Two thicker layers.	Still	
Two to three thin layers.		1.2	More than two thicker layers.	Still	
One to two thicker layers.	Moving	1.2			
Three to four thin layers.	or	1.3			
More thin/thicker layers.	Still	1.4			
	Without influence	…			
Thick blanket.		1.8			
+		…			
Clothing combined.		…			
		2.4			
Lying on		1.8			
+		…			
covered by		…			
dry leaves.		2.7			

* The listed values apply to bodies of average weight (reference: 70 kg), in an extended position on a 'thermally indifferent' base.
From Henssge C. Death time estimation in case work. I. The rectal temperature time of death nomogram. *Forensic Sci Int* 1988;**38**:209–236.

also gives the 95 per cent confidence limits according to Tables 6.15 and 6.16 and points to high uncertainty of the result when the temperature difference between rectum and surrounding is too low. Some adjustment is reminded in cases of known fever or hypothermia. The influence of the kind of supporting base on the corrective factor according to Table 6.19 is not taken into account just as the dependence of corrective factors on the body weight according to Table 6.20 or equation 6.10. In such cases adjustment is necessary.

W. Schweitzer MD (Zürich) implemented a pHp written program (http://www.swisswuff.ch/calculators/todeszeit.php). The appended three tables analogous to Tables 6.18, 6.19 and 6.20 assist in choosing an appropriate empirical corrective factor that also takes into account the supporting base and the dependence of corrective factors on the body weight (Figure 6.32). The generally used initial temperature at death of the order of 37.2°C can be changed if indicated. The result can be rounded to arbitrary 'smallest output

Table 6.19 Influence of the kind of supporting base on the corrective factor

Supporting base		Clothing?	Corrective factor
Indifferent	Usual floor of rooms, dry soil, lawn, asphalt.	Yes/no	
Insulating	Excessively thickly upholstered.	Thick	+0.1
		Thin	+0.3
		No	+1.3
	Mattress (bed), thick carpet.	Yes	+0.1
		No	+1.1/+1.2
	About 2 cm wettish leaves.	No	+1.3
	About 2 cm totally dry leaves.	No	+1.5
Accelerating	Concrete, stony, tiled.	Thick	−0.1
		Very thin	−0.2
		No	−0.75

Table 6.20 Chart of the dependence of corrective factors on the body weight*

Cooling conditions	4	6	8	10	20	30	40	50	60	70	80	90	100	110	120	130	140	150
										1.3								
Clothing,	1.6	1.6	1.6	1.6	1.5					**1.4**					1.3	1.2	1.2	1.2
more layers	2.1	2.1	2.0	2.0	1.9	1.8				**1.6**				1.4	1.4	1.4	1.3	1.3
Bedspread	2.7	2.7	2.6	2.5	2.3	2.2	2.1	2.0		**1.8**			1.6	1.6	1.6	1.5	1.4	1.4
	3.5	3.4	3.3	3.2	2.8	2.6	2.4	2.3		**2.0**		1.8	1.8	1.7	1.6	1.6	1.5	1.5
	4.5	4.3	4.1	3.9	3.4	3.0	2.8	2.6	2.4	**2.2**	2.1	2.0	1.9	1.8	1.7	1.7	1.6	1.6
Clothing +	5.7	5.3	5.0	4.8	4.0	3.5	3.2	2.9	2.7	**2.4**	2.3	2.2	2.1	1.9	1.9	1.8	1.7	1.6
bedspread	7.1	6.6	6.2	5.8	4.7	4.0	3.6	3.2	2.9	**2.6**	2.5	2.3	2.2	2.1	2.0	1.9	1.8	1.7
Feather bed	8.8	8.1	7.5	7.0	5.5	4.6	3.9	3.5	3.2	**2.8**	2.7	2.5	2.3	2.2	2.0	1.9	1.8	1.7
	10.9	9.8	8.9	8.3	6.2	5.1	4.3	3.8	3.4	**3.0**	2.8	2.6	2.4	2.3	2.1	2.0	1.9	1.8

Real body weight (kg) — Average range

(see Table 6.1)

* The average range of body weight, which is the base of the corrective factors 'known by experience' (Table 6.18), has been chosen at 70 kg (bold numbers). Below a corrective factor of 1.4 (up to 0.75), the dependence on the body weight can be neglected.

From Henssge C. Rectal temperature time of death nomogram: dependence of corrective factors on the body weight under stronger thermic insulation conditions. *Forensic Sci Int* 1992;**54**:51–56.

unit [minutes]' (e.g. 30 minutes). The given 95 per cent tolerances are in accord with Tables 6.15 and 6.16.

The commercial Windows-operated program of C.A. Henssge MD (Magdeburg) [63] (http://www.AMAsoft.de) is flexible and interactive. Instead of an exact single value, a range for ambient temperature and corrective factor can be entered alternatively because in many cases it is impossible to appoint exact values to the found circumstances at the scene. A range of body weight first estimated

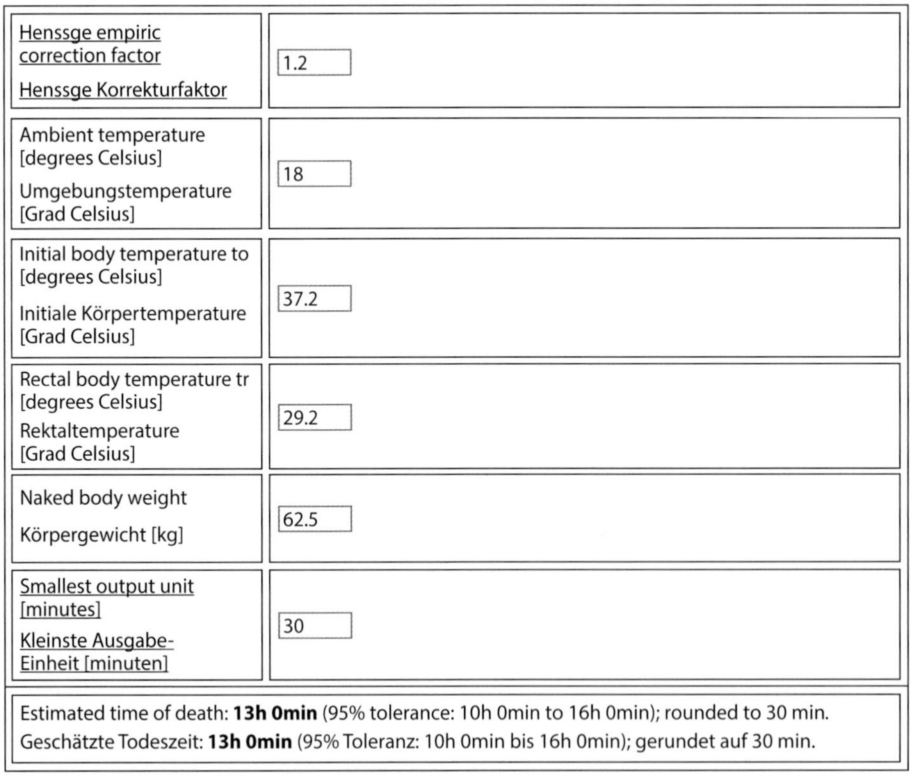

Henssge empiric correction factor / Henssge Korrekturfaktor	1.2
Ambient temperature [degrees Celsius] / Umgebungstemperatur [Grad Celsius]	18
Initial body temperature to [degrees Celsius] / Initiale Körpertemperatur [Grad Celsius]	37.2
Rectal body temperature tr [degrees Celsius] / Rektaltemperatur [Grad Celsius]	29.2
Naked body weight / Körpergewicht [kg]	62.5
Smallest output unit [minutes] / Kleinste Ausgabe-Einheit [minuten]	30

Estimated time of death: **13h 0min** (95% tolerance: 10h 0min to 16h 0min); rounded to 30 min.
Geschätzte Todeszeit: **13h 0min** (95% Toleranz: 10h 0min bis 16h 0min); gerundet auf 30 min.

Figure 6.32 Example of Schweitzer's free online program. (Courtesy of W. Schweitzer, http://www.swisswuff.ch/calculators/todeszeit.php)

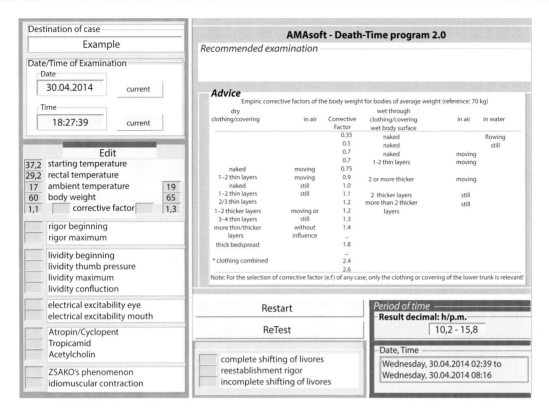

Figure 6.33 Computation of a case example by the PC program of C.A. Henssge (http://www.AMAsoft.de) with ranges of body weight, ambient temperature and corrective factor [63].

at the scene can also be entered (Figure 6.33; compare with Figures 6.38 and 6.40). Two superimposed tables analogous to Tables 6.18 and 6.19 assist in choosing an appropriate empirical corrective factor that also takes into account the supporting base where required. The adjustment of corrective factors in dependence on the body weight (see Table 6.20) operates automatically according to equation 6.10 whenever it is required. The generally used starting temperature at death of the order of 37.2°C can be changed if there is a history of fever during life. In addition, the program involves some non–temperature-based methods/criteria within a compound method (see Chapter 10). When the temperature-based nomogram method must not be used because of contrary circumstances, the examination of the body should instead begin with any of the non–temperature-based methods/criteria. The result is displayed in hours post mortem decimal as well as in date and time.

2. By means of nomogram (Figures 6.34 and 6.35) [58,59]. The calculation of the period since death by a computer program should be the preferred method of implementation of nomogram forms nowadays because it has more convenient handling, provides more accurate results and avoids significant errors caused by using potentially distorted scales of

reproduced nomograms [24]. For the first step (see Figure 6.36), the points of the scales of the measured rectal temperature (e.g. 27°C in the left margin) and ambient temperature (e.g. 15°C in the right margin) have been joined by a straight line, which crosses the diagonal of the nomogram at a specific point. For the second step, a second straight line must be drawn passing through the centre of the circle (below left of the nomogram) and the intersection of the first line and the diagonal (Figure 6.37). The second line crosses the semicircles, which represent the different body weights, each with a calibration of the death time. The time since death (e.g. 13.5 hours post mortem) can be read off at the intersection of the semicircle of the given body weight (e.g. 70 kg). The body weight used can be the real (chosen standard conditions of cooling) or the corrected body weight (using corrective factors). The second straight line touches the outermost semicircle, where the permissible variation of 95 per cent can be seen respectively levelling off the range of reliability. In bodies found under standard conditions of cooling, the figures 'standard (naked-still air)' are true (see Table 6.15). The figures 'using corrective factors' should be used when the body is found under cooling conditions differing from the chosen standard (see Table 6.16).

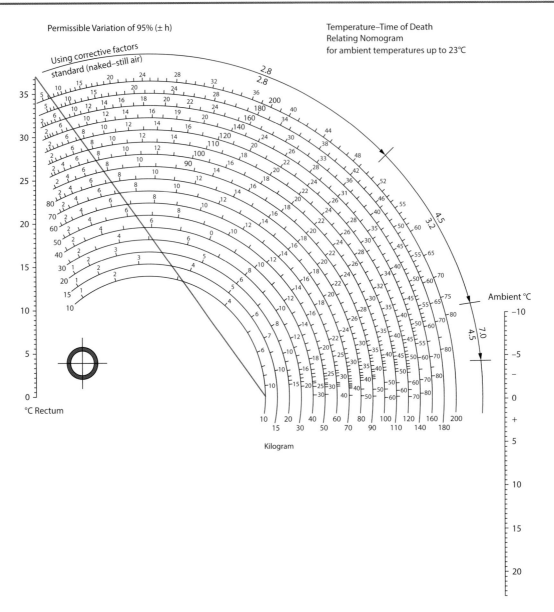

Figure 6.34 Nomogram for reading off the time of death from a single measurement of rectal and ambient temperature and from the body weight for ambient temperatures up to 23°C according to equation 6.14. Without any corrective factor the nomogram is related to the chosen standard conditions of cooling. Reproduction of this form can provoke erroneous results by even slight distortion of the scales [24]. Download and print the original form at http://www.rechtsmedizin.uni-bonn.de/dienstleistungen/for_Med/todeszeit

■ Application of the 'nomogram method' in casework

The estimation of the time since death at the scene of death using the nomogram-form (see Figures 6.34 to 6.37) or computation by means of a computer program requires:

1. Single measurement of the 'deep' rectal temperature.
2. Estimation of the body weight.
3. Evaluation of the mean ambient temperature.
4. Evaluation of the corrective factor, if necessary.
5. Consideration of the features where the method must not be used.
6. Calculation of the interval of death.

The nomogram form itself (or equations 6.14 and 6.15) is the result of experimental body coolings under chosen standard conditions of cooling reported earlier.

The chosen standard conditions of cooling are defined as follows:

- Naked body with dry surfaces.
- Lying extended on the back.

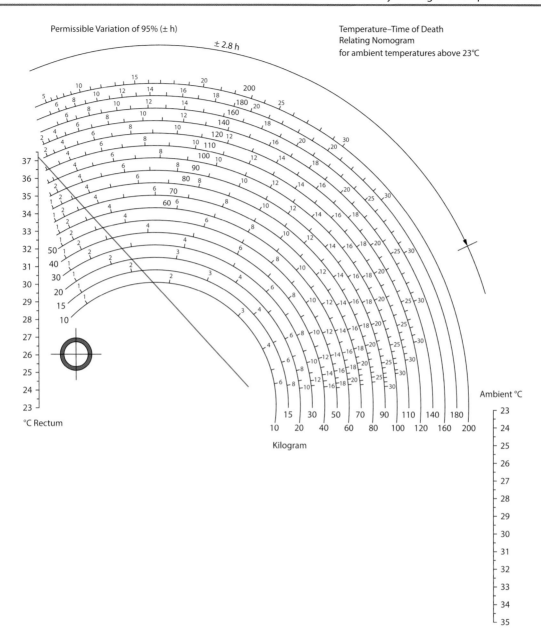

Permissible Variation of 95% (± h)

± 2.8 h

Temperature–Time of Death
Relating Nomogram
for ambient temperatures above 23°C

°C Rectum

Kilogram

Ambient °C

Figure 6.35 Nomogram for reading off the time of death from a single measurement of rectal and ambient temperature and from the body weight for ambient temperatures above 23°C according to equation 6.15. Without any corrective factor the nomogram is related to the chosen standard conditions of cooling. Reproduction of this form can provoke erroneous results by even slight distortion of the scales [24]. Download and print the original form at http://www.rechtsmedizin.uni-bonn.de/dienstleistungen/for_Med/todeszeit

- On a thermally indifferent base.
- In still air.
- In surroundings without any source of strong heat radiation.

If a body is found under conditions similar or comparable to the chosen standard conditions of cooling, the time of death can be computed or read off according to the measured deep rectal temperature, the mean ambient temperature and the body weight. Provided it is made as exactly as possible, the time of death read from the nomogram closely approaches the computed time. The given permissible variation of 95 per cent at the outermost semicircle 'standard (naked–still air)' corresponds to the data of Table 6.15 and Figures 6.27 and 6.28.

If the cooling conditions differ from the chosen standard, they have to be taken into account by evaluating a corrective factor. The real body weight must be multiplied by the evaluated corrective factor. The time of death has to be read from the nomogram at the semicircle of the corrected body weight. The permissible variation of 95 per cent at the outermost semicircle 'using corrective factors'

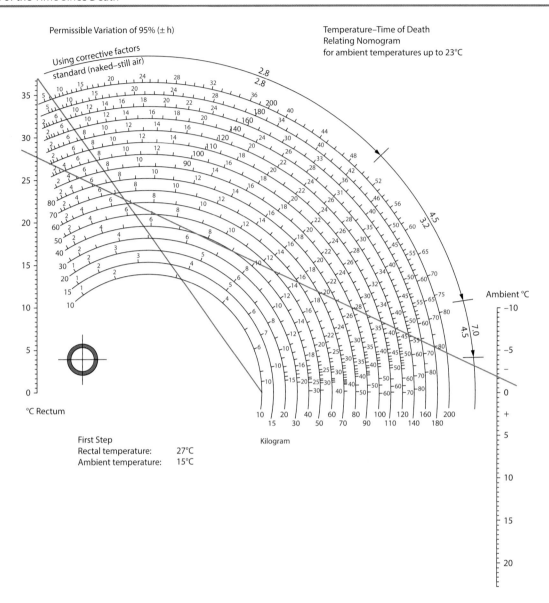

Figure 6.36 The use of the nomograms. First step [60]. Reproduction of this form can provoke erroneous results by even slight distortion of the scales [24]. Download and print the original form at http://www.rechtsmedizin.uni-bonn.de/dienstleistungen/for_Med/todeszeit

is then valid corresponding to Table 6.15 and Figures 6.29 and 6.30. By analogy, *B* must be calculated by equation 6.5 when computing the time of death.

The successful use of the nomogram method requires experience, as with any medico-legal procedure. It is very easy to read off the time since death from the nomogram or to compute it. However, especially after computing the time of death without adding the permissible variation of 95 per cent, this gives the impression of high accuracy, which leads to the danger of misuse and misinterpretation.

First, the estimation of the time since death by any method of examination of the body is really the task of a forensic pathologist.

Second, the indicated value read from the nomogram or the computed time of death, is a mean value – a misleading part of the full result. *The interval limited by the*

permissible variation of 95 per cent is the one and only result: the death occurred, with the probability of 95 per cent, within this interval. A more precise indication of the interval since death cannot be obtained according to all the results of scientific investigations. A central mean value must not be offered (see Figure 6.33).

Third, when using the nomogram method, the interval of death that is obtained is calculated using factors that are themselves either measures or evaluations. *It is possible to use the right rules but obtain the wrong results if the factors are wrong. The most important thing is to analyze these factors carefully at the scene of the crime. Fragmentary analysis of the facts at the scene often result in significant false estimation of the period since death.*

The estimation of the body weight at the scene of death is a question of personal experience. A serious mistake

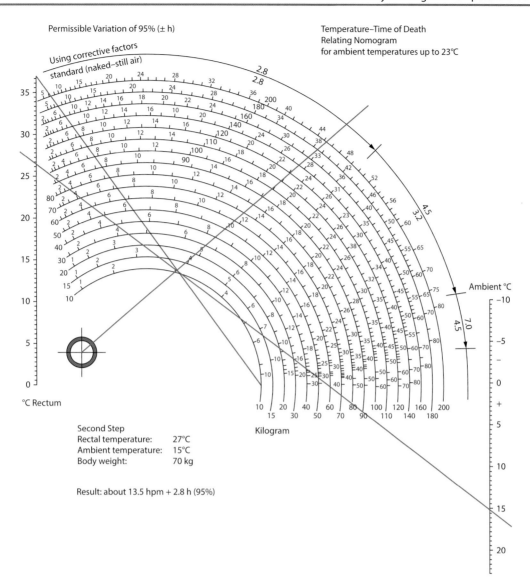

Figure 6.37 The use of the nomograms. Second step [60]. Reproduction of this form can provoke erroneous results by even slight distortion of the scales [24]. Download and print the original form at http://www.rechtsmedizin.uni-bonn.de/dienstleistungen/for_Med/todeszeit

could be remedied quickly by weighing the body after its removal from the scene.

In the following subsection, evaluation of the 'mean ambient temperature' and of the 'corrective factor', as well as consideration of the features where the method must not be used, are discussed in more detail.

To enable handling of the method, it is referenced to special cases of a field study that are listed in Tables 6.17 and 6.21. The field study [66] includes 72 consecutive cases of an inspection of the scene of crime by a forensic pathologist before autopsies were carried out. The period of death was estimated by using the temperature-based nomogram method as a primary method (see Table 6.17), followed by the use of other non–temperature-based methods to confirm or improve the primary result (see Chapter 10).

Evaluation of the mean ambient temperature

Theoretically, equations 6.1, 6.14 and 6.15 require a constant ambient temperature. In fact, the mean ambient temperature of the whole period between the time of death and the time of investigation is employed [60,65]. The actual measured ambient temperature at a scene of crime need not necessarily be the mean. At first, the actual ambient temperature should be measured close to the body, and particularly at the same level above the base. It is recommended that not only the air temperature be measured but also the temperature of the underlying surface itself – if possible probing into the earth, into gaps between stones or beneath a carpet. If there are differences among ambient temperatures around the body, take the mean or use the range (Figures 6.38 and 6.39).

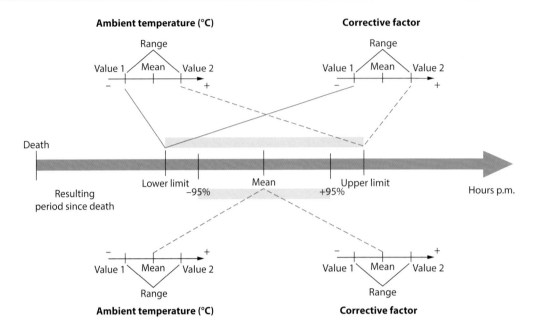

Figure 6.38 Scheme of the resulting periods since death using: (mode 1) mean values of the elevated ranges of ambient temperature and corrective factor and adding the empirical permissible variation of 95 per cent (see Tables 6.15 and 6.16); and (mode 2) the upper and lower brackets of the evaluated ranges of ambient temperature and corrective factor. If the evaluated ranges of both ambient temperature and corrective factor are very wide, the resulting period since death using mode 2 calculation may be greater than that using mode 1 calculation. It is recommended that both modes of calculation be applied and to use the wider period since death for expert opinion.

Furthermore, it is advisable to measure the temperature of the wider surroundings of the body, for example in the next room, the corridor and the landing, respectively, to obtain a view of temperature distribution (e.g. case 26 in Table 6.17). Some additional observation is necessary: in a closed room, look for the heating system and note its operating state (e.g. case 13 in Table 6.17). Were the windows and doors open or closed when the body was found? What about the outside temperature or sunshine through windows, and its possible influence on the room temperature (e.g. cases 44, 54 and 56 in Table 6.17)? The course of the ambient temperature from night (time of death) into day (finding the body) should be taken into account for evaluation of the mean ambient temperature of the period in question (e.g. cases 27, 42, 49 and 56 in Table 6.17). If the body is found outside, contact the weather station and ask for hourly temperatures and periods of rain, wind and sunshine (e.g. cases 11 and 42 in Table 6.17). Later, for example in court, this can be an advantage if the ambient temperature comes into question. Then consider the mean ambient temperature during the interval between death and the examination of body. The actual measured ambient temperature(s) and the concomitant temperature-related circumstances allow an evaluation of the required mean ambient temperature of the period in question, at least as a range in most cases (see Figure 6.38).

If ambient temperature *decreases* more or less continuously, its mean value for the period in question can be used successfully. A continuous *increase* of the ambient temperature is more problematic if a long death time comes into question (see later). The difference between rectal and ambient temperature should then be considered. If there is only a small difference, the method should not be used. The progression of cooling can be estimated quickly by calculation of the value of Q (equations 6.1, 6.14 or 6.15). Conversely, the calculated mean of the ambient temperature can be used if the progression of cooling is still low ($Q > 0.5$).

When a range of ambient temperature is applied, two death times are computed or read from the nomogram – a shorter time corresponding to the lower ambient temperature, and a longer time corresponding to the higher ambient temperature (see Figures 6.38 and 6.39).

A peculiarity is a sudden great change in ambient temperature. Two murder cases in which the bodies had been transported from high ambient temperatures (scene of the crime) to low ambient temperature (place of finding the body) were the reason for cooling experiments with a sudden decrease and increase of ambient temperature of the order of 15°C in the course of the cooling process [5]. The experiments were performed with the aforementioned cooling dummies. In the case of a sudden *decrease* in ambient temperature, after cooling in a higher ambient temperature (about 21°C) for several hours to about 4°C, a second 'temperature plateau' occurred that was shorter than the known plateau at the beginning of body cooling. The second plateau at the beginning of the second cooling phase in a sudden decreased ambient temperature required a lower value of the constant A (1.15) compared with the

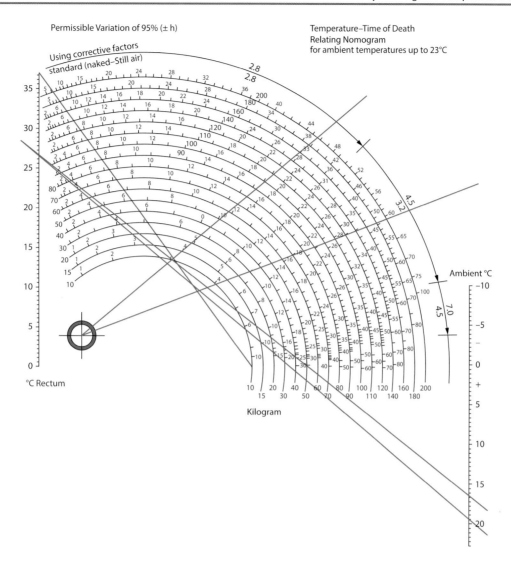

Figure 6.39 The use of the nomogram in a case with ranges of the ambient temperature (17°C to 20°C) and the corrective factor (1.2 to 1.5) of a real body weight of 75 kg corresponding to corrected body weights between 90 and 110 kg [60].

known value (1.25) at the beginning of cooling. The period since death could be computed if the body was transported at a known time from a known high level of ambient temperature to a low ambient temperature by means of the following three-step procedure (Figure 6.40).

Step 1

Going from the dummy temperature (T_{r1}) at any time of the second cooling phase (t_1) in low ambient temperature (T_{a2}), the body temperature (T_{r2}) at the known time (t_2) of rapid decrease of the ambient temperature can be calculated by transforming equation 6.14 using a value of 1.15 for the constant A:

$$T_{r2} = \frac{T_{r1} - T_{r2}}{Q} + T_{r2} \tag{6.16}$$

with

$$Q = 1.15 \times \exp[B \times (t_1 - t_2) - 0.15$$
$$\times \exp\left[\frac{1.15 \times B}{0.15} \times (t_1 - t_2)\right] \tag{6.17}$$

Step 2

Using the calculated body temperature (T_{r2}) at the known moment of moving the body according to equations 6.17 and 6.18, the unknown period ($t_2 - t_3$) of the first cooling phase in the known higher ambient temperature (T_{a1}) can be calculated by the standard method, either nomographically or by computing as usual according to equation 6.15.

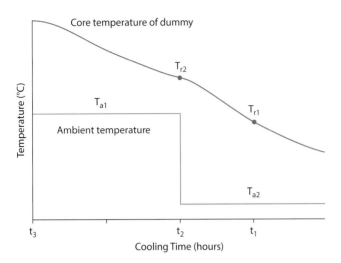

Figure 6.40   The scheme for the three-step procedure.

Step 3

The whole cooling period (tw) analogous to the period since death results from the addition of times of both cooling phases:

$$t_1 - t_3 = (t_1 - t_2) + (t_2 - t_3) \tag{6.18}$$

The errors of the calculated cooling times were within the known confidence limits of the method. The estimated period of death calculated by the three-step procedure was in agreement with the investigated period in the murder cases. One experimental online cooling curve of a body cooling for the first 10 hours at an ambient temperature of 22.5°C, and for the next 9 hours at 7.8°C, could also be sufficiently modelled by the three-step procedure.

In contrast, Althaus and I [5] were not able to model mathematically the cooling curves of the experiments with a sudden increase of ambient temperature from 4°C to 21°C. Nevertheless, an engineering induced team [19] provided a four-step procedure to estimate the cooling period analogous to the period of death in the dummy experiments with sudden increase of ambient temperature [5]. The main principle is to compute a theoretical body temperature T'_r at the time of temperature measurement t_1 that would have been measured if no sudden increase of ambient temperature had taken place. That results in a difference ΔT between the measured temperature T_r and the lower theoretical temperature T'_r.

$$\Delta T = T_r - T'_r \tag{6.19}$$

This difference is caused by the sudden increase of ambient temperature from T_{a1} to T_{a2} at t_2. A standardization of ΔT with respect to its cause, the increase ΔT_a, is denoted by R. In its mathematical expression the whole cooling time t is replaced by the known cooling period after the sudden increase of ambient temperature $t_1 - t_2 = \Delta t$. The denotation of t follows Figure 6.40.

Step 1

$$R = A \exp[B(\Delta t - d)] - (A - 1)\exp\left[\frac{AB}{A - 1}(\Delta t - d)\right] \tag{6.20}$$

with $d = \dfrac{0.07}{B}$

B according to equation 6.5 ; 6.14 A = 1.25

Step 2

$$\Delta T = \Delta T_a (1 - R) \tag{6.21}$$

Step 3

$$T'_r = T_r - \Delta T \tag{6.22}$$

Step 4

This step involves estimation of the whole cooling time t analogous to the time since death by the standard method of equation 6.14 with T'_r and T_{a1} by means of computation or nomographically.

The cooling times of the dummy experiments [5] could be calculated without systematic error within small confidence limits as demonstrated by the histograms of errors [19].

The study may provide evidence that the period since death can be calculated by the four-step procedure if the ambient temperature undergoes a rapid increase at a known time from a known level to a higher level.

Evaluating the corrective factor

The experience of all the experimental body and dummy cooling reported earlier is shown in Tables 6.18 to 6.21. The listed corrective factors are valid for typical situations whenever a body is found in a roughly extended position, or sitting.

The corrective factor for cooling conditions in air that differ from the standard conditions should be evaluated under three aspects:

1. Clothing/covering of the lower trunk, dry (left-hand side) or 'wet-through' (right-hand side).
2. Resting or moving air.
3. Type of supporting base (accelerating or decelerating) compared with 'indifferent'.

Should the occasion arise, it is useful to re-examine the experimental background that provided the corrective factors listed in Table 6.18:

1. With the exclusively radial transfer of heat from the body to surroundings (as well as the probe site within the rectum) in mind, only the clothing or covering and other special cooling conditions (the ground, wetness, wind) of the lower trunk are relevant for evaluating the corrective factor.

Table 6.21 Data of paired cases

Case	Cooling conditions	Correction factor		Real body weight (kg)	Ambient temperature (°C)		Rectal temperature (°C)	Time estimated		Time ascertained		Comment
		Mean	Range		Measured	Used		lower limit (hpm)	upper limit (hpm)	lower limit (hpm)	upper limit (hpm)	
6	LB on bed, covered with two thick blankets together about 30 cm thick, night dress, short panty.	2.4	2.0–2.8*	89	20.6/20.6	19.6/21.6	36.9	02.0	07.6	01.8	15.0	*Because of strong insulation condition and high body weight: adaption according to Table 6.3: 1.8–2.5.
7	Room, hanging at door, short panty.	1.05	1.0–1.1	78	20.6/20.6	19.6/21.6	35.0	03.0	08.6	01.8	15.0	The wife was strangled by the husband, who committed suicide by hanging thereafter.
36	Apartment house, stony staircase, LP, thicker pyjamas.	1.0	0.9–1.1	62	15.6/16.1	15.5/16.5	33.1	03.0	08.6	07.1	08.1	The mother and her 3-year-old son were killed by the culprit.
37	Room, floor, carpet, thicker pyjamas, disposable nappies.	1.5	1.3–1.7*	14	15.8/16.3	15.5/16.5	28.3	02.5	08.1	06.8	07.8	*There is no experience with one-way nappies concerning the correction factor. The used range was speculated. Because of strong insulation condition and low body weight the correction factor of 1.7 was adapted to 2.2 according to [61].
46	Windowless basement room, LP on tiled floor, jeans, bodice.	1.0	0.9–1.1	57	22.5/23.0	22.5–23.0	32.8	04.9	10.5	05.8	06.1	The woman was killed by the man who committed suicide immediately thereafter.
47	Windowless basement room, leaned back sitting on a pail with a dust-filled bag on it, jeans, short panty.	1.3*	1.2–1.4*	77	as 46	as 46	35.5	03.5	09.1	07.3	07.6	*The pail with a dust-filled bag on it looks like a stronger thermic insulation.
70	Room, sitting position on thick upholstered couch, back and left region of the lower trunk leaning against thick cushions, pyjamas, pants, in front open bathing-gown.	1.3	1.2–1.4	96	18.0/19.0	18.0/19.0	33.5	08.5	14.1	04.0	17.5	The man committed suicide at an unclear time after having killed his wife at a time that could be exactly investigated.
71	Room, LL, floor, carpet, pyjamas, briefs.	1.2	1.1–1.3	64	18.0/19.0	18.0/19.0	26.5	14.4	23.4	17.2	17.7	

hpm, hours post mortem; LB, lying back; LL, lying in a lateral position; LP, lying prone.

From Henssge C, Althaus L, Bolt J, Freislederer A, Henssge CA, Hoppe B, Schneider V. Experiences with a compound method for estimating the time since death. I. Rectal temperature nomogram for time since death. Int J Legal Med 1999;**113**:303–319.

2. The corrective factors listed in Table 6.18 were investigated experimentally on bodies lying on a simple covered stretcher, which was declared to be a 'thermally indifferent' base. Different grounds such as floor, asphalt and dry lawn (e.g. cases 11, 55 and 64 in Table 6.17) dummy experiments have shown that insulating bases may require corrective factors up to 1.3, and excessively heat-conducting bases to 0.5 in naked bodies (see Table 6.10). Therefore, the base on which the body lies should be checked for both its thermal conductivity and its heat capacity. For example, thin sheet metal has a high conductivity but a low heat capacity, and so will not markedly accelerate body cooling. In contrast, the concrete floor of a cellar has both a higher conductivity and capacity. The cooling of a naked body will be accelerated according to a corrective factor of 0.75. The effect of the type of base on clothed bodies seems to be diminished more (thicker clothes) or less (thin clothes). Instructive examples in Table 6.17 are cases 15, 26, 28 and 46 for accelerating bases and cases 47, 48, 62 and 70 for insulating bases.

3. The position of the body (i.e. whether it is extended or crouched) influences cooling. Exact data are not yet known.

4. The influence of even slow but permanently moving air on body cooling is significant as long as the body is naked or is only thinly clothed (covered) or if the surface of the naked or clothed (covered) body is wet through. Therefore, attention should be paid to even slightly moving air (e.g. cases 25, 43 and 72 in Table 6.17).

5. The corrective factors listed in Table 6.18 were investigated on bodies of average body weight. Systematic investigations of the cooling of different-sized dummies under various conditions resulted in a clear dependency of the corrective factors on body weight in cases of a low or high body weight and, at the same time, higher thermic insulation conditions [61]. Higher body weights need lower factors and, *vice versa,* lower body weights need higher factors, as listed in Table 6.18. Insulation conditions that require a corrective factor up to 1.3 according to the experience on bodies of medium body weights (see Table 6.18) – reference 70 kg – can be used independently of the real body weight. Table 6.20 should be used whenever a special case requires a corrective factor of 1.4 or greater, according to Table 6.18, and the body weight exceeds 80 kg or is less than 60 kg at the same time. In such a case, evaluation of the corrective factor should be made, in the first instance, relative to the actual cooling conditions by experience from average body weights (e.g. Table 6.18). The corrective factor chosen in the first instance must be applied to the real high or low body weight either by Table 6.20 or by equation 6.10. Using equation 6.10 removes the need for interpolation. One of the previously mentioned computer programs, http://www.AMAsoft.de (see Figure 6.33), automatically takes into account this adaptation whenever the body weight and the corrective factor according to Table 6.18 require it. Examples can be seen in Table 6.17 (cases 6 and 66) and Table 6.20 (case 37).

6. As in many cases involving cooling conditions significantly different from standard conditions, the initial commitment to an exact corrective factor is impossible, and it is advisable to choose a range for the corrective factor (see Figures 6.38 and 6.39). If it is necessary to use Table 6.20 or equation 6.10, the threshold values of that chosen range of corrective factors must be modified. Once the time of death has been taken from the nomogram at two corrected body weights, the result is a range for the time of death (see Figures 6.38 and 6.39).

Example: A scene may lead to the choice of a range of corrective factors, perhaps between 1.8 and 2.2; the choice is based on experience of particular conditions (e.g. a bedspread) for an average body weight (see Table 6.18). The actual body weight may be evaluated to approximately 20 kg. Using Table 6.20, a corrective factor range of 2.4 (from 1.8) to 3.6 (from 2.2) would be the result. Using equation 6.10, the exact range would be 2.3 to 3.4. The corrected weight, taking the bedspread in the case of a 20-kg body into account, would range between 50 and 70 kg. If the ambient temperature is 18°C and the rectal temperature is 29°C, the range of the time of death would be 9.4 hours (50 kg) to 12.6 hours (70 kg) according to the nomogram, corresponding to 11 ± 1.6 hours. However, this range of the time of death resulting from the range of corrective factor is smaller than the ± 2.8 hours permissible variation of 95 per cent given by the nomogram (see Figures 6.38 and 6.39). We recommend, in all cases, using the wider range (11 ± 2.8 hours) in official statements to avoid misleading the investigation. In fact, it is impossible to limit that range without loss of reliability. The previously mentioned computer programs operate according to this recommendation. On the contrary, the use of additional methods for estimating the time of death is recommended (see Chapter 10).

A few cases of the bodies of babies and infants covered with a bedspread may confirm the data of Table 6.20. The victims of a triple murder were a baby (3.2 kg), a child (8.1 kg) and their mother (44 kg). The bodies of the children were found in bed, fully clothed and covered by a thick bedspread. The body of the mother was found lying on a bed, clothed in ski trousers and covered partly by a bedspread. The time of death would be met exactly in the case of the 3.2-kg body by nomographical read-off of the time of death using a corrective factor of 9.0, which corresponds to 2.8 in the case of a 70-kg body (see Table 6.20). The real time of death would be recorded by the upper limit of the permissible variation of 95 per cent (2.8 hours) to the examined time applying a corrective factor of 4.0, which corresponds to 2.0 in the case of a 70-kg body. Corrective factors of between 7.0 (2.7 at 70 kg) and 3.0 (1.9 at 70 kg) would be correct for the 8.1-kg body. In the case of the 44-kg body, the real time of death would be recorded by the application of 3.2 (1.9 at 70 kg) and 1.4 (1.4 at 70 kg) as corrective factors. The three cases can be solved sufficiently by the combined application of Tables 6.18 and 6.20. Further actual cases (numbers 36 and 37 in Table 6.21) may also confirm adoption of the corrective factor in dependence of the body weight in cases of strong thermic insulation conditions according to equation 6.10 (see Table 6.20).

7. Evaluating the corrective factor of body weight for special cooling conditions differing from the chosen standard conditions is often the most difficult problem, particularly when clothing or covering, special bases, moving air and wetness overlap. The difficulty can be avoided by complying with the previously mentioned order of the three aspects in evaluating the corrective factor, namely: (1) clothing or covering; (2) resting or moving air; and (3) accelerating or decelerating base. The difficulty can be further avoided if, instead of a point value, a range of corrective factors is chosen appropriate to the actual cooling conditions (see Table 6.18 and Figures 6.38 and 6.39). Instructive examples are cases 15, 22, 27 and 54 in Table 6.17.

Known changes of cooling conditions

If the changes in cooling conditions are known, they can often be taken into account without loss of reliability and without a significant reduction in accuracy. The one common situation is a change of the cooling conditions by the investigators before the temperature measurements can be made.

For example, a thick bedspread was taken off a body 1 hour before the temperature measurement. Nevertheless, a corrective factor of about 1.8 (see Table 6.18) was used for calculating the death time. Although the drop of the rectal temperature starts to become steeper during the 1 hour after the bedspread was removed from the body, the resulting error will be negligible because it is additive (compare the lower graphs in Figure 6.13; 26 to 28 hours post mortem). Certainly, if such a significant change of the cooling conditions has lasted several hours, it can no longer be neglected. The probable cooling curve should then be reconstructed from the time of temperature measurements by using a computer.

Sometimes, the ambient temperature is significantly changed by the person who found the body, or by the investigators (e.g. closing or opening windows, using special lamps that heat a small room quickly), a short time before temperature measurement. If the ambient temperature was changed 1 or 2 hours before body temperature measurement, body cooling becomes accelerated or decelerated after the change of ambient temperature, and the resulting error will again be negligible so far as the ambient temperature before its change is used.

A second temperature plateau provides a lag of the 'reaction' of the rectal temperature curve (see the example in Figure 6.40). If such a significant change of the ambient temperature has lasted for several hours, the range or the mean ambient temperature should be used as discussed earlier.

Uncertainty in the value of corrective factors

There is often uncertainty about point values of mean ambient temperature, body weight and, especially, corrective factors for special cooling conditions. It is a good strategy to evaluate possible upper and lower limits (see Figure 6.38). The nomogram (see Figure 6.39) or a computer program helps in this calculation by taking a range of each factor. The available computer program [63] requires range on principle.

Example (see Figure 6.39): For a body of 75 kg actual body weight and a rectal temperature of 27°C, evaluate a mean ambient temperature between 17°C and 20°C and a corrective factor between 1.2 and 1.5 for special clothing. Using the nomogram, draw 2 × 2 straight lines: connect a 27°C rectal temperature with both 17°C and 20°C. Now draw two more lines crossing the semicircles. Read off the time since death on both lines at the two intersections of the following semicircles: 75 × 1.2 = 90 kg and 75 × 1.5 = 112.5 (110) kg. The result will be four values for a death time: about 19, 23.5, 23 and 28.5 hours post mortem. Thus, it could be stated that death occurred between 19 and 28.5 hours before the time of investigation, which means 23.5 ± 4.5 hours. This example also demonstrates clearly that the given permissible variation at the outermost semicircle (± 4.5 hours; see Figure 6.39) includes some uncertainties.

This method is recommended if the points of contact (mean ambient temperature, corrective factor, body weight at scene) are not closely defined, so that a range must be taken into account.

The computer program http://www.AMAsoft.de generally computes the period of death in two ways [63] (see Figures 6.38 and 6.39):

1. The time of death is computed using the mean values of the chosen ranges of corrective factor, and mean ambient temperature, respectively. The period of death results by adding the empirical permissible variation of 95 per cent (see Tables 6.10 and 6.13).

2. In addition, the period of death is computed using the lower and upper brackets of the evaluated ranges

of ambient temperature and corrective factor, thus giving the lower and the upper limit of the period of death.

If the second method results in a wider range of the period than the first method, it is used as the final result (see Figure 6.38). There were some such cases in the previously mentioned field study [66] (e.g. cases 42, 49 and 56 in Table 6.17).

When the method must not be used

This method cannot be used, however, under a number of conditions. Having analyzed the situation at the scene carefully, it must be decided whether this approach is feasible:

1. Strong radiation. There is no experience in taking solar or other radiation into account. If a body is found with direct sun on its surface, the situation is apparent. If a body is found at a place where the sun is not actually shining, the question of sun radiation must be checked, to establish whether direct sun radiation on the body may have been possible. For example, a body was found at night in a closed room lying on the floor near the southwest window. Using the apparent factors – especially the darkness – a death time of early afternoon was given. Because at this time the body would have been in direct sun radiation, we did not give any statement concerning the time of death. Situations such as this are open to inappropriate use of any temperature method. Conversely, a short period of direct sun radiation on the body just before examination is not a contraindication to the method.

2. Uncertain severe change of cooling conditions. In contrast to methods with multiple temperature measurements at the scene for direct estimation of the individual values of the required constants, the nomogram method with a single measurement of rectal temperature can still be used when even severe changes of the cooling conditions occur for a short period before examination, if they can be reconstructed in relation to time and type (see earlier). If the changes in the cooling conditions are assumed but are really unknown in extent and direction, the method must not be used. A common situation of this type is a presumed severe change of cooling conditions during the interval between discovering the body and the beginning of the examination by the crime police.

   Example: A body of 51 kg was found lying on its back, extended in a room on the floor. It was clothed only with a gown open at the front. Even the crime police could not decide later whether the windows and the doors were originally open because the body was found 4.5 hours previously. The actual measured room temperature was 12.4°C. The radiator in the room felt warm. The room thermostat showed 21°C and the heating system was found to be working. The rectal temperature was 21°C. If the windows and doors were open during the whole time interval since death occurred, the mean room temperature would have been similar to the actual measured temperature of about 12°C. A corrective factor of 0.75 for permanently moving air should be applied (51 kg corrected 38 kg). The death time interval would have been 12.5 ± 2.8 hours (95 per cent) according to the nomogram. Conversely, supposing the windows and doors had been closed between the moment of death and finding the body 4.5 hours before examination, the mean room temperature until examination would have been close to 21°C; its fall to 12.4°C must have developed only when windows and doors were opened 4.5 hours before. A special corrective factor (still air) would then be out of the question. In this case, no reliable reading from the nomogram could be made because of the 21°C figure of both the ambient and the rectal temperature. Later on, the death time could have been calculated as 27 hours before examination at the scene in accord with the following reconstruction. The body cooling had not yet reached the ambient temperature (about 21°C) when the unidentified person found the body and opened the windows and doors. If the rectal temperature was about 24°C at this moment, the mean nomographic death time would be 23 hours (51 kg; corrective factor 1.0; ambient temperature 21°C). During the following 4.5 hours with changed cooling conditions, the rectal temperature fell to the measured 21°C. This example demonstrates the advice to 'analyze carefully the factors at the scene' before giving an estimate of death time. No special knowledge is necessary, but only general physical thinking about the carefully analyzed situation at the scene.

3. Unusual cooling conditions. This point is not only a matter of formally selecting a corrective factor (from Table 6.18) for the special cooling conditions, but is also a matter of personal experience. In cases of unusual cooling conditions without any personal experience, the examination at the scene should still be performed. Nevertheless, a statement of the time since death cannot be given from this method (e.g. cases 31 and 45 in Table 6.17). After a test cooling of the dummy, an opinion can be given later on whether the question of death time becomes of greater importance (see later).

4. Repeated extensive climatic changes. The method must not be used if repeated extensive climatic changes have occurred that do not allow the evaluation of representative mean figures for ambient temperature and corrective factors for the whole period between death and investigation.

5. Transported body. If the place where the body was found is not the same as the place of death, the method must not be used except when both the place of death and the date of transportation of the body are known. This is uncommon, but the circumstances of transportation become apparent later on. Therefore, the examination of the body at the place where it was found should still be made. Under certain circumstances, a restricted statement of the time since death can be given to support the investigation.

It is strongly recommended not to use the method after the removal of the body to the mortuary if there is only reported information about the place where the body was found. Conversely, there are no arguments against measurement of the rectal temperature and examination of the other methods estimating the time since death after the removal of the body to the mortuary, provided the forensic investigator has already inspected the scene of crime and the period of the transportation has not been too long. Marty and Baer [104] investigated the influence on body cooling of storing bodies in a closed compartment such as a coffin, a closet or a car boot. Whereas storing a body in a closet or a car boot did not affect the cooling rate significantly, bodies stored in a wooden coffin showed a lower cooling rate corresponding to a mean corrective factor of 1.2 (variation 1.0 to 1.3).

6. Suspicion of general hypothermia. See earlier and Figure 6.26. An example of suspected malignant hyperthermia is shown in case 33 in Table 6.17.

Special problems

Besides the questions referred to earlier, some further problems are encountered.

High ambient temperature

As discussed in connection with constant A and its uncertain dependence on the ambient temperature, it is emphasized that the nomogram (see Figure 6.35) and equation 6.15 for ambient temperatures above 23°C are based on the data from De Saram *et al.* [35]. Among our own data on experimental body cooling, there are no cases that cooled in ambient temperatures above 23°C. In the casework of a multicentre study ($n = 46$) [2] are seven cases where the ambient temperature was above 23°C. In the field study (n = 72) [66] reported earlier (see Tables 6.17 and 6.21) are seven cases where the mean ambient temperature was above 23°C (e.g. cases 48 and 66 in Table 6.17) and four further cases where the upper bracket of the range of ambient temperature was above 23°C. The estimated death times of these cases using the nomogram of Figure 6.35 or equation 6.5 with the 1.11 value of constant A are in accord with the true times of death. However, more experience of body cooling in high ambient temperatures has yet to be gained.

Fever at death

In our cooling experiments reported earlier, we had some cases with fever at death (see Figure 6.25). The errors caused by fever are included in the given permissible variations of 95 per cent and are greatest for the first postmortal hours, decreasing later (see Table 6.13 and Figure 6.26). By computation, the temperature at death can be changed from 37.2°C to a higher figure when adequate investigation or autopsy findings suppose fever at death. When using the nomogram form, the difference between the supposed temperature at death and the normal 37.2°C must be subtracted both from the measured rectal temperature and from the ambient temperature (e.g. case 33 in Table 6.17).

Longer agony

If there is a long period between the time of fatal injury and death, the estimate of the time since death should be supplemented by emphatically warning the investigators of a possibly longer interval. Stating only the time since death in cases of a possible longer period of agony can lead to a misunderstanding. In addition, the nomographically estimated time of death may be loaded with a greater error because the regulation of body temperature can be markedly disturbed during agony, either from a central fever or from hypothermia. In the latter case, cooling may develop even more quickly during agony than on a dead body. During agony, the circulation acts as convectional heat transfer from the centre of the body to the surface. At the same time, the regulation of homeostasis of body temperature by additional heat production can be reduced. A clear decision on whether a longer period of agony comes into question or not can be made only after autopsy. The preliminary examination of the body at the scene may suggest a very short agony, even if this is not the case. An immediate autopsy after the procedure at the scene is the best way to recognize such a mistake. The stated death time can be corrected quickly after autopsy before misleading the investigation. Later on, the findings of toxicological (e.g. ratio of metabolites) or histological (e.g. age of wounds, signs of organ shock) examination may provide evidence of a distinct interval between fatal injury and death.

Accuracy of calculated time since death

In 1990, Albrecht *et al.* [2] published a multicentre study on the accuracy of calculated time since death. The range of accuracy stated previously (see Figures 6.27 to 6.30) at the outermost circle of the nomogram results from experimental body cooling under controlled conditions in various research institutes.

Representative assessments of accuracy in using the nomogram method at the scene are difficult to obtain because of technical problems. A single forensic pathologist does not deal with sufficient cases to constitute a scientific study. Therefore, a multicentre study was made using 11 forensic pathologists from 6 forensic institutes in Germany, Austria and Switzerland [2]. Seventy-six cases were examined at the scene. All bodies were later examined by autopsy. The cooling conditions at the scene varied over a wide range corresponding to evaluated corrective factors between 0.3 (bodies found in flowing water) and 2.1 (thick bedspread). Ambient temperatures varied between −6°C and 26°C. The differences (nomographically estimated − actual interval of death) were calculated as follows (Figure 6.41). Because the investigated time of death was known with certainty in most cases, the mean figure and the upper and the lower limits of this interval were related to the mean of nomographically estimated time of death. In consequence, 3 values of error (dt 1, dt 2 and dt 3) of each case entered into the statistical analysis of error. The 76 cases were divided into 2 groups.

Group I

These 46 cases had clearly defined points of contact. The standard deviation of the differences between nomographic and actual death times resulted in ± 1.3 hours, equivalent to permissible variation of 95 per cent of ± 2.6 hours (Figures 6.42 and 6.43). The progress of cooling corresponded in 37 cases to values of $Q > 0.5$, and in 9 cases the cooling was more advanced, corresponding to values

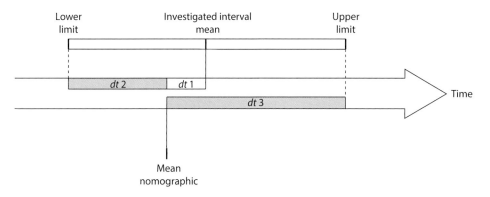

Figure 6.41 Differences between nomographically calculated time of death and mean (dt 1), lower limit (dt 2) and upper limit (dt 3) of the investigated time of death used in the statistical analysis of errors. (Data from Albrecht A, Gerling I, Henssge C, Hochmeister M, Kleiber M, Madea B, Oehmichen M, Pollak St, Püschel K, Seifert D, Teige K. Zur Anwendung des Rektaltemperatur- Todeszeit-Nomogramms am Leichenfundort (German, English summary). *Z Rechtsmed* 1990;**103:**257–278.)

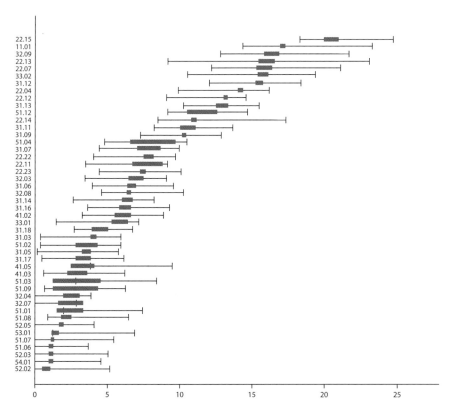

Figure 6.42 The thin bars represent the nomographically calculated interval according to the permissible variation of 95 per cent given at the nomogram, and the thick bars represent the investigated interval of death in group I of casework. (Data from Albrecht A, Gerling I, Henssge C, Hochmeister M, Kleiber M, Madea B, Oehmichen M, Pollak St, Püschel K, Seifert D, Teige K. Zur Anwendung des Rektaltemperatur-Todeszeit-Nomogramms am Leichenfundort (German, English summary). *Z Rechtsmed* 1990;**103:**257–278.)

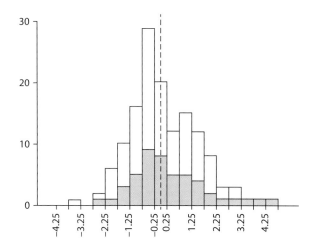

Figure 6.43 Histogram of errors of all the 46 cases of group I according to Figures 6.41 and 6.42.

of $0.5 > Q > 0.2$. There was no trend towards increased errors with advance of cooling, as expected theoretically and from experimental body coolings.

In 20 cases, the real death time was less than 4 hours. Among these were 5 cases in which the nomographic death time did not agree closely with the actual time, but did not contradict it. These cases could be explained by the problem of stated 37.2°C for *To,* as discussed earlier. The errors may be avoided by means of examining the mechanical and electrical excitability of muscles (see Chapter 10). Separating the 26 cases with a real death time greater than 4 hours, the standard deviation was ± 1 hour – equivalent to a permissible variation of ± 2 hours (Figures 6.44 and 6.45), which is significantly smaller than both the total group I and that suggested by the nomogram. The latter

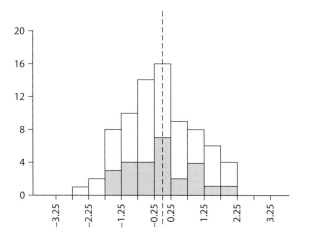

Figure 6.44 Histogram of errors of that part of the cases of group I having investigated death times greater than 4 hours (26 cases; compare with Figure 6.45). (Data from Albrecht A, Gerling I, Henssge C, Hochmeister M, Kleiber M, Madea B, Oehmichen M, Pollak St, Püschel K, Seifert D, Teige K. Zur Anwendung des Rektaltemperatur- Todeszeit-Nomogramms am Leichenfundort (German, English summary). *Z Rechtsmed* 1990;**103:**257–278.)

result seems to indicate lower errors in casework than in experimental body coolings. This rather surprising result could be explained by the previously discussed 'pre-analytic' error inherent in experimental body cooling but usually absent in casework. Nevertheless, the results of this group confirm the reliability of the nomogram method within the 95 per cent permissible variation.

Group II

These additional 30 cases had uncertain corrective factors. The nomographic death time interval does not agree with the real investigated interval in 5 cases, thus demonstrating that an estimate of the death time should not be given at all where points of contact are unsure (Figure 6.46).

In 1999, Henssge *et al.* [66] published a single-centre field study on the experiences with a compound method for estimating the time since death at the scene in 72 consecutive cases. The computer-assisted nomogram method [63] was used as the primary method (examples in Table 6.17 and 6.21), followed by non–temperature-based methods [67] (see Chapter 10).

The reliability of the estimated period since death by the temperature-based nomogram method could be considered in 60 cases where the period of death could be determined by the police investigations with certainty. In all these cases, the estimated period since death was consistent with the investigated period. In 50 cases, the estimated period since death corresponded completely to the investigated period, and partially in 10 cases. In the latter 10 cases, death could have occurred within the overlapping range between the estimate and the investigated period.

In each of 4 cases 2 bodies were found at the same scene, and the question of the sequence of deaths arose. These paired cases (see Table 6.21) provide evidence for the degree of differentiation that is achieved with the nomogram method. Despite the different rectal temperatures, congruent periods of death resulted because of different cooling conditions and body weights (cases 6/7, 36/37 and 46/47). In the paired cases 36/37 and 46/47, the police investigation ascertained nearly simultaneous death of the 2 persons. In the paired case 6/7, the police investigation could not verify the times of death. In the paired case 70/71, the time of the wife's death could be exactly verified by the investigation, but the time of the husband's death remained unclear. In contrast to the other 3 paired cases, the different cooling conditions and body weights did not compensate the different rectal temperatures, with the result that different periods since death were calculated at the 95 per cent level of permissible variation.

Reconstruction of body cooling

When a body is found under special cooling conditions where there is no experience of a corrective factor, test cooling of a 37°C heated dummy at the place and under the

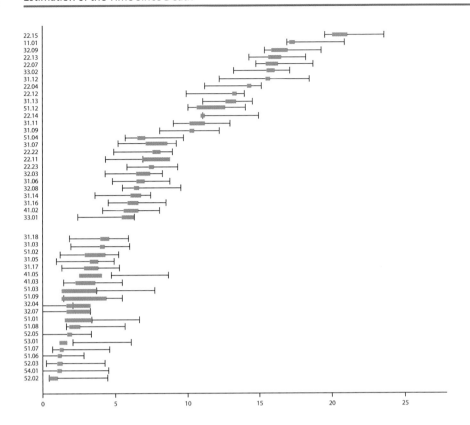

Figure 6.45 The thin bars represent the nomographically calculated time of death but with interval according to the permissible variation of 95 per cent of that part of casework having investigated death times greater than 4 hours (see Figure 6.44). The thick bars represent the investigated interval of death. The calculated interval does not agree with the investigated interval in case numbers 41.05, 51.01 and 53.01.

special conditions where the body was found can provide evidence of the true corrective factor. Before a dummy can be used for such a reconstruction, its cooling under the chosen standard conditions must be investigated by several test coolings. As a result of these tests (see Figure 6.2), the weight of the body can be calculated (equation 6.3), and this is replaced by the dummy. This weight stands for the chosen standard conditions of cooling. It acts as the real body weight *(bw)* in calculating the corrective factor according to equation 6.4. The weight resulting from the test cooling under the special conditions at the place where the body was actually found acts as *bw calc* in equation 6.4.

The additional measurement of heat flow and temperatures on the surfaces of body, especially on the supporting surface, may assist the detection of special influencing factors of the body cooling (see Figures 6.19 to 6.21), including the influence of heat radiation.

Besides additional measurements concerning the body cooling in special cases, it is recommended in all cases to apply other, simple methods in addition to the nomogram method [67]; these are described in Chapter 10.

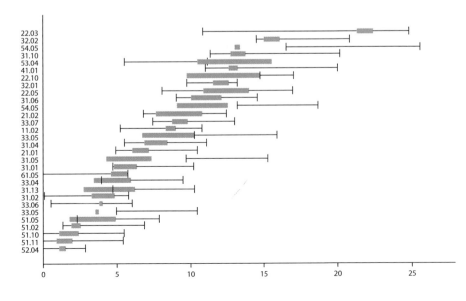

Figure 6.46 Nomographically calculated (thin bars) and investigated interval of death (thick bars) of group II including 30 cases with recognizable unsure point of contact.

Investigation of central brain temperature

Beyond our investigation of the rectal temperature probe site, we investigated the central brain temperature. The theory of modelling the central brain temperature mathematically is the same as described in connection with the rectal temperature (see equation 6.1).

The central brain temperature was recorded in 53 bodies, stored at nearly constant ambient temperatures between 10°C and 30°C in still air. The measurements were started on average 1.6 hours post mortem and were continued for 8 to 50 hours. The diameters of the temperature probes were 0.5 and 1 mm. The probes were inserted via the upper part of the superior orbital fissure into the brain with a depth of half the sagittal diameter of the head. The computation of the time of death according to equation 6.1 (Tr replaced by Tb = brain temperature) with average values for the starting temperature, To (37.2°C), and the constants B (−0.127) and A (1.135) provided margins of error for the 95 per cent tolerance limits of ± 1.5 hours up to 6.5 hours post mortem, ± 2.5 hours between 6.5 and 10.5 hours post mortem, and ± 3.5 hours between 10.5 and 13.5 hours post mortem. Compared with the margins of error based on rectal body cooling (see Figures 6.27 to 6.30 and Tables 6.15 and 6.16), a more precise estimation of the time of death can be obtained up to 6.5 hours post mortem only. For practical applications, a 'brain temperature–time of death nomogram' was constructed (Figure 6.47). The nomogram is related only to 'standard conditions' of cooling (see earlier). Even uniformly moving air alters the time relations – the constant B changes from −0.127 to −0.158 [65]. The cooling coefficient B was also influenced by the amount of hair. Nevertheless, taking this into account, the estimated time of death did not become significantly more accurate. Other influencing factors have not yet been fully investigated. The often expressed opinion that the cooling curve of the brain would be less affected by factors that could affect the cooling of other temperature probe sites [20,94] cannot be confirmed, either physically or empirically. Nevertheless, this concept may be correct because the head is less often clothed or covered than the trunk.

Inserting temperature probes on both sides via the upper part of the superior orbital fissure, the measured brain temperatures differed by up to 1.5°C, corresponding to a difference of computed death times up to 1 hour. This result required further studies into the optimal way to insert the probes into the centre of the brain. The best method of obtaining a well-standardized probe site was found by Ratermann [122] to be as follows: the probe is placed on the palpebral conjunctive of the lower eyelid within the temporal part of the first medial third of the infraorbital margin at an angle of 50 to 60 degrees to the nasal septum (Figure 6.48). Using this technique, and using an insertion depth of half the sagittal diameter of the head, the temperature probe will be situated at the centre of the brain. The temperature differences

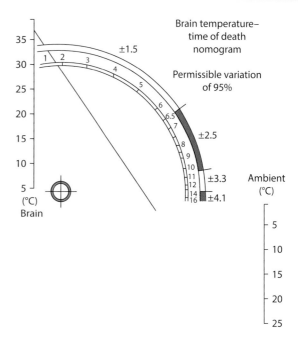

Figure 6.47 Central brain temperature–time of death nomogram related to 'standard conditions' of cooling. For the first step the points of the scales of the measured brain temperature (in the left margin) and ambient temperature (in the right margin) have been connected by a straight line, which crosses the diagonal of the nomogram at a particular point. The second step is to draw a second straight line through the centre of the circle, below left of the nomogram, and the intersection of the first line and the diagonal. The latter touches the outermost semicircle where the permissible variation of 95 per cent can be seen (see Figures 6.36 and 6.37).

between probes on both sides will be only minutely variable. In a study of 25 bodies using this procedure, the margin of error for the 95 per cent tolerance limits of computed time of death was ± 1.3 to 6.5 hours post mortem.

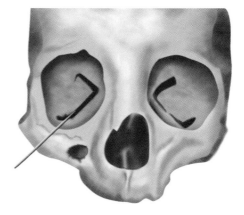

Figure 6.48 Standardized method of inserting the temperature probe into the 'centre' of brain providing more instant positioning than other procedures of insertion. (Data from Ratermann J. *Postmortale Hirntemperaturmessungen zur Todeszeitbestimmung – Untersuchungen zur Insertionstechnik der Temperaturmesssonden.* Münster, Germany, University of Münster, MD thesis, 1986.)

Combined brain and rectal temperatures

Estimating the time of death on the basis of simultaneous measurements of brain and rectal temperatures on 21 bodies cooling under standard conditions, the following margins of error for the 95 per cent tolerance limits were obtained [70]. Up to 6.5 hours post mortem, the most precise computation of time of death was achieved by the exclusive application of brain temperature, which gave a time of death within ± 1.5 hours. Between 6.5 and 10.5 hours post mortem, the brain-rectum combined computation of time of death balanced in the ratio of 6:4 (Figure 6.49) was the most precise, at ± 2.4 hours. Beyond 10.5 hours post mortem, the most precise computation of time of death was achieved by exclusive application of rectal temperature, and gave a time of death within ± 3.2 hours. These data agree well with those of a series of 53 bodies [68] that was based on the brain temperature only, as well as of the series that was based on the rectal temperature only.

Integrating equation 6.1 applied to brain temperature and then again to rectal temperature with an equation common to both by dividing them into each other eliminates the starting temperature, *To*:

$$\frac{Tb - Ta}{Tr - Ta} = \frac{1.135\exp(-0.127 \times t) - 0.135\exp(-1.0677 \times t)}{1.25\exp(B \times t) - 0.25(5 \times B \times t)}$$

(6.23)

where *Tb* is brain temperature; *Tr* is rectal temperature; *Ta* is ambient temperature; *B* is constant; and *t* is time of death (hours) (see equations 6.1, 6.2, 6.14 and 6.15).

This procedure may avoid major errors, for example, in cases involving fever in the occurrence of death, as in 2 cases in the previously mentioned series. The rectal

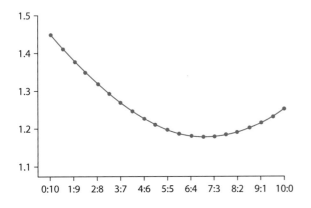

Figure 6.49 Relationship between standard deviation of errors of the computed time of death (ordinate) and the ratio of the balance of brain to rectal temperatures (abscissa) in combined computation of the time of death during the interval from 6.5 to 10.5 hours post mortem corresponding to the standardized temperature 'Q' (equation 6.1) of the brain. (Data from Henssge C, Frekers R, Reinhardt S, Beckmann E-R. Determination of time of death on the basis of simultaneous measurement of brain and rectal temperature (German, English summary). *Z Rechtsmed* 1984;**93**:123–133.)

temperature, first measured 2 hours post mortem, was 38°C in both cases. The fever-induced errors of computed death times in the later period when the rectal temperature had fallen below 37°C was reduced from about 3 hours (underestimation) to about 1 hour and virtually 0 hours, respectively.

6.2 Finite element method in temperature-based death time determination

■ *Michael Hubig, Holger Muggenthaler and Gita Mall*

■ Physical methods in temperature-based death time determination

One of the main targets of forensic medicine in homicide cases is death time determination. Various methods estimate the time of death by evaluating postmortem changes of physiological body parameters [65]. A long history of forensic casework culminated in the realization that postmortem core temperature decline is the most reliable of those parameters. The general guiding idea is to use a temperature-time diagram showing the postmortem temperature progression of the body core: the *model curve* T(t).

All temperature-based death time determination methods differ merely in the way of calculating the model curve T(t). Because decline of body temperature cannot be measured on site, the model curve must be known beforehand. Body core temperature and the parameter values necessary for calculating the model curve such as ambient temperature, body mass and height or clothing are measured or determined at the crime scene. Once the model curve T(t) is calculated from the parameters, the time difference between death and core temperature measurement – called *time since death* t_S – can be determined starting from the measured *core temperature* T_M on the abscissa and reading t_S from the ordinate. This can be expressed by a simple formula:

$$T(t_S) = T_M$$

(6.24)

Although this strategy is easily realized in a time-temperature diagram (Figure 6.50), given the model curve T(t), it is complicated in most cases to solve equation 6.24 directly numerically by computing:

$$t_S = T^{-1}(T_M)$$

(6.25)

Two classes of methods to calculate a model curve T(t) can be differentiated: the so-called *mathematical approaches* and the *physics-based approaches*. Although the mathematical approaches use general knowledge of physical cooling processes as well as information about

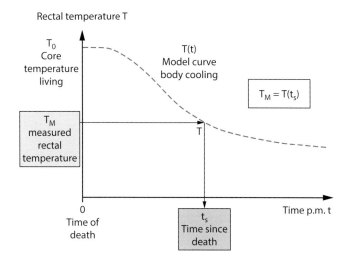

Figure 6.50 The model curve in death time estimation. Temperature time diagram for body core cooling based death time estimation. T(t) (dashed curve) body core temperature as a function of time t starting at the core temperature (T_0) of the living. Death time estimation: Horizontally moving from left to right starting at the measured rectal temperature T_M on the abscissa until the model curve is met. Then moving orthogonally down on the time axis, which is gauged to have 0 at the time of death, to read t_s, the time since death estimate.

the general geometrical form of cooling curves, the physics-based approaches try to implement the physics of body cooling completely by taking into account the different heat exchange mechanisms, the geometry of the special cooling scenario and the material properties of the cooling body, as well as the thermodynamically relevant parts of the scene. Mathematical approaches use fitting parameters not directly tied to physical measurements to compute the model curve (e.g. the corrective factor in the method of Marshall and Hoare and Henssge, described in part 6.1 of this chapter). This often leads to problems in the estimation of those parameters because the values derive for somehow fuzzily defined classes of cooling scenarios. Physics-based methods, in contrast, use only measurable parameters of thermodynamics and are frequently affected by the problem that not all values can be achieved at the crime scene a posteriori and therefore must be reasonably estimated.

A typical example of the mathematical death time estimation–type approaches is the method of Marshall and Hoare with the parameters of Henssge, also called the nomogram method, which is presented in part 6.1 of this chapter. In contrast, the finite element method (FEM) described in this discussion is typical of the physics methods class.

■ The physics of body cooling

Body cooling – like all cooling processes of objects in our universe – can be described as a physical process. The physical quantity relevant in body cooling is the temperature field T(r,t), which is a function of the three coordinates

in space r = (x,y,z) and the time coordinate t. The temperature field states the temperature T(r,t) for every location r at a specified time t. For computational purposes in FEM, the temperature T(r,t) has to be specified on an absolute scale starting from absolute zero at −273°C. Therefore, the scale of choice for this purpose is the *Kelvin* scale with the unit °K. A temperature value expressed in the Kelvin scale can be easily transformed to the centigrade scale by changing the unit °K to °C and subtracting 273°C.

If the temperature field $T_0 = T(r, t_0)$ is known at a certain time t_0 for all relevant locations r in space, the theory of thermodynamics allows to compute the temperature field T = T(r,t) for all times t later than t_0. The temperature field T_0 is called the *initial condition* of the actual cooling problem. For example, the temperature field of the body at the moment of death is supposed to be known beforehand (e.g. from literature or measurements); this temperature field is usually part of the initial condition of a cooling problem in death time determination. Because the region Ω in space that is relevant for the cooling problem considered is bounded, we have to define the temperature field T for all relevant times t in the time interval I of interest on the boundary ∂Ω of the region Ω. This partial fixing of the temperature field T on the boundary ∂Ω of the relevant region Ω is called the *boundary condition* of the cooling problem. In case of a body cooling problem in death time determination, the relevant region Ω may be a room where the boundary ∂Ω consists of the walls, the ceiling and the floor and the temperature has to be fixed throughout the whole cooling process as a boundary condition.

The science of *thermodynamics* represents the time evolution of the cooling process by a solution T(r,t) of the so-called *heat equation* (see [13] or [28]), which in the general case of body cooling is a second order partial differential equation, under the relevant initial and boundary conditions.

Heat transfer mechanisms

Three main mechanisms are considered for body cooling: *conduction, convection* and *radiation*. Although the first two can be interpreted as pure mechanical processes on a microscopic scale, the last mechanism, radiation, includes mechanics and electrodynamics. In our representation of heat transfer mechanisms relevant for body cooling, we rely mainly on the books by Cengel [28], Gerthsen and Vogel [47] and Alonso and Finn [3].

The last section of this chapter part does not deal with heat transfer mechanism *per se* but with a mechanism of postmortem heat production in the body. Nevertheless, we see the solution to discuss the postmortem heat source in this section on heat transfer mechanisms as adequate because convection and radiation are at play in the FE model as heat sinks.

The microscopic theory of thermodynamics discovered and quantified the interpretation of a medium's temperature essentially as the mean velocity of its particles. Quantum mechanics later showed that a certain temperature of a medium leads to a specific spectrum of quantum leaps of the outer electrons in the hull of its constituent atoms and therefore to irradiation of electromagnetic waves.

Heat conduction means heat flux from a static medium into another static medium. The terminus static is used to emphasize that no macroscopic movement (e.g. a flux phenomenon in a fluid) is involved in this heat transport mechanism. Conduction is governed by the heat equation, which interprets heat flux as a sort of energy transport phenomenon. In principle, conduction can be fully understood by applying the conservation of energy principle and the proposition that heat flux power is proportional to the temperature difference between start and destination, which shall be demonstrated here in a simple linear case: Let R be a rod with cross section A and length L, and let further T_1 be the temperature at the right end of the rod R and T_2 be the temperature at the left end. The rod R shall consist of a homogeneous material of *conductivity* λ with a unit of W/(°K m). The heat power of conductivity between the right and the left end of the rod can be quantified as:

$$P_{\text{cond}} = A \cdot \lambda \cdot \frac{T_1 - T_2}{L} \qquad (6.26)$$

This means that P_{cond} is proportional to the cross section A, to the temperature difference $T_1 - T_2$ and inversely proportional to the length L of rod R. The proportionality constant is the conductivity λ.

Convection is the term used for heat energy transfer from a stationary medium into a medium with non-zero average particle velocity. Usually, the moving target medium of heat transport is a *fluid*, which can be a gas as well. Body cooling in moving air is a good example of convective heat transfer: Heat is transferred from the skin as the stationary medium into the surrounding air, which is moved by wind and represents the moving fluid. Because of the intricate nature of convective heat transfer processes involving fluid dynamics, the thermodynamic theory of convection is the most complex of all heat transfer mechanism theories and can be applied only in a linearized and approximated form. The convection process depends on the following parameters of flow in the target fluid:

- Dynamic viscosity μ [kg/(m sec)].
- Mass density ρ [kg/m³].
- Coefficient of volume expansion β [1/°K].
- Specific heat c [kJ/(kg°K)].
- Free stream fluid velocity v_E [m/second].
- Thermal conductivity λ [W/(°K m)].

When the convection process has reached a steady state, a temperature gradient in the fluid can be registered: Most of the fluid in the free stream region is of temperature T_E but near the surface of the stationary medium the fluid temperature rises continuously and monotonously with falling distance to the surface up to the surface temperature T_S. We can interpret this as the existence of a thin *film* of fluid near the surface where the temperature gradient changes with changing distance from the surface. For computational purposes a so-called *film temperature* T_F is introduced as the mean of T_E and T_S:

$$T_F = (T_S + T_E)/2 \qquad (6.27)$$

An analogous film of fluid can be imagined for the fluid velocity, which depends on the distance to the surface only near the surface, where the velocity v of the fluid drops continuously from the free stream velocity v_E to the value 0 directly on the surface.

Fluid dynamic distinguishes two types of flows, known as *flow regimes: laminar flows* and *turbulent flows*. Flow regimes can be characterized by purely kinematic criteria: A laminar flow is a highly ordered motion with smooth streamlines, whereas a turbulent flow is a highly disordered motion with strong velocity vector fluctuations in time and space and curly streamlines. Turbulent flows usually lead to faster mixing of the fluid and therefore mostly increase heat transfer in comparison with laminar flows.

Because of the highly complex nature of flow phenomena, the convective heat power P_{conv} is approximated as a linear function of the temperature difference $T_E - T_S$ with good results. The proportionality constant of this approach is called *convection coefficient* h. The dependency of h on the geometry of the scenario (i.e. the shape of the cooling stationary surface and the direction of the fluid flow) is expressed in the formulae by two terms:

- The characteristic length δ, a constant depending solely on the specific geometry of the convection scenario (e.g. if the scenario is a cooling cylinder of diameter D with a fluid flowing orthogonally to the rotational axis around the cylinder, the characteristic length is $\delta = D$).
- A function f connecting the so-called Nusselt number Nu (see equations 6.30 to 6.32) to the Prandtl number Pr (see equation 6.33) and the Reynolds number Re (see equation 6.34) or the Grashof number Gr (see equation 6.35).

Both quantities can be found in tables containing specific scenario geometries in textbooks (e.g. [28]).

The theory of thermodynamics differentiates two types of convection: *natural convection* where the movement of the target fluid is caused by buoyancy forces and *forced convection* if the target medium is moved by other forces. Because of the complex nature of the mechanisms involved, the convective heat transfer power P_{conv} is modelled as a linear approximation called *Newton's law of cooling* to the heat transfer equation:

$$P_{\text{conv}} = h \cdot A \cdot (T_S - T_E) \tag{6.28}$$

In equation 6.28, the symbol h stands for *the convection heat transfer coefficient,* A is the area through which convective heat transfer takes place, the temperature of the cooling stationary surface is named T_S and T_E is the fluid temperature sufficiently far from the surface. Numerical computation of the convective heat transfer coefficient is done via the *Nusselt number Nu:*

$$h = Nu \cdot \frac{\delta}{\lambda} \tag{6.29}$$

The symbol Nu in equation 6.29 is for the Nusselt number, λ the heat conductivity of the fluid and δ the characteristic length of the cooling scenario. Three dimensionless quantities Pr, Re and Gr, called numbers, are most important for computation of the Nusselt number Nu. In case of forced convection we have a functional dependency:

$$Nu = f(Pr, Re) \tag{6.30}$$

whereas in case of free convection we may write:

$$Nu = f(Pr, Gr) \tag{6.31}$$

The function f depends on the geometry of the cooling scenario as mentioned earlier and has to be measured or taken from textbooks such as those by Cengel [28] or from original literature [32].

If both mechanisms, forced and free convection, are involved in one cooling scenario, a common Nusselt number Nu has to be computed depending on the Nusselt numbers Nu_{forced} and Nu_{free} for the forced convection and the free convection part of the scenario, respectively. The following formula was yielded by evaluation of experimental data. The plus sign stands for the case where the mixing forced and free flows have the same direction, whereas the minus sign is valid if the free flow and the forced flow have opposite directions:

$$Nu = \left(Nu_{\text{forced}}{}^n \mp Nu_{\text{free}}{}^n\right)^{1/n} \tag{6.32}$$

The parameter n = 3 is used for horizontal surfaces, whereas n = 4 better matches the cases of vertical surfaces.

Nu is a function of the *Prandtl number Pr,* which can be interpreted as the ratio between molecular quasi-diffusivity of momentum and the molecular diffusivity of heat in the fluid. This interpretation leads to the formula:

$$Pr = \frac{\mu \cdot c}{\lambda} \tag{6.33}$$

which can be expressed as Pr being proportional to the dynamical viscosity μ, the specific heat capacity c and inversely proportional to the conductivity λ of the fluid.

In case of forced convection, the *Reynolds number Re* describes the flow regime. It is defined as the ratio between inertia forces and viscous forces in the fluid. This leads to the following formula for the Reynolds number Re:

$$Re = \frac{\rho \cdot v_E \cdot \delta}{\mu} \tag{6.34}$$

A large Reynolds number means that inertia forces are large in comparison to viscous forces. Therefore, a large Reynolds number indicates that viscous forces are too weak to preserve ordered motion of the fluid, which leads to rapid and random changes of the local velocity vector in the fluid. The result is a turbulent flow. Conversely, a small Reynolds number leads to an ordered and thus laminar flow. For a given fluid and a given flow scenario a critical Reynolds number Re_{crit} can be found separating laminar flows from turbulent flows.

The *Grashof number Gr* governs the flow regime in case of free convection just as the Reynolds number does in case of forced convection. In analogy to the definition of the Reynolds number, it is defined as the ratio of buoyancy force and viscous force in the fluid. Transformation of this definition leads to the following formula for the Grashof number Gr:

$$Gr = \frac{g \cdot \beta \cdot (T_S - T_E) \cdot \rho^2 \cdot \delta^3}{\mu^2} \tag{6.35}$$

As in forced convection, a critical Grashof number Gr_{crit} can be found for a specific free convection cooling scenario meaning that for $Gr > Gr_{\text{crit}}$ the flow is turbulent and laminar otherwise. For example, for the cooling process of a vertical plate, the critical Grashof number Gr_{crit} is about 10^9.

Radiation is the third mechanism to be considered in body cooling. A so-called *black body,* which has a surface of area A absorbing all electromagnetic waves of all frequencies and reflecting none of them, of a specific surface temperature T irradiates with a power $P_{\text{black body}}$ described by the famous *Stefan-Boltzmann law:*

$$P_{\text{black body}} = A \cdot \sigma \cdot T^4 \tag{6.36}$$

The factor σ in the equation is the *Stefan-Boltzmann constant:*

$$\sigma = \frac{4}{15} \cdot \pi^5 \cdot \frac{k^4}{c^2 \cdot h^3} = 5.6703 \cdot 10^{-8} W/(m^2 \cdot {}^\circ K^4) \tag{6.37}$$

Radiation heat transfer includes not only energy loss by radiation but also the absorption of thermal radiation arriving at the surface from other surfaces that in some cases even belong to the same body. This, among other aspects, makes radiation heat transfer a complicated task for computation. The other cause is that most real bodies are not black bodies in the technical sense: They reflect a certain proportion of irradiation and absorb the other part. This fact is taken into account by using *emissivity* factors ε_i for all approximately plane homogeneous surfaces of a scenario. The factor ε_i is the quotient of the radiation power emitted by the surface and the radiation power emitted by a black body surface of equal geometry at the same temperature. This factor actually depends on the radiation frequency. In practical computations, the *grey body approximation* is often used; it states that the irradiation spectrum of the real surface A_i of temperature T can be generated by multiplying the spectrum of the black body of temperature T by ε_i. Additionally, it is assumed that the surface A_i is *opaque*, which means not transparent, and that it does not reflect radiation but backscatters it *diffusively*.

Another point to be considered is the position of every surface A_i in space relative to the positions of all other surfaces A_1, ..., A_n involved in the scenario. This is done by *view factors* $VF(A_i, A_k)$ for each pair A_i, A_k of surfaces in the scenario. The view factor $VF(A_i, A_k)$ is defined as the quotient of the radiation amount leaving surface A_i hitting surface A_k and the overall amount leaving surface A_i. This factor is used to compute the ratio of the radiation leaving surface A_i and striking surface A_k.

Let A_1 and A_2 be two surfaces of area A_1 and A_2, of temperatures T_1 and T_2 and emissivities ε_1 and ε_2 respectively. Let $VF(A_1, A_2)$ be the view factor of this scenario, then the power irradiated from surface A_1 on A_2 can be computed as:

$$P_{1,2} = A_1 \cdot VF(A_1, A_2) \cdot \sigma \cdot \left(\varepsilon_1 \cdot T_1^4 - \varepsilon_2 \cdot T_2^4 \right) \qquad (6.38)$$

It is a well-known fact that heat-producing mechanisms in the body do not come to an abrupt halt when the heart stops (see [93] and [99]). Different causes of this postmortem *inner energy production* are discussed in the literature. The overall thermodynamic effect is modelled in FEM death time determination by attributing a fast decreasing heat power P_{inner} to certain compartments of the human body in an FEM cooling scenario model. A physiologically plausible approach models the overall inner energy production of the body as an exponentially dropping function of time:

$$P_{inner}(t) = P_0 \cdot \exp(-\alpha \cdot t) \qquad (6.39)$$

The inner energy production rate P_0 at the time of death was assumed to be the basal metabolic rate (see, e.g. [88]) multiplied by the body mass m, whereas the factor α, which determines half-life, was fitted [Mall, Eisenmenger 2005] using the cooling model of Marshall and Hoare to a value of $\alpha = 0.0000770164$ second^{-1}. The inner energy production rate is implemented in the FE model as a power density varying in the different body compartments (see [147]): 60 per cent of the basal metabolic rate are attributed to the trunk core, 18 per cent to the muscles, 17 per cent to the brain and 5 per cent to the connective tissue and the skeleton.

Differential equation of heat transfer

This section relies on the textbooks by Steinbuch [145], Baehr and Stephan [13] and Thomas [156].

Essentially, heat transfer processes can be seen as energy transport phenomena that are governed by a sort of diffusion equation. The temperature field T(r,t) is modelled as a function of space r and time t, which is differentiable two times. It is essential to define a specific spatial range Ω, where the heat equation shall be solved resulting in the temperature field T(r,t) with the location vector r in the range Ω. Deriving a differential equation for the quantification of body cooling starts from the well-known *basic equation for heat transfer* of Fourier, which states that the stream density of heat energy at location r is proportional to the gradient grad T(r,t) of the temperature field T(r,t) at this location r. The proportionality constant $\lambda(r,t)$ is as usual in body cooling applications, a scalar function of space and time and is called *conductivity*. Introduction of another material constant, which is called the *specific heat capacity c,* stating how much heat energy is necessary for warming up a mass unit of a specific material by 1°K, turns out to be necessary to eliminate the heat stream density. The specific heat capacity c is a function $c(r,t)$ of space and time as well as the mass density $\rho(r,t)$. Applying the Gaussian integral theorem eventually leads to the well-known *homogeneous heat equation*. Additionally, considering the role of *heat sources* and *sinks* in the heat energy transportation process by introducing *heat source and sink densities p(r,t)* results in the *general inhomogeneous form of the heat equation:*

$$\text{(P)} \qquad \frac{\partial}{\partial t} T = \frac{\lambda}{c \cdot \rho} \cdot \Delta T + \frac{1}{c \cdot \rho} \cdot p \qquad (6.40)$$

The Laplace operator Δ applied to the temperature field T(r,t) is an abbreviation for the following sum of second order spatial partial derivations of T(r,t):

$$\Delta T(r,t) = \frac{\partial^2 T}{\partial x^2}(r,t) + \frac{\partial^2 T}{\partial y^2}(r,t) + \frac{\partial^2 T}{\partial z^2}(r,t) \qquad (6.41)$$

The spatial position vector r has the components x, y and z. In equation (P) the symbol ρ stands for the mass density. The symbol p represents the heat power density of all heat generating or heat consuming entities in the spatial range Ω of the equation. The transport process equation (P) models heat conduction only, so processes such as warming by irradiation or cooling by convection have to be coped with by implementing specifically designed heat sources or sinks at the locations in Ω, where radiation heat transfer or convective warming or cooling takes place. This can be done because the heat powers of those processes are known from equations 6.28 and 6.38. The heat power (equation 6.39) of postmortem energy production is modelled as a heat source in (P) as well.

To yield a unique solution T(r,t) of the inhomogeneous heat equation (P) in the spatial range Ω for all points of a time interval I = *[t$_0$,t$_1$]* of interest, we need to specify *initial conditions*: one has to define the temperature field $T_0(r)$ = T(r,t$_0$) at the beginning t$_0$ of the cooling process for every point r in the spatial range Ω:

$$\text{(I)} \qquad \forall r \in \Omega: T(r,t_0) := T_0(r) \qquad (6.42)$$

The second condition to guarantee uniqueness of the solution of the cooling problem is connected to the edge ∂Ω of the spatial range Ω. Because the FEM cannot compute T(r,t) on an infinite space, we have to specify the bounded region Ω as definition range for the temperature field T(r,t). On the edge ∂Ω of Ω the solution cannot be computed, it has to be specified as a function T_∂(r,t) – called the *boundary condition* – a priori for r in ∂Ω and for all points t in the time interval I = *[t$_0$,t$_1$]* of this process:

$$\text{(B)} \qquad \forall t \in \left[t_1,t_1\right]: \forall r \in \partial\Omega: T(r,t) := T_\partial(r,t) \qquad (6.43)$$

The three conditions (I), (B) and (P) together are now sufficient for the existence and uniqueness of a solution T(r,t) in the range Ω and for all times t in I.

■ Solving the heat equation

As sources for the material presented in this section, we mention the textbooks by Steinbuch [145] and Zienkiewicz and Taylor [177]. The following presentation is only loosely based on these texts.

From the theory of partial differential equations, we know that there is a unique solution to the boundary and initial value problem posed by ((I),(B),(P)). Nevertheless, it is impossible to find exact formulae for such solutions in most practical cases. This is *a fortiori* true in the real body cooling cases, which are relevant in homicide cases. Since the beginning of the computer age, there have been several approaches to compute good approximations to solutions of problems such as ((I),(B),(P)). The finite difference scheme and the boundary element method have to be named in this context. One of the most effective and widely used methods is the FEM, which was developed in the 1960s and 1970s. It provides a general approximation method for vector fields, which leads in a natural way to an approach for computing approximate solutions of partial differential equations such as (P) under conditions (I) and (B).

The finite element method

In the next paragraphs, the term *mathematically easy* is used extensively. A function is called mathematically easy if it and all its derivations of sufficiently high order can be computed by hand in a finite and exact form. This implies that the function itself and also its necessary derivations can be easily implemented in a computer program.

The first step of the FEM is to find a discrete approximation of the temperature field T(r,t), which is defined on the spatial range Ω at a certain point t in the relevant time interval I. For this purpose, the range Ω is approximated by a spatial volume E, which is assembled of small volumes E$_1$, ..., E$_N$ (Figure 6.51). Every small volume E$_n$ can be described as the result of a mathematically easy transformation f$_n$ = (f$_n^x$, f$_n^y$, f$_n^z$), called *element transformation*, with the three vector components f$_n^x$, f$_n^y$, f$_n^z$, which maps Euclidean space IR^3 into itself. The element transformation f$_n$ is applied to an elementary mathematical volume E*, which is called the *pre-element* (e.g. of the unit cube or of a tetrahedron in IR^3) (Figure 6.52) to generate the volume E$_n$:

$$E_n = f_n(E^*) \qquad (6.44)$$

The vertices e*$_1$, ..., e*$_k$ of the volume E* are called *pre-nodes* of E$_n$, whereas their images e$_1$: = f$_n$(e*$_1$), ..., e$_k$: = f$_n$(e*$_k$) under the transformation f$_n$, which are the vertices of E$_n$, are called *nodes* of E$_n$. For every node index k there is a mathematically easy function h*$_k$ defined on E*, which maps E* into the real numbers IR. The function h*$_k$ takes the value 1 on the pre-node e*$_k$ and the value 0 on all other pre-nodes e*$_j$ of E*. Moreover, for all indices k the value h*$_k$(r*) of the function h*$_k$ is falling monotonously with rising distance between e*$_k$ and the point r* in E*. The functions h*$_1$, ..., h*$_K$ are called *pre-shape functions*. One can define *shape functions* on any E$_n$ by 'pulling back' the point r in E$_n$, where the shape function h$_k$ is to be defined, to the volume E* via f$_n^{-1}$ and applying the pre-shape functions h*$_k$ from E* to E$_n$ via the function f$_n$:

$$h_k(r) := h^*_k\left(f_n^{-1}(r)\right) \qquad (6.45)$$

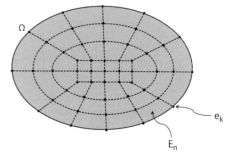

Figure 6.51 Finite element (FE) model of a two-dimensional ellipsoid. For convenience, the domain Ω of interest, modelled here, has the simple geometric shape of an ellipsoid and is two dimensional only. FE models in real case work are mostly more complex and three dimensional. The domain of interest Ω is shown in blue, the shapes of the elements E$_n$ are shown as dashed lines and the nodes e$_k$ are dots.

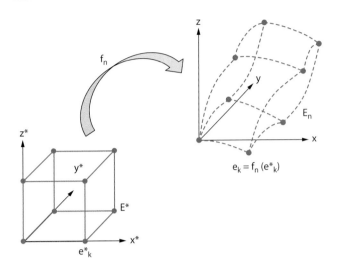

Figure 6.52 Element transformation. A cuboid pre-element E* (drawn lines) with the pre-nodes e_1^*, ...,e_8^*, presented in the lower left corner, is transformed via the element transformation f_n into the element E_n (dashed lines) with the nodes e_1, ..., e_8, shown in the upper right corner, which is a distorted image of the pre-element. Each pre-node e_k^* is mapped to its counterpart e_k via f_n.

A volume E_n together with its nodes e_k and its shape functions h_k and its element transformation f_n is called a *finite element*. For convenience we will often use the term 'finite element E_n'.

For any function g* on E*, assigning a real number g*(r*) to each r* in E*, the pre-shape functions h_k^* on E* can be used to generate a simpler function g*# on E* which approximates g*, if g* is sufficiently smooth on E*:

$$g^{*\#}(r^*) := \sum_{k=1}^{K} g^*(e_k^*) \cdot h_k^*(r^*) \tag{6.46}$$

This means to compute an approximate g*# of g* by a linear combination of g*'s values $g^*(e_k^*)$ on the pre-nodes of E* with the values of the pre-shape functions $h_k^*(r^*)$ as weights. This idea can be applied to a function g (e.g. temperature distribution T) with a range in the real numbers on the volume E_n analogously:

$$g^\#(r) := \sum_{k=1}^{K} g(e_k) \cdot h_k^*(r) = \sum_{k=1}^{K} g(e_k) \cdot h_k^*(f_n^{-1}(r)) \tag{6.47}$$

To apply this idea to partial differential equation solving it is necessary to define the approximation of a partial derivation of a function g from E_n into the set IR of the real numbers. This can be done consistently by defining it as the partial derivative of the approximation g# with respect to the metavariable ξ, which can be the variable x, y or z:

$$\left(\frac{\partial g(r)}{\partial \xi}\right)^\# := \frac{\partial g^\#(r)}{\partial \xi} \tag{6.48}$$

Computing this formula with the help of the chain rule and of definition 6.47 the partial derivations of the pre-shape functions h_n as well as of the inverted element transformations f_n^{-1} appear. In the following we will use matrix representation for convenience. Note that all matrices are defined for only one element E_n initially. This is indicated by appending the index 'n' onto the matrix names. Later we will use the matrices' names without index n indicating that all matrices X_n – where 'X' can be 'H', 'B', 'T' or 'J' – of the same type for all finite elements E_1, ..., E_N are concatenated in an obvious way by the enumeration of the shape functions h_k^n of the elements E_n to assemble the matrix X for the whole cooling system from the K x K - element matrices X_n and from matrices of the same dimensions K x K filled with 0s. The K x K - matrices completely filled with zeros are represented simply by the single symbol 0 in equation 6.49:

$$X = \bigcup_{n=1}^{N} X_n := \begin{pmatrix} X_1 & \cdots & 0 \\ \vdots & \ddots & \vdots \\ 0 & \cdots & X_N \end{pmatrix} \tag{6.49}$$

Analogously vectors related to the whole cooling system are assembled from the specific element vectors. For example the concatenation T^+ of the element-related temperature vectors T_n^+ defined in equation 6.54 is defined simply by putting all components of all vectors T_n^+ in a column vector T^+ following the scheme $T^+ = (T_1^+, ..., T_N^+)^T$.

We define the vector H_n of the shape functions h_k evaluated at r in E_n and the vector H_n^* of the pre-shape functions h_k^* evaluated at r* with r = $f_n(r^*)$ by:

$$H_n(r) := (h_1(r) \ldots h_K(r)) \tag{6.50}$$

$$H_n^*(r^*) := (h_1^*(r^*) \ldots h_k^*(r^*)) \tag{6.50*}$$

Their derivations $B_n = H_n'$ and $B_n^* = H_n^{*\prime}$, evaluated at r in E_n and r* in E* respectively are therefore:

$$B_n(r) := H_n'(r) := \begin{pmatrix} \dfrac{\partial h_1(r)}{\partial x} & \cdots & \dfrac{\partial h_K(r)}{\partial x} \\ \dfrac{\partial h_1(r)}{\partial y} & \cdots & \dfrac{\partial h_K(r)}{\partial y} \\ \dfrac{\partial h_1(r)}{\partial z} & \cdots & \dfrac{\partial h_K(r)}{\partial z} \end{pmatrix} \tag{6.51}$$

$$B_n^*(r^*) := H_n^{*\prime}(r) := \begin{pmatrix} \dfrac{\partial h_1^*(r^*)}{\partial x^*} & \cdots & \dfrac{\partial h_K^*(r^*)}{\partial x^*} \\ \dfrac{\partial h_1^*(r^*)}{\partial y^*} & \cdots & \dfrac{\partial h_K^*(r^*)}{\partial y^*} \\ \dfrac{\partial h_1^*(r^*)}{\partial z^*} & \cdots & \dfrac{\partial h_K^*(r^*)}{\partial z^*} \end{pmatrix} \tag{6.51*}$$

For computing derivations the *Jacobi matrix* $J_n(r^*)$ of the spatial partial derivatives of the element transformation f_n

evaluated at the point $r^* = f_n^{-1}(r)$ in E^* and its inverse $J_n(r^*)^{-1}$, which is identical to the matrix of the partial derivations of the inverted element transformation f_n^{-1}, at the location vector r is useful:

$$J_n(r) := \begin{pmatrix} \dfrac{\partial f_n^x(r^*)}{\partial x^*} & \dfrac{\partial f_n^y(r^*)}{\partial x^*} & \dfrac{\partial f_n^z(r^*)}{\partial x^*} \\[1.5ex] \dfrac{\partial f_n^x(r^*)}{\partial y^*} & \dfrac{\partial f_n^y(r^*)}{\partial y^*} & \dfrac{\partial f_n^z(r^*)}{\partial y^*} \\[1.5ex] \dfrac{\partial f_n^x(r^*)}{\partial z^*} & \dfrac{\partial f_n^y(r^*)}{\partial z^*} & \dfrac{\partial f_n^z(r^*)}{\partial z^*} \end{pmatrix} \tag{6.52}$$

$$J_n^{-1}(r) := \begin{pmatrix} \dfrac{\partial f_n^{-1x}(r)}{\partial x} & \dfrac{\partial f_n^{-1y}(r)}{\partial x} & \dfrac{\partial f_n^{-1z}(r)}{\partial x} \\[1.5ex] \dfrac{\partial f_n^{-1x}(r)}{\partial y} & \dfrac{\partial f_n^{-1y}(r)}{\partial y} & \dfrac{\partial f_n^{-1z}(r)}{\partial y} \\[1.5ex] \dfrac{\partial f_n^{-1x}(r)}{\partial z} & \dfrac{\partial f_n^{-1y}(r)}{\partial z} & \dfrac{\partial f_n^{-1z}(r)}{\partial z} \end{pmatrix}$$

$$= J_n(r)^{-1} := \begin{pmatrix} \dfrac{\partial f_n^x(r^*)}{\partial x^*} & \dfrac{\partial f_n^y(r^*)}{\partial x^*} & \dfrac{\partial f_n^z(r^*)}{\partial x^*} \\[1.5ex] \dfrac{\partial f_n^x(r^*)}{\partial y^*} & \dfrac{\partial f_n^y(r^*)}{\partial y^*} & \dfrac{\partial f_n^z(r^*)}{\partial y^*} \\[1.5ex] \dfrac{\partial f_n^x(r^*)}{\partial z^*} & \dfrac{\partial f_n^y(r^*)}{\partial z^*} & \dfrac{\partial f_n^z(r^*)}{\partial z^*} \end{pmatrix}^{-1} \tag{6.53}$$

The *determinant* of the Jacobi matrix $J_n(r^*)$ is $|J_n(r^*)|$.

If finally the vector T_n^+ of the values $T(e_1,t), \ldots, T(e_K,t)$ of the temperature field $T(r,t)$ at the node points $e_1, \ldots, e_K$ of E_n is defined (with the script 'T' indicating transposition of the vector) as:

$$T_n^+(t) := \left(T(e_1,t), \ldots, T(e_K,t) \right)^T \tag{6.54}$$

we can write the approximating field $T^\#(r,t)$ as well as the approximation $(\text{grad } T)^\#$ of its *spatial gradient* grad T and the time derivations $(\partial T / \partial t)$ approximation $(\partial T/\partial t)^\#$ in matrix form:

$$T^\#(r,t) := H(r) \cdot T^+(t) \tag{6.55}$$

$$(grad\, T)^\#(r,t) := B(r) \cdot T^+(t) \tag{6.56}$$

$$\left(\frac{\partial T}{\partial t} \right)^\#(r,t) := H(r) \cdot \left(\frac{\partial T^+}{\partial t} \right) \tag{6.57}$$

The second step of FEM is to transform the partial differential equation (P) into an equation that can be solved with the finite and essentially linear numerical methods that can be implemented on computers. Using Green's integral theorem and a weak representation of the equation with the help of test functions, formula (P) is transformed to an equation, where the finite element approximations, yielded in the first step, can be inserted. This leads to the following form of the partial differential equation, which is stated here for the sake of simplicity in the homogeneous form:

$$c \cdot \rho \cdot \left(\int_\Omega H^T H \, d\Omega \right) \cdot \left(\frac{\partial T^+}{\partial t} \right) + \lambda \cdot \left(\int_\Omega B^T B \, d\Omega \right) \cdot T^+ = 0 \tag{6.58}$$

In this equation, the integrals over the region Ω are pure spatial integrations referring to the variable r. Further, it is obvious that the functions to be integrated $H^T H$ and $B^T B$ are solely dependent on the shape functions h_k; they do not depend on the actual temperature field T or on its derivations.

For convenience we introduce the following abbreviations:

$$C := \lambda \cdot \left(\int_\Omega B^T B \, d\Omega \right) \tag{6.59}$$

$$M := c \cdot \rho \cdot \left(\int_\Omega H^T H \, d\Omega \right)$$

The matrix C is called the conductivity matrix and M is called the heat capacity matrix.

Both of the integrals in equation 6.59 have the same integration range Ω, which consists of the element regions E_ns set union. The set union sign U is used here, in contrary to equation 6.49, in its conventional denotation:

$$\Omega := \bigcup_{n=1}^N E_n \tag{6.60}$$

Therefore, C and M can be represented as the following sums, where the set union symbol U has to be interpreted as assembling a matrix from the element matrices:

$$C := \bigcup_{n=1}^N \lambda_n \cdot \left(\int_{E_n} B_n{}^T B_n \, dE_n \right)$$

$$M := \bigcup_{n=1}^N c_n \cdot \rho_n \left(\int_{E_n} H_n{}^T H_n \, dE_n \right) \tag{6.61}$$

Using the transformation theorem for integrals, the integrations in equation 6.61 can be computed via the Jacobi matrices J_n and the element transformations f_n as integrations on the pre-element E^* for all elements E_n:

$$C := \bigcup_{n=1}^N \lambda_n \cdot \left(\int_{E^*} J_n^{-1T} \cdot B_n^{*T} \cdot B_n^* \cdot J_n^{-1} |J_n| dE^* \right)$$

$$M := \bigcup_{n=1}^N c_n \cdot \rho_n \left(\int_{E^*} H_n^{*T} \cdot H_n^* |J_n| dE^* \right) \tag{6.62}$$

Additionally, introducing the heat source and sink power density $p(r,t)$, the vector p_n^+ of its values on the nodes of element E_n, the vector p^+ of all node values and the approximation equation p ≈ H p⁺ after inserting equation 6.62 into equation 6.58 yields the *FEM heat equation* for the inhomogeneous case:

$$M \cdot \left(\frac{\partial T^+}{\partial t} \right) + C \cdot T^+ = H \cdot p^+ \qquad (6.63)$$

The FEM heat equation represents a major step for approximately solving the original partial differential equation system ((P),(B),(I)) because the equation contains *no more spatial derivations* of the temperature field. Only an ordinary differential equation system of first order is left that can be numerically treated.

Implementation of the finite element method

Given the FEM heat equation, it is now possible to compute an approximated solution by using a finite difference method for time integration of the system where only linear algebra operations have to be used in every time step.

■ The body cooling finite element model

Generating an FE model of the human body for death time determination via body cooling was performed for the first time by G. Mall [96] in her habilitation thesis. The FE models used at the Forensic Medicine Institute in Jena, Germany up to 2014 are derived from this model. Modelling and pre-processing were done with the *FEM-Preprocessor* MENTAT, which also performs features of post-processing and is currently distributed by the MSC Software Company Munich, Germany. The program allows users to define an FE model interactively by constructing three-dimensional geometrical objects, setting nodes and defining element areas, element types and material properties. The program also allows users to define a start temperature field $T_0(r,t)$ of the body as initial condition (I) and to define boundary conditions (B) such as the ambient temperature $T_A(r,t)$ or ground temperature. The preprocessor transforms input data into the actual FEM input data file, which contains the whole information in a purely numerical style (e.g. the nodes are transferred to its coordinate tuples). The FEM computation consists of the computation of the heat capacity matrix M and the conductivity matrix C for the whole scenario, in stating the FE heat equation in the general inhomogeneous form that takes into account all the boundary conditions and in solving the FE heat equation. These steps are performed by the *FE processor* program, which is the software MARC from MSC. The result of its computations is a sequence of temperature field approximations $T^\#(r,t_j)$ that give for each of J+1 time steps $t_0, t_1, \ldots, t_J$ the node temperatures $T^+(r,t_j)$ at any node location of the whole model. This information is passed back to the pre-processor/postprocessor, which allows the user to visualize and check the results.

Mapping the cooling scenario: geometry

The human body was approximated by elementary geometrical forms. The forms were filled with approximately 8000 solid, nearly exclusively cuboid, 8-node so-called HEX-8 elements, which are the elements E_n, determining the element area E_n as well as the shape functions h_k, in our earlier explanations. Using the fact that the human body has a median-sagittal symmetry approximately, it was possible to perform the FE computations for half of the body, thus saving a huge amount of computing time (which was more important in the 1990s than it is now). The *meshing,* which means setting the nodes (~10 000) and relating them to elements, was done exclusively manually. The complex body anatomy geometry prevented the use of automatic meshing software.

The original FE model (Figures 6.53 and 6.54), from which application models can be derived by scaling the spatial dimensions, had a length of 2 m, a (half) trunk width of 0.2 m and a sagittal depth of 0.2 m. The inner elements have a mean edge length of approximately 0.025 m. The whole body is covered by a layer of solid cuboid elements, maximally 0.005 m thick, representing the skin except the part on the symmetry plane. On the skull, this layer covers another layer, 0.01 m thick, that represents the skull bone. The model is lying on its 'back' with arm and leg slightly abducted. The arm and leg were modelled with semi-ellipsoid cross sections.

As support surface of the substrate, a trough, consisting of a 0.01-m-thick element layer matching the body contours, was generated. This trough can be thickened by scaling, and its material properties can be adapted to the actual underground of a case by changing the material properties. The projection of the trough onto the x-y-plane is a rectangle. The models of body and trough together include approximately 10 000 elements and approximately 13 000 nodes.

For the FE model presented, we differentiated the tissue compartments in the human body, which are represented in Table 6.22, together with their numbers of elements and their volume proportion in the FE model.

Thermodynamical properties of biological materials

All the thermodynamical constants given in this discussion are taken from the literature (e.g. [28] and [37]). The FEM presupposes the knowledge of the relevant material constants for the case scenario considered. In practical casework, we are confronted with the difficulties of gaining reliable values for the materials relevant for the cooling process. In many cases, one has to rely on published parameter values of similar materials or must estimate

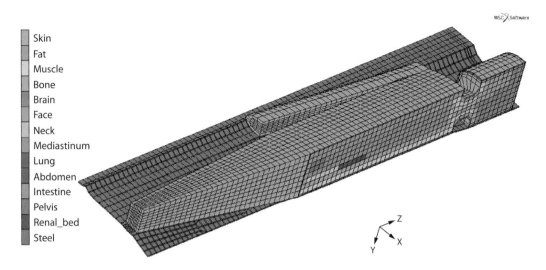

Figure 6.53 Finite element (FE) model of cooling body: outside view. FE model representing the cooling body in dorsal position, legs parallel, arms parallel to trunk. The shapes of the pre-elements used are mostly cuboids. Only some prism-shaped pre-elements were applied. The body is lying on a thin plate perfectly matching the dorsal shape of the body to generate good contact for heat conduction. (Courtesy of MSC Software, Munich, Germany.)

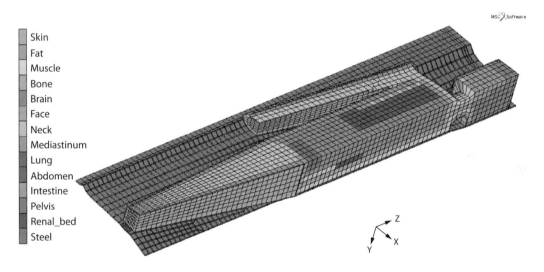

Figure 6.54 Finite element (FE) model of cooling body: view with ventral layers removed. Ventral layers of body elements are removed from the FE body cooling model to show inner features of the model. The structures modelled are coloured and listed on the scale on the left side of the image. (Courtesy of MSC Software, Munich, Germany.)

values and make reasonable assumptions. Each of the three parameters λ, c, ρ is dependent on the location r in the scene (Table 6.23).

Heat conductivity λ is defined as the heat transfer rate through a unit thickness of the material per unit area per unit temperature difference.

Defining specific heat c of a material means stating the energy required to raise a unit mass of a substance by one temperature unit.

The mass density ρ, measuring mass per volume, seems to be the most uncomplicated physical quantity in the heat equation at first sight. In principle, for any object of homogeneous consistency, immersion of an object into water yields the volume, and weighing the object leads to the mass. However, because the individual body can deviate a great deal from the standardized mean body geometry and in many cases there is no access to individual organs of the body, even this parameter ρ can be unknown.

A special role is played by the radiation connected emissivity ε. It takes values between 0 and 1, and it measures the ratio of emitting radiation power of the real surface and the black body under equal temperature conditions. The values of this parameter have to be taken from literature as well.

In real casework, we are confronted with the problem of identifying and separating homogeneous regions in the body *(segmentation problem)* and assigning material properties to them. Currently, the solution consists of using

124 Estimation of the Time Since Death

Table 6.22   Body compartments with numbers of elements and volume proportion

Body tissue	Number of elements	Volume proportion (%)
Skin	2740	10.3
Fat tissue	1798	26.2
Muscle	2019	28.0
Skeleton	680	10.0
Brain	174	4.2
Face soft tissue	91	2.3
Cervical organs	14	0.2
Mediastinum	104	2-6
Lungs	220	5.0
Upper abdominal organs	97	2.2
Gastrointestinal tract	259	6.0
Renal bed	42	0.8
Retroperitoneum	47	1.2
Pelvic organs	43	1.0
Sum	8328	100

Table 6.23   Body compartments with heat conductivity λ, specific heat capacity c and mass density ρ

Body tissue	λ [W m^{-1}°C^{-1}]	c [J kg^{-1}°C^{-1}]	ρ [kg m^{-3}]
Skin*	0.47	3680	1085
Fat tissue	0.21	2300	920
Muscle	0.51	3800	1085
Skeleton	0.75	1700	1357
Brain	0.49	3850	1080
Facial soft tissue	0.51	3245	1056
Cervical organs	0.48	3363	1006
Mediastinum	0.47	3375	1033
Lungs	0.28	3520	560
Upper abdominal organs	0.48	3730	1080
Gastrointestinal tract	0.46	3346	933
Renal bed	0.39	3158	1026
Retroperitoneum	0.51	3800	1085
Pelvic organs	0.49	3350	1008

* The emissivity ε of the skin was assumed to be ε = 0.95, a value that can be found in Cengel [28].

published anatomical knowledge and data about organ geometry in the human body, as well as material constants published in the biomechanics [37] and physiology literature [147,165] or elsewhere [34]. The more desirable solution, to have a computed tomography body scan of a body in a real case and automatically generate an individual FE model from it, has not yet been realized.

For the model presented, the material constants of single organ parts could be taken from the literature. Because the FE model should not include too many details for computational capacity reasons, it was often necessary

to combine several organs to one compartment. So every material property of any compartment was assembled as linear combination of the material properties of its components with the volume proportions as weight factors (which are given in parentheses in the following listings). For the face soft tissue, the material properties of eyes (one sixth), connective tissue (one third), muscle (one third) and fat (one sixth) were used, whereas the cervical organs were composed of oesophagus (one fourth), trachea (one fourth), thyroid (one fourth) and connective tissue (one fourth). For the mediastinum, a mixture of heart (one half), trachea (one sixth), esophagus (one sixth) and connective tissue (one sixth) was used, the upper abdominal organs were assumed to consist of liver (three fourths) and spleen (one fourth) and the gastrointestinal tract of stomach (one sixth), bowel (two thirds) and fat (one sixth). The renal bed was combined of kidney (two thirds) and fat (one third), the pelvic organs compartment of bladder (one half), connective tissue (one fourth) and muscle (one fourth), whereas the retroperitoneum was assumed to consist of muscle by 100 per cent.

Starting the cooling process: initial conditions

Solving a differential equation needs a fixed initial condition $T_0(r) = T(t_D,r)$ at the time of death t_D as a starting point. In practical casework, the temperature distribution $T_0(r)$ of the cooling body is, strictly speaking, unknown. For many cases, a reasonable guess can be made by assuming the standard mean temperature field $T(r)$ in the living body, as published in the physiology literature. This approach does not take into account singular circumstances (e.g. fever, hypothermia or strong physical stress at the time of death t_D). It is usually adequate to assume that there is a temperature gradient from the body core to the peripheral body parts.

For the initial condition temperature field $T_0(r)$ in a case of body cooling at room temperature the results of [88] can be assumed. Additionally, we set the temperature of the body core at 37.2°C as in Marshall and Hoare [101–103]. The resulting temperature field of the body model is shown in Figure 6.55. Table 6.24 shows the values used for $T_0(r)$.

The initial temperature field of those parts of the scenario not belonging to the body (e.g. the floor or the surrounding air) should be measured. If there is no further information about the latter temperature field but the statement that the scenario was not heated up or cooled down by external causes (e.g. a heating system switched on during the cooling process or a window opened during investigations but some hours before temperature measurement), it can be reasonable to assume that the scenario without the cooling body was in a temperature steady state. Then the room air temperature T_A can be taken as a raw approximation for the initial condition temperature field $T_0(r) = T_A$ of the scenario's non-body parts.

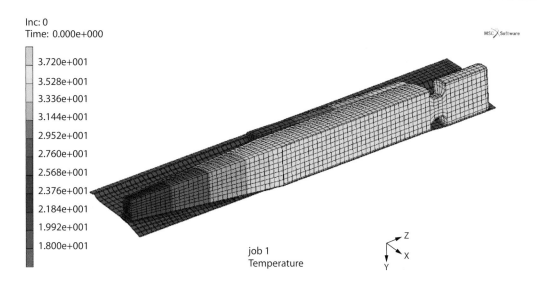

Inc: 0
Time: 0.000e+000

MSC Software

3.720e+001
3.528e+001
3.336e+001
3.144e+001
2.952e+001
2.760e+001
2.568e+001
2.376e+001
2.184e+001
1.992e+001
1.800e+001

job 1
Temperature

Figure 6.55 Initial condition: temperature field of the living. Finite element (FE) body cooling model with temperature field T_0 of the living as initial condition to heat equation solving. The local temperature $T_0(r)$ which is originally given in the nodes locations only is interpolated between nodes at every location r over the whole FE model. Temperatures in °C are colour coded as depicted in the scale on the left side. (Courtesy of MSC Software, Munich, Germany.)

Table 6.24 Initial temperature node sets in the body with number of nodes and initial temperature T_0

Node set	Number of nodes	Temperature T_0 [°C]
Head (outer).	355	35
Head (middle).	254	36
Head (inner).	450	37.2
Neck (outer).	60	35
Neck (middle).	45	36
Neck (inner).	60	37.2
Trunk (outer).	816	35
Trunk (middle).	854	36
Trunk (inner).	1873	37.2
1: Arm (outer)/Arm (inner).	60/139	35/36
2: Arm (outer)/Arm (inner).	36/132	34/35
3: Arm (outer)/Arm (inner).	64/132	33/34
4: Arm (outer)/Arm (inner).	64/132	32/33
5: Arm (outer)/Arm (inner).	64/132	31/32
6: Arm (outer)/Arm (inner).	64/132	30/31
7: Arm (outer)/Arm (inner).	64/132	29/30
8: Arm (outer)/Arm (inner).	64/132	28/29
9: Arm (outer)/Arm (inner).	33/33	27/28
1: Leg (outer)/Leg (inner).	107/345	35/36
2: Leg (outer)/Leg (inner).	128/324	34/35
3: Leg (outer)/Leg (inner).	128/324	33/34
4: Leg (outer)/Leg (inner).	128/324	32/33
5: Leg (outer)/Leg (inner).	128/324	31/32
6: Leg (outer)/Leg (inner).	128/324	30/31
7: Leg (outer)/Leg (inner).	128/324	29/30
8: Leg (outer)/Leg (inner).	128/324	28/29
9: Leg (outer)/Leg (inner).	81/81	27/28

Connecting the cooling process to the world: boundary conditions

Solution of the initial and boundary value problem ((I),(B),(D)) involves defining boundary conditions in the sense of (B) for the whole duration of the cooling process. This means specifying the temperature field $T_\partial(r)$ for all locations r on the boundary $\partial\Omega$ of the range considered. For example, this could mean assigning a fixed and constant temperature T_∂ for all points r on the walls (modelled as two-dimensional objects) of a small room where cooling takes place, during all times t for which the cooling process is computed: $T_\partial(r,t) = T_\partial$. In most cases, the boundary condition (B) assigns a constant temperature T_A to the surrounding air and neglects the minor effect of air heating by body cooling.

The problem of setting boundary values reflects the more basic problem of choosing a finite range Ω for the scenario of body cooling. In principle, the range Ω could be modelled as the whole earth and its atmosphere. This is certainly absurd because time, storage and computing capacity are finite and costly in most application cases. Therefore, one takes advantage of the fact that in some distance to the cooling, body temperature effects, caused by body cooling, cannot be detected anymore. The usual solution is to implement the range Ω's boundary $\partial\Omega$ in at least such a distance of the cooling body. An erroneous choice of the boundary $\partial\Omega$ can be the source of major errors in computing death time. If, for example, a cooling body is situated on a stony and wet cellar floor, which is a good heat conductor, it would be fallacious to choose part of the boundary $\partial\Omega$ to be the surface of the cellar and to assign a constant temperature (far below the body core temperature of 37.2°C) to it. This would lead to a heat flow from the body into the cellar that is not slowed down by the warming of the part of the ground directly below the body. Therefore, this heat flow would be much too strong, leading to accelerated cooling and to death time estimation $t_D^{\wedge}$ that is too late ($t_D^{\wedge} \gg t_D$) in comparison with the true time of death t_D. The correct solution would have been to model a part of thickness D of the cellar in Ω and to include its outer walls as a part of $\partial\Omega$. It would have been necessary to model several Ωs with different values of D (e.g. D = 0.25 m, D = 0.5 m and D = 1.0 m) to test whether the outer walls of the cellar heat up essentially at a given D value. For the final computation, such a value of D would have been chosen to fix the cooling scenario.

Reconstructing time since death

Once the model described in the previous sections matches the complete initial and boundary value problem ((P), (I), (B)), the FE computation can be started. As was already mentioned, the result of the solving process is a series of temperature fields $(T(r,t_j))_j = 1,...,J$, where each $T(r,t_j)$ describes the temperature distribution on the spatial region Ω containing the cooling body (Figure 6.56). Let now r_M be a node in the FE model corresponding to the top of the rectal temperature probe during rectal temperature measurement at the crime scene that produces the value T_M. By extracting the point series $(t_j, T(r_M,t_j))_j = 1,...,J$ from the series of temperature fields $(T(r,t_j))_j = 1,...,J$ and applying interpolation of the point series $(t_j, T(r_M,t_j))_j = 1,...,J$ the model curve $T(t)$ can be reconstructed, which gives the deep rectal temperature at any time t in the interval $[t_0, t_j]$. Because $t_0 := 0$ is set in the FE calculation, we can now read time since death t_S directly from the model curve $T(t)$ diagram by looking up the value t_S which satisfies the equation:

$$T(t_S) = T_M \tag{6.64}$$

as described at the beginning of this chapter part.

■ Model validation

As for all parts or applications of theories in science there is no verification for cooling models. This is a direct consequence of Popper's epistemology. The only possibility to be reasonably sure that a scientific method actually works is to have as many tests as possible in practical situations, where viability can be checked. This tactic is called validation. The FE-based death time determination is in a comparably comfortable situation with respect to validation. The heat equation (P) as well as the algorithms for computing all heat transfer mechanisms were tested in many varying scenarios. The situation for the FEM in thermodynamics seems to be even better. Since its development in the 1960s and 1970s, there have been legions of applications to technical problems, where the predictions

of the FEM could be directly compared with measurements. The only part of the temperature and FE-based death time estimation to be validated is the FE model of the cooling body itself.

Validation of any cooling model can be done by comparison with real cooling cases, as well as with established models in scenarios where they are known to work well. In the next section, the matching of FEM to the well-established Marshall and Hoare model is shown in four hypothetical case scenarios. The subsequent section presents comparisons with real cooling cases.

One major problem in the FEM validation of body cooling is that real cases regularly show special conditions that have to be implemented in the FE model. For example, the FE model of a very obese body must be generated starting from the original model by adding layers of fat tissue under the skin. The model of a body half covered by a blanket will be constructed by adding additional element layers onto the skin layer. Such 'handmade model variants' involve an immense expenditure of work in every single case. Therefore, the validation of a large number of cases, necessary to compute quantitative statistical measures (e.g. confidence intervals) is extremely costly. The next stage of the FEM death time estimation method development will involve automatic or semi-automatic FEM mesh generating from computed tomography or magnetic resonance images bypassing this bottleneck.

Comparison with the model of Marshall and Hoare

For the comparison of FEM, the model of Marshall and Hoare [101–103] was chosen. This model takes into account the cooling body's height, which at first sight seems to be an important geometrical parameter: It determines not only the 'linear distribution' of body mass in the direction of the body's main axis but also the body's surface area. Because FEM takes into account the body constitution, a model with the parameters body mass m and body height L seems to be adequate. The *model of Marshall and Hoare*, like the *model of Henssge,* is a double exponential model of the following form:

$$\frac{T(t) - T_A}{T_0 - T_A} = \frac{p}{p - Z} \cdot e^{-Z \cdot t} - \frac{Z}{p - Z} \cdot e^{-p \cdot t} \tag{6.65}$$

where the following parameter values were fixed: The parameter Z depends on the *size factor S:*

$$Z = 0.0573 + 0.000625 \cdot S$$

with the size factor S being defined by the quotient of body surface area estimate A given in cm² and body mass m in kg:

$$S = 0.8 \cdot \frac{A}{m}$$

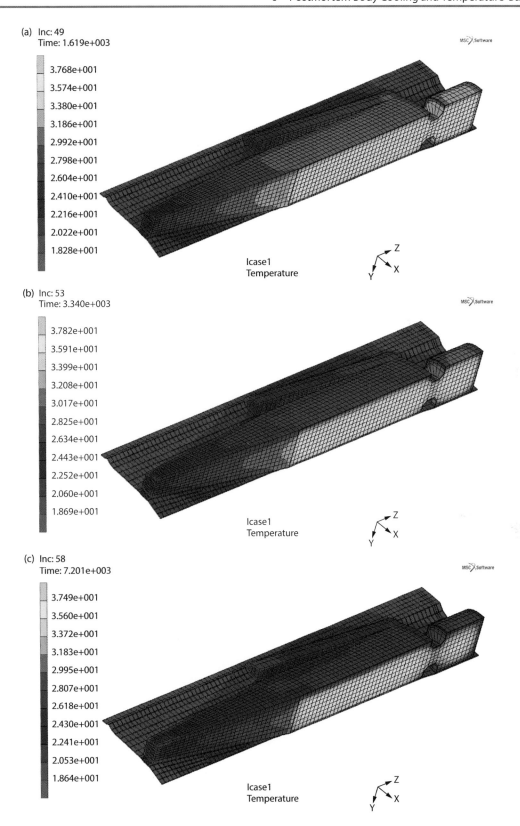

Figure 6.56 Phases of body cooling: time evolution of the body's temperature field. (a) to (h) represent the finite element (FE) output of eight successive states of body cooling. The FE body model is shown with the temperature field T(r, t) at different times t of the cooling process. Interpolation and colour coding of the temperature field T(r, t) is analogous to Figure 6.55. (a) Time t = 1619 seconds = 0.45 hour. (b) Time t = 3340 seconds = 0.93 hour. (c) Time t = 7201 seconds = 2.00 hours. (d) Time t = 10 900 seconds = 3.03 hours. (e) Time t = 24 860 seconds = 6.91 hours. (f) Time t = 53 970 seconds = 14.99 hours. (g) Time t = 82 730 seconds = 22.98 hours. (h) Time t = 115 100 seconds = 31.97 hours. (Courtesy of MSC Software, Munich, Germany.) (*Continued*)

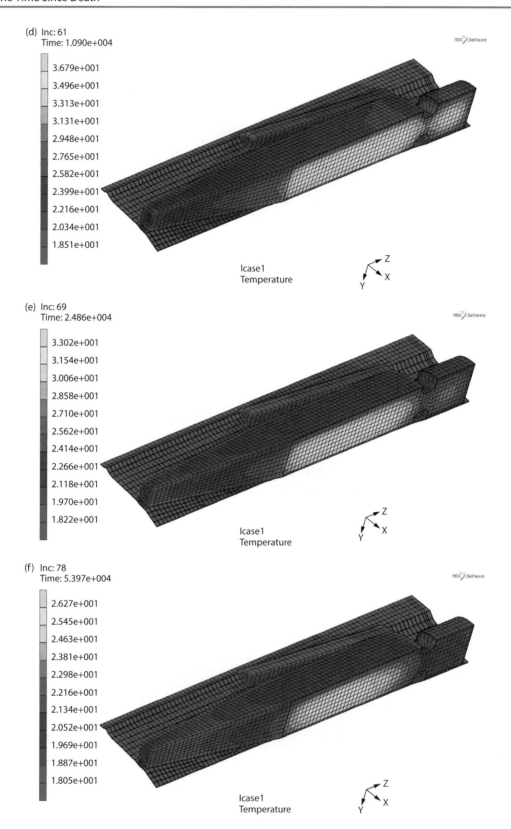

Figure 6.56 (*Continued*) Phases of body cooling: time evolution of the body's temperature field. (a) to (h) represent the finite element (FE) output of eight successive states of body cooling. The FE body model is shown with the temperature field T(r, t) at different times t of the cooling process. Interpolation and colour coding of the temperature field T(r, t) is analogous to Figure 6.55. (a) Time t = 1619 seconds = 0.45 hour. (b) Time t = 3340 seconds = 0.93 hour. (c) Time t = 7201 seconds = 2.00 hours. (d) Time t = 10 900 seconds = 3.03 hours. (e) Time t = 24 860 seconds = 6.91 hours. (f) Time t = 53 970 seconds = 14.99 hours. (g) Time t = 82 730 seconds = 22.98 hours. (h) Time t = 115 100 seconds = 31.97 hours. (Courtesy of MSC Software, Munich, Germany.) (*Continued*)

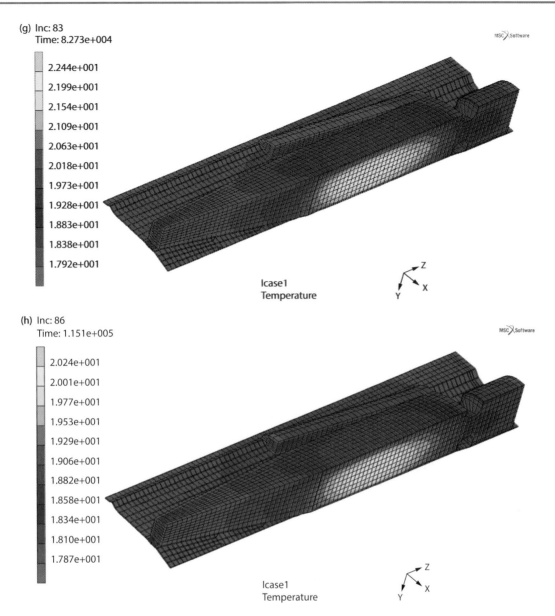

(g) Inc: 83
Time: 8.273e+004

MSC Software

2.244e+001
2.199e+001
2.154e+001
2.109e+001
2.063e+001
2.018e+001
1.973e+001
1.928e+001
1.883e+001
1.838e+001
1.792e+001

lcase1
Temperature

(h) Inc: 86
Time: 1.151e+005

MSC Software

2.024e+001
2.001e+001
1.977e+001
1.953e+001
1.929e+001
1.906e+001
1.882e+001
1.858e+001
1.834e+001
1.810e+001
1.787e+001

lcase1
Temperature

Figure 6.56 (*Continued*) Phases of body cooling: time evolution of the body's temperature field. (a) to (h) represent the finite element (FE) output of eight successive states of body cooling. The FE body model is shown with the temperature field T(r, t) at different times t of the cooling process. Interpolation and colour coding of the temperature field T(r, t) is analogous to Figure 6.55. (a) Time t = 1619 seconds = 0.45 hour. (b) Time t = 3340 seconds = 0.93 hour. (c) Time t = 7201 seconds = 2.00 hours. (d) Time t = 10 900 seconds = 3.03 hours. (e) Time t = 24 860 seconds = 6.91 hours. (f) Time t = 53 970 seconds = 14.99 hours. (g) Time t = 82 730 seconds = 22.98 hours. (h) Time t = 115 100 seconds = 31.97 hours. (Courtesy of MSC Software, Munich, Germany.)

In the formula for the size factor S, the body surface estimate A is computed using the DuBois formula (see, e.g. [88]):

$$A = 0.007184 \cdot L^{0.725} \cdot m^{0.425}$$

The parameter p is given together with a value p_{min}, which leads to a temperature curve $T_{min}(t)$ lying below the model curve $T(t)$ as a lower boundary and a value p_{max} with a corresponding temperature curve $T_{max}(t)$ as an upper bound.

$$p = 0.4, \quad p_{min} = 0.275, \quad p_{max} = 0.6$$

Rectal cooling curves T(t) were computed for four different cooling scenarios varying three important parameters: ambient temperature T_A, body mass m and body height L. The scenario was cooling of the naked body on a steel trolley lying on the back with stretched legs and arms parallel to the body. The surrounding air was assumed to be static and the parameters of the four scenarios were as follows:

M1. $T_A = 18°C$, $m = 80$ kg, $L = 1.75$ m (Figure 6.57 (a)).
M2. $T_A = 8°C$, $m = 80$ kg, $L = 1.75$ m (Figure 6.57 (b)).
M3. $T_A = 13°C$, $m = 61$ kg, $L = 1.60$ m (Figure 6.57 (c)).
M4. $T_A = 13°C$, $m = 103$ kg, $L = 1.90$ m (Figure 6.57 (d)).

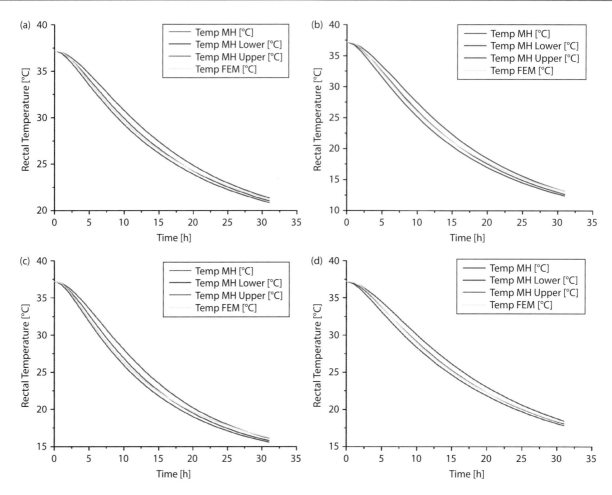

Figure 6.57 Validation with Marshall and Hoare model: cooling curves. The time-temperature diagrams show the rectal cooling curve (in red), as well as the upper and lower boundary curve (both in blue) of the Marshall and Hoare (MH) model for a test scenario Mi (with i = 1, 2, 3, 4) and the finite element (FE)-generated model (FEM) curve (in yellow) for the same scenario Mi for comparison. The four scenarios M1 to M4 vary in ambient temperature T_A, body mass m and body length L. (a) Scenario M1: $T_A = 18°C$, m = 75 kg, L = 1.75 m. (b) Scenario M2: $T_A = 8°C$, m = 75 kg, L = 1.75 m. (c) Scenario M3: $T_A = 13°C$, m = 61 kg, L = 1.60 m. (d) Scenario M4: $T_A = 13°C$, m = 103 kg, L = 1.90 m.

Figure 6.57 shows the resulting FEM computed rectal cooling curves (yellow), the Marshall and Hoare model curve T(t) (red) and the lower and upper Marshall and Hoare boundary curve (blue) of the scenarios M1 to M4. The resulting FE curve T(t) approximates the Marshall and Hoare curve well in all cases. In all the scenarios, the lower and upper boundary curves are not crossed by the FEM curve. For times of up to 25 hours post mortem, the back calculation results can be seen to be of the order of magnitude of 1 hour or less.

Comparison with real body cooling

For real case validation of the FE model, cooling experiments were conducted in the Munich Institute of Legal Medicine by Gita Mall and Inga Sinicina in the years 2003 to 2007. The bodies of suddenly deceased persons whose times of death were well documented were transferred into a climate chamber in the institute where their cooling processes could be plotted by rectal and skin thermometers

in a chamber that held the air temperature at the constant level T_A measured and documented at the death scene. The experiments are described in Muggenthaler *et al.* [110]. For comparison, the rectal temperature curves measured in the chamber are represented together with the FEM-generated model curve.

To demonstrate FE model validation, we chose two cases of very similar body constitution from literature [109]. Case 1 was used to calibrate the FE model to the specific body constitution by changing the thickness of the subcutaneous fat layer of the torso, so that the simulation results matched the corresponding experimental rectal temperature curve for case 1. The calibration result is shown in Figure 6.58 (a), where the solid black line represents the measured data and the dashed line stands for the FEM-computed result. Although the result is very good – up to 45 hours post mortem (hpm) there are back calculation errors of order smaller than 2 hours only – one can notice local systematic deviations of the FEM-computed rectal temperature-time curve from the one yielded by

(a)

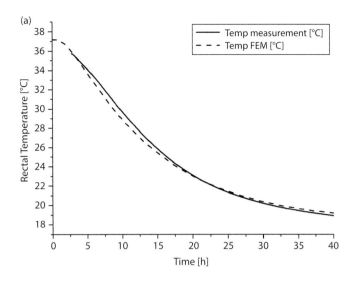

(b)

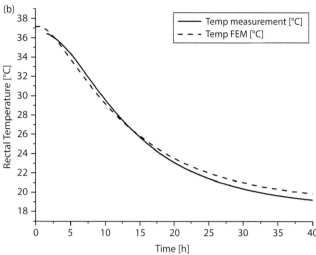

Figure 6.58 Calibration and validation on similar cases of experimental cooling. Time-temperature diagrams of two similar cooling cases. Case 1 is used to calibrate the finite element (FE) model by changing the thickness of the subcutaneous fat layer of the torso. The model was used unchanged for case 2 because both individuals had very similar body constitutions. The diagrams show the measured (drawn line) and the FE method (FEM)-computed (dashed line) rectal temperature-time curves. (a) Case 1: calibration. (b) Case 2: validation.

measurement. For example, the FE-generated curve lies consistently below the measured curve between 5 and 20 hours post mortem, a typical deviation that probably is caused by a structural model mismatch: The inner geometry and the material parameters of the FE model do not exactly represent the real cooling body. For validation purposes, the modified model was then scaled and adapted to the boundary conditions for case 2, and a simulation was performed without any further model modifications.

The environmental conditions of our validation cases (unclothed body, normal constitution, ambient temperature constant at about 18°C) are close to Henssge's standard conditions (see, e.g. [65]), which correspond to a corrective factor value $C = 1$. According to the experimental setup, the support was modelled as a flat steel basin representing the surface of the steel trolley used in the experimental measurements.

Case 1 was a male subject of 1.64 m body height and 64 kg body weight. He committed suicide in a bathtub by shooting himself immediately after announcing his suicide via telephone. This led to the discovery of the body only some minutes after death. The constant ambient temperature was 18°C, and the body lay in the bathtub in an approximately dorsal position. The time t_D between death and start of the rectal temperature measurement in the climatic chamber was $t_D = 2$ hours 44 minutes.

The male subject of case 2 died on a public staircase and was discovered immediately. He had a body height of 1.68 m, and his body weighed 65.3 kg. The ambient temperature was 18.7°C, and the time delay between death and the start of measurement was $t_D = 1$ hour 40 minutes.

Figure 6.58 (b) shows the temperature-time courses measured in the climatic chamber (solid lines) and calculated with the FE model (dashed lines). The curves in Figure 6.58

(b) represent the FE model validation. The FE simulation–derived cooling curve exhibits strong correlation with the corresponding experimental data. Nevertheless, the matching is poorer than in the calibration diagram Figure 6.58 (a), which had to be expected. Maximum back calculation error can be bounded to values smaller than 3 hours for times of up to 30 hours post mortem. As in the calibration diagram, the locally systematic deviations are noticeable, which have to be attributed to structural model mismatch.

■ Finite element error analysis

The field of FE error analysis can be split into three subfields. The first is *numerical stability* of the FE algorithm: Numerical stability is a necessary condition for the algorithm to produce reasonable results, but it does not guarantee the results to be correct. The second topic is errors in the input data caused by measurement (e.g. flaws in rectal temperature measurement value or deviations of the model geometry from the cooling scenario). Those errors are called here *input data error*. The last subject area comprises errors generated by the so-called *model error*, which is a lack of the model assumptions to match the real world conditions of the modelled scenario. This type of error may come from simplifying assumptions (e.g. the approximation of the convection constant to be independent of the actual surface temperature where the convection takes place). It is discussed earlier in the context of structural model mismatch. Frequently, this kind of error leads to a *systematic deviation* of the estimated value – the time of death – from the true value.

A problem arising from time integration step of FEM is the choice of appropriate time step widths Δt. Because computation time rises with diminishing time step size Δt, it would be convenient to have large step sizes. Conversely, approximation error and computational error grow with increasing step size. An analogous argument shows that very small mesh widths Δx are computationally unfeasible, although they yield better approximation results.

The numerical stability of the FEM depends on a condition (see, e.g. [156,177]) connecting the maximum allowed spatial mesh width Δx between two neighboring nodes of the same element to the maximum allowed time step size (Δt):

$$\Delta t \leq \frac{1}{4} \cdot \left(\frac{\lambda}{c \cdot \rho} \right) \cdot \Delta x^2 \qquad (6.66)$$

FE calculations regularly need tests of *convergence*. This means testing whether the result of the FE computations is independent of the mesh width and from the time step size. Convergence testing is usually done by doubling the element number for testing element size convergence by subdivision of elements and decreasing the maximum time step size. If those two operations lead to a calculated cooling curve that is identical – in sufficient approximation – to the cooling curve calculated with larger element size and larger time steps, the model is assumed to be convergent for practical purposes.

Investigating the input data error of a method means finding out the amount of change in the output data of the method caused by a given change in the input data. This is the classical form of the *error propagation problem*, which could be answered for FEM in principle by an approach derived using the Gaussian error propagation formula. This approach allows computing the input data error as the standard deviation of the estimated quantity – the time since death – as a function of the standard deviations of the input data. In case of FEM, the numerical computation of the partial derivations necessary for an actual evaluation is a practical problem.

The model error, which quantifies the models matching to the physics represented, requires comparison of the computation results with the real world measurements. Controlling the model error is usually called *validation*. It must be taken into account that the naïve comparison of computation and measurement results usually comprises both sorts of errors: the model error and the input data error. In case of the FE model, the validation step using the model of Marshall and Hoare (see earlier), as well as the real case validation (discussed earlier), combines both types of errors.

■ Application examples

The four typical cases of FEM application given here were taken from the paper by Mall *et al.* [96a]. These investigators

demonstrated the applicability of the FEM-based death time estimation in cases of non-standard conditions. Case A made it necessary to model an abrupt change of the body's position during cooling. For case B, an abrupt change in ambient temperature was modelled. In case C and in case D, clothing had to be modelled.

Case A

A 30-year-old woman was found dead in front of her apartment at 7:35 p.m. The body was fully clothed with a slip, brassiere, thin long-sleeved pullover of cotton-like material, jeans, nylon knee-high socks, ankle-high boots and an outdoor quilted anorak, which was open in front. The body was found in a ventral position and was turned to a dorsal position around 7:50 p.m. by the emergency doctor. The emergency doctor testified the death. The deep rectal temperature was measured at 12:00 p.m. with 29.7°C.

The environmental temperature at the same time was 16.6°C. The body height was 1.69 m. The body weighed 57.9 kg. The victim had last been seen alive at 3:30 p.m. Furthermore, the postmortem rigidity that had been broken at the crime scene in the left cubital joint had strongly recurred.

The standard FE model was scaled according to the actual body height (1.69 m) and mass (57.7 kg) by applying a scaling factor in z-direction and a different scaling factor in x- and y-directions. The standard thermal tissue properties were attributed to the tissue compartments. The clothing of the upper part of the body was modelled by a 2.5-mm-thick element layer with the thermal material properties of cotton to account for the cotton-like pullover. The quilted anorak was modelled on the back and around the arms with two element layers, the inner 30 mm thick with the thermal material properties of cellulosic insulation material and the outer 2.5 mm thick with the thermal material properties of polyester. The trousers were modelled by a 2.5-mm-thick element layer with the material properties of cotton and the bootees by a 5-mm-thick element layer with the material properties of leather. The standard initial temperature field with a temperature gradient of 37°C in the core and 27°C at the surfaces of the distal extremities was implemented. The nodes at the clothing surface were set to room temperature (20°C) because the victim had presumably been in her apartment before death. Natural convection and heat loss by thermal radiation were modelled. The initial amount of the internal energy production or the basal metabolic rate was converted to a heat flux density by division by the body volume and produced the standard initial heat flux density (1250 W/m³), which was distributed in the standard manner to the different compartments (750 W/m³ to the core, 225 W/m³ to the muscle, 212.5 W/m³ to the brain and 62.5 W/m³ to the skeletal system).

The standard internal power decrease rate was implemented. First, an FE analysis was performed, assuming a ventral position throughout cooling from death until the rectal temperature measurement produced a time since death of 7.5 hours. Then an analysis was performed, assuming a ventral position for 3 hours and then a dorsal position producing slightly longer times. The FE results would correspond to a time of death of around 4:15 p.m.

The perpetrator meanwhile confessed to have killed the victim between 4:00 and 4:30 p.m.

Case B

An 18-year-old man was found dead beside a street on a small asphalt path at 6:40 a.m. At 9:00 a.m. the deep rectal temperature was measured at 22.3°C. According to meteorological data from a nearby weather station, the air temperature was about 5°C during the night, the wind velocity (measured at a height of 10 m) was around 2 m/second and there was almost no rain. The victim had been last seen alive at 8:55 p.m. some 50 km away. A witness observed the perpetrator stopping the car, presumably to deposit the victim on the side of the street, at 11:00 p.m. The body was fully clothed with a thick woollen pullover, T-shirt, jeans, briefs, socks and shoes. The body had a length of 1.87 m and a mass of 68.3 kg.

The standard FE model was again scaled to the actual body length and body mass. The thick woollen pullover was realized by a 5-mm-thick element layer with the thermal properties of wool, the jeans by a 2.5-mm-thick element layer with the thermal properties of cotton and the shoes by a 5-mm-thick element layer with the thermal properties of leather. The standard initial temperature field with a maximum core to shell gradient from 37°C to 27°C was assumed. The standard initial energy production with the standard decrease rate was implemented. Then two different cooling phases were analyzed: the first phase during the transportation in the car and the second phase after deposition outside. In the first phase, room temperature (20°C) and natural convection were assumed. In the second phase, the outside temperature of 5°C and forced convection were assumed. The wind velocity was estimated with 0.25 m/second near the ground at the location where the body was found. According to formulae from the literature, convection coefficients between 4.5 W/(m²°C) and 6.1 W/(m²°C) were calculated. Alternative analyses were performed, with the first transportation phase lasting 1 or 2 hours. The assumption of a 1-hour transportation phase produced a total time since death of 11 hours, which would correspond to a time of death at 10:00 p.m. and deposition of the body at 11:00 p.m. The assumption of a 2-hour transportation phase produced a time since death of 11.5 hours, which would correspond to a time of death at 9:30 p.m. and deposition of the body at 11:30 p.m.

The perpetrator meanwhile confessed to have met the victim at 9:00 p.m. and killed him between 9:00 and 10:00 p.m. and deposited the victim at 11:00 p.m., corresponding to the observations of the witness.

Case C

A 49-year-old woman was found dead in her apartment at 8:45 a.m. The deep (insertion of the probe: 10 cm) rectal temperature was measured at 12:15 a.m. at 30.9°C. The environmental temperature was 23.5°C, and the ground temperature was 22.0°C. There was no sun or other irradiation. The body was fully clothed with a cotton pullover, undershirt, jeans, underpants, socks and shoes. The body height was 1.60 m, the body mass 48.7 kg.

The standard FE model was scaled to the actual body height and mass. The pullover was modelled by a 3-mm-thick element layer with the thermal properties of cotton, the jeans by a 2.5-mm-thick element layer with the thermal properties of cotton as well and the shoes by a 5-mm-thick element layer with the thermal properties of leather. The standard tissue properties, the standard initial temperature field and the standard internal energy production were implemented. Natural convection and radiation heat loss were modelled.

The development of the temperature fields over 12 hours was analyzed and evaluated at the node corresponding to the measurement site of the deep rectal temperature. A time since death of 8 hours was read from the model curve, which would correspond to a time of death around 4:15 a.m.

Investigations had meanwhile shown that the perpetrator was busy on the telephone till 4:00 a.m. and then went to the victim.

Case D

A 60-year-old man was found dead in his apartment at 6:00 p.m. The deep rectal temperature was measured at 10:00 p.m. at 27.1°C. The victim had been last seen alive at 8:20 p.m. the evening before. The body lay in a ventral position and was clothed with shirt, undershirt, trousers, underpants and socks. The underpants and trousers were dragged down below the buttocks. The ground (floor heating) was covered with a carpet. The room temperature was 25°C. The body height was 1.78 m, the body mass 83.3 kg.

The individually scaled standard FE model was complemented with a 2.5-mm-thick element layer for the clothing with the material properties of cotton. The standard tissue properties, the standard initial temperature field and the standard internal energy production were implemented. Natural convection and radiation heat loss were modelled.

The temperature fields were analyzed over 32 hours. A time since death of 25 hours could be read from the model curve, which would correspond to a time of death around 9:00 p.m. The perpetrators meanwhile confessed to have entered the apartment at 8:30 p.m.

6.3 The use of temperatures recorded from the external auditory canal for the estimation of the postmortem interval

■ *Guy Rutty*

Over the years, numerous authors have published research on the use of the external auditory canal (EAC) in both animals and humans for the recording of temperature to estimate a postmortem interval (PMI) [8–12,27,62,82,114,119,131,133–135]. This chapter part summarizes this published literature and draws on the doctorate work of Rutty [132], which remains to date the largest body of work on the use of the ear for the estimation of the PMI, to illustrate how a temperature recorded from the EAC can be used to estimate a PMI and the problems that may be encountered.

■ Anatomy of the external ear

Before considering how a temperature may be taken from the EAC or applied for the purpose of estimating the PMI, one should understand the anatomy of the ear and why, for example, in clinical medical practice, the taking of a temperature from the ear to record 'core' body temperature has become common practice in both the pre-hospital and the in-hospital environment.

The human ear is composed of three parts: the external ear, consisting of the auricle or pinna and the EAC; the middle ear or tympanic cavity; and the inner ear or labyrinth [142]. In this discussion, it is the external ear that needs to be considered further.

In terms of the embryology of the external ear, the auricle commences development at the sixth week of gestation, when a series of external 'hillocks' develops on the dorsal margins of the first and second branchial arches. Of these six mesenchymal thickenings, the majority of the auricle develops from the second branchial arch, with the tragus developing from the first arch. These structures fuse together, resulting in the individual variation in the shape of the final auricle. The auricle then shifts its position in relation to the developing mandible from a ventrocaudal to a dorsocranial position. This again accounts for malpositioned ears. The typical relief structure of the auricle then forms during the third to sixth month of development [140]. The EAC also develops from the dorsal portion of the first branchial arch. The primary external meatus forms in the eighth week as the first branchial pouch deepens towards the tympanic cavity. This forms the outer third of the canal, which is initially separated from the first pharyngeal

pouch, from which the tympanic cavity arises, by a pad of mesoderm. This remains in place up to the 21st week. The plug is then hollowed out, and the inner cells degenerate. By the seventh month, the canal is completely formed. The residual medial cells of the epithelial plug become the outer layer of the tympanic membrane [85].

The auricle or pinna is an external elastic cartilaginous structure, covered by skin, which serves to collect air vibrations for the purpose of hearing. It is composed of the following parts: the outer ridge or helix, the inner ridge or antihelix, the inferior lobule, the tragus and the concha. In addition to these main landmarks are a number of other anatomically defined points. The skin of the auricle turns inward into the EAC. The outer part of the canal is elastic cartilage with the inner part composed of bone of the tympanic plate. The canal serves to conduct sound waves to the tympanic membrane. Although the tympanic membrane and the contents of the middle ear are of adult size at birth, the EAC continues to develop up to about the age of 9 years. Initially, the canal is straight, with the tympanic membrane in a horizontal position. Over the next 9 years, the characteristic 'S' shape of the canal develops, and the membrane becomes oriented at approximately a 45-degree angle to the horizontal plane (Figure 6.59). These bends divide the EAC arbitrarily into three sections, the first and second being the cartilaginous sections and the third the bony section [76]. In an adult, the canal is approximately 2.5 cm long (the anteroinferior wall is longer, at 3.1 cm), tapering towards the tympanic membrane where the diameter is narrowest, at approximately 0.5 cm. The volume of the EAC, in the adult, is approximately 0.85 ml.

The external and middle parts of the ear are separated by the tympanic membrane. The membrane is composed of three layers: an outer layer of squamous epithelium, a middle layer of fibrous tissue and an inner layer of columnar epithelium. The membrane is roughly circular, approximately 0.074 mm thick, 1.0 cm high and 0.8 cm wide. In the adult it is oriented obliquely, facing downward, forward and laterally at approximately a 45-degree angle to the floor of the canal. The handle of the malleus (bone of the middle ear) is attached to the inner surface. The blood supply to the external surface of the membrane is from the deep auricular artery. The internal surface receives blood from the stylomastoid branch of the posterior auricular artery and from the tympanic branch of the maxillary artery. Venous drainage is to the external jugular vein, the transverse sinus and the veins of the dura mater.

■ Human thermoregulation

Humans are mammals and homeotherms: by this one means that, under a number of conditions, humans are able to maintain a normal, steady-state temperature. This is achieved by the central regulation of body temperature

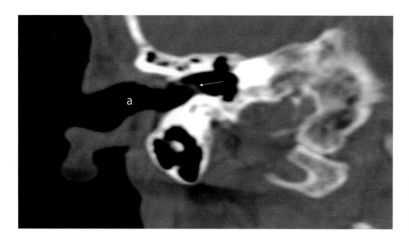

Figure 6.59 Computed tomography scan showing the typical 'S' shape of an adult external auditory canal (a) with the tympanic membrane at an approximate 45-degree angle to the floor of the canal (arrow).

mediated through receptors located within the hypothalamus. Humans maintain their temperature within a range with the internal 'thermostat' set between 36.9°C and 37.1°C, which in turn regulates core temperature between 35.5°C and 37.5°C [14]. Humans have a 'core temperature' (i.e. the temperature within the body). This is different from the 'shell temperature', which is the temperature of the skin and underlying subcutaneous tissue [158].

Body temperature is maintained by balancing heat production against heat loss. The temperature-regulating area of the body is found in the pre-optic area of the hypothalamus. This area has input from the temperature receptors of the skin and mucous membranes, as well as the internal central thermoreceptors of the hypothalamus. When the temperature of the blood increases, it causes peripheral vasodilation, perspiration and decreased metabolism. In contrast, if the blood temperature falls, then vasoconstriction, shivering and an increase in the metabolic rate occur.

The central parts of the body are kept at 'core temperature', which is regulated by gaining or losing heat from the outer aspects. However, as noted earlier, humans are not only homeotherms but also rhythmic creatures. By this one means that our body temperature follows a circadian rhythm (i.e. it fluctuates up and down during the 24-hour day [115]). This raises the questions of what do we mean by a 'core temperature' and what should it be?

Humans are usually considered to have an average body temperature of 37°C (98.6°F); this value is credited to Wunderlich, who claimed to have analyzed 1 million axillary temperatures from 25 000 patients [172]. Wunderlich is also credited with indicating that there is a potential range of core temperature and that the body temperature is at its lowest between 02:00 and 08:00 hours and at its peak between 16:00 and 19:00 hours (i.e. the circadian rhythm) [95]. In addition to this diurnal variation, the core temperature is said to be higher in blacks than in whites, and in girls and women compared with boys and men, in part attributed to the menstrual cycle. The core temperature is affected by one's environment and by the clothes one

is wearing [83,92,141]. The temperature is different when one is resting and asleep compared with during exercise, when the temperature may be up to 1°C higher than the resting temperature [167]. It can also be affected by the use of drugs including alcohol and caffeine, bright light and atmospheric pressure [123,149,151,170]. These observations are important if using a 'core temperature' within a PMI calculation. Because most PMI algorithms are based on a starting temperature of 37°C, if this is not the case, then the result of the calculation will be incorrect.

■ Ear thermometry

Although Benzinger and Taylor [17] are cited in almost all publications on the recording of temperatures from the EAC as the original authors who drew attention to the ability to record body core temperature from the EAC, it was in fact Williams and Thompson who had first described a device to measure body temperature from the EAC [169]. They described the use of a Western Electric V611 thermistor, which was incorporated into a plastic ear mould, moulded to the contour of the EAC so that it was insulated from the environmental temperature, to record the temperature of the EAC in one patient, in one ear during the night. The temperatures obtained were approximately 0.25°C lower than simultaneous readings taken from the sublingual region. This temperature is within the range reported in more recent publications, which report that the EAC temperature may be between 0.06°C and 0.74°C lower than the sublingual temperature [164].

The reason that Benzinger is credited with the first reporting of core temperatures from the EAC, and not Williams and later Carlson, is because these two previous authors had measured the temperature of the ear canal and not the tympanic membrane. The 1963 paper by Benzinger and Taylor [17] described how three different types of fixation method were used to apply a thermocouple to the tympanic membrane. The temperatures were then recorded and compared with those from the anterior ethmoid sinus, anterior wall of the sphenoid sinus and Rosenmüller's fossa. The hypothesis was put forward that, because the tympanic membrane receives the same blood supply from the internal carotid artery, which then goes on to supply the hypothalamus, which in turn regulates core temperature, the tympanic temperature is a more accurate representation of core temperature than are other sites, specifically the rectum, a hypothesis reiterated by Benzinger in 1969 [16]. Benzinger reported that the tympanic temperature was approximately 1.5°C lower than the rectal temperature but was easy to obtain, was reproducible and showed consistent patterns of response to external warming or cooling.

These types of contact probes were used in clinical practice into the 1970s, although patient discomfort and complications such as perforation of the tympanic membrane restricted their use [161]. During the 1980s, the design of the probe was altered. Work originally undertaken by the US National Aeronautics and Space Administration aerospace program studies of the EAC as a potential site of temperature measurement in astronauts was incorporated into civilian medical applications such that by 1991 at least six makes of the new so-called 'infrared tympanic thermometers' (ITTs) were available on the market [7,44].

■ Clinical infrared thermometry

Infrared thermometry uses the 'black box' principle in which for each wavelength the maximum amount of radiation depends only on the temperature of the emitter (the 'black box') and is a precise value [38]. The emissivity of a surface is the ratio of emitted radiation to radiation emitted by a black box at the same temperature. Thus, if you know the emissivity geometry and the spectrum of radiation, it is possible to derive the temperature of a surface. In the case of infrared thermometry, the wavelengths are 0.7 to 20 µm. Following this principle, the ITT uses a thermopile to detect infrared emissions from the tympanic membrane and then calculates the body temperature as a function of the intensity of the infrared radiation detected.

The first commercially available ITT was produced in 1986 by Intelligent Medical Systems (Carlsbad, California) and was aptly named the FirstTemp thermometer [18]. This first design comprised a hand-held probe attached by a cable to a desktop unit containing a calibration system, microprocessor, A-D converter, power supply, display and a charger. The probe was covered by a disposable tip/cover and was inserted into the ear canal, where it detected the temperature over a 1- to 2-second interval. Built-in offsets allowed for the estimation of oral, rectal or core temperature. The device was expensive and heavy, and it consumed a lot of power, although it became popular, especially within the paediatric community. It was replaced in 1991 by the Genius infrared thermometer (Genius IT).

Modern day ITTs share a similar design structure with the Genius IT. They consist of an otoscope-like probe tip covered by a disposable polyethylene speculum cover, a probe handle housing the infrared sensor, a microprocessor and a calibration mechanism. The temperature is displayed usually via an integral liquid crystal display in either centigrade or Fahrenheit. The probe is inserted into the EAC, and the scan button is depressed. The emitted radiation is sensed over a 1- to 2-second period, and then the temperature is displayed. These thermometers are quick to use and have a reduced risk of cross-patient infection compared with other types of thermometers [25]. Before commercial use, the Genius IT was calibrated against the National Physical Laboratory–calibrated mercury-in-glass thermometer scaled to 0.1°C. It was designed to give rapid temperature readings in an operating range of 27.5°C to 40°C.

Problems with clinical infrared thermometry readings

Following the introduction of infrared thermometry into clinical practice, several publications compared different makes of ITs, and it began to become apparent that there may be potential problems related to the accuracy of the readings with these types of thermometers [77,105,112]. The first problem lay in the name of the thermometer itself. Although these ITs were originally called infrared 'tympanic' thermometers, it soon became apparent that because of the probe's wide view of the EAC, the thermometers were reading heat radiated from the skin of the wall of the EAC as well as that of the tympanic membrane. Given that it was considered that a heat gradient existed within the EAC, this would lead to the potential underestimation of the temperature if the probe was not fully inserted or directed towards the tympanic membrane [45]. Thus, although the most accurate reading is obtained if the probe is aimed at the anterior inferior aspect of the tympanic membrane, in light of the realization of the source of the majority of the radiation, in the latter 1990s the term 'tympanic' was dropped, and the name was changed to 'infrared thermometers' (ITs) [154].

The next problem concerned the choice of ear from which to take the reading. Although not statistically significant, there can be a temperature difference of up to 0.47°C between the left and right EAC [54]. In a normothermic child or adult, this temperature difference does not matter, but it becomes important during the assessment of febrile illness, in which this small difference could lead either to the diagnosis being missed or to its being overdiagnosed.

It then became questioned whether or not the temperature of the EAC represents core temperature because it was found that there could be up to a 1.2°C difference between the EAC temperature reading and readings at other conventional sites such as the rectum, bladder, oesophagus, pulmonary artery, axilla and sublingual areas [15,22,33,39, 40,46,73,87,106,124,127,163,175].

Finally, it was considered whether or not local and systemic variables influenced the temperature readings. The probe itself is of a rigid, non-variable design, whereas the human EAC changes in size and shape with the age of the subject. The EAC of the neonate is small and straight, whereas that of the adult is longer and curved. Hence it was found that errors in temperature recording could occur when the thermometers were used with neonates, compared with infants and compared with adults [113,126,152].

Because the probe must be inserted such that the sensor looks at the tympanic membrane, operator training becomes important [116,153]. A more accurate temperature reading may be achieved with the use of the ear tug [118,159]. The probe itself is at a lower temperature than the inside of the EAC. This can lead to a lowering of the temperature in the EAC when the probe is inserted and can cause the formation of water droplets on the probe window, which can again alter the temperature reading [86].

Any obstruction present within the EAC could affect the ability of the sensor to see the tympanic membrane. Hair does have an effect on the temperature, as does impacted wax (cerumen), but non-impacted wax is said to have no effect on infrared radiation detection within the EAC [36,43,125,173]. Local infection, particularly otitis media, does not appear to have a significant effect on the readings, although if the tympanic membrane is bulging because of the presence of fluid or middle ear infection, this may alter the readings [79,84,117,150]. The application of local cream or removal of grommets has no effect, but local scarring, as a result of alteration in local blood flow, can change temperature readings [26,157]. An episode of vertigo causes the temperature to rise [107].

The next variables to be considered are the effect of the environmental ambient temperature and the effect of wind on the face. It has been shown that a rise in environmental ambient temperature from 18°C to 35°C results in falsely high temperature readings from the EAC [29,55,56,176]. These false readings have been reported by other authors, who also draw our attention to the observation that a lower ambient temperature does not significantly affect the EAC temperature reading [144]. Kahyaoglu et al. [81] considered that this could be caused by an effect on the ear lobe and an alteration of blood flow through it. In a series of experiments observing the effects of crying on the EAC, these investigators found that the auricle would go red during an episode of crying as a result of increased blood flow, but the temperature within the EAC remained unaltered [81]. The other potential environmental variable is that of the effect of hot and cold wind on the face. Sato et al. [136] reported that if the face and neck were warmed or cooled by hot or cold wind, there was no alteration in the EAC temperature, although this finding was disputed by Thomas et al. [155],

who found that if one fanned air onto the face, there was a fall in EAC temperature.

Remaining with variables within the head and neck area, if one consumes a hot or cold drink or smokes a cigarette, then this will result in an alteration of the oral temperature [168]. However, EAC temperature has not been reported to date to be influenced by these potential variables [130].

Many publications report the effect of hypothermia or hyperthermia and exercise on the temperature within the EAC [52,53,148,162,174]. These reports have shown that, in the case of hypothermia, the EAC temperature remains stable and can be used to take a temperature reading. However, in hyperthermia and during periods of exercise, the rectal temperature rises but the EAC temperature does not follow this rise and can thus yield a falsely low result. This phenomenon is thought to be caused by the local physiological effect known as selective countercurrent cooling of the brain. As core temperature rises, the body reacts by keeping the brain cool.

Finally there are miscellaneous reports touching on the temperature in the EAC. In patients with meningitis, the EAC temperature has been reported to be higher than the expected core temperature. In persons with a spinal cord injury where the afferent input to the hypothalamus may be altered, this may in turn affect the efferent messages for shivering, sweating and vasoconstriction and may alter both core temperature and EAC temperature [31]. The sex and age of the individual may have an influence because it has been reported that children and women have higher resting EAC temperatures than do men [30]. The natural circadian rhythm of body temperature results in the EAC temperature at its lowest at approximately 02:00 hours, with a steady rise throughout the day until 18:00 hours, when it drops down through the evening to its lowest point at 02:00 hours again [30]. Sato et al. [136] also noted that foot bathing altered the temperature recording from the EAC. Wright et al. [171] used the ability of the IT to record local temperatures to record the temperature of intravenous fluid bags and found that they could be used as long as the temperature remained under 40°C [98].

■ Early human cadaveric experimental data

As far as the author can ascertain, the first proposal for the use of temperatures recorded from the EAC to estimate a PMI was made by Baccino et al. [11] at a meeting in Paris in 1991. Although referenced in the group's later paper, to the author's knowledge this meeting presentation is not accessible within the published literature (personal communication, 2014). The first published reference to the use of the EAC for estimation of a PMI is in the 1991 edition of Knight's *Forensic Pathology* [89]. In this edition, it was suggested that the ear can be used as an alternative site for recording a temperature for estimating the PMI [89]. However, this suggestion was unreferenced.

In 1992, Nokes *et al.* [114] were the first to publish in the peer-reviewed literature research concerning the use of the outer ear as a means of determining the postmortem period in human corpses. Five cadavers on entering the mortuary were stripped, weighed and measured. In each case a calibrated thermocouple was inserted into the EAC to a point just in front of the tympanic membrane, and the temperature was measured every 15 minutes for a constant period of time. The resulting cooling curves showed a consistently shaped cooling curve without an initial plateau (Figure 6.60).

From these curves, Nokes *et al.* [114] developed the following formula:

$$t1 = \frac{\left(ln\theta_0 - ln\theta_1\right)\Delta t}{\left(ln\theta_1 - ln\theta_2\right)}$$

where $\Delta t = t_2 - t_1$.

In this logarithmic equation, $(ln)\theta_0$ is the original temperature of the outer ear at the time of death, and t_1 and t_2 are arbitrary times after death.

During this work, these investigators realized that the outer ear temperature in life cannot be assumed to be 37°C. Through readings taken from five healthy living volunteers, Nokes *et al.* [114] reported that the outer ear temperature in life ranged between 35°C and 36°C, which led them to adopt 35.5°C as the temperature at death for their calculations. However, in doing this, they observed errors between the actual and estimated PMI and considered this

assumption to be a major source of error in their calculations. They also questioned whether or not a single exponential equation could be applied to the calculation with knowledge of the temperature plateau effect known to affect calculations derived from the rectum. Having raised this question, they considered it highly unlikely that such a plateau existed with the ear. These investigators also questioned the possibility of environmental factors influencing the temperature. In view of their observations, they concluded that the errors present in their experiments rendered the ear an unsuitable site for temperature-based PMI calculations.

Despite the suggestion of Nokes *et al.* [114] regarding the unsuitability of the EAC as a temperature recording site, this did not deter future researchers.

■ Animal cadaveric experimental data

Two research groups now appear to have arisen, each working independently of each other. The first group was in France and was led by Baccino, the second was in the United Kingdom and was led by Rutty. Baccino's early work was focussed on humans but evolved using an animal model, as discussed later. Rutty, conversely, initially revisited the work of Nokes *et al.* using an animal model. Starting in 1994 and presenting the first data on the use of ITTs for recording temperatures from the EAC in the postmortem period in 1996 [135], this work formed the basis of Rutty's doctoral studies.

Working with the UK Ministry of Defence, Veterinary and Remount Services, Rutty was permitted access to five British Army male German shepherd dogs who were euthanized for veterinary reasons. Following the administration of intravenous sodium pentobarbitone, each deceased animal was immediately transported to a secure room on the Ministry of Defence base and was placed on an examination table (i.e. no significant time elapsed between death and transportation of the body). The temperature within the room was essentially the same as the outside ambient temperature and was subject to ambient temperature variation. In each dog the following were recorded: ambient room temperature using the thermocouple; wind speed over the body using a digital anemometer; rectal temperature using the thermocouple; and right external ear canal temperatures using a First Temp Genius Tympanic Thermometer (Sherwood Medical) and an Ototemp Veterinary Infrared Tympanic Temperature Scanner (Henry Schein Rexodent, London), as well as the thermocouple (i.e. three readings per time period). Only one reading was taken from each site with each thermometer at each time period. Readings were taken hourly for the first 6 hours and every two hours from 6 to 12 hours, and then in two cases readings were taken from the EAC only at 22 and 24 hours.

From this work, and similar to the work of Nokes *et al.* [114], a postmortem temperature plateau was not

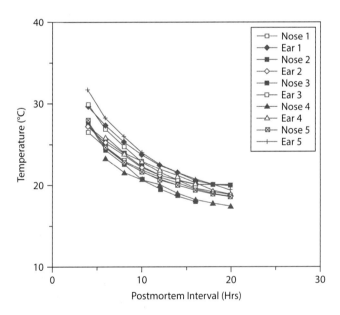

Figure 6.60 Postmortem cooling curves for five corpses with the nose and ear used as temperature measurement sites. (From Nokes LDM, Flint T, Jaafar S, Knight BH. The use of either the nose or outer ear as a means of determining the post-mortem period of a human corpse. *Forensic Sci Int* 1992;**54**:153–158.)

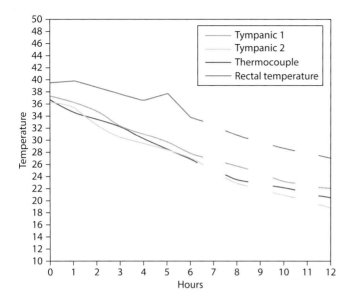

Figure 6.61 External auditory canal and rectal temperature (°C) for time (hours) for a dog. (From Rutty GN. *The Use of Temperatures Recorded From the External Auditory Canal in the Estimation of the Time Since Death.* Sheffield, University of Sheffield, medical doctorate thesis, 2001, as modified in Rutty GN. The estimation of the time since death using temperatures recoded from the external auditory canal. Part I. Can a temperature be recorded and interpreted from this site? *Forensic Sci Med Pathol* 2005;**1**:41–51.)

observed in the temperature recorded from the dogs' ears (Figure 6.61). The starting and subsequent ear temperatures were shown to be consistently lower than the rectal temperatures, an observation reported both in animals [111] and in humans (see earlier).

When the ear temperatures were applied to the rule of thumb algorithm (see part 6.1 of this chapter), the PMI was overestimated in every case. However, one has to take into account the difference between the ear and the rectal temperatures at any given time. Thus, the rule of thumb was modified to take account of these differences, first by using the difference between the two readings for each individual case and then by using a constant derived from the mean temperature difference between the rectal and ear temperatures for all dogs at all time periods.

$$\text{PMI} = (\text{EAC } t0 \text{ °C}) - (\text{EAC } t1 \text{ °C} + C) + 3$$

where $t0$ is the temperature at the time of death, $t1$ is the temperature at a time period after death and C is the constant derived from the mean difference between the rectal and EAC temperatures during the postmortem period.

The subsequent calculation still overestimated the PMI, although the time generated was closer to the known actual time. The ear temperatures were then applied in an unmodified manner to the other published algorithms. By using this data set, the best results, either on their own or as a range, were obtained from both Henssge nomograms, especially the nomogram for the brain [68].

This early animal work supported the earlier observations of Nokes *et al.* [114] with regard to the temperature plateau. Unlike the work of Nokes *et al.*, however, it suggested that it could be possible to apply temperatures recorded from the ear to previously published PMI methods, but the operator had to take into account the difference between the rectal and ear temperatures at death that would affect calculations using methods designed for use with rectal temperatures.

In 2007, Baccino *et al.* [9] published work on the cooling rates of pig heads submerged in water. These investigators undertook two sets of experiments. The first was designed to consider whether the isolated pig head ear and brain temperatures behaved after death in a similar manner to those of the intact pig cadaver, and, having concluded that they did, these investigators then used nine pairs of isolated pig heads in air and water in temperatures ranging from 0°C to 20°C to study ear and brain temperatures. From this work, these investigators supported Rutty's doctorate observations in humans that the head was less affected by variables [135] than other temperature recording sites, further suggesting it to be a more reliable body region for PMI estimation. Baccino *et al.* also supported the previous work of Henssge reporting that cooling rates in water were quicker than those in air and also showed in pigs that tympanic cooling is almost equal to cerebral cooling, although these workers pointed out that this finding cannot be extrapolated to humans because of differences in pig ear anatomy and brain size.

In 2009, Proctor *et al.* [119] published their observations of postmortem cooling curves in 16 dogs with recordings made using temperature probes and a data logger. Aural temperatures were recorded using a probe inserted 4 cm into the EAC for 32 hours in still air. The temperature graph for all dogs is shown in Figure 6.62. Similar to others' work, Proctor *et al.* observed that the temperature in the EAC was lower than that of the rectum. Within the paper's discussion, the first three paragraphs appeared to convey the authors' confusion about why this observation occurred. Although these investigators suggested a number of reasons for this occurrence, they did not make reference to the previous published work of Rutty [133,135], who observed the same phenomenon in his canine research. They did, however appear to realize the lack of a plateau stage of EAC cooling, as observed by previous authors.

■ Human cadaveric experimental data

In 1993, Baccino *et al.* [12] made a presentation at the Dusseldorf meeting of the International Association of Forensic Sciences on temperatures from the outer ear and time of death. Like Nokes *et al.* earlier and Rutty later, they reported that temperatures from the EAC did not show a postmortem plateau. Unlike Nokes *et al.*, however, Baccino *et al.* [12] reported that the use of a single temperature

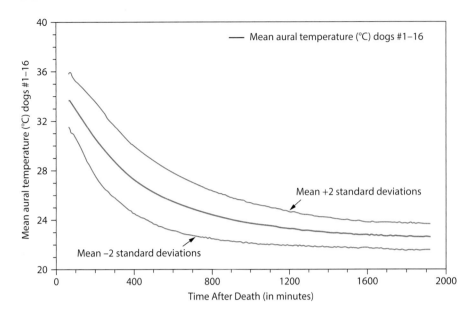

Figure 6.62 Data logger mean aural temperature readings (°C) for all dogs every 5 minutes (n = 16). (From Proctor KW, Kelch WJ, New JC. Estimating the time of death in domestic canines. *J Forensic Sci* 2009;**54**:1433–1437.)

reading from the EAC showed a higher correlation with the actual PMI than with a single temperature measurement from the liver.

In 1996, Baccino *et al.* [10] published the first substantive research on the use of the outer ear temperature to estimate a time since death; these investigators had presented the data at the 1994 American Academy of Forensic Sciences meeting in San Antonio, Texas. Using a research cohort of 138 hospital deaths with known times of death, transported to the mortuary within 60 to 180 minutes of death, and by using a thermistor thermometer, these investigators measured the temperature in the rectum and in both EACs during an actual postmortem period of 60 to 1115 minutes. The corpses were divided into 4 groups, with group 1 stored at 0°C to 5°C, group 2 stored between 6°C and 10°C, group 3 stored from 11°C and 15°C and group 4 stored between 16°C and 23°C. The temperatures recorded were applied to both multivariate and linear regression formulae, the latter of which provided an 'interval' formula:

$$\text{PMI (min)} = A \, (37°C - OE \, T°) + B$$

where *OE* is the temperature in the EAC. Baccino *et al.* reported that because they were not able to maintain the corpses at temperatures higher than 23°C to avoid decomposition, the formula required modification to take this into account. It was thus modified to:

$$\text{PMI (min)} = A \, OE \, T° + B \text{ ambient } T° + C$$

with the correlation coefficient of 0.9 and a standard deviation of 127 minutes. This was named the 'global' equation for EAC temperatures.

For the research cohort (138 corpses) Baccino *et al.* reported that the correlation coefficient (r) values for the EAC method always provided better correlation with the

time of death no matter what the ambient temperature was compared with the rectal temperature or other methods investigated in their paper (Table 6.25). These investigators observed that the estimated PMI calculated from EAC temperatures differed from the actual by less than 1 hour in 77 per cent of cases when using the EAC temperature alone and in 93 per cent of cases when using the multivariate equation.

In a letter to the editor following publication, Rutty [131] supported the work of Baccino *et al.* but drew to their attention other variables that may influence temperatures from the EAC and concluded with recommending caution, at this time, in obtaining and interpreting temperatures recorded from this site. Their response to this letter [8] addressed these concerns and also those of Henssge [62], who criticized the 'interval' and 'global' formulae for using constants that were not defined and thus could not be known to others. Baccino, in his response, informed us that the reason that this was done was that there were commercial obligations related to those formulae for a prototype thermometer described at the end of the original paper. He did, however, provide an exampled formula for an ambient temperature range of 16°C to 23°C, which had been presented at a meeting in France:

$$\text{PMI (min)} = 56.44 \, [37°C - OE \, T°C] - 150$$

$$66\% \text{ confidence interval} = \pm 25\%$$

$$95\% \text{ confidence interval} = \pm 40\%$$

Following this work, between 1996 and 1999 Rutty collected scene and ambient temperature and humidity data, as well as serial ambient, EAC and rectal temperatures every 15 minutes from 600 human cadavers in the supine position. The ambient room temperature, the temperature

Table 6.25 Research sample: results of linear regression analysis of relationship between actual and estimated postmortem interval using six methods*

Methods		Ambient temperature intervals			
		0–5°C (n = 34)	6–10°C (n = 34)	11–15°C (n = 33)	16–23°C (n = 37)
Outer ear temperature	r	0.88	0.95	0.76	0.73
	SD (min)	190	18	113	52
Rectal temperature	r	0.82	0.84	0.65	0.28
	SD	37	31	105	123
Vitreous K$^+$	r	0.73 (NS)	0.68	0.58	0.40
	SD	224	117	184	108
CSF K$^+$	r	0.76 (NS)	0.51 (NS)	0.38 (NS)	0.74
	SD	198	166	190	29
Plasma log Na$^+$/K$^+$	r	0.63	0.46	−0.12 (NS)	−0.55
	SD	257	297	11	42
Plasma log Cl$^-$	r	0.44 (NS)	−0.03 (NS)	−0.0027 (NS)	0.004 (NS)
	SD	299	249	190	132

* Rule of thumb 1: postmortem interval (h) = (rectal temperature at time of death [°F] – rectal temperature at T1 [°F])/1.5; rule of thumb 2: postmortem interval (h) = (rectal temperature at time of death [°C] – rectal temperature at T1 [°C]) + 3.

Cl$^-$, chloride; CSF, cerebrospinal fluid; K$^+$, potassium; Na$^+$, sodium; NS, not significant; r, correlation coefficient; SD, standard deviation.

From Baccino E, De Saint Martin L, Schuliar Y, Guilloteau P, Le Rhun M, Morin JF, Leglise D, Amice J. Outer ear temperature and time of death. *Forensic Sci Int* 1996;**83**:133–146.

within both EACs and the rectal temperature were recorded over a minimal period of 60 minutes (maximum, 225 minutes) by using a logging thermometer (HI 92840C logging thermometer, Hanna Instruments, Leighton Buzzard) with an APK1 air probe for each EAC and an LPK1 general probe for the rectum and ambient temperature (supplier: Hanna Instruments). It was found that there was no statistical difference between the temperatures recorded from either EAC with the body in the supine position. The second observation was that the rectal temperature was always found to be higher than that of the EAC (Figure 6.63). The EAC was also found to cool at a rate of approximately 0.5°C per hour, whereas the rectum cooled by 0.7°C per hour.

The time of death was known in 127 of cases because the death had been witnessed by either a relative/spouse or by a member of the general public. The following methods were used to estimate a PMI using an EAC temperature: rule of thumb, Henssge nomogram for the rectum [60], Henssge nomogram for the brain [68], Al-Alousi temperature ratio method [1] and the method of De Saram [35]. The rule of thumb overestimated the PMI using both rectal and EAC temperatures. This was more pronounced with the EAC temperatures. If a constant derived from the difference between the rectal and EAC temperatures was added to the equation, then the value approached, but still overestimated, the actual PMI. When EAC temperatures were applied to the Henssge nomograms, the rectal nomogram significantly overestimated the time, whereas the brain nomogram reduced this overestimation. When the Al-Alousi algorithm was used, the rectal values underestimated the time since death, whereas the

EAC overestimated them again, and in the case of the algorithm of De Saram both the EAC and rectal values underestimated the PMI [132].

Although the general observations made by Rutty were similar to those made by Baccino and others with regard to the use of EAC temperatures and previously published formulae, Rutty identified that the use of the K probes used with the logging thermometer may have caused a number of problems. First, although the EAC probes were chosen specifically because of their perforated ends, which recorded the temperature only within this area of the probe, the shafts were made of metal. Thus, when they were inserted into the EAC, they were at room ambient temperature and required a period of stabilization. He postulated that this may have resulted in heat exchange between the EAC and the metal of the probe. The perforations of the probes were observed to become clogged with wax and required regular cleaning, which was difficult to perform. Finally, the placement of the probes was dependent on the skill of the operator, and thus it was possible that some probes were not fully inserted into the EAC.

Chronologically, the next group to visit the concept of using the EAC for estimating the PMI was that of Kanawaku *et al.* [82] from Japan. This group used a computer simulation to analyze the cooling pattern of the EAC in a body placed in a nearly constant environment. Using computed tomography images from a single head, these investigators built a three-dimensional human head model. Thermophysical properties, initial condition and boundary condition were all postulated and calculations made based on an unsteady heat transfer equation using

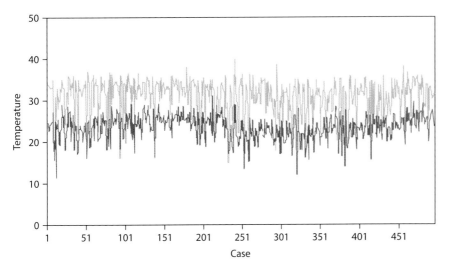

Figure 6.63 A plot of the rectal (green) and mean external auditory canal (red) temperatures (°C) for all cases. (From Rutty GN. *The Use of Temperatures Recorded From the External Auditory Canal in the Estimation of the Time Since Death.* Sheffield, University of Sheffield, medical doctorate thesis, 2001, as modified in Rutty GN. The estimation of the time since death using temperatures recoded from the external auditory canal. Part I. Can a temperature be recorded and interpreted from this site? *Forensic Sci Med Pathol* 2005;**1**:41–51.)

a finite element method to solve the equation. The cooling process was calculated for a 13-hour period. To verify the model, they continuously recorded temperatures from a single case using a temperature data logger and sensor over a 17-hour period. Again, this group observed in the test subject that EAC cooling followed a single exponential curve. In terms of the computer simulation, it was observed that at a heat transmission coefficient of 6 W/m²°C, the simulation cooling curve nearly overlapped that of the case study (Figure 6.64). These workers concluded that measuring a temperature from the EAC at a scene of death was easy and that, assuming the body was relatively fresh, a useful result could be expected to be generated for the estimation of the PMI.

Finally, in 2009 Cattaneo *et al.* [27] revisited the work of Rutty to consider whether an ITT could be used to record temperatures from the EAC of cadavers. Recording multiple EAC temperatures from 25 cadavers at set intervals between 10 and 20 hours following arrival at the mortuary with 2 different types of commercially available ITs, these investigators confirmed the previous work of Rutty that cadaveric EAC temperatures could be recorded with such devices and that the ear temperatures in both ears were similar when recorded with the 2 devices (i.e. in a supine body, the side from which the EAC temperature is recorded is not significant).

■ Variables that could influence a postmortem interval calculation

Several concerns have been raised over the years by researchers about possible influences over temperatures recorded from the EAC, both clinically (see earlier) and in cadavers. Baccino *et al.* [10] suggested that in the presence of otorrhagia or if the body is lying on its side with one ear in close contact with a surface, then an EAC temperature should not be recorded. Further concerns were raised

by Rutty [131] in his letter on Baccino's work. Cattaneo *et al.* [27] were concerned over the influence that blood or perforation of the tympanic membrane may have if a probe, rather than an infrared device, was used. Finally, Kanawaku *et al.* [82] questioned whether the length of hair on the scalp may have an influence on head cooling, although Henssge had previously advised, in terms of postmortem brain temperature, that the estimated time of death did not become significantly more accurate even if the amount of hair was considered.

In the series of 600 cadavers studied by Rutty, he considered the role of a number of possible variables on EAC temperatures on 2 data sets: 499 cadavers where the wind speed was below the level of detection for the anemometer and 127 cases where the time of death was known. The variables assessed for both groups were gender, body weight, body length, absence or presence of clothing, whether the body was covered or not at the scene, whether the body was wet or dry, environmental humidity at the scene and mortuary, body position at the scene, head position at the scene and wind speed over the body. For 100 random cadavers, Rutty also assessed the distribution of head hair, the estimated length of the hair, the head circumference, the ear pinna and lobe morphology, ear index [41], skull bone thickness [128,129] and brain weight. For 99 cases, the length of each EAC was measured. For a further 70 cases, the EAC measurements were derived from clinical computed tomography scans. The degree of atheroma within the right and left common carotid arteries below and at the bifurcation, as well as to the internal and external carotid arteries immediately above the bifurcation, were assessed in 103 paired vessels. Finally, a small data set considering the effect of body activity, position and drinking of hot fluids was assessed on living volunteers [132,134].

The results for the 499 and 127 data sets identified 3 variables that could have an influence on the temperature from the EAC. Within the 127 data sample, the wearing of

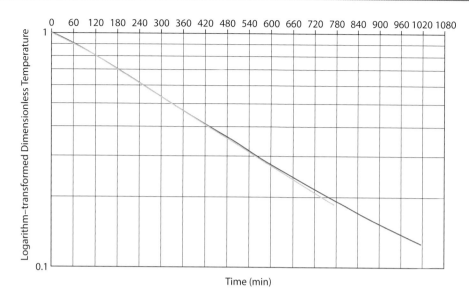

Figure 6.64 Logarithm-transformed curves for the case subject and the model. Red dotted line, simulation case; Blue dotted line, measured case. (From Baccino E, Guilloteau P, Le Moigne E, Schuliar Y. Postmortem delay determination: interest of the outer ear temperature. Paper presented at the 13th International Association of Forensic Sciences meeting, Dusseldorf, Germany, 1993.)

a dress, the humidity of the mortuary and whether a body was found indoors or outside were identified as statistical influences, but because they were not found to be so in the larger data set they were dismissed. However, in the 499 cases, the only significant variable that was found potentially to influence the EAC temperature was the position of the body at the scene. The cadavers were categorized into those lying on their back, front, right side or left side. Unlike the suggestion made earlier by Baccino *et al.*, there was no significant difference between the temperature within the right and left EAC for body position. A difference was observed, however, between the rectal and mean EAC temperatures for the bodies on their back compared with the other positions, although this was influenced by the small numbers of cases found on their front and sides compared with those on their back.

For 101 cadavers, a fan was used to generate wind across the head and body. This was shown to have no effect on the temperatures recorded from the EACs. In 34 cases, cadavers had been refrigerated before assessment, and thus the starting EAC temperature was below ambient temperature. It was observed that the EAC temperatures rose over a 120-minute period to approach ambient temperature.

In the case of head hair, no significant effect was observed, even if the external auditory meatus was covered by hair. Similarly, ear shape and lobe attachment, head circumference, brain weight, skull bone thickness and the degree of atheroma within the carotid arteries had no effect on EAC temperatures. Considering the EAC length, in any individual there may be a difference between the left and right side, but this was not found to be statistically different. This could be an important observation because the EAC is expected to have a temperature gradient within the canal between the external ambient temperature and the tympanic membrane. Thus, the choice of thermometer to take an EAC reading becomes important, as discussed elsewhere.

In the living, the temperature within the EAC was found to vary with the time of day and activity. Interestingly, this appeared to be related to mental, rather than physical, activity. It was also found to rise after drinking a hot drink. Unlike the cadaver work and in support of Baccino *et al.*, the EAC in contact with the ground when lying on one side was found to be warmer than the EAC exposed to ambient temperature. This was a time-dependent effect with a difference of 0.1°C at 1 minute, 0.6°C at 5 minutes and 0.9°C after 10 minutes for an unsupported head.

■ Application in practice

There are two sources of research to draw on in terms of application of temperatures recorded from the EAC for estimating a PMI. The first is that of the test cases of Baccino *et al.* [10] from the 1996 published study. Having established the 'interval' and 'global' formulae, Baccino *et al.* applied these along with two variants of the rule of thumb formula and the Henssge nomogram to a test population comprising 141 corpses with an actual PMI of 120 to 1330 minutes. As with their research data set, these investigators again separated the data into four ambient temperature groups. They reported that the 'interval' and 'global' formulae using temperatures from the EAC provided better results than using the rule of thumb and Henssge nomogram with temperatures recorded from the rectum, particularly for ambient temperatures over 15°C and postmortem periods up to 20 hours (Table 6.26). However, they pointed out that in their opinion EAC temperatures could be used in the presence of otorrhagia or if the body is lying on its side with one ear in close contact with a surface. If the postmortem period is more than 15 hours, from this work they recommended that an EAC temperature should not be used. These workers promoted the use of EAC temperatures at the scene for simplicity, lack of a disturbing effect on evidence gathering and better accuracy.

Between 1996 and 1999, Rutty [132] recorded single reading temperatures from both EACs and the rectum, as well as the ambient temperatures by using a First Temp Genius Tympanic Thermometer (Sherwood Medical) and an alcohol-in-glass thermometer for 80 unselected suspicious and homicide death scenes and autopsies that he attended. An ambient temperature could be recorded with the infrared thermometer as long as it was above 17°C. However, the value was found always to be significantly higher than that of the traditional glass thermometer. As was later verified by the work of Cattaneo *et al.* [13] it was found that there was no significant difference between the temperatures within both EACs when both were measured using either the IT or the alcohol-in-glass thermometer.

In the majority of cases, the rectal temperature was higher than its equivalent EAC temperature. This difference may be explained by the knowledge that in life the temperature in the EAC is lower than in the rectum. Thus, the temperature at the time of death at the two sites may not be the same. Although the rectum may (or may not) be 37°C, the EAC temperature may be lower. In addition, if we consider the 'cooling curve' observed from the dog and human research discussed earlier, we can anticipate that the EAC will, unlike the rectum, show no lag phase before cooling. Thus, we can redraw our theoretical cooling curves for the two sites to explain potentially the difference in the temperatures at the two sites at any given time (Figure 6.65).

This was also found to have a thermometer-dependent variant because the temperature in the EAC tended to be higher if measured with the tympanic rather than the alcohol-in-glass thermometer. This observation will affect any subsequent PMI estimation using an EAC temperature. An explanation for this can be hypothesized in the way that the two thermometer types record temperatures within the EAC (Figure 6.66).

Table 6.26 Effect of postmortem interval length on the results of five algorithms applied to a test sample (n = 141)*

PMI (min)		Ambient temperature intervals		
		≤420 (7 h) (n = 43)	≤600 (10 h) (n = 79)	≤900 (15 h) (n = 128)
Actual (PMIA)		274 ± 87	377 ± 134	521 ± 210
Estimated (PMIE)				
Outer ear temperature	'Interval'	264 ± 110	355 ± 171	462 ± 204
	'Global'	296 ± 113	366 ± 176	467 ± 206
Rectal temperature	Rule of thumb 1	116 ± 145	194 ± 243	308 ± 237
	Rule of thumb 2	276 ± 121	342 ± 202	436 ± 214
	Hennsge	138 ± 127	166 ± 117	280 ± 174
Error				
Mean (PMIA − PMIE min)				
Outer ear temperature	'Interval'	10 ± 111	21 ± 139	59 ± 146
	'Global'	−22 ± 127	10 ± 167	54 ± 102
Rectal temperature	Rule of thumb 1	158 ± 173	182 ± 234	213 ± 209
	Rule of thumb 2	2 ± 153	35 ± 201	84 ± 188
	Hennsge	130 ± 168	201 ± 157	256 ± 161
Relative (Error/PMIA %)				
Outer ear temperature	'Interval'	−1 ± 44	2.5 ± 39	7 ± 33
	'Global'	−16 ± 51	−4 ± 47	3 ± 40
Rectal temperature	Rule of thumb 1	51 ± 65	48 ± 61	42 ± 49
	Rule of thumb 2	−12 ± 65	0 ± 59	8.5 ± 48
	Hennsge	39 ± 73	48 ± 55	46 ± 43

* Rule of thumb 1: postmortem interval (h) = (rectal temperature at time of death [°F] – rectal temperature at T1 [°F])/1.5; rule of thumb 2: postmortem interval (h) = (rectal temperature at time of death [°C] – rectal temperature at T1 [°C]) + 3.

min, minimum; PMI, postmortem interval.

From Baccino E, De Saint Martin L, Schuliar Y, Guilloteau P, Le Rhun M, Morin JF, Leglise D, Amice J. Outer ear temperature and time of death. *Forensic Sci Int* 1996;**83**:133–146.

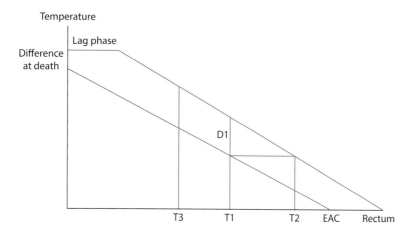

Figure 6.65 The theoretical cooling slopes for the rectum and the external auditory canal (EAC) showing a rectal plateau before temperature decline. Temperature °C. T1, time (hours) of reading from EAC; T2, equivalent rectal temperature at T1; T3, EAC temperature at rectal temperature T1; D1, difference between rectal and EAC temperature at T1. (From Rutty GN. *The Use of Temperatures Recorded From the External Auditory Canal in the Estimation of the Time Since Death*. Sheffield, University of Sheffield, medical doctorate thesis, 2001, as modified in Rutty GN. The estimation of the time since death using temperatures recoded from the external auditory canal. Part I. Can a temperature be recorded and interpreted from this site? *Forensic Sci Med Pathol* 2005;**1**:41–51.)

Using the temperatures recorded from the rectum and both EACs with the different instruments, the PMI was now estimated using several previously published formulae. An 'actual' estimation of the time since death, which was based on information available at the time of the autopsy, was available in a total of 62 cases. For up to approximately 16 hours after death, the centigrade rule of thumb calculation for all sites and instruments tended to overestimate the PMI, whereas this calculation underestimated the PMI after approximately 16 hours. The IT significantly overestimated the PMI more than the rectal temperature, and the alcohol-in-glass thermometer was even more pronounced. The PMI could, however, be more closely estimated by introducing a constant to the calculation derived from the total mean difference between the rectal and EAC temperatures, although it still tended to overestimate the true PMI.

The temperatures were then applied to the Henssge nomogram for the rectum and the brain. The infrared temperatures from the EAC overestimated the PMI in the majority of cases. However, using those cases where there was certainty of the actual PMI, applying infrared EAC temperatures to the brain nomogram predicted the 'actual' time in 77 per cent of cases (Figures 6.67 and 6.68) [134].

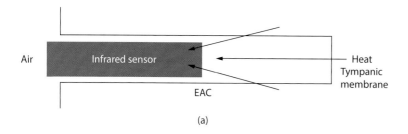

(a)

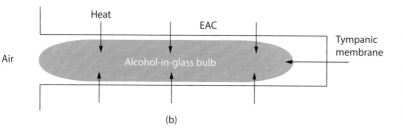

(b)

Figure 6.66 Hypothesized reason why there is a difference between the readings from the external auditory canal (EAC) with the different types of thermometer. (a) = infrared, (b) = alcohol-in-glass. (From Rutty GN. *The Use of Temperatures Recorded From the External Auditory Canal in the Estimation of the Time Since Death*. Sheffield, University of Sheffield, medical doctorate thesis, 2001.)

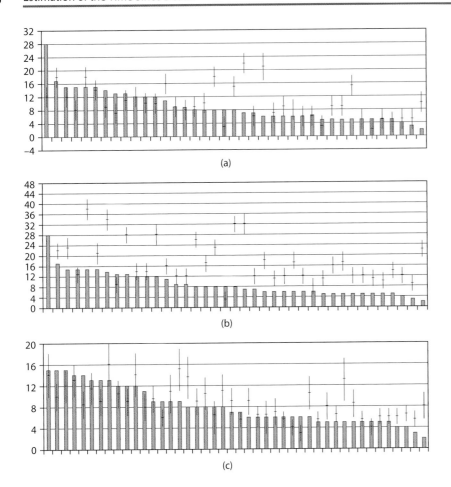

(a)

(b)

(c)

Figure 6.67 Plot of the 'actual' time since death (blue box) with the estimated time since death including the 95 per cent confidence limits for cases used with the Henssge nomogram for the rectum ((a) and (b)) and the brain (c) for the rectal and infrared right external auditory canal values. (From Rutty GN. The estimation of the time since death using temperatures recoded from the external auditory canal. Part II. Using single temperatures from this site to estimate the time since death with consideration of environmental and body "factors" that could affect the estimation. *Forensic Sci Med Pathol* 2005;**2:**113–123.)

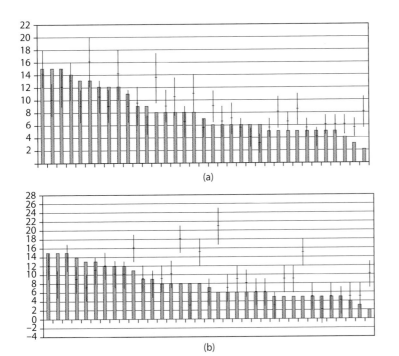

(a)

(b)

Figure 6.68 Plot of the 'actual' time since death (blue box) with the estimated time since death including the 95 per cent confidence limits for 35 rectal and infrared right external auditory canal values used with both the Henssge nomogram for the rectum (a) and the brain (b). (From Rutty GN. The estimation of the time since death using temperatures recoded from the external auditory canal. Part II. Using single temperatures from this site to estimate the time since death with consideration of environmental and body "factors" that could affect the estimation. *Forensic Sci Med Pathol* 2005;**2:**113–123.)

■ Summary

Decades have passed since the concept of using temperatures recorded from the EAC was first postulated. During this time a wealth of evidence has been collected from a number of study centres in the United Kingdom, Europe and Japan that independently reached comparable conclusions. Recording a temperature from the EAC can be undertaken quickly and easily without contamination of more critical evidence, for example, in the case of a sexual assault, by using a variety of thermometers including commercially available infrared thermometers. The thermometer used influences the temperature value. Unlike the rectum, the EAC has no discernible postmortem plateau phase, it follows a linear regression cooling curve and the temperatures can be applied to published algorithms. However, the PMI estimations generally overestimate the value unless a constant is applied to take into account the difference between the rectal temperature and the EAC temperature at any given time or a specific formula such as that of Baccino *et al.* [10] is used. When an EAC-specific formula is used, the published literature supports that the PMI calculation is more accurate than that derived from the rectum. If an infrared thermometer is used along with the Henssge nomogram for the brain, the estimates should be correct in 77 per cent of cases. Apart from the choice of thermometer and daily temperature variations, the only variable that has to be taken into account is which EAC is nearer the ground.

References

1. Al-Alousi LM, Anderson RA, Land DV. A non-invasive method for postmortem temperature measurements using microwave probe. *Forensic Sci Int* 1994;**64**:35–46.

2. Albrecht A, Gerling I, Henssge C, Hochmeister M, Kleiber M, Madea B, Oehmichen M, Pollak St, Püschel K, Seifert D, Teige K. Zur Anwendung des Rektaltemperatur- Todeszeit-Nomogramms am Leichenfundort (German, English summary). *Z Rechtsmed* 1990;**103**:257–278.

3. Alonso M, Finn EJ. *Physik.* Amsterdam, Addison-Wesley, Inter European Editions, 1977.

4. Altgassen X. *Untersuchungen zum 'postmortalen Temperaturplateau' an Abkühlkurven von Kunstkörpern.* Cologne, Germany, University of Cologne, MD thesis, 1992.

5. Althaus L, Henssge C. Rectal temperature time of death nomogram: sudden change of ambient temperature. *Forensic Sci Int* 1999;**99**:171–178.

6. Althaus L, Stückradt S, Henssge C, Bajanowski T. Cooling experiments using dummies covered by leaves. *Int J Legal Med* 2006;**121**:112–114.

7. Anonymous. Infrared ear thermometry. Health Devices 1991;**20**:431–441.

8. Baccino E. response to Dr. Rutty's letter re: 'Outer ear temperature and time of death'. *Forensic Sci Int* 1997;**87**:173.

9. Baccino E, Cattaneo C, Jouineau C, Poudoulec J, Martrille L. Cooling rates of the ear and brain in pig heads submerged in water: implications for post-mortem interval estimation of cadavers found in still water. *Am J Forensic Med Pathol* 2007;**28**:80–95.

10. Baccino E, De Saint Martin L, Schuliar Y, Guilloteau P, Le Rhun M, Morin JF, Leglise D, Amice J. Outer ear temperature and time of death. *Forensic Sci Int* 1996;**83**:133–146.

11. Baccino E, Frammery MF, Guedes Y, Morin JF, Barthelemy L. *Détermination de l'heure du décès sur les lieux: apports respectifs de la mesure de la température tympanique et hépatique.* Paris, Société de Médecine Légale et de Criminologie de France, 1991.

12. Baccino E, Guilloteau P, Le Moigne E, Schuliar Y. Postmortem delay determination: interest of the outer ear temperature. Paper presented at the 13th International Association of Forensic Sciences meeting, Dusseldorf, Germany, 1993.

13. Baehr HD, Stephan K. *Wärme- und Stoffübertragung,* Berlin, Springer, 1996.

14. Bartlett EM. Temperature measurement: why and how in intensive care. *Intensive Crit Care Nurs* 1996;**12**:50–54.

15. Beckstrand RL, Wilshaw R, Moran S, Schaalje GB. Supralingual temperatures compared to tympanic and rectal temperatures. *Pediatr Nurs* 1996;**22**:436–438.

16. Benzinger M. Tympanic thermometry in surgery and anesthesia. *JAMA* 1969;**209**:1207–1211.

17. Benzinger TH, Taylor GW. Cranial measurements of internal temperature in man. In: Herzfeld CM (ed.), *Temperature: Its Measurement and Control in Science and Industry.* New York, Reinhold, 1963, pp 111–120.

18. Betta V, Cascetta F, Sepe D. An assessment of infrared tympanic thermometers for body temperature measurement. *Physiol Meas* 1997;**18**:215–225.

19. Bisegna P, Henssge C, Althaus L, Giusti G Estimation of the time since death: sudden increase of ambient temperature. *Forensic Sci Int* 2008;**176**:196–199.

20. Brinkmann B, May D, Riemann U. Post mortem temperature equilibration of the structures of the head (German, English summary). *Z Rechtsmed* 1976;**78**:69–82.

21. Brinkmann B, Menzel G, Riemann U. Environmental influences to postmortem temperature curves (German, English summary). *Z Rechtsmed* 1978;**81**:207–216.

22. Brogan PA. Tympanic thermometry: poor correlations. *Clin Pediatr (Phila)* 1993;**32**:699–670.

23. Brown A, Marshall TK. Body temperature as a means of estimating the time of death. *Forensic Sci* 1974;**4**:125–133.

24. Burger E, Dempers, J, Steiner S, Shepherd R. Henssge nomogram typesetting error. *Forensic Sci Med Pathol* 2013;**9**:615–617.

25. Burke K. The tympanic membrane thermometer in paediatrics: a review of the literature. *Accid Emerg Nurs* 1996;**4**:190–193.

26. Castle S, Toledo S, Daskal L, Norman D.C. The equivalency of infrared tympanic membrane thermometry with standard thermometry in nursing home residents. *J Am Geriatr Soc* 1992;**40**:1212–1216.

27. Cattaneo C, Di Giancamillo A, Campari O, Orthmann N, Martrille L, Domeneghini C, Jouineau C, Baccino E. Infrared tympanic thermography as a substitute for a probe in the evaluation of ear temperature for post-mortem interval determination: a pilot study. *J Forensic Leg Med* 2009;**16**:215-–17.

28. Cengel YA. *Heat Transfer: A Practical Approach.* New York, McGraw-Hill, 1998.

29. Chamberlain JM, Grandner J, Rubinoff JL, Klein BL, Waisman Y, Huey M. Comparison of a tympanic thermometer to rectal and oral thermometers in a pediatric emergency department. *Clin Pediatr (Phila)* 1991;**30**(4 Suppl):24–29.

30. Chamberlain JM, Terndrup TE, Alexander DT, Silverstone FA, Wolf-Klein G, O'Donnell R, Grandner J. Determination of normal

ear temperature with an infrared emission detection thermometer. *Ann Emerg Med* 1995;**25**:15–20.

31. Chu A, Burnham R.S. Reliability and validity of tympanic temperature measurement in persons with high spinal cord injury. *Paraplegia* 1995;**33**:476–479.

32. Colin J, Houdas Y. Experimental determination of coefficient of heat exchange by convection of human body. *J Appl Physiol* 1976;**22**(1):31–38.

33. Darm RM, Hecker RB, Rubal BJ. A comparison of noninvasive body temperature monitoring devices in the PACU. *J Post Anesth Nurs* 1994;**9**:144–149.

34. de Dear RJ, Arens E, Hui Z, Oguro M. Convective and radiative heat transfer coefficients for individual human body segments. *Int J Biometeorol* 1997;**40**:141–156.

35. De Saram G, Webster G, Kathirgamatamby N. Post-mortem temperature and the time of death. *J Crim Law Criminol Police Sci* 1955;**46**:562–577.

36. Doezema D, Lunt M, Tandberg D. Cerumen occlusion lowers infrared tympanic membrane temperature measurement. *Acad Emerg Med* 1995;**2**:17–19.

37. Duck FA. *Physical Properties of Tissue*. London, Academic Press, 1990.

38. Edge G, Morgan M. The Genius infrared tympanic thermometer: an evaluation for clinical use. *Anaesthesia* 1993;**48**:604–607.

39. Erickson RS, Kirklin SK. Comparison of ear-based, bladder, oral and axillary methods for core temperature measurement. *Crit Care Med* 1993;**21**:1528–1534.

40. Erickson RS, Woo TM. Accuracy of infrared ear thermometry and traditional temperature methods in young children. *Heart Lung* 1994;**23**:181–195.

41. Farkas LG. Anthropometry of normal and anomalous ears. *Clin Plast Surg* 1978;**5**:401–412.

42. Fiddes FS, Patten TD. A percentage method for representing the fall in body temperature after death. Its use in estimating the time of death. *J Forensic Med* 1958;**5**:2–15.

43. Flo G, Brown M. Comparing three methods of temperature taking: oral mercury-in-glass, oral Diateck and tympanic First Temp. *Nurs Res* 1995;**44**:120–122.

44. Fraden J. Infrared electronic thermometer and method for measuring temperature. 1989. US Patent 4 797 840.

45. Fraden J, Lackey RP. Estimation of body sites temperatures from tympanic measurements. *Clin Pediatr (Phila)* 1991;**30**(4 Suppl 4):65–70.

46. Freed GL, Fraley JK. Lack of agreement of tympanic membrane temperature assessments with conventional methods in a private practice setting. *Pediatrics* 1992;**89**:384–386.

47. Gerthsen C, Vogel H. *Physik: Ein Lehrbuch zum Gebrauch neben Vorlesungen*. Berlin, Springer, 1993.

48. Green MA, Wright JC. Postmortem interval estimation from body temperature data only. *Forensic Sci Int* 1985;**28**:35–46.

49. Green MA, Wright JC. The theoretical aspects of the time-dependent Z equation as a means of postmortem interval estimation using body temperature data only. *Forensic Sci Int* 1985;**28**:53–62.

50. Grober H, Erk S, Grigull U. *Wärmeübertragung*. Berlin, Springer, 1957.

51. Gruner K. *Todeszeitbesimmung aus der Rektaltemperatur*. Berlin, Humboldt University, medical thesis, 1985.

52. Hansen RD, Olds TS, Richards DA, Richards CR, Leelarthaepin B. Infrared thermometry in the diagnosis and treatment of heat exhaustion. *Int J Sports Med* 1996;**17**:66–70.

53. Harasawa K, Kemmotusu O, Mayumi T, Kawano Y. Comparison of tympanic, esophageal and blood temperatures during mild hypothermic cardiopulmonary bypass: a study using an infrared emission detection tympanic thermometer. *J Clin Monit* 1997;**13**:19–24.

54. Hasel K, Erickson R. Effect of cerumen on infrared ear temperature measurement. *J Gerontol Nurs* 1995;**21**:6–14.

55. Hashizume Y. Fluctuations of rectal and tympanic temperatures with changes of ambient temperature during night sleep. *Psychiatry Clin Neurosci* 1997;**51**:129–133.

56. Henker R, Ciyne C. Comparison of peripheral temperature measurements with core temperature. *AACN Clin Issues* 1995;**6**:21–30.

57. Henssge C. Precision of estimating the time of death by mathematical expression of rectal body cooling (German, English summary). *Z Rechtsmed* 1979;**83**:49–67.

58. Henssge C. Estimation of death-time by computing the rectal body cooling under various cooling conditions (German, English summary). *Z Rechtsmed* 1981;**87**:147–78.

59. Henssge C. Temperatur-Todeszeit-Nomogramm für Bezugsstandardbedingungen der Leichenlagerung. *Kriminal Forens Wiss* 1982;**46**:109–115.

60. Henssge C. Death time estimation in case work. I. The rectal temperature time of death nomogram. *Forensic Sci Int* 1988;**38**:209–236.

61. Henssge C. Rectal temperature time of death nomogram: dependence of corrective factors on the body weight under stronger thermic insulation conditions. *Forensic Sci Int* 1992;**54**:51–56.

62. Henssge C. Concerning the paper by Baccino et al., entitled: 'Outer ear temperature and time of death'. *Forensic Sci Int* 1997;**87**:169.

63. Henssge CA. *Beitrag zur Standardisierung eines komplexen Verfahrens zur Todeszeitbestimmung am Leichenfundort: Interaktives Computerprogramm*. Essen, Germany, University of Essen, MD thesis, 1999. http://www.AMAsoft.de

64. Henssge C, Brinkmann B. Todeszeitbestimmung aus der Rektaltemperatur. *Arch Kriminol* 1984;**174**:96–112.

65. Henssge C, Madea B. *Methoden zur Bestimmung der Todeszeit an der Leiche*. Lübeck, Schmidt-Römhild, 1988.

66. Henssge C, Althaus L, Bolt J, Freislederer A, Henssge CA, Hoppe B, Schneider V. Experiences with a compound method for estimating the time since death. I. Rectal temperature nomogram for time since death. *Int J Legal Med* 1999;**113**:303–319.

67. Henssge C, Althaus L, Bolt J, Freislederer A, Henssge CA, Hoppe B, Schneider V. Experiences with a compound method for estimating the time since death. II. Integration of non-temperature-based methods. *Int J Legal Med* 1999;**113**:320–331.

68. Henssge C, Beckmann ER, Wischhusen F, Brinkmann B. Determination of time of death by measuring central brain temperature (German, English summary). *Z Rechtsmed* 1984;**93**:1–22.

69. Henssge C, Brinkmann B, Püschel K. Determination of time of death by measuring the rectal temperature in corpses suspended in water (German, English summary). *Z Rechtsmed* 1984;**92**:255–276.

70. Henssge C, Frekers R, Reinhardt S, Beckmann E-R. Determination of time of death on the basis of simultaneous measurement of brain and rectal temperature (German, English summary). *Z Rechtsmed* 1984;**93**:123–133.

71. Henssge C, Hahn S, Madea B. Praktische Erfahrungen mit einem Abkühlungsdummy (German, English summary). *Beitr Gerichtl Med* 1986;**44**:123–126.

72. Henssge C, Madea B, Schaar U, Pitzken C. Die Abkühlung eines Dummy unter verschiedenen Bedingungen im Vergleich zur Leichenabkühlung (German, English summary). *Beitr Gerichtl Med* 1987;**45**:145–149.

73. Hicks MA. A comparison of the tympanic and axillary temperatures of the preterm and term infant. *J Perinatol* 1996;**16**:261–267.

74. Hiraiwa K, Kudo T, Kuroda F, Ohno Y, Sebetan IM, Oshida S. Estimation of postmortem interval from rectal temperature by use of computer-relationship between the rectal and skin cooling curves. *Med Sci Law* 1981;**21**:4–9.

75. Hiraiwa K, Ohno Y, Kuroda F, Sebetan IM, Oshida S. Estimation of postmortem interval from rectal temperature by use of computer. *Med Sci Law* 1980;**20**:115–125.

76. Huber GC. *Piersol's Human Anatomy.* 9th ed. Philadelphia, JB Lippincott, 1930, p 1488.

77. Jakobsson J, Nilsson A, Carlsson L. Core temperature measured in the auricular canal: comparison between four different tympanic thermometers. *Acta Anaesthesiol Scand* 1992;**36**:819–824.

78. James WRL, Knight BH. Errors in estimating time since death. *Med Sci Law* 1965;**5**:111–116.

79. Jolin SW, Howell JM, Milzman DP, Stair TO, Butzin CA. Infrared emission detection tympanic thermometry may be useful in diagnosing acute otitis media. *Am J Emerg Med* 1995;**13**:6–8.

80. Joseph A, Schickele E. A general method for assessing factors controlling postmortem cooling. *J Forensic Sci* 1970;**15**:364–391.

81. Kahyaoglu O, Babka I, Demirci C, Boyer D. Effect of crying on infrared tympanic temperature measurement in pediatrics. *Clin Pediatr (Phila)* 1997;**36**:48–49.

82. Kanawaku Y, Kanetake J, Komiya A, Maruyama S, Funayama M. Computer simulation for post-mortem cooling processes in the outer ear. *Leg Med* 2007;**9**:55–62.

83. Kato M, Ando T, Yamashita Y, Tokura H. Thermophysiological effects of two different types of clothing under warm temperatures. *Appl Human Sci* 1995;**14**:119–124.

84. Kelley B, Alexander D. Effect of Otitis Media on infrared tympanic thermometry. *Clin Pediatr (Phila)* 1991;**30**(4 Suppl):46–48.

85. Kelley KE, Mohs DC. The external auditory canal. *Anat Physiol Otolaryngol Clin North Am* 1996;**29**:725–739.

86. Kiesow LA, Hurely C. Fogging in infrared tympanic and ear thermometry. *Ann Intern Med* 1995;**122**:634–635.

87. Klein DG, Mitchell C, Petrinec A, Monroe MK, Oblak M, Ross B, Youngblut JM. A comparison of pulmonary artery, rectal and tympanic membrane temperature measurement in the ICU. *Heart Lung* 1993;**22**:435–441.

88. Klinke R, Silbernagl SA (eds.). *Lehrbuch der Physiologie.* Stuttgart, Germany, Thieme, 1994.

89. Knight B. The pathophysiology of death. In: Knight B (ed.). *Forensic Pathology.* London, Edward Arnold, 1991, p 76.

90. Knörle T. *Normierungsvarianten für die Wärmeflussmessung an einem Kunstkörper.* Cologne, German, University of Cologne, MD thesis, 1991.

91. Koppes-Koenen KM. *Untersuchungen zum parameterfreien Verfahren der Todeszeitbesimmung aus Körpertemperaturen von Green und Wright.* Cologne, Germany, University of Cologne, MD thesis, 1991.

92. Li X, Tokura H. Acclimatization effect on the evening fall in core temperature under influence of two types of clothing. *Experientia* 1996;**52**:613–615.

93. Lundquist F. Physical and chemical methods for the estimation of the time of death. *Acta Med Leg Soc* 1956;**9**:205–213.

94. Lyle HP, Cleveland FP. Determination of the time of death by body heat loss. *J Forensic Sci* 1956;**1**:11–23.

95. Mackowiak PA, Wasserman SS, Levine MM. A critical appraisal of 98.6°F, the upper limit of normal body temperature, and other legacies of Carl Reinhold August Wunderlich. *JAMA* 1992;**268**:1578–1580.

96. Mall G. *Temperaturgestützte Bestimmung der Todeszeit mit Hilfe der Methode der Finiten Elemente, Habilitationsschrift.* Munich, Ludwig-Maximilians University 2000.

96a. Mall G, Eisenmenger W. Estimation of time since death by heat-flow Finite-Element model part II: application to non-standard cooling conditions and preliminary results in practical casework. *Legal Medicine* (Tokyo). 2005 Mar;**7**(2):69–80.

97. Mall G, Hubig M, Beier G, Eisenmenger W. Energy loss due to radiation in postmortem cooling. Part A. Quantitative estimation of radiation using the Stefan-Boltzmann Law. *Int J Legal Med* 1998;**111**:299–304.

98. Mall G, Hubig M, Beier G, Büttner A, Eisenmenger W. Energy loss due to radiation in postmortem cooling. Part B. Energy balance with respect to radiation. *Int J Legal Med* 1999;**112**:233–240.

99. Mall G, Hubig M, Beier G, Büttner A, Eisenmenger W. Supravital energy production in early post-mortem phase: estimate based on heat loss due to radiation and natural convection. *Legal Med* 2002;**4**:71–78.

100. Malt M. *Das Abkühlverhalten eines Kunstkörpers unter Berücksichtigung seines Wärmeflusses.* Cologne, Germany, University of Cologne, MD thesis, 1991.

101. Marshall TK, Hoare FE. Estimating the time of death. I. The rectal cooling after death and its mathematical expression. *J Forensic Sci* 1962;**7**:56–81.

102. Marshall TK, Hoare FE. Estimating the time of death. II. The use of the cooling formula in the study of post mortem body cooling. *J Forensic Sci* 1962;**7**:189–210.

103. Marshall TK, Hoare FE. Estimating the time of death. III. The use of the body temperature in estimating the time of death. *J Forensic Sci* 1962;**7**:211–221.

104. Marty W, Baer W. Cooling of cadavers in a coffin (German, English summary). *Rechtsmedizin* 1993;**3**:51–53.

105. Matsukawa T, Hanagata K, Miyaji T. A comparison of four infrared tympanic thermometers with tympanic membrane temperatures measured by thermocouples. *Can J Anaesth* 1996;**43**:1224–1228.

106. Milewski A, Ferguson KL, Terndrup TE. Comparison of pulmonary artery, rectal and tympanic membrane temperatures in adult intensive care patients. *Clin Pediatr (Phila)* 1991;**30**(4 Suppl):13–16.

107. Moriya K, Sekitani T, Yamashita H, Mizokami H. Tympanic membrane temperature in a patient with vertigo. *Acta Otolaryngol Suppl* 1993;**506**:24–25.

108. Mueller B. Das Verhalten der Mastdarmtemperatur der Leiche unter verschiedenen äusseren Bedingungen. *Dtsch Z Gesamte Gerichtl Med* 1938;**29**:158–162.

109. Muggenthaler H, Hubig M, Mall G. Heat-flow finite-element models in death time estimation. In: Turk EE (ed.). *Forensic Pathology Reviews*, vol. 6, Berlin, Springer Science + Business Media, 2011, pp 259–275.

110. Muggenthaler H, Sinicina I, Hubig M, Mall G. Database of postmortem rectal cooling cases under strictly controlled conditions: a useful tool in death time estimation. *Int J Legal Med* 2012;**126**(1):79–87.

111. Myers M.J, Henderson M. Assessment of two devices for measuring tympanic membrane temperature in swine, dairy cattle and dairy calves. *J Am Vet Med Assoc* 1996;**208**:1700–1701.

112. Newbold J. Evaluation of a new infrared tympanic thermometer: a comparison of three brands. *J Pediatr Nurs* 1991;**6**:281–283.

113. Nobel JJ. Infrared ear thermometry. *Pediatr Emerg Care* 1992;**8**:54–58.

114. Nokes LDM, Flint T, Jaafar S, Knight BH. The use of either the nose or outer ear as a means of determining the post-mortem period of a human corpse. *Forensic Sci Int* 1992;**54**:153–158.

115. Park SJ, Tokura H. Effects of two types of clothing on the day-night variation of core temperature and salivary immunoglobulin A. *Chronobiol Int* 1997;**14**:607–617.

116. Petersen MH, Hauge HN. Can training improve the results with infrared tympanic thermometers? *Acta Anaesthesiol Scand* 1997;**41**:1066–1070.

117. Pontious Sl, Kennedy A, Chung K, Burroughs TE, Libby LJ, Vogel DW. Accuracy and reliability of temperature measurement in the emergency department by instrument and site in children. *Pediatr Nurs* 1994;**20**:58–63.

118. Pransky SM. The impact of technique and conditions of the tympanic membrane upon infrared tympanic thermometry. *Clin Pediatr (Phila)* 1991;**30**(4Suppl):50–52.

119. Proctor KW, Kelch WJ, New JC. Estimating the time of death in domestic canines. *J Forensic Sci* 2009;**54**:1433–1437.

120. Prokop O. Die Abkühlung der Leiche. In: Prokop O, Gohler W (eds.). *Forensische Medizin.* Berlin, Verlag Volk und Gesundheit, 1975.

121. Rainy H. On the cooling of dead bodies as indicating the length of time that has elapsed since death. *Glasgow Med J* (new series) 1868;**1**:323–330.

122. Ratermann J. *Postmortale Hirntemperaturmessungen zur Todeszeitbestimmung – Untersuchungen zur Insertionstechnik der Temperaturmesssonden.* Münster, Germany, University of Münster, MD thesis, 1986.

123. Roeggla G, Roeggla M, Binder M, Roeggla H, Muellner M, Wagner A. Effect of alcohol on body core temperature during cold-water immersion. *Br J Clin Pract* 1995;**49**:239–240.

124. Rogers J. Evaluating tympanic membrane thermometry. *Nurs Times* 1992;**88**:52.

125. Rohrberg M, Fritz U, Braun U. Temperaturmessung im Gehorgang: Verleich eines Infrarot-thermometers mit konventionellen Temperatursonden und Evalation klinischer einfuegroeen auf die infrarot-messund. *Anasthesiol Intensivmed Notfallmed Schmerzther* 1997;**32**:409–413.

126. Romano MJ, Fortenberry JD, Autry E, Harris S, Heyroth T, Parmeter P, Stein F. Infrared tympanic thermometry in the pediatric intensive care unit. *Crit Care Med* 1993;**21**:1181–1185.

127. Romanovsky AA, Quint PA, Benikova Y, Kiesow LA. A difference of 5°C between ear and rectal temperatures in a febrile patient. *Am J Emerg Med* 1997;**15**:383–385.

128. Ross AH, Jantz RL, McCormick WF. Cranial thickness in American females and males. *J Forensic Sci* 1998;**43**:267–272.

129. Ross MD, Lee KAP, Castle WM. Skull thickness in black and white races. *S Afr Med J* 1975;**50**:635–838.

130. Roth NR, Verdile VP, Grollman LJ, Stone DA. Agreement between rectal and tympanic membrane temperature in marathon runners. *Ann Emerg Med* 1996;**28**:414–417.

131. Rutty GN. Concerning the paper by Baccino et al., entitled: 'Outer ear temperature and time of death'. *Forensic Sci Int* 1997;**87**:171–172.

132. Rutty GN. *The Use of Temperatures Recorded From the External Auditory Canal in the Estimation of the Time Since Death.* Sheffield, University of Sheffield, medical doctorate thesis, 2001.

133. Rutty GN. The estimation of the time since death using temperatures recoded from the external auditory canal. Part I. Can a temperature be recorded and interpreted from this site? *Forensic Sci Med Pathol* 2005;**1**:41–51.

134. Rutty GN. The estimation of the time since death using temperatures recoded from the external auditory canal. Part II. Using single temperatures from this site to estimate the time since death with consideration of environmental and body "factors" that could affect the estimation. *Forensic Sci Med Pathol* 2005;**2**:113–123.

135. Rutty GN, Smith NC, Rutty JE. The use of infrared thermometry for determination of time since death in the early post mortem period. *J Pathol* 1996;**179**(Suppl);13A.

136. Sato KT, Kane NL, Soos G, Gisolfi CV, Kondo N, Sato K. Reexamination of tympanic membrane temperature as a core temperature. *Appl Physiol* 1996;**80**:1233–1239.

137. Schwarz F, Heidenwolf H. Le refroidissement post mortem: sa signification quant à l'heure du décès. *Intern Pol Rev* 1953;**8**:339–344.

138. Sellier K. Determination of the time of death by extrapolation of the temperature decrease curve. *Acta Med Soc* 1958;**11**:279–302.

139. Shapiro HA. The post-mortem temperature plateau. *J Forensic Med* 1965;**12**:137–141.

140. Siegert R, Weerda H, Remmert S. Embryology and surgical anatomy of the auricle. *Facial Plastic Surg* 1994;**10**:232–243.

141. Smith DL, Petruzzello SJ, Kramer JM, Misner JE. The effects of different thermal environments on the physiological and psychological responses of firefighters to a training drill. *Ergonomics* 1997;**40**:500–510.

142. Snell RS. The ear. In: *Clinical Anatomy for Medical Students.* Boston, Little, Brown and Company, 1981, pp 709–720.

143. Stadtmüller K. *Zur Todeszeitbestimmung aus der Leichenabkühlung: Die Normierung der Abkühlgeschwindigkeit unterschiedlicher Körper auf verschiedene äussere Bedingungen.* Cologne, Germany, University of Cologne, MD thesis, 1991.

144. Stavem K, Saxholm H, Smith-Erichsen N. Accuracy of infrared ear thermometry in adult patients. *Intensive Care Med* 1997;**23**:100–105.

145. Steinbuch R. *Finite Elemente – Ein Einstieg.* Berlin, Springer, 1998.

146. Stipanits E, Henssge C. Präzisionsvergleich von Todeszeitrückrechnungen ohne und mit Berücksichtigung von Einflussfaktoren (German, English summary). *Beitr Gerichtl Med* 1985;**43**:323–329.

147. Stolwijk JAJ, Hardy JD. Control of body temperature. In: Lee DHK, Falk HL, Murphy SD (eds.). *Handbook of Physiology,* Sect. 9: *Reactions to Environmental Agents.* Bethesda, Maryland, American Physiological Society, 1977.

148. Stone JG, Young WL, Smith CR, Solomon RA, Wald A, Ostapkovich N, Shrebnick DB. Do standard monitoring sites reflect true brain temperature when profound hypothermia is rapidly induced and reversed? *Anesthesiology* 1995;**82**:344–351.

149. Szpak D, Groszek B, Obara M, Kusiak K. Thermoregulatory dysfunction secondary to acute ethanol poisoning. *Przegl Lek* 1995;**52**:281–283.

150. Talo H, Macknin ML, Mendendrop SV. Tympanic membrane temperatures compared to rectal and oral temperatures. *Clin Pediatr (Phila)* 1991;**30**(4 Suppl):30–33.

151. Tanabe M, Shido O. Changes in body core temperatures and heat balance after abrupt release of lower body negative pressure in humans. *Int J Biometerol* 1994;**38**:48–54.

152. Terndrup T, Milewski A. The performance of two tympanic thermometers in a pediatric emergency department. *Clin Pediatr (Phila)* 1991;**30**(4 Suppl):18–23.

153. Terndrup T, Rajik J. Impact of operator technique and device on infrared emission detection tympanic thermometry. *J Emerg Med* 1992;**10**:683–687.

154. Terndrup T, Crofton DJ, Mortelliti AJ, Kelley R, Rajk J. Estimation of contact tympanic membrane temperature with a noncontact infrared thermometer. *Ann Emerg Med* 1997;**30**:171–175.

155. Thomas KA, Savage MV, Brengelmann GL. Effect of facial cooling on tympanic temperature. *Am J Crit Care* 1997;**6**:46–51.

156. Thomas JW. *Numerical Partial Differential Equations: Finite Difference Methods.* New York, Springer, 1998.

157. Tomkinson A, Roblin DG, Quine SM, Flanagan P. Tympanic thermometry and minor ear surgery. *J Laryngol Otol* 1996;**110**:454–455.

158. Tortora GJ, Anagnostakos NP. *Principles of Anatomy and Physiology.* London, Harper & Row, 1990, pp 815–821.

159. Tourangeau A, MacLeod F, Breakwell M. Tap in on ear thermometry. *Can Nurse* 1993;**89**:24–28.

160. Unland M. *Ein Modell zur Bestimmung der Todeszeit aus dem Wärmefluss.* Cologne, Germany, University of Cologne, MD thesis, 1991.

161. Wallace CT. Perforation of the tympanic membrane: a complication of tympanic thermometry during anesthesia. *Anesthesiology* 1974;**41**:290–291.

162. Walpoth BH, Galdikas J, Leupi F, Muehlemann W, Schlaepfer P, Althaus U. Assessment of hypothermia with a new tympanic thermometer. *J Clin Monit* 1994;**10**:91–96.

163. Weiss ME, Poeltler D, Gocka I. Infrared tympanic thermometry for neonatal temperature assessment. *J Obstet Gynecol Neonatal Nurs* 1994;**23**:798–804.

164. Wells N, King J, Hedstrom C, Youngkins J. Does tympanic temperature measure up? *MCN Am J Matern Child Nurs* 1995;**20**:95–100.

165. Werner J, Buse M. Temperature profiles with respect to inhomogeneity and geometry of the human body. *J Appl Physiol* 1988;**65**(3):1110–1118.

166. Wessel H. *Leichenabkühlung bei Bettlagerung.* Münster, Germany, University of Münster, MD thesis, 1989.

167. White MD, Cabanac M. Exercise hyperpnea and hyperthermia in humans. *J Appl Physiol* 1996;**81**:1249–1254.

168. White N, Baird S, Anderson DL. A comparison of tympanic thermometer readings to pulmonary artery catheter core temperature readings. *Appl Nurs Res* 1994;**7**:165–169.

169. Williams RJ, Thompson RC. A device for obtaining a continuous record of body temperature from the external auditory canal. *Science* 1948;**108**:90–91.

170. Wright K, Badia P, Myers BL, Plezler SC, Hakel M. Caffeine and light effects on nighttime melatonin and temperature levels in sleep-deprived humans. *Brain Res* 1997;**747**:78–84.

171. Wright RO, Jay GD, Becker BM, Linakis JG. Use of infrared thermometry to measure lavage and intravenous fluid temperature. *Am J Emerg Med* 1995;**13**:281–284.

172. Wunderlich C. *Das Verhalten der Eiaenwarme in Krankenheiten.* Leipzig, Germany, Otto Wigand, 1868.

173. Yaron M, Lowenstein SR, Koziol-McLain J. Measuring the accuracy of the infrared tympanic thermometer: correlation does not signify agreement. *J Emerg Med* 1995;**13**:617–621.

174. Yeo S, Scarbough M. Exercise-induced hyperthermia may prevent accurate core temperature measurement by tympanic membrane thermometer. *J Nurs Meas* 1996;**4**:143–150.

175. Yetman RJ, Coody DK, Stewart M, Montgomery D, Brown M. Comparison of temperature measurements by an aural infrared thermometer with measurements by traditional rectal and axillary techniques. *J Pediatr* 1993;**122**:769–773.

176. Zehner WJ, Terndrup TE. The impact of moderate ambient temperature variance on the relationship between oral, rectal and tympanic membrane temperatures. *Clin Pediatr (Phila)* 1991;**30**(4 Suppl):61–64.

177. Zienkiewicz OC, Taylor RL. *The Finite Element Method,* vols. 1 and 2. London, McGraw-Hill, 1997.

7 Autolysis, Putrefactive Changes and Postmortem Chemistry

The early signs of death (postmortem lividity, rigor mortis) together with the supravital reactions are of great importance for estimating the time since death. Immediately following the early signs of death, the later postmortem changes develop, which cannot strictly be separated from the early changes. Later postmortem changes lead not only to the decomposition of a corpse but also in some cases to its preservation. Endogenous processes resulting in decomposition are autolysis, putrefaction and decay, whereas exogenous factors include animal predation, exposure to the elements and mechanical injury. Late postmortem changes may appear in chronological order in a cadaver as a result of changes in the surrounding conditions. However, if a corpse is exposed to separate environmental conditions by its position, quite different processes of decay may occur simultaneously.

7.1 Autolysis (self-digestion)

■ *Burkhard Madea and Gerhard Kernbach-Wighton*

Autolysis is defined as the destruction of tissues and organs by their own enzymes. As a result of membrane destruction, the lysosomes discharge hydrolytic enzymes, which are activated by the low pH value in the cytosol: acid phosphatase, acid ribonuclease, acid desoxyribonuclease, cathepsin, collagenase and many other enzymes. They play a decisive role in the self-destruction of cell structures. Organs, such as the pancreas, which are already rich in enzymes during life, are thus subject to very quick cell digestion after death, as are the gastric mucosa and the adrenal medulla. Because of a breakdown of cell membranes with a postmortem equalization of the concentration of substances that were unequally distributed in the different compartments during life, potassium increases and sodium and chloride concentrations decrease in extracellular fluid after death. As a result of anaerobic glycolysis, lactic acid concentrations rise, whereas pH values fall. Substantial factors in the progression of autolytic changes are the inner milieu of the cadaver at the time of death and the surrounding temperature. As bacteria continuously penetrate the tissues, autolysis is finally superseded by the processes of putrefaction and decomposition.

■ Putrefaction

Contrary to autolysis, putrefaction is defined as a 'heterolytic' alkaline, colliquative process on a reductive basis caused by bacteria. This extensive chemical process is accompanied by both visual (bloating) and olfactory (foul ammoniacal odours) features resulting from the generation of gases (hydrogen sulphide, hydrocarbons) and the release of ammonia. Bloating is especially seen in tissues with low turgor, such as the eyelids, mouth, and tongue, which may become monstrously swollen (Figure 7.1). The abdomen may also be extremely bloated as a result of gas accumulation. The production of gas is the main reason that drowned bodies float to the surface of water after some time. There are intrinsic and extrinsic factors influencing the onset and extent of the postmortem changes (Table 7.1) [185]. As a result of the buildup of sulph-haemoglobin, the abdominal wall shows greenish discolouration, beginning in the lower right belly (because oxygen is required for the buildup of sulph-haemoglobin). The discolouration may then expand to the entire surface of the body.

The spread of bacteria in the veins of the subcutaneous tissue and haemolysis of red blood cells cause venous marbling of the skin (Figure 7.2). A further characteristic of putrefaction is the formation of putrefaction transudates (accumulation of fluids leaking out of the dermis with blister formation). During putrefaction, hair and nails loosen and can easily be dislodged. In the course of putrefaction, liquefaction of fatty tissues finally occurs. Because of the breakdown of proteins, biogenic amines (e.g. putrescine, cadaverine, histamine, choline) may accumulate, as well as cadaveric alkaloids, referred to as ptomaines ('cadaveric poisons'). However, although ptomaines have muscarinic atropine-like effects, they are not 'toxic'. During bacterial proteolysis, certain amino acids such as delta-aminovaleric acid or gamma-aminobutyric acid can be found in the brain and liver and may be used to make a rough estimate of the time elapsed since death. Further changes arising from gas accumulation are the formation of so-called 'foam' organs and the discharge of putrefactive fluids from the mouth, nose, anus and genitals. In pregnant women, the pressure from putrefactive gas may cause the fetus to be expelled through the genitalia, a phenomenon known by the term 'coffin birth'. The progression of putrefaction even in a constant ambient temperature is so variable that no conclusion can be drawn about the time of death (Table 7.2) [12].

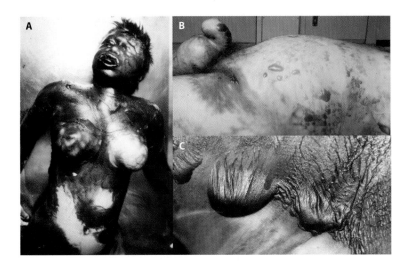

Figure 7.1   Bloating of tissues (A, B), discolouration (A) and putrefactive blisters of the skin (B, C).

Table 7.1   Intrinsic and extrinsic factors influencing onset and extent of postmortem changes

Acceleration of onset and extent of postmortem changes
• Death occurred in a hot, moist environment or under high ambient temperatures.
• Body surface was insulated by warm clothing or other covering.
• Considerable time interval elapsed after death until artifactual cooling of the body.
• Subject was overweight or had a high fat content.
• Subject suffered from or died of underlying infection or sepsis.
• Subject was intoxicated (e.g. with illicit drugs such as heroin).
• Subject suffered from or died of open wounds (perforating/penetrating trauma such as multiple accidental injuries, stab wounds, gunshot wounds, impalement injuries) or during surgical procedures.
Deceleration of onset and extent of postmortem changes*
• Death occurred in a cold, dry environment or under low ambient temperatures.
• Subject was scantily dressed, naked or undressed shortly after death.
• Subject was stored in a cooling device (refrigerator, freezer) shortly after death.

* These factors slow the speed of postmortem changes but in general do not alter the underlying postmortem biological processes.

Data from Tsokos M. Post mortem changes and artefacts during the early post mortem interval. In: Tsokos M (ed.). *Forensic Pathology Reviews*. Totowa, New Jersey, Humana, 2005, pp 183–237.

Table 7.2 gives only rough indications for the sequence of putrefactive changes in cadavers exposed above ground at relatively narrow ranges of temperatures (Table 7.3 gives indications of putrefaction in bodies exposed to air) [94].

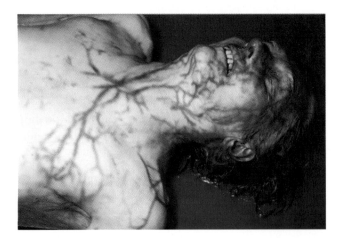

Figure 7.2   Venous marbling.

A rule of thumb that goes back to the Berlin forensic physician Johann Ludwig Casper (1796–1864) – named Casper's rule – says that 1 week in air equals 2 weeks in water equals 8 weeks buried in the ground [26]. Casper's rule thus relates the decomposition process to different environmental conditions (air, water, earth), but does not allow a precise determination of time of death.

Chemistry of putrefaction

Putrefaction is a bacterial process that starts with the normal microbial flora of the skin and the mucous membranes. Of particular importance are streptococci and various species of *Proteus*, whose flagellant motility enables these bacteria to spread quickly over an organism. Catabolic putrefying processes comprise proteins, carbohydrates and lipids. Protein breakdowns yield amino acids, which are then either de-aminated into their corresponding acids or decarboxylated into analogous amines by which the end products ammonia and carbon dioxide are created. The aromatic

Table 7.2 Morphological changes in the putrefaction phase: aboveground exposure at 20°C to 24°C (68°F to 75°F) without insect infestation*

Indication	Interval after death
Initial greenish discolouration on abdominal skin.	1–2 days
Cutaneous venous marbling.	2–4 days
Beginning of film-like slippage of the epidermis.	5–6 days
Loss of pigmentation in the stratum germinativum.	6–8 days
Putrefactive blisters and putrefactive transudates in the body cavities.	8–14 days
Putrefactive emphysema in the subcutis.	8–14 days
Bloating of abdominal cavities.	8–14 days
Diffusion of all fluids, collapse of organs.	Usually not until months later
Beginning of mummification with dehydration of soft tissues.	Usually not until months later

* This table gives only rough indications for the sequence of putrefaction effects in cadavers exposed above ground at a relatively narrow range of temperature. Numerous variations are possible, depending on the body's build, the underlying surface, coverings, terminal illness and other factors.

Data from Berg S. Todeszeitbestimmung in der spätpostmortalen Phase. In: Brinkmann B, Madea B (eds.). *Handbuch Gerichtliche Medizin*, vol. 1 Berlin, Springer, 2004, pp 191–204.

amino acids phenylalanine, tyrosine and tryptophan yield p-cresol, phenol, skatole and indole, which have been identified as main olfactory components of putrefaction. By anaerobic glycolysis, one molecule of glucose yields two molecules of lactic acid. Various bacteria, among them

Table 7.3 Progression of the putrefaction of bodies in air, at a temperature of about 20°C

Interval after death	Indication
1–2 days	Green discolouration of abdominal wall; softening of eyeballs.
3–5 days	Dark green discolouration of large parts of the abdominal wall; some patchy green discolourations of the skin of other body regions; haemorrhagic fluid leaking out from mouth and nostrils; marbling.
8–12 days	Whole body surface dark green; face, neck and thoracic wall partly reddish green; bloating of abdomen, scrotum and face; fingernails still fixed; hair loose, beginning to peel.
14–20 days	Whole body green or reddish brownish; bloating of the whole body; blisters, partly filled with putrefactive fluid, partly bursting with desiccation of the dermis; eyes (iris, pupils, sclerae) red-brown discolouration; fingernails peeling.

Data from Naeve, cited in Madea B. *Die Ärztliche Leichenschau.* 2nd ed. Berlin, Springer, 2006.

clostridia, may, through alcohol fermentation, break down monosaccharides into alcohol, so that typical putrefactive alcohols are created in the cadaver. Lipids are broken down by hydrolases, esterases and catalases into their components [11,20,101,110,111]. Even putrefied bodies may be preserved very well under special circumstances, especially when they are hermetically submerged or when decomposition is interrupted or at least considerably delayed by wrapping the body or parts of the body in plastic bags or vinyl (Figure 7.3). Experimental investigations on the influence of vinyl materials on postmortem alterations in rabbit and mice cadavers kept in plastic bags of different air volumes (3 litres/5 pints, 1 litre/1 3/4 pints, no air) at room temperature resulted in clearly delayed decomposition of these cadavers, with the volume of air within the bag clearly of greatest importance for the progression of putrefaction.

■ Decomposition

Although putrefaction is a mainly anaerobic bacterial reduction process, decomposition is dominated by aerobic microbiological processes that may create pungent, rotten odours originating from the metabolic products of oxidation. Decomposition is a dry, acidic process on an oxidative basis, which leads to the splitting off of acids (carbonic acid, phosphoric acid, sulphuric acid). At the beginning of decomposition, large patches of fungus may form on the skin and mucous membranes (Figure 7.4).

Period up to skeletonization

The period up to skeletonization shows great variability, depending on the storage conditions of the body. This concept is expressed by Casper's rule (defined earlier), which says that a cadaver lying on the ground decomposes more quickly than one lying in water or underground, although the ratios

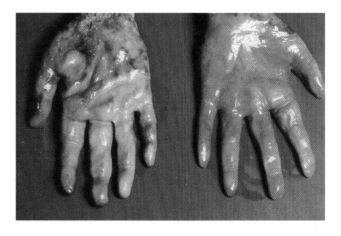

Figure 7.3 Hands of a homicide victim 2 years after the murder. The body was wrapped in several plastic bags. Although the epidermis is completely lost, dactyloscopic identification was possible.

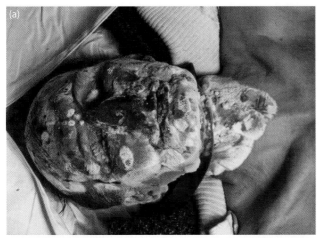

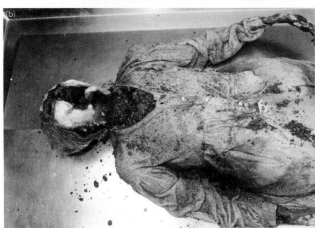

Figure 7.4 (a) Decomposition with patches of fungus on the face. (b) Advanced decomposition after exhumation with fungus patches on the skin.

Casper gave are certainly also subject to numerous varying conditions. Corpses lying on the surface of the ground are, as a rule, skeletonized within 1 year, and after 2 years the bones are completely free of soft tissues. A considerable proportion of soft part reduction during the summer months results from maggot infestation and animal predation. Under such conditions, a cadaver can be completely skeletonized within a few weeks (Figure 7.5). In the case of a body lying underground, the time required for skeletonization essentially depends on the composition of the soil. Under normal conditions, in a usually water-permeable, aerated soil at a depth between 1 and 2 m (3 feet 3 inches to 6 feet 6 inches), about 5 to 7 years are needed until skeletonization is complete, although considerably longer periods can also be observed. In warmer climates, the period needed for skeletonization to occur is normally shorter. Results of exhumations in the past few years indicated, however, that even after burial periods of 5 to 7 years, some bodies, in addition to clothing, were often found to be well preserved; in some cases, the internal organs including the gastrointestinal tract were still intact. Bodies buried in crypts or sarcophagi may undergo mummification (see later). Special conditions apply to burials in mass graves.

Even if many bodies are buried together at the same time, each body may display quite different degrees of decomposition; bodies lying on the periphery are usually extensively decomposed, whereas bodies lying more in the centre may display good preservation of soft tissues with pronounced grave wax formation. The bones of bodies lying above ground are, as a rule, completely skeletonized after 1 to 2 years; they show no remnants of soft tissues and no traces of cartilages or tendons. Remnants of soft tissues may still be found up to the second decade after burial in inhumed bodies, more rarely after the third or fourth decade. Remains of clothing may be preserved even longer [11,13,110,111].

■ Animal predation

In the very early postmortem interval (PMI), there may already be traces of animal predation, not only from rats or mice, or – in water – crabs and fish, but also from dogs and cats. Mice typically gnaw away the epidermis and leave characteristic gnawing marks (Figure 7.6).

Large areas of soft tissue damage may be caused, particularly by dogs. This damage can be explained by the dog's wish to provoke a reaction from its lifeless owner, first by licking the face, and then, when there is no result, behaving instinctively, by biting and later mutilating the owner.

■ Preservation processes in cadavers

Although autolysis, putrefaction and decomposition lead to dissolution and disintegration of the body down to its bones and tendons, the body may be preserved under special environmental conditions. Such preservation processes include mummification and adipocere formation. Preservation of the body can also be found in bog bodies and permafrost bodies.

Mummification

Mummification usually occurs when the water of the body's tissues evaporates in response to dryness of the environment and good ventilation. Mummification through natural processes may occur in bodies buried in churches or crypts (e.g. the lead cellar of Bremen Cathedral in Germany), but it is also seen in bodies that have lain at home, indoors, for some time before being discovered. Through mummification, the skin dries out into a hard, leathery state. The dehydration sometimes causes the body to be fixed in the position it was assumed to have been in at the onset of death (Figure 7.7). Furthermore, there is substantial weight loss as a result of desiccation and shrinking of tissues. It is especially a rapid loss of water that contributes to mummification, such as occurs by storage in dry, drafty air or on a warm and dry ground (Figure 7.8). Mummification leading to a leather-like, hard stiffening of the skin may, under appropriate

Figure 7.5 Advanced skeletonization of the skull after 1 week of lying on the surface in the wood in summer.

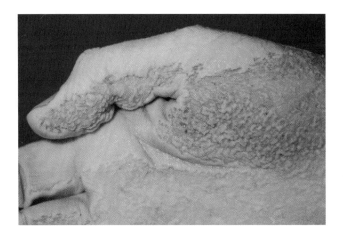

Figure 7.6 Gnawing marks in the epidermis of the hands by mice.

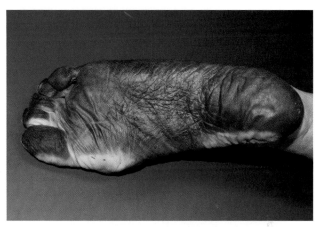

Figure 7.8 Mummification of a whole foot sole within 3 days after death.

Decomposition of the body in the grave – saponification

A body buried in soil should be reduced to a skeleton after 15 to 20 years, at the latest. As is well known, skeletons may remain preserved for a much longer period of time (several centuries). Whether a corpse has largely decomposed within this time, however, also depends on the properties of the soil – its mineral composition and aeration – and on groundwater conditions. For these reasons, only those sites that have appropriate soil should be used for cemeteries. Examples of unsuitable sites are grounds in which the coffins are actually lying in groundwater or where the zone of decay constantly or temporarily contains groundwater and areas subject to flooding by bodies of water in public use. Nevertheless, under such conditions, a particular preservation process known as saponification – the formation of adipocere, or grave wax – may occur. Saponification can be observed in bodies that have lain in a completely or partially hermetic damp environment (e.g. water corpses and corpses in damp graves). During the formation of adipocere, unsaturated fats

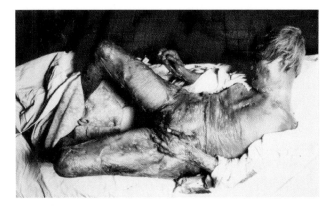

Figure 7.7 Mummification of a body in a fixed position. The man was lying on the couch of his apartment for half a year after death while doors and windows were open (in autumn and winter).

environmental conditions, commence relatively quickly (after 2 to 3 days), starting at the extremities (fingers, tips of nose and chin, ears, skin over the cheekbones); pronounced mummification, however, as a rule, is not detectable until after several weeks [5,11,13,48,81,110,111].

(oleic acids) are converted into saturated fats (palmitic and stearic acids). Saponification begins in the skin after about 6 weeks and in muscles after around 3 to 4 months. Entire extremities may be converted into adipocere, although this requires several months to years (Figure 7.9). The term adipocere (*adeps,* fat; *cera,* wax) goes back to Fourcroy (1789) and Thouret (1792), who, during the closure of a cemetery in Paris, noticed that the bodies buried there, some of them in groups, had not 'wasted away', but had been preserved in the same characteristic way.

The German word *Fettwachs* ('fat wax') is still commonly used, although the substance contains neither fats (glycerin esters of higher fatty acids) nor waxes (esters between long-chain fatty acids and univalent alcohols), but instead contains higher fatty acids with C-chain lengths between 12 and 20. Macroscopically, fatty tissues are first converted into a greyish-white greasy mass, which later shows a waxy consistency. As a rule, adipocere begins to form in warmer water after around 1 to 2 months. The final state may result in conversion of soft body tissues into a hard shell of adipocere; if this happens in a limb, the central long bone sits loosely, such as in a tube of grave wax. For an entire body to convert into an adipocere corpse may take more than a year; its final state is also called a 'plaster corpse' because of its crumbly, hard consistency [53,89,94–98,110,111,132,136,143,150].

Permafrost bodies

Extensive body preservation may also be observed in permanently frozen ground. Permafrost bodies have been found in northern Canada (e.g. in the early 1980s). The bodies in question had been members of the Franklin expedition in the 1840s. The cadaver found in the Hauslabjoch area of the Italian Alps ('Ötzi') is a famous frozen body from central Europe [10,60,70,81,110,111,171–173].

Bog bodies

In bog bodies, the effects of humic acid include bone demineralization, the tanning of soft tissues and a typical reddish dying of the hair. Because of the preservation of the body surfaces of bog corpses, it is often possible to collect significant evidence of the circumstances of death and the cause of death. Along with the presence of tannin and humic acid, a third important factor is the oxygen-poor peaty soil, which suppresses putrefaction processes and thus contributes to the good preservation of bog bodies [137,191,197,198].

■ Accumulated degree days to estimate the postmortem interval from decomposed human remains

Megyesi *et al.* [119] attempted to estimate the PMI interval from decomposed human remains by using accumulated degree days (ADDs). Because soft tissue decomposition is a sequential process with numerous small changes occurring throughout, these investigators scored decomposition in three specific areas of the body:

1. The head and neck, including the cervical vertebrae.
2. The trunk, including the thorax, pectoral girdle, abdomen and pelvis.
3. The limbs, including the hands and feet (Tables 7.4 to 7.6).

Tables 7.4 to 7.6 define the categories and stages of decomposition for each of the anatomical regions along with the assigned point value [119].

The stages of decomposition were slightly different for each of the three anatomical areas.

The scores of each of the three anatomical regions are combined to produce a total body score (TBS). The TBS for the cases reported by Megyesi *et al.* [119] (n = 68) ranged from 3 (fresh) to 53 (dry bones).

The ADDs were calculated as follows: all average daily temperatures above 0°C for all days from death and

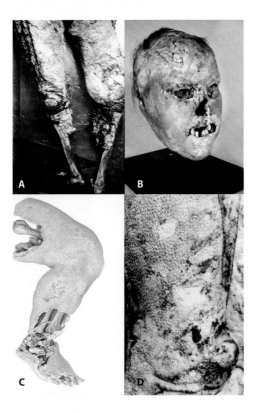

Figure 7.9 Saponification. (a) Soft tissues of the thighs were converted into hard shells of adipocere with the long bones hanging loosely. (b) Saponification of the head. (c) The leg of a newborn child, with saponification; after lying in flowing water for several months, the outer shapes of the legs were preserved; the chalk-like brittle mass, which looks like a stiff tube, contains loose bones. The muscles are missing. (d) The texture of the fat nodules in the subcutaneous fatty tissue was fixed by adipocere formation (état mamelonné).

Table 7.4 Categories and stages of decomposition of the head and neck

A. Fresh	
1 point	1. Fresh, no discolouration.
B. Early decomposition	
2 points	1. Pink-white appearance with skin slippage and some hair loss.
3 points	2. Grey to green discolouration; some flesh still relatively fresh.
4 points	3. Discolouration and/or brownish shades, particularly at edges; drying of nose, ears and lips.
5 points	4. Purging of decompositional fluids out of eyes, ears, nose and mouth; some possible bloating of neck and face.
6 points	5. Brown to black discolouration of flesh.
C. Advanced decomposition	
7 points	1. Caving in of flesh and tissues of eyes and throat.
8 points	2. Moist decomposition with bone exposure less than one half that of the area being scored.
9 points	3. Mummification with bone exposure less than one half that of the area being scored.
D. Skeletonization	
10 points	1. Bone exposure of more than half of the area being scored with greasy substances and decomposed tissue.
11 points	2. Bone exposure of more than half the area being scored with desiccated or mummified tissue.
12 points	3. Bones largely dry, but retaining some grease.
13 points	4. Dry bone.

Data from Megyesi MS, Nawrocki SP, Haskell NH. Using accumulated degree-days to estimate the postmortem interval from decomposed human remains. *J Forensic Sci* 2005;**50**(3):618–626.

Table 7.5 Categories and stages of decomposition of the trunk

A. Fresh	
1 point	1. Fresh; no discolouration.
B. Early decomposition	
2 points	1. Pink-white appearance with skin slippage and marbling present
3 points	2. Grey to green discolouration; some flesh still relatively fresh.
4 points	3. Bloating with green discolouration and purging of decomposition fluids.
5 points	4. After bloating, following release of abdominal gases, with discolouration changing from green to black.
C. Advanced decomposition	
6 points	1. Decomposition of tissue producing sagging of flesh; caving in of the abdominal cavity.
7 points	2. Moist decomposition with bone exposure less than one half that of the area being scored.
8 points	3. Mummification with bone exposure less than one half that of the area being scored.
D. Skeletonization	
9 points	1. Bones with decomposed tissue, sometimes with body fluids and grease still present.
10 points	2. Bones with desiccated or mummified tissue covering less than one half of the area being scored.
11 points	3. Bones largely dry, but retaining some grease.
12 points	4. Dry bone.

Data from Megyesi MS, Nawrocki SP, Haskell NH. Using accumulated degree-days to estimate the postmortem interval from decomposed human remains. *J Forensic Sci* 2005;**50**(3):618–626.

discovery were summed up. Temperatures below 0°C were always recorded as zero, because freezing temperatures severely inhibit biological processes. The TBS range of the investigated cases is shown in Table 7.7 [119]. The ADDs for all cases ranged from 27.1 to 3320.9, with a mean of 439.01 degree days.

By log-transforming both ADDs and PMI and by squaring TBS, an effective linear regression can be produced (Figures 7.10 and 7.11).

To predict the time of death for a new forensic case, one would first calculate the TBS for the individual by using the scoring strategy. Using several equations derived from the statistical analysis of their material, the time of death can be calculated together with 95 per cent confidence limits. The conclusion of the authors is that methods for determining the PMI from decomposition that take into account the temperature experienced after death produce more accurate estimates of the time of death than do methods that ignore accumulated temperatures. The proposed decomposition scoring system should be used cautiously only on

complete adult-sized remains that have not been burned, buried or submerged. The pilot study found that more than 80 per cent of the observed variation in human decomposition could be accounted for by the combination of elapsed time and temperature as it is reflected in ADDs. The proposed method should be further investigated not only by anthropologists but also within a forensic context [99].

Predicting the postmortem submersion interval for human remains recovered from water by using decompositional time tables incorporating accumulated degree days

As long known, bodies decomposing in water show soft tissue modifications similar to those of bodies decomposing on land (see also part 7.4 of this chapter). However, the visual markers appear at different time intervals, mainly because of ambient temperatures. For bodies decomposing on land, Megyesi *et al.* [119] developed an equation for calculating ADDs. This system measures a process of decomposition as the summation of progressive numerical

Table 7.6   Categories and stages of decomposition of the limbs

	A. Fresh
1 point	1. Fresh, no discolouration

	B. Early decomposition
2 points	1. Pink-white appearance with skin slippage of hands and/or feet.
3 points	2. Grey to green discolouration; marbling; some flesh still relatively fresh.
4 points	3. Discolouration and/or brownish shades, particularly at edges; drying of fingers, toes and other projecting extremities.
5 points	4. Brown to black discolouration; leathery appearance of skin.

	C. Advanced decomposition
6 points	1. Moist decomposition with bone exposure less than one half that of the area being scored.
7 points	2. Mummification with bone exposure of less than one half of the area being scored.

	D. Skeletonization
8 points	1. Bone exposure over one half the area being scored; some decomposed tissue and body fluids remaining.
9 points	2. Bones largely dry, but retaining some grease.
10 points	3. Dry bone.

Data from Megyesi MS, Nawrocki SP, Haskell NH. Using accumulated degree-days to estimate the postmortem interval from decomposed human remains. *J Forensic Sci* 2005;**50**(3):618–626.

Table 7.7   Characteristics of decomposition and corresponding total body score range

Decomposition characteristics	Total body score range
Purging from facial orifices.	8–13 (n = 19)
Bone exposure of head less than one half.	14–26 (n = 34)
Bloating of abdomen.	11–19 (n = 34)
Bone exposure of thorax.	20–35 (n = 24)
Bone exposure of limbs.	21–35 (n = 22)

Data from Megyesi MS, Nawrocki SP, Haskell NH. Using accumulated degree-days to estimate the postmortem interval from decomposed human remains. *J Forensic Sci* 2005;**50**(3):618–626.

scores (i.e. TBS), based on the appearance of three separate regions: the head, the trunk and the limbs.

Heaton *et al.* [65] assessed and scored postmortem decomposition by using described stages of decomposition observed on the head, the torso and the limbs (Tables 7.8 to 7.10). Eight stages of decomposition were identified for both the face (FADS) and the body (BADS), and nine stages were identified for the limbs (LADS). Thus, a total aquatic decomposition score (TADS) of 25 can be produced. From the 148 cases studied, TADS scores ranging from a score of 3 (no apparent decomposition) to 25 (complete decomposition – skeletonization and disarticulation) were calculated. The ADDs were calculated for 144 cases by summarizing the average temperatures for each 24-hour-period for the number of days that made up the postmortem submersion interval (PMSI).

$$ADD = \sum \text{Average daily temperature}$$
$$\text{(degrees Celsius) for the entire PMSI}$$

The values for ADD ranged from 0.04 to 2151. There is an almost linear correlation between the TADS and the log ADD (Figure 7.12).

ADDs have a significant and essentially identical correlation with decomposition at each of the study sites. Bodies in water for a prolonged length of time at cooler temperatures and those subjected to warmer temperatures for a shorter time showed similar rates of decomposition.

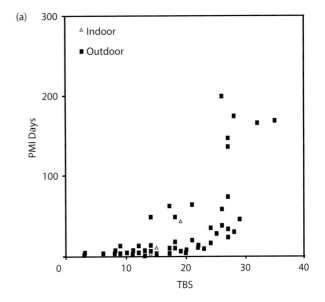

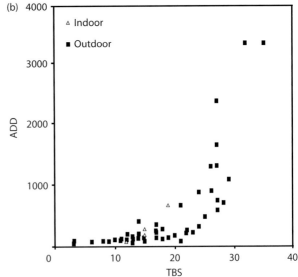

Figure 7.10   (a) Scatter of postmortem interval (PMI) versus total body score (TBS) (n = 68). (b) Scatter plot of accumulated degree days (ADD) versus TBS (n = 68).

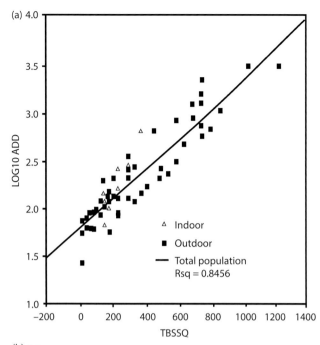

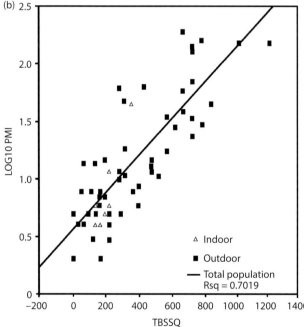

Figure 7.11 (a) LOG10-transformed postmortem interval (PMI) versus total body score squared (TBSSQ) with a regression (n = 66). (b) LOG10-transformed accumulated degree days (ADD) versus TBSSQ with a regression (n = 66).

Once ADDs have been predicted from the TADS, the PMSI can be inferred by summarizing the average daily temperatures from the date the body was recovered retrospectively until the estimated ADD value is reached. This should indicate the time frame in which the body entered the water. Table 7.11 presents calculated predictions as confidence intervals for all values of TADS between 5 and 25 [65].

Table 7.8 Descriptive stages for decomposition observed in the face and the assigned facial aquatic decomposition score

FADS	Description
1	No visible changes.
2	Slight pink discolouration, darkened lips, goose pimpling.
3	Reddening of face and neck, marbling visible on face; possible early signs of animal activity or predation concentrated on the ears, nose and lips.
4	Bloating of the face, green discolouration, skin beginning to slough off.
5	Head hair beginning to slough off, mostly at the front; brain softening and liquefaction; tissue becoming exposed on face and neck; green-black discolouration.
6	Bones becoming exposed, concentrated over the orbital, frontal and parietal regions, with some exposure of the mandible and maxilla; early adipocere formation.
7	More extensive skeletonization on the cranium; disarticulation of the mandible.
8	Complete disarticulation of the skull from the torso; extensive adipocere formation.

FADS, facial aquatic decomposition score.

From Heaton V, Lagden A, Moffatt C, Simmons T. Predicting the postmortem submersion interval for human remains recovered from U.K. waterways. *J Forensic Sci* 2010;**55**(2):302–307.

Table 7.9 Descriptive stages for decomposition observed on the torso and the assigned body aquatic decomposition score

BADS	Description
1	No visible changes.
2	Slight pink discolouration, goose pimpling.
3	Yellow-green discolouration of abdomen and upper chest; marbling; initiation in internal organs of decomposition and autolysis.
4	Dark green discolouration of abdomen, mild bloating of abdomen, initial skin slippage.
5	Green-purple discolouration; extensive abdominal bloating, tense to touch; swollen scrotum in males; exposure of underlying fat and tissues.
6	Black discolouration; bloating becoming softer; initial exposure of internal organs and bones.
7	Further loss of tissues and organs; more bone exposed; initial adipocere formation.
8	Complete skeletonization and disarticulation.

BADS, body aquatic decomposition score.

From Heaton V, Lagden A, Moffatt C, Simmons T. Predicting the postmortem submersion interval for human remains recovered from U.K. waterways. *J Forensic Sci* 2010;**55**(2):302–307.

7.2 Eye changes after death

■ *Burkhard Madea and Claus Henssge*

■ Electrolyte concentrations in vitreous humour

Autolysis starts with the cessation of energy metabolism in the cell and causes dissolution of the chemical, physical

Table 7.10   Descriptive stages for decomposition observed in the limbs and the assigned limb aquatic decomposition score

LADS	Description
1	No visible changes.
2	Mild wrinkling of skin on hands and/or feet, possible goose pimpling.
3	Skin on palms of hands and/or soles of feet becoming white, wrinkled and thickened; slight pink discolouration of arms and legs.
4	Skin on palms of hands and/or soles of feet becoming soggy and loose; Marbling of the limbs, predominantly on upper arms and legs.
5	Skin on hands/feet starting to slough off; yellow-green to green-black discolouration on arms and/or legs; initial skin slippage on arms and/or legs.
6	Degloving of hands and/or feet, exposing large areas of underlying muscles and tendons; patchy sloughing of skin on arms and/or legs.
7	Exposure of bones of hands and/or feet; muscles, tendons and small areas of bone exposed in lower arms and/or legs.
8	Bones of hands and/or feet beginning to disarticulate; bones of upper arms and/or legs becoming exposed.
9	Complete skeletonization and disarticulation of limbs.

LADS, limb aquatic decomposition score.

From Heaton V, Lagden A, Moffatt C, Simmons T. Predicting the postmortem submersion interval for human remains recovered from U.K. waterways. *J Forensic Sci* 2010;**55**(2):302–307.

Table 7.11   Total aquatic decomposition score and the predicted accumulated degree days and confidence intervals, back transformed from the logarithmic model

TADS	Predicted ADDs	Lower 95% confidence interval	Upper 95% confidence interval
5	13.16	3.550	45.88
6	17.70	4.825	61.52
7	23.79	6.552	82.58
8	31.99	8.889	110.9
9	43.01	12.05	149.2
10	57.83	16.31	200.8
11	77.76	22.07	270.5
12	104.5	29.82	364.9
13	140.6	40.26	492.6
14	189.0	54.31	665.6
15	254.1	73.18	900.3
16	341.7	98.51	1219
17	459.4	132.5	1652
18	617.7	178.0	2241
19	830.5	238.9	3043
20	1117	320.4	4135
21	1501	429.3	5625
22	2019	574.7	7659
23	2714	768.6	10 437
24	3649	1027	14 235
25	4906	1371	19 432

ADDs, accumulated degree days; TADS, total aquatic decompositional score.

From Heaton V, Lagden A, Moffatt C, Simmons T. Predicting the postmortem submersion interval for human remains recovered from U.K. waterways. *J Forensic Sci* 2010;**55**(2):302–307.

and morphological integrity of the body. Cessation of active membrane transport and loss of selective membrane permeability are direct consequences of the energy breakdown. With the loss of selective membrane permeability, diffusion of ions according to their concentration gradients begins. The time course of the autolytic processes is determined by many factors:

- Local anatomical factors (proximity of gallbladder, oesophagus, stomach, duodenum).

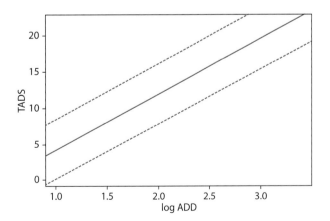

Figure 7.12   95 per cent confidence intervals around the regression slope as predicted by the model. Predicting the postmortem submersion interval for human remains recovered from UK waterways. ADD, accumulated degree days; TADS, total aquatic decomposition score.

- Tissue- and cell-specific peculiarities.
- Biochemical factors (rate of glycolysis).
- Further antemortem and postmortem factors influencing the 'interior milieu', especially temperature and pH.

As different tissues – and even the same tissues – at different topographical locations within the body have varying energy depots and rates of glycolysis, so too the duration of supravital activity varies considerably. As a result, the starting point and the time course (velocity of autolytic processes among different tissues, the same tissues at different locations of the body, as well as interindividually among different persons) differ widely.

Therefore, the following conclusions can be drawn concerning autolytic processes dependent on the time since death. Without strict differentiation of the structures investigated, the location of a collection of specimen temperature and antemortem factors (especially those that may affect postmortem pH), the range of scatter of the autolytic parameter investigated will be wide and will rise considerably with an increasing PMI. This is true for most investigations dealing with autolytic processes and analyses regarding time since death. These issues are reviewed by Schleyer [159,160,162,163] and Coe [30–37] and therefore are not addressed here again.

Loss of selective membrane permeability

The equalization of the concentration differences of ions in different compartments begins during and after the supravital period.

The equalization of concentration differences after the loss of selective membrane permeability follows Fick's first law of diffusion:

$$\overset{\circ}{m} = D \times \frac{F}{d} \times (C1 - C2) = D \times \frac{F}{d} \times c$$

where $\overset{\circ}{m}$ is the diffusion stream; D is the diffusion coefficient, dependent on the medium and the particles diffusing; c is the concentration difference; F is the surface of the diffusion medium; d is the diameter; and $C1$, $C2$ is concentration in compartments 1 and 2.

Because of its isolated topography compared with blood and cerebrospinal fluid (CSF), and because of its resistance to microbiological contamination with bacterial degradation and biochemical structures, vitreous humour is a very suitable medium for postmortem concentration studies [7,92,101,201].

The most favoured parameter studied is vitreous potassium (K^+), which diffuses post mortem from the retina (and to a lesser extent from the lens) into the vitreous body [15]. Animal experiments [15] have shown that supravital metabolism may be maintained for 15 minutes at 37°C. Even during life, there are concentration gradients within and between the intraocular fluid compartments [15,16] (Figure 7.13), with a K^+ inflow from the lens and an outflow into retinal vessels. In dogs and rabbits, the highest intraocular fluid concentration of K^+ was found in the posterior chamber and in cats in the anterior segment of the vitreous. The latter finding can be explained only by active K^+ transport across the lens [16]. The K^+ outflow from vitreous to retinal vessels seems to be purely diffusion because the K^+ concentration of the posterior vitreous is higher than that of the plasma dialysate. Post mortem, the K^+ gradient at the vitreous-retina interface reverses, with the lowest concentrations probably at the centre of the globe until diffusion equilibrium is achieved.

A striking finding was reported by Pau [134]. Although the K^+ content of the vitreous body was estimated to be 18 to 19 mg/dl, Pau noted that the vitreous layer adjacent to the retina contained about 100 mg/dl, which means that the whole vitreous behaves like a body fluid, but the vitreous layer acts as a body tissue. Whether this higher K^+ concentration of the layer is the result of electrochemical binding to the chemical substrate (tropocollagen, hyaluronic acid) is still unknown. These two findings (vitreous K^+ gradients and higher concentrations of the layer) already play an important role in the removal of vitreous humour and further pre-analytical procedures.

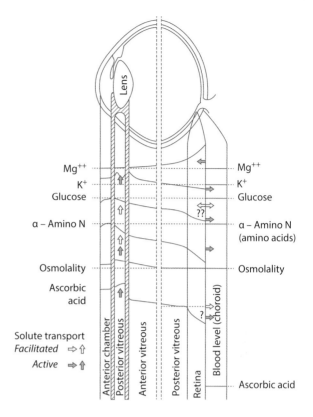

Figure 7.13 Schematic presentation of the gradients of some solute concentrations and total osmolality in the intraocular fluid system of a typical mammalian eye. The blood levels are shown by the dotted line and by the value given for the choroid. K^+, potassium; Mg^{++}, magnesium.

The following recommendations of Coe [36] concerning vitreous sample acquisition should be strictly adhered to:

'Vitreous humour should be obtained by means of needle and small syringe with suction applied gradually. The use of Vacutainer tubes with their strong initial suction commonly causes fragments of retina or other tissues to contaminate the specimen and such particulate matter will distort biochemical values. With care, over 1 ml of vitreous humour can usually be aspirated from each eye, even in newborn infants. Centrifugation with the use of the supernatant portion prevents clogging of fine tubing used in most current analytical instruments. All the vitreous that can be extracted should be withdrawn as there is variation in the concentration of many solutes between the vitreous humour next to the retina and that obtained from the centre of the globe.'

Only crystal-clear, colourless vitreous humour should be used for analysis. With the onset of decomposition, the fluid becomes cloudy and brownish. Further analytical and pre-analytical recommendations were published by Blana *et al.* [17], Coe and Apple [37], Thierauf *et al.* [183] and other sources [12,87,93,127,181,182].

Short review of the literature on vitreous potassium

The relationship between the rise of K⁺ concentration in the vitreous humour and the time since death has been established by numerous authors [1–4,6, 18,22–24,27–37,43,49–51,54,57,61,64,68,71,74–77,80,82,85–88,93,102,104–108,111,116,122,124–127,131,133,141,152,155,163,165–168,170,175–182,185,203] (see the excellent historical review by Coe and Table 7.12). The most exciting results were presented by Sturner [178], 1 on a random sample of 54 bodies observed up to 100 hours post mortem; the 95 per cent confidence limits of the K⁺ concentration were only ± 9.5 hours.

The linear rise of vitreous K⁺ and the PMI up to 104 hours post mortem were described by the following regression:

$$[K^+] = 5.476 + 0.14 \text{ h}, \quad \text{or} \quad h = 7.14[K^+] - 39.1$$

Follow-up investigations (see Table 7.12) could not confirm these 95 per cent confidence limits and revealed – even in the group of sudden or traumatic deaths – a much wider range of scatter. Figure 7.14, for example, shows the range of scatter of the values found by Hughes [71] with a regression line and 95 per cent confidence limits given by Sturner [179].

Figure 7.15 shows the values found by Coe [29] – only persons with normal electrolyte concentrations 6 hours before death are included – and the regression line and 95 per cent confidence limits given by Sturner [178]. In both instances, the values found do not fit into the 95 per cent confidence limits given by Sturner. However, one of the fundamental results of Sturner's investigation is that there are different 95 per cent confidence limits in the group of sudden or traumatic deaths and hospital deaths. Further important results were presented by Adelson et al. [1], who were able to show that the duration of the terminal episode also has a great influence on the range of scatter of K⁺ concentration over the PMI.

In cases with a terminal episode of less than 6 hours, the scatter was much smaller than in cases with a terminal episode lasting more than 6 hours. The great obstacle in using the K⁺ concentration in vitreous humour as an aid in estimating the time since death is the variation in 95 per cent confidence limits given by different authors. In a PMI of up to roughly 100 hours, these limits vary between ± 9.5 hours and ± 40 hours; in the early PMI of up to 24 hours, they vary from ± 6 hours to ± 12 hours (Figure 7.16).

The statistical parameters of the regression line vary correspondingly: (1) the K⁺ concentration at the moment of death as the intercept of regression lines between 5 and 8 mmol/l; and (2) the rise of K⁺ concentration per hour between 0.1 and 0.238 mmol/l (Table 7.13).

The slope given by Adjutantis and Coutselinis [2] is as steep as 0.55 mmol/l per hour. Coe [29] found the slope in the first 6 hours to be 0.332 mmol/l per hour, which was much steeper than for the whole investigated period

(0.1625 mmol/l per hour). In more than 100 individuals, sampling of the 2 eyes was made at different times, and the slopes for individual pairs ranged from 0.085 to 0.450 mmol/l per hour [29]. Differing individual slopes have also been reported by Madea et al. (Figure 7.17) [104].

Adjutantis and Coutselinis [2] confirmed the findings of an interindividual variation of the slope of K⁺ concentration over the PMI and recommended a timed removal of vitreous humour of both eyes at an interval of 3 hours and calculation of the time since death along the individual slope on a 'normal value' of K⁺ concentration at the moment of death (3.4 mmol/l). Death time estimation in the first 12 hours would be possible within an accuracy of ± 1.1 hour.

The reasons for these confusing results concerning regression parameters and the precise estimation of death time are not clear because all authors claimed to have considered the same careful sample taking and pre-treatment of samples before analysis.

Factors influencing the postmortem rise of vitreous potassium

Some reasons for the different regression parameters, especially the slope, have been identified:

- The duration of the terminal episode [1,104].
- The composition of the random sample of deaths: hospital cases, coroner cases (Table 7.14) [54,104,122,178].
- A much steeper slope in cases with raised urea values [104,106].
- Ambient temperatures (Figure 7.18) [15,23,24,34,80, 152,166–168].
- Possible influence of alcohol at the moment of death [179].
- Distribution of cases of the PMI.
- Instrumentation used to measure the concentrations (Figure 7.19) [17,37,181–183].
- Linear relationship between vitreous K⁺ and the PMI. This is obviously not a simple straight line but is biphasic, with a steeper slope in the first 6 hours than for prolonged times [29].
- Age. The level of vitreous K⁺ rises much more rapidly in infants than it does in adults, possibly because of a smaller diameter of the infant vitreous globe [36].

Our own investigations on vitreous K⁺ were based on the following hypothesis: One reason for the varying range of scatter in the different studies may be electrolyte imbalances at the moment of death. Unlike in experimental studies, in casework information about the electrolyte status before death is lacking. Therefore, for investigations on vitreous humour, it would be valuable to perform measurements of different parameters, some of which act as an internal standard. This should give information about homeostasis of electrolytes – mainly K⁺ – at the moment of death. Such an internal standard should have a small

Table 7.12 Summary of investigations on vitreous potassium

Reference	PMI	n	Intercept (K⁺ mmol/l)	Slope (K⁺ mmol/l per hour)	Correlation coefficient (r)	95% confidence limits	Random sample	Comment
Jaffe [74]	Up to 125 h	31					17–81 years; no cases with uraemia or electrolyte imbalances.	K^+ concentration related to logarithm of time; no significant differences between refrigerated bodies and those kept at room temperature.
Adelson et al. [1]	24 h	209	5.36 I: 5.27 II: 5.72	0.17 0.16 0.18		±10 h ±5.75 h ±12 h	I: Agonal event < 6 h. II: Agonal event > 6 h.	Straight line relationship between vitreous K^+ and PMI.
Sturner [178] Sturner and Gantner [180]	Up to 108 h	54	5.48	0.14	0.987	±9.5 h	Coroner cases	PMI = 7.14 K^+ −39.1.
Hughes [71]	Up to 117 h	135				±20 h	55 coroner cases. 80 hospital deaths.	Rise of K^+ could not be correlated with sufficient consistency with PMI.
Hansson et al. [61]	3–310 h	203	8	0.17		±40 h		In 180 cases with a PMI up to 120 h, linear rise of vitreous K^+.
Leahy and Farber [86]	30 h	52					Hospital patients; patients dead on arrival.	Vitreous K^+ concentrations appear to rise erratically after death.
Lie [88]	2–95 h	88	5.48	0.14		±3.6 h (1 SD)	Hospital cases.	Very good agreement with Sturner; slope, intercept and SD according to Henry and Smith: 'standard deviation calculated from author's data as variance from Sturner and Ganther's line of best fit'.
Marchenko [116]	6–48 h	300				Death time estimation possible within 3–6 hours.	Age 29–70 years.	Estimation of time since death possible within ±3 h.
Coe [29]	100 hpm	160	I: 4.99 II: 6.19	0.332 0.1625		±12 hours in the first day after death.	Hospital patients with normal electrolytes within 6 h of death and medical examiner cases.	I: PMI <6 h. II: PMI >6 h. Individual slope may vary between 0.085 and 0.45 mmol/l.
Krause et al. [82]	230 h	262			0.7	Range of scatter between 9 and 107 h for K^+ values between 5 and 28 mmol/l.		$K^+ = 2.96 + 1.65\sqrt{h}$ $h = \left[\dfrac{K - 2.96}{1.65}\right]^2$ Exponential rise of K^+ over the PMI.
Stegmaier [175]	82 h	98				±12		

(Continued)

Table 7.12 (*Continued*) Summary of investigations on vitreous potassium

Reference	PMI	n	Intercept (K^+ mmol/l)	Slope (K^+ mmol/l per hour)	Correlation coefficient (r)	95% confidence limits	Random sample	Comment
Adjutanis and Coutselinis [2]	12 h	120	3.4 (taken from literature).	0.55 for the first 12 hours.		~±3.3		Timed bilateral withdrawal (interval 3 h) reveals a rise in precision of death time estimation from ±3.3 to ±2.2 h.
Komura and Oshiro [80]	≈30 h	90			0.78–0.92 (according to ambient temperature).			Linear relationship between vitreous K^+ and PMI, slope being steeper in ambient temperatures of 26°C –29°C than in 13°C –17°C.
Foerch et al. [50]		>50						Linear correlation between vitreous K^+ and PMI.
Blumenfeld et al. [18]	11–77 h	127			0.63	±26 h	127 children, age 1 hour–13 years.	K^+ increases with increasing PMI in an essentially linear fashion.
Forman and Butts [51]		82	4.8	0.21	0.787			Linear relationship between potassium level and PMI; y = 4.75 x = 22.8.
Schoning and Strafuss [166–168]	48 h	60 (dogs)					Mongrel dogs.	Rise of K^+ temperature dependent.
Choo-Kang et al. [28]		105	9.67	0.09	0.85			
Balasooriya et al. [6]		59						Comparing vitreous K^+ values of both eyes, 18.6% of the results varied by more than 10% from the mean.
Farmer et al. [49]	24–120 h		238 mg/l	4.752	0.98			
Stephens and Richards [176]	35 h	1427	6.324	0.238		±20 h	Newborn–90 years.	
Madea et al. [104]	130 h	I: 170 II: 138 III: 107	5.99 5.88 5.48	0.203 0.188 0.186	0.86 0.89 0.91	±34 h ±22 h ±20 h	I: Entire sample (clinical and forensic pathology). II: Urea < 100 mg/dl. III: Urea < 100 mg/dl and terminal episode <6 h.	
Sparks et al. [170]	≈60 h	91			0.87	±10.5 within the first day.		Concomitantly the levels of 3-MT were studied in the putamen of the brain; combining K^+ and α3-MT determinations the accuracy of predicting PMI may be raised to ±8 h for individuals not dying of organic heart disease.
Schmidt [165]	88.5 h		5.35	0.17	0.83	±24.8	Sudden natural and traumatic death (forensic pathology).	

Table 7.12 (*Continued*)   Summary of investigations on vitreous potassium

Reference	PMI	n	Intercept (K⁺ mmol/l)	Slope (K⁺ mmol/l per hour)	Correlation coefficient (r)	95% confidence limits	Random sample	Comment
Montaldo *et al.* [122]	≈80 h	289	6.805 6.1–6.99	0.1652 0.15–0.20		±15 ±8 to ±23	Violent or unsuspected death.	K⁺ over the PMI in the entire sample and in various subgroups was analysed; subgroups were formed according to age, sex, type of death, autopsy findings and climatic conditions (see Table 7.14).
Gamero *et al.* [54]	24 h	60					Coroner cases.	Best correlation between K⁺ and PMI in cases dying of acute trauma with a PMI <17 h.
Rognum *et al.* [152]	120 h	87	5.8	0.17: 5°C 0.20: 10°C 0.25: 15°C 0.30: 23°C				Repeated sampling of vitreous humour (twice each eye); the higher the environmental temperature, the steeper the slope of vitreous K⁺.

K⁺, potassium; 3-MT, 3-methoxytyramine; PMI, postmortem interval; SD, standard deviation.

standard range in life, be stable post mortem and have a close relationship with electrolyte metabolism.

Search for an internal standard of electrolyte homeostasis at the moment of death

Materials and methods

Vitreous humour was sampled from 270 consecutive cases with an accurately known time of death [104,106,107].

In the forensic case group (n = 187), the sudden deaths were mainly caused by coronary artery disease, head injury, traffic accidents, fall from height or other situations.

In contrast, in the pathology group (n = 83), death occurred after chronic lingering disease (i.e. cancer, infectious diseases, renal failure, cardiac failure after myocardial infarction) (Table 7.15 and Figures 7.20 and 7.21).

After admittance to the mortuary, most of the bodies were kept at +15°C, but some of them were kept at +5°C. In all cases, vitreous humour from both eyes was completely aspirated at the same time by using a 10-ml syringe and a 20-gauge needle. Any specimens that were not crystal clear were rejected. Most of the samples were stored frozen at

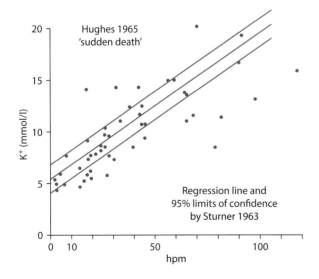

Figure 7.14 Fifty cases of sudden death published by Hughes [71] with a regression line and 95 per cent confidence limits by Sturner [178]. K⁺, potassium.

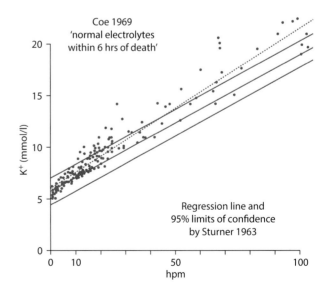

Figure 7.15 Vitreous potassium (K⁺) values of normal individuals plotted against time since death with a regression line of all values having a postmortem interval longer than 6 hours (dashed line) [29] and regression line and 95 per cent confidence limits (solid line) [178]. hpm, hours post mortem.

95% limits of confidence

	PMI (h)	95% ± h
Sturner (1963)	104	9.5
Stegmaier (1971)	85	16
Hughes (1965)	100	20
Hansson (1966)	120	40
Coe (1969)	24	12
Adelson (1963)	24	10

12 terminal episodes > 6 h

6 terminal episodes < 6 h

Figure 7.16 Potassium in vitreous humour. Different 95 per cent confidence limits quoted in the literature for the early and later postmortem interval (PMI).

Table 7.13 Differing statistical parameters of the regression line as quoted in the literature

Reference	n	Intercept (mmol/l)	Slope (mmol/l per hour)
Sturner [178]	54	5.960*	0.132*
		5.600	0.140
Adelson *et al.* [1]	209	5.360	0.170
Hansson *et al.* [61]	108	8.000	0.170
Lie [88]	88		0.140
Coe [29]	160	4.990	0.332 (first 6 h)
		6.190	0.1625 (over 6 h)
Adjutantis and Coutselinis [2]			0.550 (for the first 12 h)
Stephens and Richards [176]	1427	6.342	0.238
Madea *et al.* [104]	170	5.880	0.190

* The author's own calculations on Sturner's material with differences from Coe's statement. In cases with vitreous potassium of both eyes, the mean value was used for regression analysis. The slope varies between 0.132 and 0.238 mmol/l per hour.

−70°C until analytical determinations could be performed. After thawing, the samples were centrifuged for 10 minutes at 3000 rpm, according to Adjutantis and Coutselinis [2]. The supernatant was then used for determinations. In all cases, there was enough material for the following parameters to be measured: K^+, sodium, chloride, urea, calcium. In some cases, creatinine was also determined. Sodium, K^+, chloride and calcium were determined using ion-sensitive electrodes. Because the linearity of the K^+ electrode of the Hitachi 705 system used in this investigation was confined to 10.9 mmol/l, most samples had to be measured once more after correct dilution with ion-free water.

Urea was determined using an enzymatic method according to Gutman and Bergmeyer [58]. The presence of ammonia did not affect the results. Creatinine was measured using the kinetic (Jaffe) method [9]. In all instances, right and left eye aspirates were analyzed independently.

Results and discussion

Differences between eyes/timed bilateral withdrawal

Because the left and right eye aspirates were determined independently, some remarks are made on the differences between the eyes. There were deviations of up to 10 per cent in the single values from the mean value, even in the early PMI (Figure 7.22). These percentage deviations of the single values of each eye from the mean value are not related to the time since death or the mode of death. These findings are in good accord with those of Stegmaier [175], but they are not as marked as those reported by Balasooriya *et al.* [6] (Table 7.16). We have also obtained similar differences between the eyes for sodium, chloride and calcium. Because we used the same pre-treatment for samples as did Adjutantis and Coutselinis [2] before analysis, these differences of the K^+ concentrations between the eyes do not allow us to use the method of Adjutantis and Coutselinis [2]. It consists of determining the individual slope up to 12 hours post mortem after aspiration of vitreous humour of both eyes at different time intervals to obtain a more precise estimation of time since death. Another argument against their method is that the K^+ values in vitreous humour from both eyes obtained at different times after death (3 to 4 hours apart) are within the normal range of scatter of values obtained at identical times after death (see Figure 7.17). Correspondingly, Schleyer [163] mentioned that he could not confirm the results of Adjutantis and Coutselinis [2] by using their formula.

Urea as an internal standard

Although there are differences for single K^+ values taken at identical times, the statistical parameters of K^+ concentrations over the time since death for each eye do not differ from those of the mean value for both eyes: the regression lines are identical. Therefore, for further statistical analysis, only the mean values of both eyes were used.

Figure 7.23 shows the K^+ values of 270 cases (mean values of both eyes) plotted against time after death. There is a linear relationship between K^+ concentrations and time after death up to 120 hours. The slope is 0.20 mmol/l per hour; the intercept is 6.10 mmol per hour.

The 95 per cent confidence limits in this entire group – which consists of both sudden traumatic deaths and hospital deaths – are ± 25.51 hours up to 120 hours post mortem (Table 7.17).

The first step to reduce these 95 per cent confidence limits was to look at the question of which of the other parameters could indicate an antemortem imbalance of

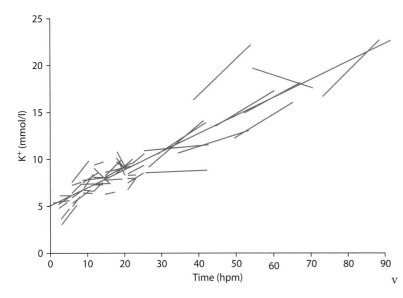

Figure 7.17 Potassium (K+) values of 53 cases of both eyes; vitreous humour of both eyes withdrawn at different time intervals after death (intervals between aspiration 2 to 3 hours, 4 to 5 hours and 12 to 24 hours). The 'rise' of the K+ concentration of vitreous humour obtained at different time intervals is within the normal range of scatter of values obtained at identical times after death. hpm, hours post mortem.

metabolism. Sodium, calcium, chloride, urea and creatinine are stable in the PMI for up to 120 hours after death (Figures 7.24 to 7.28). Figures 7.27 (a) and (c) show a marked increase of urea in many cases and are indicative of antemortem urea retention. That these high urea values result from antemortem retention and not from postmortem changes was shown by Coe [29], who compared urea values obtained from each eye at different time intervals after death. The differences in the values did not exceed 5 mg/dl, even in the cases with very long intervals between two samples. Thus, vitreous urea nitrogen can be used as an internal standard because it is stable post mortem and has a close relationship with electrolyte metabolism. In the next step, all cases having a vitreous urea nitrogen level higher than 100 mg/dl were excluded from the entire group of K+ values to check whether, in this diminished random

Table 7.14 Regression parameters and 95 per cent confidence limits in the entire sample and various subgroups according to the mode and cause of death

Mode and cause of death	n	Intercept K+ (mmol/l)	Slope (mmol/l per hour)	95% confidence limits
Total number	289	6.805	0.1652	15
≤60 years	176	6.677	0.1657	14
>60 years	113	6.636	0.1663	16
Sudden death	138	6.683	0.1652	16
Violent death	151	6.661	0.1666	16
Sudden death ≤60 years	29	6.609	0.1727	14
Sudden death >60 years	42	6.183	0.1722	17
Violent death ≤60 years	111	6.801	0.1656	13
Violent death >60 years	40	6.663	0.1665	16
Sudden cardiac death ≤60 years	36	6.867	0.1803	17
Sudden cardiac death >60 years	31	6.383	0.1835	23
Violent asphyxial death	26	6.470	0.1689	12
Other violent death	125	6.692	0.1653	16
Death in winter	60	6.989	0.1626	16
Death in summer	74	6.567	0.1715	11
Violent death ≤60 years in winter	25	6.999	0.1500	21
Violent death ≤60 years in summer	34	6.100	0.2015	8

K+, potassium.

From Montaldo B, Umani Ronchi G, Marchiori A, Forgeschi M, Barbato M. La determinatione della concentrazione del potassio nel'umor vitreo: verifica di un methodo strumentale tanatocronologico. *Riv Ital Med Leg* 1989;**11**:180–199.

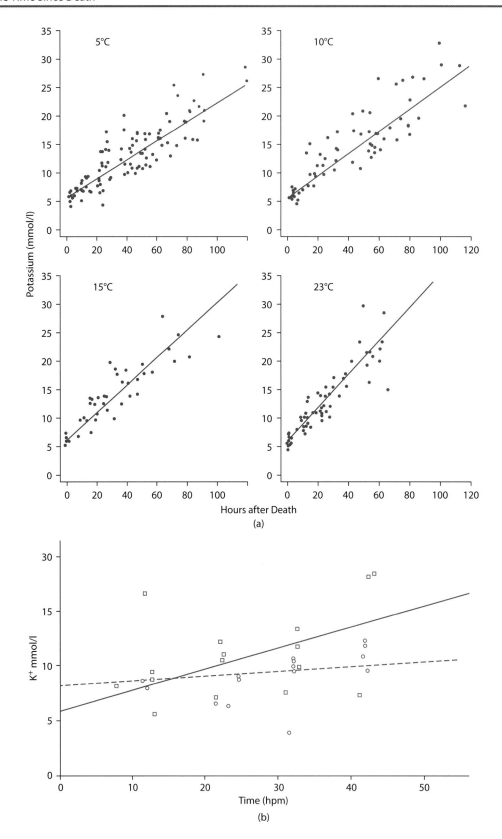

(a)

(b)

Figure 7.18   (a) Scatter plots of vitreous humour potassium (K⁺) levels in subjects kept at 5°C, 10°C, 15°C and 23°C after death (the median slopes being 0.17 (5°C), 0.20 (10°C), 0.25 (15°C) and 0.30 (23°C) mmol/l per hour). The median slopes are indicated by lines [152]. (b) 32 K⁺ values from 24 bodies brought within 3 hours of death into ambient temperatures of 5°C (squares) and 20°C (circles) [23].

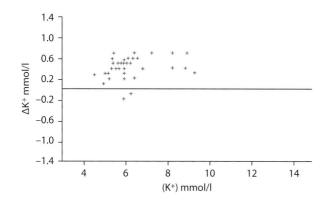

Figure 7.19 Differences of potassium (K⁺) concentrations determined with ion-specific electrodes and flame photometry (ion-specific electrodes minus flame photometry) over the K⁺ concentrations determined with ion-specific electrodes (calculation on the material of Coe and Apple [37]). Determination with ion-specific electrodes reveals slightly higher values than with flame photometry.

Table 7.15 Composition of the random sample (n = 270) with regard to the cause of death

Cause of death	Forensic pathology	Clinical pathology	Total
Neoplasms	3	32	35
Accidents	47	3	50
Fall from height	21		21
Hanging	5		5
Myocardial infarction	71	21	92
Pulmonary thromboembolism	1	2	3
Cerebral infarction/cerebral bleeding		5	5
Liver or renal failure	3	7	10
Gunshot	7		7
Intoxication	8		8
Burns	4		4
Other	17	13	30
Total	187	83	270

sample, there is a closer connection between K⁺ concentrations and time since death. In 42 cases of the entire group, there were vitreous urea nitrogen levels greater than 100 mg/dl (see Table 7.17).

In the diminished group (n = 228), the intercept was 6.02 mmol/l, and the slope 0.18 mmol/l per hour. The 95 per cent confidence limits up to 120 hours post mortem were reduced from ± 25.51 to ± 21.78 hours.

The difference in the 95 per cent confidence limits of the entire group and of the diminished sample is significant. All patients with a urea level greater than 100 mg/dl had had chronic diseases. The different 95 per cent confidence limits in the entire group and in the diminished group are in general in good accord with Sturner's report, which highlighted that coroner cases of sudden and traumatic death showed a better correlation between K⁺ concentration and time since death than did hospital cases.

In a third step, we excluded all cases with urea values greater than 70 mg/dl (see Table 7.17). However, the improvement in accuracy was not significant compared with the first step of elimination.

Creatinine as an internal standard

The value of creatinine as an internal standard was also checked. Creatinine and vitreous K⁺ levels were determined in 170 cases. Different creatinine values were chosen as limiting values (Table 7.18). The comparison of urea and creatinine as an internal standard showed that urea is more sensitive (see Table 7.18). The combination of limiting values for urea levels lower than 70 mg/dl and creatinine values lower than 1 mg/dl revealed the most precise death time estimation with 95 per cent confidence limits of ± 15 hours in the time interval up to 120 hours post mortem. Considering from our random sample only sudden traumatic deaths (n = 71), and excluding all cases with urea values greater than 70 mg/dl, revealed a significant reduction in the 95 per cent confidence limits from ± 22.34 to ± 17 hours (see Table 7.18; Figures 7.29 and 7.30).

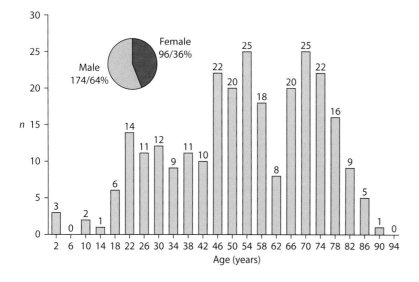

Figure 7.20 Distribution of the authors' random sample with regard to gender and age.

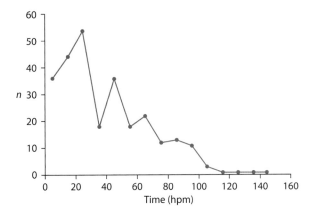

Figure 7.21 Distribution of the postmortem interval of the authors' random sample (n = 270). hpm, hours post mortem.

The result of these steps of elimination to obtain a closer relationship between K^+ and time since death is that, by these means, a separation into cases with and without severe disturbances of metabolism is possible. Depending on the information obtained from the corpse in question – no other knowledge about health before death should be necessary – one can choose the reference for estimating time since death with different 95 per cent confidence limits (Table 7.19; see also Tables 7.17 and 7.18). A limiting value for urea of 100 mg/dl – which has been chosen arbitrarily – seems to be sufficient to separate cases with and without disturbances of metabolism at the moment of death.

Our conclusion that vitreous urea nitrogen is the most suitable internal standard of the disturbed homeostasis of electrolyte metabolism is confirmed by our augmented study.

Recommendations for further studies

Several internal and external factors have been identified that govern the postmortem rise of vitreous K^+. The rise of vitreous K^+ in different temperature groups must be studied further to have reference material for casework. However, further studies on vitreous K^+, in our opinion, make sense only if all the external and internal factors influencing the postmortem increase of K^+ are taken into consideration. For these studies, more case material is necessary not only to determine the effect of influencing factors but also to obtain useful statistical parameters to be applied in casework.

Rognum et al. [153] published a paper on the postmortem increase of vitreous hypoxanthine (Hx) in comparison with vitreous K^+; the vitreous humour was collected by repeated sampling. The scatter of the K^+ values was greater than for Hx. However, our own preliminary studies give contrary results, with the scatter of levels for Hx being greater than those for K^+ [108]. Perhaps by combining both methods and performing a multiple linear regression analysis, the procedure for the estimation of death time can be improved.

Which formula should be used in casework?

In his historical review, Coe [36] asked whether vitreous K^+ could be considered to have any value for the forensic pathologist at the present time. He recommended the test, and we share his opinion. Vitreous K^+ is only of limited value for estimating the time since death in the first 24 hours post mortem because other methods (e.g. body cooling, electrical excitability of skeletal muscles, chemical excitability of the iris) work quite satisfactorily in this postmortem period, but the value of vitreous K^+ may increase with an increasing PMI, especially when the body has lain in a low to moderate environmental temperature. However, Coe proposed as the simplest procedure the well-known equation developed by Sturner [178]:

$$PMI = 7.14 \times K^+ \text{ concentration} - 39.1$$

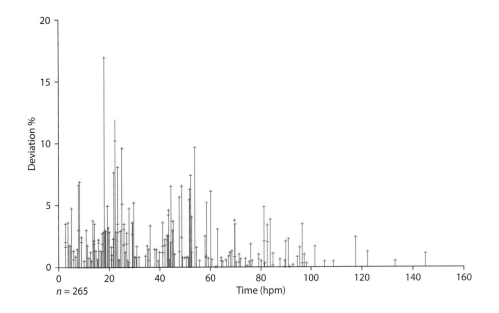

Figure 7.22 Histogram showing the percentage deviation of the single potassium values of each eye from the mean value of both eyes. hpm, hours post mortem.

Table 7.16   Percentage difference in results of potassium, sodium and urea in each eye expressed as a percentage of the mean result*

Potassium difference	<4%	4–10%	>10%
n	29 (240)	19 (23)	11 (2)
%	49.2 (90.5)	32.2 (8.7)	18.6 (0.8)
Sodium difference	**<2%**	**2–5%**	**>5%**
n	35 (173)	18 (56)	6 (36)
%	59 (65)	31 (21.1)	10 (13.5)
Urea difference	**<6%**	**6–12%**	**>12%**
n	27 (217)	11 (27)	9 (20)
%	57 (82.2)	23 (10.2)	19 (7.6)

* Authors' data in parentheses.

Data from Balasooriya BAW, Hill CAS, Williams AR. The biochemistry of vitreous humour: a comparative study of the potassium, sodium and urate concentration in the eyes at identical time intervals after death. *Forensic Sci Int* 1984;**26:**85–91.

Although the slope in Sturner's material is the flattest reported in the literature (see Table 7.13), Coe stated that results obtained from this formula are most satisfactory when the ambient temperature in which the body has lain is less than 50°F, and he emphasized that results even under these conditions may be inexact. The 95 per cent confidence limits will be much greater than ± 4 hours on the first day and will increase with an increasing PMI. However, clear values for the precision of estimating the time since death (95 per cent confidence limits) using the Sturner formula are lacking. Madea *et al.* [107] compared the suitability and precision of death time estimation of the Sturner formula with their own equation with a much steeper slope (Figure 7.31). In 100 cases, mostly sudden traumatic or natural death with a short terminal episode and an ambient temperature lower than 50°F, the time since death was extrapolated using both the Sturner formula:

$$PMI = 7.14 \times K^+ \text{ concentration} - 39.1$$

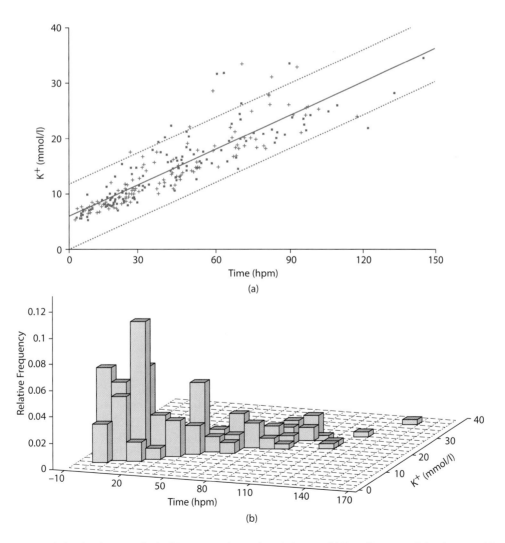

(a)

(b)

Figure 7.23   (a) Potassium (K⁺) value (mean value) of 270 cases plotted against time since death. This entire sample includes forensic and hospital cases. (b) Two-dimensional distribution of K⁺ values and postmortem interval. hpm, hours post mortem.

Table 7.17 Urea as internal standard: statistical parameters of the entire sample and the subgroups*

		Urea <100 mg/dl	Change (%)	Urea <70 mg/dl	Change (%)
n	270 (170)	228 (138)	−15.5	206	23.7
Intercept	6.10 (5.99)	6.02 (5.88)	−1.3	5.92	−2.9
Slope	0.20 (0.2033)	0.18 (0.1877)	−10	0.18	−10.0
Correlation coefficient (r)	0.89 (0.86)	0.91 (0.89)	+2.2	0.93	+4.5
Variance (s^2_{yx})	8.57	5.09	−40.6	4.09	−47.7
Standard deviation (s_{yx})	2.93 (3.42)	2.25 (2.62)	−23.2	2.02	−31.0
95% confidence limits (h)	± 25.51 h (± 34)	± 21.78 h (± 22)	−14.6	± 20.4 h	−21.3

* Data in parentheses are from Madea B, Henssge C, Honig W, Gerbracht A. References for determining the time of death by potassium in vitreous humour. *Forensic Sci Int* 1989;**8:**231–243.

and our own formula:

$$PMI = 5.26 \times K^+ \text{ concentration} - 30.9$$

From the deviation between real and extrapolated time since death, statistical parameters of precision of death time estimation were calculated. In a second step, we calculated the time since death for all cases in our random sample (n = 270) with a PMI of more than 30 hours and a urea value of less than 100 mg/dl (n = 109) by using Sturner's equation. This random sample is comparable to Sturner's material, in respect of cause and manner of death. Using the Sturner equation, there is a systematic deviation between real and extrapolated time since death (Figure 7.32 and Table 7.20). The mean difference between real and extrapolated time since death is 15 hours in the group of 100 cases compared with only −0.26 hours using our own equation. In the group of cases with a PMI of more than 30 hours and with urea values lower than 100 mg/dl, the mean difference (x) rises to 26 hours and the 95 per cent confidence limits to ± 41 hours (Figure 7.33 and Table 7.21). This means that these parameters cover nearly the whole investigated PMI. The systematic overestimation of the time since death using Sturner's equation was expected: the reason is the flat slope (see Figure 7.31). Nearly all studies with larger case material reveal a much steeper slope between 0.17 and 0.238 mmol/l per hour. Therefore, when using the vitreous K⁺ level to estimate the time since death, equations with a steeper slope than that reported by Sturner should be preferred to avoid systematic overestimations of the time since death.

Estimating the time since death with a slope of 0.19 mmol/l per hour and an intercept of 5.88 mmol/l (which is almost the same as the intercept calculated from Sturner's material of 5.96 mmol/l) provides an estimation of the time since death with no systematic deviations. The 95 per cent confidence limits are ± 20 hours up to 100 hours post mortem.

Other equations on PMI estimation are shown in Table 7.22.

A comparison of the precision of death time estimation using these different formulas is still missing.

Re-analysis of original data and construction of a local regression model

Lange *et al.* [85] re-analysed the data of six studies on the rise of vitreous K⁺ comprising 790 cases total [1,29,71,104,175,178]. This re-analysis revealed that:

- The relationship between vitreous K⁺ and PMI is not completely linear.
- The residual variability of vitreous K⁺ as a function of PMI is not constant.

Therefore, these investigators developed a new approach for modelling vitreous K⁺ and PMI that accommodated non-linearities and changing residual variability. At first, a local regression model – specifically a loess smooth curve – was fitted separately to the data from each of the six studies. The data of all six studies were then combined to yield a single loess curve with 95 per cent confidence limits (Figure 7.34).

The estimated loess curve and confidence limits were then used in an inverse prediction method to construct low, middle and high PMI estimates at given values of vitreous K⁺ (Table 7.23).

The reliability of estimated PMI decreases with an increasing K⁺ concentration. However, PMI estimates are more precise over the entire range of vitreous K⁺ and PMI than are estimates obtained from any single study alone. For K⁺ values lower than 7 mmol/l, the extent of the lower and upper 95 per cent confidence limits is ± 1 hour. For K⁺ values greater than 7 mmol/l but less than 12 mmol/l, the extent of these confidence limits is ± 2 hours. For a K⁺ value greater than 12 mmol/l and less than 18 mmol/l, the extent is ± 3 hours, whereas for a value greater than 18 mmol/l, the extent is ± 5 hours. For concentrations greater than18 mmol/l, the extent is even greater.

However, because of the much greater variability of the single K⁺ concentrations of the included studies from the 'single loess curve' with its 95 per cent confidence limits, the reliability of the statistical evaluation remains unclear. Obviously, the 95 per cent confidence limits concern the 'single loess curve' and not the deviations of the single values from the 'single loess curve'.

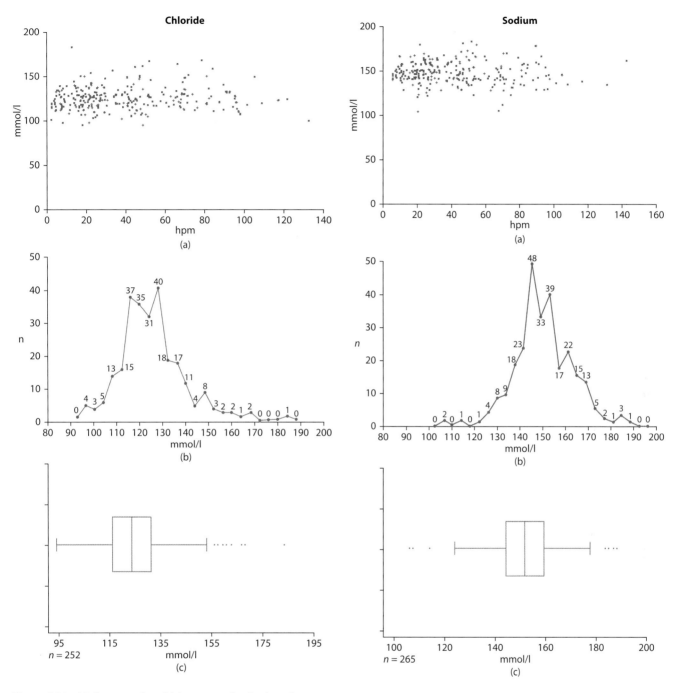

Figure 7.24 (a) Concentration, (b) frequency distribution of concentration and (c) box plots of chloride concentration. The rectangular box contains 50 per cent of all values found, marked by the upper and lower quartile. The box is divided by the median in two parts. The lines on the right and the left of the box correspond to the 90 per cent confidence interval and the median. The distribution becomes evident from the box plots.

Figure 7.25 (a) Concentration, (b) frequency distribution of concentration and (c) box plots of sodium concentration. The rectangular box contains 50 per cent of all values found, marked by the upper and lower quartile. The box is divided by the median in two parts. The lines on the right and the left of the box correspond to the 90 per cent confidence interval and the median. The distribution becomes evident from the box plots.

Re-evaluation of the data of Lange and associates

To re-evaluate the validity of the table of Lange *et al.* [85] (see Table 7.23) from 523 cases with measured K^+ concentrations and known time since death, 492 cases (94 per cent) were selected [102]. In these 492 cases, the K^+ concentrations were within a 10 per cent interval (±5 per cent) around the increasing K^+ values given by Lange *et al.* (see Table 7.23).

Of the selected 492 cases, 153 had a PMI within the predicted PMI for the given K^+ concentration, and 339 lay outside the interval (Table 7.24) [102].

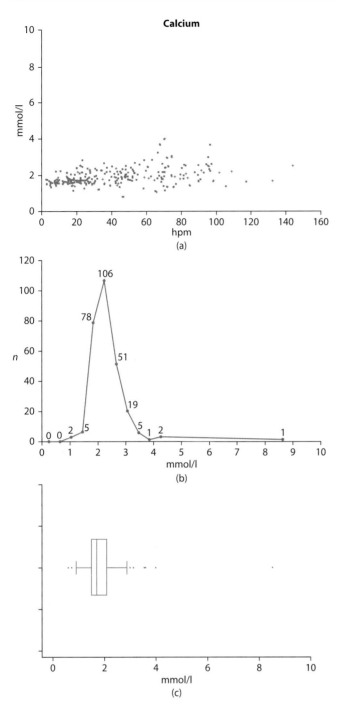

Figure 7.26 (a) Concentration, (b) frequency distribution of concentration and (c) box plots of calcium concentration. The rectangular box contains 50 per cent of all values found, marked by the upper and lower quartile. The box is divided by the median in two parts. The lines on the right and the left of the box correspond to the 90 per cent confidence interval and the median. The distribution becomes evident from the box plots.

There has been a mean difference of −6 hours between estimated time since death according to Table 7.23 and actual time since death and a standard deviation of ± 12 hours.

Figure 7.35 shows a widening gap between estimated and actual time since death with an increasing K⁺

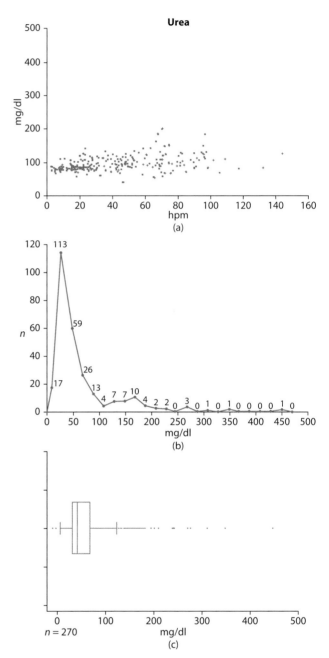

Figure 7.27 (a) Concentration, (b) frequency distribution of concentration and (c) box plots of urea concentration. The rectangular box contains 50 per cent of all values found, marked by the upper and lower quartile. The box is divided by the median in two parts. The lines on the right and the left of the box correspond to the 90 per cent confidence interval and the median. The distribution becomes evident from the box plots.

concentration corresponding to an increasing time since death.

It can be concluded that the calculation of the time since death based on the table published by Lange et al. [85] (see Table 7.23) reveals a systematic overestimation of the time since death, and the accuracy of death time estimation cannot be confirmed [102].

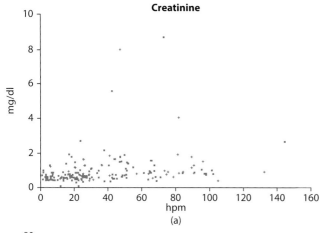

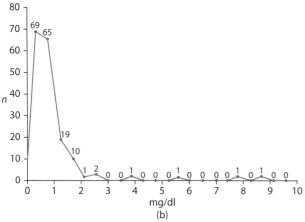

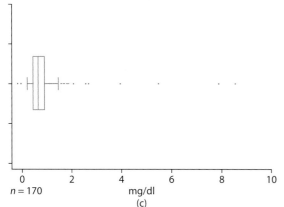

Figure 7.28 (a) Concentration, (b) frequency distribution of concentration and (c) box plots of creatinine concentration. The rectangular box contains 50 per cent of all values found, marked by the upper and lower quartile. The box is divided by the median in two parts. The lines on the right and the left of the box correspond to the 90 per cent confidence interval and the median. The distribution becomes evident from the box plots.

Accuracy of estimating the time since death by using the potassium concentration as independent valuable

Since the 1970s, reports on the rise of the K+ concentration in vitreous humour have been published, with different statements concerning the accuracy of death time estimation. Although in most investigations the PMI has been used as the independent variable and K+ concentration as the dependent variable for regression analysis between PMI and K+ concentration, it has been suggested to use the K+ concentration as the independent variable for regression analysis [124,127]. Changing variables would lead to a higher accuracy in death time estimation. This hypothesis has meanwhile been checked on independent cases with K+ and Hx in vitreous humour. Linear regression with the K+ or Hx concentration as an independent variable has revealed a slightly more accurate death time estimation compared with linear regression with PMI as the independent variable (Table 7.25). Thus, for example, the accuracy could have been improved from ± 25.96 to ± 23.27 hours by using the K+ concentration as the independent variable [102].

Multiple linear regression analysis

Multiple linear regression analysis uses, apart from vitreous K+, further time-dependent changing vitreous analytes. By using the multiple linear regression formula:

$$PMI = 24.64 + (4.3741 \times K^+) - (0.278 \times Na^+) - (0.065 \times urea) - (1.08 \times \log glucose)$$

95 per cent confidence limits of ± 14 hours could be achieved (Figure 7.36). Using K+ alone, the 95 per cent confidence limits on the same sample (n = 85) were ± 16.2 hours. Therefore, it can be concluded that, by using multiple linear regression analysis, a slight increase in the precision of death time estimation can be achieved.

■ Hypoxanthine

Elevated Hx values resulting from tissue hypoxia have been demonstrated by several authors in different body fluids (plasma, urine, CSF, fetal scalp blood) [47,55,62,63,75,102, 108,113–115,118,124,127,139,140,142,151–153,156,157, 169]. These elevated Hx values are thought to be good markers of hypoxia, mainly in paediatric cases [62,63,113– 115,118,139,140,142,151,153,157,158,169]. The increase of Hx during hypoxia is thought to be caused by the following three mechanisms:

1. An increased concentration of cellular adenosine monophosphate.
2. A decreased transformation of Hx into uric acid.
3. Inhibition of xanthine oxidase (Figure 7.37).

In 1957, Praetorius et al. [142] reported a postmortem rise of Hx in CSF, and there are some reports on the postmortem elevation of Hx in skeletal muscle as an aid for estimating the time since death. A 1991 study [152] of a then

Table 7.18   **Creatinine as internal standard and creatinine compared with urea as internal standard in a random sample of 170 cases**

Statistic parameters		Creatinine <2 mg/dl	Creatinine <1.5 mg/dl	Creatinine <1.2 mg/dl	Creatinine < 1.0 mg/dl
Creatinine as internal standard (n)	170	163	154	142	133
Intercept	6.19	6.20	6.25	6.13	5.99
Slope	0.19	0.18	0.18	0.18	0.18
Correlation coefficient (r)	0.93	0.94	0.94	0.95	0.95
Variance (s^2_{yx})	4.39	3.37	3.20	2.79	1.62
Standard deviation (s_{yx})	2.10	1.84	1.79	1.67	
95% confidence limits (h)	± 19.89	± 18.08	± 17.99	± 16.94	± 16.22
Statistic parameters		**Urea <100 mg/dl**	**Urea <70 mg/dl**	**Urea <70 and Creatinine <1 mg/dl**	
Urea as internal standard compared with creatinine (n)	170	146	135	127	
Intercept	6.19	6.06	5.90	5.87	
Slope	0.19	0.187	0.18	0.18	
Correlation coefficient (r)	0.93	0.95	0.96	0.96	
Variance (s^2_{yx})	4.39	2.58	2.25	2.22	
Standard deviation (s_{yx})	2.10	1.60	1.50	1.49	
95% confidence limits (h)	± 19.89	± 16.33	± 15.22	± 14.99	

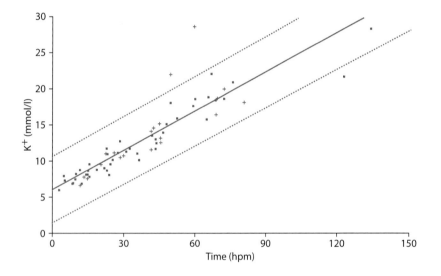

Figure 7.29 Potassium (K^+) values in cases of sudden traumatic death (n = 71). hpm, hours post mortem.

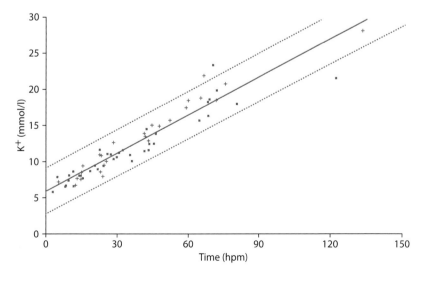

Figure 7.30 Potassium (K^+) values in cases of sudden traumatic death; elimination of all cases with urea values greater than 70 mg/dl. Significant rise in the precision of death time estimation. hpm, hours post mortem.

Table 7.19 Urea values lower than 70 mg/dl as an internal standard in cases of sudden traumatic death

Value	Entire sample	Urea <70 mg/dl
n	71	68
Intercept	6.0	6.0
Slope	0.18	0.177
Correlation coefficient (r)	0.90	0.94
Variance (s^2_{yx})	5.341	2.528
95% confidence limits	22.72	17.14

new biochemical method for estimation of postmortem time on 87 cases revealed the following:

- A linear rise of Hx in vitreous humour in the PMI up to 120 hours post mortem (hpm).
- A dependency of the slope of rise of vitreous Hx on temperature (the higher the ambient temperature, the steeper the slope).
- A strong correlation between vitreous Hx and vitreous K^+ values.
- A smaller range of scatter of the vitreous Hx than the vitreous K^+ values.

These results are based on 368 vitreous samples taken from 87 cases; 2 samples were taken from each eye, and 4 values per case were obtained.

The authors suggested further investigations on vitreous Hx in comparison with vitreous K^+. These investigations are indeed necessary because there are no statistical

parameters on the precision of death time estimation by vitreous Hx compared with vitreous K^+.

Materials and methods

Our own investigations [108] were performed on 92 bodies with a known time since death. Each globe was punctured only once, and the whole vitreous humour was withdrawn. Each sample was analyzed independently. In these 92 cases, the vitreous humour of both eyes was withdrawn at the same time post mortem.

In an additional 43 cases, vitreous humour of both eyes was withdrawn at timed intervals, ranging from 2 to 20 hours after death. The CSF samples were obtained by single puncture of the cisterna cerebello-medullaris.

The cases used for this study were all adults who had died either suddenly of natural causes, with a brief terminal episode, or of traumatic causes, also with a brief terminal episode.

The K^+ concentration was determined using ion-selective electrodes, and the Hx concentration was determined using a high-performance liquid chromatography method analogous to that of Rognum et al. [152].

Results and discussion

Vitreous humour

The vitreous samples of both eyes taken at the same time post mortem showed a good correlation of Hx and K^+

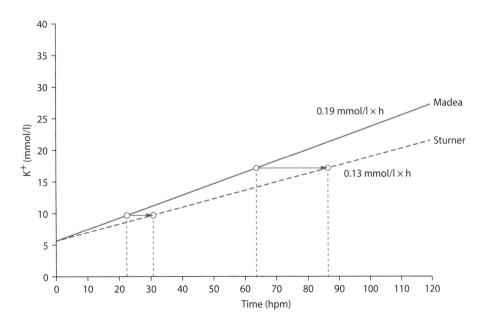

Figure 7.31 Vitreous potassium (K^+) level over the postmortem interval (in hours [hpm]). Regression lines of Sturner and of the authors' own material. The intercept of both regression lines is nearly identical, but the slope varies between 0.13 mmol/l per hour (Sturner [178]) and 0.19 mmol/l per hour (authors' material). The much flatter slope of Sturner's regression for the same K^+ values causes a systematic overestimation of the time since death compared with the authors' regression. This overestimation increases with an increasing postmortem interval.

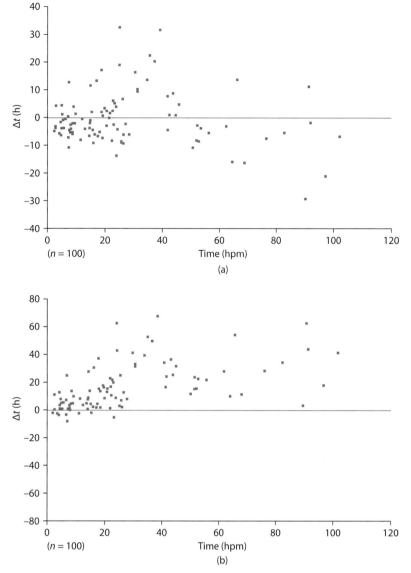

Figure 7.32 Deviations between extrapolated and real time since death (Δt in hours) over the postmortem interval for 100 independent cases in the postmortem interval from 3 to 100 hours post mortem (hpm). (a) Deviations using the authors' formula; no systematic deviations. (b) Deviations using the Sturner equation: systematic overestimation of the time since death.

Table 7.20 Mean differences, standard deviation and 95 per cent confidence limits (in hours) between real and extrapolated time since death for 100 independent cases in the postmortem interval of 3 to 100 hours, using Sturner's and the authors' own equations for extrapolating the time since death

	Sturner's equation*	Authors' equation
n	100	100
$\bar{x}$	15.35	−0.258
SD	± 16.43	± 0.56
95% confidence limits	± 32.76	± 19.06

* Data from Sturner WQ [178].

$\bar{x}$, mean differences; SD, standard deviation.

values. For statistical analysis, the mean values of the K^+ and Hx concentrations from both eyes were used.

Hx increased in a linear mode over the PMI; the linear rise began immediately post mortem rather than after a certain 'stable interval' of some 48 to 72 hours, as originally described (Figure 7.38). This immediate postmortem rise of Hx concentration is in good accord with experimental animal findings of Gardiner et al. [55] and the findings of Rognum et al. [152].

The K^+ concentration increases linearly, as has long been known (Figure 7.39), and it has a much stronger correlation with the time since death than the Hx concentration (correlation coefficient [r] = 0.925 for K^+ compared with r = 0.714 for Hx). The 95 per cent confidence limits are ± 17 hours for vitreous K^+ and ± 32 hours for vitreous Hx (Table 7.26).

The conclusion of Rognum et al. [152] that the scatter of levels is greater for K^+ than for Hx cannot be confirmed based on our own material [see also 102, 124 and 127].

In cases with timed bilateral withdrawal of vitreous humour (intervals from 2 to 20 hours), there are great interindividual differences in the rise of Hx concentrations. As is already known for vitreous K^+, there may be greater differences between the concentrations in both eyes, even

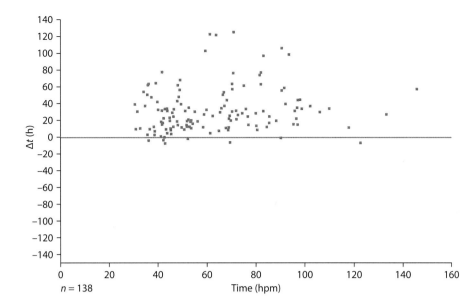

Figure 7.33 Deviations between real time (Δt) and estimated time since death over the postmortem interval in hours for 109 cases with a postmortem interval of more than 30 hours and vitreous urea values below 100 mg/dl. Extrapolation of the time since death with Sturner's equation [178].

when samples are withdrawn at the same time. This is also true for the Hx concentration. Indeed, if there are greater differences between both eyes, the later sample may have an even lower Hx concentration than the earlier sample.

Table 7.21 Mean difference, standard deviation and 95 per cent confidence limits (in hours) between real and extrapolated time since death for 109 cases with a postmortem interval of more than 30 hours and a vitreous urea value lower than 100 mg/dl

	Sturner's equation
n	109
	PMI >30 h
	Urea <100 mg/dl
$\bar{x}$	26.68
SD	± 20.88
95% confidence limits	± 40.92

Data from Sturner [178].

$\bar{x}$, mean differences; SD, standard deviation.

The differences between the results from our study [108] and those of Rognum et al. [152] on vitreous Hx and K+ are apparent. However, because we have used similar methods and the random samples consisted of comparable cases, an explanation for this discrepancy is not straightforward. One reason may be seen in the repeated sample taking, with disturbance of the vitreous concentration gradient. During life, in mammalian eyes, there are concentration gradients for several parameters among the different intra-ocular fluid compartments. After death, new gradients are established, mainly between the retina and the centre of the globe. Therefore, for biochemical analysis it is mandatory to aspirate the whole of the vitreous humour. Repeated sample taking disturbs the diffusion gradient and establishes a drainage effect, as described by Schourup [169] and by Dotzauer and Naeve [47] in their studies on CSF.

Rognum and Saugstad [151] seemed to be aware of this drainage effect in another study on vitreous Hx values in cases of sudden infant death syndrome. Although

Table 7.22 Formulae for determining postmortem interval (hours) with potassium concentration (mmol/l)

Reference	Equation obtained*	Formula proposed
Sturner [178]	y = 0.14 x + 5.6	PMI = 7.14 [K+] − 39.1
Adelson et al. [1]	y = 0.17 x + 5.36	-
Hansson et al. [61]	y = 0.17 x + 8	-
Coe [29]	y = 0.332 x + 4.99 (x < 6h)	-
Coe [29]	y = 0.1625 x + 6.19 (x ≥ 6h)	-
Adjutanis and Coutselinis [2]	y = 0.55 x + 3.14	-
Stephens and Richards [176]	y = 0.238 x + 6.342	-
Madea et al. [104]	y = 0.19 x + 5.88	PMI = 5.26 [K+] − 30.9
James et al. [75]	y = 0.23 x + 4.2	PMI = 4.32 [K+] − 18.35
Muñoz Barús et al. [127]	y = 0.17 x + 5.60	PMI = 3.92 [K+] − 19.04
Jashnani et al. [76]		PMI = 1.076 [K+] − 2.815

* y is potassium (K+); variable x is postmortem time/interval (h).

PMI, postmortem interval.

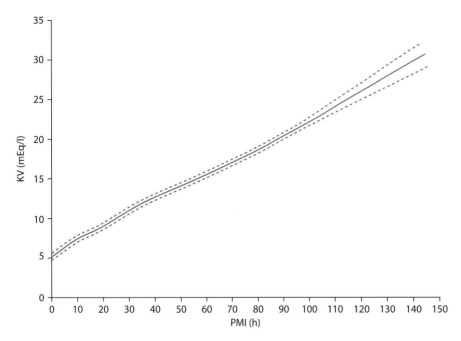

Figure 7.34 The estimated relationship between vitreous potassium (KV) and postmortem interval (PMI) for six studies, with 95 per cent lower and upper confidence limits. (From Lange N, Swearer ST, Sturner WQ. Human postmortem interval estimation from vitreous potassium: an analysis of original data from six different studies. *Forensic Sci Int* 1994;**66:**159–174.)

Table 7.23 Estimated values of postmortem intervals for various increasing values of potassium obtained from combining all 790 cases and the loess procedure

Measured vitreous potassium concentration mmol/l	Estimated PMI (h)		
	Lower 95% confidence limit value	Mean value	Upper 95% confidence limit value
5.9	2	3	4
6.4	3	5	6
7.0	6	7	8
7.5	8	10	12
8.0	11	13	15
8.5	14	16	19
9.1	18	21	22
10.1	23	25	27
11.1	29	30	32
12.1	33	35	38
13.0	39	41	44
13.9	44	47	50
14.9	51	54	57
15.9	58	61	64
17.0	66	69	72
18.3	74	77	81
19.7	81	85	90
21.1	89	94	100
22.6	98	103	111
24.2	106	113	123

From Lange N, Swearer ST, Sturner WQ. Human postmortem interval estimation from vitreous potassium: an analysis of original data from six different studies. *Forensic Sci Int* 1994;**66:**159–174.

Table 7.24 Overview of cases (n = 492) with potassium concentrations within 10 per cent around the mean values according to Lange *et al.* (see Table 7.23)*

		Frequency	Percentage
Cases within the postmortem interval corresponding to the potassium concentration according to Table 7.23.	No	n = 339	68.9%
	Yes	n = 153	31.1%
	Total	N = 492	100.0%

* The postmortem interval (PMI) was calculated for the respective K+ according to Table 7.23; 339 PMIs were outside the PMI according to Table 7.14, and 153 were inside.

From Madea B, Rödig A. Time of death dependent criteria in vitreous humor: accuracy of estimating the time since death. *Forensic Sci Int* 2006;**164:**87–92.

each globe was punctured twice, the Hx values of the second sample were found to be too high. These authors reported that, 'Multiple sampling during hypoxaemia was attempted, but this procedure led to artificially high values of hypoxanthine compared with control values from the left eye … and the procedure had to be abandoned' [139]. These authors added that, 'Furthermore, in the group in which sampling was started early after death, there was a slight tendency for the Hx increase to be greater at the second sampling within the same eye. This increase could be attributable to a certain degree of tissue mutilation during the sample procedure'.

A second possible reason for the different results may be that not only does Hx increase post mortem in vitreous humour and CSF as a result of irreversible circulatory arrest, anoxaemia and diffusion, but also, during vital hypoxia, 'there is an accelerated catabolism of adenosine monophosphate to hypoxanthine which accumulates in tissues and body fluids [151]'.

In 1975, increased levels of plasma Hx were reported in newborn infants with clinical signs of intrauterine hypoxia

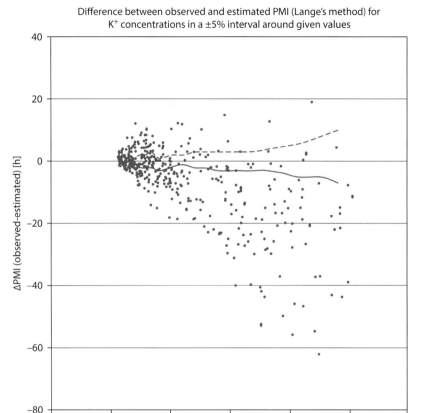

Difference between observed and estimated PMI (Lange's method) for K+ concentrations in a ±5% interval around given values

---

—— Lower 95% value of estimated PMI (Lange's method) relative to given mean
--- Upper 95% value of estimated PMI (Lange's method) relative to given mean
•   Distance of observed PMI from mean estimated PMI according to Lange et al.

Figure 7.35   Deviations between real and extrapolated time since death over the potassium (K+) concentration. Each point represents the difference between the observed postmortem interval (PMI) and estimated PMI according to Lange *et al*. Those cases with K+ concentrations in a ±5 per cent interval around the given concentrations were included. The two lines represent the upper and lower value of the 95 per cent confidence interval according to Lange *et al*. [85] relative to the given means [102].

Table 7.25   **Regression parameters of the linear regression for estimating the time since death from vitreous potassium: correlation coefficient, standard deviation and 95 per cent confidence limits***

| Data | Own cases (N = 170) | | Cases from Muñoz Barús *et al*., 2002 (N = 171) | |
	[K+]-dependent variable	PMI-dependent variable	[K+]-dependent variable	PMI-dependent variable
Rise (PMI/K+)	4.76	3.82	5.78	3.81
Intercept (PMI)	−29.05	−16.46	−32.28	−18.15
Mean value of residues (real minus calculated)	0.055	0.000	−0.014	0.000
Standard deviation (h)	13.25	11.87	4.36	3.54
95% confidence limits	± 25.96	± 23.27	± 8.55	± 6.94
PMI (h)	Up to 133		Up to 23	
Correlation coefficient (r²)	0.801		0.660	

* Compared are precisions of estimating the time since death on two random samples with [K+] as dependent or independent variable. Own sample and cases by Muñoz Barús *et al*. (n = 176).

[K+], potassium concentration; PMI, postmortem interval.

From Madea B, Rödig A. Time of death dependent criteria in vitreous humor: accuracy of estimating the time since death. *Forensic Sci Int* 2006;**164**:87–92.

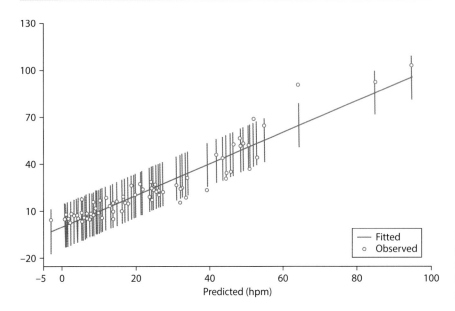

Figure 7.36 By multiple regression analysis, the calculated time since death over the real time since death. The vertical lines represent the 95 per cent confidence limits. hpm, hours post mortem.

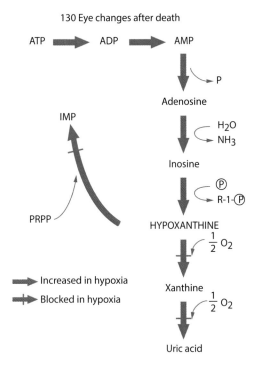

Figure 7.37 Cellular mechanisms for an increase of hypoxanthine concentration during hypoxia. ADP, adenosine diphosphate; AMP, adenosine monophosphate; ATP, adenosine triphosphate; IMP, inosine monophosphate; NH$_3$, ammonia; P, phosphate; PRPP, 5-phospho-a-d-ribosyl pyrophosphate. (From Saugstad OD. Hypoxanthine as a measurement of hypoxia. *Pediatr Res* 1975;**9**:158–161.)

during labour, compared with newborn infants after normal delivery. These increased values were interpreted as being caused by hypoxia, and the Hx accumulation in plasma was seen as a sensitive parameter of hypoxia.

The increase in Hx levels in different body fluids has been confirmed by several working groups. The vital elevation resulting from hypoxia is a factor of about 2.5 to 5, but it is rarely 10 or more. Compared with this vital elevation, the postmortem rise has a 66-fold increase [55], which is much more marked. However, if hypoxia during life causes a marked increase in vitreous Hx, this may of course result in a greater scatter of postmortem Hx values than of K$^+$ values.

The postmortem rise of vitreous K$^+$ is mainly caused by diffusion from the retina into the centre of the globe, whereas Hx is a postmortem degradation product of the adenine nucleotide metabolism. Hx is formed by the process of several enzymatic reactions (see Figure 7.37), and it then diffuses along the concentration gradient. In theory, it could be expected that a parameter such as a postmortem increase that is solely the result of diffusion would correlate much more strongly with the time since death than would a parameter that increases in response to vital or postmortem degradation and diffusion. Meanwhile, different formulae for determining PMI (hours) with Hx (μmol/l) have been proposed (Table 7.27) [75,102,108,127,152].

In CSF, there is an exponential rise of the Hx concentration, with the steepest slope during the first 15 hours post mortem (Figure 7.40). This steep rise during the early PMI is apparent from the results of Praetorius *et al.* [142], who found a more than 100-fold increase of Hx and xanthine values in CSF during the time interval up to 36 hours post mortem.

Manzke *et al.* [114] observed no significant differences in the oxypurine concentrations of CSF samples during the first 3 days post mortem (the samples were reserved during autopsy), but these authors clearly obtained their samples too late. Immediately after death, a rapid and marked rise of Hx in CSF occurs, and an equilibration seems to be achieved after about 20 hours. An exponential rise has also been reported in CSF K$^+$ levels. Among several other components of CSF examined by Schourup [169], the steepest rise occurs within the first few hours post mortem, and equilibration is achieved after about 15 hours.

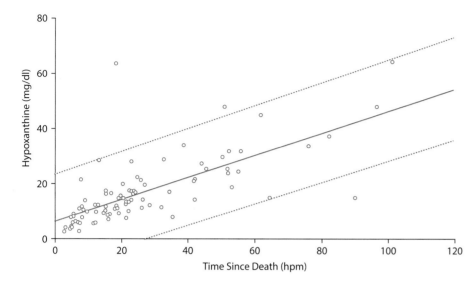

Figure 7.38 Hypoxanthine concentration in vitreous humour over the time since death (hours post mortem [hpm]), with 95 per cent confidence limits.

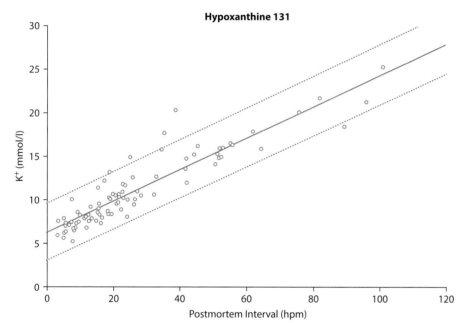

Figure 7.39 Potassium (K⁺) concentration over the postmortem interval (hours post mortem [hpm]), with 95 per cent confidence limits.

The mean normal value for CSF Hx in newborn infants was found to be 3.6 (range, 1.8 to 5.5) mmol/l, whereas that in adults was 1.8 (range, 0.6 to 5.1) mmol/l [62,63].

Compared with the rise of Hx in CSF that occurs as a consequence of hypoxia, the postmortem rise and the postmortem Hx levels are much more marked. Neither CSF K⁺ nor CSF Hx concentrations can be recommended for practical

Table 7.26   Statistical parameters on the precision of estimating the postmortem interval by vitreous hypoxanthine and potassium

	Hypoxanthine	Potassium
n	92	92
Correlation coefficient (r)	0.7138	0.925
Intercept (a)	3.6991	6.3177
Slope (b)	1.293	0.179
95% confidence limits	± 30.1	± 16.3

Table 7.27   Formulae for determining postmortem interval (hours) with hypoxanthine (μmol/l)

Reference	Equation obtained*	Formula proposed
Rognum *et al.* [152]	$y = 4.2\,x + 7.6$ at 5°C	
	$y = 5.1\,x + 7.6$ at 10°C	
	$y = 6.2\,x + 7.6$ at 15°C	
	$y = 8.8\,x + 7.6$ at 23°C	
Madea *et al.* [108]	$y = 1.29\,x + 3.69$	
James *et al.* [75]	$y = 3.2\,x - 0.15$	PMI = 0.31 [Hx] + 0.05
Muñoz *et al.* [127]	$y = 3.01\,x + 26.45$	PMI = 7.14 [Hx] + 0.17

* y is hypoxanthine; variable x is the postmortem interval (h).

Hx, hypoxanthine; PMI, postmortem interval.

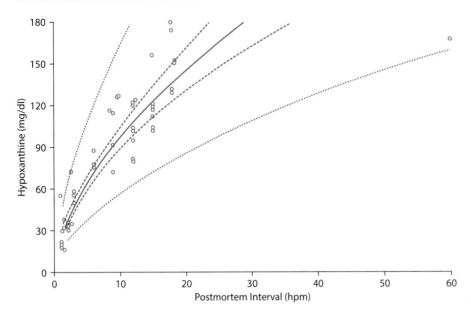

Figure 7.40 Increase of hypoxanthine in cerebrospinal fluid over various postmortem intervals. An equilibration is achieved after 15 to 20 hours post mortem (hpm).

use in death time estimation because the 95 per cent confidence limits are wide, and they also increase with increasing PMI. Other methods function satisfactorily during this early PMI, for up to 20 hours.

7.3 Cerebrospinal fluid chemistry

■ Burkhard Madea and Claus Henssge

Postmortem changes of cerebrospinal fluid (CSF) electrolytes are caused by autolytic changes of cell membranes with resulting greater permeability, so that intracellular ions of higher concentrations diffuse out into the extracellular fluid, whereas ions with a higher extracellular concentration decrease as a result of the increased volume of distribution. Postmortem changes of CSF electrolytes are based mainly on hypoxic damage of the choroid plexus.

The investigations of Schleyer on chloride and magnesium concentrations in CSF [160], of Schleyer and Janitzki on inorganic phosphorus in CSF [164] and of Dotzauer and Naeve on sodium and calcium concentrations in CSF [164] revealed that determination of these parameters is of no use in estimating the time since death – not even in the early postmortem interval (PMI). Calcium showed a tendency to increase in the later PMI, and sodium decreased with increasing PMI. Mason et al. [117] were the first to report on a relationship between time since death (t) and potassium (K+) concentration [K+] (in mmol/l) in cisternal fluid with the following regression:

$$[K^+] = 48.56 + 61.45 \lg t$$

and a standard deviation of ± 9.4 mg K+/100 ml.

This standard deviation is equivalent to a halving or doubling of the time since death calculated from the cisternal fluid K+. Neither Mason et al. [117] nor Dotzauer and Naeve [47] recommended cisternal fluid electrolyte determination for estimating the PMI.

A postmortem increase of K+ was also reported by Naumann [130] and by Murray and Hordynsky [128]. The latter authors drew the following conclusions from their investigations on 46 bodies in the time interval from 2 to 24 hours post mortem:

1. Spinal fluid cannot be compared with cisternal fluid because of the obvious divergent gradients of diffusion.
2. The concentrations of sodium, magnesium and calcium have no obvious relationship with the time since death.
3. The amount of K+ increases at a constant rate in relation to the temperature of the body.
4. Severe infections or toxic processes that exist for an extended period before death influence the subsequent rate of diffusion.

Schleyer's [160] results show, in addition to the previous studies on cisternal fluid K+, a great scatter of values over the PMI. According to Schleyer, bloody cisternal fluid does not show excessively high K+ values [159]. Further studies on CSF K+ concentrations, with similar results, were published by Fraschini et al. [52], Paulson and Stickney [135] and Weischer [197].

In spite of these disappointing results, Urban and Tröger [186–190 and personal communication, R. Urban, 1987] carried out extensive investigations on CSF electrolytes. The results were obtained from cases of sudden death. From 147 bodies, cisternal fluid was withdrawn repeatedly at half-hourly intervals; from 143 bodies, only 1 sample was taken. Rectal temperatures were taken simultaneously. As expected from the literature, the concentrations of calcium and magnesium showed no correlation with the time since death. Sodium concentrations decreased exponentially during the first 20 hours post mortem; 2 subgroups kept at ambient temperatures of 5°C and 20°C showed no differences (Figure 7.41).

The exponential rise of cisternal fluid K⁺ during the first 20 hours post mortem showed a stronger relationship with the time since death (Figure 7.42). This rise of K⁺ was also not influenced by the environmental temperature. In Figure 7.42, the single values are plotted with 98 per cent confidence limits. During the first 10 hours, the variation was ± 1 hour, with the exception of four individuals dying of liver failure or uraemia. All the other cases were sudden deaths. Figure 7.42 (b) appears to indicate that the rise of cisternal K⁺ is not influenced by the environmental temperature. Urban and Tröger [189] could reduce the deviations between real and extrapolated time since death from ± 1.5 hours during the first 15 hours post mortem to −0.75 to +1 hour by taking the actual rectal temperature and the cooling velocity into consideration. In 1987, the authors presented a 'Potassium – time since death nomogram' and claimed 95 per cent confidence limits of ± 1.4 hours, which are wider than the published variations of ± 1 hour up to 10 hours post mortem.

In 1987, 95 per cent confidence limits of death time estimation from cisternal fluid K⁺ of ± 2.36 hours up to 15 hours post mortem were reported. By taking the temperature into consideration, these limits could be reduced to ± 1.4 hours for the interval up to 15 hours post mortem; during the interval up to 10 hours post mortem, the 95 per cent limits were ± 1.03 hours. Urban found a strong linear correlation between the estimated time since death based on cisternal K⁺ and the estimated time since death based on rectal temperature by using the nomogram method of Henssge (see part 6.1 of Chapter 6) (Figure 7.43). The author assessed cisternal K⁺ to be the most precise method of death time estimation in the early PMI because the 95 per cent confidence limits are only ± 1.4 hours compared with ± 2.8 hours using Henssge's nomogram method. The high correlation between death time estimation from cisternal K⁺ and body temperatures strengthens the value of combining different methods for a reliable statement on the time since death.

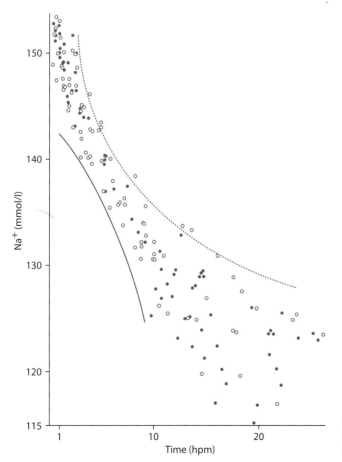

Figure 7.41 Temperature dependency of the decrease of the sodium (Na⁺) concentration in cisternal fluid over the postmortem interval. Open circles, ambient temperature of 5°C; closed circles, ambient temperature of 20°C. There is no temperature dependency. hpm, hours post mortem.

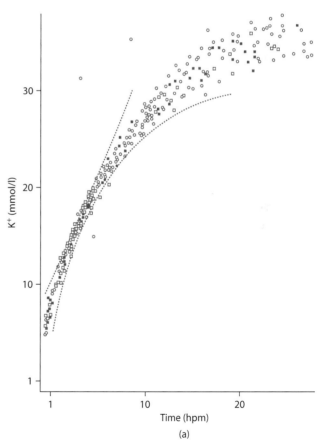

(a)

Figure 7.42 (a) Exponential rise of cisternal fluid potassium (K⁺) over the postmortem interval with cause of death. Closed squares, throttling, manual strangulation; closed circles, asphyxiation, drowning; open circles, cardiac failure: pulmonary thromboembolism, myocardial infarction; open squares, cardiac failure: shooting, stabbing; stars, liver failure, uraemia; four cases with liver failure/uraemia showed a marked deviation. (b) Rise of K⁺ for two different environmental temperatures: squares, 5°C; circles, 20°C. hpm, hours post mortem. *(Continued)*

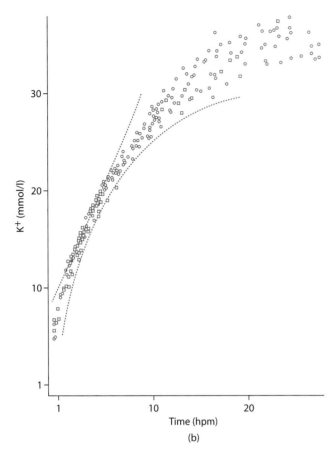

(b)

Figure 7.42 (*Continued*) (b) Rise of K+ for two different environmental temperatures: squares, 5°C; circles, 20°C. hpm, hours post mortem.

Urban and Tröger [186,188] recommended the application of his method for all cases except the following:

- Intracranial/intracerebral bleeding with haemorrhage into ventricles or cisterns.
- Chronic lingering disease with electrolyte imbalances.
- Death from hypothermia.

The value of these investigations on the increase of cisternal K+ are without any doubt because Urban has, unlike other authors, studied the cisternal K+ concentration during its steepest rise and not during the interval when the equilibrium had already been achieved.

However, succeeding authors (Madea *et al.* [101,105] and Wiesböck *et al.* [200]) found a much wider range of scatter even in cases of sudden death (Figure 7.44). Comparing the raw data of Mason *et al.* [117] with Urban's results (Figure 7.45), Mason's values taken serially from 8 bodies show a greater scatter of values, although Mason *et al.* [117] claimed to have eliminated all cases with diseases that could influence serum K+.

In the 46 cases of Murray and Hordynsky [128] (Figure 7.46), as well as in Schleyer's cases [159], there is a much wider range of scatter than was found by Urban. However, the random sample of the latter authors included cases with causes of death such as encephalitis, glomerulonephritis, chronic hepatitis, stroke and bronchopneumonia, which may cause an antemortem dysregulation of electrolyte homeostasis.

The discrepancies between our results and those of Urban cannot be explained by differences in the random

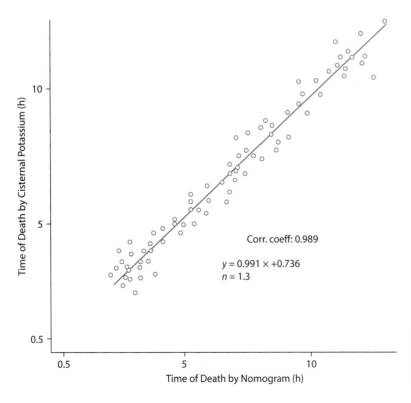

Corr. coeff: 0.989

$y = 0.991 \times +0.736$
$n = 1.3$

Figure 7.43 Correlation between estimated time since death from potassium concentration in cisternal fluid and rectal temperature (using the nomogram method of Henssge).

samples because we studied cases of sudden death exclusively. Our sample consisted mostly of natural deaths, whereas Urban's group consisted of traumatic deaths such as strangulation, throttling, shooting and stabbing, which he was in part able to investigate within 1 hour after death.

According to Urban, the differences in taking the samples (single sample taking or repeated sample taking) cannot be taken into consideration as a cause of the different scatter: he found no systematic differences in the scatter of K^+ values between single sample taking and repeated sample taking (unlike Schourup [169]).

The cause of the discrepancies in the scatter of values remains unclear, and further studies are necessary to clarify this situation. At present, we cannot recommend the use of the method of Urban and his narrow 98 per cent confidence limits.

7.4   Estimation of duration of immersion

■ *Elke Doberentz and Burkhard Madea*

The estimation of the time of immersion is a common problem in forensic medicine. The factors that govern the rate of decomposition in water and the time in which the signs of immersion are developing were identified long ago:

- The water temperature, the most important factor.
- The osmolarity of the water (fresh water, salt water).
- The bacterial content of the water (e.g. body found in a settling basin of a sewage plant).
- Stagnant water – running water.

Decomposition, of course, proceeds much faster in warm water than in cold water.

For the estimation of the time of immersion 'in water of average temperature climates' some rules of thumb have been developed, for example [79]:

1. No wrinkling of the finger pads is present: up to a few hours.
2. Wrinkled fingers, palms and feet: from half a day to 3 days.
3. Early decomposition, often first in the dependent areas of head and neck, abdomen and thighs: 4 to 10 days.
4. Bloating of face and abdomen with marbling of veins and peeling of epidermis on hands and feet and slippage of the scalp: 2 to 4 weeks.
5. Gross skin shedding, muscle loss with skeletal muscle, partial liquefaction: 1 to 2 months.

In the German literature, the rules of thumb for estimation of immersion [48,123,144] are similar to those in the English literature [56,78,79,112,138,174]. However, the reliability and validity of these rules are low. According to

Spitz (147), wrinkling of the skin cannot be used to determine the period of time a body was in the water. In the last 3 decades several authors have worked on the progression of washerwoman's skin depending on water temperature, osmolarity and other factors [112,145,193,195,196]. However, these investigations have never gained practical relevance because in the very early postmortem interval (PMI) other methods such as body cooling give quite satisfying results [68,69].

In the 1960s, a German forensic pathologist developed a table for the estimation of the time interval of immersion by taking into account the actual water temperature and morphological findings of bodies immersed in water identified during the external or internal examination [146–149]. This chart is part of German textbooks [25,95], but it seems to be relatively unknown in the English literature.

■ Correlation of water temperature and stages of putrefaction

The original investigations of the forensic pathologist Reh on 277 bodies recovered from the River Rhine with known

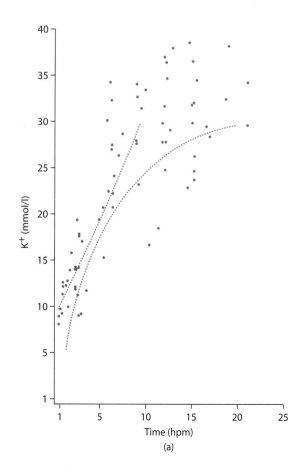

Figure 7.44 (a) Potassium (K^+) concentration over the postmortem interval (PMI) (n = 76); sudden deaths; 98 per cent confidence limits by Urban. Although the sample consists only of sudden deaths, the range of scatter is much wider than that in Urban's sample. (*Continued*)

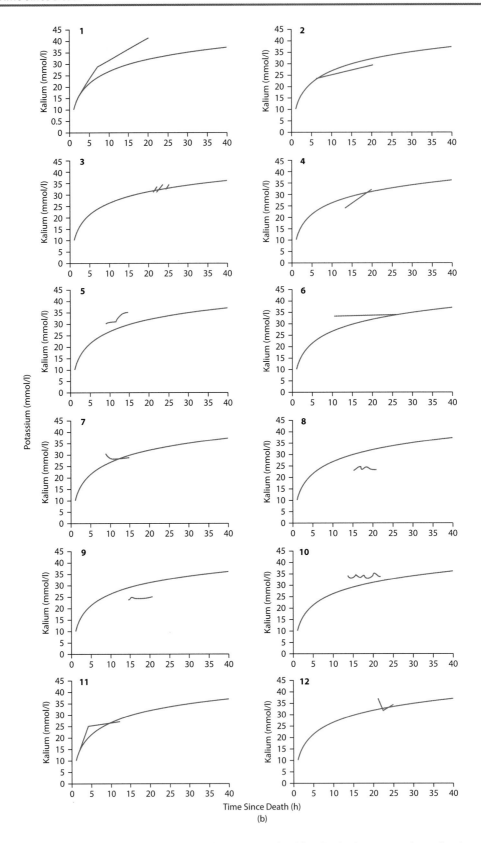

Figure 7.44   (*Continued*) (b) Individual courses of cisternal K⁺ levels in 12 cases of sudden death after repeated sample taking (ambient temperature 5°C) over the time since death. The regression curve was calculated from 76 independent K⁺ values (single sample taking). The 'rise' of cisternal K⁺ is irregular; in some cases there is a drop of the potassium concentration (cases 7, 8, 10, 12), even in the early PMI (case 7). hpm, hours post mortem. (From Wiesböck J, Josephi E, Liebhart E. Intraindividuelle Kaliumverschiebungen im Liquor cerebrospinalis nach dem Tod. *Beitr Gerichtl Med* 1989;**47**:403–405.)

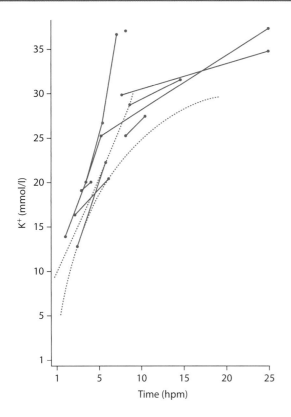

Figure 7.45 Potassium (K⁺) values (from Mason *et al.* [117]) with 98 per cent confidence limits. Nineteen values were taken from 8 bodies. hpm, hours post mortem.

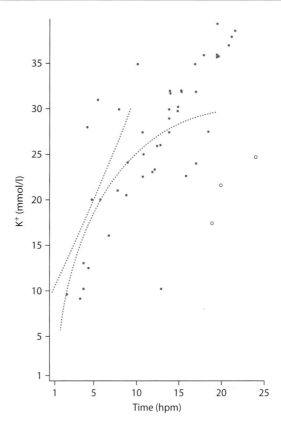

Figure 7.46 Forty-six potassium (K⁺) values (from Murray and Hordynsky [128]) with 98 per cent confidence limits by Urban. In 3 cases, only spinal fluid was available; this fluid has systematically lower potassium values than cisternal fluid. hpm, hours post mortem.

PMIs were carried out to answer the question whether there is any correlation between time of immersion and water temperature on the one hand and signs of death, signs of immersion and stages of putrefaction on the other [146,147].

The corpses were mainly recovered from the Rhine and Rhine harbour in Düsseldorf, Germany (70 per cent), with a smaller percentage (30 per cent) from other stagnant or running waters, lakes and (swimming-) pools.

Only those bodies were taken into consideration that were brought into a mortuary or a low environmental temperature (4°C, to prevent further putrefaction) immediately after recovery. Bodies of newborns or small children were excluded.

The external examination was normally carried out 2 to 3 days after recovery of the body, which is a common time interval between recovery and legal autopsy in Germany.

Certain criteria concerning autolysis, putrefaction and maceration were taken into consideration in each case (see Table 7.28).

The water temperature at the place and time of recovery – taken 0.5 to 1 m below the water surface – was considered as well.

Figure 7.47 shows the average annual water temperatures of the River Rhine in Düsseldorf from 1961 to 1964 and of the River Danube in Vienna from 1897 to 1910. Although the temperatures of the River Danube are slightly lower

than those of the Rhine (lowest difference in March: 1°C; highest difference from August to February: >1.8°C), the curves are almost identical.

However, within 1 month, the water temperature can vary considerably even in one place, and it can vary even more among different sites of the same river. Therefore, Reh considered the average water temperature for each month from 1961 to 1964.

In stagnant waters, the temperature is a little higher than in running waters.

Reh examined 277 corpses and established the following chronological order for the development of the signs of death and stages of putrefaction:

- Washerwoman's skin.
- Loosening of rigor mortis.
- Bloating and discolouration of the body.
- Loosening and loss of skin, hairs and nails, with loss of toenails last.
- Inner findings: transudate in pleural cavity greater than 500 ml.
- Heart without blood and liquefaction of brain.

A definite stage of putrefaction is achieved earlier in higher water temperatures.

Table 7.28 Reh's table to estimate the minimum time interval of immersion*

Ø	Month	Jan.	Feb.	March	April	May	June	July	Aug.	Sept.	Oct.	Nov.	Dec.
	Median water temperature (C) of the month according to measurements of Reh	3.5°	3.9°	5.8°	9.9°	13.0°	17.4°	18.6°	18.6°	17.3°	13.2°	8.8°	4.7°
	Signs of putrefaction												
1.	Marbling	32	25	16 (23)	9–10	4–5	2	1–2	2	3	4–5	10	17
2.	Distension of tissues by gas	35	25	16 (23)	10	4–5	2–3	2	3	3–4	7	10	17
3.	Discolouration of the body	35	25	16 (23)	(14)	4–5	2	2	3	3–4	7	10	17
4.	Peeling of the epidermis	35	25	16 (23)	(16)	4–5	3	2	3	3–4	7	10	17
5.	Hair loss	35	25	16 (23)	10–12	4–5	2–3	2–3	3	3–4	7	10	17
6.	Hands: beginning of wrinkling	(1)	(1) 28–30	(12 h)			(6 h)			2 h		2 h	(1)
7.	Nails become loose	>35	(40) 30–32	23	16	5	2–3	3	3	3–4	11	17	28
8.	Peeling of skin in glove form	35	(45)	23	16	10	3	3	3-4	4	7	20	28
9.	Nail loss	>53	45	30 (40)	21	14	8	3	4	10	>11	20	>35
10.	Feet: beginning of wrinkling	(1)	(1)	(12 h)	(1)		(6 h)	½ h		2 h		2 h	(1)
11.	Nails become loose	>53	40	26 (35)	17	10	5	3	4	8	12	17	28
12.	Peeling of skin	>53	60	35	16	10	5	3	5–6	8–9	>11 (14)	20	28
13.	Nail loss	>53	>60	53	>35	>28	>10	3	>10	>10	>11	>20	>35
14.	Transudate in pleural cavities†	35	25 (40)	18 (35)	10	5	3–4	3	3	11	5	>20	
15.	Heart without blood	>39	32–34 (40)	23	14–15	9	4	3	3	5	11	20	28
16.	Brain liquefied	35	30 (40)	(23)	14–	5	3–4	3	3	6	10	17	28

* Minimum time of immersion in days; maximum time in days shown in parentheses.

† >500 ml in adults.

Modified from Reh [147].

In Figure 7.48, the dependency of putrefaction on water temperature and time of immersion is shown for three criteria:

- Bloating of the body (gas emphysema).
- Liquefaction of brain.
- Loosening of toenails.

For all three criteria, the minimal time interval is given, and it becomes evident that decomposition is accelerated in higher water temperatures. Although in March loosening of toenails or liquefaction of brain requires a time interval of more than 20 days (minimum, 24 to 26 days), the minimum time interval in July is only 2 to 4 days.

Rhine in Düsseldorf, 1961–1964
Danube in Vienna, 1897–1910

Figure 7.47 Average annual water temperatures of the River Rhine in Düsseldorf from 1961 to 1964 and of the River Danube in Vienna from 1897 to 1910.

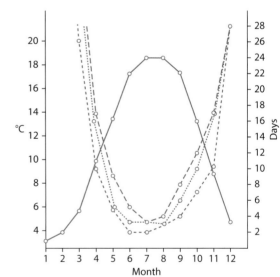

Bodies were kept for 2 to 3 days in the mortuary

Mean water temperature of the Rhine
Minimum time for gas emphysema
Minimum time for liquefaction of brain
Minimum time for loosening of toe nails

Figure 7.48 The dependency of putrefaction on water temperatures and times of immersion.

The second factor is that the different signs of putrefaction take place simultaneously.

■ Table for estimating the minimum time interval of immersion

From the average water temperatures for each month and the stages of decomposition, Reh developed a table with the minimum time intervals of immersion (Table 7.28). The left column contains the signs of decomposition (numbers 1 to 16), and the heading shows the months. Every month correlates with an average monthly water temperature (shown in the line below the month).

As many criteria as possible should be used for estimating the minimum time interval since death. With more than only one or two criteria, the result becomes more reliable. Every sign of putrefaction is correlated with a minimum time in which this sign can develop. This means, for example, that marbling can be found after a minimum of 32 days in January. After determining the signs of putrefaction and considering the several minimum times for each sign, the longest minimum time of all – the sign developing last – will be the minimum time for immersion in water. For example, the body shows marbling (32 days in January) and a liquefied brain (35 days in January) – the minimum time interval of immersion is 35 days because only after 35 days is brain liquefaction seen. The maximum time of

immersion can also be determined: a heart without blood can be found after more than 39 days. If the heart contains blood, the body was not immersed for 39 days. Our example has a minimum time of immersion of 35 days and maximum time of immersion of 39 days. A better estimation of the immersion time can be made and help to support the investigations by using the chart instead of the old rules of thumb.

For estimating the minimum time interval of immersion, the average water temperature that is closest to the actual water temperature at the time of recovery is considered and not the water temperature of the actual month. Reh proposed using the water temperature of the day of recovery for an estimation [146,147]. With this table, not only can the minimum time interval of immersion be estimated, but also the maximum interval can be estimated by considering those criteria that have not yet developed in the corpse.

If in June marbling, bloating and discolouration have developed, and the nails are loose but not lost, it may be concluded that the interval of immersion is more than 3 days but less than 8 days.

Further examples are given in Tables 7.29 to 7.34.

It has been recorded during recent years that the water temperature of the Rhine has exceeded the temperatures indicated by Reh, especially in summer. Nevertheless, a careful estimation of the minimal time interval of immersion is possible if the highest temperature given in the table is considered.

Table 7.29   Example to estimate the minimum time interval of immersion*

	Month	Jan.	Feb.	March	April	May	June	July	Aug.	Sept.	Oct.	Nov.	Dec.
Ø	Median water temperature (C) of the month according to measurements of Reh	3.5°	3.9°	5.8°	9.9°	13.0°	17.4°	18.6°	18.6°	17.3°	13.2°	8.8°	4.7°
	Signs of putrefaction												
1.	Marbling	32	25	16 (23)	9–10	4–5	2	1–2	2	3	4–5	10	17
2.	Distension of tissues by gas	35	25	16 (23)	10	4–5	2–3	2	3	3–4	7	10	17
3.	Discolouration of the body	35	25	16 (23)	(14)	4–5	2	2	3	3–4	7	10	17
4.	Peeling of the epidermis	35	25	16 (23)	(16)	4–5	3	2	3	3–4	7	10	17
5.	Hair loss	35	25	16 (23)	10–12	4–5	2–3	2–3	3	3–4	7	10	17
6.	Hands: beginning of wrinkling	(1)	(1) 28–30	(12 h)			(6 h)			2 h		2 h	(1)
7.	Nails become loose	>35	(40) 30–32	23	16	5	2–3	3	3	3-4	11	17	28
8.	Peeling of skin in glove form	35	(45)	23	16	10	3	3	3–4	4	7	20	28
9.	Nail loss	>53	45	30 (40)	21	14	8	3	4	10	>11	20	>35
10.	Feet: beginning of wrinkling	(1)	(1)	(12 h)	(1)		(6 h)	½ h		2 h		2 h	(1)
11.	Nails become loose	>53	40	26 (35)	17	10	5	3	4	8	12	17	28
12.	Peeling of skin	>53	60	35	16	10	5	3	5–6	8–9	>11 (14)	20	28
13.	Nails lost	>53	>60	53	>35	>28	>10	3	>10	>10	>11	>20	>35
14.	Transudate in pleural cavities†	35	25 (40)	18 (35)	10	5	3–4	3	3	11	5	>20	
15.	Heart without blood	>39	32–34 (40)	23	14–15	9	4	3	3	5	11	20	28
16.	Brain liquefied	35	30 (40)	(23)	14–16	5	3–4	3	3	6	10	17	28

* Minimum time of duration of immersion in days; maximum time in days shown in parentheses. Shaded areas show minimum time of immersion 10 days; in reality 5 days.

† >500 ml in adults.

Table 7.30   Example to estimate the minimum time interval of immersion*

Month	Jan.	Feb.	March	April	May	June	July	Aug.	Sept.	Oct.	Nov.	Dec.
Ø Median water temperature (C) of the month according to measurements of Reh	3.5°	3.9°	5.8°	9.9°	13.0°	17.4°	18.6°	18.6°	17.3°	13.2°	8.8°	4.7°
				Signs of putrefaction								
1. Marbling	32	25	16 (23)	9–10	4–5	2	1–2	2	3	4–5	10	17
2. Distension of tissues by gas	35	25	16 (23)	10	4–5	2–3	2	3	3–4	7	10	17
3. Discolouration of the body	35	25	16 (23)	(14)	4–5	2	2	3	3–4	7	10	17
4. Peeling of the epidermis	35	25	16 (23)	(16)	4–5	3	2	3	3–4	7	10	17
5. Hair loss	35	25	16 (23)	10–12	4–5	2–3	2–3	3	3–4	7	10	17
6. Hands: beginning of wrinkling	(1)	(1) 28–30	(12 h)			(6 h)			2 h		2 h	(1)
7. Nails become loose	>35	(40) 30–32	23	16	5	2–3	3	3	3–4	11	17	28
8. Peeling of skin in glove form	35	(45)	23	16	10	3	3	3–4	4	7	20	28
9. Nail loss	>53	45	30 (40)	21	14	8	3	4	10	>11	20	>35
10. Feet: beginning of wrinkling	(1)	(1)	(12 h)	(1)		(6 h)	½ h		2 h		2 h	(1)
11. Nails become loose	>53	40	26 (35)	17	10	5	3	4	8	12	17	28
12. Peeling of skin	>53	60	35	16	10	5	3	5–6	8–9	>11 (14)	20	28
13. Nail loss	>53	>60	53	>35	>28	>10	3	>10	>10	>11	>20	>35
14. Transudate in pleural cavities[†]	35	25 (40)	18 (35)	10	5	3–4	3	3	11	5	>20	
15. Heart without blood	>39	32–34 (40)	23	14–15	9	4	3	3	5	11	20	28
16. Brain liquefied	35	30 (40)	(23)	14–16	5	3–4	3	3	6	10	17	28

* Minimum time of duration of immersion in days; maximum time in days shown in parentheses. Shaded areas show 2 to 3 days.

† >500 ml in adults.

Good experiences with Reh's table have been reported. The chart is much better than the formerly used rules of thumb and takes the actual water temperatures into account [91].

However, the following requirements have to be met to avoid miscalculations: the bodies should have been kept at a low environmental temperature (4°C) 2 to 3 days after recovery if the signs of death and stages of putrefaction have been observed 2 to 3 days after recovery. If the examination is carried out immediately after recovery, the table can be applied as well, but the bodies must not have been

Table 7.31   Example to estimate the minimum time interval of immersion*

Month	Jan.	Feb.	March	April	May	June	July	Aug.	Sept.	Oct.	Nov.	Dec.
Ø Median water temperature (C) of the month according to measurements of Reh	3.5°	3.9°	5.8°	9.9°	13.0°	17.4°	18.6°	18.6°	17.3°	13.2°	8.8°	4.7°
				Signs of putrefaction								
1. Marbling	32	25	16 (23)	9–10	4–5	2	1–2	2	3	4–5	10	17
2. Distension of tissues by gas	35	25	16 (23)	10	4–5	2–3	2	3	3–4	7	10	17
3. Discolouration of the body	35	25	16 (23)	(14)	4–5	2	2	3	3–4	7	10	17
4. Peeling of the epidermis	35	25	16 (23)	(16)	4–5	3	2	3	3–4	7	10	17
5. Hair loss	35	25	16 (23)	10–12	4–5	2–3	2–3	3	3–4	7	10	17
6. Hands: beginning of wrinkling	(1)	(1) 28–30	(12 h)			(6 h)			2 h		2 h	(1)
7. Nails become loose	>35	(40) 30–32	23	16	5	2–3	3	3	3–4	11	17	28
8. Peeling of skin in glove form	35	(45)	23	16	10	3	3	3–4	4	7	20	28
9. Nail loss	>53	45	30 (40)	21	14	8	3	4	10	>11	20	>35
10. Feet: beginning of wrinkling	(1)	(1)	(12 h)	(1)		(6 h)	½ h		2 h		2 h	(1)
11. Nails become loose	>53	40	26 (35)	17	10	5	3	4	8	12	17	28
12. Peeling of skin	>53	60	35	16	10	5	3	5–6	8–9	>11 (14)	20	28
13. Nail loss	>53	>60	53	>35	>28	>10	3	>10	>10	>11	>20	>35
14. Transudate in pleural cavities[†]	35	25 (40)	18 (35)	10	5	3–4	3	3	11	5	>20	
15. Heart without blood	>39	32–34 (40)	23	14–15	9	4	3	3	5	11	20	28
16. Brain liquefied	35	30 (40)	(23)	14–16	5	3–4	3	3	6	10	17	28

* Minimum time of duration of immersion in days; maximum time in days shown in parentheses. Shaded areas show >20 days; really 25 days.

† >500 ml in adults.

Table 7.32 Example to estimate the minimum time interval of immersion*

	Month	Jan.	Feb.	March	April	May	June	July	Aug.	Sept.	Oct.	Nov.	Dec.
Ø	Median water temperature (C) of the month according to measurements of Reh	3.5°	3.9°	5.8°	9.9°	13.0°	17.4°	18.6°	18.6°	17.3°	13.2°	8.8°	4.7°
	Signs of putrefaction												
1.	Marbling	32	25	16 (23)	9–10	4–5	2	1–2	2	3	4–5	10	17
2.	Distension of tissues by gas	35	25	16 (23)	10	4–5	2–3	2	3	3–4	7	10	17
3.	Discolouration of the body	35	25	16 (23)	(14)	4–5	2	2	3	3–4	7	10	17
4.	Peeling of the epidermis	35	25	16 (23)	(16)	4–5	3	2	3	3–4	7	10	17
5.	Hair loss	35	25	16 (23)	10–12	4–5	2–3	2–3	3	3–4	7	10	17
6.	Hands: beginning of wrinkling	(1)	(1) 28–30	(12 h)			(6 h)			2 h		2 h	(1)
7.	Nails become loose	>35	(40) 30–32	23	16	5	2–3	3	3	3–4	11	17	28
8.	Peeling of skin in glove form	35	(45)	23	16	10	3	3	3–4	4	7	20	28
9.	Nail loss	>53	45	30 (40)	21	14	8	3	4	10	>11	20	>35
10.	Feet: beginning of wrinkling	(1)	(1)	(12 h)	(1)		(6 h)	½ h		2 h		2 h	(1)
11.	Nails become loose	>53	40	26 (35)	17	10	5	3	4	8	12	17	28
12.	Peeling of skin	>53	60	35	16	10	5	3	5–6	8–9	>11 (14)	20	28
13.	Nail loss	>53	>60	53	>35	>28	>10	3	>10	>10	>11	>20	>35
14.	Transudate in pleural cavities[†]	35	25 (40)	18 (35)	10	5	3–4	3	3	11	5	>20	
15.	Heart without blood	>39	32–34 (40)	23	14–15	9	4	3	3	5	11	20	28
16.	Brain liquefied	35	30 (40)	(23)	14–16	5	3–4	3	3	6	10	17	28

* Minimum time of duration of immersion in days; maximum time in days shown in parentheses. Shaded areas show >2 to 3 days; really 3 to 4 days, June, water temperature 21°C.

[†] >500 ml in adults.

Table 7.33 Example to estimate the minimum time interval of immersion*

	Month	Jan.	Feb.	March	April	May	June	July	Aug.	Sept.	Oct.	Nov.	Dec.
Ø	Median water temperature (C) of the month according to measurements of Reh	3.5°	3.9°	5.8°	9.9°	13.0°	17.4°	18.6°	18.6°	17.3°	13.2°	8.8°	4.7°
	Signs of putrefaction												
1.	Marbling	32	25	16 (23)	9–10	4–5	2	1–2	2	3	4-5	10	17
2.	Distension of tissues by gas	35	25	16 (23)	10	4–5	2–3	2	3	3–4	7	10	17
3.	Discolouration of the body	35	25	16 (23)	(14)	4–5	2	2	3	3–4	7	10	17
4.	Peeling of the epidermis	35	25	16 (23)	(16)	4–5	3	2	3	3–4	7	10	17
5.	Hair loss	35	25	16 (23)	10–12	4–5	2–3	2–3	3	3–4	7	10	17
6.	Hands: beginning of wrinkling	(1)	(1) 28–30	(12 h)			(6 h)			2 h		2 h	(1)
7.	Nails become loose	>35	(40) 30–32	23	16	5	2–3	3	3	3–4	11	17	28
8.	Peeling of skin in glove form	35	(45)	23	16	10	3	3	3–4	4	7	20	28
9.	Nail loss	>53	45	30 (40)	21	14	8	3	4	10	>11	20	>35
10.	Feet: beginning of wrinkling	(1)	(1)	(12 h)	(1)		(6 h)	½ h		2 h		2 h	(1)
11.	Nails become loose	>53	40	26 (35)	17	10	5	3	4	8	12	17	28
12.	Peeling of skin	>53	60	35	16	10	5	3	5–6	8–9	>11 (14)	20	28
13.	Nail loss	>53	>60	53	>35	>28	>10	3	>10	>10	>11	>20	>35
14.	Transudate in pleural cavities[†]	35	25 (40)	18 (35)	10	5	3–4	3	3	11	5	>20	
15.	Heart without blood	>39	32–34 (40)	23	14–15	9	4	3	3	5	11	20	28
16.	Brain liquefied	35	30 (40)	(23)	14–16	5	3–4	3	3	6	10	17	28

* Minimum time of duration of immersion in days; maximum time in days shown in parentheses. Shaded areas show >3 days <8 days.

[†] >500 ml in adults.

Table 7.34 Example to estimate the minimum time interval of immersion*

	Month	Jan.	Feb.	March	April	May	June	July	Aug.	Sept.	Oct.	Nov.	Dec.
Ø	**Median water temperature (C) of the month according to measurements of Reh**	3.5°	3.9°	5.8°	9.9°	13.0°	17.4°	18.6°	18.6°	17.3°	13.2°	8.8°	4.7°
	Signs of putrefaction												
1.	Marbling	32	25	16 (23)	9–10	4–5	2	1–2	2	3	4–5	10	17
2.	Distension of tissues by gas	35	25	16 (23)	10	4–5	2–3	2	3	3–4	7	10	17
3.	Discolouration of the body	35	25	16 (23)	(14)	4–5	2	2	3	3–4	7	10	17
4.	Peeling of the epidermis	35	25	16 (23)	(16)	4–5	3	2	3	3–4	7	10	17
5.	Hair loss	35	25	16 (23)	10–12	4–5	2–3	2–3	3	3–4	7	10	17
6.	Hands: beginning of wrinkling	(1)	(1) 28–30	(12 h)			(6 h)			2 h		2 h	(1)
7.	Nails become loose - *not yet*	>35	(40) 30–32	23	16	5	2–3	3	3	3–4	11	17	28
8.	Peeling of skin in glove form	35	(45)	23	16	10	3	3	3–4	4	7	20	28
9.	Nail loss	>53	45	30 (40)	21	14	8	3	4	10	>11	20	>35
10.	Feet: beginning of wrinkling	(1)	(1)	(12 h)	(1)		(6 h)	½ h		2 h		2 h	(1)
11.	Nails become loose – *not yet*	>53	40	26 (35)	17	10	5	3	4	8	12	17	28
12.	Peeling of skin	>53	60	35	16	10	5	3	5–6	8–9	>11 (14)	20	28
13.	Nails lost	>53	>60	53	>35	>28	>10	3	>10	>10	>11	>20	>35
14.	Transudate in pleural cavities[†]	35	25 (40)	18 (35)	10	5	3–4	3	3	11	5	>20	
15.	Heart without blood	>39	32–34 (40)	23	14–15	9	4	3	3	5	11	20	28
16.	Brain liquefied	35	30 (40)	(23)	14–16	5	3–4	3	3	6	10	17	28

* Minimum time of duration of immersion in days; maximum time in days shown in parentheses. Shaded areas show >4 days <10 days; really 5 days.

[†] >500 ml in adults.

exposed to environmental temperatures for a longer period. However, it must be ensured that there is no time interval between death and immersion. Having this in mind and taking into account as many criteria as possible, a careful estimation of the minimum and maximum time intervals of immersion can be made.

In 1977, Reh *et al.* [149] published, as an addition to the table, diagrams (temperature and time diagrams for different stages of putrefaction and maceration) that also allow an estimation of the minimum interval of immersion. These diagrams are based on observations on 395 bodies recovered from water. The requirements are the same as for the tables.

Reh stated in this paper that there is no difference between running and stagnant water in the chronological development of the parameters of putrefaction and maceration. The main point to consider is the water temperature at the time of recovery.

Evaluation of the data of Reh

The aim of a 2010 evaluation study was to evaluate the validity and reliability of Reh's table for the estimation of the time of immersion that was developed in the 1960s [44]. For this purpose, we evaluated retrospectively the autopsy protocols of 73 bodies from the years 1993 to 2007 mainly recovered from the River Rhine or other running

waters and some lakes. In all cases, the time interval since the persons had been missing had exactly been known. In all cases, relatives had noticed the disappearance in a timely manner (e.g. the children had disappeared, or older people had disappeared from a residential facility for older adults). From police records and further investigations by the police, it was assumed that the time since the persons had been missing and the time of immersion had been more or less identical. The collected data included gender, age, last time seen alive, length of time missing, time of recovery, state of decomposition and signs of immersion, place of recovery, depth of water, water temperature, cause of death, toxicological findings and blood alcohol concentration. In all cases, comparable to Reh's original method, the examination had taken place a few days after recovery, and the bodies had been kept at low environmental temperatures.

The signs of putrefaction were marked in Reh's table to determine the minimum time of immersion by using the average water temperatures of the month (according to Reh's table) in which the body was recovered without regard to the real water temperatures.

Finally, the estimated minimal time interval of immersion was compared with the real missing time. In those cases in which the estimated time of immersion exceeded the missing time, the average monthly water temperatures in Reh's table were compared with the real water temperatures from official sources (agency of water management) and with the real water temperatures on the day of recovery and the average water temperature during the missing time [196]. The official water temperatures of every day are determined by different water temperatures measured on several times during the course of the day.

Furthermore, in 33 cases from 1999 to 2005, the time of immersion was estimated with the aid of Reh's table by using the real water temperatures from the day of recovery and, for comparison, by using the average water temperature during the missing time. The basis of the analysis was the nearest average water temperatures in Reh's table without taking into account the actual month.

Finally, we compared the actual water temperatures of the River Rhine (from 1999 to 2007) with the average monthly water temperatures of that river from 1961 to 1964.

■ Results

Most of the bodies were found in the River Rhine, and others were found in smaller rivers, ponds or (swimming-) pools. Bodies were found all through the year but at high percentages during the months of January, June and July (Figure 7.49). Although it is within the bounds of possibility that the time of immersion could be shorter than the missing time, the opposite is quite impossible. In 49 cases, the chart gave quite reliable results, with the estimated time of immersion and the missing time in accord. In 12 cases, the time of immersion was underestimated compared with the time the person had been missing.

The greatest differences were found in these cases:

- Missing time 70 days, minimum time interval of immersion (according to Reh's table) 6 days.

- Missing time 97 days, minimum time of immersion 35 days.
- Missing time 54 days, minimum time of immersion 10 days.

However, in 12 cases, according to Reh's table the time of immersion exceeded the time the persons had been missing by more than 3 days when the estimation of the time of immersion was based on the average monthly temperature without taking into account the real water temperatures (Figure 7.50 and Table 7.35). Eight of these 12 bodies were found in the River Rhine, 4 in smaller tributaries. The greatest difference was 29 days (see Table 7.35):

- Water temperature from Reh's table: 5.8°C in March.
- Real average water temperature at the missing time: 7.1°C.
- Real water temperature on the day of recovery: 6.6°C.

Important differences were also found in case 7 (Table 7.36). The difference was 25 days. The real water temperature during the missing time had been higher than the average monthly water temperature in Reh's table:

- Water temperature from Reh's table: 3.9°C in February.
- Real average water temperature at the missing time: 7.9°C.
- Real water temperature on the day of recovery: 8.8°C.

In cases 4 and 10 (see Table 7.35), the times of immersion were overestimated for 11 and 10 days, respectively. In both cases, the average monthly water temperatures in Reh's chart were higher than the real water temperatures on the days of recovery and the average water temperature during the missing times.

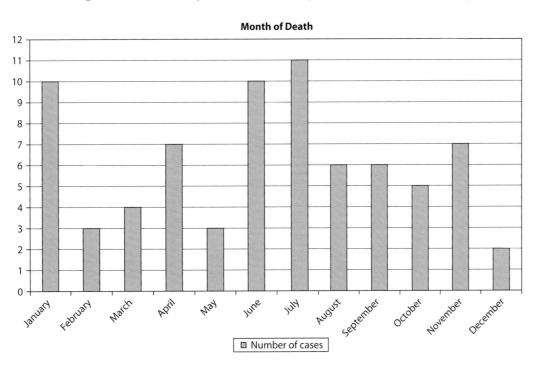

Figure 7.49 Monthly distribution of the 73 bodies recovered from water.

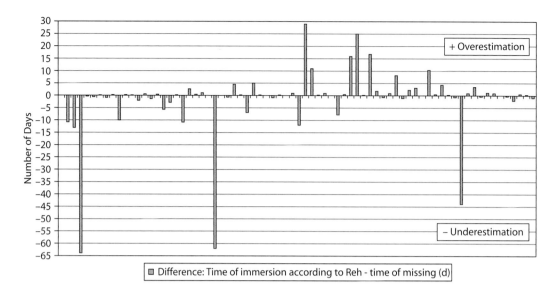

Figure 7.50 Difference between times of immersion according to Reh and the real missing times in 73 cases.

In cases 2 and 6 (see Table 7.35), no real water temperatures were available.

In 33 further cases, the actual water temperatures, instead of the average monthly water temperatures, were taken into account for the estimation of the times of immersion; again, in 14 cases, the times of immersion according to Reh's table exceeded the time the persons had been missing (see Table 7.36). The maximum time difference was 32 days (missing time 3 days – time of immersion based on the actual water temperature on the day of recovery and also on the average water temperature of 35 days).

Interestingly, in most of these cases, no difference between times of immersion based on the actual water temperature on the day of recovery compared with the average monthly water temperature was found. The reason is that in these cases the actual and the average water temperatures had been nearly identical.

In one case (case 8), the water temperature on the day of recovery was remarkably higher than the average monthly water temperatures in Reh's table:

- The maximum average monthly water temperature from Reh's table is 18.6°C (for July and August).
- Real water temperature on the day of recovery: 25.9°C.
- Real average water temperature during the missing time: 25.13°C.

■ Discussion

In cases with a long PMI, the minimum time interval of immersion can be underestimated, especially if signs of putrefaction attributed to a defined water temperature are

Table 7.35 Time of immersion was longer than the missing time in 12 cases

Case	River	Missing time (days)	Duration of immersion according to Reh (days)	Difference Reh – missing time (days)	Real water temperature on the day of recovery (°C)	Average monthly water temperature in Reh's table (°C)	Average water temperature during the missing time (°C)
1	Rhine	3.56	8.0	4.44	23.3	17.3	23.1
2	Sieg	15.02	20.0	4.98	—	8.8	—
3	Rhine	24.00	53.0	29.0	6.6	5.8	7.1
4	Rhine	2.95	14.0	11.05	9.7	9.9	9.2
5	Rhine	37.13	53.0	15.87	8.0	3.9	4.4
6	Sieg	6.17	23.0	16.83	—	5.8	—
7	Rhine	15.01	40.0	24.99	8.8	3.9	7.9
8	Rhine	1.79	10.0	8.21	24.1	18.6	24.1
9	Mosel	6.82	10.0	3.18	14.5	13.2	15.9
10	Rhine	12.74	23.0	10.25	3.5	5.8	4.3
11	Rhine	35.73	40.0	4.27	13.7	9.9	9.3
12	Mosel	2.72	6.0	3.28	22.3	17.3	22.1

Table 7.36 Estimated time of immersion in 33 cases on the basis of the water temperatures of the day of recovery and the average water temperature during the known missing time

Case	Missing time (days)	Water temperature of the day of recovery (°C)	Duration of immersion according to Reh (days)	Average water temperature (°C)	Duration of immersion according to Reh (days)	Difference Reh – missing time for water temperature day of recovery	Difference Reh – missing time for average water temperature
1	12.7	3.7	30.0	4.38	28.0	17.3	22.3
2	0.05	12.65	0.5	12.65	0.5	0.45	0.45
3	35.73	13.7	11.0	11.2	21.0	−20.73	−24.73
4	0.92	22.12	0.03	20.88	0.03	−0.89	−0.89
5	54.0	22.9	3.0	17.62	10.0	−44.0	−44.0
6	1.06	8.55	0.08	8.67	0.08	−0.98	−0.98
7	3.0	19.7	6.0	19.46	6.0	3.0	3.0
8	1.79	25.9	—	25.13	—	—	—
9	15.01	5.1	30.0	5.45	30.0	14.99	14.99
10	37.12	8.0	20.0	5.9	53.0	−17.12	15.88
11	0.65	7.9	0.08	7.9	0.08	−0.57	−0.57
12	7.05	14.0	9.0	13.87	9.0	1.95	1.95
13	2.94	9.7	35.0	9.18	35.0	32.06	32.06
14	24.0	6.6	53.0	7.1	53.0	29.0	29.0
15	0.05	15.9	0.08	15.9	0.08	0.03	0.03
16	0.89	8.3	0.08	8.35	0.08	−0.81	−0.81
17	4.0	19.9	4.0	19.96	4.0	0	0
18	0.08	20.7	0.02	20.7	0.02	−0.06	−0.06
19	1.08	7.1	0.08	7.15	0.08	−1.0	−1.0
20	19.0	13.8	20.0	13.55	20.0	1.0	1.0
21	3.6	22.5	4.0	22.7	4.0	0.4	0.4
22	0.62	16.8	0.08	17.05	0.08	−0.54	−0.54
23	0.9	22.1	0.02	22.35	0.02	−0.88	−0.88
24	3.0	21.1	4.0	20.8	4.0	1.0	1.0
25	9.0	16.8	0.25	16.7	0.25	−8.75	−8.75
26	0.5	10.9	2.0	11.0	2.0	1.5	1.5
27	1.0	8.8	0.08	8.65	0.08	−0.92	−0.92
28	5.0	19.0	4.0	19.3	4.0	−1.0	−1.0
29	3.1	22.8	4.0	21.8	4.0	0.9	0.9
30	2.7	22.3	4.0	21.3	4.0	1.3	1.3
31	6.8	16.2	6.0	16.1	6.0	−0.8	−0.8
32	72.1	7.6	53.0	7.2	53.0	−19.1	−19.1
33	0.1	24.0	0.25	24.0	0.25	0.15	0.15

found fully developed. In these cases, it has to be kept in mind that Reh's chart allows estimation only of the minimum time interval of immersion.

By using the chart correctly (on the basis of the real water temperatures), the missing time can also be overestimated. In 14 cases (of 33 cases; see Table 7.36), the determined times of immersion exceeded the real missing times. The water temperatures (on the day of recovery and the average water temperatures of the missing time) have been related to the nearest average monthly water temperature from Reh's chart. This point may be problematic because nearly identical water temperatures can be found in the chart (e.g. in July or August with 18.6°C or June and September with 17.3°C and 17.4°C), but they are related to different maximum and minimum time intervals of immersion. It is supposed that

Reh respected the water temperatures of the preceding months (with lower or higher water temperatures). This is of significance only when a body is immersed for longer than 1 month. In cases 4 and 10, the estimated minimum time of immersion exceeded the known missing time, although the water temperature in Reh's table was higher than the real water temperature. If the estimation is based on a higher water temperature (Reh's table) even though the water temperatures had been lower, the time of immersion will be underestimated because in relation to the higher temperatures, not all signs of putrefaction have developed.

Reh proved for the first time a statistical correlation between putrefactive changes and water temperature. Based on this correlation, he developed a chart to estimate the minimum time of immersion. The estimations were based on the water temperatures at the day of recovery. However, using the water temperature of the day of recovery can reveal totally inaccurate conclusions because the water temperatures during the whole time of immersion can be higher or lower. Especially when the immersion time is comparatively long, fluctuation of water temperatures can be observed, and the water temperature on the day of recovery may not be representative of the water temperature during the whole time of immersion. This becomes evident from Figure 7.51, in which original water temperatures over 20 days at the turn of the years 2002 to 2003 are shown. The water temperature on the day of recovery (2.9°C) is about 4°C lower than the average temperature (6.8°C). By using the water temperature on the day of recovery, the *estimated* time of immersion would be much longer than the *real* time of immersion. The water temperature on the day of recovery is the average water temperature on the day the body was found, as measured by an official water company.

In contrast, in two cases (cases 4 and 10; see Table 7.30) we found an overestimation of the time of immersion, although the average monthly water temperature in Reh's chart was higher than the water temperature on the day of recovery and the average water temperature during the time the individual was missing.

Another problem is the recommendation to use average monthly temperatures for the estimation of duration of the immersion. If, for example, the water temperature on the day of recovery is 13.1°C, nearly the same temperature can be found in May (13.0°C) and October (13.2°C) in Reh's table. Although there is only a slight difference of the

average temperature, the estimated times of immersion differ widely. Our analyses revealed that in some cases the actual water temperatures have been more than 7°C higher than the average monthly temperatures reported by Reh. The rise of the water temperatures of the River Rhine is also illustrated in Figures 7.52 and 7.53. Today, the average monthly water temperatures of the River Rhine measured near Bonn are approximately 2°C higher than in the 1970s and 3°C to 4°C higher than the average monthly water temperatures in Reh's table. Climate changes, as well as direct anthropogenic influences (industrial waters, power stations), may have contributed to an increase of the water temperature in the River Rhine. There are also considerable annual fluctuations in the average monthly water temperatures (Figure 7.54). The normal water level of the Rhine ranges between 200 and 550 cm [83], relating to the measuring stations along the Rhine.

Furthermore, we compared the average monthly water temperatures according to Reh's table with the actual water temperatures of the River Rhine for the years 1999 to 2007. The analysis is confined to this time period because digital and online data have been available only since 1999. Today's average monthly water temperatures of the River Rhine range about 4°C higher than in the 1960s (Table 7.37; see Figure 7.53).

Since 1978, the water temperature of the River Rhine increased by about 1.2°C [195]. Although this increase seems to be minor, there are considerable monthly and yearly climate changes with an influence on water temperatures (see Figures 7.52 and 7.54). Even fluctuations of about 8.0°C per year can be found.

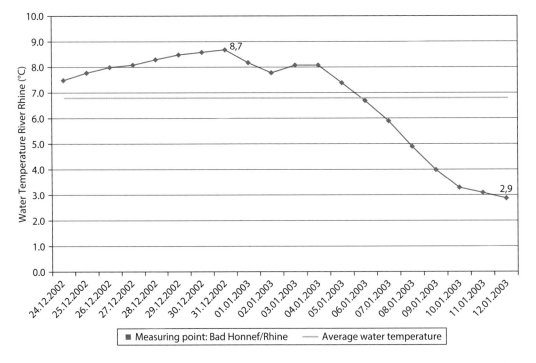

Figure 7.51 Example of the fluctuations of water temperatures during a period of 20 days (original water temperatures of the River Rhine from 24 December 2002 to 12 January 2003). (From Doberentz E, Madea B. Estimating the time of immersion of bodies found in water: an evaluation of a common method to estimate the minimum time interval of immersion. *Rev Esp Med Leg* 2010;**36**(2):51–61.)

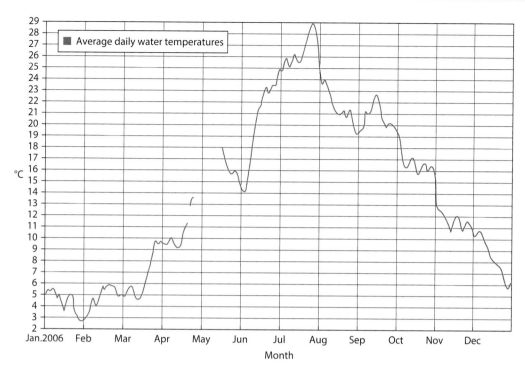

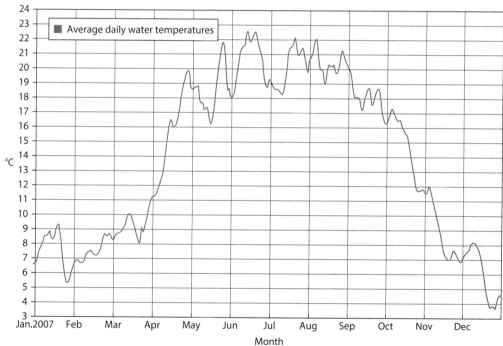

Figure 7.52 Water temperatures (°C) of the River Rhine measured near Bonn in 2006 and 2007. (From Landesumweltamt NRW. *Jahresbericht 2007, Jahresbericht 2007, Klimawandel.* http://www.lanuv.nrw.de/ veroeffentlichungen/jahresberichte/jabe2007/jabe2007S17S24.pdf, Jahresbericht 2007, Klimawandel, http://www.lanuv.nrw.de, 23.11.2008.)

■ Conclusions

The development of Reh's chart for the estimation of the minimum time of immersion of a body represented real progress because definite putrefactive changes and water temperature were taken into account. Therefore, Reh's chart replaced the old and unreliable rules of thumb for the estimation of the duration of immersion. However, overall water temperatures have increased since the 1960s. For higher water temperatures (>20°C), Reh's table is unreliable and further investigations are necessary, especially for higher water temperatures regarding the correlation between temperatures and progression of putrefaction. For

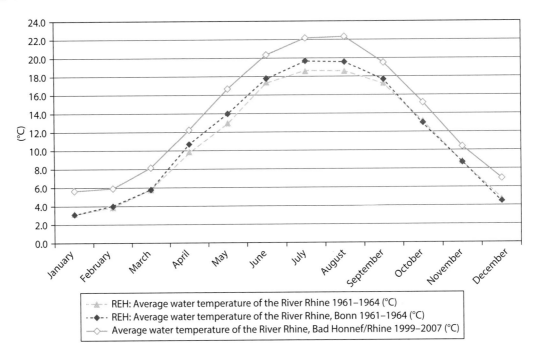

Figure 7.53 Average monthly water temperatures of the River Rhine from 1961 to 1964 and from 1999 to 2007. (From Doberentz E, Madea B. Estimating the time of immersion of bodies found in water: an evaluation of a common method to estimate the minimum time interval of immersion. *Rev Esp Med Leg* 2010;**36**(2):51–61.)

lower water temperatures, the given chart can be used even today. However, the actual measured water temperature on the day of recovery should be used for estimating the time of immersion; such data are available at agencies of water management. If a longer time of immersion is assumed or if considerable variations of water temperatures have to be taken into account, the average temperature during the missing time should be used.

Because of monthly fluctuations of the water temperature, it is not advisable to estimate the time of immersion based on data of the month of recovery without regard to the daily water temperatures.

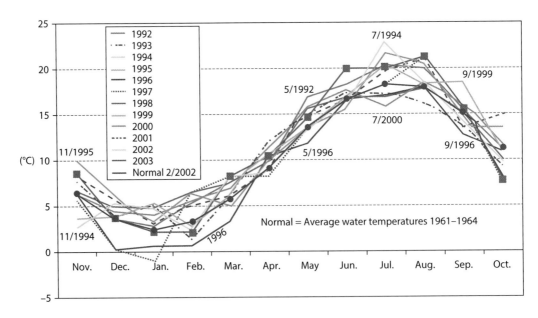

Figure 7.54 Average monthly water temperatures of the years 1992 to 2003 of the River Rhine, weather station Düsseldorf. (From Landesumweltamt NRW. *Jahresbericht 2003: Das hydrologische Jahr und das aussergewöhnliche Niedrigwasser des Rheins im Sommer.* http://www.lanuv.nrw.de/veroeffentlichungen/jahresberichte/2003/jabe03_s47.pdf2003, http://www.lanuv.nrw.de, 23.11.2008.)

Table 7.37 Average monthly water temperatures of the Rhine from 1961 to 1964 and 1999 to 2007

Month	Jan.	Feb.	March	April	May	June	July	Aug.	Sept.	Oct.	Nov.	Dec.
Average water temperature of the River Rhine, Bonn 1961–1964 (°C)	3.1	4.0	5.8	10.7	14.0	17.8	19.7	19.6	17.7	13.0	8.7	4.5
Reh: average water temperature of the River Rhine 1961–1964 (°C)	3.5	3.9	5.8	9.9	13.0	17.4	18.6	18.6	17.3	13.2	8.8	4.7
Average water temperature of the River Rhine, Bad Honnef/ Rhine, 1999–2007 (°C)	5.7	5.9	8.2	12.3	16.7	20.4	22.2	22.3	19.5	15.2	10.4	7.0

■ Recommended procedure

When finding a body immersed in water, it is necessary to measure the water temperature immediately on the same day. The water temperature depends on the type of water. For larger rivers, water temperatures on each day are available from the associated agencies of water management.

With the water temperature on the day of recovery and the signs of decomposition and putrefaction, an estimation of the time of immersion can be made by using Reh's chart. The water temperature on the day of recovery must be allocated to the closest average monthly water temperature from Reh's chart. If a longer time of immersion is suspected (e.g. advanced signs of putrefaction during the cold winter months), it could be useful to check the water temperatures during the last few weeks, because there can be significant variations in water temperatures. An alternative time of immersion can therefore be estimated.

7.5 H³-Magnetic resonance spectroscopy

■ *Frank Musshoff and Burkhard Madea*

As described before for the estimation of the early postmortem interval (PMI) of 1 to 1.5 days, various methods are well established. For the later PMI, the accuracy of procedures is clearly lower [67,93]. Under these circumstances, the common indicators for the estimation (i.e. rigor mortis, livor mortis or the body's core temperature) will have reached steady state in most cases. Especially when putrefactive changes are apparent, only a rough estimation of the PMI is possible based on subjective experience of the forensic pathologist, but this is not a scientifically sound method.

In the twentieth century, various chemical tests were developed for an estimation of PMIs in the late postmortem phase by identifying und quantifying by-products of the decomposition of the body, including substances in the soil underneath the decomposing corpse [192]. Some studies concentrated on specific groups of metabolites (e.g. fats [46] or proteins [20,121]).

Early in the 1970s, extensive experimental work was carried out on protein degradation during putrefaction in various organs by Bonte [19,21]. It was speculated that the initially lagging proteolytic changes were caused by catalysis of autoenzymes, whereas bacteriological processes were thought to be responsible for a distinct acceleration from the twentieth day after death. At this time period, some amino acid concentrations showed a marked increase, which was followed by maximal bacterial growth that ultimately led to a sudden regression of special amino acids. Amines simultaneously appeared.

These findings were pursued by Daldrup [41], who took into account that interindividual differences in brain tissue composition are very small and that the skull represents a natural barrier against external factors. Daldrup proposed a method for the estimation of PMIs on the basis of amino acid concentrations in the brain that was based on empirical findings [38–40]. In an experiment, a corpse had been kept at room temperature (16°C to 23°C) for more than 48 days; at regular intervals, brain samples were taken, and the content of free amino acids and related compounds were analysed. It could be demonstrated that in a period from 4 to 20 days post mortem, the PMI could be calculated from the concentrations of α-aminobutyrate (ABU), γ-aminobutyrate (GABA) and glutamic acid (GLU) in the brain according to the following formula:

$$T \sim \ln\left(\frac{ABU + GABA}{GLU} + 1\right)$$

where T is the postmortem time lapse (days) and ABU, GABA and GLU are the concentrations in micromoles per gram (µmol/g) wet tissue of the corresponding amino acids. In a period from 4 to 20 days post mortem, nearly a linear correlation was found (Figure 7.55).

The procedure is based on GLU reactions, specifically proteolysis and α-decarboxylation as well as γ-decarboxylation (Figure 7.56). In the range of about 17.5°C to 25°C, which guarantees bacterial growth and metabolism, the method was described as independent of ambient temperature. It was demonstrated that in addition to the

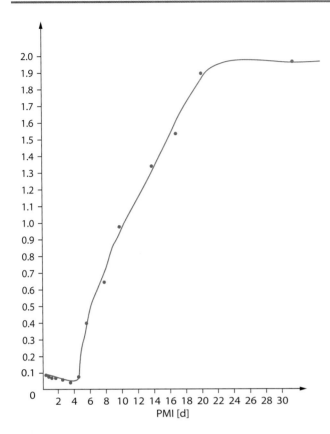

Figure 7.55 Correlation between the postmortem interval (PMI) and the Daldrup formula calculated from the concentrations of α-aminobutyrate (ABU), γ-aminobutyrate (GABA) and glutamic acid (GLU) according to Daldrup [40].

temperature, a pH between 6 and 7.2 is essential for high proteolytic activity. The brain samples from the cortex or parts of the putrefied brain mush can be taken without any special precaution during routine autopsy. The results of an experiment were supported by some practical cases where the PMI was well or reasonably well known.

However, these methods never gained real practical relevance. For one thing, they are time consuming, and labor-intensive chemical analysis is required. Moreover, most of these procedures attempted to characterize PMI by a few parameters, or even by just one specific parameter, which led to poor correlation as a result of interindividual differences.

In 2002, first results concerning postmortem decomposition of brain tissue were described by using proton magnetic resonance spectroscopy (^{1}H-MRS) in a sheep head model and in selected human cases [72]. At first, changes in the concentrations of metabolites usually present *in vivo* and the appearance of previously reported decay products were observed. At about 3 days post mortem, new metabolites including free trimethylammonium (fTMA), propionate (PROP), butyrate (BUT) and iso-butyrate (iBUT) started to appear *in situ* (Figure 7.57). Observed metabolites and time course were comparable in sheep and human brain tissues. These findings could be confirmed using isolated whole heads of young pigs, in which the time course of spectral changes was observed within 3 weeks [8]. *In situ* ^{1}H-MRS was considered as a possibly useful tool for the estimation of PMIs. Scheurer *et al.* [158] proposed mathematical functions to describe the time course of characteristic metabolites in decomposing brain (sheep head model) up to 3 weeks post mortem. In a first step, analytical

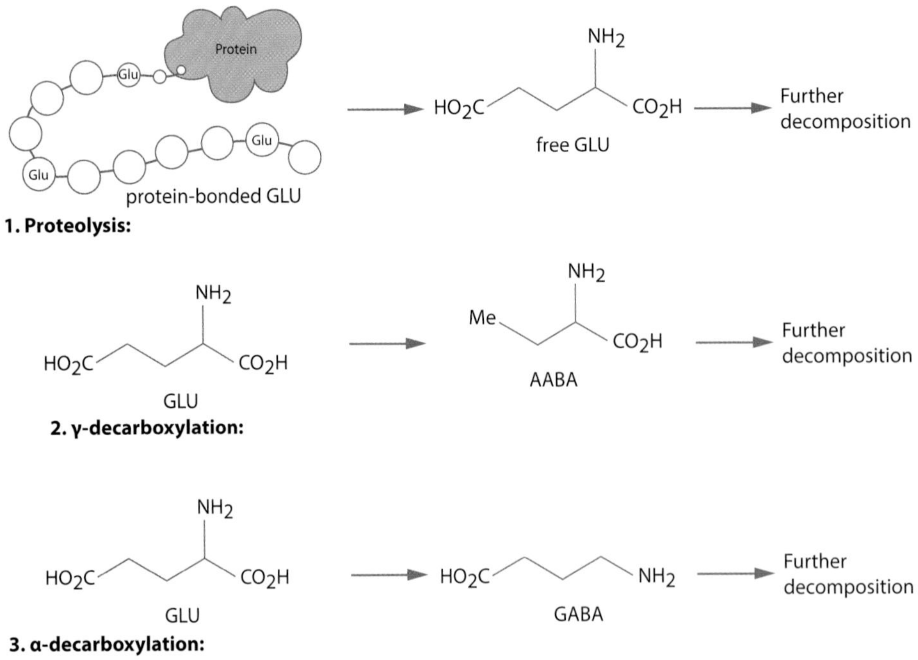

1. Proteolysis:

protein-bonded GLU → free GLU → Further decomposition

2. γ-decarboxylation:

GLU → AABA → Further decomposition

3. α-decarboxylation:

GLU → GABA → Further decomposition

Figure 7.56 Reactions of glutamic acid (GLU) in the brain during decomposition. AABA, α-aminobutyrate; GABA, γ-aminobutyrate.

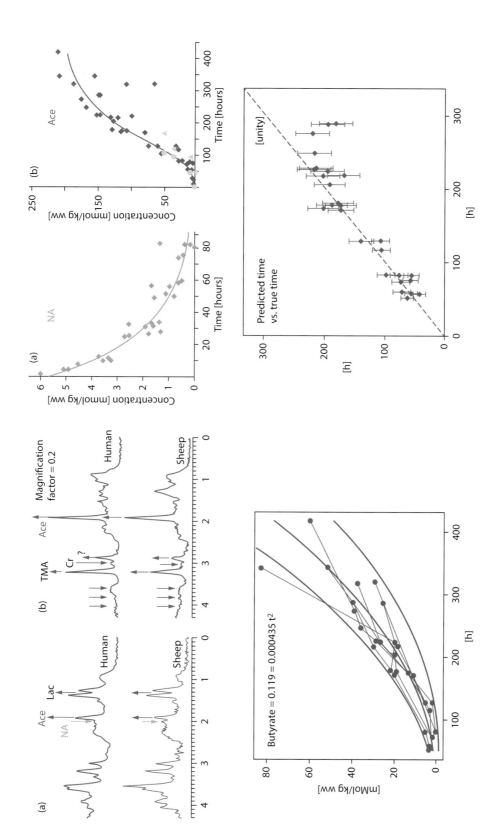

Figure 7.57   (a) Human and sheep spectra measured a) 2 days and b) 7 days post mortem. (b) Time course of a) NA (N-acetyl-aspartate) and b) Ace (acetate) concentration. (c) Concentration changes of butyrate over time post mortem. (d) Correlation of predicted time versus true time (±2 SD). Lac, lactate; TMA, trimethylammonium. ((a) and (b) from Ith M, Kreis R, Scheurer E, Dirnhofer R, Boesch C, Using ¹H-MR spectroscopy in forensic medicine to estimate the post-mortem interval: a pilot study in an animal model and its application to human brain. *Proc Int Soc Magn Reson Med* 2001;**9**:388; (c) and (d) from Scheurer E, Ith M, Dietrich D, Kreis R, Huesler J, Dirnhofer R, Boesch C. Statistical evaluation of time-dependent metabolite concentrations: estimation of post-mortem intervals based on in situ ¹H-MRS of the brain. *NMR Biomed* 2005;**18**:163–172. These figures were reproduced by kind permission of the authors and International Society for Magnetic Resonance in Medicine.)

Table 7.38 **The parameterized model functions used to describe the time courses of various metabolites according to Scheurer _et al._**

Variable	Model (time [t] in h)	Concentration limits for prediction [mmol/kg$_{ww}$]	Time limits for fit (h)
Acetate (ACE)	$f(t) = \dfrac{138}{1 + exp\left[-(t - 153)/35.1\right]}$	ACE <70	t < 400
Alanine (ALA)	$f(t) = 3.27 + 0.000435 * t^2$	ALA <20	t < 200
Butyrate (BUT)	$f(t) = 0.119 + 0.000435 * t^2$	BUT <70	50 < t < 400
Free trimethylammonium (fTMA)	$f(t) = -7.25 + 0.205 * t$	fTMA <30	50 < t < 200
Propionate (PROP)	$f(t) = -1.93 + 0.0851 * t$	PROP <30	20 < t < 400

Data from Scheurer E, Ith M, Dietrich D, Kreis R, Husler J, Dirnhofer R, Boesch C. Statistical evaluation of time-dependent metabolite concentrations: estimation of post-mortem intervals based on _in situ_ ¹H-MRS of the brain. _NMR Biomed_ 2005;**18**:163–172.

mathematical functions were proposed to describe the time courses of 10 metabolites in the decomposing brain (Table 7.38).

Subsequently, the inverted functions were used to predict PMIs based on measured metabolite concentrations. Individual PMIs calculated from five different metabolites (acetate [ACE], alanine [ALA], BUT, fTMA, PROP) were then pooled. Being weighted by their inverse variances (var):

$$PMI_{estimated} = \frac{\sum_i PMI^i_{individual} \Big/ var_i}{\sum_i 1 \Big/ var_i}$$

The variance of this weighted prediction (PMI$_{estimated}$) was calculated as follows:

$$var\left(PMI_{estimated}\right) = \frac{1}{\sum_i 1 \Big/ var_i}$$

Correlation coefficient and average variance calculated from this formula for the combination of ACE, ALA, BUT, fTMA and PROP were 0.928 and 113, respectively. In the case of sheep experiments, individual PMIs calculated gave a good correlation up to 250 hours post mortem. Additionally, results could be transferred to human cases. However, the bodies were measured only at one point in time and were stored at 4°C for between 20 and 70 hours before MR examination. The same working group then studied the effect of ambient temperature, which could be reliably included in the PMI determination [73]. These results have not yet been transferred to human cases. In addition, a Chinese group of investigators proposed a mathematical model for the estimation of PMIs by using ¹H-MRS at different temperatures [202].

It has to be considered, that for the preliminary experiments isolated heads of animals were used, which were prepared by closing the spinal canal with plasticine, fixing in a plastic holder and storing in a plastic container or bag. In a comparison of the metabolic changes in an isolated whole head and a head of an intact animal, different results were obtained [129]: Gas bubbles occurring

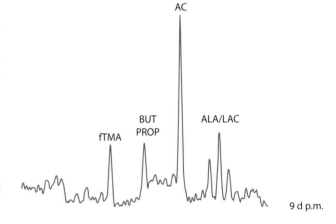

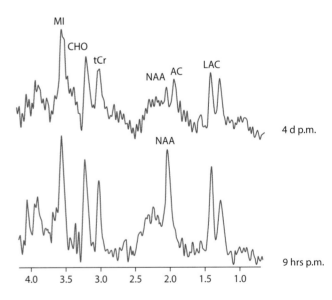

Figure 7.58 Metabolic decomposition in an isolated brain of a sheep measured by proton magnetic resonance spectroscopy on a 1.5-T magnetic resonance system (TR/TE 2500/25 ms) 9 hours, 4 days and 9 days post mortem (p.m.). The data of other groups were highly reproducible (AC, acetate; ALA, alanine; BUT, butyrate; CHO, choline; fTMA, free trimethylamine; LAC, lactate; MI, myo-inositol; NAA, N-acetyl-aspartate; PROP, propionate; tCr, total creatine), according to Musshoff _et al._ [129].

in the brain tissue after 6 to 7 days in the isolated animal head and after 4 to 5 days in the head of the whole animal complicated the selection of a voxel entirely within homogeneous brain tissue and impaired spectroscopic measurements at longer PMIs. During short PMIs, spectra obtained from the isolated head (Figure 7.58) showed signals already described by others and also occurring in healthy living brain, such as the singlets of N-acetyl-aspartate (NAA) at 2.01 ppm, (total) creatine (tCr) at 3.02 ppm and a single peak of bound TMA, mainly including choline compounds (CHO) at 3.19 ppm [120]. After a short time, the methyl (CH$_3$)doublets of lactate (LAC) at 1.33 ppm and ALA at 1.47 ppm appeared. Nine hours post mortem, ACE was detected only as a small upfield shoulder of the NAA peak. At longer PMIs, ACE became the predominant peak, and additional signals evolved for succinate at 2.41 ppm and fTMA at 2.88 ppm, whereas other metabolites such as NAA, tCr and LAC disappeared.

In conclusion, the animal model appeared highly reproducible and in principle can be seen as a useful tool for further studies. However, quite different results were revealed by investigation of the metabolic alterations in the brain of the whole animal. Spectra showed differences already 48 hours post mortem, but especially after longer PMIs (Figure 7.59). Fifteen days post mortem, mainly fTMAs and LAC were found in the intact animal, but no further metabolites such as ACE, PROP, ALA and BUT, which were used for the mathematical model for the estimation of PMIs as described earlier [73,158]. These metabolites were detectable only in the isolated animal head 15 days post mortem. However, significant differences in metabolic alterations during postmortem decomposition in the brain were demonstrated between the animal model with isolated heads and the intact animal. Decomposition in the intact animal appeared faster and probably different compared with the model with isolated heads, as a result of bacterial invasion from the gastrointestinal tract,

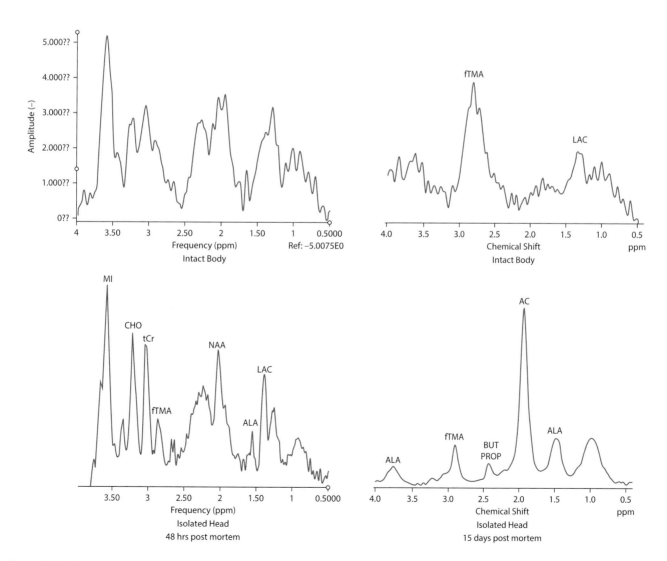

Figure 7.59 Proton magnetic resonance spectroscopy of sheep brain; analysis of an intact body and an isolated head 48 hours and 15 days post mortem (AC, acetate; ALA, alanine; BUT, butyrate; CHO, choline; fTMA, free trimethylamine; LAC, lactate; MI, myo-inositol; NAA, N-acetyl aspartate; PROP, propionate; tCr, total creatine), according to Musshoff *et al.* [129].

which can reach the brain in a few days in a cadaver. The significance of putrefiers such as *Clostridium sordelli* for the estimation of the PMI had been demonstrated by Bonte [20] and by Daldrup and Huckenbeck [42] several years earlier.

However, the investigation of postmortem decomposition by ¹H-MRS may represent a real progress in research. The procedure allows non-invasive chemical analysis *in situ* with quantitation of analytes, as well as longitudinal studies of postmortem changes with reproducible results. Influencing factors such as temperature and temperature-dependent invasion ability of bacteria can be easily studied, but in further studies intact bodies should be used instead of isolated heads. Old questions in forensic medicine such as death time estimation can benefit from recent developments in modern imaging systems.

References

1. Adelson L, Sunshine I, Rushforth NB, Marnkoff M. Vitreous potassium concentration as an indicator of postmortem interval. *J Forensic Sci* 1963;**8**:503–514.

2. Adjutantis G, Coutselinis A. Estimation of the time of death by potassium levels in the vitreous humour. *Forensic Sci Int* 1972;**1**:55–60.

3. Ahi RS, Garg V. Role of vitreous potassium level in estimating postmortem interval and the factors affecting it. *J Clin Diagn Res* 2011;**5**:13–15.

4. Ashima M, Agrawal YK. An overview of methods used for estimation of time since death. *Aust J Forensic Sci* 2011;**43**(4):275–285.

5. Aufderheide AC. *The Scientific Study of Mummies.* Cambridge, Cambridge University Press, 2003.7.1

6. Balasooriya BAW, Hill CAS, Williams AR. The biochemistry of vitreous humour: a comparative study of the potassium, sodium and urate concentration in the eyes at identical time intervals after death. *Forensic Sci Int* 1984;**26**:85–91.

7. Balazs EA, Denlinger JL. The vitreous. In: Dawson, H (ed.). *The Eye*, vol. 1a. 3rd ed. London: Academic Press, 1984, pp 533–589.

8. Banaschak S, Rzanny R, Reichenbach JR, Kaiser WA, Klein A. Estimation of postmortem metabolic changes in porcine brain tissue using ¹H-MR spectroscopy: preliminary results. *Int J Legal Med* 2005;**119**:77–79.

9. Bartels H, Böhmer M, Heirli C. Serum-Kreatinin-Bestimmung ohne Enteiweissung. *Clin Chim Acta* 1972;**37**:193–197.

10. Beattie O, Geiger J. *Der eisige Schlaf. Das Schicksal der Franklin-Expedition.* Munich, Germany, Piper, 1992. (Originally published *Frozen in Time: The Fate of the Franklin Expedition.* London, Bloomsbury Publishing, 1987.)

11. Berg S. Leichenzersetzung und Leichenzerstörung. In: Mueller B (eds.). *Gerichtliche Medizin,* vol. 1. Berlin, Springer, 1975, pp 62–106.

12. Berg S. Todeszeitbestimmung in der spätpostmortalen Phase. In: Brinkmann B, Madea B (eds.). *Handbuch Gerichtliche Medizin,* vol. 1. Berlin, Springer, 2004, pp 191–204.

13. Berg S, Rolle R, Seemann H. *Der Archäologe und der Tod, Archäologie und Gerichtsmedizin.* Munich, Germany, Verlag C. J. Bucher, 1981.

14. Berman ER, Voaden M. The vitreous body. In: Graymore CN (ed.). *Biochemistry of the Eye.* London, Academic Press, 1970, pp 373–471.

15. Bito LZ. Intraocular fluid dynamics I: Steady state concentration gradients of magnesium, potassium and calcium in relation to the sites and mechanisms of ocular cation transport processes. *Exp Eye Res* 1970;**10**:102–116.

16. Bito LZ. The physiology and pathophysiology of intraocular fluids. In: Bito LZ, Davson H, Fenstermacher JD (eds.). *The Ocular and Cerebrospinal Fluids.* London, Academic Press, 1977, pp 273–289.

17. Blana SA, Musshoff F, Hoeller T, Fimmers R, Madea B. Variations in vitreous humor chemical values as a result of pre-analytical treatment. *Forensic Sci Int* 2011;**210**:263–270.

18. Blumenfeld TA, Mantell CH, Catherman RL, Blanc WA. Postmortem vitreous humour chemistry in sudden infant death syndrome and in other causes of death in childhood. *Am J Clin Pathol* 1979;**71**:219–223.

19. Bonte W. Der postmortale Eiweiss-Katabolismus. *Beitr Gerichtl Med* 1975;**33**:57–75.

20. Bonte W. *Der postmortale Proteinkatabolismus. Experimentelle Untersuchungen zum Problem der forensischen Leichenzeitbestimmung.* Göttingen, Germany, Habilitation Schrift, 1978.

21. Bonte W, Bleifuss J, Volck J. Experimental investigations in postmortem protein degradation. *Forensic Sci* 1976;**7**:9–22.

22. Bortolotti F, Pascali JP, Davies GG, Smith FP, Brissie RM, Tagliaro F. Study of vitreous potassium correlation with time since death in the postmortem range from 2 to 110 hours using capillary ion analysis. *Med Sci Law* 2011;**51**:S20–S23.

23. Bray M. The eye as a chemical indicator of environmental temperature at the time of death. *J Forensic Sci* 1984;**29**:396–403.

24. Bray M. The effect of chilling, freezing and rewarming on the postmortem chemistry of vitreous humour. *J Forensic Sci* 1984;**29**:404–411.

25. Brinkmann B, Madea B. *Handbuch Gerichtliche Medizin,* vol. 1. Berlin, Springer, 2004.

26. Casper JL. *Atlas zum Handbuch der gerichtlichen Medizin.* 3rd ed. Berlin, Verlag von August Hirschwald, 1860.

27. Chandrakanth HV, Kanchan T, Balaraj BM, Virupaksha HS, Chandrashekar TN. Postmortem vitreous chemistry: an evaluation of sodium, potassium and chloride levels in estimation of time since death (during the first 36 h after death). *J Forensic Leg Med* 2013;**20**:211–216.

28. Choo-Kang E, McKoy C, Escoffrey C. Vitreous humour analytes in assessing the postmortem interval and the antemortem clinical status. *Wiss Med J* 1983;**32**:23–26.

29. Coe JI. Postmortem chemistries on vitreous humour. *Am J Pathol* 1969;**51**:741–750.

30. Coe JI. Further thoughts and observations on postmortem chemistries. *Forensic Sci Gaz* 1973;**5** 2–6.

31. Coe JI. Postmortem chemistries on blood with particular reference to urea nitrogen, electrolytes and bilirubin. *J Forensic Sci* 1974;**19**:33–42.

32. Coe JI. Postmortem chemistry: Practical consideration and a review of the literature. *J Forensic Sci* 1974;**19**:13–42.

33. Coe JI. Postmortem chemistry of blood, cerebrospinal fluid and vitreous humour. In: Wecht CH (ed.). *Legal Medicine Annual.* New York: Appleton-Century-Crofts, 1976, pp 53–91.

34. Coe JI. *Definition and Time of Death: Modern Legal Medicine, Psychiatry and Forensic Science.* Philadelphia, FA Davis, 1980.

35. Coe JI. Postmortem biochemistry of blood and vitreous humour in pediatric practice. In: Mason JK (ed.). *Pediatric Forensic Medicine and Pathology.* London, Chapman & Hall Medical, 1989, pp 191–203.

36. Coe JI. Vitreous potassium as a measure of the postmortem interval: an historical review and critical evaluation. *Forensic Sci Int* 1989;**42**:201–213.

37. Coe JI, Apple FS. Variations in vitreous humour chemical values as a result of instrumentation. *J Forensic Sci* 1985;**30**:828–835.

38. Daldrup T. Die Bedeutung der Bildung von α- und γ-Aminobuttersäure während der Fäulnis von eiweisshaltigem menschlichem Organmaterial. Eine Möglichkeit der Todeszeitbestimmung? *Beitr Gerichtl Med* 1979;**40**:379–382.

39. Daldrup T. Zur Kinetik des postmortalen bakteriellen Glutaminsäurestoffwechsels im Gehirn. *Z Rechtsmed* 1981;**86**:195–203.

40. Daldrup T. Praktische Erfahrungen mit der Leichenalterbestimmung durch Auswertung bakterieller Stoffwechselprodukte. *Z Rechtsmed* 1983;**90**:19–25.

41. Daldrup T. *Die Aminosäuren des Leichengehirns.* Stuttgart, Germany, Enke, 1984.

42. Daldrup T, Huckenbeck W. Bedeutung des Fäulnisbakteriums Clostridium sordellii für die Leichenaltersbestimmung. *Z Rechtsmed* 1984;**92**:121–125.

43. Deokar RB, Shendarkar AT, Patil SS. Estimation of the time since death by means of changes in the eye: vitreous humour calcium levels. *Int J Healthcare Biomed Res* 2013;**1**:141–146.

44. Doberentz E, Madea B. Estimating the time of immersion of bodies found in water: an evaluation of a common method to estimate the minimum time interval of immersion. *Rev Esp Med Leg* 2010;**36**(2):51–61.

45. Dolinak D, Matshes E, Lew E: *Forensic Pathology.* Burlington, Massachusetts, Elsevier Academic Press, 2005.

46. Döring G. Postmortaler Lipidstoffwechsel. *Beitr Gerichtl Med* 1975;**33**:76–84.

47. Dotzauer G, Naeve W. Vergleichende Untersuchungen über den Natrium- und Kaliumgehalt im Serum wie im Liquor postmortem. *Dtsch Z Gerichtl Med* 1960;**49**:406–419.

48. Dotzauer G, Tamaska L. Hautveränderungen an Leichen. In: Marchionini (ed.). *Handbuch der Haut- und Geschlechtskrankheiten* (Ergänzungswerk, vol. 1, T1). Springer: Berlin, Heidelberg, 1968.

49. Farmer JG, Benomran F, Watson AA, Harland WA. Magnesium, potassium, sodium and calcium in postmortem vitreous humour from humans. *Forensic Sci Int* 1985;**27**:1–13.

50. Foerch JS, Forman DT, Vye MV. Measurement of potassium in vitreous humour as an indication of the postmortem interval. *Am J Clin Pathol* 1979;**72**:651–662.

51. Forman DT, Butts J. Electrolytes of the vitreous humour as a measure of the postmortem interval. *Clin Chem* 1980;**26**:1024.

52. Fraschini F, Muller E, Zanoboni A. Postmortem increase of potassium in human cerebrospinal fluid. *Nature* 1963;**98**:1208.

53. Gaedke J. *Handbuch des Friedhofs und Bestattungsrechtes.* 9th ed. Cologne, Germany, Heymanns, 2004.

54. Gamero JJ, Romero JL, Arufe MI, Vizcaya MA. Incremento de la concentración de potasio en humor vitreo en functión del tiempo postmortem. *Riv Ital Med Leg* 1990;**12**:785–801.

55. Gardiner EE, Newberry RC, Keng JY. Postmortem time and storage temperature affect the concentrations of hypoxanthine, other purines, pyrimidines, and nucleosides in avian and porcine vitreous humor. *Pediatr Res* 1989;**26**:639–642.

56. Gee DJ. Drowning. In: Polson CJ, Gee DJ, Knight B (ed.). *The Essentials of Forensic Medicine.* 4th ed. Oxford, Pergamon Press, 1985, pp 421–448.

57. Girela E, Villanueva E, Irigoyen P, Girela V, Hernández-Cueto C, Peinado JM. Free amino acid concentrations in vitreous humour and cerebrospinal fluid in relation to the cause of death and postmortem interval. *J Forensic Sci* 2008;**53**(3):730–733.

58. Gutman I, Bergmeyer HU. *Methods of Enzymatic Analysis, vol. IV,* 2nd ed. New York, Academic Press, 1974, p 1794.

59. Haberda A, v Hofmann R. *Lehrbuch der gerichtlichen Medizin.* 11th ed. Berlin, Urban und Schwarzenberg, 1927.

60. Haglund WD, Sorg MH. *Forensic Taphonomy.* Boca Raton, Florida, CRC Press, 1997.

61. Hansson LMA, Uotila U, Lindfors R, Laiho K. Potassium content of the vitreous body as an aid in determining the time of death. *J Forensic Sci* 1966;**11**:390–394.

62. Harkness RA. Review: hypoxanthine, xanthine and uridine in body fluids. Indicators of ATP depletion. *J Chromatogr* 1988;**429**:255–278.

63. Harkness RA, Lund RJ. Cerebrospinal fluid concentrations of hypoxanthine, xanthine, uridine and inosine: high concentrations of the ATP metabolite, hypoxanthine, after hypoxia. *J Clin Pathol* 1983;**36**:1–8.

64. Harper DR. A comparative study of the microbiological contamination of postmortem blood and vitreous humour samples taken for ethanol determination. *Forensic Sci Int* 1989;**43**:37–44.

65. Heaton V, Lagden A, Moffatt C, Simmons T. Predicting the postmortem submersion interval for human remains recovered from U.K. waterways. *J Forensic Sci* 2010;**55**(2):302–307.

66. Henry JB, Smith FA. Estimation of the postmortem interval by chemical means. *Am J Forensic Med Pathol* 1980;**1**:341–347.

67. Henssge C, Madea B. Estimation of the time since death. Forensic Sci. Int. 2007;**165**:182–184.

68. Henssge C, Brinkmann B, Püschel K. Todeszeitbestimmung durch Messung der Rektaltemperatur bei Wassersuspension der Leiche. *Z Rechtsmed* 1984;**92**:255–276.

69. Henssge C, Knight B, Krompecher T, Madea B, Nokes L. *The Estimation of the Time Since Death in the Early Postmortem Period,* 2nd ed. London, Edward Arnold, 2002.

70. Höpfel F, Platzer W, Spindler K *Der Mann im Eis,* vol. 1. Bericht über das internationale Symposium 1992 in Innsbruck, Veröffentlichungen der Universität Innsbruck. Innsbruck, Austria, University of Innsbruck, 1992, p 187.

71. Hughes W. Levels of potassium in the vitreous humour after death. *Med Sci Law* 1965;**150**:150–156.

72. Ith M, Bigler P, Scheurer E, Kreis R, Hofmann L, Dirnhofer R, Boesch C. Observation and identification of metabolites emerging during postmortem decomposition of brain tissue by means of *in situ* ¹H-magnetic resonance spectroscopy. *Magn Reson Med* 2002;**48**:915–920.

73. Ith M, Scheurer E, Kreis R, Thali M, Dirnhofer R, Boesch C. Estimation of the postmortem interval by means of ¹H-MRS of decomposing brain tissue: influence of ambient temperature. *NMR Biomed* 2011;**24**:791–798.

74. Jaffe FA. Chemical postmortem changes in the intraocular fluid. *J Forensic Sci* 1962;**7**:231–237.

75. James RA, Hoadley PA, Sampson BG. Determination of postmortem interval by sampling vitreous humour. *Am J Forensic Med Pathol* 1997;**18**(2):158–162.

76. Jashnani KD, Kale SA, Rupani AB. Vitreous humor: biochemical constituents in estimation of postmortem interval. *J Forensic Sci* 2010;**55**(6):1523–1527.

77. Klein A, Klein S. *Todeszeitbestimmung am menschlichen Auge.* Desden, Germany, Dresden University, MD thesis, 1978.

78. Knight B. *Forensic Pathology.* 2nd ed. London, Edward Arnold, 1996.

79. Knight B. *Legal Aspects of Medical Practice.* 3rd. ed. London, Churchill Livingstone, 1982.

80. Komura S, Oshiro S. Potassium levels in the aqueous and vitreous humour after death. *Tohoku J Exp Med* 1977;**122**:65–68.

81. Krause D. Späte Leichenveränderungen. In: Brinkmann B, Madea B (eds.). *Handbuch Gerichtliche Medizin*, vol. 1. Berlin, Springer, 2004, pp 150-170.

82. Krause D, Klein A, Meissner D, Roitzsch E, Herrmann WR. Die Bedeutung der Kaliumkonzentration im Glaskörper menschlicher Augen für die Todeszeitbestimmung. *Z Arztl Fortbild* 1971;**65**:345–348.

83. Landesumweltamt NRW. *Jahresbericht 2003: Das hydrologische Jahr und das aussergewöhnliche Niedrigwasser des Rheins im Sommer.* http://www.lanuv.nrw.de/veroeffentlichungen/jahresberichte/2003/jabe03_s47.pdf2003, http://www.lanuv.nrw.de, 23.11.2008.

84. Landesumweltamt NRW. *Jahresbericht 2007, Jahresbericht 2007, Klimawandel.* http://www.lanuv.nrw.de/veroeffentlichungen/jahresberichte/jabe2007/jabe2007S17S24.pdf, Jahresbericht 2007, Klimawandel, http://www.lanuv.nrw.de, 23.11.2008.

85. Lange N, Swearer ST, Sturner WQ. Human postmortem interval estimation from vitreous potassium: an analysis of original data from six different studies. *Forensic Sci Int* 1994;**66**:159–174.

86. Leahy MS, Farber R. Postmortem chemistry of human vitreous humour. *J Forensic Sci* 1967;**12**:214–222.

87. Lendoiro E, Cordeiro C, Rodríguez-Calvo MS, Vieira DN, Suárez-Penaranda JM, López-Rivadulla M, Munoz-Barús JI. Applications of tandem mass spectrometer (LC-MSMS) in estimating the postmortem interval using the biochemistry of the vitreous humour. *Forensic Sci Int* 2012;**223**:160–164.

88. Lie JT. Changes of potassium concentration in vitreous humour after death. *Am J Med Sci* 1967;**254**:136–142.

89. Lötterle J, Schmierl G, Schellmann B. Einfluss der Bodenart auf die Leichendekomposition bei langen Liegezeiten.*Beitr Gerichtl Med* 1982;**40**:197–201.

90. Madea B. Leichenzerstückelung mit ungewöhnlicher Konservierung der Leichenteile. *Arch Kriminol* 1994;**193**:72–78.

91. Madea B. Estimation of duration of immersion. *Nord Rettsmed* 2002;**8**:4–10.

92. Madea B. Muscle and tissue changes after death. In: Henssge C, Knight B, Krompecher T, Madea B, Nokes L (eds.). *The Estimation of the Time Since Death in the Early Postmortem Period.* 2nd ed. London, Edward Arnold, 2002, pp 134–208.

93. Madea B. Is there recent progress in the estimation of the postmortem interval by means of thanatochemistry? *Forensic Sci Int* 2005;**151**:139–149.

94. Madea B. *Die Ärztliche Leichenschau.* 2nd ed. Berlin, Springer, 2006.

95. Madea B. *Praxis Rechtsmedizin.* 2nd ed. Berlin, Springer, 2007.

96. Madea B. *Handbook of Forensic Medicine.* Chichester, John Wiley & Sons, 2014.

97. Madea B. *Praxis Rechtsmedizin: Befunderhebung, Rekonstruktion und Begutachtung.* 3rd ed. Berlin, Springer, 2014.

98. Madea B, Brinkmann B (eds.). *Handbuch Gerichtliche Medizin,* vol. 2. Berlin, Springer, 2003.

99. Madea B, Doberentz E. Commentary on Heaton V, Lagden A, Moffatt C, Simmons T. Predicting the postmortem submersion interval for human remains recovered from U.K. waterways. *J Forensic Sci* 2010;**55**(2):302–307. *J Forensic Sci* 2010;**55**(6):1666–1667.

100. Madea B, Henssge C. Informationswert der Kaliumkonzentration in Glaskörperflüssigkeit für die Todeszeit – Präzisionsgewinn durch Erfassung antemortaler Dysregulationen? *Beitr Gerichtl Med* 1987;**45**:151–155.

101. Madea B, Musshoff F. Postmortem biochemistry. *Forensic Sci Int* 2007;**165**:165–171.

102. Madea B, Rödig A. Time of death dependent criteria in vitreous humor: accuracy of estimating the time since death. *Forensic Sci Int* 2006;**164**:87–92.

103. Madea B, Cremer U, Schiwy-Bochat KH. Leichenverbergung durch Einmauern und Einbetonieren. *Arch Kriminol* 2003;**212**:129–140.

104. Madea B, Henssge C, Honig W, Gerbracht A. References for determining the time of death by potassium in vitreous humour. *Forensic Sci Int* 1989;**8**:231–243.

105. Madea B, Henssge C, Püschel K, Honig W. Wie zuverlässig ist die Todeszeitbestimmung aus der Kaliumkonzentration in Zisternenliquor? *Beitr Gerichtl Med* 1988;**46**:375–381.

106. Madea B, Henssge C, Staak M. Postmortaler Kaliumanstieg in Glaskörperflüssigkeit: Welche Parameter sind als Indikatoren einer vitalen agonalen Elektrolytdysregulation geeignet? *Z Rechtsmed* 1986;**97**:259–268.

107. Madea B, Herrmann N, Henssge C. Precision of estimating the time since death by vitreous potassium: comparison of two different equations. *Forensic Sci Int* 1990;**46**:277–284.

108. Madea B, Käferstein H, Hermann N, Sticht G. Hypoxanthine in vitreous humour and cerebrospinal fluid: a marker of postmortem interval and prolonged (vital) hypoxia? Remarks also on hypoxanthine in SIDS. *Forensic Sci Int* 1994;**65**:19–31.

109. Madea B, Kreuser C, Banaschak S. Postmortem biochemical examination of synovial fluid: a preliminary study. *Forensic Sci Int* 2001;**118**(1):29–35.

110. Madea B, Preuss J, Musshoff F. Vom blühenden Leben zu Staub – Der natürliche Kreislauf von Werden und Vergehen. In: Wieczorek A, Tellenbach M, Rosendahl W (eds.). *Mumien – Der Traum vom ewigen Leben.* Mainz, Germany, Philipp von Zabern, 2007, pp 5–22.

111. Madea B, Preuss J, Musshoff F. From flourishing life to dust: the natural cycle of growth and decay. In: Wieczorek A, Rosendahl W (eds.). *Mummies of the World.* Munich, Germany, Prestel, 2010, pp 14–29.

112. Mant AK. *Taylor's Principles and Practice of Medical Jurisprudence.* London, Churchill Livingstone, 1984.

113. Manzke H, Dörner K, Grünitz J. Urinary hypoxanthine, xanthine and uric acid excretion in newborn infants with perinatal complications. *Acta Paediatr Scand* 1977;**66**:713–717.

114. Manzke H, Krämer M, Dörner K. Postmortem oxypurine concentrations in the CSF. In: Nyhan WL, Thompson LF, Watts RWE (eds.). *Purine and Pyrimidine Metabolism in Man. V. Festschrift for JE Seegmiller.* New York, Plenum Press, 1986, pp 587–591.

115. Manzke H, Staemmler W. Oxypurine concentration in the CSF in children with different diseases of the nervous systems. *Neuropediatrics* 1981;**12**:209–214.

116. Martchenko HP. Veränderungen des Kaliumgehaltes der Glaskörperflüssigkeit in Abhängigkeit von der Todeszeit. *Gerichtl Med* 1966;**61**:295.

117. Mason JK, Klyne W, Lennox B. Potassium levels in the cerebrospinal fluid after death. *J Clin Pathol* 1951;**4**:231–233.

118. Meberg A, Saugstad OD. Hypoxanthine in cerebrospinal fluid in children. *Scand J Clin Lab Invest* 1978;**38**:437–440.

119. Megyesi MS, Nawrocki SP, Haskell NH. Using accumulated degree-days to estimate the postmortem interval from decomposed human remains. *J Forensic Sci* 2005;**50**(3):618–626.

120. Michaelis T, Helms G, Frahm J. Metabolic alterations in brain autopsies: proton NMR identification of free glycerol. *NMR Biomed* 1996;**9**:121–124.

121. Mittmeyer HJ, Strebel KH. Experimentelle Untersuchungen zur forensischen Liegezeitbestimmung durch Elektrofokussierung von löslichen Muskelproteinen. *Z Rechtsmed* 1980;**85**:235–240.

122. Montaldo B, Umani Ronchi G, Marchiori A, Forgeschi M, Barbato M. La determinatione della concentrazione del potassio nel'umor vitreo: verifica di un methodo strumentale tanatocronologico. *Riv Ital Med Leg* 1989;**11**:180–199.

123. Mueller B. *Gerichtliche Medizin.* 2nd ed., vol. 1. Berlin, Springer, 1975.

124. Muños JI, Suárez-Peñaranda JM, Otero XL, Rdríguez-Calvo MS, Costas E, Miguéns X, et al. A new perspective in the estimation of post-mortem interval (PMI) based on vitreous. *J Forensic Sci* 2001;**46**(2):209–214.

125. Muñoz Barús JI, Febrero-Bande M, Cadarso-Suárez C. Flexible regression models for estimating post-mortem interval (PMI) in forensic medicine. *Stat Med* 2008;**27**:5026–5038.

126. Muñoz Barús JI, Rodríges-Calvo MS, Suárez-Penaranda JM, Vieira DN, Cadarso-Suárez C, Febrero-Bande M. PMICALC: An R code-based software for estimating post-mortem interval (PMI) compatible with Windows, Mac and Linux operating systems. *Forensic Sci Int* 2010;**194**:49–52.

127. Muñoz Barús JI, Suárez-Penaranda JM, Otero XL, Rodríguez-Calvo MS, Costas E, Miguénes X, Concheiro L. Improved estimation of postmortem interval based on differential behaviour of vitreous potassium and hypoxanthine in death by hanging. *Forensic Sci Int* 2002;**125**:67–74.

128. Murray EF, Hordynsky W. Potassium levels in the cerebrospinal fluid and their relation to duration of death. *J Forensic Sci* 1958;**3**:480–485.

129. Musshoff F, Klotzbach H, Block W, Traeber F, Schild H, Madea B. Comparison of post-mortem metabolic changes in sheep brain tissue in isolated heads and whole animals using ^{1}H-MR spectroscopy: preliminary results. *Int J Legal Med* 2011;**125**:741–744.

130. Naumann HN. Cerebrospinal fluid electrolytes after death. *Proc Soc Biol Med* 1958;**98**:16–18.

131. Odrizola A, Riancho JA, de la Vega R, Agudo G, Garcia-Blanco A, Cos de E, Fernandez F, Sanudo C, Zarrabeitia MT. miRNA analysis in vitreous humor to determine the time of death: a proof-of-concept pilot study. *Int J Legal Med* 2013;**127**:573–578.

132. Padosch SA, Dettmeyer R, Kröner L, Preuss J, Madea B. An unusual occupational accident: fall into a sewage plant tank with a lethal outcome. *Forensic Sci Int* 2005;**149**:39–45.

133. Passos MLC, Santos AM, Pereira AI, Santos RJ, Santos AJC, Saraiva MLMFS, Lima JLFC. Estimation of postmortem interval by hypoxanthine and potassium evaluation in vitreous humor with a sequential injection system. *Talanta* 2009;**79**:1094–1099.

134. Pau H. Betrachtungen zur Physiologie und Pathologie des Glaskörpers. *Graefes Arch Ophthalmol* 1951;**152**:201–247.

135. Paulson G, Stickney D. Cerebrospinal fluid after death. *Confin Neurol* 1971;**33**:149–162.

136. Petersohn F. Rechtsmedizinische Feststellungen an einer 3 Jahre in Plastik gehüllten Kindesleiche. *Beitr Gericht Med* 1972;**29**:351–358.

137. Pieper P. Moorleichen. In: Beck H, Geuenich D, Steuer H (eds.). *Reallexikon der Germanischen Altertumskunde,.vol 20.* Berlin, Walter De Gruyter, 2002, pp 222–229.

138. Polson CJ, Gee D, Knight B. *Essentials of Forensic Medicine.* 4th ed. Oxford, Pergamon Press, 1985.

139. Poulsen JP, Oyasaeter S, Rognum TO, Saugstad OD. Hypoxanthine, xanthine, and uric acid concentrations in the cerebrospinal fluid, plasma, and urine of hypoxemic pigs. *Pediatr Res* 1990;**28**:477–481.

140. Poulsen JP, Rognum TO, Oyyasaeter S, Saugstad OD. Changes in oxypurine concentrations in vitreous humor of pigs during hypoxemia and postmortem. *Pediatr Res* 1990;**28**:482–484.

141. Pounder DJ, Carson DO, Johnston K, Orihara Y. Electrolyte concentration differences between left and right vitreous humor samples. *J Forensic Sci* 1998;**43**(3):604-607.

142. Praetorius E, Poulsen H, Dupont H. Uric acid, xanthine and hypoxanthine in the cerebrospinal fluid. *Scand J Clin Lab Invest* 1957;**9**:133–137.

143. Preuss J, Brünig J, Madea B. Artifizielle Enterdigung durch Witterungseinflüsse. *Rechtsmedizin* 2004;**14**:14–19.

144. Prokop O, Göhler W. *Forensische Medizin.* 3rd ed. Stuttgart, Germany, Gustav Fischer, 1976.

145. Püschel K, Schneider A. Die Waschhautentwicklung in Süss- und Salzwasser bei unterschiedlichen Temperaturen. *Z Rechtsmed* 1985;**95**:1–18.

146. Reh H. Anhaltspunkte für die Bestimmung der Wasserzeit. *Dtsch Z Gerichtl Med* 1967;**59**:235–245.

147. Reh H. *Diagnostik des Ertrinkungstodes und Bestimmung der Wasserzeit.* Düsseldorf, Germany, Triltsch, 1969.

148. Reh H. Über den frühpostmortalen Verlauf der Waschhaut an den Fingern. *Z Rechtsmed* 1984;**92**:183–188.

149. Reh H, Haarhoff K, Vogt CD. Die Schätzung der Todeszeit bei Wasserleichen. *Z Rechtsmed* 1977;**79**:261–266.

150. Rodriguez WC, Bass WM. Decomposition of buried bodies and methods that may aid in their location. *J Forensic Sci* 1985;**30**(30):836–852.

151. Rognum TO, Saugstad OD. Hypoxanthine levels in vitreous humor: evidence of hypoxia in most infants who died of sudden infant death syndrome. *Pediatrics* 1991;**87**:306–310.

152. Rognum TO, Hauge S, Oyasaeter S, Saugstad OD. A new biochemical method for estimation of postmortem time. *Forensic Sci Int* 1991;**51**:139–146.

153. Rognum TO, Saugstad OD, Oyasaeter S, Olaysen B. Elevated levels of hypoxanthine in vitreous humor indicate prolonged cerebral hypoxia in victims of sudden infant death syndrome. *Pediatrics* 1988;**82**:615–618.

154. Rothschild MA, Schmidt V, Pedal I. Leichenlipid. Unterschiedliche Entstehungsarten erschweren zusätzlich die Abschätzung der Leichenliegezeit. *Arch Kriminol* 1996;**197**:165–174.

155. Rumran NK, Bardale RV, Dongre AP. Postmortem analysis of synovial fluid and vitreous humour for determination of death interval: a comparative study. *Forensic Sci Int* 2011;**204**(1–3):186–190.

156. Saugstad OD. Hypoxanthine as a measurement of hypoxia. *Pediatr Res* 1975;**9**:158–161.

157. Saugstad OD, Olaisen B. Postmortem hypoxanthine levels in the vitreous humor: an introductory report. *Forensic Sci Int* 1978;**12**:33–36.

158. Scheurer E, Ith M, Dietrich D, Kreis R, Husler J, Dirnhofer R, Boesch C. Statistical evaluation of time-dependent metabolite concentrations: estimation of post-mortem intervals based on *in situ* ^{1}H-MRS of the brain. *NMR Biomed* 2005;**18**:163–172.

159. Schleyer F. *Postmortale klinisch-chemische Diagnostik und Todeszeitbestimmung mit chemischen und physikalischen Methoden.* Stuttgart, Germany, Thieme, 1958.

160. Schleyer F. Untersuchungen über die Beziehungen der postmortalen Chlor- und Magnesiumkonzentration in Liquor und Plasma zu Leichenalter und Todesursache. *Frankfurt Z Pathol* 1959;**69**:644–648.

161. Schleyer F. Determination of the time since death in the early postmortem interval. In: Lundquist F (ed.). *Methods of Forensic Science,* vol. 2. New York, Interscience Publishers, John Wiley and Sons, 1963, pp 253–293.

162. Schleyer F. Neuere Erkenntnisse über agonale und frühpostmortale chemische Vorgänge in den Körperflüssigkeiten. *Dtsch Z Gesamte Gerichtl Med* 1967;**59**:48–57.

163. Schleyer F. Wie zuverlässig ist die Kaliumbestimmung im Glaskörperinhalt als Mittel zur Todeszeitschätzung? *Z Rechtsmed* 1973;**71**:281–288.

164. Schleyer F, Janitzki U. Untersuchungen über den postmortalen Phosphatgehalt von Liquor und Serum in Beziehung zum Leichenalter. *Dtsch Z Gesamte Gerichtl Med* 1959;**49**:229–234.

165. Schmidt V. *Postmortale Elektrolytbestimmungen in Glaskörperflüssigkeiten und Liquor zur Todeszeitbestimmung.* Hamburg, Germany, Institute of Forensic Medicine medical dissertation, 1988.

166. Schoning O, Strafuss AC. Determining time of death of a dog by analysing blood, cerebrospinal fluid and vitreous humour collected postmortem. *Am J Vet Res* 1980;**41**:955–957.

167. Schoning P, Strafuss AC. Postmortem biochemical changes in canine vitreous humour. *J Forensic Sci* 1980;**25**:53–59.

168. Schoning P, Strafuss AC. Postmortem biochemical changes in canine cerebrospinal fluid. *J Forensic Sci* 1980;**25**:60–66.

169. Schourup K. *Dodstidsbestemmelse pa grundlag of postmortelle cisternevaedskevorandringer og detpostmortelle temperaturfald.* (English Summary: Determination of the time since death.) Copenhagen, Danks Vindenskabs, medical dissertation, 1950.

170. Sparks DL, Oeltgen PR, Kryscio RJ, Hunsaker JC, III. Comparison of chemical methods for determining the postmortem interval. *J Forensic Sci* 1989;**34**:197–206.

171. Spindler K. *Der Mann im Eis: Die Ötztaler Mumie verrät die Geheimnisse der Steinzeit.* Munich, Germany, C Bertelsmann, 1993.

172. Spindler K, Rastbichler-Zissernig E, Wilfing H, Zurnedden D, Nothdurfter H. *Der Mann im Eis: Neue Funde und Ergebnisse.* Vienna, Springer, 1995.

173. Spindler K, Wilfing H, Rastbichler-Zissernig E, Zurnedden D, Nothdurfter H, *Human Mummies: A Global Survey for the Status and the Techniques of Conservation.* Vienna, Springer, 1996.

174. Spitz WU. *Medicolegal Investigation of Death.* 3rd ed. Springfield, Illinois, Charles C Thomas, 1993.

175. Stegmaier K. *Untersuchungen über die postmortale Kaliumkonzentration in Glaskörperinhalt und Kammerwasser und ihre Beziehung zur Todeszeit.* Marburg, Germany, Marburg University, MD thesis, 1971.

176. Stephens RJ, Richards RG. Vitreous humour chemistry: the use of potassium concentration for the prediction of the postmortem interval. *J Forensic Sci* 1987;**32**:503–509.

177. Sturner WQ. Die gerichtmedizinische Bedeutung der Glaskörperflüssigkeit. In: Vamosi M (ed.). *Aktuelle Fragen der gerichtlichen Medizin II. Wiss Beitr Univ Halle-Witten*berg 1965, pp 57–62.

178. Sturner WQ. The vitreous humour: postmortem potassium changes. *Lancet* 1963;**1**:807–808.

179. Sturner WQ, Dowdey ABC, Putman RS, Dempsey JL. Osmolality and other chemical determinations in postmortem human vitreous humour. *J Forensic Sci* 1972;**18**:387–393.

180. Sturner WQ, Gantner GE. The postmortem interval: a study of potassium in the vitreous humor. *Am J Clin Pathol* 1964;**42**:137–144.

181. Tagliaro F, Bortolotti F, Manetto G, Cittadini F, Pascali VL, Marigo M. Potassium concentration differences in the vitreous humour from the two eyes revisited by microanalysis with capillary electrophoresis. *J Chromatogr A* 2001;**924**:493–498.

182. Tagliaro F, Manetto G, Cittadini F, Marchetti D, Bortolotti F, Marigo M. Capillary zone electrophoresis of potassium in human

vitreous humour: validation of a new method. *J Chromatogr B* 1999;**733**:273–279.

183. Thierauf A, Musshoff F, Madea B. Post-mortem biochemical investigations of vitreous humor. *Forensic Sci Int* 2009;**192**:78–92.

184. Tsokos M. Post mortem changes and artefacts during the early post mortem interval. In: Tsokos M (ed.). *Forensic Pathology Reviews.* Totowa, New Jersey, Humana, 2005, pp 183–237.

185. Tumram NK, Bardale RV, Dongre AP. Postmortem analysis of synovial fluid and vitreous humour for determination of death interval: a comparative study: *Forensic Sci Int* 2011;**204**:186–190.

186. Urban R. *Elektrolytbestimmung im Liquor cerebrospinalis – mathematische Analyse experimenteller Befunde unter Berücksichtigung forensisch relevanter Einflussfaktoren zur Todeszeitbestimmung im frühpostmortalen Intervall.* Hanover, Germany, Habilitation Schrift, 1987.

187. Urban R, Tröger HD. Einfluss der Todesursache auf die Leichenliegezeitbestimmung im Zisternenliquor. Vortrag 17. Jahrestreffen der Arbeitsgemeinschaft Nordund Westdtsch. *Rechts*med 1986.

188. Urban R, Tröger HD. Todeszeitbestimmung im frühpostmortalen Intervall – Kalium–Todeszeit-Bezugsnomogramm. Vortrag 66. Jahrestagg. *Dtsch Gesamte Rechtsmed* 1987:8.

189. Urban R, Tröger HD. Todeszeitbestimmung Möglichkeiten und Grenzen der Elektrolytbestimmung im Leichenliquor. *Beitr Gerichtl Med* 1987;**45**:157–161.

190. Urban R, Tröger HD, Krüger HJ. Todeszeitbestimmung im früh-postmortalen Intervall durch Elektrolytbestimmung im Zisternenliquor. Vortrag 64. Jahrestagg. *Dtsch Gesamte Rechts*med 1985;7–11 September, Hamburg.

191. Van der Sanden, W. *Mumien aus dem Moor – Die vor- und frühgeschichtlichen Moorleichen aus Nordwesteuropa.* Amsterdam, Batavian Lion International, 1996.

192. Vass AA, Bass WM, Wolt JD, Foss JE, Ammons JT. Times since death determination of human cadavers using soil solution. *J Forensic Sci* 1992;**37**:1236–1253.

193. Waterlevel Rhein. http://www.wetteronline.de/pegel.htm, 07.412.2009.

194. Weber W. Zur Waschhautbildung der Fingerbeeren. *Z Rechtsmed* 1978;**81**:63–66.

195. Weber W. Flüssigkeitspenetration durch Leistenhaut. *Z Rechtsmed* 1982;**88**:185–193.

196. Weber W Laufkötter R. Stadien postmortaler Waschhautbildung – Ergebnisse systematischer qualitativer und quantitativer experimenteller Untersuchungen. *Z Rechtsmed* 1984;**92**:277–290.

197. Weischer K. *Biochemische Liquoruntersuchungen an Leichen.* Münster, Germany, Münster University, MD thesis, 1982.

198. Wieczorek A, Rosendahl W (eds.). *Mumien – Der Traum vom ewigen Leben.* Mainz, Germany, Philipp von Zabern, 2007.

199. Wieczorek A, Rosendahl W (eds.). *Mummies of the World.* Munich, Germany, Prestel, 2010.

200. Wiesböck J, Josephi E, Liebhart E. Intraindividuelle Kaliumverschiebungen im Liquor cerebrospinalis nach dem Tod. *Beitr Gerichtl Med* 1989;**47**:403–405.

201. Wurster U, Hoffmann K. Glaskörper. In: Hockwin O (ed.). *Biochemie des Auges.* Stuttgart, Germany, Enke, 1985, pp 100–134.

202. Yang TT, Li ZW, Liu L, Zhen N. [Estimation of postmortem interval with single-voxel proton ¹H-MR spectroscopy at different temperature]. *Fa Yi Xue Za Zhi* 2008;**24**:85–89 (in Chinese).

203. Yogiray V, Indumati V, Kodliwadmath MV. Study of vitreous humour to assess the postmortem interval and cause of death. *J Forensic Med Toxicol* 2008;**9**:171–174.

8 Gastric Contents and Time Since Death

Burkhard Madea and Bernard Knight

The state of digestion and distribution of the last meal in the stomach and the upper intestine have long been proposed as a method for estimating the time since death [6,11,15,16,19,20,28,29]. The volume of the stomach contents compared with the volume of the last meal and the transportation distance into the small intestine must be known. Even if the volume of the last meal is not known from the type of meal (e.g. breakfast, lunch), rough estimations of the time of day when death occurred may be possible.

Estimations of the time since death based on stomach contents are often also required because the police did not call for a forensic pathologist to be present at the scene of a crime [4].

The state of digestion and the transportation rate of food from the stomach to the duodenum depend on several antemortem (anatomical, physiological, psychological, pathological, agonal, type of food) factors, which contribute to the great intraindividual and interindividual variability of gastric emptying. Therefore, it is not astonishing that diverging estimates on the time of death in relation to the last meal have been made by different pathologists in the same case. Estimations considering all circumstances should be made only with great reservation. Digestion itself does not cease with death but progresses after death; the state of digestion is therefore of only little value in estimating the time since death.

Opinions on this topic vary from author to author, but the following random extracts from standard English language textbooks indicate that strong evidential value can rarely be placed on the use of gastric contents in timing death.

'The state of digestion of the stomach contents and bowel may be used as an additional means of fixing the hour of death in relation to the last meal. Most elaborate tables have been prepared of the time taken by the stomach to digest certain articles of diet, but these are wholly unreliable. The rate of digestion varies in different persons and gastric and intestinal activity is much retarded in cases of trauma and insensibility. Even without the paralysis of movement that is common to grave injury or deep insensibility, the process of emptying of the stomach may be much delayed' (Simpson [27]).

'If undigested food is found in the stomach at a postmortem examination, it is often claimed that the deceased must have died within 3–4 hours of his last meal. This claim is of limited value as there are great individual variations in the emptying time of the stomach. As the rate of digestion is variable and as it is not possible to determine the degree of digestion

of various foods from a naked-eye examination of the stomach contents, little reliance can be placed upon estimates of the post-mortem interval which are based upon the apparent state of digestion. Gastric digestion may continue post-mortem, this creating further difficulties' (Gordon et al. [10]).

'Attempts to fix this time (of death) based solely on examination of the stomach contents are unsatisfactory even when allowance is made for the factors which either hasten or retard digestion; allowance must always be made for individual variation. ...the foregoing (purported times of emptying), however, cannot be relied upon nor should it be relied upon, as crucial evidence which purports to fix the time of death within narrow limits' (Polson et al. [24]).

'The rate of emptying of the stomach is so variable that it cannot be used to give any certain indication of the time that has elapsed between the last meal and the death. The state of the stomach and its contents might, however, help in making a decision when, for example, death could have taken place at two or more times. When a person dies in bed after taking supper, an empty stomach would point to death having occurred towards the end of the night, rather than earlier. If there is food in the stomach of a person found dead one morning on the kitchen floor, it might point to death after breakfast, rather than before it' (Camps [7]).

'Never to be disregarded are the variations which exist in the speed with which food normally passes through the gastrointestinal tract of different persons. Moreover, emotional upsets can produce changes in gastrointestinal motility. Thus psychogenic pylorospasm can prevent normal departure of a meal from the stomach for several hours. At the opposite, extreme hypermotility caused by emotional disturbance can result in hurried transit of food and chyme through the gut with resultant diarrhoea.

The physical and chemical facets of digestion are beset by so many imponderable and uncontrollable variables *in vivo*, that one cannot rely on the extent of mechanical dissolution and chemical breakdown of the gastric content, to help reach a reasonable estimate as to how long food was present in the stomach. Careful consideration of these factors indicates that one must be extremely wary about making statements about the time since death in relation to the last known meal on the basis of the "amount of digestion" of the gastric contents' (Adelson [1]).

'In conclusion, the emptying of the stomach is a complex multifactorial process and its evaluation for determining the time of death requires caution and careful review of all limiting factors. Consideration must also be given to the possibility of one or more close consecutive meals' (Spitz [30]).

'For many years, pathologists have argued over the reliability of the state of digestion of gastric contents as an indicator of the time between the last meal and death, the leading case in modern times being that of Truscott in Canada. There is now almost a consensus that with extremely circumscribed exceptions, the method is too uncertain to have much validity' (Knight [14]).

'Thus this study demonstrates that the gastric emptying of either liquids or solids is subject to relatively wide differences in the same and different individuals, even if the same meal is ingested. If in addition to this we add differences in the weight, caloric content and composition of the meal we would see even greater differences in half-emptying time' (Di Maio and Di Maio [8]).

■ Is there postmortem transport of gastric contents?

Previously published reports claimed that postmortem transport of gastric contents to the duodenum occurs; these reports were based on animal experimental observations of postmortem electrical and pharmacological excitability of gastric smooth muscles and volume-dependent peristalsis of the gastric wall [9,13]. When pressure was applied to the gastric wall with high filling volumes of the stomach, contractions of the wall were observed [9].

Our own animal experiments [17,18] were carried out to answer the following questions under the following circumstances (Tables 8.1 to 8.4).

Table 8.1 Postmortem gastric emptying: observation of stomach and small bowel under direct view

Material	Method
10 rats (HAN-SPRD, body weight about 100 g); no feeding 2 days before death; anaesthesia with ether; death from KCl IV (5×) or ether/O₂ deficiency (5×).	Immediately after circulatory arrest: • Opening of the abdomen. • Pinching off the pylorus. • Positioning of a stomach sound. • Instillation of blue gelatine into the stomach. • Removing the clamp. In no case post mortem was there peristaltic transport of gastric contents into the duodenum.

IV, intravenously; KCl, potassium chloride.

Table 8.2 Observing the stomach and small bowel under direct view: dependence of antemortem transport on survival time

Material	Method
4 rats (HAN-SPRD, body weight about 100 g); anaesthesia with ether.	During anaesthesia: • Positioning of a stomach sound. • Instillation of blue gelatine into the stomach. • Survival time 2, 5, 10, 20 min; then • Death due to KCl IV. • Opening of the abdomen. Transport distance into the small bowel depending on the survival time: 2 min – 2 cm. 20 min – 15 cm. No postmortem gastric emptying, but postmortem transport of small bowel content did occur.

IV, intravenously; KCl, potassium chloride.

Table 8.3 Observing stomach and small bowel under direct view: effect of prostigmin on postmortem transport

Material	Method
4 rats (HAN-SPRD, body weight 200 g); no feeding 2 days before death; anaesthesia with ether; death from KCl IV (2×) and exsanguination.	• 4 min before death, 0.28 ml prostigmine given IV. • Opening of the abdomen immediately after circulatory arrest. • Pinching off the pylorus. • Positioning of a stomach sound. • Instillation into the stomach. • Removing the clamp. No postmortem transport of gastric contents.

IV, intravenously; KCl, potassium chloride.

Table 8.4 Postmortem gastric emptying: radiological control of gastric transport

Material	Method
10 rats (HAN-SPRD), body weight 150–180 g; no feeding for 1 day before death (7×); feeding immediately before death (3×); prostigmine IV 5 min before circulatory arrest (2×); death by ether/O₂ deficiency.	• Immediately after circulatory arrest, instillation of barium sulphate into the stomach by a stomach sound (3–5 ml, 10°C). • Radiological controls taken (anteroposteriorly and laterally) of the abdomen immediately after circulatory arrest, 10–15 min post mortem, 30 min post mortem (see Figure 8.1 (a) and Figure 8.2 (a)). • 2 hours post mortem: preparation of stomach and small bowel (see Figure 8.1 (b and c) and Figure 8.2 (b)). No postmortem transport of gastric contents (neither barium sulphate nor solid stomach contents).

IV, intravenously.

1. Is there any postmortem transport of stomach contents applied immediately after circulatory arrest to the stomach?
2. Is there any transport of stomach contents (gelatine) applied before death, depending on survival time?
3. Is there any effect of prostigmine on postmortem peristalsis?
4. Is there any effect of feeding before death?

The stomach and small bowel were observed under direct vision after opening the abdomen, or the stomach contents (barium sulphate) were seen by means of a radiological control. In all cases, preparation of the stomach and small bowel was carried out 2 hours post mortem.

Although peristaltic twitchings of the stomach were visible under direct view, no case of peristaltic emptying of the gastric contents was observed after death.

Even in the cases of feeding immediately before death, there was no transport of food to the duodenum (Figure 8.1). Correspondingly, when the whole stomach was filled with barium sulphate, no transport to the duodenum occurred (Figure 8.2). Postmortem peristaltic transport of the small bowel contents may occur during the first minutes after death.

Under intravenous prostigmine, there was also no peristaltic gastric emptying, although the peristaltic twitchings may have been stronger. Depending on the survival time, liquid stomach contents (coloured gelatine) applied 2 to 20 minutes before death may have been transported to the duodenum. Overall, there was no evidence of any functionally relevant postmortem gastric peristalsis with postmortem transport of the gastric contents.

The 'fastener' function of the pylorus clearly remains stable after death. These findings correlate with those found at autopsy by the German pathologist, Ludwig Aschoff (1921), who was able to perform autopsies at about 30 minutes after death during the First World War. Aschoff always found the pylorus fastened, whereas the supravital contraction of the pylorus occurred without relaxation, followed by rigor mortis [2].

Another argument for the postmortem stable fastener function of the pylorus, and against postmortem gastric emptying, is that in cases of newborn infants who survived only for a few minutes, air may be found in the stomach but not in the small bowel. Furthermore, in the

(b)

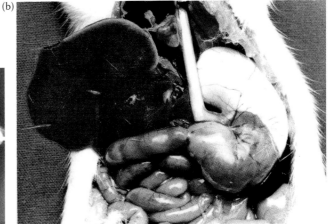

(a)

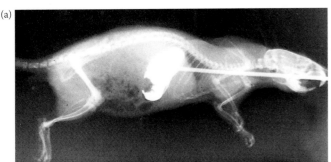

(c)

Figure 8.1 Stomach filled with barium sulphate; in the distal stomach solid food fed before death. No transport either of food or of barium sulphate into the duodenum. (a) Radiographic control. (b) Stomach and small bowel *in situ*. Pylorus fastened. (c) Stomach and duodenum after preparation.

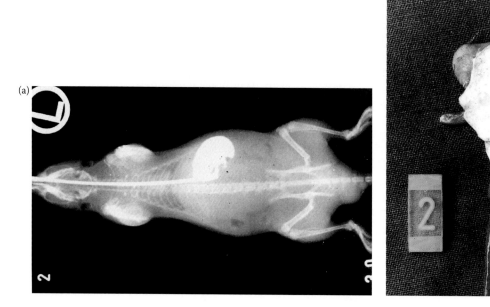

Figure 8.2   The whole stomach filled with barium sulphate. No transport into the duodenum. (a) Radiographic control. (b) Stomach and duodenum after preparation.

previously mentioned investigations that claimed post-mortem peristaltic emptying of gastric contents, this could be observed only when high pressures were applied to the stomach wall.

■ Gastric emptying pattern

Gastric emptying has been studied and quantified since the 1980s by using different methods (radiological, intubation-aspiration, radioisotopes, ultrasound, absorption kinetics of orally administered solutes, ferromagnetic traces) [12,20–22].

Liquids leave the stomach much more rapidly than do solids. For liquids, gastric emptying clearly follows an exponential function, but solids show a linear emptying pattern. A mixed meal shows an exponential emptying pattern, with the emptying time itself depending on the volume and composition of the last meal(s) and with carbohydrates, proteins and lipids leaving the stomach in that order. The following gastric emptying times have been cited in the literature:

- One to 3 hours for a light, small-volume meal.
- Three to 5 hours for a medium-sized meal.
- Five to 8 hours for a large meal.

Data relating to the gastric emptying pattern of solids and liquids are based on radionuclide studies (Table 8.5), but in the older German literature, tables were provided that indicated how rapidly different liquids, vegetables and mixed meals leave the stomach (Table 8.6).

Table 8.5   Solid and liquid gastric emptying in normal subjects assessed by dual isotopic radionuclide methods

Authors	No. of subjects	Meal size (g)	Solids 50% emptying time (min)	Liquids 50% emptying time (min)
Fischer *et al.* (1982)	20	380	100 ± 4	30 ± 3
Heading *et al.* (1976)	10	185	120 ± 6	45 ± 4
Horowitz *et al.* (1984)	22	250	78 ± 4	19 ± 1
Moon *et al.* (1981)	8	300	77 ± 5	38 ± 4
	8	900	146 ± 26	81 ± 12
	10	1692	277 ± 44	178 ± 22
Wright *et al.* (1993)	31	410	87 ± 9	63 ± 6

Modified from Horowitz M, Pounder DJ. Gastric emptying: forensic implications of current concepts. *Med Sci Law* 1985;**25**:201–214.

It should be kept in mind that different anatomical and functional disorders cause either delayed or rapid gastric emptying (Table 8.7). For example, in cases of raised intracranial pressure, gastric emptying may cease for several days. Püschel [25] reported data relating to solid stomach contents found at autopsy 10 days after scalding, 5 days after subdural haematoma, 9 days after scalding, 11 days after polytrauma and even a bolus death 14 days after subdural haematoma with entirely parenteral nutrition.

Table 8.6 Solid and liquid gastric emptying according to Pensold and Stinzing

Food leaving stomach	Quantity (g)
1–2 hours	
Water	100–200
Carbon dioxide, water	220
Tea	200
Coffee	200
Cocoa	200
Beer	200
Light wines	200
Milk (boiled)	100–200
Beef tea	200
2–3 hours	
Coffee with cream	200
Cocoa with milk	200
Wine	200
Water, beer or boiled milk	300–500
Egg (uncooked), scrambled or boiled	100
Beef/sausage	100
Boiled fish	200
Cauliflower	150
Potatoes	150
Cherries	150
White bread	70
Asparagus (boiled)	150
3–4 hours	
Date	100
Bread	40
Boiled chicken	220–230
Beef, boiled or uncooked	250
Ham, boiled or uncooked	160
Roast veal	100
Rice	150
Apple	150
Bean	150
Spinach	150
4–5 hours	
Ham, fatty	120
Eggs (5)	—
Beefsteak, roasted	250
Hare, roasted	150
Goose, roasted	250
Canard, roasted	280
Herring, salted	200
Lentils (porridge)	150
Peas (porridge)	200

From Tröger HD, Baur C, Spann KW. *Mageninhalt und Todeszeitbestimmung.* Lübeck, Schmidt-Römhild, 1987.

Table 8.7 Aetiology of delayed and rapid gastric emptying

Transient delayed gastric emptying.

- Postoperative illness.
- Acute viral gastroenteritis.
- Hyperglycaemia.
- Drugs: morphine, anticholinergics, levodopa, beta-adrenergic agonists, nicotine.
- Stress: labyrinthine stimulation, cold, pain, pectin supplementation.

Chronic gastric stasis.

- Diabetes mellitus.
- Postsurgical – truncal vagotomy with pyloroplasty and antrectomy.
- Gastro-oesophageal reflux.
- Anorexia nervosa.
- Progressive systemic sclerosis.
- Chronic idiopathic intestinal pseudo-obstruction.
- Amyloidosis.
- Myotonia dystrophica.
- Familial dysautonomia.
- Dermatomyositis.
- Tachygastria.
- Paraplegia.
- Idiopathic myocardial infarction.
- Acute abdomen.
- Laparotomy.
- Physiological: liquids, acid, lipids, left-side position.

Rapid gastric emptying.

- After gastric surgery.
- Vagotomy.
- Antrectomy/subtotal gastrectomy.
- Zollinger–Ellison syndrome.
- Duodenal ulcer disease.
- Reserpine.
- Physiological: liquids, hunger.

Data from Horowitz M, Pounder DJ. Gastric emptying: forensic implications of current concepts. *Med Sci Law* 1985;**25**:201–214; and Tröger HD, Baur C, Spann KW. *Mageninhalt und Todeszeitbestimmung.* Lübeck, Schmidt-Römhild, 1987.

Horowitz and Pounder [12] summarized their review on gastric emptying as follows:

1. Simultaneously ingested liquid, digestible solid and non-digestible solid foods leave the stomach at different rates.
2. The emptying pattern of low-calorie liquids approximates a mono-exponential (volume-dependent) process that results primarily from the motoric activity of the proximal stomach.
3. The emptying of digestible solids usually occurs much more slowly than that of liquids and approximates a linear pattern following an initial lag period. It is primarily dependent on the motor activity of the distal stomach.
4. The emptying of larger, non-digestible particles chiefly occurs during the interdigestive periods, as a specific result of gastric motor activity.

5. Meals of higher osmotic and caloric content are emptied more slowly.
6. There is a substantial variation in emptying rates in normal subjects, and this variation may even be altered by diseases.

■ Estimation of time of death from gastric contents

From the examination of the stomach contents, only a rough estimation can be derived, and this may extend over a few hours. According to Horowitz and Pounder [12], only the solid components of a mixed solid and liquid meal should be considered, and the weight of the stomach contents should be compared with the estimated weight of the last meal and reference made to the known 50 per cent emptying times for the solid components of meals of various sizes (see Table 8.5).

Tröger *et al.* [31] compared the gastric contents (volume) found at autopsy with time and volume of last meals on an autopsy collective of 47 cases (sudden and unexpected death, exclusion of brain tumours, gastro-intestinal tract surgery, intoxication, alcoholism). The

gastric contents (as per cent volume of the last meal) were plotted against the survival time. Only a gastric content weight of more than 10 g was considered, and a regression line and 90 and 98 per cent confidence limits were calculated (Figure 8.3) [3].

The following conclusions were derived from the graph:

- If 90 per cent of the last meal is still found in the stomach, the last food intake was probably within the last hour before death, with 98 per cent confidence limits of 3 to 4 hours.
- At autopsy, if 50 per cent of the volume of the last meal is found in the stomach, the last food intake was about 3 to 4 hours before death, with 98 per cent confidence limits of not less than 1 hour and not more than 10 hours.
- If only 30 per cent of the last meal is found, the last food intake was about 4 to 5 hours before death, with 98 per cent confidence limits not less than 1 to 2 hours and not more than 10 to 11 hours.

The data shown in Figure 8.3 are valid only for mixed food. If the volume of the last meal is not known exactly, tables for the calculation of restaurant portions have been published by Tröger *et al.* [31].

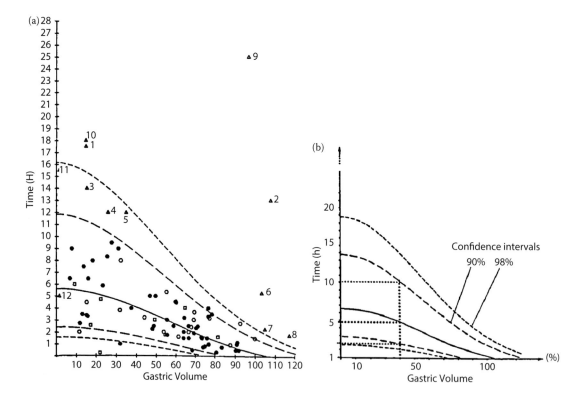

Figure 8.3 (a) Relation between gastric volume of a mixed meal in per cent of ingested volume and time after food intake with regression line, 90 and 98 per cent limits of confidence. Whole sample consists of 48 cases. Closed circles, normal cases; open circles, alcohol concentration between 0.3 and 3.18 per cent (n = 17); squares, death after hospitalization (n = 8); triangles, special cases (intoxication, trauma to the head). (b) Procedure in practice. From the stomach content in per cent of the ingested volume, an estimation of the survival period can be made. (From Baur C, Spann KW, Tröger HD, Schuller E. Magenfüllung und Todeszeitpunkt. *Beitr Gerichtl Med* 1980;**38**:193–197.)

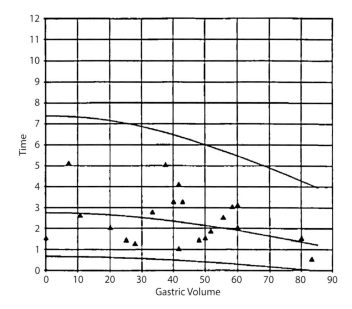

Figure 8.4 Pure carbohydrate food: rest volume in per cent of ingested volume plotted against the survival period after food intake. Regression line and 90 per cent limits of confidence. (From Tröger HD, Baur C, Spann KW. *Mageninhalt und Todeszeitbestimmung.* Lübeck, Schmidt-Römhild, 1987.)

Pure carbohydrate food leaves the stomach earlier than does mixed food. Therefore, a specialized graph was also derived for pure carbohydrate food (gastric contents in relation to the volume of the last meal) as well (Figure 8.4), and a graph is also available for baby food (Figure 8.5). Because of the small sample sizes, confidence limits could not be calculated, and in the actual case only mean values could be estimated.

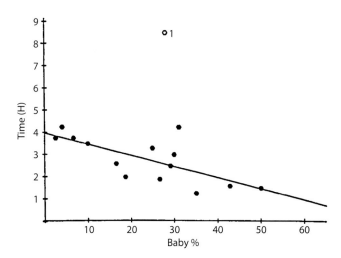

Figure 8.5 Babies up to 10 months – rest volume in per cent of the ingested volume in relation to the time since food intake. One case of fatal intoxication. (From Tröger HD, Baur C, Spann KW. *Mageninhalt und Todeszeitbestimmung.* Lübeck, Schmidt-Römhild, 1987.)

Practical procedure

In practical terms, the stomach contents at autopsy (mixed food with evidence of meat, carbohydrates, vegetables) are weighed and compared with the volume of the last meal. If the volume of the last meal is not known exactly, the gastric contents can be compared with typical restaurant portions. The remaining volume, expressed as a percentage of the ingested volume, provides the mean survival time after food intake, with the corresponding confidence limits. The actual case must be comparable to the case from which the graph was calculated.

For mixed food, these graphs are advantageous when estimating the time since death because the confidence limits derived from casework material can be used, and subjective rough estimations can be avoided. For the identification of food ingredients in stomach contents, the use of microscopic and/or immunological identification methods may be necessary, and these methods have been described in detail in a monograph [31]. For special identification methods, experts must be consulted.

To examine gastric contents, an additional sieve analysis is recommended [26], using a sieve tower. This equipment consists of a collecting basin and four sieves, each with a 20-cm diameter, which can be fitted together. The mesh diameters of the four sieves are 6.3, 4, 2 and 1 mm, respectively.

After weighing the gastric contents, the whole volume is placed into the upper sieve (6.3-mm mesh). If the contents are viscous, water will be added; this permits the contents to be separated into one liquid and up to four solid phases, and these can be further analyzed as appropriate (Figures 8.6 and 8.7).

■ Conclusions

It is thus apparent that the factors affecting gastric emptying are multiple and complex. Brophy *et al.* [5] tested the same subjects on different days with identical meals and liquids. These investigators showed marked variation even in the same individual at different times; the half-emptying times of solids ranged between 29 and 92 minutes, whereas for orange juice the times varied between 12 and 30 minutes.

Attempting to use the *state of digestion,* rather than the quantity of food, as a measure of time since ingestion is even more fraught with uncertainty. Assessing the stage of digestion in terms of time is subjective and almost impossible because virtually no one has any standardized control data for matching. Moreover, the original nature of the meal is usually unknown, so the appearance of the stage of digestion of, say, porridge and bread would be utterly different, at 1 hour from swallowing, from that of meat and raw root vegetables.

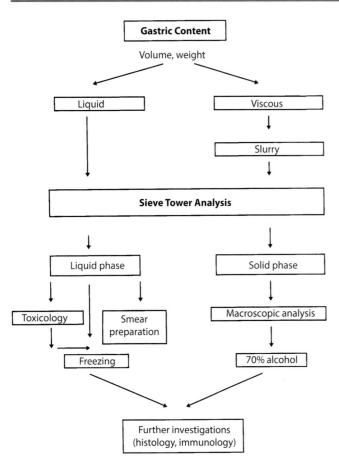

Figure 8.6 Sieve tower analysis of gastric contents allowing further preparation and investigation of the various phases of gastric content. (From Rabl W, Sigrist T. Auftrennung des Mageninhaltes mittels Siebturm-Technik. *Arch Kriminol* 1992;**189:**164–168.)

Figure 8.7 Solid phase of gastric contents consisting of vegetables (mixed salad) with only slight digestion. Victim stabbed soon after food intake (1 to 2 hours).

In summary, the quantity and digestive appearance of gastric contents are modified by the following factors:

- The total quantity of food taken at a meal.
- Additional 'snacks' taken between meals, especially from the modern habit of 'grazing', frequently on quick 'convenience' foods. Where frequent snacking occurs, food may still be in the stomach when the meal under consideration arrives.
- The ratio of solid to liquid in the meal and later 'top-ups' of liquids or solids.
- The carbohydrate and fat contents compared with more inert fibres, etc.
- Marked variations among individuals.
- Variations in the same individual from day to day (Brophy *et al.* [5]).
- Dramatic variations resulting from psychogenic and endocrine factors of emotion, fear, pain, anger, shock and trauma – with or without unconsciousness.

From the foregoing discussion, it is readily apparent that there is a whole range of variable factors making it impossible to use stomach contents as definitive evidence in estimating the time since death.

Even generalizations so often used by pathologists and other medical witnesses can be wildly incorrect, sometimes to the detriment of justice. However eminent a pathologist may be, his or her expertise on this matter is of necessity limited. This pathologist may have conducted thousands of postmortem examinations, in each one of which the stomach contents have been noted. However, in most cases, the issue of the time since death does not need to be considered. Also in most cases, the time and nature of the last meal are unknown and are usually of no interest. So, where does the medical witness obtain the sometimes dogmatic evidence that he or she delivers in court with such pontifical gravitas?

It may be true that for the majority of persons, the 'average meal' leaves the stomach in something between 30 minutes and 3 hours. However, these persons are not subjects of a forensic examination that is necessitated by a violent crime that may have all the connotations of emotion, fear, injury, etc. that are well known to disrupt the digestive process. In addition, the 'majority of persons' leaves a very sizeable minority, whose gastric emptying may lie well outside the so-called 'normal' parameters. Because proof in a criminal case must be 'beyond reasonable doubt', this leaves only little scope for firm testimony based on such shifting sands as gastric physiology.

Unfortunately for defence counsel, the value of such evidence tends to be one-sided – in other words, the unreliability of timing of death from stomach contents allows it to be legitimately claimed, in almost all situations, that death *could* have occurred during the period alleged by the prosecution – whereas the same evidence can virtually never be used to claim that it *could not* and thus remove the time of death into a period of alibi. This negative trend may be persuasive when added to other evidence, even though it has no probative value. A prime example of this is the Truscott case, described here.

■ A case history: Steven Truscott

The best-known instance where the estimation of time since death based on the postmortem evaluation of stomach contents became a matter of international controversy is that of Steven Truscott.

In 1959 in Ontario, Canada, a 14-year-old boy was accused of sexually assaulting and strangling a 12-year-old girl, Lynne Harper. He was found guilty and was sentenced to be hanged, although on appeal several months later, this sentence was reduced to life imprisonment. Disquiet about his conviction led an investigative journalist, Isobel Lebourdais, to write a book on what was claimed to be an injustice; subsequently, a considerable political furore developed.

In 1966, the case was re-heard at the Supreme Court, and many forensic experts from Canada, the United States and Britain gave evidence, mainly on the reliability of estimating the time of death from gastric contents. These experts included Professor Milton Helpern from New York, Professor Francis Camps and Professor Keith Simpson from Britain, Dr Charles Petty (Baltimore, Maryland), Dr Frederick Jaffe (Toronto, Canada), Dr Sam Gerber (Cleveland, Ohio), Mr John Funk (Toronto, Canada) and Dr Noble Sharpe (Toronto, Canada). The Supreme Court upheld the conviction, and Truscott served about 10 years in prison and, on his release, assumed a new identity. The case remained in the public eye, however, with television and press coverage at intervals. In 2001, Steven Truscott declared his intention of clearing his name. He claimed that he was innocent of the crime for which he was convicted more than 40 years ago, and further expert medical opinion was being sought. The circumstances indicated that Truscott had only a period of 45 minutes in which he could have committed the crime; Lynne Harper was seen alive at 7:15 p.m., and Truscott was back home with numerous witnesses at 8:00 p.m. on the evening in question. The body was not discovered until 41 hours later, and a postmortem examination was carried out 48 hours later, 2 days after the girl was last seen alive. The pathologist was Dr John Penistan, a hospital histopathologist who also performed medico-legal autopsies. He gave evidence to the effect that, based on rigor mortis, hypostasis and stomach contents, the time of death lay within a 30-minute interval, 2 days previous to the autopsy.

The facts relating to the gastric contents were that the girl ate a meal of turkey, cranberry sauce, peas, potatoes and pineapple pudding between 5:30 and 5:45 that evening. There were other foods also on the table, but it is not known whether she took those, nor was there any knowledge of what fluids were taken.

The pathologist recorded that the stomach contents consisted of 'approximately one pint (568 ml)', although the evidence of two other doctors who examined the material in the forensic laboratory was that the volume was about 300 ml.

The material was described by Dr Penistan in his autopsy report as 'poorly masticated, only slightly digested food, including peas, onion, corn and a few shreds of apparent meat'. The forensic scientist, Mr Funk, described it as being of the consistency of 'a thick stew'. Dr Noble Share, a medically qualified forensic scientist, said it was like 'a lumpy porridge'.

Dr Penistan's actual words in his autopsy report, to which he adhered during the trial, were as follows:

'Note on time of death; this opinion, which would place the time of death between 7:15 and 7:45 p.m. on 9 June 1959, is based on the following observations and assumptions:

The extent of decomposition which is entirely compatible with death approximately 45 hours prior to identification, having regard to the environmental and climatic conditions.

The extent of rigor mortis. This had almost passed off – a finding again compatible with death at the suggested time.

The limited degree of digestion and the large quantity of food in the stomach. I find it difficult to believe that this food could have been in the stomach for as long as 2 hours unless some complicating factor was present, of which I have no information. If the last meal was finished at 5:45 p.m., I would therefore conclude that death occurred prior to 7:45 p.m. The finding would be comparable (sic) with death as early as 7:15 p.m.'

Although Dr Penistan actually concludes with an opinion that death was *consistent* (although he uses the word 'comparable') with occurring as early as 7:15 p.m., his earlier phraseology was that the findings were *indicative* of death occurring between 7:15 and 7:45 p.m. This opinion was repeated throughout the trial and the later Supreme Court hearing, both by Dr Penistan and by those expert witnesses who supported his view – in spite of the defence witnesses and lawyers forcibly indicating that the medical evidence also allowed death to have taken place well outside those unreasonably narrow limits.

Although there was considerable other non-medical evidence involved in this case, there is no doubt that dogmatic adherence to unreliable pathological findings, which retrospectively placed the time of death within a 30-minute bracket from an autopsy 2 days later, contributed to the death sentence being passed on a 14-year-old boy.

References

1. Adelson L. *The Pathology of Homicide.* Springfield, Illinois, Charles C Thomas, 1974.
2. Aschoff L. Diskussionsbemerkung zu Mangold E: Über Automatie, Erregbarkeit und Totenstarre in verschiedenen Teilen des Froschmagens. *Dtsch Med Wochenschr* 1920;**16**:447–448.
3. Baur C, Spann KW, Tröger HD, Schuller E. Magenfüllung und Todeszeitpunkt. *Beitr Gerichtl Med* 1980;**38**:193–197.
4. Berg S. Der Beweiswert der Todeszeitbestimmung (Überlebenszeit). *Beitr Gerichtl Med* 1969;**25**:61–65.
5. Brophy CM, Moore JG, Christian PE, Egger MJ, Taylor AT. Variability of gastric emptying measurements in man employing standardized radiolabeled meals. *Dig Dis Sci* 1986;**31**:799–806.
6. Camps FE. Establishment of the time of death: a critical assessment. *J Forensic Sci* 1959;**4**:73–82.
7. Camps FE (ed.). *Gradwohl's Legal Medicine.* 3rd ed. Bristol, John Wright, 1976, p 98.
8. DiMaio D, DiMaio VJM. *Forensic Pathology.* New York, Elsevier, 1989, pp 36–42.
9. Forster B, Hummelsheim G, Döring G. Tierexperimentelle Untersuchungen über die postmortale Magenperistaltik bei Leuchtgas- und Parathion-Vergiftung. *Dtsch Z Gerichtl Med* 1965;**56**:148–159.
10. Gordon I, Shapiro HA, Berson SD. *Forensic Medicine: A Guide to Principles.* 3rd ed. Edinburgh, Churchill Livingstone, 1988, p 56.
11. Holczabek W. Zur Untersuchung des Magen-Darmtraktes für die Todeszeitbestimmung. *Beitr Gerichtl Med* 1961;**21**:23–27.
12. Horowitz M, Pounder DJ. Gastric emptying: forensic implications of current concepts. *Med Sci Law* 1985;**25**:201–214.
13. Joachim H. *Probleme der frühen Todeszeitbestimmung und die sogenannten supravitalen Reaktionen im Tierversuch.* Freiburg, Germany, Habil. Schrift, 1976.
14. Knight B. *Forensic Pathology.* 2nd ed. London, Edward Arnold, 1996, pp 89–90.
15. Knight B. The use of gastric contents in estimating time since death. In: Henssge C, Knight B, Krompecher T, Madea B, Nokes L. *Estimation of the Time Since Death in the Early Postmortem Period.* 2nd ed. London, Edward Arnold, 2002, pp 209–215.
16. Legge C. *The Use of Gastric Contents in Estimating Time Since Death.* London, Queen Mary University of London, Master of Science in Forensic Medical Sciences thesis, 2011.
17. Madea B, Oehmichen M, Henssge C. Postmortaler Transport von Mageninhalt. *Z Rechtsmed* 1986;**97**:201–206.
18. Madea B, Oehmichen M, Henssge C. *Postmortale Magenperistaltik? Festschrift Prof Spann.* Berlin, Springer, 1986, pp 200–205.
19. Merkel H. Über Mageninhalt und Todeszeit. *Dtsch Z Gerichtl Med* 1922;**1**:346–358.
20. Modi JP. *Medical Jurisprudence and Toxicology.* Bombay, Tripathi, 1957.
21. Moore JG, Christian PE, Brown JA, Brophy C, Datz F, Taylor A, Alazraki N. Influence of meal weight and caloric content on gastric emptying of meals in man. *Dig Dis Sci* 1984;**29**:513–519.
22. Moore JG, Christian PE, Coleman RE. Gastric emptying of varying meal weight and composition in man. *Dig Dis Sci* 1981;**26**:16–22.
23. Moore JG, Tweedy C, Christian PE, Datz FL. Effects of age on gastric emptying of liquid-solid meals in man. *Dig Dis Sci* 1983;**28**:340.
24. Polson CJ, Gee DJ, Knight B. *The Essentials of Forensic Medicine.* 4th ed. Oxford, Pergamon Press, 1985, pp 32–33.
25. Püschel K. Nüchternheitsgebot und Aspirations prophylaxe aus rechtsmedizinischer Sicht. *AINS* 1996;**31**:248–250.
26. Rabl W, Sigrist T. Auftrennung des Mageninhaltes mittels Siebturm-Technik. *Arch Kriminol* 1992;**189**:164–168.
27. Simpson CK (ed.). *Taylor's Principles and Practice of Medical Jurisprudence.* 12th ed. London, J & A Churchill, 1965, p 210.
28. Sonderegger W. *Zeitbestimmungen nach biologisch-medizinischen Methoden in dem Gebiet der Rechtsmedizin.* Zürich, Medical dissertation, 1916.
29. Sorge A. Die Verwertung des Mageninhaltes zur Bestimmung der Todeszeit und der Zeit der letzten Nahrungsaufnahme. *Z Medizinal Beamte* 1904;**17**:373–390.
30. Spitz WU. *Spitz & Fisher's Medicolegal Investigation of Death.* 3rd ed. Springfield, Illinois, Charles C Thomas, 1993, pp 28–31.
31. Tröger HD, Baur C, Spann KW. *Mageninhalt und Todeszeitbestimmung.* Lübeck, Schmidt-Römhild, 1987.

Immunohistochemical Methods as an Aid in Estimating the Time Since Death

Burkhard Madea

Immunohistochemical detection of insulin, thyroglobulin and calcitonin

Although morphological methods of death time estimation are of no practical value in forensic practice, there seems to be some change by the application of immunohistochemistry methods [1–6]. Wehner and colleagues studied whether a positive immunoreaction to various antigens such as insulin, thyroglobulin or calcitonin is correlated with the time since death [2–6]. The philosophy behind these investigations is that with an increasing postmortem interval, the tertiary structure of the antigen undergoes postmortem changes, and as a result of protein denaturation, stainings become negative. For example, the colloid and the follicular cells of the thyroid give a positive immunoreaction for thyroglobulin until 5 days post mortem, whereas none of the cases older than 13 days shows such a reaction (Figure 9.1). A negative reaction therefore means that a body has been dead for more than 6 days, and positive reaction means that a body has been dead for less than 12 days.

The pancreatic β-cells from up to 12-day-old corpses produce a positive immunoreaction towards insulin in all cases, whereas no corpse older than 30 days shows such a

reaction. This means that in a case of negative immunoreaction, the time since death can be assumed to be more than 12 days before the autopsy. When there is a positive stain, the death must have occurred a maximum of 29 days earlier.

Calcitonin was always detectable in c-cells of the thyroid up to 4 days, and in bodies older than 13 days there was always negative staining.

The results of the immunohistochemical detection of insulin, thyroglobulin and calcitonin are summarized in Table 9.1.

Meanwhile, a chart was developed to give a rough estimation of the time since death by immunohistochemical methods (Figures 9.2, 9.3 and 9.4).

Table 9.1 Immunohistochemical detection of insulin, thyroglobulin and calcitonin according to Wehner [2–6]

	Positive staining	Negative staining
Insulin	Up to 12 days in all cases	>30 days in all cases
Thyroglobulin	Up to 5 days in all cases	>13 days in all cases
Calcitonin	Up to 4 days in all cases	>13 days in all cases

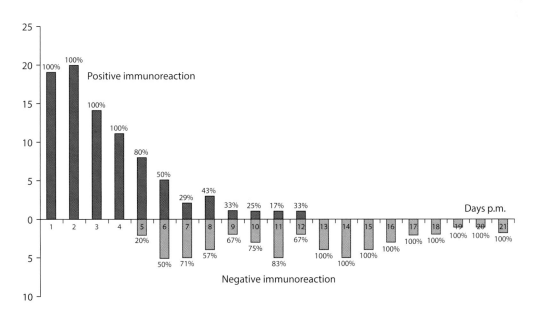

Figure 9.1 Overview of the time dependency of the stainability of thyroglobulin.

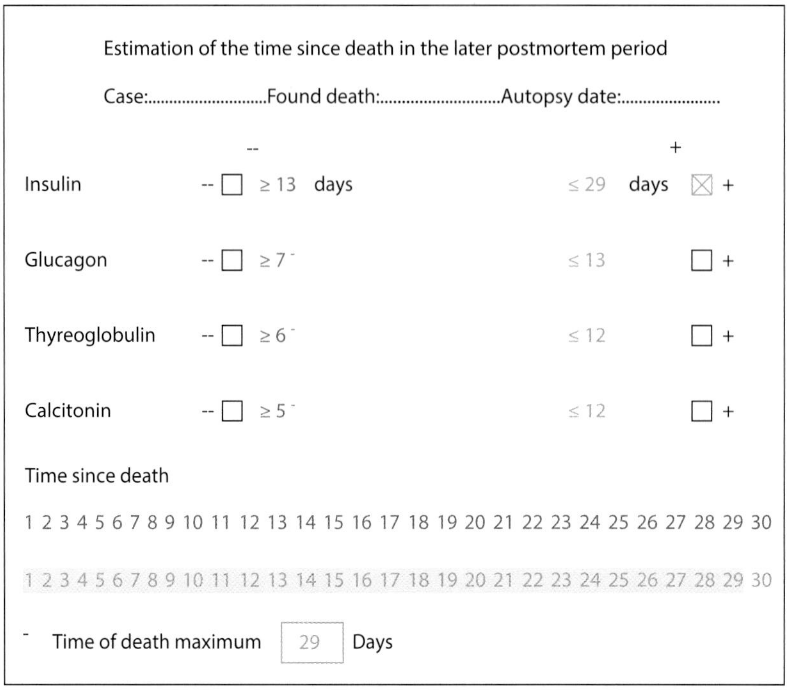

Figure 9.2 Positive immunoreaction of insulin: time since death maximal 29 days.

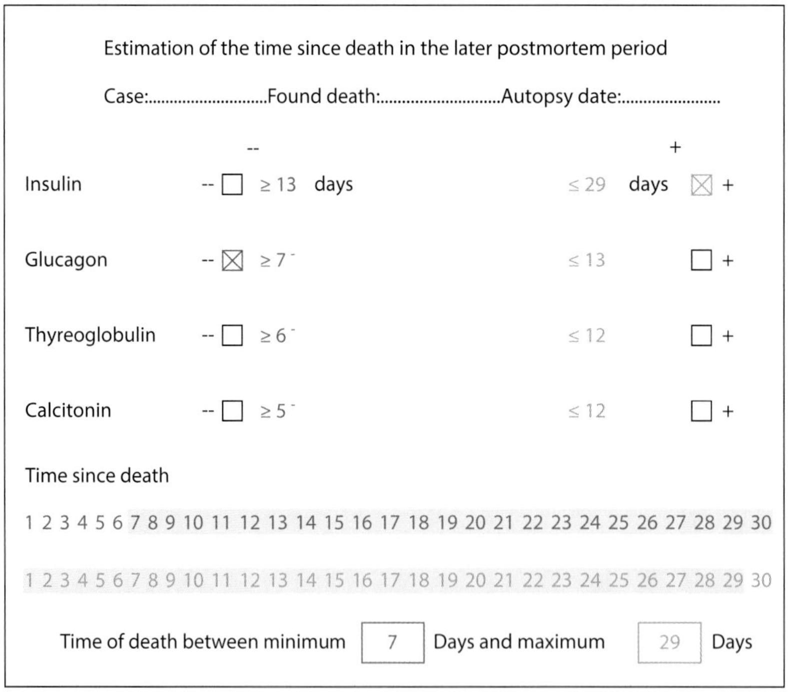

Figure 9.3 Additional investigation of glucagon with a negative immunoreaction: delimitation of the time since death between 7 and 29 days.

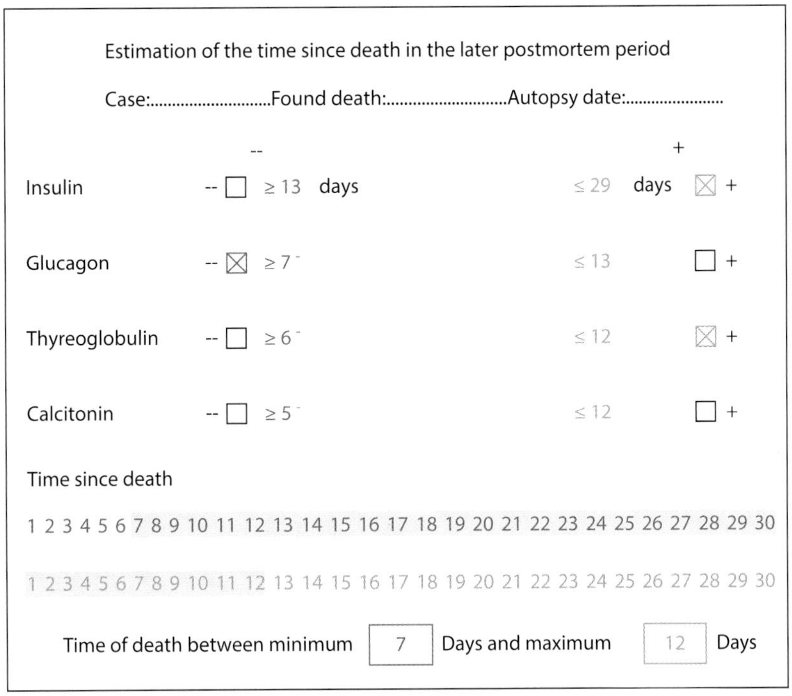

Figure 9.4   Additional investigation of thyroglobulin with a positive immunoreaction: further delimitation between 7 and 12 days.

▪ Conclusions

The immunohistochemical detection of antigens allows only a very rough estimation of the time since death, which may be helpful in single cases. However, these time limits may change in different environmental conditions. Control studies on independent case material are still missing.

References

1. Madea B. Is there recent progress in the estimation of the postmortem interval by means of thanatochemistry? *Forensic Sci Int* 2005;**151**:139–149.

2. Wehner F. Die Eingrenzung der Leichenliegezeit im spätpostmortalen Intervall. Neue Ansätze mittels immunhistochemischer Verfahren. *Med Welt* 2009;**11–12**:402–406.

3. Wehner F, Wehner HD, Schieffer MC, Subke J. Delimitation of the time of death by immunohistochemical insulin detection in pancreatic β-cells. *Forensic Sci Int* 1999;**105**:161–169.

4. Wehner F, Wehner HD, Schieffer MC, Subke J. Delimitation of the time of death by immunohistochemical detection of thyroglobulin. *Forensic Sci Int* 2000;**110**:199–206.

5. Wehner F, Wehner HD, Subke J. Delimitation of the time of death by immunohistochemical detection of calcitonin. *Forensic Sci Int* 2001;**122**:89–94.

6. Wehner F, Wehner HD, Subke J. Delimitation of the time of death by immunohistochemical detection of glucagon in pancreatic β-cells. *Forensic Sci Int* 2002;**124**:241–248.

10 Practical Casework

10.1 Integration of different methods in casework

■ *Claus Henssge and Burkhard Madea*

The great interindividual variability of the postmortal changes as a consequence of many influencing factors restricts the accuracy of death time estimation and, if the limits of confidence of a method are not exactly known, impairs the reliability. Because no single method allows a sufficiently exact and reliable estimation of the interval of death in any particular case, it is recommended that several different methods are used. The selection of methods requires some consideration of the level of investigation and the consequent expenditure of effort.

The following scheme of integration of different methods is recommended for estimating the time of death in casework at the scene. The guidelines are as follows:

1. Whenever possible, use measurements instead of subjective evaluations.
2. Avoid a 'mean value' for the resulting time of death; instead, always offer a 'range' (i.e. the minimum and maximum limits).
3. Take into account important influencing factors on each criterion.
4. Use no more methods in a particular case than are potentially useful.
5. Give a preliminary statement of the interval of death at the scene.
6. The reliability of a stated range of time since death is more important than attempting to give an unrealistically narrow range.

The examination of the body at the scene usually begins with the use of the temperature-based method by using the nomogram as described in Chapter 6, part 6.1. The margins of error of this method can be reduced in many cases by using the following methods, although they themselves have wider margins of error. In a few cases, where the temperature-based method must not be used because of contrary circumstances, those methods should still be used.

■ Time-relevant criteria of different methods

Development of rigor

For more detailed information, see Chapter 4.

Hitherto, the grade of rigor has generally been evaluated subjectively for estimating the time of death in casework

of human bodies. Measurement with a special device is uncommon for a variety of reasons [1,3,22]. The description of the stages of the subjectively evaluated rigor differs from author to author [2,17,18]. For our purposes, only those stages of rigor that are relevant to the time of death are of interest. According to the statistical analysis by Mallach [17,18] of the data in the literature, this is given only for the following stages: 'beginning', 'full development', 'duration' and 'complete resolution' of rigor. The latter two stages are not relevant because of their late postmortal onset of 57 (± 14) hours post mortem and 76 (± 32) hours post mortem, respectively. The stages of rigor are not exactly described either by Mallach [17,18] or in the only other experimental reports of Von Hofmann [11] in 1876 and 1877. (All the other data of Mallach's statistical analyses are figures from textbooks without any experimental basis.) 'Beginning' may mean 'you can observe slight rigor in the joints'. 'Full development' or 'complete development' (shortened to 'maximum' in Tables 10.1 to 10.3) may mean 'rigor is strongly developed in all joints'. There is a third useful marker – the re-establishment of rigor after breaking it. The re-established rigor is less strong than it was before breaking. To avoid a false-positive result, it is necessary to ensure that rigor was broken completely by fully moving the elbow joint several times. A negative result should be stated only if the examined joint had not been manipulated (e.g. by transport or removal of clothing) between breaking the rigor and examination for re-establishment.

Table 10.1 Rigor related to the time of death (hpm)

Stage	Mean	Standard deviation	Limits* Lower	Limits* Upper
Beginning	3	2	0.5	7
Maximum	8	1	2.0	20
Re-establishment			2.0	8

* Lower and upper limits of variance computed from literature data (1811–1960) [17].

Table 10.2 Hypostasis related to the time of death (hpm)

Stage	Mean	Standard deviation	Limits* Lower	Limits* Upper
Beginning	0.75	0.5	0.25	3
Confluence	2.50	1.0	1.00	4
Maximum	9.50	4.5	3.00	16
Thumb pressure	5.50	6.0	1.00	20
Complete shifting	3.75	1.0	2.00	6
Incomplete shifting	11.00	4.5	4.00	24

* Lower and upper limits of variance computed from literature data (1905–1963) [17].

Table 10.3 Probability of a time interval of ± 0.1 hour around the mean value of the time since death (examples) related to the standard deviation

Criterion stage	Mean	Standard deviation	Probability*
Hypostasis			
Complete shifting	3.75	1.0	0.08
Thumb pressure	5.50	6.0	0.01
Maximum	9.50	4.5	0.02
Incomplete shifting	11.00	4.5	0.02

* The probabilities were computed according to equation 10.1 for a time interval of ± 0.1 hour (12 minutes) around the mean.

The death time relationship of these three suitable marks of rigor can be seen in Table 10.1.

Lividity

For more detailed information, see Chapter 5.

Subjective methods are also employed for the evaluation of lividity. Attempts to make the evaluation of lividity objective [12,13] were not generally accepted in practical work until recently. Data in the literature – exceptionally figures from textbooks without experimental basis – were analyzed statistically by Mallach [17,18], for the following degrees of lividity (see Tables 10.2 and 10.3): 'beginning', 'confluence', 'maximum of expansion and intensity' (shortened to 'maximum'), 'complete displacement by slight pressure' (using the thumb; shortened to 'thumb pressure'), 'complete shifting' and 'incomplete shifting' after turning the body over. Complete shifting means that lividity disappears completely in the upward-facing parts of the body after turning it over and then appears in the downward parts; this is apparently dependent on the death time and may take from a few minutes to up to 1 hour. Incomplete shifting means that lividity fades only in the upward-facing parts and appears only slightly in the downward-facing parts after turning the body over. The maximum stage of lividity should be stated only after a second examination carried out later, especially in cases where bleeding had occurred. The criterion 'complete shifting' can be observed at the scene frequently when the body, or even parts of it, had been moved to a new position in the course of the investigative procedure. 'Incomplete shifting' is found to be more likely at autopsy if the body had been transported in another position than that examined at the scene. Two other criteria – 'incomplete displacement after strong pressure' and 'only small fading after turning the body' – were not taken into account because they do not bring further information to the early death time interval in which we are interested.

The reason for non-displacement and non-shifting of lividity is not the early diffusion of haemoglobin, as supposed formerly, but rather the haemoconcentration by loss of fluid that penetrates the wall of those vessels related to the hydrostatic pressure, as shown by Hilgermann [10].

Mechanical excitability of skeletal muscle

For more detailed information, see Chapter 3.

Sufficient data are given in the literature on the two phenomena of postmortal mechanical excitability:

1. Tendon reaction, or Zsako's phenomenon, described first by Zsako [23] and examined as follows [21]: Striking at the lower third of the quadriceps femoris muscle about 10 cm above the patella with a reflex hammer causes an upward movement of the patella because of a contraction of the whole muscle.

2. Idiomuscular contraction (bulge), tested as described by Dotzauer [4] and Prokop [21]: Striking at the biceps brachii muscle with the back of a knife causes a muscular bulge at the point of contact resulting from local contraction of the muscle. The related times of death listed in Table 10.4 are taken from Popwassilew and Palm [19]. The muscular bulge is maintained for some hours if the examination takes place several hours post mortem, as is usually the case, when adenosine triphosphate (ATP) levels are low. Nevertheless, to avoid a false-negative result, one should carefully check whether a local contracture appears after striking the muscle, but immediately disappears again, as may happen in the very early postmortem period in response to high levels of ATP.

The electrical excitability of skeletal muscle

For more detailed information, see Chapter 3.

An extensive literature on this subject has accrued since the 'second' start of the investigations in this field by Prokop [20]. We refer here only to the results of the extensive experimental material of Klein and Klein [14] on 447 bodies. Because the type of electrical stimulus used influences the muscle reaction, the following data of death time are related to stimulation by 'rectangular-like' impulses of a duration of a 'few milliseconds' in a repetition rate of 30 to 70 per second and an amplitude of 50 volts (resistance 1 kOhm) [14]. A small battery-operated generator with constant-current rectangular impulses of 30 mA, 10-ms duration and a frequency of 50 per second is now available commercially (for details, see: j-peschke. homepage.t-online.de). The time data shown in Table 10.4 can be transferred when using this device.

Needle electrodes are inserted 5 to 7 mm deep into the nasal part of the upper eyelid at a distance of 15 to 20 mm (Figure 10.1). The grade of reaction is divided into six degrees according to the spread of the reaction of the mimic muscles. The strongest reaction (degree VI) is obtained if the reaction includes the upper and lower eyelids, forehead and cheek. In the minimal reaction (degree I), only a small local fascicular contraction of the nasal angle of the upper

Table 10.4 Chronological arrangement of the lower and upper limits of the time since death related to the different stages of the cited methods according to literature data*

Parameter checked	Answer		Answer	
	↓		↓	
	Result reduction of the lower limit (t ≥hpm)		Result reduction of the upper limit (t ≤hpm)	
Lividity				
Beginning?	Yes	0.0	No	3.0
Confluence?	Yes	1.0	No	4.0
Thumb pressure?	No	1.0	Yes	20.0
Complete shifting?	No	2.0	Yes	6.0
Maximum?	Yes	3.0	No	16.0
Incomplete shifting?	No	4.0	Yes	24.0
Rigor mortis				
Beginning?	Yes	0.5	No	
Re-establishment?	No	2.0	Yes	9.5
Maximum?	Yes	2.0	No	20.0
Mechanical excitability				
Zsako's phenomenon?	No	0.0	Yes	2.5
Idiomuscular contraction?	No	1.5	Yes	13.0
Electrical excitability				
Eye VI?	No	1.0	Yes	6.0
Eye V	No	2.0	Yes	7.0
Eye IV?	No	3.0	Yes	8.0
Eye III?	No	3.5	Yes	13.0
Eye II?	No	5.0	Yes	16.0
Eye I?	No	5.0	Yes	22.0
Orbicularis oris muscle?	No	3.0	Yes	11.0
Chemical excitability				
Iris				
Atropine/cyclopentolate	No	3.0	Yes	10.0
Mydriaticum Roche (tropicamide)?	No	5.0	Yes	30.0
Acetylcholine?	No	14.0	Yes	46.0

* The upper limit of 8 hours related to re-established rigor was replaced by 9.5 hours according to a newer finding [9].

From Madea B, Henssge C. *Estimation of the Time Since Death: Integration of Different Methods.* Digest of the International Meeting of P.A.A.F.S. and Police Medical Officers, Wichita, Kansas, August 10–14, 1987.

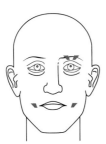

Figure 10.1 Position of insertion of electrodes for facial stimulation.

eyelid appears (Figure 10.2). In addition, the electrodes can also be inserted 10 mm from each corner of the mouth.

We extracted the data in Table 10.4 from the original data produced by Klein and Klein [14] and computed the permissible variation of 95 per cent [5]. In cases with haematoma or emphysema of the eyelid, the time figures are much greater; in cases of a long terminal episode, the time figures are much smaller than those given in Table 10.4 [14]. At present, and regardless of the criticisms [5,15], this method seems to be the most suitable of all the reported 'electrical'

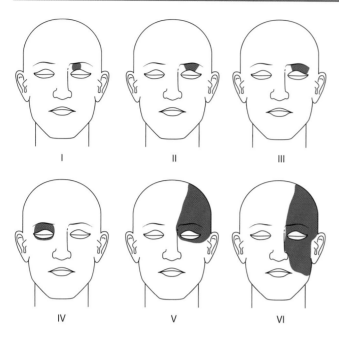

Figure 10.2 Degrees of reaction following electrical stimulation of facial muscles.

methods for casework. Apart from the nomogram method, it is more useful than any of the other methods reviewed in this volume (see Table 10.7).

The chemical excitability of the iris

For more detailed information, see Chapter 3.

From the extensive literature in this field we refer only to the systematic investigations of Klein and Klein [14] on 5765 eyes of 3979 bodies. From these results, we used the data listed in Table 10.4. To examine this reaction, about 0.5 ml of the solution is injected subconjunctivally at the limbus corneae [14]; the concentration used is not important (e.g. 5 per cent). The onset of the reaction begins between 5 and 30 minutes after the injection, and it lasts at least 1 hour. Acetylcholine (miosis) and noradrenaline (mydriasis) have the same time interval of postmortem reaction. However, the effect of acetylcholine is more reliable, and the application of noradrenaline is preferable only if the starting width of the pupil is small. The so-called double reaction, first miosis (e.g. acetylcholine), followed by mydriasis (e.g. atropine) on the same eye, or vice versa, gives no further time information than each reaction separately (using both eyes) (all according to Klein and Klein). To avoid mistakes, it is recommended that the starting diameter of the pupil is measured with a slide caliper to determine whether there was a reaction or not.

■ Arrangement of data

As we concluded earlier in this section, there is no statistical evidence for the use of *mean* values of the time since

death in a special case. Remembering the mathematical relationship between the probability of a short time interval ($X < X_k$) around the mean (x) and the standard deviation (SD):

$$\text{Prob } (X < X_k) = X - x/\text{SD} \qquad (10.1)$$

there is only a very small probability that the mean values will be accurate because of the great SDs (examples shown in Table 10.3).

In compliance with this, the mean value of the idiomuscular contraction (6.9 hours post mortem) occurred in only 6 per cent of the cases of an experimental study [4]. To avoid great errors in our statements of the time since death, we have to avoid the use of mean values. Therefore, we recommend only the use of the upper and lower time limits of any criterion as the basis of statements. In the example of the idiomuscular contraction sought by striking the biceps muscle, no case was reported as having had idiomuscular contraction after the 13th hour post mortem. In no case was this reaction missed before 1.5 hours post mortem. This means that, if the reaction occurs, we can say only that the time since death must be less than 13 hours. If there is no reaction, we can state only that the time since death must be greater than 1.5 hours. Integrating the results of all examinations in the same manner, the greatest figure of any lower limit and the smallest figure of any upper limit reduce the interval within which the death occurred – with a high probability of at least 95 per cent.

From this point of view, and for practical purposes, data are best arranged chronologically, according to the lower and the upper limits (see Table 10.4).

■ Principle of using a special chart

For casework, we rearranged the data of Table 10.4 into a special chart (Figure 10.3), which facilitates the choice of the subsequently helpful criteria in an actual case. In the example in Figure 10.3, the examination began with measurement of the rectal temperature, followed by use of the nomogram method. The result was 4.5 hours post mortem (lower limit) and 10.1 hours post mortem (upper limit). The lower limit can be confirmed or improved only by a criterion with a higher figure for its lower limit. Looking at the chart, in the left-hand column we can quickly find only two criteria that could improve the lower limit: the electrical excitability if there is a negative result; and the chemical excitability of the iris by tropicamide (Mydriaticum Roche, Hoffmann La Roche), also if there is a negative result. The upper limit (10.1 hours post mortem) can be confirmed or improved only by a criterion with a lower figure for its upper limit. We can quickly find the possibly helpful criteria on the chart, in the right-hand column: the electrical excitability, again if there is a reaction of degree IV (or V or VI); or the

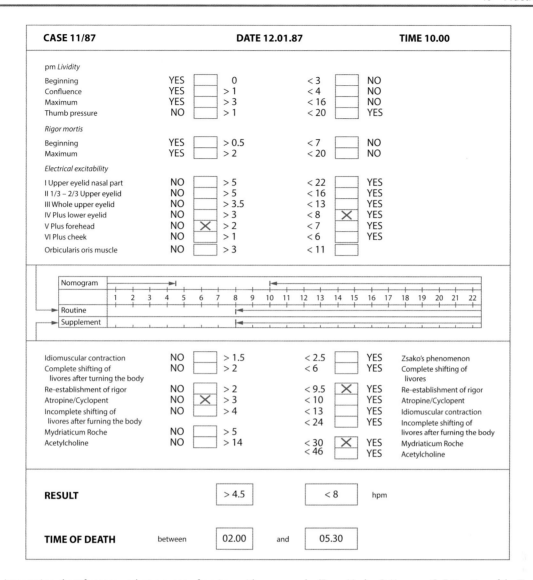

Figure 10.3   Integrating chart for casework at a scene of a crime with an example. (From Madea B, Henssge C. *Estimation of the Time Since Death: Integration of Different Methods.* Digest of the International Meeting of P.A.A.F.S. and Police Medical Officers, Wichita, Kansas, August 10–14, 1987.)

chemical excitability of the iris by atropine or cyclopentolate (Cyclopent, United Pharmacies) if there is a reaction and the re-establishment of the rigor after breaking if it occurs. We examined the electrical excitability of the mimic muscles and the chemical excitability of the iris by atropine (one side) and by Mydriaticum Roche (other side), and we broke the rigor of one elbow joint. The other criteria need not be examined because they could not help in this case. (We always routinely examine the stages of rigor and hypostasis.)

The results of the examined criteria are put into the chart (see Figure 10.3). Only the electrical excitability (degree IV) and the re-established rigor were helpful: they reduced the upper time limit of the temperature-based nomogram result from 10 to 9.5 hours post mortem (re-establishment) and further to 8 hours post mortem (degree IV). The chemical examinations did not provide an improvement in this case. In so far as this example is typical, the electrical

examination gives rather more of an improvement than the other criteria (see Table 10.7). The final result in this case is as follows: with a high probability (95 per cent), the death occurred between 4.5 and 8 hours before the examination. The computer program http://www.AMAsoft.de automatically leads the procedure of examining the body at the scene according to this logistic (Figure 10.4) after performing all mathematical operations of the nomogram method (see Figure 6.33). The computer program was evaluated in a field study [8,9].

■ Experiences in casework

In 32 cases with investigated death times between 2 and 13 hours, both the nomogram and the electrical excitability of mimic muscles were used (Figure 10.5 and Table 10.5) [16]. The results provide evidence that the range of death times

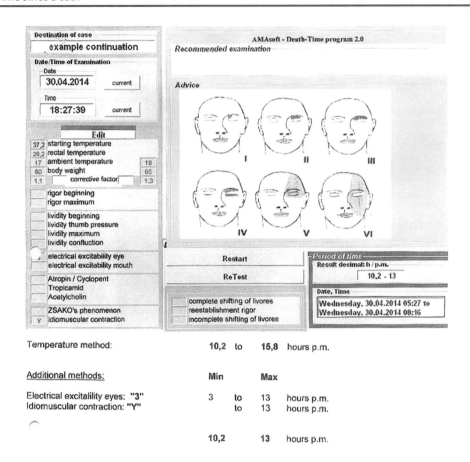

Temperature method: 10,2   to   15,8   hours p.m.

Additional methods: **Min**   **Max**

Electrical excitalility eyes: "3"   3   to   13   hours p.m.
Idiomuscular contraction: "Y"   to   13   hours p.m.

                                             10,2   **13**   hours p.m.

Figure 10.4   Case example (see Figure 6.33) of using the PC program http://www.AMAsoft.de for continuative examination of the non–temperature-based criteria according to this logistic.

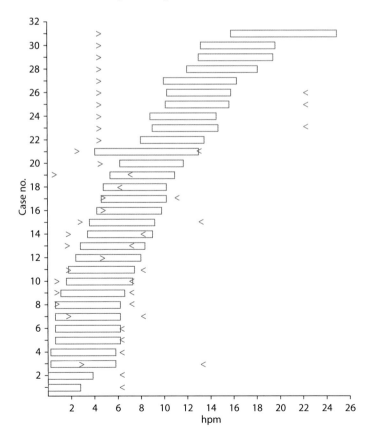

Figure 10.5 Combined application of the temperature-based nomogram and the electrical excitability for determining the time since death [16]. Case numbers are according to Table 10.5. Boxes: death time estimation by the nomogram method (lower and upper 95 per cent limits of confidence; see Table 10.5). > < Death time information based on the degree of electrical excitability. For instance, degree III positive (case 15) not only reveals the information that the time since death is <13 hpm but also means degree IV negative and therefore that the time since death is 3 hpm. Especially during the time period from 3 to 8 hpm, combining electrical excitability with the nomogram method reveals a more precise death time estimation than using one method alone. The real time since death was always within the calculated time since death.

Table 10.5 Death-time estimation from body temperature (using the nomogram) and the degree of electrical excitability

No.	Cause of death	Time of investigation	T_R	T_A	Body weight	f	Death-time estimation (nomogram)	Degree of electrical excitability	Death-time estimation (hours)
1	Female, 44 years, 3 homicidal shotgun wounds of the neck	13.20	37.2	35.5	60	0.5	0–2.8	VI	<6
2	45 years, male, suicidal shotgun wound of the head	13.30	37.1	17	70	1.2	0–3.8	VI	<6
3	30 years, female stab wounds of the heart	16.10	35.6	14.5	54	1.1	0.2–5.8	III	>3<13
4	53 years, female, stab wounds of the neck and chest	15.55	36.5	18.5	74.3	1.2	0.2–5.8	VI	<6
5	Male suicidal shotgun injury of heart and lung	03.15	36	20.9	56	1.2	0.6–6.2	VI	<6
6	48 years, male, homicidal stab wounds of the chest	01.45	36.1	24.8	80	1	0.6–6.2	VI	<6
7	6 years, female, blunt force injury to the skull	06.15	26.4	2.3	19.8	1	0.6–6.2	IV	>2<8
8	80 years, female, coronary artery disease	16.20	36.7	23.6	71	1.9	0.6–6.2	V	>1<7
9	42 years, male, stab wounds of the neck	19.30	36.5	17.7	62.5	1.9	1–6.6	V	>1<7
10	20 years, female, fatal heroin intoxication	20.45	33.2	20.7	36.3	1	1.6–7.2	V	>1<7
11	35 years, female, stab wounds of chest and neck	04.25	33.3	9.5	60	1	1.8–7.4	IV	>2<8
12	72 years, female, homicidal strangulation	19.00	34.8	19.7	60.1	1.2	2.4–8	I neg.	>5
13	29 years, male, homicidal gunshot wound of the heart	10.25	34.7	18	75	1.05	2.8–8.4	V	>1<7
14	39 years, female, homicidal gunshot wound of the skull	09.20	34.9	21.5	75.5	1.1	3.4–9	V	>1<7
15	14 years, male, homicidal gunshot wound of the skull	09.00	33.4	20	61.2	1	3.6–9.2	III	>3<13
16	22 years, female, blunt force injury to skull and neck	04.45	32.1	20.6	50	1	4.2–9.8	I neg.	>5
17	45 years, female, alcoholic bleeding from gastric erosions	08.00	30.2	21.5	35.4	1	4.6–10.2	I orb. oris +	>5<11
18	44 years, male, homicidal shotgun wound of the heart	03.15	34.4	22.8	80	1	4.6–10.2	VI	<6
19	58 years, male, homicidal blunt force injury of the skull	13.15	28.3	6	65	1	5.4–11	V	>1<7
20	Homicidal stab wounds of the neck	11.15	32.9	24	71.5	1.1	6.2–11.8	I neg.	>5

(Continued)

Table 10.5 (*Continued*) Death-time estimation from body temperature (using the nomogram) and the degree of electrical excitability

No.	Cause of death	Time of investigation	T_R	T_A	Body weight	f	Death-time estimation (nomogram)	Degree of electrical excitability	Death-time estimation (hours)
21	3 years, female, drowning	00.30	26.2	22.9	16	1	4.1–13.1	III orb. oris +	>3<11
22	56 years, male, homicidal blunt force injury of the skull	10.45	33.2	22.5	90	1	8–13.6	I neg.	>5
23	Female, homicidal stab wounds of the neck	11.00	30.6	23.5	59.8	1.1	9–14.6	I	>5<22
24	Male, homicidal stab wounds of the neck	11.30	33.6	22.9	97.5	1.1	9.2–14.8	I neg.	>5
25	Male, homicidal stab wounds of the chest	12.10	32.7	21.5	87	1.2	10.2–15.8	I neg.	>5
26	79 years, female, throttling	04.00	31	21.8	65	1.2	10.4–16	I	>5<22
27	Female accidental traumatic asphyxia	12.30	25.9	19.6	42	1	10–16.4	I neg.	>5
28	Female, throttling	19.10	25.7	16.1	64	1	12–18.2	I neg.	>5
29	39 years, male, stab wounds of the neck	10.10	27.5	18	75.5	1	13–19.4	I neg.	>5
30	22 years, female, homicidal gunshot wound of the chest	23.20	26.5	19.1	62.6	1–1.2	13.2–19.6	I neg.	>5
31	73 years, female, homicidal strangulation	13.00	27.5	18	74	1.3	15.9–24.9	I neg.	>5
32	41 years, male, chronic alcoholism, pneumonia	12.05	38.9	24	72	1	—	IV orb. oris + thenar+++	>2<8

+, positive; *f*, corrective factor; neg., negative; orb. oris, orbicularis oris; T_A ambient temperature (°C); T_R rectal temperature (°C).

From Madea B, Henssge C. Electrical excitability of skeletal muscle postmortem on casework. *Forensic Sci Int* 1990;**47:**207–227.

resulting from the temperature nomogram becomes smaller in some cases by application of the method of electrical excitability of facial muscles according to Figure 10.2. Nevertheless, in the other cases the self-confidence of the investigator in his or her opinion on the time since death increases by using 2 independent methods with a common result. In addition, the 32 investigated cases confirmed the results of Klein and Klein [14].

Two special cases [7] may demonstrate that factors influencing the time course of electrical excitability in a contrary direction to body cooling may mislead or confuse the investigator when they are not taken into account (Figures 10.6 and 10.7).

In the case of Figure 10.6, the temperature-based nomogram method showed the death time interval to be from 8.8 to 14.3 hours, corresponding to 26.6°C rectal temperature, 10°C ambient temperature and 72 kg body weight. Rigor mortis had not begun, and electrical excitability showed a full reaction (degree VI) resulting in a death time of less than 7 and 6 hours, respectively. These results excluded each other. The suspicion of fatal hypothermia, as a result of purple-red patches of discolouration of the skin on and around the elbow and knee joints, was confirmed by autopsy findings such as haemorrhagic erosions of the stomach and

haemorrhage of the pancreas and its ductus. The fatal hypothermia explains the contrary results of death time estimation between the temperature-based nomogram method and the electrical excitability method: the hypothermia simulated a long time since death because of the fall in central body temperature during life. The nomogram method must not be used in such a case (see Chapter 6.1). Electrical excitability is not influenced by hypothermia. The investigated time of death was really 2.5 hours.

In the other special case (see Figure 10.7), there was a large difference in the electrical excitability of the right and left eyelids. The right upper eyelid had emphysema resulting from an incised wound in the glabella region. Because of the higher figure obtained for death times with regard to the degree of electrical excitability in cases with emphysema or fresh haemorrhage [14], the reaction of the right eyelid (degree III) cannot be used as an upper limit of death time (13 hours). The investigated time since death was really 15 hours.

The experiences with the complete 'integrated method' used in a field study of 72 consecutive cases at the scene were published [8,9]. Subsequent to the use of the temperature nomogram as primary method (see Tables 6.1.17 and 6.1.21), the non–temperature-based methods (see

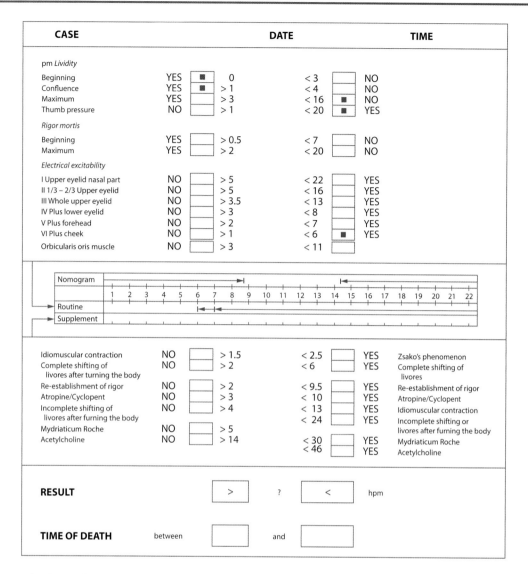

Figure 10.6   Example of using the integrating chart (see text).

Table 10.4, Figure 10.3 and Figure 10.4) were selectively used to improve (or at least confirm) the range of death times resulting from the temperature nomogram. The case-oriented selection of the additional methods followed the principle discussed earlier (see Figure 10.3), and it was supported by the interactive notebook program (http://www. AMAsoft.de) discussed earlier in this chapter. The program defines the term 'confirmation of the range of death time resulting from the temperature nomogram' as follows [6]: To confirm the upper and lower time limits obtained by the primary nomogram method, an additional criterion is requested only if its time limit is 20 per cent or at least 1 hour higher, or 20 per cent or at least 1 hour lower, respectively (Figure 10.8).

Using this logistic, only those criteria were used that could be potentially helpful in the actual cases examined. In 3 cases, none of the required examinations could be performed because of the particular situation at the scene.

In several cases the required additional examinations could be performed only incompletely. Nevertheless, the range of death time as estimated by the nomogram method became smaller by application of additional methods in 49 cases (examples in Table 10.6). In a further 6 cases, the additional methods confirmed the time limits obtained by the temperature method. In 3 of 4 cases where the temperature method should not be used, the period since death was estimated by the non–temperature-based methods exclusively (see Table 10.6). As expected, the electrical examination gave rather more of an improvement, but the other criteria also contributed to improvement in many cases (Table 10.7). As can be seen from the examples in Table 10.6, the developing cascade of stepwise limitation of the period since death by examination of each further criterion contributes to the self-confidence of the investigator in his or her opinion on the period since death. The application of the integrated method including the nomogram method and the

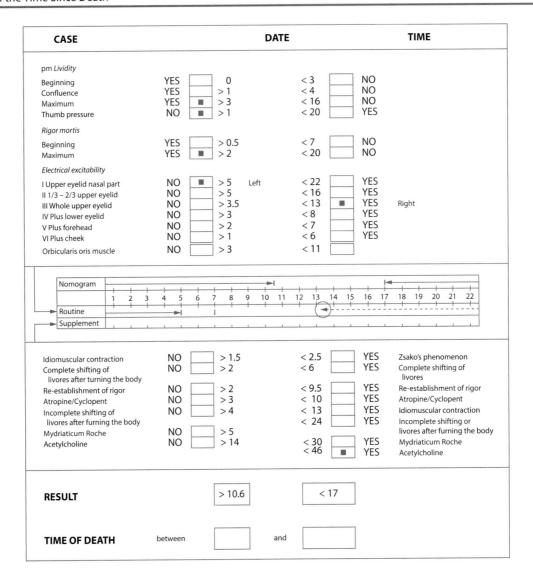

Figure 10.7   Example of using the integrating chart (see text).

additional non–temperature-based criteria led to total spans of the period since death in the order of 1.5 hours in 5 cases, and up to 3.5 hours in a further 15 cases. In only 1 of the 72 cases (case number 23 in Table 10.6) did the upper limit of the estimated period since death concluded from the re-establishment of rigor (8 hours post mortem) contradict the time of death investigated by the crime police (9.4 hours post mortem). However, the upper limits of the period since death concluded from the nomogram method (11.7 hours post mortem) and from the criterion mydriasis of iris to atropine (10 hours post mortem) were not in contradiction. The case gives cause for replacing 8 hours post mortem with 9.5 hours post mortem concerning the upper limit of re-established rigor in Tables 10.1 and 10.4 and in Figures 10.3, 10.6 and 10.7).

The field study clearly demonstrates the usefulness of estimating the period since death in the early postmortem period by application of the 'integrated method' described in this volume.

■ Discussion

It must be emphasized that the proposed system is not the result of simultaneous measurements of experimental investigations, but rather is based only on separate data from the literature. Most of the data are again not the result of experimental investigations, but figures taken from textbooks. Therefore, not all cited limits will be the last word. For example, case number 23 in Table 10.6 points to a higher upper time limit of the criterion re-establishment of rigor (9.5 hpm) than the literature-based 8 hpm (see Tables 10.1 and 10.4).

Nevertheless, these data chosen and arranged from statistical and practical points of view are now evaluated in two field studies with simultaneous examination of the combined temperature-based nomogram method and the electrical excitability [16], as well as of combinations of all the parts of the integrated method [7,8].

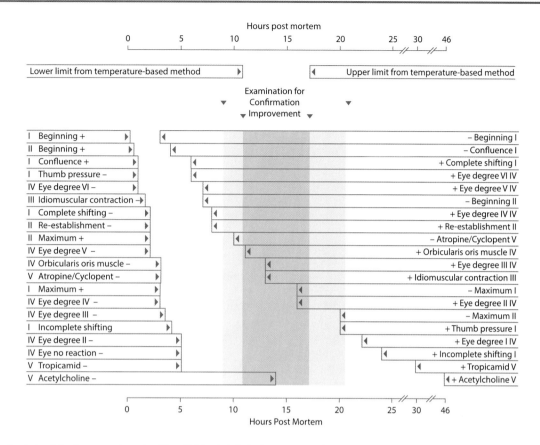

Figure 10.8 Logistic of the 'integrated method' (see Table 10.4). Only those criteria that can improve or confirm the time limits from the nomogram method should be used in an actual case.

Using the proposed combined method in casework at the scene, in several cases we were able to assist the criminal investigation in its earliest stage. In other cases, the additional examination of the listed criteria did not provide reduced limits for the nomogram reading. The overall result is an estimation of a time interval within which the death occurred – longer or shorter – but reliable within at least 95 per cent limits if the instructions about using the nomogram and the other methods are followed. We believe that this is the best we can do at present, when giving a statement concerning the time of death.

10.2   Conditional probability in death time estimation

■ Stefan Potente

The conditional probability distribution (CPD) approach integrates additional information, namely the time interval in which death is at all possible to have occurred, into the nomogram interval.

Henssge's nomogram method for the estimation of time since death uses a normally distributed 2 standard deviation (SD) interval in hours since measurement as target.

In contrast, additional methods, namely supravital reactions and properties of lividity and rigor as described in the compound method (CM), aim at excluding certain time ranges. Here, findings may lead to statements about minimum or maximum hours since death.

The same principle is applied in police investigation where the time when the deceased was last seen alive and the time the body was found are checked regularly, and additional information such as way-time calculations, telecommunication data and such can be taken into account in a broader approach to the circumstances surrounding death.

When combining nomogram method results with said limitations to the time when death is at all possible to have occurred, effects on probability concerning the nomogram method findings have not yet been taken into account. In other words, 'under the condition that death might have occurred between time X and Y', a given death time interval estimated using the nomogram method may hold considerably different properties than without said conditions. Conversely, when conditions are discarded or taken out of the consideration, the unconditional death time interval will hold the properties of the 'regular', unconditional nomogram death time interval.

Table 10.6 Examples of cases in which the non–temperature-based methods provided a reduction and/or a confirmation of the lower and/or upper limit of the period since death obtained by the nomogram method

Case number	Estimation lower limit (hpm)	Method/criterion	Upper limit (hpm)	Method/criterion	Ascertainment lower limit (hpm)	Upper limit (hpm)	Comments
4	2.0	Cooling by nomogram method	7.6	**Cooling by nomogram method**	5.8	6.3	
	3.0	Lividity maximum	11.0	Electr. excit. orbic. oris m.			
	4.0	Lividity no incomplete shifting	10.0	Mydriasis to atropine			
	5.0	**No electr. excit. eye**	8.0	Rigor re-establishment			
			7.0	Electr. excit. eye V			
			6.0	Lividity complete shifting+			
15	0.3	Cooling by nomogram method	5.9	**Cooling by nomogram method**	4.3	4.5	+After repeated examination at autopsy 2 h later.
	1.0	Electr. excit. eye NO VI	13.0	Idiomuscular contraction			
	1.0	Lividity confluence	11.2	Cooling by nomogram method			
	2.0	Rigor maximum+	11.0	Electr. excit. orbic. oris m.			
	3.0	**Lividity maximum+**	10.0	Mydriasis to atropine			
			8.0	**Electr. excit. eye IV**			
20	3.5	Electr. excit. eye NO III	10.0	Mydriasis to atropine	2.8*	9.8+	+Missing for 9.8 h. *Finding the body 2.8 h before examination.
	5.6	**Cooling by nomogram method**	**8.0**	**Cooling by nomogram method**			
21	5.0	No electr. excit. eye	30.0	Mydriasis of iris to Mydriaticum Roche (tropicamide)	?	?	*The body found lying prone was transported lying back; the incomplete shifting of lividity was observed at autopsy. +Survival of the fatal pressure on the neck for at least 30 min up to 3 h; some contravascular emigration of polymorphic leucocytes in the subcutaneous fat of the ligature mark.
	18.1+	Cooling by nomogram method	29.9	Cooling by nomogram method			
			24.0+	Lividity incomplete shifting*			
23	3.0	Lividity maximum	13.0	Electr. excit. eye III	9.3	9.4	+Being inconsistent with the time of investigation.
	3.0	Electr. excit. eye NO IV	11.7	Cooling by nomogram method			
	6.1	**Cooling by nomogram method**	10.0	Mydriasis of iris to atropine			
			8.0	**Rigor re-establishment+**			

(Continued)

Table 10.6 (Continued) Examples of cases in which the non–temperature-based methods provided a reduction and/or a confirmation of the lower and/or upper limit of the period since death obtained by the nomogram method

Case number	Estimation lower limit (hpm)	Method/criterion	Upper limit (hpm)	Method/criterion	Ascertainment lower limit (hpm)	Ascertainment Upper limit (hpm)	Comments
26	2.0	Electr. excit. eye NO V	11.9	Cooling by nomogram method	7.4	7.4	
	2.0	Rigor no re-establishment	**8.0**	**Electr. excit. eye IV**			
	6.3	**Cooling by nomogram method**					
28	3.0	No electr. excit. orbic. oris m.	16.0	Electr. excit. eye II	6.6	6.9	
	3.5	Electr. excit. eye NO I	10.0	Mydriasis of iris to atropine			
	3.5	Cooling by nomogram method	9.1	Cooling by nomogram method			
	5.0	**No mydriasis of iris to Mydriaticum Roche**	**8.0**	**Rigor re-establishment**			
34	1.0	Lividity confluence	8.9	Cooling by nomogram method	4.8	5.5	
	2.0	Electr. excit. eye NO V	8.0	Electr. excit. eye IV			
	3.3	**Cooling by nomogram method**	**6.0**	**Lividity complete shifting**			
40	3.0	No electr. excit. orbic. oris m.	14.5	Cooling by nomogram method	7.5*	12.3+	*Finding the body.
	5.0	No electr. excit. eye	**10.0**	**Mydriasis of iris to atropine**			+Infliction of the stab wounds.
	8.9	**Cooling by nomogram method**					
44	0.5	Rigor beginning	13.0	Electr. excit. eye III			
	1.0	Lividity confluence	11.0	Electr. excit. orbic. oris m.			
	1.1	Cooling by nomogram method	8.0	Rigor re-establishment			
46	**3.0**	**Electr. excit. eye NO IV**	**6.7**	**Cooling by nomogram method**	3.6	4.3	Same scene as 47.
	3.0	No mydriasis of iris to atropine	13.0 13.0	Idiomuscular contraction			
	3.0	No electr. excit. orbic. oris m.	10.5	Electr. excit. eye III			
	4.9	Cooling by nomogram method	8.0	Rigor re-establishment			
			6.0				
47	2.0	Rigor maximum			5.8	6.1	Same scene as 46; examination 1.5 hours later than 46.
	3.0	Lividity maximum					
	5.0	**No mydriasis of iris to Mydriaticum Roche**		**Lividity complete shifting**			

(Continued)

Table 10.6 (Continued) Examples of cases in which the non–temperature-based methods provided a reduction and/or a confirmation of the lower and/or upper limit of the period since death obtained by the nomogram method

Case number	Estimation lower limit (hpm)	Method/criterion	Upper limit (hpm)	Method/criterion	Ascertainment lower limit (hpm)	Upper limit (hpm)	Comments
	3.5	Cooling by nomogram method	10.0	Mydriasis of iris to atropine			The man shot first the woman and then himself in the presence of witnesses: 'Contemporarily' proved.
	5.0	**Electr. excit. eye NO II**	**9.1**	**Cooling by nomogram method**	**7.3**	**7.6**	
48	3.0	Lividity maximum					+This finding would provide an extraordinarily small range of the period since death. As a precaution, the statement at the scene did not take this criterion into account.
	5.0	No electr. excit. eye					
	8.8	**Cooling**	**14.4**	**Cooling**	**11.0**	**14.0**	The upper limit of the time since death investigated later on (14.0 hpm) was identical to the lower limit of the estimated period since death based on this criterion.
	14.0+	No miosis of iris to acetylcholine					
52	1.4	Cooling by nomogram method	11.0	Electr. excit. orbic. oris m.			
	2.0	Rigor maximum	8.0	Electr. excit. eye IV			
	2.0	Electr. excit. eye NO V	8.0	Rigor re-establishment			
	3.0	**Lividity maximum**	**7.0**	**Cooling by nomogram method**	**3.6**	**4.8**	
57	5.0	No electr. excit. eye					
	5.0	No mydriasis of iris to Mydraticum Roche					
	11.6	Cooling by nomogram method	20.0	Lividity positive thumb pressure			
	14.0	**No miosis of iris to acetylcholine**	**17.2**	**Cooling by nomogram method**	**3.2**	**18.7**	
58	5.0	Electr. excit. eye NO II	24.0	Lividity incomplete shifting+			+The body found lying prone was transported lying back; the incomplete shifting of lividity was observed at autopsy.
			20.1	Cooling by nomogram method			
	13.7	**Cooling by nomogram method**	**20.0**	**Lividity positive thumb pressure**	**14.3**	**16.1**	

(Continued)

Table 10.6 (Continued) Examples of cases in which the non–temperature-based methods provided a reduction and/or a confirmation of the lower and/or upper limit of the period since death obtained by the nomogram method

Case number	Estimation lower limit (hpm)	Method/criterion	Upper limit (hpm)	Method/criterion	Ascertainment lower limit (hpm)	Upper limit (hpm)	Comments
59	1.8	Cooling by nomogram method					
	1.5	No idiomuscular contraction	8.0	Electr. excit. eye IV			
	2.0	Electr. excit. eye NO V	8.0	Rigor re-establishment			
	3.0	**No mydriasis of iris to atropine**	**7.4**	**Cooling by nomogram method**	**2.4**	**4.5**	
63			13.0	Idiomuscular contraction			
	3.0	Lividity maximum	11.2	Cooling by nomogram method			
			8.0	Rigor re-establishment			
	5.6	**Cooling by nomogram method**	**7.0**	**Electr. excit. eye V**	**6.7**	**7.1**	
67	3.0	No mydriasis of iris to atropine					
	3.0	No electr. excit. orbic. oris m.					
	3.5	Electr. excit. eye NO III	16.0	Electr. excit. eye II			
	4.9	Cooling by nomogram method					
	5.0	**No mydriasis of iris to Mydriaticum Roche**	**10.5**	**Cooling by nomogram method**	**9.3**	**10.3**	
68	2.0	Electr. excit. eye NO V	15.9	Lividity maximum			
	3.0	Lividity maximum					
	6.9	**Cooling by nomogram method**	**8.0**	**Electr. excit. eye IV**	**5.7**	**11.2**	
69			11.0	Electr. excit. orbic. oris m.			
			10.0	Mydriasis of iris to atropine			
	1.7	Cooling by nomogram method	7.3	Cooling by nomogram method			
	3.0	**Lividity maximum**	**6.0**	**Electr. excit. eye VI**	**3.1**	**3.4**	
71	5.0	No electr. excit. eye	23.4	Cooling by nomogram method			
	14.4	**Cooling by nomogram method**	**20.0**	**Lividity positive thumb pressure**	**17.2**	**17.7**	

(Continued)

Table 10.6 (Continued) Examples of cases in which the non–temperature-based methods provided a reduction and/or a confirmation of the lower and/or upper limit of the period since death obtained by the nomogram method

Case number	Estimation lower limit (hpm)	Method/criterion	Upper limit (hpm)	Method/criterion	Ascertainment lower limit (hpm)	Ascertainment upper limit (hpm)	Comments
72			9.5	Cooling by nomogram method			+Observed at the scene after turning the body from lying prone to lying back.
	2.0	Electr. excit. eye NO V	8.0	Electr. excit. eye IV			
			8.0	Rigor re-establishment			
	3.9	**Cooling by nomogram method**	**6.0+**	**Lividity complete shifting+**	5.1	5.4	
Cases where the nomogram method must not be used							
31	1.0	Lividity confluence	10.0	Mydriasis of iris to atropine			Because of the particular circumstances, the temperature-based nomogram method could not be used.
	3.0	**Electr. excit. eye NO IV**	**8.0**	**Rigor re-establishment**	4.8	5.3	
38	0.5	Rigor beginning	11.0	Electr. excit. orbic. oris m.			The temperature-based method was not used because of heat exposure by a room fire.
			10.0	Mydriasis of iris to atropine			
	1.0	**Electr. excit. eye NO VI**	**7.0**	**Electr. excit. eye V**	3.0	?	
45	1.0	Lividity confluence					The temperature method was not used because of the particular cooling conditions/
	2.0	Rigor maximum					
	3.0	No electr. excit. orbic. oris m.	10.0	Mydriasis of iris to atropine			
	5.0	**Electr. excit. eye NO II**	**8.0**	**Rigor re-establishment**	4.5	7.5	

+, positive; electr. excit., electrical excitability; orbic. oris m., orbicularis oris muscle.

Table 10.7   Number of instances where a criterion of a non–temperature-based method led to improvement or confirmation of the upper or lower limit of the period since death estimated from body cooling

Method/criterion	Improvement	Confirmation
Electrical excitability eye	33	18
Electrical excitability orbicularis oris muscle	6	5
Mydriasis of iris to atropine	9	3
Mydriasis of iris to tropicamide (Mydriaticum, Roche)	4	1
Miosis of iris to acetylcholine	1	2
Rigor beginning	5	4
Rigor maximum	3	0
Rigor re-establishment	6	7
Idiomuscular contraction	1	1
Lividity beginning	0	0
Lividity confluence	6	3
Lividity maximum	9	3
Lividity complete displacement by thumb pressure	3	0
Lividity complete shifting after turning over	5	5

■ Explaining maths in court – a thought experiment

Statements about probability, probability distribution and effects of certain changes in the setting can be difficult to explain to judges and juries. However, one should try to do so properly, thereby avoiding the (incorrect) impression that the expertise was just 'black magic with numbers' and something very theoretical applied to a very practical problem.

Even though the underlying maths may not be easily understood by the layperson, the problem as such may well be illustrated using analogies.

It has been shown to be helpful to illustrate the concept of normal distribution by using a (hypothetical) distribution of body height or intelligence quotient (IQ) while presenting the well-known bell-shaped curve. One may then proceed by applying this concept to real life problems, such as the design of car seats, the size of army uniforms to be held in stock and the problem of test design in high school education.

The next step would be to set a limitation to one of the systems just explained, for example, the IQ distribution in the general public. The author prefers the example of IQ distribution:

The IQ may be normally distributed with an expected value of 100 and 1 SD width of 10. Thus, 95.45 per cent (2 SD) of the population will fall into the IQ range of 80 through 120, with less than 2.5 per cent being 'more intelligent' or 'less intelligent'.

Consider Mr Smith (IQ 125), who challenges random people on the street for being smarter, the odds being clearly in favour of Mr Smith (Figure 10.9).

Consider Mr Smith moving his scheme to a MENSA meeting. MENSA is an organization of highly intelligent people, with an IQ of 120 being the minimum IQ for joining. Will Mr Smith have the same kind of success as on the streets?

Another good example is height distribution in the whole population, which will be reflected in a population of rollercoaster riders. In a random seating of a very long (never-ending if you will) rollercoaster, the height distribution should reflect the bell-shaped curve neatly. What will happen to this population when for technical reasons only people taller than 176 cm are allowed to take the ride?

Whatever example is chosen, the minimum (take home) message should include the following: (a) limitations or conditions will reflect on probability; and (b) once the conditions are taken out of the equation, everything goes back to its normal, unconditional state.

■ Assumptions and conditions in conditional probability distribution construction

Technically, from a strictly mathematical analytical point of view, every single death time interval estimated via

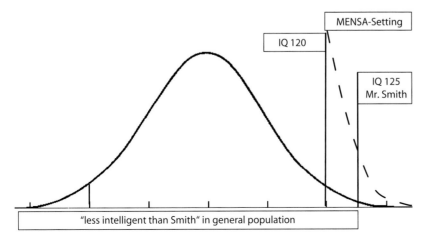

Figure 10.9 Example: 'Mr Smith'. In the general population, Mr Smith outsmarts most people. Under MENSA conditions (only IQ 120 and up), the area under the curve, representing probability, shows a very different picture.

the nomogram method is false because the unconditional interval by definition does not take into account that at time T0, when temperature was taken, the person was dead already. *Technically,* there is always a probability unequal to zero attributed to the time after rectal temperature for death time estimation was taken.

In most practical settings, this does not constitute any problem. In *ultra-early death time estimation,* however, when rectal temperature is taken shortly after death and cooling has just set in, passing the plateau, this may constitute a very practical problem, when a death time interval is calculated that overlaps in larger parts with the time after measurement and this larger part is then simply 'cut off' without further consideration of the probability.

Before constructing the CPD interval, a regular, unconditional nomogram interval is either calculated or derived graphically.

The conditions that are to be applied to it should be laid out separately first, so they may be discussed separately in court, especially if different versions may have to be constructed. It has proven useful to handle this part of the presentation very much like testimony considering blood alcohol levels (different amounts of consumed drinks, different sizes of glasses and so on), so all parties in the trial or investigation may state an opinion on one or the other assumption and may find agreement. A good example may be way-time calculations (a receipt is found stating that the victim purchased some product at time x, 5 miles from the crime scene – there may be different assumptions as to the earliest time of death depending on the mode of travel).

After both the unconditional nomogram method interval and the assumptions are laid out, the assumptions may then be applied to the unconditional death time interval to compile the CPD interval.

Compiling the conditional probability distribution interval

For compilation of the CPD interval, a computer spreadsheet is provided. The conditions in terms of upper and lower limits (e.g. 'found dead' and 'last seen alive') are entered. The probabilities of the areas cut off using those limitations are calculated. The remaining time interval where 'death is possible to have occurred' is then multiplied using the reciprocal value of the sum of cut-off probabilities to construct the conditional probability distribution, because after applying the limitations or conditions, the probability of the remaining interval (where 'death is at all possible to have occurred') must hold 100 per cent.

With the new distribution constructed, the spreadsheet will then find the smallest possible interval holding 95.45 per cent probability, doing so by finding the modus (peak) of the distribution and spreading to both sides until either a limitation is hit or the interval holds 95.45 per cent probability.

The results are produced as a new 95.45 per cent interval. Information on the unconditional interval in the light of limitations is also given. Most commonly, the unconditional interval will not hold 95.45 per cent probability when limitations are taken into account.

Case examples

'58-year-old man found dead at 08:02 on a forest path. Rectal temperature of 28.3°C in combination with 3°C ambient temperature and 65-kg body weight suggest a death time interval of 7.6 ± 2:8 hours before measurement (13:15 on 24 November 2009).

Re-establishment of rigor indicates a death time less than or equal to 8.0 hours; grade V reaction to electrical stimulation of facial muscles indicates a death time less than or equal to 7.0 hours. The upper boundary was cut off accordingly.

The death time interval was interpreted to be between 06:15 and 08:27. Confession of the perpetrator stated a time of death at 06:30.'

The unconditional construction of the nomogram method interval reveals a death time interval between 2:51 a.m. and 8:27 a.m. (5.6 hours width) with an attributed probability of 95.45 per cent.

When applying the CM method as usual, in this case introducing a maximum time since death of 7 hours before measurement as a result of findings in electrical stimulation, the resulting interval is 6:15 a.m. to 8:27 a.m. (2.2 hours width). However, this interval does not hold 95.45 per cent, but a mere 93.19 per cent.

The CPD interval, representing 95.45 per cent, stretches from 6:15 a.m. to 8:40 a.m. (2.43 hours' width).

The example, however, so far has not exploited all the information available. The information of finding the body dead at 8:02 a.m. (5.22 hours before measurement) must be introduced as well.

In the CM approach, theoretically at least, the introduction of data will transform into a death time interval between 6:15 a.m. (electrical stimulation) and 8:01 a.m. (finding of body 1 minute later). The interval width of 1.78 hours contains a probability of 100 per cent because death cannot have occurred any time outside of the interval.

When applying CPD, the known probability distribution is integrated into the calculation, and a smaller 95.45 per cent death time interval considering the known limitations is constructed, ranging from 6:15 a.m. to 7:51 a.m. (1.6 hours' width).

To highlight the benefits of CPD, we assume a variation of the previous case example:

'A group of young drug addicts has a party in the forest. One youngster leaves the group at 07:55 to urinate in the bushes. At 08:02 a police officer patrolling the forest path finds the youngster crouched over the dead body of an elderly gentleman. The wallet of the elderly man is found in the young man's possession. The young man claims that he did not harm the gentleman but rather found him already dead and took the money for drugs.'

Without CPD, the probability of intervals cannot be addressed properly in this case. Without implementation of the time of finding the body (08:02), the information is cluttered and possibly misleading, because one death time interval stated as 06:15 to 08:30 wrongly suggests the youngster's time of absence as being 'well inside the likely death time interval'.

However, we know that the body was found at 08:02, and we know it was dead for a maximum time of 7 hours before measurement.

A true 95.45 per cent interval from 06:15 to 07:51 shows that the youngster was less likely to be the killer, and the police should be informed that the case could be more complex than the first impression may have indicated.

It must be stated, of course, that interpretation of interval probability in respect to alibi should be handled with utmost care: had the youngster been the true killer and had he left the group at an earlier time (say, between 06:20 and 06:40), the probability of that time interval would have been rather 'small' as well. So probability of time intervals should not be confused with probability of guilt.

Using a dedicated Excel spreadsheet, it is easy to construct a variety of real or hypothetical cases. It also comes in handy when different versions are to be calculated such as way-time calculations assuming different modes of transport, different witness accounts about the last time the victim was seen alive and even variations of expert opinions. In addition, a quick calculation using the spreadsheet may be used to demonstrate certain information as practically irrelevant (e.g. that a runaway teen was last seen alive 3 weeks before finding the body).

It is often rewarding to look closely at case files and police statements in search of clues regarding 'possible time interval of death'. In one case, the author was able to calculate a CPD interval partly based on the following information:

Two children returned from school around 2 p.m. to find the door of the apartment (fourth floor) closed; their mother did not open it. The children assumed that their mother had gone out to buy groceries and would soon return, so they sat on the stairs by the door to wait for her. After they had waited for 4 hours, a neighbour offered to open the apartment door by using a credit card to let the children in. As they entered, they found the mother dead. She had been stabbed multiple times.

In constructing the CPD interval, 2 p.m. was used as latest possible death time because survival time in this particular case was neglectable, and no one had left the apartment after 2 p.m.

■ Results

There may be different results with varying degrees of change from unconditional to conditional probability distributions. In any case the conditional interval will show the correct 94.45 per cent interval considering the conditions or limitations applied.

1. No change in respect to practical usability

This is a usual result when the conditions or limitations introduced are rather weak, meaning that the time intervals cut-off did not hold much probability to begin with. This is easily understood from both a logical point of view and a mathematical point of view because, for example, in a body that has almost hit equilibrium with its environment, the information 'found exactly at 2 p.m. this afternoon' will not change the picture. Mathematically, a limitation at the far end 'tail portion' of the graph holds very little probability, so the reciprocal value to be multiplied with will be very close to 1, rendering the result to be changed only minimally. As a rule of thumb, conditions or limitations should fall into the unconditional 94.45 per cent interval on at least one side to yield practical results (Figure 10.10).

Otherwise the results, when calculated for actual time intervals, transfer to very small values, such as 1 minute or even just seconds, holding no practical value for investigations or use in court. However, when conditions are known, the CPD approach should be used in any case, if only to show that in fact the calculations do not yield significant results (Figure 10.10).

2. The conditional interval is smaller than the unconditional interval simply 'cut off'

This happens when the time interval determined to be 'impossible death time' by limitations is significant but does not exceed 50 per cent. In this case, simply cutting off the unconditional interval will result in an interval that holds more than 95.45 per cent probability; even 100 per cent is possible (imagine a wide 95.45 per cent interval that includes both the time of last seen alive and found dead). However, because 95.45 per cent is the standard in the nomogram method, one could either state the interval's probability in respect to conditions or calculate a new CPD 95.45 per cent interval that will be considerably smaller (Figure 10.11).

3. There is no change in interval width

In rare cases, there is no change in interval width when comparing the CPD interval with the unconditional interval that is simply cut off by limitations (Figure 10.12). This happens when the cutoff takes place exactly at the modus, the peak point of the distribution curve, and exactly 50 per cent is cut off. From a logical point of view, the proportions

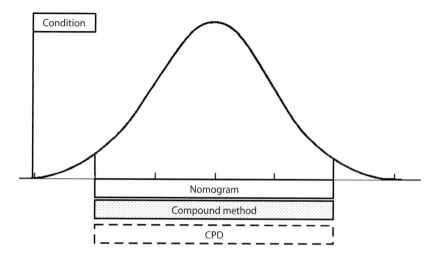

Figure 10.10 When limitations are introduced that lie far outside the 2-SD range, they do not cut off significant probability and therefore do not significantly alter probability distribution. The width of the interval derived by conditional probability distribution (CPD) does not reduce significantly.

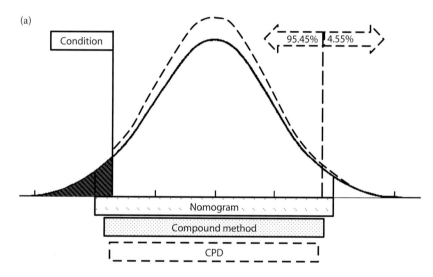

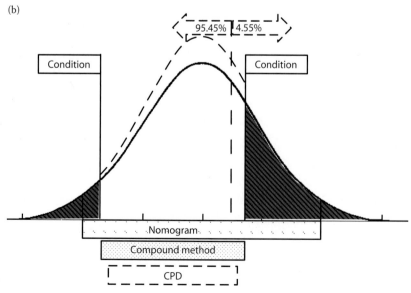

Figure 10.11 (a) When less than 50 per cent of probability is excluded using conditions (shaded area), the compound method interval will hold more than 95.45 per cent probability. Integrating the conditional probability distribution (CPD, dashed curve) will calculate interval width for 95.45 per cent probability and therefore further reduce interval width. (b) With restrictions to both sides of the probability distribution (shaded areas), each reaching inside the 2-SD range, the interval probability of the compound method interval reaches 100 per cent. Integrating the CPD (dashed curve) will calculate interval width for 95.45 per cent probability and therefore further reduce interval width.

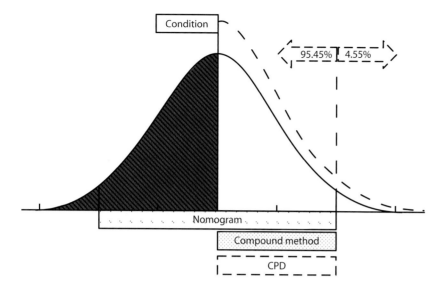

Figure 10.12 In the rare case of a condition excluding exactly 50 per cent of probability on one side of the modus, the compound method interval and conditional probability distribution (CPD) interval are equal in location and probability. Note, however, because the CPD (dotted line) is no longer symmetrical, probability will gradually diminish in growing distance to the modus.

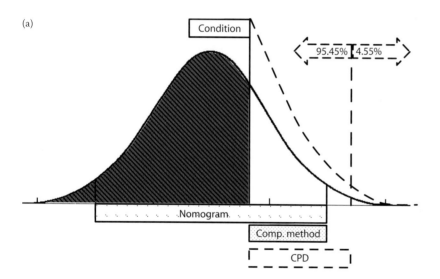

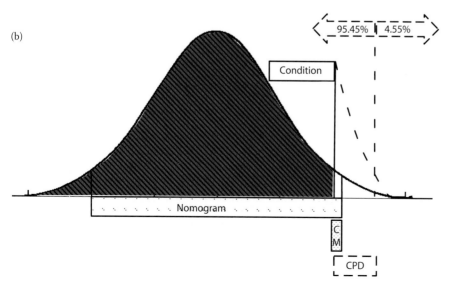

Figure 10.13 (a) When more than 50 per cent of probability is excluded by conditions, the resulting compound (comp.) method interval will hold less than 95.45 per cent probability. Therefore, when calculating the conditional probability distribution (CPD) interval holding 95.45 per cent probability, the CPD interval width must be larger compared with the compound method interval. (b) Under extreme conditions, when limiting conditions reach closely to the 2-SD boundary of the nomogram interval, the resulting compound method (CM) interval may be extremely narrow, holding extremely low probability at the same time. The CPD interval holding 95.45 per cent probability therefore is much wider than the compound method interval.

are not changed in this setting, when simply taking one half of the area inside and outside the interval away. It is, however, important to remember, and to show on the graph, that the conditional 95.45 per cent interval no longer resembles a bell shape or any peaked curve at all for that matter, but probability will fall (or rise) rapidly in respect to one border. For example, it may be reasonable to state that a person who was last seen alive leaving a party was killed more likely shortly after that point in time than later.

4. The conditional probability distribution interval is larger than the unconditional interval simply 'cut off'

This happens when the time interval determined to be 'impossible death time' by limitations does exceed 50 per cent (Figure 10.13). Those cases can change the picture in the most dramatic way up to the point where the area outside the unconditional interval, which was simply cut off, yields a higher probability of death having occurred than the area of a falsely stated 'death time interval'.

For demonstration and as a proof of concept, the CPD method was applied to a set of external data [2a]. Henssge *et al.* applied the CM to 72 crime scene cases in a field study. For 53 of these cases the CM data were given in detail, with 1 case tested twice over time (leading to a total of 54). The CPD method was applied to all 53 cases.

The CPD algorithm achieved a narrowing of the death time interval compared with the CM interval in 43 of 53 cases. The range of improvement was between −0.01 per cent and −15.21 per cent (between 0 per cent and 5 per cent in 9 cases, between 5 per cent and 10 per cent in 24 cases and more than 10 per cent in 10 cases). The 6 cases with no narrowing achieved by CM were all narrowed using CPD (between −1.75 per cent and −8.52 per cent). In 9 cases, the dismissal in CM was so large that the probability in the given CM interval was less than 95.45 per cent (between 47.38 per cent and 94.87 per cent). The true 95.45 per cent-interval for these cases calculated using CPD was therefore wider compared with the CM interval (between +2.71 per cent and +309.17 per cent). However, in those cases the resulting CPD intervals were all smaller than the original nomogram method interval (between −51.79 per cent and −71.43 per cent). In 9 cases, no information was provided about the time the person was found dead or was last seen alive, respectively. In retrospect, this information could have been obtained easily and could have led to further improvements when using CPD.

References

1. Beier G, Liebhardt E, Schuck M, Spann M. Measurement of rigor mortis on human skeletal muscles in situ [in German, with English summary]. *Z Rechtsmed* 1977;**79**:277–283.

2. Berg S. *Grundriss der Rechtsmedizin*. Munich, Germany, Müller und Steinicke, 1984.

2a. Biermann FM, Potente S. The deployment of conditional probability distributions for death time estimation. *Forensic Sci Int* 2011 Jul 15;210(1–3):82–6. doi: 10.1016/j.forsciint.2011.02.007. Epub 2011 Mar 5.

3. Forster B, Ropohl D, Raule P. A new formula for the measurement of rigor mortis: the determination of the FFR-Index [in German, with English summary]. *Z Rechtsmed* 1977;**80**:51–54.

4. Dotzauer G. Idiomuskulärer Wulst und postmortale Blutung. *Dtsch Z Gerichtl Med* 1958;**46**:761–771.

5. Henssge C. *Methoden zur Bestimmung der Todeszeit*. Berlin, Humboldt University, MD thesis, 1982.

6. Henssge CA. *Beitrag zur Standardisierung eines komplexen Verfahrens zur Todeszeitbestimmung am Leichenfundort: Interaktives Computerprogramm*. MD thesis. Essen, Germany, University of Essen, MD thesis, 1999. http://www.AMAsoft.de

7. Henssge C, Madea B. Determination of the time since death: body heat loss and classical signs of death – an integrated approach. *Acta Med Leg Soc* 1988;**I**:9.

8. Henssge C, Althaus L, Bolt J, Freislederer A, Haffner HT, Henssge CA, Hoppe B, Schneider V. Experiences with a compound method for estimating the time since death. I. Rectal temperature time of death nomogram. *Int J Legal Med* 2000;**113**:303–319.

9. Henssge C, Althaus L, Bolt J, Freislederer A, Haffner HT, Henssge CA, Hoppe B, Schneider V. Experiences with a compound method for estimating the time since death. II. Integration of non–temperature-based methods. *Int J Legal Med* 2000;**113**:320–331.

10. Hilgermann R. *Histochemische Untersuchungen zur Frage der Diffusions-Totenflecke*. Marburg, Germany, Marburg University, MD thesis, 1973.

11. Hofmann EV. Die forensisch wichtigsten Leichenerscheinungen. *Vierteljahresschr Gerichtl Med* 1876;**25**:229–261 and 1877;**26**:17–40.

12. Hunnius PV. *Das Verhalten der Totenflecken bei quantitativen Druckmessungen in Abhängigkeit vom Leichenalter*. Tübingen, Germany, Dissertation, 1973.

13. Hunnius PV, Mallach HJ, Mittmeyer HJ. Quantitative pressure measurements of livores mortis relative to the determination of the time of death [in German, with English summary]. *Z Rechtsmed* 1973;**73**:235–244.

14. Klein A, Klein S. *Die Todeszeitbestimmung am menschlichen Auge*. Dresden, Germany, Medical Akademy, MD thesis, 1978.

15. Madea B, Henssge C. *Estimation of the Time Since Death: Integration of Different Methods*. Digest of the International Meeting of P.A.A.F.S. and Police Medical Officers, Wichita, Kansas, August 10–14, 1987.

16. Madea B, Henssge C. Electrical excitability of skeletal muscle postmortem on casework. *Forensic Sci Int* 1990;**47**:207–227.

17. Mallach HJ. Zur Frage der Todeszeitbestimmung. *Berl Med* 1964;**18**:577–582.

18. Mallach HJ, Mittmeyer HJ. Rigor mortis and livores. [in German, with English summary]. *Z Rechtsmed* 1971;**69**:70–78.

19. Popwassilew J, Palm W. Über die Todeszeitbestimmung in den ersten 10 Stunden. *Z Arztl Fortbildung* 1960;**54**:73–77.

20. Prokop O. *Lehrbuch der gerichtlichen Medizin*. Berlin, VEB Verlag Volk und Gesundheit, 1960.

21. Prokop O. Supravitale Erscheinungen. In: Prokop O, Göhler W (eds.). *Forensische Medizin*. Berlin, Verlag Volk und Gesundheit, 1975, pp 1, 27.

22. Schuck M, Beier G, Liebhardt E, Spann W. On the estimation of lay-time by measurements of rigor mortis. *Forensic Sci Int* 1979;**14**:171–176.

23. Zsako S. Die Bestimmung der Todeszeit durch die muskelmechanischen Erscheinungen. *Munch Med Wochenschr* 1916;**3**:82.

11 Forensic Entomology

Saskia Reibe

In forensic entomology, which is the application of entomological science in medico-legal cases, arthropods, mainly insects, are treated as objective evidence in criminal investigations. Of main interest are insects that rely on decomposing tissue such as a dead body as feeding or breeding sites.

A dead body needs to be viewed as a system. It is influenced by numerous variables, such as ambient temperature or degree of exposure, which in turn influence insect colonization. These variables also interact with and influence each other.

After collecting the insects from a corpse, analyzing their developmental stage and calculating their age by using the respective ambient temperature profile, a forensic entomologist can give reliable information about a minimum postmortem interval (PMI). This is especially important in cases that are more than a few days old, where traditional medico-legal methods fail to give an accurate estimate [12].

A main question for forensic entomologists is estimating the PMI. The textbook scenario to answer this question involves an open space, summer temperatures, no rain and a person who falls dead on the spot during daylight. In this scenario blowflies would be attracted to the body within the first hour after death. These early visitors are looking for a convenient spot to deposit their egg patches. They will choose an area of the body that provides easy access to food for their offspring. This means the area should not be likely to dry out or be subject to predators. In general, the body's natural orifices are preferred choices for oviposition, and hatching larvae start feeding on the decomposing tissue. Eventually, bacteria will have broken down most of the tissue catalyzed by insect activity and temperature, thus resulting in a corpse that will be fully infested by feeding larvae (Figure 11.1).

■ Identification of insects

A reliable estimation of a PMI involving entomological evidence can be guaranteed only if the identification of the insect species collected in association with the corpse or the surroundings is accurate. A cheap and convenient method for reliable species identification is a morphological technique using appropriate identification keys. The only pieces of equipment necessary for morphological species determination are a dissecting microscope with a proper light source and a reliable identification key. Although insect identification is a skill every experienced forensic entomologist should have, it requires extensive practice. However, it may be impossible to identify

a specimen by means of its morphology (e.g. as a result of damage). In such cases, it may be preferential to use molecular identification tools. To ensure correct species identification, established molecular methods were transferred to the forensic field [4,23,24,28]. Analysis of mitochondrial DNA (mtDNA), and particularly of the cytochrome oxidase I gene (COI), appears to be a useful tool in species identification among the sub-families of Calliphoridae [10,11,29,31].

■ Blowfly development

The developmental stages of a blowfly (Figure 11.2) can indicate the PMI [5,16,30], as a function of temperature [20]. During their feeding stages, the blowfly larvae undergo two periods of moulting while their body size and weight increase constantly. Once a critical amount of food has been metabolized, the larvae leave the food source to enter the next developmental stage. This significant part of blowfly development is the pupal stage in which the larvae undergo metamorphosis and are re-programmed to become adult flies. The duration of this stage is, like the rest of the development, temperature dependent, but in general it takes up about half of the total development period. The larvae's growth rate depends on their body temperature, which is directly influenced by environmental conditions such as the ambient temperatures and the heat generated by maggot aggregations [22]. In addition, each species has its own temperature-dependent growth rate.

■ Influence of temperature

Insects are poikilothermic organisms. Their body temperature changes with ambient temperature. The metabolic rate of poikilotherm animals shows the same temperature dependency as the reaction kinetics in a biochemical system: the rate of a chemical reaction is increased twofold for each rise of 10°C in temperature (van't Hoff's reaction-rate-temperature rule). For insect development, a relationship between ambient temperature and duration of developmental processes has long been known. There is a temperature zone where the development rate is optimal; furthermore, temperature thresholds exist below or above that optimum where no development will take place. During the twentieth century, significant effort was made to describe larval growth correctly and to find a function best representing the temperature-dependent growth rate [15]. Several empirical and physiochemical formulations

Figure 11.1 Body infested with blowfly larvae.

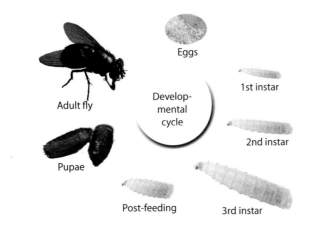

Eggs

1st instar

Develop-
mental
cycle

Adult fly

2nd instar

Pupae

Post-feeding

3rd instar

Figure 11.2 Overview of blowfly development.

of development were proposed, and two were discussed in particular by Sharpe and De Michele in 1977 [21] to present the reaction kinetics of poikilotherm development: the day-degree or temperature summation rule and the non-linear temperature inhibition model. The day-degree summation rule assumes that the rate of development (reciprocal of development curve) is proportional to temperature:

$$k = b(T - T0)$$

where k is the rate of development, b is a constant, T is the ambient temperature and T0 is a species-specific value, the so-called development zero, which is the x-intercept (i.e. an extrapolation of the linear approximation of the reciprocal of time for development).

■ Estimation of postmortem interval

The term 'postmortem interval' can be misleading when it is used in forensic entomology. The age of insect larvae feeding on a corpse can indicate a time frame of how long the corpse has been infested with insects. However, a person can already be infested while still alive. Examples include a neglected person who smokes and who has severe wounds of the leg [6] and, as reported from soldiers in the First World War, wounds that would have led to amputation if blowfly larvae had not fed on the necrotic tissue to clean the wounds [18]. In contrast, a person can be long dead and the larvae can still be only a few days old when the corpse was originally stored in a place with no access for the insects and was placed outside just a few days before the finding. Therefore, one must take into account every aspect before giving a statement about a PMI. In the latter case, if the insect evidence does not fit the decomposition stage of the corpse, the police can use that piece of information and can additionally use the information about how long the corpse has been exposed to insect activity. However, from the insect evidence alone, no reliable information can be given about the PMI in that case. Therefore, forensic entomologists refer to their estimations as minimum PMI (PMImin) (Figure 11.3).

One way to estimate a PMImin is to calculate the age of the most highly developed insect (e.g. blowfly) larvae that are feeding on the corpse and thereby giving a minimum time interval the person has been infested by insect larvae. This estimation is possible only if the calculation is done for larvae of the first colonization wave. If the life cycle of the first larvae has already been completed and the adult flies continued oviposition on the corpse, it is safe to calculate only the time of the first completed life cycle. The basis of larval age calculation is their temperature-dependent development. This implies accurate knowledge of the temperature at the time and place of larval development.

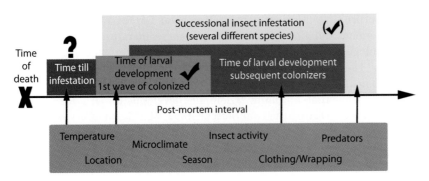

Figure 11.3 Schematic overview of the postmortem interval estimation process based on insect infestation. The estimation of time between death and the first insect infestation is highly challenging. The grey box contains a selection of factors that influence decomposition and insect activity simultaneously.

One method to approximate the ambient temperature is to record the temperature values at the desired place for a few days and compare them with data recorded at the nearest weather station. A regression analysis is applied to both data sets to obtain a formula that can be used to transform the data from the weather station covering the desired time frame into the temperature values that most likely influenced the developing larvae. In addition to temperature, the second requirement for calculating a PMImin based on larval age is the correct identification of the species, and the third requirement is the determination of the developmental progress of the collected larvae. Hence, determination of the stage (very rough estimation of age) or the length of the maggots is required, depending on the reference data set and the method that is to be used for the further calculation.

In forensic casework, two different methods are frequently used to calculate a PMImin. The correlation between larval developmental rate and temperature is well established, and all models include this factor (Figure 11.4 (a)).

The first method uses isomegalen or isomorphen diagrams, in which the lengths and the developmental stage of the larvae are combined as a function of time and mean ambient temperature in a single diagram [19]. According to its originators, this method is optimal only if the body and therefore the larvae were not undergoing fluctuating temperatures (e.g. in an enclosed environment where the temperature was nearly constant).

The second method of calculating a PMImin estimates the accumulated degree days (ADDs) or accumulated degree hours (ADHs). ADH values represent a certain number of 'energy hours' that are necessary for the development of insect larvae. The degree-day or degree-hour concept assumes that the developmental rate is proportional to the temperature within a certain species-specific temperature range [13]. However, the relationship of temperature and development rate (reciprocal of development time) is typically curvilinear at high and low temperatures and is linear only in between these extremes.

The formula for calculating ADH is as follows:

$$ADH = T \cdot (\theta - \theta_0),$$

where T is the development time, θ is the ambient temperature, and the minimum developmental threshold temperature, θ_0, is a species-specific value, the so-called development zero, which is the x-intercept (i.e. an extrapolation of the linear approximation of the reciprocal of time for development).

This value has no biological meaning; it is the mathematical consequence of using a linear regression analysis [13]. One basic condition for using the ADH method is that the ADH value for completing a developmental stage stays constant within certain temperature thresholds. For example, a developmental duration for finishing a certain stage of 14 days at 25°C results in 238 ADDs when a base temperature of 8°C is assumed. A developmental duration of 19 days at 21°C results in 231 ADDs; both ADD-values are in the same range.

In general, the ADH method seems to give good results only when the larvae of interest have been exposed to temperatures similar to those used in generating the reference value applied in the PMI calculation [2]. Moreover, the temperature range in which the development rate is actually linear is not wide enough to cover all temperatures during a typical summer in a temperate climate zone. Furthermore, neither developmental durations nor base temperatures for development have been calculated for most species in different geographical regions. The method must therefore be applied with caution. In addition, it is highly problematic that uncertainties for temperature measurements from a crime scene cannot be taken into account in either model. It is difficult to determine the actual temperature controlling the larvae at a real crime

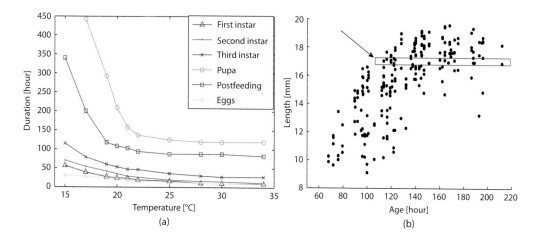

Figure 11.4 (a) Blowfly larval development as a function of temperature. (b) Scatterplot of blowfly larvae of different ages and sizes. The red box shows the distribution of larvae of the same length but different ages.

scene. Because temperature is the variable that most influences development, it is crucial to consider it as accurately as possible. The standard procedure is to use temperatures of the nearest weather station for the desired time frame and correct them by applying a regression starting from temperatures measured at the crime scene, when taking the larvae as evidence [3]. The corrected values still contain uncertainties that cannot be accounted for by the methods currently used for PMImin determination. No information exists for either model about the quality of the method or the error intervals of the calculated PMImin. In general, the greatest problem is the lack of data on the development of certain species, and especially data from different countries, because of the geographical variation in thermal requirements for insect development [14].

Calculation of PMImin also relies on determining the progress through the development cycle. Currently, this is achieved using morphological features. Figure 11.4 (b) shows the limitations of this approach: single data points illustrate the length of sampled larvae and their corresponding age. The box highlights larvae of 17 mm long and shows that the actual age of the larvae (which is used to estimate PMImin) has a very wide distribution from approximately 100 hours old to more than 200 hours old. Therefore, there is an obvious need to develop a more sophisticated and sensitive method to model developmental progress, to improve estimation of PMImin. Early efforts to integrate developmental gene expression patterns seem promising, but they have not been tested to ensure precise and applicable results in a judicial setting [7,25,26].

Another way to calculate PMImin is to use more sophisticated mathematical models that actually base their calculations on the non-linear development of blowfly larvae. Although the general consensus is that these models are not necessarily better than the previously described methods, their use should not be dismissed immediately. In 2010, a method was developed that models blowfly development based on exponential functions describing the growth curves [19]. A computer program was written that is able to use an individual temperature profile, calculate larval development for each temperature value at any desired time step and add them up to a total development time. The foremost advantage over the established methods is the additional information about the accuracy of the calculation. In addition, it is impossible to include uncertainties about the parameter in the calculation, which will influence the calculation and cannot be neglected. However, there is still a need to improve this new model and validate its use. Results of the method are shown in the case report section (first case report of suicide).

Succession

The composition of insect species present on a corpse at any given time point can be an indicator of the time frame the corpse has already been infested. Different decomposition stages of carcass attract different insect species, which also attract a range of predators. The species infesting a corpse can be manifold, and several factors influence their behaviour. Not only does the decomposition stage have an impact, but also season, temperature, microclimate, location of the body and so on can influence the succession pattern. This makes it difficult to estimate a time frame because it is impossible to conclude that species x arrives at a corpse only after time y. However, an experienced forensic entomologist who performed various field experiments observing pig carcasses at different locations, temperatures and seasons and who sampled insects from many real cases can draw conclusions from succession data if the ambient parameters are known. It is important to understand that it is impossible to use reference data published on succession experiments from regions, countries, microclimates and so on that differ from the finding situation of the case scenario in question because these data are not representative or applicable.

Sampling of insects from bodies

Here are eight simple rules to collect insect evidence:

1. Use a container that can be tightly closed so that no liquid will leak out of it.
2. Use a sheet of paper and a pencil, rip off some paper, label it with date, name and case number and put the labeled piece of paper inside the container (*really* use a *pencil* – ink from pens will be washed off by alcohol).
3. Sample the insects from the body and place them in the container (not more than half full); use forceps, a spoon or hands (the evidence is not likely to become contaminated or destroyed) (Figure 11.5).

Figure 11.5 Sampling of insect larvae in a glass container by using just the hands.

4. Optional: Pour hot, nearly boiling water in the container filled with the entomological evidence and discard the water after 1 to 2 minutes, keeping the evidence inside the container.
5. *Mandatory*: Fill the container with 70 to 80 per cent ethanol or similar alcohol.
6. Close the container.
7. Repeat using more containers if you want to sample more specimens.
8. Sample as diversely as possible (regarding different specimens and locations on the body).

■ Case reports

All cases described here were examined by autopsy in the Institute of Forensic Medicine, Bonn, Germany, and the insects were sampled and analyzed by the author.

Suicide

In July 2009, a young man was found hanging from a tree in a small forest near an urban area (Figure 11.6). The man could be identified without doubt, and his mother had reported him missing 3 days earlier, after she had found a suicide note in his bedroom. The body was transported to the Institute of Forensic Medicine nearby and was cooled at 4°C until autopsy. At time of the autopsy, it had been 147 hours since the mother last saw her son alive. During autopsy, larvae were sampled from the body and were

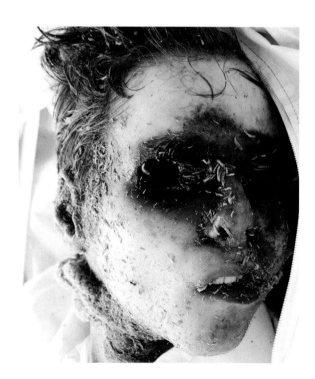

Figure 11.6   Blowfly larvae feeding in the facial region of the body; the eyes are already eaten away.

immediately killed in nearly boiling water. After discarding the water, the larvae were stored in 80°C ethanol. Species identification revealed that the larvae were *Calliphora vicina,* a typical first-wave colonizer in Germany. The largest larvae sampled measured 12.5 mm and were in early third instar stage. The PMImin was calculated using the ADH method and also using the new computer-simulated method mentioned previously. The acquired temperature data (hourly records) from a nearby weather station were used without revising them. ADH calculation resulted in a PMImin of 139 hours, meaning that the hanging took place in the afternoon of the day the young man went missing. The computer-simulated model resulted in a larval age of 145 hours, which shifted the time of the death to the morning, shortly after his mother had last seen her son. The standard deviation of the calculation was ± 3 hours. This example shows first that the calculation based on entomological evidence can be very precise and second that a more complicated, computer-based model can be a reasonable alternative to the linear model.

Skeleton in forest

At the end of July 2009, a nearly skeletonized body was found on a steep, bushy embankment under a highway bridge. The bones were partly held together by dried connective tissue. The skull was found separately, after it had rolled down the embankment and into a parking lot. The bones were nearly free of insect infestation, but below the dried scalp a few larvae of an unknown beetle species were collected, and at the connective tissue larvae of the fly species *Piophila casei* were sampled. The police wanted to clarify whether the body had most likely been lying on the embankment since earlier the same year or since the year before, to check the records of missing persons. During autopsy, it was established that the body was female and most likely of an older age.

Because the temperatures in this part of Germany did not rise to values that promote insect activity before the beginning of April 2009, it could be assumed that blowfly larvae would have fed on the body since then at the earliest, imagining a scenario where the body had been exposed in the same year. That would imply that the larvae had eaten away most of the body tissue and left the connective tissue to dry, all within 3 to 4 months. Moreover, the body must have been naked, and the number of maggots must have been immense. By implication, this would lead to very wet and 'marked' soil, as well as a massive amount of pupal cases at the finding site. However, after visiting the site and investigating the area and the corresponding soil, no such evidence could be found. The soil was dry and loose, and no pupal cases or tissue residuals could be detected. In Figure 11.7, a side-by-side comparison of the found skeleton (left) and the image of an 80-kg pig exposed in the open during summertime for 2 months is shown. It becomes apparent that the probability of an exposure

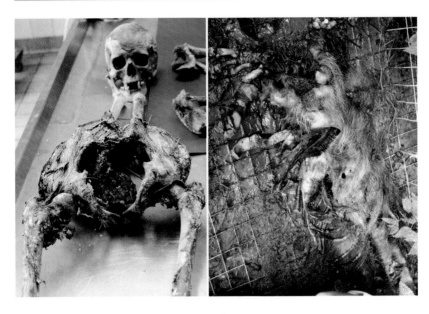

Figure 11.7 Left: Skeletonized body exposed for 10 months. Right: An 80-kg pig exposed for 2 months during summertime.

time of the body in question is not very high for a period of about 3 to 4 months.

In conclusion, the entomological report stated that there is a high probability that the corpse was exposed at least during the summer of the previous year or even earlier than that.

After a few months the police could identify the body. The investigation revealed that the person had suffered from dementia and had run away, naked, from her nursing facility in summer 2008 and was reported missing. In this case report it becomes obvious that even the absence of insect involvement can be objective evidence for a forensic entomologist.

Dismembered body

In September 2008, dog walkers found pieces of a dismembered body in a grove near the suburbs (Figure 11.8). The body parts were brought in plastic bags to the Institute of Forensic Medicine and inspected. Blowfly larvae were already crawling out of the bags. In the first bag was half a torso, two pieces of the lower legs und various small body pieces. All pieces were heavily infested with feeding blowfly larvae. One day later the police found the left arm and the head after they searched the surrounding area. At this time the identity of the corpse was unknown; it was apparent only that it was a middle-aged woman. The police ordered an estimation of the PMImin based on entomological evidence to limit the time interval for records of missing persons. For the estimation, larvae were used that were sampled on the first day the body pieces were brought to the Institute. The species was identified as *Calliphora vicina.* The finding place was investigated, and a data logger was put out to record the temperature hourly over a period of 24 hours to compare these records with the data recorded by the Institute of Metrology of the University of Bonn. The

temperature values used for the PMImin estimation were adjusted accordingly. The PMImin estimation resulted in a time period of 5 days (start of the insect infestation on the Saturday morning before finding the first body parts). The estimation implied oviposition in the early hours of Saturday morning. Because blowflies usually do not oviposit at night, it could not be determined exactly whether the eggs were deposited Saturday morning or Friday very late in the evening. The entomological report stated that the sheer number of wounds and the amount of blood after the dismembering would have been very strong triggers for the blowflies to deposit their eggs. Because the location of the actual dismembering was unknown at the time, it could not be investigated whether the blowflies had started oviposition at the crime scene or after the placement of the body outside at the finding place.

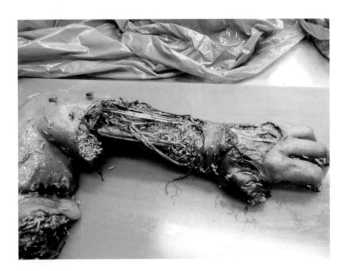

Figure 11.8 One of many body parts found in a forest after dismemberment.

Shortly afterwards the police could identify the victim and investigated her house. It became apparent that the killing and the dismembering took place in the house of the victim because a large amount of blood and more body parts were found inside and outside of the house. The partner of the victim was on the run and became a suspect immediately. Eventually, he was captured in the Netherlands and confessed to the crime. He stated that on Friday evening he and his partner started fighting and he stabbed her to death. Afterwards, to cover up his crime, he wanted to bury the body in the garden, but the pit he dug was too small, so he dismembered the body and took several body pieces outside the property, where they were finally found.

Winter suicide indoors

In January 2009, a woman was found dead in her apartment. She was found on a mattress on the floor and was dressed in thin capri pants, a T-shirt and woollen socks. Most of her body was mummified, and her face was partly skeletonized (Figure 11.9). The police investigated the case and determined that she had not been seen for 40 days.

The body was brought to the Institute for Forensic Medicine, and an autopsy was performed during which insect samples were collected. Empty pupal cases of *Lucilia sericata* sticking to the socks were sampled. A live specimen of *Necrobia rufipes* was crawling out of the clothes. Additionally, empty pupal cases and dead adult species of *Megaselia scalaris* were collected. After the abdominal cavity was opened, thousands of larvae and pupae of *M. scalaris* were revealed.

The police report stated that the temperature in the room where the body was found was 21°C. It was assumed that the temperature remained almost constant because the windows were closed and the shutters were down. For *Lucilis sericata* the minimum developmental time at 21°C is 16 days [9]. It is unclear how soon the flies could enter the room and infest the body [17]. Presumably they were active on the corpse shortly after death because the body dried out later, which is not an attractive state for blowfly larvae. *Megaselia scalaris* completes development at a 12:12 photoperiod after about 37 days [27]. Because the period that the dead woman had been missing was about 40 days, PMImin estimation based on developmental data of *M. scalaris* was much more

accurate than calculating the developmental time of *L. sericata*. It is also known that *M. scalaris* can reach corpses in closed room scenarios and even inside tightly knotted plastic bags very quickly because the specimens are very small and can usually infest a body only if they do not have to compete against the much larger blowflies [18].

Winter suicide outdoors

In December 2007, the body of a man was found on the waterfront of a lake in the outskirts of a rural area near Bonn, Germany. He had been reported missing about a month before the finding and was reported to have left a mental health institution without being dismissed. His body was clothed and partly hidden under bushes. In the autopsy report it was stated that no typical signs of decomposition were present, and livor mortis could be observed only sparsely (Figure 11.10, left). The cause of death was bleeding to death after cutting the throat. Furthermore, it was concluded to be a suicide. During the investigation of the oral cavity, several blowfly larvae of different sizes were revealed (Figure 11.10, right). During autopsy, living larvae were collected and placed on a feeding substrate to rear them at constant 25°C until adult flies would emerge. This was done for two reasons; first, it is easier to identify the species based on the adult fly; and second, it would reveal the remaining developmental time until pupation and thus make a larval age calculation more reliable. The species was identified as *Calliphora vomitoria*. Ames and Turner [1] published an ADH value of 5638 from egg to pupation for this species. Analyzing the daily temperature measurements of the nearest weather station and calculating a daily mean temperature accounted for the temperatures that influenced larval development during the time the body lay at the lake. For this calculation it was essential to take into consideration that on several days the daily mean temperature fell under the lower developmental threshold. Calculating the ADHs using the mean ambient temperature and excluding days with temperatures below the developmental threshold revealed as a starting point of larval development a time frame of 1 or 2 days after the man went missing. Usually, insects of central Europe are not overly active in November and December because the temperatures are very low. However, on the days the man went missing,

Figure 11.9 State of a body found indoors after 40 days.

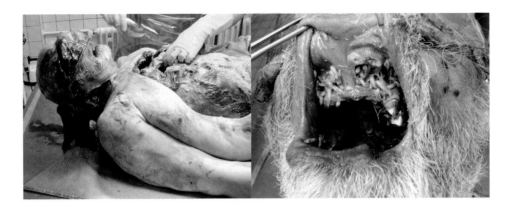

Figure 11.10 State of a body found outdoors after a missing period of about a month during wintertime.

it was unusually warm, which may have provoked certain insect activity. The results of the autopsy concluded a much shorter PMI that could have led to the question what happened between the days the man went missing and death occurred. However, the results of the entomological analysis supported the much more likely scenario that he had left the mental institution and killed himself shortly afterwards.

References

1. Ames C, Turner B. Low temperature episodes in development of blowflies: implications for postmortem interval estimation. *Med Vet Entomol* 2003;**17**:178–186.

2. Anderson GS. Minimum and maximum development rates of some forensically important Calliphoridae (Diptera). *J Forensic Sci* 2000;**45**:824–832.

3. Archer MS. Rainfall and temperature effects on the decomposition rate of exposed neonatal remains. *Sci Justice* 2004;**44**:35–41.

4. Benecke M. Random amplified polymorphic DNA (RAPD) typing of necrophageous insects (Diptera, Coleoptera) in criminal forensic studies: validation and use in practice. *Forensic Sci Int* 1998;**98**:157–168.

5. Benecke M. Six forensic entomology cases: description and commentary. *J Forensic Sci* 1998;**43**:797–805, 1303.

6. Benecke M, Josephi E, Zweihoff R. Neglect of the elderly: forensic entomology cases and considerations. *Forensic Sci Int* 2004;**146**(Suppl):S195–S199.

7. Boehme P, Spahn P, Amendt J, Zehner R. Differential gene expression during metamorphosis: a promising approach for age estimation of forensically important *Calliphora vicina pupae* (Diptera: Calliphoridae). *Int J Legal Med* 2013;**127**:243–249.

8. Büchner F. *Pläne und Fügungen: Lebenserinnerungen eines deutschen Hochschullehrers.* München/Berlin, Urban und Schwarzenberg, 1965.

9. Grassberger M, Reiter C. Effect of temperature on *Lucilia sericata* (Diptera: Calliphoridae) development with special reference to the isomegalen- and isomorphen-diagram. *Forensic Sci Int* 2001;**120**:32–36.

10. Harvey ML, Gaudieri S, Villet MH, Dadour IR. A global study of forensically significant calliphorids: implications for identification. *Forensic Sci Int* 2008;**177**:66–76.

11. Harvey ML, Mansell MW, Villet MH, Dadour IR. Molecular identification of some forensically important blowflies of southern Africa and Australia. *Med Vet Entomol* 2003;**17**:363–369.

12. Henssge C, Madea B. Estimation of the time since death in the early post-mortem period. *Forensic Sci Int* 2004;**144**:167–175.

13. Higley LG, Haskell NH. *Insect Development and Forensic Entomology in Forensic Entomology: The Utility of Arthropods in Legal Investigations.* Boca Raton, Florida, CRC Press, 2009, pp 389–405.

14. Honek A. Geographical variation in thermal requirements for insect development. *Eur J Entomol* 1996;**93**:303–312.

15. Janisch E. Die Leben- und Entwicklungsdauer der Insekten als Temperaturfunktion. *Z Wissenschaft Zool* 1928;**132**:176–186.

16. Keh B. Scope and applications of forensic entomology. *Annu Rev Entomol* 1985;**30**:137–154.

17. Reibe S, Madea B. How promptly do blowflies colonise fresh carcasses? A study comparing indoor with outdoor locations. *Forensic Sci Int* 2010;**195**:52–57.

18. Reibe S, Madea B. Use of *Megaselia scalaris* (Diptera: Phoridae) for post-mortem interval estimation indoors. *Parasitol Res* 2010;**106**:637–640.

19. Reibe S,, Doetinchem PV, Madea B. A new simulation-based model for calculating post-mortem intervals using developmental data for *Lucilia sericata* (Dipt.: Calliphoridae). *Parasitol Res* 2010;**107**:9–16.

20. Sharpe P, Hu L. Reaction kinetics of nutrition dependent poikilotherm development. *J Theor Biol* 1980;**82**:317–333.

21. Sharpe P, DeMichele D. Reaction kinetics of poikilotherm development. *J Theor Biol* 1977;**64**:649–670.

22. Slone D, Gruner S. Thermoregulation in larval aggregations of carrion-feeding blow flies (Diptera: Calliphoridae). *J Med Entomol* 2007;**44**(3):516–523.

23. Sperling FA, Anderson GS, Hickey DA. Partial sequencing of the cytochrome oxydase b subunit gene I: a tool for the identification of European species of blow flies for postmortem interval estimation. *J Forensic Sci* 1994;**39**:418–427.

24. Stevens J, Wall R. Species, sub-species and hybrid populations of the blowflies *Lucilia cuprina* and *Lucilia sericata* (Diptera: Calliphoridae). *Proc Biol Sci* 1996;**263**:1335–1341.

25. Tarone AM, Foran DR. Gene expression during blow fly development: improving the precision of age estimates in forensic entomology. *J Forensic Sci* 2011;**56**(Suppl 1):S112–S122.

26. Tarone AM, Jennings KC, Foran DR. Aging blow fly eggs using gene expression: a feasibility study. *J Forensic Sci* 2007;**52**:1350–1354.

27. Trumble J, Pienkowski R. Development and survival of *Megaselia scalaris* (Diptera: Phoridae) at selected temperatures and photoperiods. *Proc Entomol Soc Wash* 1979;**81**(2):207–210.

28. Wallman J, Adams M. Molecular systematics of Australian carrion-breeding blowflies of the genus *Calliphora* (Diptera: Calliphoridae). *Austr J Zool* 1997;**45**:337–356.

29. Wallman JF, Leys R, Hagendoorn K. Molecular systematics of Australian carrion-breeding blowflies (Diptera: Calliphoridae) based on mitochondrial DNA. *Invertebrate Systematics* 2005; **19**:1–15.

30. Wells JD, Lamotte LR. *Estimating the Postmortem Interval in Forensic Entomology: The Utility of Arthropods in Legal Investigations.* Boca Raton, Florida, CRC Press, 2009, pp 367–388.

31. Wells JD, Wall R, Stevens JR. Phylogenetic analysis of forensically important *Lucilia* flies based on cytochrome oxidase I sequence: a cautionary tale for forensic species determination. *Int J Legal Med Sci Law* 2007;**121**:229–233.

12 Radiocarbon Dating
Basic Principles and Applications

Wilfried Rosendahl and Doris Döppes

Scientific analysis of human remains, be they skeletal remains or mummified bodies or body parts, has major substantive importance for various disciplines, including not only archaeology but also anthropology, paleontology and forensic medicine. In addition to specific data on such finds (e.g. gender, size and age at death), postmortem interval (PMI) and geological age are also primary objects of enquiry. Whereas specific data can frequently be collected from morphological features on different bone elements (everything depending on the completeness and state of preservation), pure bone analysis cannot determine PMIs reliably. Whenever they are extant and typical for a specific period, accompanying finds such as grave goods, clothing remains or everyday objects facilitate relative dating. Depending on the age and preservation of a find, as well as the type and quality of accompanying finds, relative dates contain uncertainties of differing magnitude or imprecise time frames. This unsatisfactory situation for many of the aforementioned disciplines' scientific enquiries did not change fundamentally until the development of radiometric and chemical or physical dating methods based on natural decay chains. The method best suited for numerical or absolute dating of human skeletal remains and mummies from 50 000 years ago to the present is so-called radiocarbon or carbon-14 (^{14}C) dating. This technique was developed and applied by Willard Frank Libby from the University of Chicago at the end of the 1940s [1,14]. Libby was awarded the Nobel Prize in chemistry in 1960 for his work. The method has seen numerous improvements in measuring systems over the years. The development of the accelerator mass spectrometer (AMS) at the University of Oxford in 1977 was a particularly important advance. This equipment made it possible not only to minimize the quantity of samples required significantly but also to increase measurement speed and accuracy considerably (see Figure 12.1). Work is still being done at present to improve these parameters.

■ Basic principles

The element carbon (C) is one of the biosphere's most important chemical constituents. Organic carbon compounds are the basis for all life. Three carbon isotopes occur naturally, the stable isotopes ^{12}C (98.89 per cent) and ^{13}C (1.11 per cent) and the unstable or radioactive isotope ^{14}C (10^{-10} per cent). Radiocarbon (^{14}C) is continually produced in the upper layers of the atmosphere by the interaction of neutrons from cosmic rays with nitrogen (N) atoms. During the nuclear reaction ^{14}N(n,p)^{14}C, ^{14}N captures one neutron and releases one proton in return, thus transforming ^{14}N into radiocarbon (Figure 12.2). The average global rate of ^{14}C production is approximately 6 to 13.5 kg/year. Beta (β^-) decay causes unstable ^{14}C with a half-life of 5730 ± 40 years to decay into ^{14}N, one electron and one antineutrino. Chemically, ^{14}C acts like the other carbon isotopes and bonds with oxygen to form carbon dioxide. ^{14}C enters the biosphere through plant photosynthesis and, subsequently, the animal food chain. This is also called the carbon cycle. The ^{14}C fraction in carbon remains in equilibrium as long as a living organism is an active part of this cycle. This changes when an organism dies. No more new ^{14}C is introduced, and the initial quantity starts decaying radioactively. Its physical half-life is 5730 ± 40 years (i.e. only half of the initial ^{14}C content exists after this period and, in turn, only half of that after another 5730 ± 40 years). The maximum age limit currently determinable by AMS is approximately 50 000 years.

According to Libby's model, the ^{14}C age can be calculated with the following equation:

$$t = 8033 \cdot \ln \left({}^{14}C_0 / {}^{14}C \right)$$

where t is age, ln is natural logarithm and ^{14}C$_0$ is ^{14}C modern standard.

In 1958, De Vries demonstrated that the ^{14}C/^{12}C ratio fluctuates naturally over time. Thus, the model assumption of a spatiotemporally constant initial value of ^{14}C is not met [7]. This means that calculated ^{14}C ages are far younger than the corresponding solar or calendar years. They can deviate by significantly more than 1000 years in certain eras. There are three main causes of natural fluctuations of the atmospheric ^{14}C/^{12}C ratio. Whereas changes in the Earth's magnetic field are chiefly responsible for long-term changes [17], short-term fluctuations are governed by solar activity (the so-called De Vries effect). The exchange of carbon from various geosphere and biosphere reservoirs with the atmosphere can also cause fluctuations.

Because ^{14}C mixes in the atmosphere very rapidly, ^{14}C fluctuations become noticeable at the same time all over the world, thus eliminating the problem of varying local concentrations.

Figure 12.1 One of the most modern pieces of equipment for carbon-14 dating, the accelerator mass spectrometer of the MICADAS type at the Klaus-Tschira-Laboratory for Radiometric Dating Methods in the Curt-Engelhorn-Centre Archaeometry in Mannheim, Germany. (Photograph courtesy of W. Rosendahl, Mannheim, Germany.)

In addition to natural fluctuations, there are also anthropogenically caused changes. Named after Hans E. Suess, the 'Suess-effect' describes the impact of industrialization and the use of fossil fuels on the ^{14}C content in the atmosphere since the mid-nineteenth century [23]. Given that fossil fuels no longer contain any detectable ^{14}C because of their old age, only ^{12}C and ^{13}C are released when they are burned. This dilution causes an artificial reduction of the ^{14}C content in the atmosphere (2 to 3 pMC [per cent modern carbon]). This can give the appearance of an unduly old age and therefore must be factored in when determining age.

The 'atom bomb effect' describes another important anthropogenic influence, namely, and as the name implies, the impact on or substantial increase of atmospheric ^{14}C content from above-ground nuclear tests between 1950 and 1963. The ^{14}C content is still elevated 20 per cent today [26]. Because the values of the changes in the artificial ^{14}C content are known to the exact year, even samples after 1950 or the recent past can be radiocarbon dated very well using so-called 'bomb peak dating' (Figure 12.3). The ^{14}C content of hair, skin or tendons can be used to determine time of death accurately to approximately 2 years [11]. The values obtained are compared with those of the bomb curve. Hair is better suited because, unlike bone, it grows continuously, and thus its ^{14}C content corresponds well with the biosphere at the time of death and allows relatively precise dating. This is especially important for the application of radiocarbon dating in forensic sciences.

Under certain conditions, spatial changes of the ^{14}C ratio can also occur, which must be allowed for and corrected when taking a measurement. Isotopic fractionation deserves mention. In other words, the three carbon isotopes with different masses can move differently or be released slightly during processes in the carbon cycle (e.g. during photosynthesis in different plant groups). Furthermore, there is the reservoir effect. This effect can be observed, for instance, in milieus where the ^{14}C had a higher average half-life (e.g. in deep ocean water) [2]. Allowance must also be made for possible contamination of samples by substances with a different ^{14}C age. For instance, many Pleistocene bone finds were still prepared with bone glue at the beginning of the twentieth century. Various purification processes (e.g. Soxhlet extraction) during sample pretreatment can help minimize contamination problems.

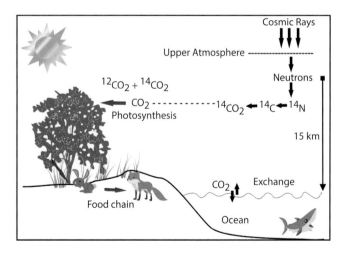

Figure 12.2 Radiocarbon cycle in the atmosphere and biosphere. (Graphic by W. Rosendahl, Mannheim, Germany.)

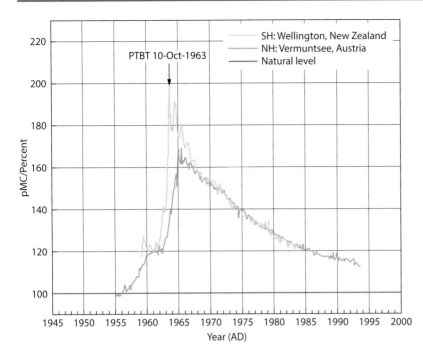

Figure 12.3 Bomb peak calibration curve. The New Zealand curve (red) is representative of the Southern Hemisphere; the Austrian curve (green) is representative of the Northern Hemisphere (data set from the Carbon Dioxide Information Analysis Center, Oak Ridge National Laboratory, Oak Ridge, Tennessee). The date of the Partial Test Ban Treaty (PTBT) is marked on the graph. (Graphic public domain, Wikipedia.) pMC, percent of modern carbon.

■ Calibration

In keeping with international consensus, the readings obtained by radiocarbon dating are denoted as the conventional ^{14}C or AMS ^{14}C age, with 1950 as the zero reference point. The measured date is specified as a numerical value with a standard deviation (± value) and followed by the symbol BP. BP stands for 'before present', meaning the reference year 1950. Thus, a ^{14}C AMS age of 2250 BP indicates that a sample has an age of 2250 ^{14}C years before 1950. Because these ^{14}C dates are known to be systematically 3 per cent too low and the temporally variable dates are also not factored into the initial ^{14}C ratio, the dates have to be calibrated or corrected and converted into calendar years. Dendrochronology (i.e. dating using certain tree species' growth rings) and varve chronology (i.e. dating using seasonally laminated marine sediment) are primarily employed for this purpose [9]. Uranium-thorium-dated speleothems from China and the Bahamas, dated coral reefs, oxygen isotope analysis of benthic Foraminifera, tephra from known volcanic eruptions and laminated Greenland ice cores have also been referenced since 2009 [18]. In principle, dates can now be calibrated to the dating limit of 50 000 years. Calibrated raw dates are indicated by calBP. Free programs that ascertain calendric dates are available or can be requested from various AMS laboratories online (e.g. http://www.calpal-online.de).

Calibrated ages are usually indicated by 1 sigma, corresponding to a confidence probability of 68.3 per cent. It rises to 95.5 per cent for 2 sigma. In such a case, measurements were taken over a longer period because enough material was available from the same sample, thus reducing the statistical error.

■ Sample material and sample pretreatment

Radiocarbon dating is used in many disciplines because it is suitable for a wide variety of materials: all organic materials such as wood, charcoal, plant remains, peat, bone, teeth, ivory, antler, hair, leather and textiles, as well as inorganic materials, including shells, corals, Foraminifera, calcareous sinter, inorganic carbon and carbon dioxide dissolved in groundwater extracted from continental and glacier ice [10].

Because contamination can occur during soil sedimentation, datable carbonaceous samples are freed from coarse impurities, and foreign carbon that can distort age is removed. Acid and alkali pretreatment separates carbonates from humins. Organic conservation substances can also distort age and are removed by the aforementioned Soxhlet extraction and ultrafiltration. Collagen, a water-insoluble structural protein, is extracted from bone. Bone was long considered to be unsuitable for ^{14}C dating because it is very porous and thus prone to exchange reactions with the groundwater. Collagen is hardly prone to exchanges. In the final step, organic samples are converted into carbon dioxide and subsequently converted into a solid graphite form.

Samples more in the milligram range are needed for measurement in an AMS. The atoms themselves are counted, not decay events as in Geiger or liquid scintillation counting. Thus, very small samples can be analysed. The graphite sample obtained is bombarded with cesium ions to obtain carbon ions. The ions of the ^{14}C isotope are separated in the accelerator according to their different masses. Age can be determined from the ratio of ^{14}C to ^{12}C. ^{13}C serves as the control for the separation processes. The values for the initial quantities, factoring in losses during sample pretreatment, are summarized in Table 12.1.

Table 12.1 Approximate amounts of sample used for the accelerator mass spectrometer technique

Material	Amount (mg)
Wood	100
Charcoal	100
Hair	20–50
Peat	50–100
Leather/skin	50–100
Textile	20–50
Plant remains	>10
Pollen	200
Bone	200–2000
Carbonate	>10

■ Radiocarbon dating in forensics: closing remarks

As explained earlier, radiocarbon dating basically provides a means for so-called 'bomb peak dating' to determine the PMI after 1950 [6,16,24,25,27]. Depending on the type of sample, however, the value of the dates is highly dependent on various parameters. Allowance must be made for uncertainties, especially when the PMIs are short. Methodologically, problems are caused by humans' individual metabolisms and the resultant different rapid assimilation and exchange of ^{14}C in various parts of the body such as hair, skin, internal organs or bones. Hair, blood and nails are best suited for radiocarbon dating because their faster and continuous metabolism causes them to assimilate and exchange ^{14}C faster, too. By comparison, bones and collagen metabolize so much more slowly that ^{14}C is exchanged only every 10 to 30 years on average [5]. This means that the ^{14}C age of bone collagen dates the last assimilation or exchange of ^{14}C rather than the age at death. This results in an unduly old age. The shorter the PMI is, the more problematic the meaningfulness of the date becomes. It is therefore advisable in such cases to perform supporting analyses and tests in addition to radiocarbon dating. In relation to the result of the dating, the potential findings can narrow down a PMI. Depending on the condition and completeness of a skeletal find, anthropological analyses as well as morphological and microscopic bone analyses could be used to determine individual age and gender [13].

■ Case studies from the Ice Age to the present

Six examples of the use of radiocarbon dating related to the basic subject of the book based on the author's current research projects are presented here. The case studies have been selected to cover different periods, from the Late Pleistocene through the recent past, and to treat different issues and methodological approaches.

Old or too old? On the dating of cave bears from Baumann's Cave in the Harz

The bone remains from Baumann's Cave in Bode Valley (Harz, Germany) have been well known since the sixteenth century. More was written about this cave than any other in the early days of natural science research. Parts of the 1950-metre-long cave are open to visitors.

Chiefly cave bears (approximately 95 per cent) were found in Baumann's Cave. Such caves are called bear caves because associated fauna is usually represented minimally. The range of fossilized fauna (e.g. steppe bison, muskoxen, reindeer, cave lions, leopards, cave hyenas, arctic foxes, wolverines, wild horses, woolly rhinoceroses, mountain hares and diverse small mammals) known from the cave confirms that the finds generally date to the last major Ice Age (Würm glaciation).

Various bones, also from cave bears, were sampled for ^{14}C dating to ascertain whether the fauna dated from an older (older than 50 000 years) or younger phase of the last Ice Age. Pretreatment revealed that the bones still contained enough collagen for dating that is basically methodologically reliable. The oldest sample was dated to 43 016 ± 814 years BP or 46 702 ± 1.681 years calBP, thus revealing that the finds date from the last half of the last Ice Age and can still be dated very well by radiocarbon analysis despite their old age [12]. This example demonstrates that allowance has to be made for relatively high standard deviations in older dates near the dating limit and that pure ^{14}C dates and calibrated ages differ significantly. This absolutely must be factored into any interpretation of the find context based on age values (Figure 12.4).

Easy to date but not a baby: an Egyptian mummy from Basel

Mummy III 8226 is a completely wrapped Egyptian mummy of a child in the Natural History Museum in Basel, Switzerland. More precise information on its provenance and entry in the collection is not available. The mummy presumably became part of the collections of the Museum of Ethnology in Basel in the nineteenth century.

The mummy's physical appearance – it has a length of 54 cm – initially suggests that it must be a baby. Not until computed tomography (CT) scans were taken did it become apparent that the bandages wrap the skeletal remains of a 3- to 4-year-old toddler rather than a baby [21]. The gender cannot be determined. The skeleton is disordered and has been shoved together. All the bones of the lower extremities – the feet are missing – have been moved to the upper body so that the upper ends of the femurs are at shoulder level.

The arrangements inside the mummy shrouds as described for the toddler are not untypical of the

Figure12.4 Cave bear skeleton in Baumann's Cave (Harz, Germany). (Photograph by W. Rosendahl, Mannheim, Germany.)

Greco-Roman era (end of the Ptolemaic Dynasty or Roman era). Importance was attached to the outer shroud in particular. Because no traces of embalming substances were found, the body was very likely subjected to decomposition until skeletonizing before it was shrouded. Afterward, the skeletal remains were laid together in a more or less orderly fashion and wrapped carefully. This could also explain the absence of various skeletal elements. Traces of partly well-preserved painting are visible on the outer surfaces of the bandages. The motifs are closely related to the pantheon of ancient Egyptian gods and their symbolism. Identification with the death deity Osiris is particularly evident.

An unpainted piece of the bandage was radiocarbon dated to verify the relative dating possible from the find context. When dating Egyptian mummies, it is essential that potential samples are free of embalming substances (resin or bitumen). This includes both body and bandages samples. Mummy III 8226 was dated to 1968 ± 21 years before the present (18 ± 21 BC), thereby providing excellent confirmation and narrowing the relative date to the Greco-Roman era (Figure 12.5).

Mother and children? An unusual South American mummy group from Mannheim

In many respects, the most important and most interesting mummified object in the Reiss-Engelhorn-Museen in Mannheim, Germany, is the group of M1 with M1a and M1b consisting of three mummies, a woman (M1) with two children. The child M1a is lying atop the stomach of the woman, who is lying on her side. Child M1b is lying beneath the woman's head. An old object label in the vitrine records the provenance as 'Toltec Indian with two

children, Mexico, from an old tumulus near Oaxaca, 1895'. Mexican provenance is highly unlikely because this type of preservation is expected only in the Andean coastal region of South America. Woollen cloth is also not expected from Mexico because the country has none of the domesticated animals from which wool is obtained. The skin's postmortem discolouration and the woman's position tend to evidence of provenance from Quiani in northern Chile.

Small bone samples were taken for ¹⁴C dating and genetic analyses to clarify age and a possible genetic relationship among the three mummies.

Both the physical features of the body and the results of the CT scans revealed that mummy M1 is a woman. The

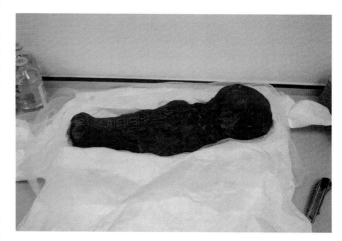

Figure 12.5 Mummy of the child III 8226 from the Natural History Museum in Basel, Switzerland. Well-preserved traces of painting and an inscription referencing the death deity Osiris are clearly visible on the surface of the bandages. (Photograph by W. Rosendahl, Mannheim, Germany.)

woman has a height of approximately 156 cm. Her individual age is between 30 and 35 years. She was probably still nursing up until her death [20]. An abnormality of her hip joint on both sides was an unusual pathological finding. It may be avascular necrosis, a disease characterized by death of part of the femur head caused by an interrupted blood supply. Because the woman is mummified exceptionally well, remains of the brain, spinal cord and contents of the large intestine have been preserved. Another abnormality is a separation of the symphysis pubis in the pelvic region, which is visible in the CT scan. This is a crack in the symphysis pubis, which probably occurred during childbirth.

The mummy of the child M1b displays the same blackish patina as the mummy M1 and is lying with its upper body beneath the mummified woman's head. Its head, first and second cervical vertebrae, hands and feet are missing. Whereas gender and height cannot be determined, the individual age can be specified as 2 to 3 years old.

As mentioned, the mummified child M1a is lying on the stomach of the mummified woman. Unlike the mummies M1 and M1b, mummy M1a does not have a blackish patina. This child can therefore be assumed to have been added to the group later. Except for the missing feet and skin blemishes in the face, this mummy is also very well preserved. Large portions of the body except for the head are wrapped in a light brown woven fabric. Some cords made of plant fibres encircle the fabric. Three-dimensional animation during the CT scans revealed that the circle of cords is a regularly knotted carry net with a wide mesh. The child's gender and height could not be determined. It was 1 to 2 years old, based on the dental status, and approximately 18 months old, based on the length of the femur. Some pathological changes were detected. There is a bone tumour on the right upper jaw. The tumour may have been caused by fibrous dysplasia, chronic abnormal growth of new bone mass. It is the most frequent bone defect to appear in childhood and youth. Fibrous dysplasia manifests not only in frequent bone fractures but also in hormone imbalance (e.g. excess growth hormones). The cause of this disease is a non-heritable genetic defect. A discernible shift of the child's teeth may be connected with the disease. The exceptionally good mummification of the child is also evident in the preservation of remains of soft tissue in the lower abdomen and in the eye sockets and remains of the brain in the skull.

Molecular genetic tests confirmed that the three mummies came from South America but did not deliver any findings about a possible mother-child relationship in the mummy group.

This question can be answered by the findings of the ^{14}C dating, however. The mummified woman M1 dates to 1095 ± 50 years AD, a significant deviation from the date of 1347 ± 30 years AD of the mummified child M1a. This confirms the suspicion raised by the different skin colouration of the mummies that this mummified child was added to the

Figure 12.6 View of the South American mummy group 'Woman With Two Children' from the Reiss-Engelhorn Museum in Mannheim, Germany. One mummified child (M1a) is lying on the woman's stomach, and another (M1b) is beneath her head. (Photograph courtesy of J. Christen, Mannheim, Germany.)

mummy group later, most likely to make it more interesting for a buyer and to obtain a better price. The mummified child M1b's age of 1206 ± 36 years AD constitutes a difference that argues against a mother-child relationship between mummies M1 and M1b. Concomitant analyses of diet revealed that mummy M1 primarily lived on a diet of fish and seafood [4]. Because ^{14}C travels more slowly in the marine cycle than in the terrestrial cycle, it is not impossible that mummy M1 was dated somewhat too old or that the date must be corrected towards the more recent date. For this reason, a mother-child relationship between these two mummies is definitely possible (Figure 12.6).

Three dates but still no age: an Asian mummy from Mannheim

Mummy M6 is a complete, light-skinned full-body mummy in an extended supine position. Impressions of a once-extant textile cushion are discernible in sections of the upper body. The collection's archive did not contain any other documents or information on this mummy's cultural geographical origins or proposed dating.

Bone and tissue samples were each taken from mummy M6 for genetic tests and ^{14}C dating to learn something about its possible geographical origins and dating. The mummy was subjected to a CT scan as the basis for a physical anthropological analysis [19].

The evaluation of the CT data revealed that it is a 15- to 17-year-old male adolescent with a height of approximately 153 cm (Figure 12.7).

Apart from a skull fracture in the right forehead, which probably occurred post mortem, the teeth in particular are pathologically striking. Several teeth in both the upper jaw and lower jaw are significantly misaligned. The incisors in the upper jaw display the shovel shape typical of Asian or Indian peoples. The wisdom teeth have not broken through yet.

Figure 12.7 Mummy (M6) with geographical origins in northeast Asia from the collections of the Reiss-Engelhorn-Museen in Mannheim, Germany. (Photograph by W. Rosendahl, Mannheim, Germany.)

The ethmoidal sinuses in the nasal cavity have survived, but the cranial cavity is completely empty and does not contain any remains of the brain. The sacroiliac joint located in the pelvic ring is dislocated on both sides. Because it transmits the entire load of the torso to the legs, the sacroiliac joint is crucially important for the mechanics of the body and overall posture. The cause of this joint defect is unknown.

Genetic tests ascertained that the mummy can, in principle, be both American and East Asian in origin [22]. This mummy's individual sequence profile rules out a Pacific origin. A specific genetic mutation, conversely, indicates a northeast Asian origin.

Unfortunately, ^{14}C dating was unable to date the mummy plausibly. The dates ascertained in three different samples (bone and tissue) are scattered over a time frame from the Late Pleistocene until early 1950. The textile impressions discernible on the mummy are not the only evidence against a Late Pleistocene age. Because we know that the mummy entered the museum with Gabriel von Max's collection in 1917, it can in no way correspond to the most recent date ascertained. Still unidentified contamination makes correct dating impossible at present.

The Bog Dog from Burlage: changing dating of a significant bog body

A peat cutter chanced on an incompletely preserved mummified dog in black peat approximately 70 cm beneath the terrace of Kloster Bog in Burlage (Cloppenburg District, Lower Saxony, Germany) in 1953 [15]. Its fur is well preserved, but all lower parts of the extremities as well as sections of its head are missing because of improper recovery. The find is a typical bog body (i.e. mummified by the bog water's special properties of chemical preservation).

Just under 70 cm in length, the so-called 'Bog Dog from Burlage' has a shoulder height of no more than 40 cm. Although the skull resembles that of a present-day German Spitz, it is significantly more elongated. The dog's build most closely resembles that of a Hovawart, the typical 'farmer's dog' since the Middle Ages. The Bog Dog's coat deviates from that of this race considerably, however. Rather than fine, long and smooth, it is only 5 to 7 cm long and bristly. A genetic analysis is scheduled soon to identify the dog's breed (Figure 12.8).

The archaeological layer was palynologically dated shortly after the discovery of the mummified dog. It was

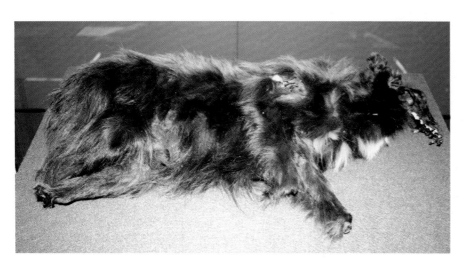

Figure 12.8 Bog Dog from black peat from Kloster Bog near Burlage in the Cloppenburg District (Lower Saxony, Germany), in the collections of the Geomuseum at the University of Münster, Germany. (Photograph by W. Rosendahl, Mannheim, Germany.)

dated to approximately 3200 years [15]. This would make it a bog body from the late Bronze Age.

As part of new testing of the Bog Dog in the German Mummy Project, a bone sample was radiocarbon dated at the Reiss Engelhorn Museum in Mannheim to verify this dating. The surprising result was that the mummified dog's age of 1544 ± 67 years AD dates it to the modern era [3]. The discrepancy between the two dates now available can be explained easily. The palynological analysis dated the archaeological layer correctly, but the dating of the mummy find proceeded from the false assumption that it had been embedded at the same time the archaeological layer formed. The new and first-time direct dating of the bog body itself revealed that the find was not embedded in older strata until much later. This example excellently demonstrates the importance of dating the find itself and not only the archaeological layer or accompanying finds.

A CT scan of the find produced more new information [3]. The skeleton turned out to be very well preserved. Nevertheless, a flattening of individual skeletal elements caused by the pressure of the applied load of the peat on the surface, as well as demineralization from the acidic surrounding soil, is discernible. Some vertebrae and ribs have disappeared from the anatomical group post mortem. In terms of individual age and gender, this is a young to young adult male dog. Finally, the Bog Dog from Burlage is the sole surviving animal bog body in the world.

Ötzi's pet? The find of a frozen, mummified hare from the alps

This unusual mummified animal was discovered in South Tyrol (Italy) in August of 2005. The location of the find was 3000 m above sea level in the Hochferner glacier in Pfitsch. At 3463 m, the Hochfernerspitze is one of the highest mountains in the Zillertal Alps. The mummified hare melted out of the hanging Hochferner glacier on the northern face in 2005. The finders, S. Landthaler and E. Zössmaier, initially brought their find to the State Hunting and Fishing Agency in Bolzano and then to the South Tyrol Museum of Archaeology, where the first tests were supposed to be performed. Even before precise determinations and dates were available, this find went through the media as 'Pfitschi' or the 'Ötzi Hare', referring to the world famous Neolithic mummy of the so-called 'Iceman', also known by the name 'Ötzi', discovered in 1992. Initial ^{14}C dating of a tissue sample yielded an age more recent than 1950. The find was therefore considered to be meaningless and more or less fell into oblivion.

New tests as part of the German Mummy Project revealed that the find is definitely an Alpine mountain hare (*Lepus timidus varronis* Miller 1901). Not only the altitude but also the longer hind legs and shorter forelegs, as well as the cross-section of the upper incisors, attest to this classification. With an average weight of 2.5 to 3 kg and a length of 460 to 560 mm, it is the smallest subspecies of mountain hare. Mountain hares are found in the Alps above 1300 m above sea level. The decline in population of this hare in the Alpine countries of Germany, France, Italy, Austria, Switzerland and Slovenia is also connected with global warming.

The mummification process in the ice (freeze drying) shrunk the mummified hare down to 350 mm. Fur has survived only in small tufts on its back and paws. Wherever the parchment-like skin is missing, the bones are still joined only by tendons. Genetic tests revealed that the hare belongs to a now unfamiliar haplogroup [8], thus giving rise to doubts about the young dating obtained in 2005. It was therefore dated a second time, this time using bone material. The result confirmed the dating. Calibration with so-called 'bomb peak dating' determined that the time of death was between 1984 and 1988 (Figure 12.9).

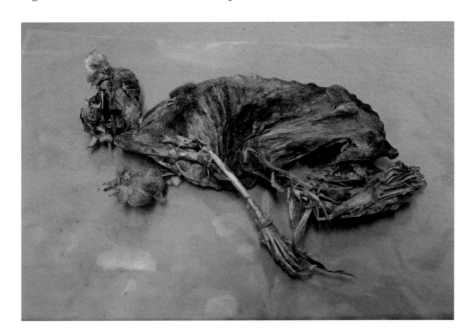

Figure 12.9 A mummified Alpine mountain hare from Hochferner glacier near Pfitsch, South Tyrol, Italy. (Photograph by W. Rosendahl, Mannheim, Germany. Object from the South Tyrol Museum of Natural History in Bolzano, Italy.)

References

1. Arnold JR, Libby WF. Age determination by radiocarbon content: checks with samples of known age. *Science* 1949;**110**:678–680.

2. Ascough PL, Cook GT, Dugmore A. Methodological approaches to determining the marine radiocarbon reservoir effect. *Prog Phys Geogr* 2005;**29**(4):532–547.

3. Bertling M, Gill-Robinson H., Rosendahl W. The Bog Dog from Burlage. In: Wieczorek A, Rosendahl W (eds.). *Mummies of the World*. Munich, Germany, Prestel, 2010, pp 298–299.

4. Bocherens H. Keratinisotopie: Antworten zu Lebensraum und Ernährung. In: Wieczorek A, Tellenbach M, Rosendahl W. (eds.). *Mumien: der Traum vom ewigen Leben*. Mainz, Germany, Zabern, 2007, pp 235–238.

5. Chisholm BS. Variation in diet reconstructions based on stable isotopic evidence. In: Price TD (ed.). *The Chemistry of Prehistoric Human Bone*. Cambridge, Cambridge University Press, 1989, pp 10–37.

6. Cook GT, Dunbar E, Black SM, Xu S. A preliminary assessment of age at death determination using nuclear weapons testing ^{14}C activity of dentine and enamel. *Radiocarbon* 2006;**48**:305–313.

7. De Vries HL. Variation in concentration of radiocarbon with time and location on earth. *Proc K Ned Akad Wet* 1958;**61**:1–9.

8. Döppes D, Gill-Frerking H, Joger U, Rosendahl W, Stümpel N. A mountain hare mummy from Zillertaler Alps. *Yearb Mummy Stud* 2014;**2**:23–29.

9. Friedrich M, Remmele S, Kromer B, Hofmann J, Spurk M, Kaiser KF, Orcel C, Küppers M. The 12460-year Hohenheim oak and pine tree-ring chronology from Central Europe: a unique annual record for radiocarbon calibration and paleoenvironment reconstructions. *Radiocarbon* 2004;**46**(3):1111–1122.

10. Geyh MA. *Handbuch der physikalischen und chemischen Altersbestimmung*. Darmstadt, Germany, WBG, 2005, pp 1–211.

11. Hodgins G, Brook GA, Marais E. Bomb-spike dating of a mummified baboon in Ludwig Cave, Namibia. *Int J Speleol* 2007;**36**(1):31–38.

12. Joger U, Rosendahl W. The Rübeland Caves (Harz Mts.): historical excavations and modern analyses. *Braunschweig Nat Schrift* 2012;**11**:55–68.

13. Knight B. *Forensic Pathology*. 3rd ed. London, Edward Arnold, 2014, pp 1–672.

14. Libby WF. *Radiocarbon Dating*. Chicago, University of Chicago Press, 1952, pp 1–124.

15. Lotze F. Vorläufige Mitteilung über einen Moorhundfund bei Papenburg a. d. Ems. *Neues Jahrbuch Geol Palaontol Monatsh* 1955;137–138.

16. Lynnerup N, Kjeldsen H, Heegaard S, Jacobsen C, Heinemeier J. Radiocarbon dating of the human eye lens crystallines reveal proteins without carbon turnover throughout life. *PLoS One* 2008;**3**(1):e1529.

17. Mazaud A, Laj C, Bard E, Arnold M, Tric E. Geomagnetic field control of ^{14}C production over the last 80 ky: implications for the radiocarbon time-scale. *Geophys Res Lett* 1991;**18**(10):1885–1888.

18. Reimer PJ, Baillie MGL, Bard E, Bayliss A, Beck JW, Blackwell PG, Bronk Ramsey C, Buck CE, Burr GS, Edwards RL, Friedrich M, Grootes PM, Guilderson TP, Hajdas I, Heaton TJ, Hogg AG, Hughen KA, Kaiser KF, Kromer B, McCormac FG, Manning SW, Reimer RW, Richards DA, Southon JR, Talamo S, Turney CSM, van der Plicht J, Weyhenmeyer CE. IntCal09 and Marine09 radiocarbon age calibration curves, 0–50000 years cal BP. *Radiocarbon* 2009;**51**:1111–1150.

19. Rosendahl W, Alt KW, Meier S, Rühli F. Eine asiatische Mumie aus den Reiss-Engelhorn-Museen. In: Wieczorek A, Tellenbach M, Rosendahl W (eds.). *Mumien: der Traum vom ewigen Leben*. Mainz, Germany, Zabern, 2007, pp 347–348.

20. Rosendahl W, Alt KW, Meier S, Rühli F, Michler E, Mitschke S, Tellenbach M. Südamerikanische Mumien aus den Sammlungen der Reiss-Engelhorn-Museen. In: Wieczorek A, Tellenbach M, Rosendahl W (eds.). *Mumien: der Traum vom ewigen Leben*. Mainz, Germany, Zabern, 2007, pp 358–366.

21. Rosendahl W, Gill-Robinson H, Hotz G, Pommerening T. The Egyptian mummies from Basel. In: Wieczorek A, Rosendahl W (eds.). *Mummies of the World*. Munich, Germany, Prestel, 2010, pp 326–328.

22. Rütze C, Forster P, Burger J. Molekulargenetische Herkunftsbestimmung von Mumien. In: Wieczorek A, Tellenbach M, Rosendahl W (eds.). *Mumien: der Traum vom ewigen Leben*. Mainz, Germany, Zabern, 2007, pp 229–233.

23. Suess HE. Radiocarbon concentration in modern wood. *Science* 1955;**122**:415.

24. Taylor RE, Suchey JM, Payen LA, Slota PJ. The use of radiocarbon (^{14}C) to identify human skeletal materials of forensic science interest. *J Forensic Sci* 1989;**34**:1196–1205.

25. Ubelacker HD. Artificial radiocarbon as an indicator of recent origin remains in forensic cases. *J Forensic Sci* 2001;**46**:1285–1287.

26. Wagner GA. *Altersbestimmung von jungen Gesteinen und Artefakten*. Stuttgart, Germany, Enke, 1995, pp 1–277.

27. Wild EM, Arlamovsky KA, Golser R, Kutschera W, Priller A, Puchegger S, Rom W, Steier P, Vycudilik W. ^{14}C dating with the bomb peak: an application to forensic medicine. *Nucl Instruments Methods Phys Res B* 2000;**172**:944–950.

13 Cross-Sectional Imaging and the Postmortem Interval

Guy Rutty and Bruno Morgan

The first documented use of X-rays in relation to the investigation of death was in 1896, when X-rays were used by Professor Schuster to assist in the investigation of a gunshot homicide in Manchester, England [6]. During the next 100 years, radiography became an important adjunct to autopsy practice, principally to facilitate identification and investigate the cause of death. In 1983, the application of computed tomography (CT), a newer radiological approach to autopsy practice, was reported [21]. However, it was not until the twenty-first century that research was initiated to apply these radiological approaches – postmortem computed tomography (PMCT) [28], postmortem magnetic resonance (PMMR) and, later, micro-computed tomography (micro-CT) – to assist with the consideration of the postmortem interval (PMI).

■ Postmortem computed tomography

Although PMCT was first proposed as a replacement to the conventional invasive autopsy in 1994 [5], it has taken more than 20 years of technical development and pioneering research at a number of centres across the world to reach today's global acceptance of the increasing role in autopsy practice of this imaging technique. Even now PMCT remains in its infancy, with many further potential applications to autopsy practice, including a potential role in the estimation of the PMI. Although numerous postmortem changes can be observed with time after death by using PMCT, there is as yet no established method whereby these changes can be used to estimate a PMI. However, that is not to say that consideration has not been given to this by several researchers using a variety of approaches and that in the future, with further research, a PMCT algorithm to estimate a minimal PMI (PMImin) interval will not emerge.

Rigor mortis

According to Levy, Harke and Mallak [23], PMCT shows no specific finding for rigor mortis assessment. These authors suggest that skeletal muscle attenuation, size and shape are not affected by rigor mortis.

Livor mortis

Some authors have considered the presence of livor mortis (also referred to as 'lividity' or 'hypostasis') as detected by PMCT. In 2002, Shiotani *et al.* [33] reported that hypostasis could be observed using PMCT within 2 hours of death in approximately half of their 126 cases. This finding corresponds to the time frame for the appearance of livor mortis on external examination of the body, and thus in theory PMCT could be used to estimate a PMImin. These investigators also described how hypostasis manifests on PMCT images as a high-density fluid level in the lumen of the heart and great vessels. These workers proposed that this appearance was caused by the gravitational separation of serum and red blood cells following the cessation of blood flow.

The separation of blood into serum and blood cells (i.e. a haematocrit effect) is now recognized to occur not only in the heart and great vessels but also in the veins, organs and tissues [23] (Figure 13.1). In the cranium, this separation occurs within the posterior sagittal sinus, straight sinus and transverse sinus, where it can be mistaken, by the unwary investigator, for acute thrombosis [23] or subarachnoid haemorrhage [39] (Figure 13.2). It can be seen with more clarity and precision using PMMR [19]. Shiotani *et al.* reported that this separation does not occur in everyone and is influenced by factors such as age, clinical anaemia, blood volume, position after death and temperature. Ishida *et al.* [12] reported that clear cardiac and great vessel hypostasis on PMCT is related to high clinical fibrinogen states before death.

In the case of body organs other than the chambers of the heart, hypostasis is best seen in the lungs when increased attenuation occurs between the dependent and non-dependent aspects (Figure 13.3). This phenomenon can be reduced with the use of ventilated PMCT [10,27].

Finally, for the skin, increased attenuation occurs between the subcutaneous fat and the dermis, with the dermis becoming thicker in the dependent parts of the body. However, to date no published research exists concerning the distribution and fixation of lividity on PMCT images over time, as has been observed and documented during the external examination of the body.

Vascular wall changes

It is now widely recognized that the so-called 'native' or non-enhanced PMCT scan is insufficient for the diagnosis of vascular-related disease, specifically coronary artery disease. The use of PMCT with angiography (PMCTA) has been proposed as the new PMCT gold standard. However, because of the changes that occur within blood vessels

269

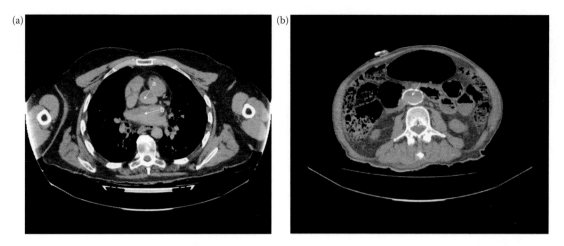

Figure 13.1   (a) Axial section of the thorax showing postmortem blood hypostasis levels within the aorta (a) and pulmonary trunk (b). (b) Axial section of the abdomen showing postmortem blood hypostasis level within the abdominal aorta (arrow).

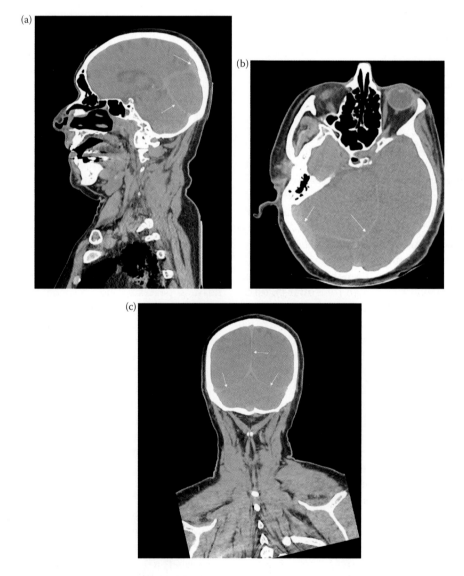

Figure 13.2   (a) Sagittal, (b) axial and (c) coronal sections of the head showing postmortem blood hypostasis (arrows) mimicking subarachnoid haemorrhage.

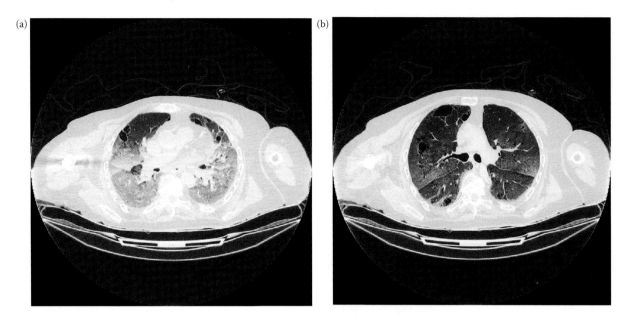

Figure 13.3   (a) Preventilated postmortem computed tomography (PMCT) and (b) postventilated PMCT axial images showing removal of the effect of postmortem hypostasis within the lungs.

after death, even with PMCTA the diagnosis of some natural diseases, such as pulmonary thromboembolus, remains difficult.

One of the changes that may occur after death is that the great vessels may collapse. This can be observed on the native, non-enhanced scan. Shiotani *et al.* [34] reported that the diameter of the ascending aorta was smaller than that of a living person. In a later study. Takahashi *et al.* [38] reported that the aorta shrunk at all anatomical levels, and these investigators also noted that the aorta became oval in the descending and abdominal parts (Figure 13.4). Ishikawa *et al.* [15] later undertook a study of the abdominal aorta just below the diaphragm in 140 cases within 5 days of death. These investigators reported a relationship between the changes in aortic shape (narrowing), which they proposed result from the action of gravity at this point, and time. Because a similar relationship was not observed in the thoracic aorta or at the bifurcation of the abdominal aorta, the investigators proposed that this relationship was caused by the variation in the support of the aorta at differing points along its length, whether by local anatomical variations or the presence of atherosclerosis. Although Ishikawa *et al.* proposed that postmortem aortic narrowing may be time related, and thus amenable for use to estimate the PMI, they highlighted several factors that must be taken into account and investigated, such as the effect of physical build, cardiopulmonary resuscitation (CPR), haemorrhage and decomposition.

Postmortem gas formation

Air and putrefactive gas (both referred to from this point onward as 'gas') are seen on PMCT within the vessels, organs, soft tissues and body cavities [23]. To date the

literature has concentrated on the source, composition and distribution of gas within the vascular system, rather than its appearance within the soft tissues [8,13,18,20,30,40].

The first sites of true putrefactive gas observed with PMCT are within the intestinal wall and the mesenteric and portal venous systems [23] (Figure 13.5). This gas then develops within all vascular spaces and potential anatomical spaces, normally in a symmetrical distribution unless there is focal or asymmetrical decomposition caused by an injury or local anatomical area of cooling or warming [23].

The principal problem when considering the presence of intravascular gas on PMCT is that it may not be derived from decomposition. Shiotani *et al.* [35] described a relationship between gastrointestinal distension attributed to CPR and the presence of hepatic portal venous gas (HPVG) observed within 2 hours of death. A similar observation was reported by Asamura *et al.* [1]. Although HPVG is associated with clinical disease such as cholangitis, cholecystitis and sepsis, as well as trauma, Shiotani *et al.* [35] reported that HPVG may be seen within 2 hours of death in the absence of CPR or local disease. A similar time frame was observed by Yamazaki *et al.* [41] in a case of death caused by ischaemic heart disease. Yokota *et al.* [42] observed gas formation within the arterial and venous system and suggested that the pattern of distribution could be used to distinguish between true postmortem gas formation and gas that associated with CPR. Egger *et al.* [7] studied the distribution of gas within the vascular compartment and proposed that it follows a specific distribution pattern. Singh *et al.* [36], through the study of a single adult case serially scanned over a 3-day period, described the progressive formation of intra-hepatic and intra-cardiac gas. These investigators illustrated how, in the absence of CPR or abdominal trauma, intra-hepatic and

(a)

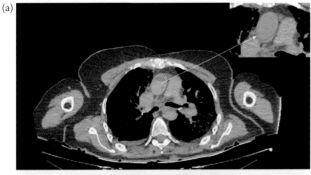

(b)

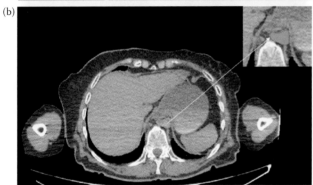

(c)

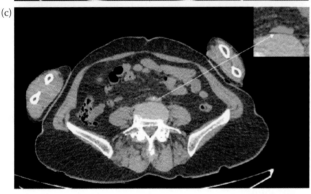

Figure 13.4 Postmortem collapse of the aorta varies depending on the anatomical position in the body. (a) Ascending aorta, (b) abdominal aorta at emergence through diaphragm and (c) abdominal aorta close to the bifurcation into the iliac vessels.

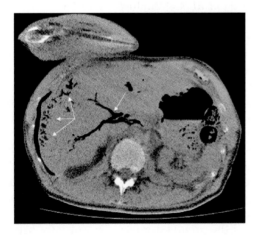

Figure 13.5 Axial image using minimum-intensity projection showing air (arrow) in the portal veins as an early postmortem change.

intra-cardiac gas can form within 7 hours and 30.5 hours, respectively, after death.

Thus, to date there is a paucity of published data related to the time frame when true putrefactive gas forms within the vascular compartment, as opposed to gas associated with CPR. Although these data suggest that a PMImin exists for this gas formation, the formation of true putrefactive gas within blood vessels cannot currently be used to predict a time since death.

Thyroid gland changes

A single study by Ishida *et al.* [14] reported changes in the thyroid gland between antemortem clinical CT and PMCT that relate to the time elapsed. This study of 50 patients dying in a tertiary care hospital identified that the density (Hounsfield units, HU) of the left and right thyroid lobes decreased after death. However, these investigators were unable to use this relationship to predict a time of death interval.

Cerebral parenchyma attenuation

Clinicians used to reporting PMCT scans will be aware that the brain has an appearance of global hypoxic injury. Blurring and loss of definition of the grey-white matter junction, decease in cerebral attenuation and sulcal effacement occur early, with complete loss of grey-white matter differentiation seen within 2 to 3 days after death [5].

Currently, only a single preliminary abstract has been published detailing the estimation of PMI by using cerebral PMCT of deceased hospital patients. Bayat and Klein [3] undertook a study of 61 cerebral PMCT scans and investigated the density (HU) of the dorsal aspects of the superior sagittal sinus, the left and right vitreous humour and the anterior and posterior horns of the left and right lateral ventricles. These cases occupied a postmortem time frame of 3.0 to 45.1 hours. The investigators observed an increase in density of the lateral ventricle regions with a strong correlation between density (HU) and the PMI (personal communication, W.M. Klein, 2014) (Figure 13.6). In the published abstract, Bayat and Klein hypothesized that this observation could be used to estimate a PMI, although validation studies would be required.

■ ¹H-magnetic resonance spectroscopy

In 2002. Ith *el al.* [16] considered the application of hydrogen proton magnetic resonance spectroscopy (¹H-MRS), as part of magnetic resonance imaging (MRI), to forensic medicine in an attempt to estimate the PMI. Studying eight abattoir-acquired decapitated sheep heads stored at 20°C and four human cadavers stored at 4°C, these investigators considered the change in four brain metabolites over an

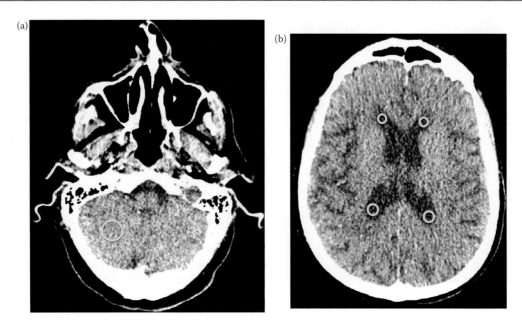

Figure 13.6   (a) Site for density measurement of the right cerebellar hemisphere at the level of nasopharynx (circle). (b) Site for density measurements of cerebrospinal fluid in the anterior and posterior horns of the most lateral part of the left and right ventricles of the brain (circles). (Courtesy of A. Bayat and W.M. Klein, Radboud University Medical Center, Amalia Children's Hospital, Nijimegen, The Netherlands.)

18-day period. They concluded that for the first 48 hours the sheep and human metabolite changes could be correlated with time, but after 3 days new metabolites appeared. Building on this work, a series of authors applied ^{1}H-MRS to both pig and sheep head models in an attempt to study metabolite change with time and at different ambient temperatures further [2,17,31]. These investigators showed that it is possible to define a single equation to describe eight metabolite concentrations as a function of PMI and ambient temperature that could be used to determine a PMI. However, once bacterial decomposition ensues, reliable PMI calculation cannot occur.

More recent work by Musshoff *et al.* [24] showed problems when using a decapitated head as the experimental model. When these authors applied ^{1}H-MRS to a whole cadaver porcine model, significant differences in time-related metabolic changes were observed between the isolated heads and the intact animals. Thus, although ^{1}H-MRS appears to be a promising avenue for the estimation of the PMI, to date insufficient data exist for ^{1}H-MRS to be reliably used to calculate a PMI in the human body.

■ Micro-computed tomography

To date micro-CT has had limited application to postmortem investigation [29], partly because of the restricted availability of this imaging modality to autopsy practitioners. Having said this, the forensic entomology work of Richards *et al.* [26] from the Natural History Museum in London showed that cross-sectional imaging using micro-CT can be applied for the estimation of a PMImin.

After death, blowflies are the first insect species to colonize the body [11]. Immature blowflies pass through three developmental stages: egg, larval and pupal. By recording the duration of development of the oldest immature stage recovered from the body, it is possible to estimate a PMImin [4]. Methods can be applied to both the larval and pupal stages to estimate a PMImin. In terms of the pupal stage, these methods have included measurement of the beginning and end of pupariation [25], as well as morphology studies that have included the use of light and scanning electron microscopy [37] and histological examination [22]. These techniques when applied to pupae are time consuming and destructive. In an attempt to overcome this problem, micro-CT has been used to facilitate the description of insect anatomy [9].

Richards *et al.* [26] applied micro-CT to examine the development of blowfly pupae (Figure 13.7). Imaging of the pupae was enhanced by staining them with iodine. By using micro-CT to investigate the internal anatomical changes during blowfly metamorphosis and by comparing the changes observed with those externally, Richards *et al.* described how micro-CT can be applied to estimate a PMImin. These investigators highlighted that micro-CT is rapid, inexpensive and non-destructive, allowing for multiple pupae to be examined at the same time. Although currently pupae are killed for the examination, these investigators suggested that, considering other work within the insect world, scanning the development of live pupae may be possible with micro-CT, thus producing more robust PMI estimation. Rutty *et al.* achieved this goal of live imaging in the production of Figure 13.7 for this book.

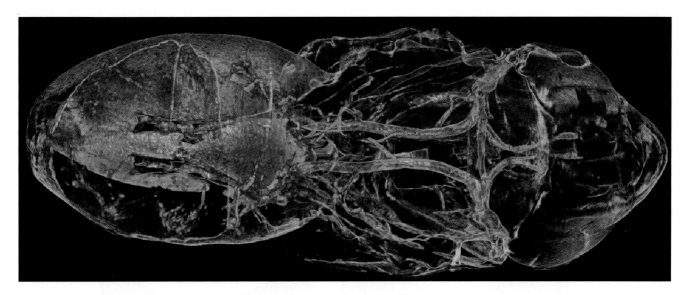

Figure 13.7   Fifteen-day-old blowfly pupa imaged live throughout pupation with micro-computed tomography showing development of adult fly structures. (Courtesy of G. Clark, Department of Engineering, University of Leicester.)

References

1. Asamura H, Ito M, Takayanagi K, Kobayashi K, Ota M, Fukushima H. Hepatic portal venous gas on postmortem CT scan. *Leg Med (Tokyo)* 2005;**7**:326–330.

2. Banaschak S, Rzanny R, Reichenbach JR, Kaiser WA, Klein A. Estimation of postmortem metabolic changes in porcine brain tissue using ¹H-MR spectroscopy: preliminary results. *Int J Legal Med* 2005;**119**:77–79.

3. Bayat A, Koopmanschap D, Klein WM. Postmortem interval: value of post-mortem cerebral CT. *J Forensic Radiol Imaging* 2014;**2**:98 (abstract 1.10).

4. Catts EP. Problems in estimating the post-mortem interval in death investigations. *J Agric Entomol* 1992;**9**:245–255.

5. Donchin Y, Rivkind AI, Bar-Ziv J, Hiss J, Almog J, Drescher M. Utility of postmortem computed tomography in trauma victims. *J Trauma* 1994;**37**:552–555; discussion 555–556.

6. Eckert WG, Garland N. The history of the forensic application in radiology. *Am J Forensic Med Pathol* 1984;**5**:53–56.

7. Egger C, Bize P, Vaucher P, Mosimann P, Schneider B, Dominguez A, Meuli R, Mangin P, Grabherr S. Distribution of artifactual gas on post-mortem multidetector computed tomography (MDCT). *Int J Legal Med* 2012;**126**:3–12.

8. Fischer F, Grimm J, Kirchhoff C, Reiser MF, Graw M, Kirchhoff S. Postmortem 24-h interval computed tomography findings on intrahepatic gas development and changes of liver parenchyma radiopacity. *Forensic Sci Int* 2012;**214**:118–123.

9. Friedrich F, Beutel RG. Micro-computed tomography and a renaissance of insect morphology. In: Stock SR (ed.). Developments in X-ray tomography VI. *Proc SPIE* 2008;**7078**:70781U.

10. Germerott T, Preiss US, Ebert LC, Ruder TD, Ross S, Flach PM, Ampanozi G, Filograna L, Thali MJ. A new approach in virtopsy: postmortem ventilation in multislice computed tomography. *Leg Med (Tokyo)* 2010;**12**:276–279.

11. Greenberg B. Flies as forensic indicators. *J Med Entomol* 1991;**28**:565–577.

12. Ishida M, Gonoi W, Hagiwara K, Takazawa Y, Akahane M, Fukayama M, Ohtomo K. Hypostasis in the heart and great vessels of non-traumatic in-hospital death cases on postmortem computed tomography: relationship to antemortem blood tests. *Leg Med (Tokyo)* 2011;**13**:280–285.

13. Ishida M, Gonoi W, Hagiwara K, Takazawa Y, Akahane M, Fukayama M, Ohtomo K. Intravascular gas distribution in the upper abdomen of non-traumatic in-hospital death cases on postmortem computed tomography. *Leg Med (Tokyo)* 2011;**13**: 174–179.

14. Ishida M, Gonoi W, Hagiwara K, Takazawa Y, Akahane M, Fukayama M, Ohtomo K. Postmortem changes of the thyroid on computed tomography. *Leg Med (Tokyo)* 2011;**13**:318–322.

15. Ishikawa N, Nishida A, Miyamori D, Kubo T, Ikegaya H. Estimation of postmortem time based on aorta narrowing in CT imaging. *J Forensic Leg Med* 2013;**20**:1075–1077.

16. Ith M, Bigler P, Scheurer E, Kreis R, Hofmann L, Dirnhofer R, Boesch C. Observation and identification of metabolites emerging during postmortem decomposition of brain tissue by means of in situ ¹H-magnetic resonance spectroscopy. *Magn Reson Med* 2002;**48**:915–920.

17. Ith M, Scheurer E, Kreis R, Thali M, Dirnhofer R, Boesch C. Estimation of the postmortem interval by means of ¹HMRS of decomposing brain tissue: influence of ambient temperature. *NMR Biomed* 2011;**24**:791–798.

18. Jackowski C, Sonnenschein M, Thali MJ, Aghayev E, Yen K, Dirnhofer R, Vock P. Intrahepatic gas at postmortem computed tomography: forensic experience as a potential guide for in vivo trauma imaging. *J Trauma* 2007;**62**:979–988.

19. Jackowski C, Thali M, Aghayev E, Yen K, Sonnenschein M, Zwygart K, Dirnhofer R, Vock P. Postmortem imaging of blood and its characteristics using MSCT and MRI. *Int J Legal Med* 2006;**120**:233–240.

20. Keil W, Bretschneider K, Patzelt D, Behning I, Lignitz E, Matz J. [Air embolism or putrefaction gas? The diagnosis of cardiac air embolism in the cadaver]. *Beitr Gerichtl Med* 1980;**38**:395–408 [in German].

21. Kranz P, Holtas S. Postmortem computed tomography in a diving fatality. *J Comput Assist Tomogr* 1983;**7**:132–134.

22. Levy M, Bautz AM. Degeneration of larval salivary glands during metamorphosis of the blowfly, *Calliphora erythrocephala meigen* (Diptera: Calliphoridae). *Int J Insect Morphol Embryol* 1985;**14**:281–290.

23. Levy AD, Harke HT, Mallak CT. Postmortem imaging. MBCT features of post-mortem change and decomposition. *Am J Forensic Med Pathol* 2010;**31**:12–17.

24. Musshoff F, Klotzbach H, Block W, Traeber F, Schild H, Madea B. Comparison of post-mortem metabolic changes in sheep brain tissue in isolated heads and whole animals using ¹H-MR spectroscopy: preliminary results. *Int J Legal Med* 2011;**125**: 741–744.

25. Richards CS, Villet MH. Data quality in thermal summation development models for forensically important blowflies. *Med Vet Entomol* 2009;**23**:269–276.

26. Richards CS, Simonsen TJ, Abel RL, Hall MJ, Schwyn DA, Wicklein M. Virtual forensic entomology: improving estimates of minimum post-mortem interval with 3D micro-computed tomography. *Forensic Sci Int* 2012;**220**:251–264.

27. Robinson C, Biggs MJ, Amoroso J, Pakkal M, Morgan B, Rutty GN. Post-mortem computed tomography ventilation: simulating breathholding. *Int J Legal Med* 2014;**128**:139–146.

28. Rutty GN, Brogdon G, Dedouit F, Grabherr S, Hatch GM, Jackowski C, Leth P, Persson A, Ruder TD, Shiotani S, Takahashi N, Thali MJ, Woźniak K, Yen K, Morgan B. Terminology used in publications for post-mortem cross-sectional imaging. *Int J Legal Med* 2013;**127**:465–466.

29. Rutty GN, Brough A, Biggs MJ, Robinson C, Lawes SD, Hainsworth SV. The role of micro-computed tomography in forensic investigations. *Forensic Sci Int* 2013;**225**:60–66.

30. Sakata M, Miki A, Kazama H, Morita M, Yasoshima S. Studies on the composition of gases in the post-mortem body: animal experiments and two autopsy cases. *Forensic Sci Int* 1980;**15**:19–29.

31. Scheurer E, Ith M, Dietrich D, Kreis R, Hüsler J, Dirnhofer R, Boesch C. Statistical evaluation of time-dependent metabolite concentrations: estimation of post-mortem intervals based on in situ ¹H-MRS of the brain. *NMR Biomed* 2005;**18**:163–172.

32. Shiotani S, Kohno M, Ohashi N, Atake S, Yamazaki K, Nakayama H. Cardiovascular gas on non-traumatic postmortem computed tomography (PMCT): the influence of cardiopulmonary resuscitation. *Radiat Med* 2005;**23**:225–229.

33. Shiotani S, Kohno M, Ohashi N, Yamazaki K, Itai Y. Postmortem intravascular high-density fluid level (hypostasis): CT findings. *J Comput Assist Tomogr* 2002;**26**:892–893.

34. Shiotani S, Kohno M, Ohashi N, Yamazaki K, Nakayama H, Ito Y, Kaga K, Ebashi T, Itai Y. Hyperattenuating aortic wall on postmortem computed tomography (PMCT). *Radiat Med* 2002;**20**:201–206.

35. Shiotani S, Kohno M, Ohashi N, Yamazaki K, Nakayama H, Watanabe K. Postmortem computed tomographic (PMCT) demonstration of the relation between gastrointestinal (GI) distension and hepatic portal venous gas (HPVG). *Radiat Med* 2004; **22**:25–29.

36. Singh MK, O'Donnell C, Woodford NW. Progressive gas formation in a deceased person during mortuary storage demonstrated on computed tomography. *Forensic Sci Med Pathol* 2009; **5**:236–242.

37. Sukontason KL, Kanchai C, Piangjai S, Boonsriwong W, Bunchu N, Sripakdee D, Chaiwong T, Kuntalue B, Siriwattanarungsee S, Sukontason K. Morphological observation of puparia of *Chrysomyanigripes* (Diptera: Calliphoridae) from human corpse. *Forensic Sci Int* 2006;**161**:15–19.

38. Takahashi N, Higuchi T, Hirose Y, Yamanouchi H, Takatsuka H, Funayama K. Changes in aortic shape and diameters after death: comparison of early postmortem computed tomography with antemortem computed tomography. *Forensic Sci Int* 2013; **225**:27–31.

39. Takahashi N, Satou C, Higuchi T, Shiotani M, Maeda H, Hirose Y. Quantitative analysis of intracranial hypostasis: comparison of early postmortem and antemortem CT findings. *AJR Am J Roentgenol* 2010;**195**:W388–W393.

40. Thali MJ, Yen K, Schweitzer W, Vock P, Ozdoba C, Dirnhofer R. Into the decomposed body: forensic digital autopsy using multislice-computed tomography. *Forensic Sci Int* 2003;**134**:109–114.

41. Yamazaki K, Shiotani S, Ohashi N, Doi M, Honda K. Hepatic portal venous gas and hyper-dense aortic wall as postmortem computed tomography finding. *Leg Med (Tokyo)* 2003;**5**(Suppl 1): S338–S341.

42. Yokota H, Yamamoto S, Horikoshi T, Shimofusa R, Ito H. What is the origin of intravascular gas on postmortem computed tomography? *Leg Med (Tokyo)* 2009;**11**(Suppl 1):S252–S255.

Index